W9-AEG-699

ALSO BY DUDLEY CLENDINEN

The Prevailing South: Life and Politics in a Changing Culture
(editor)

Homeless in America
(a book of photographs, edited by Michael A. W. Evans)

DUDLEY CLENDINEN
and
ADAM NAGOURNEY

A Touchstone Book
Published by Simon & Schuster
New York   London   Toronto   Sydney   Singapore

OUT for GOOD

The Struggle to Build
a Gay Rights Movement
in America

 TOUCHSTONE
Rockefeller Center
1230 Avenue of the Americas
New York, NY 10020

Copyright © 1999 by Dudley Clendinen and
Adam Nagourney
All rights reserved,
including the right of reproduction
in whole or in part in any form.
First Touchstone Edition 2001
TOUCHSTONE and colophon are
registered trademarks of Simon & Schuster, Inc.
Designed by Edith Fowler
Manufactured in the United States of America

10 9 8 7 6 5 4 3 2 1

The Library of Congress has cataloged the
Simon & Schuster edition as follows:

Clendinen, Dudley.
    Out for good : the struggle to build a gay rights
movement in America / Dudley Clendinen and
Adam Nagourney.
        p.   cm.
    Includes bibliographical references and index.
    1. Gay rights—United States—History.
2. Gay liberation movement—United States—
History.   3. United States—Politics and
government.   4. United States—Social conditions.
I. Nagourney, Adam.   II. Title.
HQ76.8.U5C58   1999
305.9'0664—dc21   99-12523   CIP
ISBN 0-684-81091-3
        0-684-86743-5 (Pbk)
Excerpts from The Advocate are reprinted by
permission of The Advocate, copyright 1967–1988
by Liberation Publications Inc. All rights reserved.

The authors gratefully acknowledge permission to
reprint lyrics from "United We Stand," by Tony Hiller
and Peter Simons. © 1970 Mills Music Ltd. (UK)
© Renewed. All Rights Assigned to and controlled by
EMI Mills Music, Inc. All Rights Reserved. Used
by Permission. Warner Bros. Publications U.S. Inc.,
Miami, FL 33014

FOR JEFFREY SCHMALZ, 1953–1993

Contents

Introduction:

AN INVISIBLE PEOPLE

As the nation entered the heat and uncertainty of the summer of 1969, at the end of a decade that had upended the social order, drawing whole classes of the American culture into collision with each other, one vast population remained essentially silent, unseen and strangely inert. Amid all the violence of that time—the racial murders, the political assassinations, the riots and burning cities; amid all the turmoil and change—the advent of sexual liberation, the protests against the Vietnam War, and the demands being made by African Americans and women, students and Native Americans—this was a population too shy and fearful to even raise its hand, to declare that it was present in that time, too.

Yet its members were present. They were involved in all those other protests and civil rights crusades. Some, bold and bright, grew rather famous in them. They just were not involved in their own cause yet. There were hundreds of thousands, perhaps millions, of homosexuals in the United States in the summer of 1969, and they knew they had reason to be unhappy. They had many of the same complaints that blacks and women and students did. Social causes were igniting all around them, roaring through the culture like prairie fires. Their own discontent was building. But there was only a tiny network of people stoking it, a few organizations in places like San Francisco, Los Angeles, Washington and New York. Two decades after a middle-aged man named Harry Hay had come home from a party in Los Angeles one night in 1948,

burning with the idea that homosexuals should band together in common political cause to seek equality, there were still only a few hundred souls in the
entire country who were willing to organize and protest, to show themselves in
some public way. All the vast rest of the homosexual population tended to presume, as the culture around them did, that they were flawed, and that the flaw
was theirs: a sin they should cast off, a puzzle they could solve. And so, mostly,
gay men and lesbians kept their feelings inside, identifying themselves only to
each other, if they did so at all. As a population, they existed only in the sense
that a secret exists, and is known to exist, without being acknowledged. They
did not recognize themselves as a class of people, and the larger culture did
not either.

They were, in June 1969, a secret legion of people, known of but
discounted, ignored, laughed at or despised. And like the holders of a
secret, they had an advantage which was a disadvantage, too, and which
was true of no other minority group in the United States. They were invisible. Unlike African Americans, women, Native Americans, Jews, the Irish,
Italians, Asians, Hispanics or any other cultural group which struggled
for respect and equal rights, homosexuals had no physical or cultural
markings, no language or dialect which could identify them to each other,
or to anyone else. The census didn't count them, market surveys didn't
seek them, political parties didn't court them. They had no electoral power,
no financial leverage, no legal recognition in their favor, no protection if
someone discovered their secret and fired or evicted or blackmailed them for
it. They had, as a class, much to complain about, yet they did not exist as a
class. If they existed, it was in just three ways, all in the negative: as a group of
sinners, "an abomination" in the eye of God; as a group of criminals, for
whom sex was against the law; and as a category of the mentally ill, for so the
Diagnostic and Statistical Manual of the American Psychiatric Association
defined them.

That was the condition of life for homosexuals in this country on the Friday night in June 1969 when the New York City police raided a gay bar in
Greenwich Village called the Stonewall Inn. It was a bar which had been
raided many times before. It was a population—in New York and elsewhere—
that was accustomed to raids and arrests. But that night, for the first time, the
usual acquiescence turned into violent resistance. There were stones thrown,
windows and doors broken, flames, people running in the streets. It was not
exactly the big time as riots go, but it was historic—a departure from the past.
From that night the lives of millions of gay men and lesbians, and the attitude
toward them of the larger culture in which they lived, began to change rapidly.
People began to appear in public as homosexuals, demanding respect. And
the culture began to react to them.

• • •

The modern gay rights movement which was ignited that night is the subject of this book. It is a close, sometimes intimate narrative of a gathering political movement among a group of people who had to start at zero in order to create their place in the nation's culture. It is the story of the last great struggle for equal rights in American history to this point, and it is a story which has not been told. The nation's whole history, its accumulated character, has been a melting accretion of wave after wave of such groups, each of which has had to fight for its place of respect. The gay rights movement has elements both parallel and quite different from the movements which have gone before. But the fundamental feeling, the bias which defined this population to begin with, is more subtle, more personal than any other. It is sexual. That dynamic sets up an emotional conflict, both within gay men and lesbians and within the broader culture, which is unique to the character and path of this movement. The kinds of oppression that homosexuals have experienced, the role that religion played in it, the psychological effect of it, the way gay men and lesbians do and don't relate to each other, the fractious nature of the movement, its difficulty in finding leaders and a voice—and the transcendent experience of AIDS—have all made this struggle for civil rights different from the others. It has been hard at times for those within—and for those outside—to perceive the focus of this movement, its ideology and its core. That may be because its members have been so ill-equipped to shape their own identities, or to understand themselves. They had, to begin with, no positive way to see themselves, no precedent on which to stand. And it was just as they began to develop one that they were attacked by the disease of AIDS.

That being said, it seems likely that the movement for gay identity and gay rights has come further and faster, in terms of change, than any other that has gone before it in this nation. Yet its story—the personal and political narrative of this movement—has never been told. There have been many nonfiction accounts about aspects of it. There have been individual sexual and political memoirs. There have been biographies and autobiographies. There have been metropolitan histories like Frances FitzGerald's *Cities on a Hill*, George Chauncey's *Gay New York* and Charles Kaiser's *The Gay Metropolis*. There have been periodic essays by Gore Vidal, early profiles in courage like *The Gay Crusaders* by Kay Tobin and Randy Wicker, cultural travelogues like *States of Desire* by Edmund White, oral histories like Eric Marcus's *Making History* and event histories like Martin Duberman's *Stonewall*. There have been historical and cultural anthologies like Jonathan Ned Katz's *Gay American History* and Neil Miller's *Out of the Past*, and works of personal perspective and cultural analysis like Del Martin and Phyllis Lyon's *lesbian/woman*. There have been books on gay sensibility, opera, film and writing. There has been a vast sad, angry, lyrical and also witty literature of AIDS, in fiction and nonfiction, from Larry Kramer's fiery polemics and plays, to Paul Monette's bittersweet memoirs, *Borrowed Time* and *Becoming a Man,* to Randy Shilts's simple, majestic account of the spread of AIDS, *And the Band Played On,* to Tony Kushner's Pulitzer Prize–winning drama, *Angels in America.* But no book before has attempted to follow the germ of rebellion which began with Stonewall, as it blossomed in other cities into a national political movement.

The lack of a definitive account may be because the movement itself is so young, because it has been so fragmented, because it has progressed so fast and been so transformed by AIDS. In the formulation of history, thirty years is not a long time to look back on. It took seven years, for instance, just to produce this book. But in many respects—given the kaleidoscopic changes that occurred—those three decades were a period of light years. They also followed a distinct and earlier period of the movement, a period of quite different, almost hidden character. That period—between the night in Los Angeles in 1948 when Harry Hay came home, to feverishly write his homosexual manifesto while his wife and children slept, and the night in 1969 when the riot broke out at the Stonewall Inn—was when the fundamental philosophical principles of the movement were formed and the battle lines drawn: that homosexuals were normal, too; that they were not insane; and that they had a right to enjoy love and civil liberties like any other group. Those were huge assertions, particularly in the 1950s and 1960s, when homosexuals, like Communists, were being hunted and purged from American government and society at every level. But it was a polite crusade. The case was made in pamphlets, proper demonstrations and forums of debate by the homophile leaders of that time—people like Franklin Kameny, Phyllis Lyon, Del Martin and Barbara Gittings. Some of them survived to become important figures in the struggle that followed after Stonewall, and John D'Emilio's *Sexual Politics, Sexual Communities: The Making of a Homosexual Minority in the United States, 1940–1970* remains the definitive account of that time.

But it was not until homosexuals began to adopt the tactics of other, more radical movements after the riots in New York that the struggle for gay rights gained momentum, and quicker change began to come. The story of that struggle, its pain, its jealousies, its wit and vision—its excesses and flaws—is the content of this book. It is an account which proceeds from the first night of the riots, and continues for twenty years, through 1988, when the gay rights movement was overtaken, if temporarily, by the AIDS movement. The narrative flows, as events themselves did, through the cities which became the main theaters and also occasional stages of the drama—through New York, Los Angeles, Boston, Minneapolis–St. Paul, Austin, Washington, D.C., Atlanta, Chicago, San Francisco, Miami, Seattle and New Orleans. It is a narrative which moves not just from place to place, revisiting some places again and again, as the years unfold, but from conflict to conflict and from theme to theme, as the story grows from a scattering of local struggles and personalities to a seething pattern more truly national in character. Some tensions are constant. They were present early on, and they are present now. They are the great shaping tensions of the movement. Some personalities—a very few—are constant, too. They are the main characters in this story, the recurrent threads in the fabric of events. But there are a number of other characters, too, incandescent figures who burn bright but briefly, dominating one stage or another, illuminating the issues at play and then fading in the wake of subsequent events. Almost all of them, as this history begins, are people unknown to the larger culture. But it is they who shaped this movement, and in many cases were consumed by it.

The cities which figure in this history were chosen because the events which occurred in them seemed germinal or essential in some way to the shaping of the modern gay rights movement and identity. The people in these pages are there for the same reason. After years of research they are the names and personalities who could not be left out, the ones who seemed, to the authors at least, to belong in a definitive history of the movement. That is what this book is intended to be. But it is not intended to be comprehensive. It is not an encyclopedic account. Given that this is the story of a fundamental change in national life and perspective, there are dozens—hundreds—of cities and towns which could logically be included in such an atlas. There are hundreds—thousands—of men and women who were important to events in those places. Their absence from this book—in many cases, their excision from a manuscript which was originally much larger—has been a painful part of the writing process. The decision to compress the material on San Francisco, whose history has already been well documented in other books, particularly *The Mayor of Castro Street: The Life and Times of Harvey Milk*, was difficult, too. Our hope is that this book is stronger—better balanced in proportion and detail—for being leaner.

With a movement as personal as this one, a history becomes the story of particular lives. The narrative in the pages which follow is an account weaned from nearly seven hundred different interviews with 330 of the men and women who formed this movement—or opposed it—across the country. The taped transcripts of those conversations run to millions of words. The archival material those men and women shared—the notes and journals, old letters and pamphlets pulled from the basements and attics of their lives—was buttressed by research in the Library of Congress, in regional and university archives, in independent gay and lesbian archive collections from Los Angeles to Minneapolis–St. Paul to New York; and by a careful search through thousands of copies of newspapers and magazines, both in the mainstream press and in the network of gay publications which grew up to report the events ignored by that press. Many of those publications no longer exist. Many of the men and women interviewed for this book in the last seven years no longer exist.

No other movement has been so reshaped by a plague. But no other movement has been so torn from the beginning between the sometimes conflicting goals of sexual liberation and civil rights. And no other movement, certainly, has paid so heavy a price for the freedom won. For the way in which many of them stood up for themselves, and the later courage with which they died, some of its members became heroes to their cause. That has a poignancy because this was not a cause, or a population, which began with heroes. No one homosexual was celebrated in the American culture in 1969. When young homosexuals looked for information in libraries in the summer of that year, they found clinical references and glum descriptions in journals of medicine and psychiatry, and a scattering of news items all filed under such headings as "variant," "lesbian," "pervert," "homosexual," "sodomist" and "deviate." Just one little bookstore in the country specialized in lesbian and gay books. The one nonfiction book available in the 1960s, written by a homosexual and intended for others like him in their search for identity, was *The Homosexual in America,* by Donald Webster Cory. It was a pseudonym, the cover behind which a sometime university teacher—a married man—could hide. The one commercially successful play which dealt directly with homosexuality, and which suggested that it might be better to be dead than gay, was *The Boys in the Band.*

There were two organizations in the whole country in 1969 bold enough to include the word "homosexual" in their name. And those were in San Francisco, the only city in the United States in which the political outlines of gay community had begun to form, well before Stonewall. There, in the bohemian neighborhood of North Beach, in the decade after World War II, a lively, visible gay clientele collected at a bar called the Black Cat. The police swept in, but the owner, a stubborn businessman named Sol Stoumen, fought the police raids in court as illegal under state law—and won. For a while there was a flowering of bar culture in San Francisco, and in 1961, a defiant gay waiter and cabaret performer from the Black Cat, José Sarria, ran for city supervisor, to show his incredulous friends and fans that it could be done.

But nowhere in the nation had anyone openly homosexual been elected to public office. Almost nowhere in the nation outside San Francisco, Washington and New York, in fact, was there plain talk about homosexuals in public forums or the press. There were almost no stories in general circulation newspapers or magazines about people like them, except as oddities or predators. It was the culture which defined them, and it was a relatively recent thing. Only a hundred years before, as European academics began trying to study and classify different kinds of human behavior, was the term "homosexuality" coined: a hybrid of Greek and Latin, a label for love between men.* It was only in the early 1950s, in California, that the first enduring political organizations for homosexuals had been formed, the Mattachine Society in Los Angeles for men, the product of Harry Hay's dream; and the Daughters of Bilitis in San Francisco for women. They were intended as forums to which men and women could bring their common secrets and common needs, and their hopes of educating the culture to accept them.

But the broad homosexual subpopulation had found somewhere else to meet by 1969, somewhere appropriate to its place in American society, the one institution in America where they were welcome. It was, in some ways, the perfect place for people who were pent up and yearning to let go, and had nowhere to go but public galleries, streets, bathrooms and parks. It was the one place which is everywhere available to the unconnected, the lonely, the unaccepted and unloved. It was a bar. A gay bar. Mostly, those were male bars, with a handful of separate lesbian bars for the women. In a city like Boston or Washington, there might be just one or two lesbian bars. And in small cities, there might be just one bar for everybody. Almost everywhere, they were in windowless buildings, or buildings whose windows had been covered or blacked out, and whose entries were through a solid door, usually with a peephole, guarded by bouncers. Sometimes they were downtown, but frequently, they were in old industrial or warehouse neighborhoods, away from busy areas where people might see who came and went. Always, the crowded time was night—not cocktail hour, but late, the hunting hours. The late hour, the dark, brooding building, the cars gathered around it at midnight like bees at a hive, the cut of light and sound as the door opened and closed, the appraising looks of the customers who passed on their way out—the whole scene pulsed with secret excitement and intrigue. If bars in the '60s still symbolized the rites of manhood to traditional young males, to young gay males trying to find the missing context of their lives, what a gay bar promised was

---

* Before that effort to define a condition from observed behavior, there was no such person as a homosexual. There was only language derived from the behavior—meaning the sexual act itself. Chiefly, there was sodomy, a name drawn from the Bible story of Sodom and Gomorrah, in the Book of Genesis, used to describe the sex men had with men. In the long list of commandments which God was said to have given to Moses in the Old Testament, in the Book of Leviticus, sex with various kinds of partners was condemned. The church created harsh punishments on earth for such sinners, including burning at the stake for sodomists. Later, such sin was made a crime by kingdoms, as they took power from the church by making laws in the name of the crown. Sodomy did not become a crime in English law until the reign of Henry VIII, and then, in 1533, Parliament enacted a statute making buggery, the act of anal intercourse, a felony punishable by death. Since English law was the received law of the American colonies, and since the states took much of their law after the American Revolution from the same source, Old Testament morality became the basis for most of American law governing sexual behavior.

much more: freedom, shelter, friendship, excitement, romance, seduction—escape.

But almost everywhere, those bars which represented so much to so many were owned by people who were not gay, or even sympathetic to gay life. Their drinks were overpriced and watered down, and almost nowhere were the customers allowed to dance, to touch each other suggestively, to hold each other close. It was usually illegal for men to dance together, just as it was often against the law for men to dress in women's clothes. Everyone was afraid of being entrapped and arrested. A very friendly person could easily be a cop.

To the owners, this was business, and frequently it was conducted by the one business group that was accustomed to dealing with the police, to supplying the illegitimate or illegal needs of patrons no legitimate business could serve: To a great extent, these bars were owned or run by the Mafia. Through the 1960s and into the 1970s, in most places, serving homosexuals was treated as illegal, or the bars that served them were illegal, or the police just acted as if something illegal was going on there. Because legitimate money would not invest in a liquor license and bar operation to serve a clientele which was basically illegal to begin with, the Mafia often simply operated gay bars without bothering to get a license and paid off the police. But the police also raided these bars, particularly during election cycles, sometimes calling the parents or employers of those they arrested to say that their child or employee had been found at a homosexual bar. Some people killed themselves over things like that in the 1960s. A few, in San Francisco, Washington and New York, chose to resist the pattern, demonstrating in public, seeking the support of the pulpit and of the courts. The traditional homophile groups, like the Mattachine Society, picketed outside the White House and the Pentagon and Independence Hall in Philadelphia, carrying signs and walking in a neat oval pattern. They were still doing those things in June 1969, and they were still polite.

But in places like San Francisco and Minneapolis, in words and in organization, the first signs of the next, more radical stage had begun to show. The challenge to authority, the violent police actions and the resulting riots at the Democratic National Convention in Chicago in the summer of 1968 had had a profound effect in radicalizing all the protest movements in the country. The old homophile movement was molting, and something else was emerging. No one really expected anything radical from an essentially silent, secret subculture which emerged mainly at night, to congregate in mob bars. It didn't seem the kind of crowd with anything to stand for, or any will to fight. But that, as it happened, was the place where homosexuals were most frequently attacked. So when the spark did come, perhaps it should not be surprising that it came in one of those places, at one of those times. Perhaps only in retrospect does it seem clear that this was the logical way it would happen, that the last struggle for civil rights in the twentieth century would begin with a fight at a bar.

PART ONE

Awakening

1

A FIGHT AT A BAR

June 1969, New York

Craig Rodwell was walking from Washington Square Park to his second-floor apartment on Bleecker Street in Greenwich Village when he saw the paddy wagon pulled up on Christopher Street in front of the Stonewall Inn. Instinctively, he stopped and pushed his way to the front of the crowd. There was not much of a gay movement in New York on the night of June 27, 1969, but any account of what there was would certainly have included Craig Rodwell. He was one of three members of the Mattachine Society who in 1966 had walked into a gay bar in Greenwich Village, announced that they were homosexuals and demanded drinks, challenging the bartender to defy the State Liquor Authority regulation forbidding service to people like them. That small confrontation produced a state appellate ruling in 1967 that struck down the ban, arguably the only success for the homosexual rights movement in New York for nearly an entire decade. On Thanksgiving Day that year Rodwell took the money he had earned working as a waiter at the Boatel Hotel in Fire Island Pines (where his duties included shining a flashlight on men who were dancing too closely together) and opened the Oscar Wilde Memorial Bookshop on Mercer Street, paying $115 a month in rent. For anyone who did not understand the significance of Oscar Wilde, Rodwell posted a "Gay is Good" sticker in the window, under the sign that said, "A book shop for the homophile movement." Rodwell didn't have much to put on his eight shelves inside. He did not like books or reading: He was dyslexic, had a short attention span and would come to boast that he had not read a single book in his shop. The bookstore had less to do with books than it did with the homophile movement, which is what had occupied much of Rodwell's time in New York over the past five years. And that is why, walking past the Stonewall after a night of playing cards, Rodwell had stopped to join the fight at the bar.

The next morning, Rodwell picked up the *New York Post* to see if it had reported the demonstration. It had. Rodwell paused for a minute to absorb the headline: "Village Raid Stirs Melee." The five-paragraph story noted that an attack on a homosexual bar had sparked a "near-riot." How strange, Rodwell thought, to see the word "homosexual" so near a word like "riot" in a newspaper. He recalled the demonstrations he had witnessed as a homophile activist in New York, Philadelphia, Chicago and Washington through the 1960s: small, rare, respectful, even timid, with the men wearing ties and jackets and the women in skirts. Rodwell went from his newspaper to his telephone, and spent the day giving friends his account of what had happened early that morning on Sheridan Square. By nightfall, the square was more crowded than ever, with demonstrators looking to pick up where they had left off, along with hundreds of curious onlookers, some gay and some not, who had heard of the uprising. They milled around the Stonewall, which had reopened serving only soft drinks. The police department's Tactical Patrol Force was better prepared on Saturday; about two hundred of them were lined up at the corner of Christopher Street and Greenwich Avenue, and at midnight the skirmishes had started anew. But they had a different flavor this time; there were still fires burning in trash cans, and pennies and bottles hurtling through the air, and chants of "Gay Power" and "Queen Power." But it was more like a rowdy Saturday night than a riot. Only four people were arrested that evening, compared to thirteen, including seven Stonewall employees, the night before. The fighting flared on and off through Wednesday and its complexion changed more each night. By midweek, many of the homosexuals had drifted off, replaced by an odd collection that included 1960s revolutionaries, Black Panthers, yippies and members of the Socialist Workers Party, whose cause was not necessarily homosexual rights.

As it turned out, press coverage of the Stonewall "near-riot" was fleeting: The *New York Times* devoted two nine-paragraph stories to it, each without a byline. The *Daily News,* under the headline "Homo Nest Raided, Queen Bees Are Stinging Mad," reported that the "queens" had "turned commandos and stood bra strap to bra strap against an invasion of the helmeted Tactical Patrol Force." The story continued: " 'We may have lost the battle, sweets, but the war is far from over,' lisped an unofficial lady-in-waiting from the court of the Queens. 'We've had all we can take from the Gestapo,' the spokesman, or spokeswoman, continued." According to the *News*, the Stonewall was just a little bar where homosexuals "do whatever little girls do when they get together." Even the *Village Voice*, the chronicler of the New Left, found humor rather than history in the riot at the Stonewall. "Wrists were limp, hair was primped," it reported. The bar patrons did not walk past the police, but went by with a "swish." The *Voice* later that summer disparaged the "Great Faggot Rebellion," and referred to homosexuals as "queers," "swishes" and "fags."

But for all that, there *had* been a change in the atmosphere, and if New York's straight establishment hadn't noticed it—indeed, if the overwhelming majority of homosexuals in the city and across the nation hadn't noticed it—it was instantly apparent on the shattered door of the Stonewall. Within hours after the rioters went home, a message urging calm had been painted on the front of the bar: "WE HOMOSEXUALS PLEAD WITH OUR PEOPLE TO PLEASE HELP MAINTAIN PEACEFUL AND QUIET CONDUCT ON THE STREETS OF THE VILLAGE—MATTACHINE." The Mattachine Society, with the Daughters of Bilitis for women, made up almost the entire extent of homosexual activism in New York. But by dawn, another, more dissident message had been splashed onto the front of the Stonewall: "SUPPORT GAY POWER."

The headquarters of the Mattachine Society was three miles away from the Stonewall, in a former dentist's office at 243 West End Avenue. It was here, the day after the raid, that the homophile movement of the past and the gay liberation movement of the future converged. Dick Leitsch, the executive director of the Mattachine Society, had grasped the implications of Stonewall—both for the organization he headed and for himself—and he was at his Mattachine desk first thing Saturday morning. Leitsch (pronounced LYE-tch) was the wily son of a wealthy tobacco family in Kentucky, who referred to other men as "aunties" and "she," and cared little for all the talk about civil rights that was suddenly swirling around the issue of homosexuality. There were, he liked to say, only three significant letters in the word "homosexual"—and those were *s, e* and *x*. The most prominent homosexual rights leader in New York of the time had declared that he had entered the movement "dick first," and that, "for me, homosexuality is 10 percent cause and 90 percent fun."

Leitsch was pleased to find people lining up to see him that Saturday—starting with Inspector Seymour Pine of Greenwich Village's Sixth Precinct. It was Leitsch, on those rare occasions when a homosexual contact was needed, who was sought out by TV stations and newspaper reporters, by the police department and city hall. He could even write personal letters to the handsome mayor of New York, John V. Lindsay, and know they would end up on the mayor's desk. In the days after Stonewall, Leitsch and his Mattachine Society were, as far as official New York was concerned, the only game in town. Inspector Pine was searching for help in cooling things down, so, of course, he went to see Dick Leitsch.

There were other people in the Mattachine offices after the riot, too: young homosexuals Leitsch had never encountered before. They wanted stencils to trace signs and a mimeograph to run off leaflets, and Leitsch granted all their requests. Four years earlier, Leitsch had been one of those new faces, at the vanguard of what counted as insurgency in the Mattachine Society. He had won his job then by scolding the incumbents for being timid, pledging that if he led the Mattachine Society, he would not sit by and let the New York City police continue to entrap homosexual men in public bathrooms, or the State Liquor Authority crack down on bars that openly catered to homosexuals (he went on to fulfill both promises). Leitsch was thirty-four years old, and he recalled, as he watched these new activists, the parting words of the man he defeated when he entered the leadership ranks of the Mattachine, Donald Webster Cory, the author of *The Homosexual in America.* "Well, Dick," said Cory, who came from the era when everyone, Cory included, used a pseudonym—which Leitsch had refused to do—"they call me the father of 'the homophile movement,' and homosexuals always turn on their fathers, so I should have expected this."

The other members of the Mattachine Society—neat, middle-aged men with soft bellies and trimmed short hair—were also uneasy about this strange new troop of men and women who began showing up in the days ahead, with their long hair and unkempt beards, torn blue jeans and T-shirts, and talk of gay power. Most of them kept their complaints to themselves, but Randy Wicker did not. He had marched on the draft board in New York in 1964 and the White House in 1965, and now he warned that the Stonewall agitators were in a weekend undoing all the progress the homophiles had made in a decade. He was horrified by headlines in the *Daily News,* the attention being paid to the transvestites and the Mafia-controlled bar that he, too, thought should be shut down. These new homosexuals, he complained to Leitsch, were intent on burning down their own ghetto (and hadn't the blacks done the same thing the previous year, after Robert F. Kennedy was assassinated?). Leitsch found himself quietly agreeing. The "new homosexuals" were like the black militants who had upset the moral authority of the nonviolent black leaders of the mid-1960s. Leitsch had always thought of himself, in philosophy and tone, closer to Martin Luther King, whose picture he kept on his office wall, right next to his picture of John V. Lindsay. As he surveyed the new terrain, he thought bitterly, "We're turning out just like *them*. We're getting to be like Stokely Carmichael."

• • •

On July 6, a week and a day after Stonewall, Randy Wicker climbed the stage at the Electric Circus, a discotheque in the East Village, where a rally of sorts had been called to commemorate the raid at Stonewall and the sudden new defiance that seemed afoot among many homosexuals in New York City. "We'll be open to the general public as usual, but we're especially encouraging gay people to come—and we really hope that everyone will dance together and dig one another," the club declared in a press release advertising the night. Wicker, wearing an American flag shirt and striped blue-and-white bell-bottoms, took the stage at midnight, before a crowd of mostly gay men who had passed the evening dancing to psychedelic rock music. "In years past," Wicker told them, his nasal, lilting voice floating over the room, "I would have dressed more conservatively, but tonight calls for a new approach." Then he went on to share publicly the concern he had voiced to Leitsch at the Mattachine headquarters. "Throwing rocks at windows doesn't open doors!" he declared.

Wicker would come to regret what he said that night, describing it years later as one of the great mistakes of his life. He hadn't noticed it at the time, but something about the riot at Stonewall—something about the image of homosexuals fighting back after so many years of unchallenged police raids on gay bars across the nation—had stirred an unexpected spirit among many young homosexuals. Until then, many of them had been part of the anti-war movement, the civil rights movement or the feminist movement, if they had any interest in politics at all. Now, the crowd at the Electric Circus included people wearing a button that no one remembered seeing before: "Equality for Homosexuals." Indeed, the mere fact of the evening was remarkable: it suggested that a riot which had spilled out of a two-room bar in Greenwich Village the week before was worth commemorating. Within three months Craig Rodwell would begin planning for an anniversary march and rally for New York. By the following June, there would be sizable marches in New York and Los Angeles, and smaller ones in San Francisco and Chicago. The anniversary of the Stonewall raid would become known, if unofficially, as Gay Pride Day, the last Saturday in June, a day commemorated with marches and rallies across the nation, in a celebration that would continue to swell in size for a generation.

Dick Leitsch's actions in the weeks after Stonewall echoed Randy Wicker's words at the Electric Circus: "Throwing rocks at windows doesn't open doors!" Quickly, he moved to co-opt rival groups and leaders, sending volunteers to distribute literature through Greenwich Village designed to secure the Mattachine Society's position. "Where do we go from here?" one flyer asked. It noted that "bottles have been thrown and people have been hurt," adding: "We all know that the streets cannot remain an armed camp and that further violence in the streets won't accomplish anything constructive." The leaflet called for a meeting with public officials, and said that Mattachine "stands ready to arrange a meeting." The group also distributed a three-page circular, "The Hairpin Drop Heard Around the World," written by Leitsch, that described the "first gay riots in history." The leaflet took its name from the coded language of Leitsch's generation: dropping a hairpin meant signaling that one was homosexual (mentioning one's collection of Judy Garland records, for instance). The "hairpin" leaflet caught the attention of Michael Brown, twenty-eight, a volunteer for Hubert Humphrey in 1968 who was then working at an interior decorating firm. He went to see Leitsch at the Mattachine's office, where he argued that a more aggressive response was needed. Leitsch put Brown in charge of a new Mattachine Action Committee, and called for a public forum for July 9 at the Freedom House, where the Mattachine Society held its monthly meetings.

This new group gathered by Brown—younger, more radical, new to the world of homophile politics—met in the back room of the Mattachine office, as far away from the main office as Leitsch could place them. It grew to include Marty Robinson, a kinetic, twenty-six-year-old carpenter; Jim Owles, who had been thrown out of the army for writing letters to local newspapers criticizing the Vietnam War; and Lois Hart, a former nun with a pixie haircut and wire-rimmed glasses. It also included Martha Shelley, twenty-six years old and a tomboy, with wire-rimmed glasses, short hair and a Brooklyn accent, who had just quit a social service job in Harlem and was now a secretary at Barnard College. She had joined the New York chapter of the Daughters of Bilitis eighteen months earlier, but she felt, because of her age and her politics, like a misfit there.

Leitsch had encouraged the creation of the committee, but it soon worried him. One day he overheard laughter and applause from the back room, and rushed in, his face in a tight smile. "You aren't thinking about starting another group, are you?" he asked. That was, in fact, exactly what they were talking about. Shelley appeased him with a lie: Absolutely not, she said. Her dislike for Dick Leitsch was growing daily—she considered him a misogynist, and found it repulsive that the leader of the Mattachine Society found humor in loudly inquiring, "Who opened the tuna fish?" whenever a woman walked into the room.

The Freedom House was almost two miles from the Stonewall, in a commercial district far from where most of the city's homosexuals worked or lived. The first gay community meeting after Stonewall was held there because that is where the Mattachine Society always gathered. It was a meetinghouse, and for $25 the Mattachine Society got the use of a room, no questions asked. "WE ARE NOT GOING TO TELL YOU WHAT TO DO," the Mattachine Society declared in block, stenciled letters in the leaflet inviting gay men and lesbians to attend. "Mattachine wants to know what you think can be done to secure your rights." Leitsch wanted to work quietly within the system, and he argued against the creation of any new groups that would, he said, divide the limited energies of the movement. But shortly after he called this meeting to order, Martha Shelley rose and proposed a different idea: a march and rally at Washington Square Park to protest police harassment. Leitsch wearily asked if anyone truly thought this made sense. Hands shot up across the room, so Leitsch unhappily suggested that anyone who wanted to organize the march move to a corner of the room.

The 2nd Gay Liberation Meeting, as it was called on the leaflet distributed a few days later, was held at a church on Waverly Place in Greenwich Village because Michael Brown thought that these kinds of discussions should be held where homosexuals in New York were concentrated. About two hundred people, most of them men, filled the folding chairs assembled in the large, hot room. Madolin Cervantes, the Mattachine Society's treasurer—and, Shelley noted, its only female member, and heterosexual at that—announced that Leitsch would be a few minutes late. "Now I, personally, am not gay," she said, smiling sweetly, as if anyone had had a moment's doubt. "But, believe me, *your* cause is *my* cause." Jim Fouratt listened with astonishment. The crowd had not come to hear that. Leitsch walked into the room wearing a conservative brown suit. Crisp and business-like—he could have been leading a Chamber of Commerce meeting—he went through the litany of grievances that had always been the agenda of the homophile movement: Police harassment must be ended, Leitsch said, but the homosexuals could not anger the establishment. Liberation will come through education of the public, which would lead to acceptance. Some in the crowd began to ridicule Leitsch's message. They shouted out attacks on the police, the Mafia and the Roman Catholic Church.

Madolin Cervantes called for the crowd's attention. "Well, now, I think that what we ought to have is a gay vigil, in a park. Carry candles, perhaps. A peaceful vigil. I think we should be firm, but just as amicable and sweet as. . . ."

"*Sweet?!*" Jim Fouratt jumped to his feet. He was wearing "my rock and roll drag," as he later described it—shiny leather pants, lizard boots up to his calves and a cowboy hat—and had curly blond hair to his shoulders and a drooping mustache. It was hard to believe that someone who looked so young (he had turned twenty-eight the month before) and tender could be so loud and searing. He had come directly out of the radical movement, had run with Abbie Hoffman and the yippie crowd, and had been at the Stonewall. But when Hoffman ignored his calls to come to Greenwich Village the day after the riot, Fouratt realized that any help for a gay rights movement would have to come from the people who turned out for this meeting. And when Cervantes spoke, he saw an opportunity to drive a wedge right through the center of the room.

"Sweet! Bullshit! There's the stereotype homo again, man! Soft, weak, sensitive! Bullshit! That's the role society has been forcing these queens to play and they just sit and accept it. We have got to radicalize, man! Why? Because as long as we accept getting fired from jobs because we are gay, or not being hired at all, or being treated like second-class citizens, we're going to remain neurotic and screwed up. No matter what you do in bed, if you're not a man out of it, you're going to get screwed up. Be proud of what you are, man! And if it takes riots or even guns to show them what we are, well, that's the only language the pigs understand." The room burst into applause. Leitsch tried to respond, but Fouratt roared right over him. "All the oppressed have got to unite! The system keeps us all weak by keeping us separate. Do you realize that not one straight radical group showed up during all those nights of rioting? If it had been a black demonstration, they'd have been there. We've got to work together with all the New Left." The speech was not completely accurate—other radicals had shown up at the Stonewall that night—but the sentiment hit home. With that, Fouratt led a group of several dozen out of the church and up Sixth Avenue. Once outside, Fouratt looked at Lois Hart and realized that he had not the slightest idea what to do with this anger he had whipped up. Back inside the church, Leitsch shouted for order. He was ignored.

July 1969, New York

"BROTHERS AND SISTERS!" Martha Shelley was standing on the rim of the fountain in the middle of Washington Square Park. A crowd of five hundred surrounded her, and she was speaking without any amplification. Shelley had taken responsibility for obtaining whatever permits were needed to rally at Washington Square Park and march the four blocks to the Stonewall Inn. It turned out the only permit needed was for a sound system. And Shelley, remembering that she was the loudest voice on the picket line she walked as a striking Harlem social service caseworker at the New York City Department of Welfare, decided she would rather yell than ask for a permit from the New York City Police Department. So there she was in the middle of Washington Square Park—all five feet four inches of her, as fierce as ever— bellowing at the top of her lungs, a little taken aback by how many men and women had turned up (mostly men), many wearing the lavender armbands she and Marty Robinson had handed out that morning.

"BROTHERS AND SISTERS!" Martha Shelley's voice was doing fine. "WELCOME TO THE CITY'S FIRST GAY POWER VIGIL! We're tired of being harassed and persecuted! If a straight couple can hold hands in

Washington Square Park, why can't we? We are tired of straight people who are hung up on sex!"

Shelley was at this moment still a member and former president of the Daughters of Bilitis, which had, uncomfortably and under pressure, agreed to Shelley's request to co-sponsor this rally with an equally reluctant Mattachine Society. In the weeks since the Mattachine church forum collapsed with the face-off between Jim Fouratt and Dick Leitsch, Shelley's ties to the Daughters of Bilitis had begun to unravel as well. She had gone to discuss the future of the movement with Joan Kent, who had signed Shelley up at her first DOB meeting. Kent's first instruction to Shelley at the DOB headquarters was to adopt a pseudonym, a standard DOB precaution in case the government obtained its membership records; Shelley had taken this advice (her real name was Martha Altman) and later embraced her pseudonym as her real name. Sitting in a Greenwich Village living room, face-to-face with Kent a few weeks after Stonewall, Shelley tried to explain why she thought the gay liberation struggle shared a common bond with blacks and groups she considered oppressed by society, and how this was a fight that should be fought aggressively and publicly. Kent, horrified, accused Shelley of being a Communist, repeating the word over and over again, refusing to even consider Shelley's ideas. Shelley felt no allegiance to the Communist Party, but she was drawn to the small group of gay radicals who in the weeks after Stonewall were emerging from other movements, with ideas of a gay liberation movement that people like Joan Kent and Dick Leitsch had never even considered. Shelley had never really felt much use for DOB: Her real insights into the gay struggle came not from the DOB monthly forums, with their clinical discussions about the nature of homosexuality, but from a particularly spiritual LSD trip she had taken a year earlier. And she certainly wasn't going to tell Joan Kent about that.

The rally at Washington Square Park, on July 27, came on the one-month anniversary of the Stonewall uprising, and it would turn out to be the last handoff from the vestiges of the Daughters of Bilitis and the Mattachine Society to the new movement that had risen so quickly on the streets. Martha Shelley and Marty Robinson, the principal speakers, were the bridges from the old to the new. Each had sought to nudge their respective organization onto a more radical course. Each felt increasingly out of place there—too angry, too militant, too young in an established and conservative setting. And each was beginning to step into the new wild and undefined world of gay liberation: it was louder, more demanding and less forgiving than the homophile movement—in short, very much a product of the contemporary political currents. For Dick Leitsch and Joan Kent, the fight had been, in effect, about being left alone to live a discreet life as a homosexual man or woman. But for Shelley and Robinson, and the people at the park and the first few meetings, it was about defining themselves to society as gay men and lesbians. It was here that the first early arguments of the gay liberation movement began to be framed: that discrimination against homosexuals was no different from discrimination against blacks and women; that gay men and lesbians wanted to live not quietly undisturbed, but openly and defiantly, demanding the same kinds of political and civil rights being sought by other minorities.

Marty Robinson was the representative of Leitsch and the Mattachine Society, which was co-sponsoring this "non-violent vigil to protest harassment of homosexuals." He was skinny and boyish-looking, with neatly clipped hair, sideburns down to the bottom of his ears, wearing a striped polo shirt and the even tighter blue jeans, particularly at the crotch, that would become his trademark. The fact that Robinson worked as a carpenter and wore a blue hard hat at work was a working-class badge of honor in his circles, where economic success was equated with the establishment. In truth, he was the son of a wealthy Brooklyn doctor and had flunked out of school. (When he told his parents, at age twenty, that he thought he was gay, they responded by offering to send him on a European vacation to regain his sexual bearings.)

"Gay power is here!" Robinson announced from the fountain's lip, all a-jitter and displaying the constant nervous energy that put even his friends on edge. "Gay power is no laugh. There are one million homosexuals in New York City. If we wanted to, we could boycott Bloomingdale's and that store would be closed in two weeks." (Although some in the crowd yelled "take it over," Robinson quickly regretted the remark; it played to stereotypes and distracted from his call to action.) "Let me tell you homosexuals, we've got to get organized. We've got to stand up. This is our chance." From there, the crowd marched in order through the streets, under a huge lavender banner with interlocking same-sex male and female symbols. They were singing "We Shall Overcome."

The new movement was eluding the best efforts of Dick Leitsch and Randy Wicker to harness it. In the final weeks of July, another leaflet appeared on the streets of Greenwich Village, this one with a headline which captured the new spirit and tone of an emerging gay activism. "DO YOU THINK HOMOSEXUALS ARE REVOLTING?" it asked slyly, in an off-centered, stenciled headline. "YOU BET YOUR SWEET ASS WE ARE." The leaflet went on to declare: "We're going to make a place for ourselves in the revolutionary movement." It added: "Homosexuals are coming together at last." The leaflet called for homosexuals to gather on July 31, four days after the rally at Washington Square Park, to "examine how we are oppressed and how we oppress ourselves," to fight for gay control of gay businesses, to publish a gay newspaper and to achieve other "radical ends." The meeting would be at Alternate U. on Fourteenth Street, the center for radical organizing, where Jim Fouratt and Michael Brown, who had left Leitsch's organization after Mattachine refused to support his efforts to align gay organizations with the yippies and the Black Panthers, had set up shop.

Alternate U. was in a brightly lit, second-floor industrial loft on the northern boundary of Greenwich Village. On any night there might be a class on Marxist theory or self-defense karate for women. Over the toilet paper dispenser in the women's room, someone had written the graffito "Harvard Diplomas: Take One." The place where homosexuals would be "coming together at last" was in a large meeting room at the top of a steep flight of steps, at six-thirty on a Thursday evening. Fouratt and Brown had set up six rows of folding chairs, each six across. That would prove not to be enough. A seat in the front was designated for the leader, but it quickly became apparent that this new organization would have no leader. The night was a long and discordant cascade of arguments and discussions, almost comic in its disorganization. The fifty people who showed up that night were all new faces, men and women who had never before had anything to do with the homophile movement. They were homosexuals for whom Stonewall had been a personal awakening. They were leftists who had worked against the war and radicals who had worked to overturn the government. They were social misfits by virtue of their sexuality, drawn by the provocative leaflets, for whom the organization would become a very public therapy session.

One of the few decisions the group officially made that night was to adopt the name Gay Liberation Front, which had been all but settled upon during the meetings in the back of the Mattachine headquarters, when someone had suggested finding a name with the words "Liberation Front" (from the National Liberation Front, the North Vietnamese guerrilla force). Martha Shelley suggested using the word "gay" in the name, and someone else suggested combining those words.

Before this night no other major homosexual rights group had used the word "gay" in its name; indeed, few even dared to use the word "homosexual." There was no talk among these new activists of disguising their mission with ambiguous titles—no homophile, no Mattachine, no Bilitis. In settling on "gay," the group picked a description of homosexuals that was so uncommon that Frank Kameny, the pioneering gay rights activist from Washington, D.C., routinely attached an asterisk to the word to explain that it meant homosexual whenever he included it in his writings.

In choosing "gay" the young activists explicitly rejected the word "homosexual." It was too clinical, they concluded, reducing homosexuality only to a physical act, reinforcing the notion that homosexuality was only about sex. The other notable aspect of the name was the use of the words "liberation" and "front." These activists were almost self-conscious in their attempt to link gay liberation to the other activist movements. But while the "liberation front" title was adopted, the signal that it sent—that this was a group whose concern with gay liberation was secondary to its concern about a greater social struggle—was misleading. From that very first night at Alternate U., the new radicals had been split over the question of whether the Gay Liberation Front should focus only on gay liberation, or whether it should be part of the larger political movement of the time. The Statement of Purpose, written that night by Lois Hart and Michael Brown, two of the most militant members of the group, suggested that the issue had been resolved: "We are a revolutionary group of men and women, formed with the realization that complete sexual liberation for all people cannot come about unless existing social institutions are abolished. We reject society's attempt to impose sexual roles and definitions of our nature. We are stepping outside these roles and simplistic myths. We are going to be who we are." The new Gay Liberation Front, said the statement, declared its allegiance to "all the oppressed: the Vietnamese struggle, the third world, the blacks; the workers."

Within the year that declaration would be the undoing of the Gay Liberation Front.

2

LOS ANGELES

December

Jim Kepner was a science fiction fan and had been one for as long as he had been a gay activist; he enjoyed the escape into this fantasy world of magazines, short stories and books almost as much as he enjoyed the company of other men. Once a week he would gather with science fiction fans to read and exchange notes, and afterward they would adjourn to one of the few restaurants in West Hollywood that was open late, Barney's Beanery, a chili parlor on Santa Monica Boulevard, at the eastern tip of what would one day be the city of West Hollywood. It smelled of grease, smoke and beer, and looked, even on its better days, as if it had seen better days. Its location, steps away from where a railroad had once run, in a neighborhood of cheap apartments where young actors, artists and bohemians made their homes, made it a center for West Hollywood nightlife. It also had been a magnet for homosexuals, at least until about 1953, when a sheriff's deputy stopped by to ask the owner at the time, Barney Anthony, why there were so many homosexuals congregating in his restaurant. Anthony took the hint, posting a sign that read "Fagots Stay Out," the misspelling apparently unintended. The sign, if only because of its directness, brought his restaurant far more fame than its chili ever did, including a photograph of the placard in *Life* magazine in the 1960s. Over at Barney's after the meetings, the members of the science fiction club would chatter on, but Kepner, the kind of man who liked to talk and talk and talk, would sit in silence, and when his friends would ask what was wrong, Kepner would gesture to the "Fagots Stay Out" sign.

To Kepner, and to other homosexuals who found themselves seated under the sign, the plain fact that a notice saying "Fagots Stay Out" could be on display at one of the most popular establishments in the city was just one illustration of the depth of antipathy toward homosexuals in the city where Harry Hay had founded the nation's first Mattachine Society nineteen years before. Another was the Los Angeles Police Department. In 1969 alone the Los Angeles Police Department made 3,858 arrests under the category of crime it used to prosecute homosexuals—"Sex Offenses (Except Rape or Prostitution)"—which typically referred to lewd conduct, anal copulation and oral copulation. Although the police said they were only responding to the complaints of an outraged citizenry, a study conducted several years later—the first attempt to measure the way the law was used against homosexual men in Los Angeles—found that the overwhelming majority of the arrests were made by undercover police officers on assignment, acting on their own initiative.

The statistics confirmed the anecdotal tales of Los Angeles homosexuals—almost always men, but sometimes lesbians as well—about their run-ins with police. Typical was a raid at The Little Cave, a popular gay bar on Sunset Boulevard in the Silverlake section of Los Angeles, on the festive night of Valentine's Day 1969. At the height of the evening, an officer from the Los Angeles Police Department's Rampart Division Vice Squad—dressed head to toe in black, the street cop uniform—walked through the front door and onto the stage where a band was playing, and seized the singer's microphone to make an announcement: "There are going to be some arrests. Remain silent. Don't move. Don't attempt to leave." Undercover vice officers in tight pants and sports shirts chose patrons with a tap on the shoulder and the words "You're under arrest." Seven men were tapped, lined up against the wall, handcuffed, searched and led out to waiting cars and vans. As they were leaving, one of the police officers paused, turned back around and, with a wave of his hand, instructed the band to pick up the music.

Homosexuals captured in these "conduct" sweeps made for the most difficult arrests. An arrest under Section 647(a) of the California Penal Code meant public exposure and humiliation, legal bills, sometimes jail time, and a fine. It also meant registering with the state as a sex offender. For licensed professions, such as public school teachers, a lewd conduct conviction meant the end of a career. A house burglar might just surrender, but a homosexual might flee or start punching and kicking, resistance which gave the police officers the excuse to respond even more aggressively. On New Year's Eve 1967, at a club called the Black Cat, a raid turned into a brawl between the police and patrons. One homosexual was beaten so badly his spleen was ruptured, though that did not prevent the police department from charging him with assaulting a police officer (he was acquitted). In the spring of 1969, at the Dover Hotel, a five-story brick building on South Main Street downtown, where men took off their clothes and left their doors open, a male nurse, Howard Efland, died in a struggle with vice officers who tried to arrest him. Efland was kicked and stomped as he yelled out, "Help me! My God, someone help me!" according to witnesses. It was ruled a justifiable homicide by a coroner's jury. Death was uncommon, but beatings were not, and the stories of these kinds of encounters embellished the police force's fearsome reputation. "You're goddamn right, you're going to give him a few licks if you can, after it's all done and after he's subdued," Joseph Wambaugh, the East Los Angeles vice cop turned novelist, said after he left the force.

The vice squad staked out public bathrooms at Echo Park, Lafayette Park, MacArthur Park and Pershing Square, the student unions and libraries at UCLA and USC, Sierra Hall at Los Angeles City College and the Greyhound Bus Station in Hollywood. These were known in the homosexual community as tearooms, places to go for anonymous sex. The vice cops knew this, too, and they peered from behind screens or through ceiling panels, or stood in urinals in tight pants and blue work shirts, a "cruising" ritual which was supposed to lead to sex. Other arrests were made in Griffith Park and on the deserted streets in and around Hollywood where men would drive around in circles, or park and wait. Terry Newman, a thirty-six-year-old junior high school reading teacher, slid into the passenger seat next to a man who had caught his eye on Selma Avenue one evening in West Hollywood. The man asked Newman what he "had in mind," and when Newman told him, he was surrounded and arrested. ("My God," Newman thought, "I'm going to lose my job." He was right.) A few weeks before Stonewall, police roared through a gay bathhouse, one of them yelling, "Something in here stinks. I smell faggots!" They banged on doors, looking for couples to arrest on charges of violating the anal and oral sex provisions of the penal code. One of the men locked the door to his room and curled up alone on the cot, later saying, "I knew then how Anne Frank must have felt."

The risks of hunting for sex in public places were hardly a surprise, and it was difficult to rally much public sympathy over men that even *The Los Angeles Advocate,* the tiny gay newspaper that had begun to be published in Los Angeles in 1967, snidely referred to as the "bush queens and tearoom aunties." Their behavior was condemned by the city's few openly homosexual leaders as well. "Think about your conduct," Jerry Joachim, the chairman of the gay organization PRIDE (Personal Rights in Defense and Education), wrote in an open letter to homosexuals in *The Advocate.* "We are going to ask you NOT TO CRUISE in public parks. This represents an intolerable situation to the LAPD and rightly so. PRIDE does not condone sexual activity in public places and, in fact, condemns such practices. . . . And remember, there are arrests that are justified. Our skirts are not 100% clean, and you know it." The police insisted they were simply enforcing the law. Captain Charles Crumly, head of the Hollywood vice unit, spent four hours one evening with fifteen homosexual leaders, explaining how there was no entrapment, no trumped-up charges, no harassment, no beatings. When a questioner pressed Crumly on how a vice officer distinguishes between a simple gesture of affection versus a violation of law, Crumly explained how, on first glance, a pat on the rear might seem harmless. "But when the hand lingers there over a sort of lengthy period of time, it's no longer a salutation," Crumly said, as Jim Kepner, his tie straight and his head cocked, listened from a corner. "He might reach clear up underneath and sort of not pat him on the rear but pat him on the front in reverse." *The Advocate* said that Captain Crumly's vigorous denials of activity that was so well known to Los Angeles's gay community "insults our intelligence."

"Is there harassment?" *The Advocate* editors continued. "Hell, no! With that, we have to agree. . . . Every year in Los Angeles, thousands of homosexuals are arrested and charged with lewd conduct or worse. Lawyers' fees and fines must total in the hundreds of thousands of dollars. Jobs are lost. Families are torn apart. Legitimate businessmen are put out of business. Harassment? You'd think we were talking about jay walking or parking tickets. This is persecution!" Given this environment, the fact that homosexual organizing was so feeble—in the city where Harry Hay got his start—was the source of more than a little bit of embarrassment. The editors of *The Advocate* publicly wondered why homosexual activism in San Francisco was so established while Los Angeles remained untended. Franklin Kameny, the founder of the Washington, D.C., Mattachine Society, read of a Los Angeles homosexual who told an arresting officer where he worked; the next day the man was fired. Why, Kameny demanded, was no one in Los Angeles making certain homosexuals knew they were not obligated to divulge their employer to arresting officers? "If there is any large city in the country whose homosexual community has done more than its share of crying (with good cause) and less than its share of remedial acting, it is Los Angeles," Kameny wrote *The Advocate.*

When a group of eighteen men met in a Hollywood storefront in December 1969 to form the Los Angeles Gay Liberation Front—following the example set in New York, whose activities were reported in some gay and underground newspapers at the time, inspiring a half-dozen groups of the same name to spring to life by the end of 1969—there was no question whom they would demonstrate against. The Los Angeles Police Department was too difficult a target for this inexperienced and disorganized assembly of men. But then there was Barney's Beanery. Here was a public restaurant in the part of the city with the greatest concentration of homosexuals boasting that it would not serve them. The parallels with the South, with its lunch counters posted with "no colored" signs, were obvious to the organizers of the GLF, which included more than a few people who had worked in the civil rights movement. Morris Kight, who had grown up in Comanche County in Central Texas and was now helping to organize this new GLF, shared stories of growing up in a part of the country where "No Colored" signs were standard fixtures at the local restaurant. Kight was, even by West Hollywood standards, an odd character: a fifty-year-old peace activist with sleek white hair—it had faded from a mousy brown to sheer white by his thirty-second birthday—that hung straight down to his shoulders, glasses with thick black rims around thick lenses, and a ring on each finger. He had been head of the Dow Action Committee, which demonstrated against Dow Chemical for manufacturing napalm. Kight had not joined the early homophile meetings, and had not made his homosexuality known to his leftist associates. But he was known in the city's underground homosexual community as someone to turn to for the name of a lawyer to handle a lewd conduct arrest or a doctor to discreetly treat a case of gonorrhea, or for a place to sleep. And now, in Los Angeles, he argued that this was an opportunity to appropriate the tactics that had worked so well for the civil rights movement. Why not picket Barney's Beanery? Why not walk in, sit down and just demand service?

It had taken nearly six months for the spark of Stonewall to reach Los Angeles, and when it finally did, it came not from an Angeleno but from Don Jackson, a drifter who floated from San Francisco to Bakersfield to Los Angeles, and made his living writing about gay issues for underground newspapers. Jackson had joined gay activists demonstrating in front of the *San Francisco Examiner* in 1969 to protest an article that portrayed homosexuals as "semi-males with flexible wrists and hips" who lived in "Fairyland." As a reward, he had been splattered with printer's ink dumped by two men from the top of the building, and ridiculed the next day in the *San Francisco Chronicle,* which called the demonstration a "harmless, if bizarre oddity" carried out by "willowy and long-haired" protesters who were "no match for the beefy policemen." After that, Jackson was off to Los Angeles, where he met Kight and suggested they form a gay liberation organization in southern California. Kight hesitated at first, reluctant to give up the certainty and status of the peace movement for something so risky. But Kight worked through his reservations, and the two placed a notice in the *Los Angeles Free Press* for the first meeting of the city's Gay Liberation Front. The advertisement reflected the severe threat that homosexuals faced trying to live in Los Angeles: the police department. "The oppression of gays in LA is worse than anywhere else in the Western world," Jackson wrote. "LA gays have been foundering; stunned by the reign of terror which the LAPD has brought on them. . . . A militant wave is sweeping the LA gay community. Effective leadership and organization are lacking."

The Los Angeles Gay Liberation Front was, at least at first, just as radical as the GLF in New York. It was dominated by the anti-war movement and New Left, whose younger members, as in New York, made the established homophile leaders uneasy. Even taking on Barney's Beanery struck some as extreme. "Barney has a right to say 'Fagots Stay Out,' " Don Slater, the editor of ONE, a homophile newspaper, told members of the new Gay Liberation Front. Everyone knew the restaurant didn't discriminate against homosexuals. The sign was just an "advertising gimmick," Slater said. But Barney's Beanery turned out to be exactly the kind of cause that the city's nonhomophile homosexual community could rally around: from radical members of the new GLF looking for a suitably splashy inaugural demonstration to the most moderate members of the activist community—notably, a Southern Pentecostal minister named Troy Perry, who had started a church for homosexuals the previous fall. Perry had little in common with the men who created the Gay Liberation Front, and he even supported the war in Vietnam, a position that while, perhaps, understandable for a boy raised in a religious family in the South, was completely alien in the world Perry was now moving in. "Can you see Jesus using a machine gun?" one activist demanded of Perry after he argued a pro-war position at a gay conference in San Francisco earlier in 1969. Within a few months, though, Perry had quietly changed his position on Vietnam and was comfortably working alongside the leaders of the Gay Liberation Front. Don Jackson described Perry's change of heart in a private letter to Dick Michaels, the editor of *The Advocate* in January 1970, but scrawled a request in the left-hand margin of the typewritten letter: "Please don't mention this in print. Troy has done this gracefully and quietly. I feel it would be bad public relations for both the GLF and Troy if the change is over-emphasized. It will be better to pretend that his new position is as it has always been."

Troy Perry wore his clerical collar at political demonstrations, and he was exactly the kind of figure gay activists wanted sitting at the counter of Barney's Beanery—imposing, charismatic, a striking figure at six feet two inches, with jet black hair and sideburns that jutted down to the bottom of each ear and out into his cheek. "We're not afraid anymore!" Perry had declared, a compelling figure standing in full vestment for a Sunday afternoon demonstration against the state's sodomy laws in front of the State Building in the city's deserted downtown. His audience responded with cheers and shouts of "Amen!" and he ended the rally with a prayer.

Morris Kight was at Perry's heels during these marches. He took note of how *The Advocate* blazed Perry's words—"We're not afraid anymore!"—across its front page, and made certain to call him when it came time to picket

Barney's. The demonstrations at Barney's Beanery started small in January 1970 and quickly grew, until 150 gay men and lesbians were standing on Santa Monica Boulevard. It was a circus, with men kissing men and women kissing women, and Kight chanting, "More deviation, less population!" and everyone holding hands under the occasional television light. "Gay is just as good as straight," they chanted. "Take the sign down!" When a patron leaving the restaurant informed the crowd that "I like girls, not boys," one of the lesbians retorted: "So do I, mister." At 10 p.m. one evening, six of them walked in to the counter, announced they were homosexual and asked for service. The owner, Irwin Held, bought them a round of beers.

"What does that sign mean?" Troy Perry asked Held.

"It doesn't mean anything," Held said.

"Then take it down," Perry demanded.

But Irwin Held refused. No matter what the sign said, no gay person had been denied service.

If Held had calculated that a few beers would buy him peace, he was wrong. Over the coming weeks and then months, they entered Barney's Beanery in groups of twos and threes, filling empty seats, ordering a single cup of coffee or bottle of beer and then settling in. Held tried to force them out as he watched his nightly collections plummet: He imposed price increases on the spot, presenting Perry with a $3 check for a cup of coffee. He refused to give back change and instructed his waiters to clear half-filled glasses of beer. He called the Sheriff's Office, demanding that the protesters be arrested. He even posted six similar signs across his restaurant, and printed Barney's Beanery matchbooks with the "Fagots Stay Out" slogan on the cover. Kight designated Rand Schrader, a bright, young UCLA law student who would become California's second openly gay judge a decade later, to act as the public spokesman for the demonstrators.

The Sheriff's Office soon grew weary of the calls from Held, and one evening a few officers disappeared with Held into the kitchen for a long time, until one of them came outside to the counter, where Troy Perry was sitting. What would it take to bring peace to Barney's Beanery? he asked.

"I want the sign taken down," Perry said.

The deputy returned to the kitchen and in a few moments one of Held's employees emerged and, without ceremony, tore the signs off the wall, handing them out as trophies, bringing an end to nearly three months of demonstrations.

3

NEW YORK

December

Homosexuals, it turned out, were extraordinarily hard to organize, a disturbing discovery for the experienced veterans of other political movements who joined the GLF in the months after the raid on the Stonewall. Gay men and lesbians in New York in 1969 were secretive, untrusting and scattered, and often lived at the edge of the law. Almost all the gay bars on Christopher Street prohibited the posting of leaflets, and some bartenders ejected GLF organizers for just distributing literature or talking politics to the customers. There were, until December 1, when *Gay* newspaper first began publishing stories about homosexuals, no gay periodicals in New York to tell homosexuals that a gay liberation front had been founded, to chronicle the evolving new movement or to profile its young leaders. The one newspaper the GLF organizers hoped they could count on—the *Village Voice*—displayed, in its coverage of homosexuality, a tone which ranged from sympathy to voyeurism to outright condemnation. One week after the GLF was formed, the *Voice* refused to print the word "gay" in a GLF classified advertisement seeking writing and artwork for a new gay liberation paper. The word "gay," the *Voice* executives informed GLF activists, who learned of its deletion *after* the edition was printed, was obscene and did not meet the newspaper's advertising copy standards.

There was an even more fundamental barrier to overcome. Other movements at the time organized around some shared identity—as blacks, as feminists, as opponents of the war. But the closest thing to a shared identity among homosexuals was the community of men who knew each other from the bars, bathhouses, back rooms and trucks—a group that by definition excluded women and resisted organization. How different this is, a frustrated John O'Brien thought, as he tried to get homosexuals on Christopher Street to join the Gay Liberation Front, from his work for the radical Students for a Democratic Society at Columbia University.

At the Sunday night meetings of the GLF (which began at Alternate U. and then moved fifteen blocks north to the Church of the Holy Apostles) most of the gay men and lesbians did not know each other; the only traits they were certain to share were their attraction to members of their own sex and the knowledge of society's disapproval of that behavior, a weak foundation for a movement. In addition, many of the GLF's most outspoken leaders saw gay liberation as another spoke in the revolutionary wheel, a worldview which saw discrimination against homosexuals as one more manifestation of what an early leaflet called the "root evil of our society . . . capitalism." But such abstract arguments seemed to ignore the real anguish of living as an open homosexual in the late 1960s. Bob Kohler, who came to the first GLF meetings and urged its members to rescue the young, homeless teenage boys who made their home in the spit of a park across from the Stonewall, raged at the GLF leaders when they responded to his pleading with talks of Marxist theory and class struggle. Other meetings were consumed by long arguments over whether the GLF should lend its name to a rally against the Vietnam War. The Gay Liberation Front would devote hours to debating whether to support the Black Panthers and Fidel Castro's Communist regime in Cuba, both heroes in much of the counterculture, yet both notoriously anti-homosexual.

Of all the domineering personalities in the Gay Liberation Front—responsible for setting its tone as much as its ideology—Martha Shelley and Jim Fouratt were probably the most forceful. The grave-looking lesbian from Brooklyn and the angelic, expelled monastery student from Rhode Island, who had moved through the worlds of Off-Broadway acting and 1960s radicalism and the record industry before landing at the GLF, seemed to have little in common. Still, they both were radical in their politics, products of the counterculture and contemptuous of the homophile movement. They were also both angry—belligerent, obnoxious and often disruptive. They both grew up feeling the outcast because they were homosexuals and, not incidentally, small. Martha Shelley was five feet four inches (as she put it, "five foot four on the outside; six foot five on the inside"), Fouratt barely two inches taller. Shelley and Fouratt discovered in the Gay Liberation Front, with its lack of structure and promises of equality for all, a place where they could have influence. Here, assertiveness and loudness counted more than size.

As a child, Fouratt, blond and delicate, was a natural target for the older boys at Catholic school, who would follow him with taunts of "fag" and "sissy." He was sickly, struggling with rheumatic fever and leukemia, which confined him to bed for two years. In one of those years, a regimen of cortisone shots for the leukemia ballooned his weight. Fouratt had filled his hours of free time with vivid fantasies of sexual adventures, though it was not until he was fifteen that he had a chance to act on them. Fouratt was hitchhiking the hour trip to school when he discovered he could make money, and find sexual satisfaction, with older men who offered him something else besides a ride. He went into a monastery to try to suppress his homosexual urges, but a case of crabs and the discovery by church officials of nude pictures in his bureau ended his clerical ambitions. By the time he showed up at the GLF wearing flashy and obviously expensive clothes, Jim Fouratt stood out in the room filled with men and women in jeans and T-shirts. He would drop remarks about the size of his penis and boast about his friendship with Abbie Hoffman. He ran roughshod over other less verbal GLF members and was widely disliked.

Martha Shelley was slightly overweight, wore thick glasses with thick lenses and had plain features on a round face which seldom showed a smile. She noticed she was different when she was in elementary school; her classmates would be drawing pictures of women in bridal gowns while she sketched octopuses or Martians. When she determined that she was a lesbian—after making love with a married woman she met at a judo class, as the woman's husband slept in the next room—her first frightened thought was that the whole world would guess her secret. After Stonewall, at those early meetings of the Gay Liberation Front, she suddenly felt a weight lifted off her tiny shoulders. "There was this incredible sensation of liberation that I don't have to take it anymore, I don't have to try to get your approval anymore," she said later. Shelley felt overwhelmed by anger. When anyone disagreed with her, she would yell louder and longer. People around her—particularly the men—found her fearsome. But Shelley kept yelling, even as she realized that her rage was only helping to poison the Sunday night GLF meetings.

If only because of their focus and intensity, Shelley and Fouratt helped set the tone for an organization where most of the members were coping with the personal turmoil that came, almost overnight, with trying to live as open homosexuals. And most gay people had not thought of their homosexuality as part of a larger political struggle before, which is what they were being asked to do now. These were the ingredients for an ideological and emotional carnival. On better days, GLF meetings were endless debates over, say, whether class struggle contributed to the oppression of homosexuals. But there were also evenings when Fouratt showed up in a dress, sometimes over leather pants, to demonstrate his empathy with the oppression of women. ("Wearing a dress is a revolutionary act," he declared.) Or the night Shelley grew so enraged at Bob Kohler for making what she saw as a sexist put-down of her ("I think you're getting hysterical," Kohler had said) that she challenged him to go out into an alley to slug it out. He declined.

Since the founders of the GLF knew they didn't want to be like the Daughters of Bilitis or the Mattachine Society, they strove to be as free-form as possible, or "amorphous," in the words of Lois Hart, another of its most influential early members. There would be a different leader every meeting, members could talk as long as they wanted to on any subject, at least until someone with a louder voice had something to say. In truth, they devoted so much time to practicing nonorganization that they failed to set any goals for themselves. The meetings were grim, inevitably dominated by its most verbal and radical members. Since there were no elected leaders, policy was set by whoever showed up, which meant policy pronouncements barely lasted beyond a meeting or two. The first time Nikos Diaman came to a GLF meeting, the evening began and ended with a debate over whether a heterosexual reporter from the *Village Voice* should be allowed to attend. Three weeks later the evening started and ended with the same discussion.

After a few of the mass Sunday meetings, Lois Hart proposed that GLF split into smaller cells of from five to a dozen people, devoted to specific interests, each with complete autonomy and policy-making authority. Hart, a former nun, was a small, tough-looking woman with a soft, crystalline voice; her power, which was considerable, grew from her obvious intelligence, a charisma born of her own spiritual explorations and a unique ability to silence a room full of activists. Her notion of creating smaller cells resonated with this anti-establishment group. Before long, it seemed as if every group of five people was forming a cell—from Trotskyites to transvestites. Even some of the most vocal opponents to cells—including John O'Brien and John Lauritsen, an aloof Harvard graduate who could barely contain his contempt for many lower-class members in the GLF—formed *their* own cell, Red Butterfly, a Marxist discussion group devoted, as Lauritsen put it, to "a highly intellectual form of socialism."

Drawing on the work of the feminist movement, Hart also began organizing consciousness-raising sessions, where groups of gay men and lesbians would share stories of the difficulties of being homosexual. The practice was called giving testimony; the sessions were liberating for some, but searing and disconcerting for others. Anyone who seemed reclusive would be attacked: "Speak from your gut!" As Martha Shelley later observed, "It is not a technique for dilettantes." The sessions came to dominate the Gay Liberation Front. But rather than helping to bring calm or create a sense of purpose for the organization, they siphoned time and energy out of the GLF. In this unsettled atmosphere, the GLF could only move sure-footedly in areas where it had a clear grievance or mission. Creating a newspaper was the first priority—*Gay* was largely controlled by members of the Mattachine Society—as a vehicle to communicate with one another and the public. Within a week of its first meeting, the group organized *Come Out!,* a tabloid which lasted eight editions. (Significantly, it had "no single editor or publisher" and was instead administered "collectively by its staff of gay people.") A second task became clear as the men and women shared stories of commercial exploitation in gay bars. The GLF had attempted to pressure bar owners into dropping rules against posting literature and same-sex touching. Its members would march from the Sunday night meetings to Christopher Street, flooding into a bar and announcing their presence with a wad of literature, a display of hand-holding and dancing or kissing. But even that—it was called "liberating the bars"— dealt only with symptoms. The seedy atmosphere of gay bars in New York reinforced the most depressing aspects of homosexual life. Each time they opened their doors for business, they effectively rebutted the contention that homosexuality was not something to be ashamed of.

The Gay Liberation Front decided to sponsor its own dances, at Alternate U. The responsibility for organizing them fell to Bob Kohler and Jerry Hoose. They were a strange-looking pair of friends—Kohler, forty-three, a good-looking former theatrical agent; Hoose, twenty years his junior, short, skinny and plain, who lived with his parents in Queens and prowled the trucks parked along the streets of Greenwich Village for sex. They scraped up the money to purchase enough six-packs of beer to fill a few garbage cans. Hoose persuaded a friend who rented a sound system for bar mitzvahs in Brooklyn to install a sound and light system. They handed out literature on the streets, and Hoose talked up the dances to his friends at the trucks. That night they mopped the floor, turned down the lights (the dimmer the lights, the better Alternate U. looked) and opened for business. Hoose was particularly nervous. But it was hardly two hours after they opened the door when Alternate U. became so crowded it seemed impossible to move from the top of the stairway to the window overlooking Sixth Avenue. Hoose, dazed and grinning, took in a sight he had never seen before: dancing, swaying, homosexual men and women. It was, he thought, a triumph. Indeed, the event turned out to be liberating in ways no one had considered before. It was an act of defiance, an attempt by homosexuals to seize a part of their culture from the underworld. But more than that, it provided the people who attended the dances—they instantly became a regular event, drawing larger crowds each Saturday night—a new view of the possibilities of their lives. After years of furtiveness, dancing in clubs staffed by heterosexuals who mocked their clientele, the men and women at Alternate U. held hands, danced and embraced.

Men (and some women) took off their shirts. "Who wants to go to a bar when you can get 600 dancing partners, a light show and a free coat check all for a contribution of $1.50, with drinks only a quarter?" asked *Come Out!* in a report on the dances. "Your presence," the Gay Liberation Front told its members in a newsletter after the dance, was "proof that gay people will meet outside the tired Mafioso bars in a common effort to improve their own community."

The third area where the GLF found consensus was at the doorstep of the *Village Voice*. Homosexuals had long been easy targets for ridicule in the mainstream newspapers, but gay activists found the *Voice*'s coverage particularly galling. There was little difference, Michael Brown said, between the *Voice* and the jaunty anti-homosexuality of the *Daily News*. In early September the GLF had submitted a second ad using the word "gay" to the *Voice*, this time for a September 5 dance, called the Gay Community Dance. This time, the *Voice* informed the GLF *before* publication that it was changing the ad to omit the word "gay," asserting that it would allow only the word "homophile" to appear. And at 9 a.m. on September 12, 1969, the GLF threw up the first gay picket line of the post-Stonewall era: on the sidewalk on Christopher Street in front of the *Voice*. Staged in daylight, three doors up from the Stonewall, it offered a test of how brazen the members of the new organization really were. It was one thing to make speeches in the comfort of Alternate U. It was another to walk Sheridan Square in midday, holding a picket sign that proclaimed one's sexuality. But almost a hundred people turned up at the *Voice*'s offices, surprising even the organizers. By 4:30 p.m., the sidewalks were loud and crowded as passersby, amused that the city's alternative newspaper was being picketed for bias, shouted encouragement. By the time Howard Smith, the *Voice* writer whose coverage struck some of the demonstrators as particularly noxious, announced that the paper's management would meet with three representatives from the GLF, concession seemed a foregone conclusion. At first, the *Voice* officials scolded the demonstrators for even protesting this of all newspapers. ("Sooo liberal we are," *Come Out!* sarcastically remarked later.) But the *Voice*'s publisher, Edwin Fancher, quickly bowed to most of the demands, agreeing to allow use of the words "gay" and "homosexual" in classified ads. The protesters learned of their success when one of the GLF members meeting upstairs leaned out a window and flashed a V sign to the crowd below.

But as the winter approached, the GLF meetings grew more bizarre and more paralyzed. One evening a drag queen urged the GLF to execute a puppy in front of St. Patrick's Cathedral to demonstrate the group's distress with the church's position on homosexuality. The idea was argued down. People would stand up and offer searingly personal tales about their lives, breaking down into tears, attacking other people in the room. When one person announced that the GLF should devote its session to "investigating why we are gay," Bob Kohler cut him off: "What is this fucking bullshit?" he cried. Many of the people at the GLF meetings were high on drugs, marijuana or speed usually, and a drug dealer could reliably be found during GLF meetings standing by the church bathroom. John O'Brien would stand in the back of the room, arms folded, his face frozen in what seemed to be a half-grin as he watched the performances. This was genuine psychotic behavior, O'Brien thought, and with each episode the prospect of the GLF's becoming a potent political force in New York City seemed increasingly remote. A group of pioneer activists, including Barbara Gittings, Kay Tobin and Frank Kameny, all of whom had been active through the 1960s, visited a GLF meeting one night to examine the vanguard of post-Stonewall organizing. Fouratt demanded to know what right they had to even be there. "What are your credentials?" Fouratt said. Gittings was flustered and embarrassed: Who were these people to challenge *her* credentials? Gittings found herself thinking about Fouratt's boots: They were expensive, she thought, fine patchwork leather boots, clothes that she, a librarian, could never have afforded. "I'm gay," Gittings said finally. "That's why I'm here."

Three of the original GLF members were particularly distraught at the turn of events, convinced that the GLF was talking itself into impotence. They were Marty Robinson, who had led the post-Stonewall demonstration at Washington Square Park; Jim Owles, a waifish Wall Street clerk, and Arthur Evans, a Columbia graduate student studying philosophy. Owles and Robinson had met at the first GLF meeting and had been drawn to each other, at first both for ideological and sexual reasons. They had a quick affair, but found their more enduring connection was their agreement that gay liberation should focus on gay liberation. Owles's disenchantment with the GLF grew along with the increasing influence of the consciousness-raising groups, which he viewed as a device by which the more powerful, more emotionally stable people in the group manipulated the emotionally vulnerable. Robinson was frustrated by his unsuccessful efforts to nudge the GLF into organizing *Voice*-like protests at public appearances by New York City mayoral candidates that might force them to address the gay rights issue. The GLF was crumbling, Robinson, Owles and Evans argued, because its foundation—its broad interest in a catalogue of causes—was cracked.

At the end of 1969, Jim Fouratt and Martha Shelley, representing the GLF, drove to a conference of old-line homophiles in Philadelphia. They returned, boasting of their success at disrupting this fading generation of homosexual activists. Though they had not quite succeeded in destroying the stodgy Eastern Regional Conference of Homophile Organizations (ERCHO), as the organization was known, which had been Fouratt's original intention, the members of the Gay Liberation Front seized control of the agenda from the moment the gavel came down. They were younger, louder and ruder than the older conference members, who watched, flustered and resentful, as their once-orderly annual gathering was strangled by arguments over the Vietnam War, abortion and even the right to take recreational drugs. Jim Fouratt once more shouted the Mattachine Society's Madolin Cervantes right off the stage, and when she referred to Fouratt and his followers as "naughty children," he demanded to know what a heterosexual woman was doing at a homosexual conference. By the end, the Mattachine leaders had taken to calling Fouratt "Vinegar" and "Goldilocks." The New York Mattachine delegation, in a gloomy report on "two long, exhausting days with almost nothing accomplished," said of the meeting: "Like all the radical agitators operating these days, they had laid their plans carefully and took the other organizations by surprise." Fouratt, it said without using his name, launched "vicious attacks of personal abuse" against other delegates and made himself "generally obnoxious."

A few weeks after Fouratt and Shelley returned to the chaos that was the Gay Liberation Front, a dispirited Jim Owles went to Arthur Evans's apartment to talk about their unhappiness with the GLF, and to talk over an idea they had been kicking around: Why not split off, and start a new organization, devoted only to the business of gay liberation? Within ten days, as Robinson and Owles shared an early-morning van ride down to Washington, D.C., for the Vietnam Moratorium March in November 1969, their decision to create a new group was all but final. The opportunity for a final break came when John O'Brien proposed turning over $500 in GLF dance revenues to the defense fund for the Black Panther 21. To Owles and Robinson, this was the last place a gay group should spend its money.

It was a bruising debate. Fouratt said Owles and Robinson were elitists, unconcerned about classism or the problems of women and transvestites. All they wanted, Fouratt said of Robinson and Owles, was gay power—or more precisely, white, male gay power. The GLF voted to give the money to the Panthers. "I am so frustrated," Owles said, barely audible, in what would be his farewell speech to the Gay Liberation Front. "I can't continue like this. I'm going to have to leave the organization." He and Marty Robinson walked out of the room.

4

CLIMBING THE SYSTEM

January 1970, New York

Arthur Evans had read about Stonewall in the *Village Voice*, or really, he had read right over it; the story of homosexuals rebelling at a bar was interesting, he thought, but nowhere nearly as compelling as the struggle against the Vietnam War. That the story stirred little interest in him said nothing about his sexual interests: it was his search for men that had drawn Evans to New York in 1963 after attending Brown University for three years, following the trail laid out in a *Life* magazine story that told of a colony of homosexuals in Greenwich Village. As an eleven-year-old boy in York, a factory town in south-central Pennsylvania, Evans had despondently concluded—when puberty came upon him in 1953, announcing itself with an overwhelming and sudden infatuation with his schoolmates—that he was alone in the world. Once in New York, Evans had made a mission of having sexual relations with a man, and soon enough, when eating dinner at the counter at Mama's Chicken Rib, Evans felt the touch of another leg against his. Evans quickly finished his supper and went home with the plain-looking man seated at the next stool—no matter that he felt barely a flicker of affection for him. Evans shared none of this with his companion the next morning, never mentioning he was a virgin, or the unexpected emotional completeness he felt after finally attempting what he had only fantasized about for a decade.

That the story about Stonewall barely registered on Evans said nothing as well about his political interests. They were as serious as he was, going back at least to the day in 1962 when his parents picked up the York morning newspaper and saw their son's picture on page one, at a civil rights march, a beacon of white in a photo of mostly black demonstrators in front of the York County Courthouse. At Brown University, he and his Jewish roommate had, upon learning that this school had compulsory prayer every Sunday, organized a protest at the chapel. They asked people to rise in silent protest during the prayer service, a demonstration so daring that it attracted national news coverage, including a wire story on the front page of Evans's hometown newspaper. Evans had been sent to college on a four-year scholarship to study chemistry by the Glatfelter Paper Company of Spring Grove, Pennsylvania, and its owner, a devout Christian, tried to cancel Evans's scholarship upon reading of this chapel protest. Evans turned for help to the Freethinkers Society of America, which threatened legal action, and the paper company backed off.

The reason Arthur Evans hadn't paid much attention to the Stonewall story in the *Village Voice* was that, although he considered himself a homosexual and a radical, he had always thought of those two traits as separate compartments of his life. The link had not been drawn until two months after the bar raid, when he and his lover of five years, Arthur Bell, a public relations director for Random House ten years his elder, were walking down Christopher Street, and a long-haired youth handed them a leaflet announcing a Gay Liberation Front meeting at St. John's Church. Bell and Evans had stopped by a few Mattachine Society meetings and given up on what then passed for gay liberation; it was like Sunday school, Evans thought, with Dick Leitsch chatting away to men in ties and white shirts. Now, they wandered over to the church and encountered a Village street character named Acid John sitting on the steps. Evans asked him who was inside. "It's a bunch of stoned-out faggots," Acid John said.

Evans was restless and curious, uncommonly intelligent—he was pursuing a doctorate in Greek philosophy at Columbia University—and took that as an invitation to walk inside. He was startled by what he saw at his first GLF meeting. Here were people debating the war in Vietnam, the struggle for civil rights, the women's movement and the "fight against imperialism." And they were all homosexuals. He had never seen anything like this. Until now, he had looked at other homosexuals as people to socialize with, men to have sex with. His own homosexuality had helped shape his radical views; he would say that he rejected a society which had rejected him because of his sexual desires. But he never considered that there might be a homosexual struggle per se, or that gay people could be a part of "the paradigm of resistance," as he put it in a characteristic turn of phrase which borrowed both from the street and the university. Evans attached himself to the periphery of the GLF, joining a cell called the Radical Study Group which read Marx and Engels and discussed the class implications of the oppression of homosexuals. Evans found these sessions fascinating, but before long, he also found himself agreeing when two new friends, Jim Owles and Marty Robinson, complained that time and spirit were being wasted at these dreary meetings of the Gay Liberation Front.

The three of them—Owles, Robinson and Evans—agreed that it was time, as Evans kept saying, to "hit the streets," though they arrived at that conclusion for different reasons. Owles and Robinson argued that the talk of revolution at GLF meetings missed the point; the correct response to gay oppression was to aim directly at the government—"hitting the system below the belt, rather than trying to cut the rug out from under [it] completely," as Marty Robinson put it. Owles described himself as "just an old Eugene McCarthy liberal" and he believed that homosexuals should present themselves to politicians as another oppressed class of citizens, much like blacks or women. By contrast, Evans considered himself a revolutionary and enjoyed the discussions among the radicals at the GLF. But he saw that revolutionary talk as a parlor exercise, stimulating to him, perhaps, but meaningless to the vast majority of gay people they were trying to reach. He thought of his days as an isolated teenager in York, feeling hopeless and thinking about suicide. Hadn't he convinced himself, living two hundred miles from New York City, that he was the only homosexual in the world? "They don't give a damn about politics," Evans would say of other homosexuals, talking at a breakneck clip, hands and red beard flapping, barely pausing for a breath. The way to really make people understand their oppression was to illustrate to homosexuals just how low their standing was, to appreciate the extent of anti-gay prejudice. Evans decided that an organization limited its appeal each time it took a position on another issue, driving away potential members. Arthur Evans might agree with friends in the GLF that society was "rotten to the core" and ready for revolution, but it made no sense to construct a gay liberation group on a notion that was so obviously alien to most of the men he saw every day on Christopher Street. Evans, Owles and Robinson agreed that the time had come to create an organization whose sole mission was attending to gay rights.

The Gay Activists Alliance that came out of those discussions was formally born on a Sunday afternoon four days before Christmas 1969, created by about twenty people, almost all men, sitting around on the floor of Arthur Bell's Upper East Side apartment. It would be run according to Robert's Rules of Order, with decisions made by majority rule. "Everybody has his or her say—not merely the loudest or most charismatic member," the group explained in a founding memo, the comparison with the GLF obvious if unstated. There would be fees, annual elections to choose five officials and membership requirements (attendance at a minimum of three meetings every six months). Owles would be the first president. The Gay Activists Alliance would even have a written constitution, with grand sweeping language, deliberately, almost presumptuously, evocative of the Bill of Rights. "We as liberated homosexual activists," its preamble began, "demand the freedom for expression of our dignity and value as human beings." With this statement, its founders meant to directly challenge society's accepted judgment of homosexuality as a mental illness or sin and argue that there could be an actual gay identity. The constitution was a rejection of both the assimilation strategy of the Mattachine Society and the view of the Gay Liberation Front that the homosexual struggle was a small part of a larger movement.

"Before the public conscience we demand an immediate end to all oppression of homosexuals and the immediate unconditional recognition of these basic rights." This included a "right to our feelings," perhaps the first declaration of a right "to feel attracted to the beauty of members of our own sex and to embrace those feelings as truly our own, free from any question or challenge whatsoever by any other person, institution or moral authority." And finally, the constitution addressed the central concerns that had led Owles, Robinson and Evans to this point: The new organization would be "completely and solely dedicated" to the fight for gay rights. The Gay Activists Alliance would be less ideological than Arthur Evans and others might have liked; it might, with its rules and limits, discourage debate and intellectual exploration. But that was a small price for the creation of a single-minded gay liberation force in New York City.

April 1970, New York

Bob Kohler could not believe what he was hearing. A gay rights bill? Why in the world, he asked Jerry Hoose, his colleague at the Gay Liberation Front, do we need a gay rights bill? But here it was, the winter of 1970, and the new Gay Activists Alliance was on Christopher Street, collecting signatures on petitions demanding that Councilwoman Carol Greitzer introduce a bill prohibiting discrimination against gays in employment in New York City. Kohler had been wary of the Gay Activists Alliance from the start. He noticed how few transvestites and women went to the GAA meetings; this could have been a Knights of Columbus, except the attendees happened to be gay. Kohler certainly wasn't happy when Owles showed up trying to recruit GLF members for the new organization, or about the empty chairs at GLF meetings that attested to the appeal of this new organization.

The gay rights bill that seemed so outlandish to Bob Kohler was, to Marty Robinson, Jim Owles and Arthur Evans, the perfect foundation upon which to construct a new political organization. It defined what the Gay Activists Alliance was about: winning equal treatment for homosexuals. It signaled that this new organization wanted to play within the system. More than anything, though, the founders of the GAA settled on a gay employment bill as the group's first mission because it didn't have a prayer of passing. It was not a goal but a cause around which to organize movement, with protests, petition-gathering and, hopefully, publicity. Marty Robinson thought it would nudge homosexuals out into the public and politicize them in a way that the GLF consciousness-raising groups never could. And he had some dramatic new ideas about how he might accomplish this.

On a brilliant Sunday morning that April, as a band played "The Star-Spangled Banner," Mayor John V. Lindsay of New York stepped briskly to the lectern at the front of the Metropolitan Museum of Art. The occasion was the hundredth anniversary of the founding of New York's grandest museum. Lindsay would shake the hands of the first hundred people on line—and among the people rising early that morning to make sure they were at the front of that line was Marty Robinson. Even that early, Robinson was becoming known for his dramatic confrontations of politicians, designed to provoke a response from his target, and perhaps even some attention in the local newspapers. He called them zaps, a phrase that would outlast both Robinson and the GAA by at least a generation. "I've never heard a homosexual stand up and talk that way to straight people before," said Tom Doerr, who would become Robinson's lover. "It really took my breath away." Robinson was brash, almost rude, in his dealings with what he saw as the enemy. His ideas, when it came to political tactics, were the dominant influence on the Gay Activists Alliance in its critical formative months. One of Robinson's seminal beliefs, which he stated every Thursday night at GAA meetings, was that homosexuals could only make progress by going after their presumed natural supporters—liberal politicians. He called it "climbing up the liberals." Liberals, Robinson argued, were vulnerable because although they shared the personal discomfort with homosexuality that was common to most politicians, they were also products of a political culture which urged tolerance for minorities, homosexuals presumably among them. Robinson contended that these kinds of politicians, torn between their personal feelings and their political philosophy, were uniquely vulnerable to pressure—the weak link in the fence.

There were, Robinson believed, few politicians more suited for "climbing" than Mayor Lindsay. The mayor had negotiated a quiet peace with the earlier generation of homosexual leaders, awarding the Mattachine Society's Dick Leitsch one of his most significant accomplishments, by issuing an executive order instructing his police department to stop entrapping them at public parks and toilets, and requiring solicitation arrests to be based on a complaint of a private citizen. Lindsay's support in the gay community, certainly among the old-timers, had been strong if discreet, as Leitsch explained in a personal letter he sent to Lindsay in June 1969: "Most gay bars have closed each night with the cry, 'Good night—and remember to vote for Lindsay!' " But many of the new activists, like Robinson, rejected this charitable view of Lindsay. They suspected he had ordered, or at least countenanced, the Stonewall raid in order to help his own reelection campaign. (Lindsay would later say he had no prior knowledge of it.) And the uprising at the Stonewall had not discouraged the police from raiding an illegal, after-hours, dingy basement gay bar called the Snake Pit, on West Tenth Street just off Seventh Avenue, and arresting 167 patrons. One of the patrons was a twenty-three-year-old Argentine man named Diego Vinales, who feared his arrest would force his deportation. He tried to escape custody, jumped out an open window at the police precinct and fell two stories onto a metal-picket fence. The *Daily News* ran a front-page picture of Vinales with six 14-inch iron prongs pierced through his body. Firemen used a blowtorch to sever the fence before taking Vinales, still impaled to the disconnected fence, to St. Vincent's Hospital. He survived, but the episode sent a shudder through homosexuals who saw the picture—a reminder that police interest in gay establishments, while certainly diminished since Stonewall, was still very much alive. The Gay Activists Alliance responded with a leaflet that declared: "Any way you look at it, that boy was PUSHED!! We are all being pushed!" Attendance at GAA meetings surged.

The Snake Pit raid was staged a month before Marty Robinson, wearing a blue baseball jacket, joined the line to shake Lindsay's hand at the Metropolitan Museum. As Evans watched from the sideline, Robinson skipped out of the line, walked up the steps and presented himself to the microphone at Lindsay's side. "Mr. Mayor, I'm a member of Gay Activists Alliance and I want to know when you intend to speak out on homosexual rights. . . ," he began. Robinson later complained that he never got to mention "fair employment legislation for gays in New York City" and vowed to never again waste time on introductions. Still, the police were so caught off guard by Robinson's sheer daring that it took a good ten seconds before they responded, dragging him back down the steps.

This was Lindsay's introduction to what turned into two years of skirmishes with this new breed of gay activists. One week after the Metropolitan Museum skirmish, Lindsay was confronted again as he tried to tape "With Mayor Lindsay," his Sunday evening television show, hosted by Arthur Godfrey, commemorating Earth Day. The GAA had infiltrated the hundred-person studio audience, which became apparent once the taping began. Lindsay and Godfrey were discussing the merits of one-way nonreturnable bottles, and Owles jumped up with a shout: "What about a one-way, nonreturnable mayor?" When Lindsay observed, "If you are stuck in a traffic jam, it's illegal to blow your horn," GAA member Philip Raia loudly commented: "It's illegal to blow anything!" Kay Tobin, the old-line activist who had helped to organize GAA after her difficult experience with Jim Fouratt and the GLF, added: "What good is environmental freedom if we don't have personal freedom?" It took twenty minutes before the mayor acknowledged the disruption. "My counsel, Michael Dontzin, will meet with those who want to see him outside." It was the start of negotiations that would lead a year later to Lindsay quietly endorsing legislation barring on-the-job discrimination against homosexuals.

Lindsay was only the most prominent target of the "climbing up the liberals" strategy. Jim Owles went to city hall with a bundle of petitions containing six thousand signatures urging passage of a gay rights bill—the results of the campaign that had so bewildered Kohler—and tried to deliver them to Carol Greitzer, the Greenwich Village councilwoman. She refused them. Greitzer was "icy cold," Owles reported back to his GAA colleagues: "She gave me the impression she was taking bad medicine." When Greitzer's Village Independent Democrats club gathered for a meeting at its second-floor headquarters overlooking Sheridan Square, three dozen members of the GAA were standing shoulder to shoulder against the walls. "Listen, Carol, baby, you're anti-homosexual, anti-homosexual!" Marty Robinson shouted as she walked through the door. Before Greitzer, flustered before an audience of her supporters, had a chance to respond, Arthur Evans bellowed: "If she doesn't relate to the homosexual cause, the Village Independent Democrats don't relate, and we are prepared to sit in." Sylvia Rivera, an imposing and loud six-foot drag queen who had been at the Stonewall riot, was yelling and shaking a fist as Robinson moved in for the final confrontation.

"Will you co-sponsor a bill?" Robinson demanded.

"Yes," Greitzer muttered.

"Do you accept the petitions?" Robinson said.

"Yes," Greitzer responded, reaching out a hand. It appeared to Robinson that she had been embarrassed into capitulation.

The Gay Activists Alliance displayed a flair and sophistication that had never before been seen in gay liberation. Like the Gay Liberation Front, this new organization had the energy of youth, and the street organizing experience of the radicals drawn from other political struggles. But it was also attracting gay people who had never before gone public. The more daring activists who had sprung forward in the months after Stonewall were joined by professional, middle-class homosexuals, people who understood government, business and the media, and who had connections throughout the establishment world. They found the Gay Activists Alliance as ideologically nonthreatening as its founders had hoped.

Before long, the GAA was manipulating the news as handily as any public relations firm, with behind-the-scenes guidance from people like Ronald Gold, a reporter for *Variety*, and Ethan Geto, a still-closeted press adviser to the Bronx borough president, Robert Abrams. Gold was razor-sharp, perceptive and tenacious, with a piercing nasal voice and a tendency to speak in sentences that tumbled out in bursts of mumbled words. Geto, so tall he had to duck his head coming into doorways, would often stand at the back of the GAA meetings, in a suit and tie, looking awkward and out of place, before going home to his wife. Never schedule a protest on a Friday, Geto and Gold would say—it had little chance of being noted in New York's tight Saturday newspapers. Demonstrations would have to be daring and inventive to stand out in this city, they said. So instead of merely staging a sit-in at the office of a New York City clerk who had spoken out against same-sex marriages, the GAA produced a mock gay wedding ceremony in his office, complete with invitations and a cake topped with groom-groom and bride-bride couples.

In a few cases, Gold alerted reporters in advance of upcoming protests, and even invited TV crews along to film the zaps as they happened—for publicity but also to guard against police abuse (the GAA eventually purchased its own video equipment to tape demonstrations). Ethan Geto was a behind-the-scenes director of the effort to lobby government and newspapers on behalf of the gay rights bill, working with his GAA colleagues to approach newspaper columnists, television news directors and editors. The very first New York public official to testify in favor of the gay rights bill was his boss, Bob Abrams. Geto urged Abrams to appear even as other advisers warned that supporting the bill would be politically ruinous.

The Gay Activists Alliance was able to infiltrate a Lindsay fundraiser at Radio City Music Hall after Ronald Gold used his *Variety* credentials to obtain tickets from the head of the projectionists' union. Another group of GAA members posing as journalism students touring city hall (Gold was their professor) made their way to the front of the mayor's office with a map Ethan Geto sketched for them. At Geto's instruction, one of them stood over a security button, obstructing the city hall guards as they tried to trigger the alarm when the disruption began. The GAA demonstrators latched themselves to the railing by the guards' desk with handcuffs borrowed from two of the group's leather enthusiasts.

The organization became so efficient—and so large—that its members created, straight-faced, a Committee on Committees, whose function was to act as a traffic cop, coordinating the actions of a roster that at times reached close to twenty. The spirit showed as well in the GAA's adoption of a logo, which was affixed to its press releases, newsletter, literature, T-shirts and buttons. Tom Doerr, a blond graphics designer, came up with the idea of the Lambda, the eleventh letter in the Greek lowercase alphabet, after rejecting the head of a fighting cock or an eagle out of concern that it would alienate women. The Lambda became the decade's most familiar symbol for gay liberation (it would be eclipsed by an upside-down pink triangle by the end of the 1970s). One GAA leaflet reported that the Lambda was chosen because it "symbolizes a complete exchange of energy—that moment or span of time witness to absolute activity" in chemistry and physics, a bit of GAA lore that was entirely fanciful. Doerr chose the Lambda, with its sleek downward sloping line leading to a front foot kicking upwards because he thought it was pretty. One "graphics queen's decision," as Arthur Evans later put it, gained political legitimacy. (Not that the selection was made lightly: It set off tense debate at a GAA meeting. Evans argued against it, saying, "it's too bland." Arthur Bell, with a tongue as sharp as his pen, snapped to his onetime lover: "What do you want—a hatchet in the heart?")

May 1970, Minneapolis-St. Paul

For all the excitement in New York that spring, it was a midwest university town that produced the first national media celebrities of the gay rights movement. They were Jack Baker, the leader of the gay student group, FREE (Fight Repression of Erotic Expression) and his lover, Mike McConnell, of Minneapolis. On May 18, 1970, after careful planning—and no real consultation with the other members of the group—Baker and McConnell put on jackets and ties and held a press conference to tell the Minneapolis press that they were going to get married. And then, with local reporters and cameras on hand to record the event, they walked hand in hand into the clerk of court's office in Minneapolis to apply for the marriage license. Baker, the law student, knew the state law did not specify that the two people marrying had to be of the opposite sex. He and McConnell knew they would probably be turned down for the marriage license. And they knew it could jeopardize McConnell's job—McConnell was about to begin work as head cataloguer for the University of Minnesota library branch in St. Paul, at a salary of $11,000 a year. But they had been planning this all spring: they knew they could sue and they knew that all of this was bound to make news.

It did. Before their walk to the clerk of court's office, McConnell, who came from Kansas, went to see the man who had hired him, the director of the university library, and told him that he was in town so that he and Jack Baker could apply for a marriage license. He was going back to Kansas, but he would return to begin work in July. "Well, thank you for telling me," the director said with a little smile. Two days later the clerk took their application and said he would have to get an opinion from the county attorney. The county attorney refused to grant the license on the grounds that it would "result in an undermining and destruction of the entire legal concept of our family structure in all areas of law," and the board of regents of the University of Minnesota voted to withdraw McConnell's job offer. With the help of the Minnesota Civil Liberties Union, Baker and McConnell sued for the marriage license and the librarian job. "It was very carefully thought out, and very, very carefully planned," McConnell said years later. "We didn't apply for a marriage license because we thought it would be fun to do. We did it because we thought it would have a profound impact on this culture. The most sacred institution in our country is marriage."

Baker and McConnell's campaign for the right to marry was a long way from the concerns of the founders of FREE, whose name and manifesto were about the freedom to be sexual, and whose stated goal was to overturn the sodomy laws which made gay people into criminals. For those who were coming to FREE's meetings, the freedom to dance, date, fall in love and have sex were the paramount goals. Getting married was the furthest thing from their minds. But the drama of Baker and McConnell's demand was irresistible, as was the legal issue the regents created when they withdrew their job offer. In private, the regents worried that allowing McConnell to work at the library would cost the University of Minnesota public funding and support. Regent John A. Yngve testified in federal court in Minneapolis that it would be "a terrible thing" for the university to hire McConnell because he "had publicly announced his intention to violate the law." But within a few months, in federal district court in Minneapolis, U.S. District Judge Philip Neville, dismissed that argument out of hand. "A homosexual is a human being," he wrote. Michael McConnell could not be refused a job at the University of Minnesota solely because he was homosexual. In order for the university "to reject an applicant for public employment, it must be shown that there is an observable and reasonable relationship between efficiency in the job and homosexuality." The board of regents won a stay of the judge's order while its lawyers appealed. McConnell worked part-time at various jobs. He and Jack Baker, the law student, qualified for food stamps. Their lawsuits would frame the gay rights movement in Minneapolis for the next two years.

May 1970, Los Angeles

In the spring of 1970, with the "Fagots Stay Out" battle won and the Gay Liberation Front of Los Angeles in its fifth month of existence, Morris Kight turned up at Troy Perry's parsonage, a house the Metropolitan Community Church rented on North Virgil Avenue for meetings and choir practice and where Perry lived with his mother and his boyfriend. Perry was now holding Sunday services at the 385-seat Encore Theater in Hollywood, large

enough for its 348-member congregation, quite a change since Perry first offered services for twelve people in his living room fourteen months before. In
the months since the demonstrations at Barney's Beanery, Perry and Kight
had forged an unusual alliance. Perry had never met anyone quite like Morris
Kight before, and theirs was surely the oddest collaboration between gay leaders of the early 1970s. Kight and Perry—whom Kight called "Brother
Troy"—shared a political agenda and appreciation for publicity. Perry's attractive public manner softened Kight's coarse edges—Kight appreciated
Perry's appeal and perhaps coveted it—while Kight's tenacity, grasp of political organizing and knowledge of Los Angeles gave the minister the political
expertise he lacked.

Kight was buzzing with a new project on the spring day when he turned
up at Perry's parsonage. The one-year anniversary of the riots in New York was
approaching, and Kight saw an opportunity. "We're going to celebrate the
Stonewall uprising." There would be a parade of homosexuals through Hollywood, with floats and banners and a street fair. In order to stage the march,
the organizers needed a parade permit, and for this they had to go before the
Police Commission, whose members included Chief Edward Davis, the per-
sonification of his department's animus toward homosexuals, whom he had
publicly described as "fruit," and "fairies" and as "lepers." Perry and Kight
made two tactical decisions at the outset. The first was that Troy Perry, in clerical collar, would be the one to make the case. The second was that Perry
would attempt to gloss over exactly what this parade was about. The organization would be called Christopher Street West, as "ambiguous as we could
be," even if it meant giving New York more of a nod than West Coast activists
might like (Los Angeles gay leaders were already beginning to resent the attention Stonewall earned New York in this new world of gay activism).

The Police Commission was an intimidating array of the city's white,
straight, male establishment. Perry tried, haltingly, to say they were nothing
more than an organization of taxpaying citizens, but his questioners obviously
knew better. Finally, Perry said: "We're the homosexual community of Los
Angeles," and with that piece of information on the table, Chief Davis drew
his line. "We would be ill-advised," Davis declared, "to discommode the people to have a burglars', or robbers', or homosexuals' parade." Christopher
Street West could stage a march only if it posted a $1.5 million insurance
bond to cover damage by any rioting, and reimburse the city $1,500 for the
cost of police overtime.

For the Gay Liberation Front of Los Angeles, these conditions were as
prohibitive as they were meant to be. The American Civil Liberties Union assigned a lawyer to appeal the commission's ruling. After expressing astonishment that Davis had compared homosexuals to burglars, ACLU attorney
Herbert E. Selwyn persuaded the commission to drop the insurance require-

ment. Superior Court Judge Richard Schauer soon forced the commission to drop its demand for police overtime and issued the permits. "Homosexuals," Judge Schauer declared, "are also citizens."

From the pulpit the following Sunday, Perry shared his distress at the experience. "For the first time, I really knew how it felt to be a member of a discriminated-against minority. It made me realize how little we've really accomplished. We've been at this for two years and nothing has changed." Tears rolled down his cheeks, and his congregation listened in silence, startled by the show of emotion. "These are not tears of sorrow, these are tears of joy," Perry declared. "My God is bigger than the city of Los Angeles, than the state of California, the government of the United States. I have faith that my God will move against injustice."

Don Kilhefner was, during the spring of 1970, spending almost all his time working with the Gay Liberation Front. He had dropped out of UCLA, abandoning his pursuit of a doctorate in African history and anthropology to focus on radical homosexual organizing. Kilhefner now had no source of income, so he slept in the apartment of a friend one night and on a park bench the next. He became a familiar sight with his long beard and hair pulled back, exposing a balding scalp, his black-rimmed glasses, and sandals and no socks. The GLF was meeting then at Satan's, a dance club in Silverlake, but Kilhefner had learned from years in the peace movement that an organization needs a permanent headquarters, with an address, phones, desks, filing cabinets and chairs for meetings. The spacious, second-floor Peace and Freedom Party headquarters on Vermont Avenue in Hollywood would be available after the spring elections, and Kilhefner had suggested that the GLF rent it for $210 a month, which it did. Not only did GLF now have a permanent meeting place, but Kilhefner had another place to sleep. For at least a few months, the Los Angeles Gay Liberation Front was probably the only organization in the country listed in the phone book under "Gay," and homosexuals began showing up at the offices on Vermont Avenue in Hollywood. Gypsies, Kilhefner called them, and he began to think of the GLF as an indoctrination camp to train young homosexuals in activism before sending them out, forming new gay liberation groups in their hometowns or at their colleges. (These efforts were complementing a separate campaign waged by New York's Gay Activists Alliance and Gay Liberation Front, which was dispatching teams of what it called Johnny Appleseeds, people like Rich Wandel and Arnie Kantrowitz of the GAA and Jim Fouratt, who was now working with the GAA, to drive from city to city trying to organize local GAA chapters.) Letters also came to GLF headquarters in Los Angeles looking for help. These were often moving appeals, mailed from parts of the country that people like Jim Kepner, who grew up in Texas, and Don Kilhefner, who came from Minneapolis, had never even considered to have much of a gay population—Gainesville, Florida, and Billings, Montana, and elsewhere. "I am interested in beginning a chapter of the Gay Liberation Front," wrote a man from Noblesville, Indiana. "If you would send me information about your group, how you got started and how you operate I would be most appreciative. We need as much assistance as we can get to get started properly." Before long, the GLF had a mailing list with a hundred such organizations spread across the country, and every time the Los Angeles group mimeographed a leaflet for a demonstration, they mailed out copies to homosexuals in other parts of the country.

The agenda for the Los Angeles GLF was largely set by the LAPD vice squad. The GLF made five-inch-by-two-inch fire-engine-red stickers with black type and a sketch of crossbones under a pig's snout (in place of the usual skull) and stuck them on bathroom walls and telephone poles: "WARNING! POLICE ENTRAPMENT PRACTICED HERE." And responding to the complaint Frank Kameny had made in the pages of the *Advocate* in 1968 about the failings of Los Angeles gay leaders, the GLF also issued wallet cards advising homosexuals what to do if they were arrested by vice police ("1. STAY CALM. Think before you speak. 2. NEVER RESIST PHYSICALLY. Say it in words. 3. DON'T TALK. . . . You are not required to provide your occupation or place of employment."). The GLF was intent on making it easier for gay men to have sex without fear of police arrest. There was no talk of a gay rights bill here: Whereas an attempt to rewrite law in New York City was merely unrealistic, in Los Angeles, it seemed absurd. "A waste of time," Morris Kight told his friend Morty Manford of New York's GAA, shortly after Kight and Manford, who was thirty years his junior, met at a gay conference in Chicago. "You're making enemies, not winning friends. I just don't see it as a winnable issue."

In New York, police activity seemed to decrease after every gay protest. In Los Angeles, the police were unbowed, unfazed even by the bizarre occasion when forty-five GLF members gathered outside the Rampart Police Station, beating tin cans with pencils, dropped to their knees and chanted "Raise! Raise!" in an attempt to levitate the police station several feet above the ground before making it disappear entirely. (Morris Kight, who was raised a Methodist until he announced at age six he would no longer go to church, showed up at the Rampart Police Station dressed as the pope. He later swore the station rose six feet: "The cameras loved it," he said.) The police were even unmoved by the GLF's provocative letters to Chief Davis: "Is it 'public decency' which is being outraged, or our own super-masculinity hang-ups? You dress in your leather and para-military drag, you have your phallic-symbol 'baton' stiff at your waist and your hot little motorcycle throbbing between your legs. Isn't that enough, without beatings and other sadistic games to climax your role-playing at being men?"

Still, the police seemed a lost cause. Thus, the attention turned to gay bars themselves, many of whose owners had, for reasons of self-preservation, taken it upon themselves to enforce vice squad regulations. "It's his place," Captain Charles Crumly of the LAPD vice squad said at a meeting with gay leaders about bar owners, describing the obligations of the bar owners. "He has an investment there and he certainly ought to do something about protecting it. If he permits violations to occur and arrests are made there and his license . . . is in jeopardy, it's his fault." The bar owners were super-vigilant, to the point of prohibiting even such permitted behavior as holding hands. The GLF staged a "touch-in" at a bar called The Farm; at 10 p.m. By a prearranged signal, the patrons turned to each other with an embrace and a kiss. "The Gay Liberation Front reminds you that we can hold hands, keep our arms around a friend's shoulder or waist, give a friendly kiss and not be denied these basic human rights by the bar establishment," read one leaflet. "We are treated like criminals!" the GLF declared in another. "Every time we let the bar deny us our basic human rights, we perpetuate the lie that homosexuality is wrong!" The owners of The Farm relented within a week.

June 28, 1970, New York

On a hot Sunday morning in New York, almost a year to the day after the riots in front of the Stonewall Inn, two hundred men and women waited nervously on a barricaded block off Sixth Avenue, near Sheridan Square, uncomfortable under the silent stares of the people watching from the sidewalk. Even for Greenwich Village, the sight of two hundred gay men and lesbians assembled on a Sunday morning, holding signs saying "Gay is Good," and "Gay Activists Alliance" and "Lesbians Unite" and "Daughters of Bilitis" and "Lavender Menace," was odd. Arnie Kantrowitz turned up early at the staging area and anxiously took in the small crowd. Here it was a year after Stonewall, the first Gay Pride march in New York's history, and only two hundred people had shown up? He caught sight of Marty Robinson, his friend from the Gay Activists Alliance:

"What do you think?"

"It's still too early," responded Robinson.

"Do you think there'll be enough?"

"I'll be happy if we get a few hundred."

Craig Rodwell, who had organized the march from his apartment on Bleecker Street, and from the counter of his Oscar Wilde Book Shop, had been handed a permit for the march just two hours earlier—a uniformed policeman had delivered it to his apartment. And that was only after Rodwell had made clear that the march from Greenwich Village to Central Park would occur, permit or no permit. Rodwell had come up with the notion of a Gay Pride march after returning from the previous year's "Reminder Day," the only attempt by homophile leaders at a national display of organization, in which a dozen or so gay men and lesbians, dressed in suits and skirts, marched in a circle in front of Independence Hall in Philadelphia. But the notion of such a decorous demonstration, once an act of some bravery, seemed a hopeless anachronism after Stonewall. Gay men and lesbians across the country now were beginning to march on police stations, sometimes holding hands on Christopher Street in New York and Santa Monica Boulevard in Los Angeles and in San Francisco, and confronting mayors and city councils. At a raucous convention of the Eastern Regional Conference of Homophile Organizations (ERCHO) in Philadelphia in November 1969, mostly notable for the disruptions staged by the GLF leaders from New York, Rodwell proposed the end of the Reminder Day, to be replaced by a march. (Rodwell had to overcome the concern of some of the older delegates that a march in Greenwich Village was an invitation for another riot by the young homosexuals.) The event Rodwell had in mind would not be called the Stonewall March— the last thing Rodwell wanted to celebrate was the mob-dominated culture of gay bars—but instead Christopher Street Liberation Day, the same name the Los Angeles organization had chosen. Rodwell, headstrong and not concerned with what anyone else thought of him, was the perfect person to organize it. When a radical on the march committee complained about spending $120 for a three-line advertisement in the *Village Voice* while "people are starving to death in this city," Rodwell silenced him with a motion to scrap the advertising budget and use the money to purchase hot dogs to be handed out on the Bowery.

Rodwell assumed the group's numbers would swell as it moved up Sixth Avenue toward Sheep Meadow in Central Park, where there would be a "gay-in," modeled after the yippie "be-ins." He was more worried about the pacing of the march (huge gaps that might make people think the march had ended, and go home), about how the recalcitrant New York City Police Department might handle the march, and most of all, about the threat of harassment and violence directed at the marchers. When Rodwell brought the idea to the Mattachine Society offices, one of the members had warned: "You'll get stoned. You'll get beaten to death." In the previous ten months, as much time and energy had gone into planning for what *might* happen—attacks on homosexuals—as for the logistics of the march itself. Parade marshals, including imposing men like Bob Kohler, had been trained by the Quakers in nonviolent responses to confrontation. They were taught, for example, to caution marchers to hide their jewelry and loose belts, the kind of loose items that could hurt them in attacks.

The concerns proved unfounded. There were a few eggs that rained down from the windows and a few shouts along the way. There were also contingents of people at Thirty-fourth and Forty-second Streets holding Bibles and condemning the marchers. Jean DeVente—"Mama Jean," as she was known among her male friends at GAA—was at the head of the parade, and turned her head away whenever, frequently, she heard "faggot" or "dyke" or "fuck you." But they were the exceptions. Before long, Mama Jean, a large woman, was thinking more about the seventy-five-degree temperature (why did they have to do this at the end of June?) than any threats.

The first gay march in New York covered fifty-one blocks, from Washington Square Park to Central Park, or just under three miles. It should have taken three hours to march, by the standards of other such events in the city. This took less than one hour. A reporter from the GLF newspaper, *Come Out!*, who arrived late, had to hop into a taxi to catch up with the parade he was assigned to cover. Bob Kohler and Jerry Hoose joked that this was not the first march but "The First Run." Part of the reason for this haste was that most of the marchers were a little frightened and unsure what the next block would bring. And part of it was the sheer excitement of the moment. In years to come, the march would become more of a pageant, with cheering crowds of onlookers. In 1970 the only thing that mattered was arriving safely in Central Park. Many of those who watched from the sidelines, all the way up the route, were themselves homosexuals, and the marchers, recognizing their friends, urged them to join the parade, so the contingent swelled as it moved uptown. Once they crossed the boundary into Central Park, the marchers, giggly and relieved, even chanted, "Out of the bushes and into the march." Central Park's bushes were notorious as a homosexual trysting area.

It was impossible, in the line of the parade, to get a measure of the size of the event they were staging. Sixth Avenue is flat from Greenwich Village to midtown. There were no floats or platform displays, at the insistence of Rodwell, who feared they would distract from the political significance of the day. Kantrowitz could tell that the line had thickened since the morning, but had no way of telling whether the march had even come close to the organizers' goals of several thousand. It was impossible to know—until the marchers reached the bluff that overlooked Sheep Meadow. From there, they could look ahead at Sheep Meadow where the "gay-in" was taking place, and behind them back down Sixth Avenue.

Many of the men and women who marched that day would forever remember that moment on top of the bluff. Before them lay a field of uncut grass, a blizzard of banners, dancing, pot-smoking, singing and music, a huge American flag, "gay pride" signs decorated with the Day-Glo hippie flower stickers, and men and women applauding each new arrival over the hill. And behind them—stretching out as far as they could see—was line after line after line of homosexuals and their supporters, at least fifteen blocks worth, by the count of the *New York Times,* which found the turnout notable enough to report it on the front page of the next day's paper. No one had ever seen so many homosexuals in one place before. On top of the bluff, many of these men and women, who had grown up so isolated and alone, stood in silence and cried.

The same day a march by the same name across the country, in Los Angeles, and facing perhaps greater obstacles, was also a success. With the permits in hand, Morris Kight and Troy Perry led their march through West Hollywood. By their count, 1,165 people showed up at McCadden Place at 6 p.m. on June 28 to mark the anniversary of Stonewall. There was a sound truck blasting martial music, a GLF float featuring a homosexual nailed to a black-and-white cross with a sign reading "In Memory of Those Killed by the Pigs," a GLF guerrilla theater skit with "fairies" dressed with wings being chased by vice cops with nightsticks and even an Orange County contingent hoisting a banner that said, "Homosexuals for Ronald Reagan." There was no trouble, notwithstanding the commission's concern for rioting, though this did not change Chief Ed Davis's view of things. When Christopher Street organizers, a few years later, invited the chief to come view the parade himself, Davis responded with a letter courteously declining: "While I support your organization's constitutional right to express itself on the subject of homosexuality, I am obviously not in sympathy with your views on the subject," he said. "I would much rather celebrate 'Gay Conversion Week,' which I will gladly co-sponsor when the medical practitioners in this country find a way to convert gays to heterosexuals."

September 1970, Boston

A whole school year after the Student Homophile League first began meeting at MIT in Boston, there still weren't five homosexual students willing to risk their future engineering careers by putting their names on a membership list for that or any other kind of gay student group. Weary of having to make up phony requests for meeting space at MIT or of having to meet at more liberal campuses like Boston University or Harvard, Stan Tillotson, the group's founder, had an inspiration. He asked five heterosexual friends at MIT if they would sign as members. They agreed, and an official chapter of the MIT Student Homophile League was born. Three years after Columbia University had chartered the nation's first Student Homophile League on a college campus, Tillotson had an organization to speak for, and as classes ended in May 1970, he asked permission to hold a dance open to gay students around Boston, center of the nation's largest college population.

It was the kind of breakthrough which had just been achieved by gay student groups on big campuses like the University of Minnesota and the University of Chicago, but at MIT the request landed on the desk of the dean of student affairs, Dan Nyhart. He consulted with the psychiatrist and staff of the university health service, and when the fall semester began, he turned Tillotson down. Dean Nyhart explained to the MIT student newspaper, *The Tech*, that medical science considered homosexuality "a disease." He worried that young, vulnerable students might be seduced at a homosexual dance, and solemnly noted, "the observable unhappiness that homosexuality brings to many persons. . . ."

Through the fall and winter of 1970, the controversy around "The Gay Mixer" that MIT refused to allow grew larger and larger, becoming the greatest issue of contention between the student government and the administration of the nation's preeminent school of science and engineering. The membership of the MIT Student Homophile League was phantom, but the issue was real: Did homosexual students have the same right to space as other students? It was, in a very fundamental way, one of the most basic issues of the gay rights movement, whether homosexuals could secure physical space for themselves outside the extortive world of the homosexual bars. The public streets in New York and Los Angeles had been the first battleground, the college campuses were the next. The results were uneven, but the *New York Times*, in a front-page story the following year, would recognize the tide of change. "In defiance of taboos" that blocked previous generations, the *Times* said, "thousands of college students are proclaiming their homosexuality and openly organizing 'gay' groups on large and small campuses across the country. No one knows exactly how many are involved, but in growing numbers they are forming cohesive campus organizations for educational, social and political purposes, often with official sanction and with remarkable acceptance from fellow students.

"From conversations with officials and homosexual students on half a dozen college campuses from Boston to Los Angeles, as well as reports from campus correspondents at 15 other schools," the *Times* said, "it would appear that the gay students have made substantial strides in changing attitudes. To do so, they hold dances and parties, run gay lounges and offices on campus, operate telephone hotlines for emergency problems and counseling services, publish newsletters and provide speakers to address fraternity, dormitory and faculty groups." The story was written by *Times* reporter Robert Reinhold. At twenty-nine, he was the youngest correspondent on the national staff, only a few years older than many of the students he had interviewed. His beat was college campuses. Although neither he nor any other *Times* reporter like him declared it in those years, Robert Reinhold was gay, a fact that may have helped him see the trend he reported in the story. Reinhold quoted a number of students, all of them anonymously. One was a freshman at MIT, but Reinhold found him not at MIT, but at a Student Homophile League social gathering in the basement of the Church of St. John the Evangelist. The Student Homophile League had not thrived at MIT. The officers of the student center and of the student government had supported the right of the SHL to hold a dance. The undergraduate assembly had even voted a resolution of support. But when the time came to take the administration on over the issue and risk losing, the assembly quailed, voting instead to formally declare the homosexuals' right to dance, and to abandon the issue. By December, the student government was so dispirited that it considered dissolving itself. It could not even attract a quorum to its last meeting of the year. In compensation for its weakness, its officers voted to give Stan Tillotson $500 so that the SHL could rent some hall off campus for a dance.

October 1970, New York

The Gay Activists Alliance was by the fall of 1970 the dominant gay rights activist organization in New York City, the most watched—and most imitated—in the country. As its founders had intended, most of its activities were built around pushing for a gay rights bill. The Gay Activists Alliance had committees assigned to finding examples of discrimination against homosexuals. Cases of clear-cut discrimination were not easy to find, if only because most homosexuals were not about to risk publicly claiming discrimination. The president of a New York private investigative agency, Fidelifacts, inadvertently helped the GAA when he boasted to a reporter of his agency's efficiency in alerting potential employers that applicants were homosexual. It was all part of its routine $12.50-per-candidate background check. Fidelifacts president Vincent Gillen said he knew how to spot homosexuals: "I like to go on the rule of thumb: that if one looks like a duck, walks like a duck, associates only with ducks and quacks like a duck, he is probably a duck." The next day, sixty-five members of the GAA and the Daughters of Bilitis showed up at Fidelifacts headquarters, led by Marty Robinson—dressed in an outsized duck outfit, flapping white feathers. "The important thing," Jim Owles told a handful of TV cameras and print reporters who found the spectacle irresistible, "is to draw the public's attention to the existence of Fidelifacts and other companies like it."

The GAA demonstrations came to take on an odd mixture of dead earnestness and high camp. In the fall of 1970 respected *Harper's* magazine published a cover story, "Homo/Hetero: The Struggle for Sexual Identity," by Joseph Epstein, which was a powerful condemnation of homosexuality. "If I had the power to do so," Epstein wrote, "I would wish homosexuality off the face of this earth. They are different from the rest of us. Homosexuals are different, moreover, in a way that cuts deeper than other kinds of human differences—religious, class, racial—in a way that is, somehow, more fundamental. Cursed without clear cause, afflicted without apparent cure, they are an affront to our rationality, living evidence of our despair of ever finding a sensible, an explainable, design to the world. . . . There is much my four sons can do in their lives that might cause me anguish, that might outrage me, that might make me ashamed of them and of myself as their father. But nothing they could do would make me sadder than if any one of them were to become homosexual. For then, I should know them condemned to a state of permanent niggerdom." At Arthur Bell's suggestion, the GAA responded with a coffee-and-donuts breakfast in *Harper's* office—a tea party—with the intention of engaging the magazine staff in a discussion of the Epstein article. At 9 a.m., they piled off the elevator on the eighteenth-floor office of *Harper's*, holding a coffeepot and donuts, folding metal tables and paper cups. Pete Fisher, a bright-eyed, twenty-six-year-old political theory student at Columbia University, had thought to invite along a crew from a local TV station. One GAA member stepped off the elevator to announce himself to a receptionist–switchboard operator: "Hello, I'm a homosexual. I'm here to show you what homosexuals are really like." Other GAA members started moving through the halls of *Harper's*, introducing themselves to employees— "I'm a homosexual!"—and offering coffee, donuts and a GAA pamphlet. The humor evaporated once Arthur Evans met Midge Decter, the *Harper's* editor who had worked on the piece. "It is serious and honest and was misread," she declared. "It does not reinforce anti-homosexual opinion." Evans's face quivered with anger. "You knew that this article would contribute to the suffering of homosexuals," Evans yelled. "You knew that. And if you didn't know that, you're inexcusably naive and should not be editor. If you know that those views contribute to the oppression of homosexuals, then damn you for publishing that article. We have a right to come here and hold you politically and morally responsible for it. You are a bigot and you are to be held responsible for that moral and political act!"

Everything about Evans's performance that day was calculated, and indeed, was mild by his standards. Pete Fisher watched once as Evans brought his face within an inch of Dr. Murray Rockowitz, the vice chairman of the city Board of Education's Board of Examiners, which was denying teacher's licenses to open homosexuals. Evans's arms were flailing, his shoulder-length hair and beard flopping, and he was yelling at the top of his lungs: "AN-SWER THE HOMOSEXUAL! ANSWER THE HOMOSEXUAL! AN-SWER THE HOMOSEXUAL!" He offered a similar display for Mary Lindsay, the mayor's wife, at a charity performance of *Two by Two* at the Imperial Theatre on Broadway. As a clutch of gay activists blocked the Lindsays' way into the theater, Evans stationed himself in front of her, face-to-face, this time bellowing, "End police harassment!" Mrs. Lindsay, frightened, responded by pushing Evans in the chest, trying to move him away.

In contrast to Evans, Jim Owles was aloof and distant, and even GAA members who voted for him as the organization's first president, a position he held through December 1971, saw him as rigid—"tight-little old-mannish" was how Arthur Bell put it—and hard to like. He would stand to the side as Marty Robinson or Arthur Evans dominated a meeting, rarely smiling, with the delicate and angular face of a boy, his brown hair waving over his shoulders, his eyes bright behind wire-rimmed glasses. He seemed always to be pale, summer and winter. What Owles might have lacked in imagination or personality he made up in spunk. After he threw himself, or what little there was of him, at a line of police officers trying to block GAA demonstrators from coming into city hall, he was pushed by police down the stairs, and then ran back, where he was placed under arrest. That led Marty Robinson to describe him as "the scrappiest little faggot in New York." But Owles, with his midwest accent and sensibilities, never quite fit in with the New York gay crowd. Talk of sado-masochism or fetishism made him uncomfortable, as did the habit of some GAA members to call each other "faggot" in a teasing, friendly way. Owles struck some of his colleagues as a strangely lonely character. Being the president of the Gay Activists Alliance was not a paying position, and Jim Owles welcomed secondhand clothes from friends and relied on their kindness for meals. When that failed, he took to going to local grocery stores wearing his oversized green West Point jacket and filling its pockets with steaks and vegetables. His friends didn't care about the shoplifting, but they were afraid that the GAA might be embarrassed if its president was arrested for something else besides the cause of gay rights. By his second one-year term, Owles's odd ways had isolated him in the group. Owles lost his attempt at a third term in 1971; he was so upset he ran into the bathroom and began to sob so loudly that his cries could be heard in the meeting room. He had never thought about life without being in the GAA. Within a year or so, he took a job as a night manager of a New York bathhouse.

The third major force in the group was Marty Robinson. His influence was partly a result of his sheer exuberance, which was infectious, and the novelty of many of his political ideas. For people like Pete Fisher, who had never met an openly gay person while growing up in New York's northern suburbs, Robinson's notion that being gay could be fun was startling. Robinson's influence was heightened by his good looks: he had short black hair and near-black eyes, soft and boyish in the way that was considered attractive in the early 1970s. It served him as well in politics as it did in his romantic conquests, which included many members of the GAA. He would come to the GAA meetings wearing skin-tight blue jeans and no underwear. Robinson had wanted to be a doctor like his father, tending to Hasidim in Brooklyn, until his ambition stumbled over his poor academic performance. He worked instead as a carpenter, and lived in a Greenwich Village apartment so tiny that the bathtub was in the kitchen. He was estranged from his family at an early age, partly because they never accepted that he was gay, but also, he told his friends, because they were upset with his drug use. The reason Marty Robinson always was so jittery, eyes fluttering, always out of breath—with a nervous edge that irritated people like Bob Kohler and Jerry Hoose—was that he liked to inject himself with a liquid form of speed. The influence of the speed was no doubt a source of the energy that fueled him. It might also have given him the courage to pull off some of his more daring stunts. But it made him unfocused, irritable and unpredictable—"a cat who would fly off the handle at the slightest provocation," as Arthur Bell described him. Robinson later worried that what he referred to as his "aggressive way of dealing with people" had held him back in the movement. Even apart from his drug use, Robinson acted more out of instinct than thought. Thus, he hardly ever wrote articles for the gay press or remembrances, and since he never provided an account of his accomplishments or thoughts, the details of his formative role in the Gay Activists Alliance seemed largely lost to history. By the time he died—in March 1992, his brain ravaged by speed and infection—he was so bitter at being ignored in the accounts of the gay political movement that he instructed his friends not to even mark his death with a memorial service.

5

FIRST STIRRINGS

January 1971, Minneapolis-St. Paul

The January 26, 1971, issue of *Look* magazine was devoted to a portrayal of "The American Family," and it included one unlikely tale: the story of the relationship of Jack Baker and Michael McConnell—three pages, with pictures, under the headline "The Homosexual Couple." "Not all homosexual life is a series of one-night stands in bathhouses, public toilets or gay bars, (those queer, mirror images of the swinging singles straight scene)," *Look* said. "Some homosexuals—a minority—live together in stable, often long-lasting relationships, like Baker's and McConnell's." The photographs showed Baker and McConnell applying for a marriage license, shaving in the morning, talking with their Roman Catholic priest at church and cuddling up at an evening gathering of straight friends. Baker and McConnell never missed mass on Sundays at the university's Newman Center Chapel, *Look* reported, and one Sunday, Baker stunned the congregation and the priest by asking a question in the middle of the service. "Do you feel that if two people give themselves in love to each other and want to grow together in mutual understanding, that Jesus would be open to such a union if the two people were of the same sex?" There was a collective gasp and a long pause, the story said, and then the priest finally gave his answer: "Yes, in my opinion, Christ would be open." Beneath this text was a photograph of the two holding hands as they walked down the street. And it was not a show put on for the sake of a national magazine. The readers of *Look* were given a fairly accurate portrait of the most public gay couple in the nation. "Michael and I hold hands on campus and at parties," Jack Baker told a gay interviewer, writing for a much narrower audience, at the time. "The only bad reaction was once when we were holding hands coming from mass at the campus Newman Center amidst four or five hundred people, and a guy stopped his car and yelled, 'Jesus Christ, why don't you kiss his ass?' Everyone coming out of church just stared him down. And I just said, 'Fuck off.' "

Other activists at the University of Minnesota resented the idealized couple portrayed in *Look,* and other members of FREE (Fight Repression of Erotic Expression) disliked Baker in particular. "I hate him," one said. "I'd like to slit his throat." But it did not matter. So far as the general public was concerned, Jack Baker and Mike McConnell were the closest things to national personalities that the gay liberation movement had produced, and they were forcing some people to reconsider their own notions of a homosexual. After his appearance in *Look,* Baker ran for president of the Minnesota Student Association, and his homosexuality was anything but hidden. His first campaign poster showed him posed in a shirt and tie and jeans—in a woman's high-heeled shoes. "Put Yourself in Jack Baker's Shoes," it said. He had another one that the Associated Press sent out as a wire photo from coast to coast. In it, he was standing with an American flag, a picture of Abraham Lincoln, an Italian mother and a baby, holding a Bible and an apple pie. "Jack Baker Comes Out," it said coyly, "for Things That Count!"

Baker's slogan was "Responsible Activism," and on a campus dominated by a radical student spirit, Baker himself came off as pretty dull (though, as one student remembered, "His posters were great"). But the *Minnesota Daily* endorsed him, and on April 8, Walter Cronkite told the nation that, "In Minneapolis, an admitted homosexual, Jack Baker, has been elected president of the University of Minnesota Student Association." It was the movement's first electoral victory, a triumph by a homosexual candidate with a sense of humor, and family values.

March 1971, Austin, Texas

The first Gay Liberation National Conference drew about three hundred lesbians and gay men from twenty cities—Los Angeles and Bloomington, Indiana; San Francisco and Lincoln, Nebraska; New York and Lawrence, Kansas—to the First Unitarian Church in Austin, Texas, a city whose huge university distinguished it as a progressive outpost in the South. The conference, "planned for and by gays" as the invitation pointedly noted, was the first such national gathering of radical gay activists devoted to discussion of the oppression of homosexuals. Political conferences in the twenty-one months since Stonewall had been far from satisfying: either the vestigial and listless conferences of the old homophile movements or the New Left assemblies, where homosexuals had to jostle for attention and respect. The idea for this conference had risen out of a particularly dispiriting gathering the previous fall called the Revolutionary People's Constitutional Convention, organized by the Black Panthers. Members of gay liberation fronts from New York, Austin, Chicago, Philadelphia and Boston had attended the sessions in Philadelphia and Washington, D.C., filling the halls with chants of "Gay Power" and saluting the Black Panthers as "the vanguard of the people's revolution." But there was no reciprocal gesture from the Panthers, no attempt to integrate the homosexuals' demands into the Panther platform. The lesbians had been particularly appalled at the way women were treated. Martha Shelley saw no difference between the Black Panthers and the Nazi Party: Both, she proclaimed, viewed women as little more than baby machines. Lois Hart, struggling to find common ground with a group she wished to embrace, described them in *Come Out!* as "a straight man's trip in CinemaScope and Technicolor . . . [they were] super butch. . . . Their words cracked with rage and self-righteousness." When Hart had demanded to know when the Panther convention would address gay and women's issues, someone responded: "We'll tolerate that crazy talk for 30 seconds and you'll be asked to leave." At another point, a man screamed at a group of lesbians: "Get out of here, you freaks! Get away from here, you sex freaks!"

The reception was hardly surprising. The straight leaders of the New Left were proving to be no less uncomfortable with—and no less hostile to—gays than heterosexuals in the society at large. Jim Fouratt's failed effort to enlist his friend Abbie Hoffman to come down to the Stonewall was only one example. Yippie leader Jerry Rubin's book *Do It!* was sprinkled with slurs that rankled homosexual activists. Rubin scorned school bureaucrats who "put one hand around our shoulders while the other hand gropes for our pants," and university administrators "sucking each other off in the back rooms of the University." In an "Open Letter to Jerry Rubin," Step May, an activist in Chicago, wrote: "It's one of the most anti-gay pieces of literature I've seen in current writing—Movement or otherwise." He added: "Let's free everyone, Jerry. Us homosexuals, too." Black Panther Minister of Information Eldridge Cleaver spoke often about the threat "faggots" posed to America. In New York, a Gay Liberation Front banner was ripped to shreds in a confrontation at a Vietnam Moratorium rally in Bryant Park. A young, long-haired New York GLF member, Earl Galvin, carried a "28th of June" banner up Pennsylvania Avenue at the November 1969 Vietnam Moratorium in Washington that had proved a turning point for Marty Robinson and Jim Owles. He shared with readers of *Come Out!* the reaction he drew when he explained he represented a cell from New York's Gay Liberation Front named for the anniversary of Stonewall: "The march was so full of liberals, nervous Nellies all. Most of the young men smiled slightly, tightened their sphincters, grabbed mom's hand and gravitated discreetly to another area of the street."

Both the Communist Party and the Socialist Workers Party had explicit prohibitions against homosexuality. "Homosexuality is part of the problem of a decaying society—in a planned society, you could deal with the problem medically and psychiatrically," the Communist Party's American spokesman, Charlene Mitchell, said in 1970. According to New York's John O'Brien, the SWP's youth league expelled him once its members realized he was gay (O'Brien was all muscles and swagger, and even other gay men often didn't recognize his homosexuality at first). Members of the Communist Party threatened to call the police to prevent a delegation of lesbians, carrying a banner saying "Gay Liberation Front Women," from joining a downtown Manhattan rally protesting the prosecution of Black Panther Angela Davis. When the women opened their banner in the midst of the crowd, a handful of Communist Party members produced an even larger banner which they lifted to hide the GLF contingent from newspaper photographers.

The Austin conference was planned in order to address gay issues away from the growing hostility of the New Left. As leaders of Austin Gay Liberation explained in their letter calling the conference, it had become obvious at the Black Panther's Revolutionary People's Convention that "gay people cannot adequately deal with the vital questions affecting their lives in brief caucuses associated with other conventions." But if the Austin conference proved anything, it was that outside forces were not needed to produce ideological divisions among this new generation of gay leaders. The conference demonstrated that the ideological divisions that had been displayed when New York's Gay Activists Alliance split off from the Gay Liberation Front fifteen months before were as deep as ever.

It began at the very first session, as Jim Fouratt led a group demanding the ejection of all heterosexuals at the church, including a University of Texas college newspaper reporter and members of the Socialist Workers Party. "We are not separatists!" responded one of the delegates, to huge cheers, and then a resounding vote against Fouratt's idea. Fouratt and his delegation stormed out, but returned, again and again, effectively paralyzing the conference. Finally, and devastatingly, Fouratt and his supporters shut off the electricity to the church's conference room. The remaining activists had gathered their chairs into a circle to shut out the distractions. With the lights out, Morty Manford raised his arm and flicked on a cigarette lighter, which cast off just enough light for him to watch most of the remaining delegates leave in defeat.

Arthur Evans had intended to talk Saturday about creating gay movement. But Fouratt and his supporters declared they would not let Evans and his "middle-class friends" take over the national movement, as they had done in New York. Thus, the afternoon was devoted not to an exploration of homosexual oppression, but to analyzing racism and sexism and how "none of us are free until all of us are free." The only tangible accomplishments of the gathering were an official endorsement of an upcoming anti-war rally in San Francisco and the May Day demonstrations in Washington, D.C. "This convention was originally called in order to discuss gay identity and the beginning of a national gay movement," Evans reported to the GAA on his return, his account reminiscent, in words and tone, of the angry newsletter published by members of the Mattachine Society sixteen months earlier, after Fouratt disrupted the homophile conference in Washington, D.C., "It attained neither end, largely due to the disruptive and manipulative tactics used by delegates from the Gay Liberation Front of New York."

The emerging homosexual rights movement was in some turmoil, torn between ideologies and generations, divided over mission and tactics. The issue of "homosexual rights" was coming into conflict with the sheer diversity of homosexual men and women, suggesting that the notion of a "homosexual community" was, in fact, misleading. Morris Kight was shoved and doused with beer by radical members of his own GLF after he tried to prevent them from storming the county jail during the city's first gay pride parade. A midwestern Gay Liberation conference sponsored in Minneapolis by FREE was forced by radicals to scrap its agenda of gay liberation issues to devote three days to talking about sexism, racism and the Black Panthers. The radicals objected that the convention agenda included addresses by heterosexuals and refused to allow Conrad Balfour, the Minnesota commissioner of human rights and one of the first supporters of gay rights statutes, to speak. Chicago Gay Liberation founder Henry Wiemhoff became the subject of a divisive debate in his organization over whether it was fair that he—the product of a white Chicago neighborhood—claim a draft exemption based on his homosexuality.

The movement bristled with contradictions. On one hand, Troy Perry was officiating at the marriage of two lesbians in Los Angeles, and Jack Baker and Mike McConnell were fighting in the Minnesota courts for recognition of their union. On the other, the Lesbian Workshop of the Revolutionary People's Convention was advocating the "destruction of the nuclear family," which it called a "microcosm of the fascist state, where the women and children are owned by, and their fates determined by, the needs of men in a man's world." Franklin Kameny was considering a run for Congress in Washington, while the GLF in New York was casting its lot with "oppressed peoples whenever possible in the struggle to destroy the Empire." New York's Gay Activists Alliance was negotiating a gay rights bill, but Chicago Gay Liberation leaders had concluded that "we no longer want to 'make it' in Amerika." The Los Angeles GLF Statement of Purpose didn't even get around to addressing the problem of homosexuals until after it established that it was "in total opposition to America's white racism, to poverty, hunger. . . . We oppose the rich getting richer, the poor getting poorer and we are in total opposition to wars of aggression and imperialism, whoever pursues them. We support the demands of blacks, Chicanos, Orientals, women, youth, senior citizens and others demanding their full rights as human beings."

These ideas were alien to the pragmatic and moderate mainstream homosexuals taking an interest in the movement, and to the conservative homophiles who controlled the major gay newspapers of the time. "It becomes more and more apparent," *The Advocate* wrote in an editorial, "that the so-called gay militants are not so much pro-gay as they are anti-establishment, anti-capitalist, anti-society. They lash out in all directions, destroying everything in sight—gay or straight." *The Advocate* under editor Dick Michaels tried to ignore the radical surge. When Don Jackson wrote Michaels to complain about its coverage, the *Advocate* editor responded with an attack. "If the Gay Liberation Movement founders, it will do so primarily because of one glaring fault: Hypocrisy," Michaels wrote. "It is possible for all homosexuals to favor freedom and justice for homosexuals. But it is the wildest and most improbable jump to say that therefore they should all be against the Vietnam war, against capitalism, or in favor of destroying society."

Gay newspaper in New York urged its readers not to abandon the homophile movement, since that would let the radicals get even more of a toehold, "now that the revolution is spreading among the gay masses, that less responsible people are beginning to infiltrate the homophile cause." Instead of court challenges and campaigns to change antiquated laws and win the support of mainstream politicians, "we may now discover that an increasing number of gay spokesmen will dump endless slogans in our laps. We will hear unceasing raps, merry-go-round like, about oppression/oppression/oppression and revolution/revolution/revolution. The purpose of this editorial is not to ask of *Gay*'s readers that they turn away from homophile organizations because of recent events, but rather that they support those organizations which have shown themselves to be responsible and civilized spokesmen for the community. . . . Dropping out of the civil libertarian struggle will only leave the homosexual cause in the hands of loudmouths." Frank Kameny warned that radicals were undercutting the movement: "The endless involvement some groups get into with racism and sexism is a very subtle cop-out. Blacks and women are respectable issues. It doesn't take much internal fortitude to stand up for them and fight for them. Homosexuality is not yet a respectable issue—it takes internal strength to stand up publicly and fight." No issue better illustrated the conflicts in the gay radical movement than whether to support the Black Panthers. At the height of the furor, Jim Fouratt offered an apology on behalf of the Black Panthers' use of the word, "faggot," which had made talk of a Panther-homosexual alliance seem far-fetched: "The problem," Fouratt wrote, "is that my brothers and sisters don't understand the word 'faggot' as Cleaver and many blacks use it. The word 'faggot' is used to describe any castrated male made impotent by the society." Fouratt found little agreement on that point. "Why are we going out for them?" Barbara Gittings demanded, up from Philadelphia for a Gay Activists Alliance meeting. "Why aren't we doing something for us? They don't come around for us. We should be doing something strictly for gay people."

May 1971, New York

The Gay Activists Alliance's Firehouse, an elegant, four-story, turn-of-the-century, abandoned Victorian building on Wooster Street that the GAA had rented in SoHo, a ten-minute walk from Christopher Street, symbolized the new gay spirit in New York that spring. The exceptionally deep building, with its high ceiling, iron front doors that rolled open (so the fire trucks could get out), and a facade painted with a fresh coat of fire engine red stretched out across 10,000 square feet and was ideal for the Thursday night meetings. The other two floors and the basement were suited for the smaller committee sessions and social gatherings during the week. But most of all, the building, with its white-tiled bay which stretched the width of two fire trucks, was an ideal place for a dance. And starting in May 1971, homosexuals, almost all men, began lining up on Wooster Street every Saturday night, in what overnight became the most popular gay dance club in New York. On any Saturday night, people like Arnie Kantrowitz, perched on the art nouveau–style spiral staircase at one side of the room (the staircase the firemen had used to descend to the trucks), would take in the expanse of men, over a thousand of them, shoulder to shoulder, shirtless, arms flying in the air, high on LSD or quaaludes or Seconals or black beauties or marijuana.* They were pounding sneakers on the cement floor, under flashing colored and strobe lights, and to a sound system "the Fillmore might envy," as Randy Wicker wrote in *Gay* newspaper, referring to the rock and roll concert hall across town. It was, Arthur Bell said, a "heaven's cross between Woodstock and Dante's inferno," and it was to be the progenitor of the huge gay discos that later appeared in New York. Suddenly, politics was glamorous. People who never thought of going to a GAA Thursday night meeting or a zap would line up to dance in

---

* In the spring of 1971, the GAA banned marijuana at the Firehouse dances to guard against police raids.

what was by day the headquarters of the most active gay rights group in the country and by night New York's premier gay club. The chorus boys and Broadway dancers appeared around midnight, after their curtains fell.

For the Gay Activists Alliance, this was triumph over the commercial and syndicate-controlled gay clubs, dwarfing the Gay Liberation Front's pioneering efforts at Alternate U. the year before. As a page one headline in *Gay* newspaper put it, "Gay Power Challenges Syndicate Bars: Dances Draw Large Crowds." Randy Wicker and Arthur Bell both reported a drop-off in Saturday night attendance at the usual gay haunts. And the dances became a huge source of income—in the first three weeks, the dances grossed $4,300. At its peak, the GAA collected an average of $1,786 every Saturday night, against just $501 in expenses. Without the dances, the GAA could not have afforded the monthly $1,100 cost of the Firehouse. Such large congregations of gay people inevitably attracted the attention of the local police precinct. At the very first dance, the GAA was greeted by a convoy of six police cars. "Do you have a certificate of occupancy?" an officer demanded. "No, officer, but we've applied for one," Owles responded, as Rich Wandel, the official GAA photographer and a future president, moved in and started snapping pictures. The officer wrote Owles a ticket for not having a certificate of occupancy, and then another for not having a permit to assemble. There was a third summons for violating the city noise regulations. After the police left, Owles held up the summonses and proclaimed: "See what we got, folks? Three more pieces of paper to plaster on the wall."

When Jim Owles spoke at the opening of the Firehouse in the spring of 1971, he envisioned a time when homosexuals would be able "to show straights and themselves that being gay means something more than the baths and the bars." The new Firehouse, he suggested, would stand as a center for gay culture and social life, as well as for gay activism. But as the Firehouse dances grew in popularity, some of the GAA founders began to worry that this new notion of a gay rights group concerned with social and cultural issues threatened its political existence. Homosexuals were so starved for social interaction and sex, Arthur Evans asserted, that they would rush at what GAA was offering; the group's political agenda would be trampled. Marty Robinson brooded about this as he spent twelve hours setting up for the first dance. What do music and dancing have to do with gay rights? he wondered, skeptical of "all you people who want to dance your way to liberation." This was a serious rift, and one that caught everyone by surprise. Marty Robinson and Arthur Evans were battling the members of what was appropriately labeled the Pleasure Committee, which was in charge of the dances. The GAA tried to patch over the divide by injecting some politics into its "pleasure." The constitution was changed to redefine the GAA as a political and cultural organization. Dances were built around a political theme (the first one was held in honor of the so-called Rockefeller Five, who had been arrested at a sit-in at state Republican headquarters after party leaders refused to meet with them). The GAA installed a mural, forty feet long and eight feet high, along the wall of the Firehouse, mostly made up of photos by Rich Wandel: a collage of portraits, including homosexuals clutching iron bars in anguish; Walt Whitman, Gertrude Stein and Allen Ginsberg, and photos of the group's leaders. The mural was decorated with slogans: "Gay Power," "Gay Pride" and "An Army of Lovers Can not Lose." The Saturday night dance entertainment began to include a showing, on the third floor, of videotapes of political zaps. (But to little obvious effect: no one could see the mural under the strobe lights of the dance, and the videotapes of demonstrations usually played to empty chairs.)

Still, the GAA was thriving. Membership swelled from the publicity; even better evidence of the group's success was the rising resentment from the remnants of other homosexual rights groups in New York. Bob Kohler and Jerry Hoose, who stayed with GLF until the end, refused to set foot in the Firehouse. Relations were even worse between the GAA and the Mattachine, particularly with Dick Leitsch, who attacked the Gay Activists Alliance regularly in his newspaper column on such matters as its battle against police crackdowns on after-hour bars. "To charge that this campaign is directed against the gay community can only be construed to be paranoiac or self-serving," Leitsch wrote. "In the Stonewall incident, at least the police were doing us a favor by putting out of business a group of exploiters who were exposing us to dangers of many kinds and taking us all for suckers. I don't believe it's a responsible use of gay power to defend the Mafia." The GAA responded with a testy letter, saying Leitsch "has no understanding of the new homosexual who embodies self-respect, courage and determination to seek beneficial revolutionary changes. The gay political groups of New York each tend to view themselves as being the savior of the homosexual. We do not apologize for depleting Mr. Leitsch's ego." From Los Angeles, even the editors of *The Advocate* cast an admiring eye at the New York group's success. The Los Angeles police vice squad had raided an afternoon fundraiser being held by a homosexual legal rights group, HELP (Homophile Effort for Legal Protection), and arrested twenty-two men. "If the organization has any good tacticians among its ranks—like some of the more brilliant members of New York's Gay Activists Alliance—it will turn the event into a cause celebre and a monumental legal battle from which the group would emerge stronger than ever," an *Advocate* editorial said.

GAA began to draw the attention of mainstream politicians. Bella Abzug, running for Congress from Greenwich Village, turned up at GAA meetings, and was rewarded with a standing ovation from a crowd gratified by the attention. She even took her campaign to the Continental Baths, though she had never really considered what a gay bath was until, escorted by Allen Roskoff, a young political operative and member of the GAA, she stumbled in the dark and found herself astonished as her eyes adjusted to the dim green lights. There's got to be a thousand naked men in towels out there, Abzug thought. They cheered wildly at the sight of Abzug, draped in a floor-length navy blue dress with white polka dots and a broad-brimmed Calamity Jane hat. She took a breath and, after regaining her footing, declared: "My mother thanks you for that. I'm sorry that I'm not quite dressed for the occasion."

GAA members showed up at Democratic forums, trying to force candidates to talk about gay issues. "That's the first time I've heard that question," Howard Samuels said when he and three other New York Democratic gubernatorial candidates were asked what they would do about gay employment rights. By November, two U.S. Senate candidates, Richard Ottinger, a wealthy Democrat, and Charles Goodell, a liberal Republican, endorsed civil rights for homosexuals. Arthur Goldberg, the former Supreme Court justice and that year's Democratic gubernatorial candidate against Nelson Rockefeller, first brushed off the activists when they surrounded his white limousine on the Upper West Side. "I have more important things to talk about," he said. A chant of "Answer the homosexual, answer the homosexual" swelled behind him. "Why the silence?" someone yelled.

A week before the election, he released a statement endorsing gay rights, after his campaign aides asked whether that would put an end to the GAA zaps disrupting his already losing campaign. Even Representative Mario Biaggi, a conservative Democrat, came to the Firehouse. "I've got no problem with your problem," Biaggi said. When people stood up to shout, demanding to know what he meant, a befuddled Biaggi reportedly said all he meant was that he had nothing against "homos."

The GAA's brash tactics did not always serve it well. After a 7–5 defeat of the gay employment bill by the New York City Council's General Welfare Committee in January 1972, Theodore Weiss, the Manhattan Democrat sponsoring the legislation, said the GAA's behavior "distressed all of us" and was "not helpful." Said Councilman Michael DeMarco of the Bronx, an opponent: "The homosexuals killed the bill themselves. Those who were undecided found their behavior generally repugnant in flaunting their gay liberation instead of stressing their civil rights." The attacks on Mayor Lindsay were a continual source of controversy as well. Why harass someone who is sympathetic to homosexuals? Leitsch demanded in his newspaper column. "Lindsay is an honest man with a concern for people and individual rights," Leitsch wrote. "His police commissioner . . . pulled the plainclothes cops out of the entrapment business. . . . I can't understand zapping Mayor Lindsay. He's made this city livable for us and for many other people." *Gay* newspaper published repeated editorials scoring gay activists for their attacks on Lindsay. "We do not doubt that the Gay Activists Alliance is impatient. We are all impatient. But chanting, 'Gay Power Now! Gay Power Now!' through the lobby doors of the Met, before being ushered away by benign policemen, is hardly an impressive expression of such impatience. By such tactics, we believe, demands for civil rights and social rights for homosexuals are reduced to fizzled street theatrics. They could tend to make the mayor and his administration less receptive to gay demands."

Jim Owles responded to the *Gay* editorial the following week: "Don't perpetuate the myth that only a beneficent mayor and not gay political power can ever bring benefits to our community. If the mayor is decent, he will respond; if he is callous and political, then don't defend him, defend the disenfranchised, the oppressed."

June 1971, Atlanta

In the first week of February 1971, about a hundred people, mostly male, mostly white, mostly in their twenties, had gathered for the first public Gay Liberation Front meeting in Atlanta, a meeting that would lead in June to a march marking the second anniversary of the riot in New York, the first big city gathering devoted to gay issues in that part of the country. Notice of the meeting came in *The Great Speckled Bird,* the city's counterculture newspaper, in an "Editor's Note": "If you are gay and would like to join with your gay sisters and brothers in Atlanta outside the bars, cruising sites and closets, call or write *The Bird* and find out about the Atlanta GLF that is forming. Soon we hope to have our own phone number and some sort of meeting schedule, but until then you can help us get it together by letting us know you're there." Atlanta, a year and a half behind New York, aimed to learn from the divisions that doomed the GLF. There was talk at that first meeting about avoiding the male chauvinism, about the need to include people of color, and to *do* things, not just talk.

Time and the experience of others hadn't made it any easier. In a month, the women and blacks were essentially gone. But the men did do something; they began organizing the June march. Not a Gay Pride march like the others being organized around the country, but a protest march in the style of the '60s—"against gay oppression"—with whomever they could get to join them, of whatever sexual and political persuasion. They ended up a motley group of fifty to one hundred gay liberationists, Socialist Workers, *Bird* writers, Young Socialist Alliance and National Organization for Women members, a few women's liberationists, and some people like Lorraine Fontana, walking with a friend with her baby in a stroller up Peachtree Street and across to Piedmont Park on a Sunday afternoon. The friend with the baby was a lesbian. Lorraine Fontana wasn't so sure about herself.

It wasn't easy to find things to protest that day in Atlanta. They didn't have a permit, but the police let them march. A delegation of gay liberationists called on the mayor, Sam Massell, and to their surprise, he met with them. They presented him with a list of demands—that he end police harassment of homosexuals, that he end all job discrimination against homosexuals, and that he "exert the moral and suasive influence of your office" to end social discrimination against homosexuals in Atlanta. And he told them he would help in any way he could. In the next ten days, four members of the GLF called the city personnel office to apply for jobs and asked if there was any policy against hiring homosexuals. They were told no. Mayor Massell told a reporter for the *Atlanta Constitution* that he had asked the four GLF members if they had discovered any instances of discrimination, and they said they hadn't. The *Constitution* put that news on the front page. Without an opponent, the city's few gay male activists spent time debating the meaning of gay liberation; the gay community in Atlanta still seemed based on good times in the bars, at private little Sunday brunches in Virginia Highlands and in the bushes in the parks at night. The Reverend John Gill, twenty-six, a recent graduate of the Princeton Theological Seminary and a just-licensed minister of the Metropolitan Community Church, arrived in town in November, sent by MCC founder, the Reverend Troy Perry, to build a new gay church in Atlanta. Neither the men nor the burgeoning lesbian community, which had no use for the men's bars, had much regard for the Reverend Gill or the church he was trying to create.

September 1971, Los Angeles

"Many of the goals that the Gay Liberation Front of Los Angeles started out to achieve have been achieved, and to some extent we have passed our usefulness." The announcement came from Morris Kight in the pages of *The Advocate*. News of the impending suspension of the Gay Liberation Front came as a surprise to many of its members, but the GLF of Los Angeles had been crumbling for the better part of a year. As Kight correctly noted, there was no longer much taste in Los Angeles for the kind of street activism that had seemed so exciting when they first picketed at Barney's Beanery. "Right at this moment," Morris Kight said as he announced the GLF's suspension, "I don't know where we would march; I don't know who we would march against." An effort to transform the GLF into more of a social organization—by using its headquarters as a coffeehouse—had proved to be a disaster. Forty mattresses were brought in to provide beds for homosexuals without homes, and the GLF headquarters had become a flophouse, with rampant drug and alcohol use, and scuffles among the tenants.

Divisions had grown within the ranks of GLF, and much of it centered around Kight. The organization had never quite recovered from an episode in which Don Jackson had proposed that the GLF organize a migration to Alpine County, a tiny mountain community of 450 people located 11,000 feet in the clouds by the Nevada border. Jackson argued that if only two hundred gay people quietly moved in and registered, they could take over the government. Jackson wanted to proceed discreetly, but Kight and Don Kilhefner saw it as a way to attract wide publicity, and announced the plan to create a "Gay Mecca" at a press conference on October 17, 1970. "We are simply following the advice of President Nixon and Spiro Agnew to work within the electoral process," Kilhefner said. Before long, newspaper readers across the nation could read the details of Jackson's carefully constructed plan. "It would mean gay territory," he had written. "It would mean a gay government, a gay civil service. . . . A gay district attorney [who] could choose which laws and which criminals he wishes to prosecute." Kight and Kilhefner issued press releases, called press conferences, talked up reporters, organized committees to plan the logistics of the takeover and provided regular updates on its progress. "We want," Kilhefner announced, "to have a county which we can control completely in order to establish a gay counterculture, the reason being that the society controlled by heterosexuals is too oppressive for us to establish an open homosexual life style." Kilhefner promised a reporter it would be "like Death Valley Days. Pioneers moving in. Hostile natives. Right and justice winning in the end." Kight, drawling out the double entendre, talked about the "penetration of Alpine County."

All of this whipped up exactly the publicity frenzy Kight and Kilhefner had intended: coverage from the networks, an appeal from the county leaders for intervention from Governor Ronald Reagan and, from New Jersey, a pledge of assistance from a right-wing fundamentalist, the Reverend Carl McIntire, to send in missionaries to protect Alpine County. "Homosexuality must be met head on by the Gospel," the Reverend McIntire declared. Bob Hope even mentioned it in a television comedy routine. "They actually tried to take over Alpine County out there in northern California," Hope said. "It's true! They had their own sheriff and he looked real good. He had boots, chaps, buckskin jacket and pearls. Instead of handcuffs he carried a slave bracelet." The people of Alpine County took the threat more seriously. The Alpine Hotel bar posted a sign saying, "Homo Hunting Licenses Sold Here," and the county leaders made it clear that the homosexuals would not be welcome. "When they pull in here," said Sheriff Stuart Merill, "they're going to find either a lot of snow or a lot of rattlesnakes." The word "Alpine" on a county marker on Highway 89 there was crossed off with a streak of white paint and altered to read "Queer County Line." Jackson's idea of a "gay mecca" collapsed under the weight of the attention.

After the Alpine County incident Kight's standing fell with the group.

He was strong-willed and domineering, capable of both coming up with boldly original projects and appropriating proposals of others as his own, sometimes without credit. His self-aggrandizement was chronic and, in truth, unnecessary. Morris Kight could rightfully claim to be central to almost every aspect of the post-Stonewall early gay rights movement in Los Angeles. (And despite some setbacks, he would prove to be among the most influential and enduring homosexual leaders in the city.) The ill feeling and a small coterie of enemies would shadow him for much of his life.

Like Kight, Don Kilhefner also thought that demonstrations had run their course, and he had a different idea for the future of gay organizing. Kilhefner had grown up on a farm in Lancaster in southeastern Pennsylvania, in a family of Amish Mennonites. He graduated from Penn State in 1960 and began working in the civil rights movement. He was among the very first to enlist in the Peace Corps, spending three years in a small village in Ethiopia, designing and constructing a gravity-water system. And now, at the GLF, he drew on these experiences, suggesting that the group go beyond politics and into service, helping troubled gay men and lesbians (as Bob Kohler had suggested in vain in New York). The Gay Liberation Front created a twenty-four-hour hotline; Kilhefner was moved by the anguish and turmoil of the callers, the sheer number of them. Kilhefner, Kight and another GLF member, John V. Platania, began to talk about creating a community services center for gays and lesbians. Kilhefner and Platania, who lived in a collective of radical homosexuals in Venice, would stay up late and explore the notion of how a center might work, writing it down as they went along. It would be an organization with the word "gay" in it—so people could find it in the phone book—and it would have a building. They would incorporate with the Secretary of State's Office and ask the Internal Revenue Service to recognize them as a not-for-profit corporation, so donations would be tax deductible. For once, they thought, gays could do something without worrying about permission from the police department. And there would be medical care—a VD clinic, since it was so hard for homosexuals to find discreet and courteous treatment for sexually transmitted diseases. There would be help for the homeless, and food, particularly for the teenage hustlers who made their living on Santa Monica Boulevard. The center would help homosexuals arrested on morals charges, and homosexual inmates about to be released from prison on probation or parole.

Within a few months, if anyone had trouble grasping how radical this whole notion was, all they needed to do was drive down to 1614 Wilshire Boulevard and stop in front of the rambling ten-room, falling-down Victorian mansion with the sagging porch. There was a two-foot-by-three-foot sign out front, clearly visible from the street: Gay Community Services Center. It read "like a neon billboard on Times Square," as Rand Schrader described it. In the months and years to come, many gay men and lesbians in Los Angeles would cautiously circle that block before parking and finally walking inside. The center even incorporated with the state of California, "to protect and serve, on a nonprofit basis, the individuals, both male and female, of the homosexual (hereinafter referred to as 'gay') community."

The first month's rent, in October 1971, was $325. The center's founders were broke; therapist Betty Berzon ran her first-night "growth" session there by candlelight. To pay the rent, Kight turned to Sheldon Andelson, a Beverly Hills lawyer prominent in the city and well known among other homosexuals as a lawyer more than willing to help men who had been arrested on morals charges. Before long a group in the shadow of the New Left was learning to work the establishment quite well. The sign out front helped; Lillene Fifield, for one, had seen it while driving along Wilshire Boulevard and finally convinced herself to park the car and walk in. She studied at USC, which had an institute to teach graduate students how to apply for public grants. Before long, she, Kight and Kilhefner were at the institute's second-floor offices almost every evening, writing up proposals for another government grant. The first grant—$15,000 from the Department of Health, Education and Welfare—was for a drug-abuse counseling program. The center no longer had to rely on closeted homosexuals for money. This would change the nature of gay organizing in Los Angeles in a way that Kight and Kilhefner could never have imagined.

6

SISTERS AND BROTHERS

The first rifts between the men and the women of Gay Liberation Front of New York had appeared, of all places, on the dance floor at Alternate University. The men—who were flocking in ever greater numbers to this Saturday night gay liberation party—did not notice it at first in their revelry. But women like Ellen Shumsky took in the scene at Alternate U. and saw only men—elbows and shoulders and muscles, men filling the room with flesh and the air with the smell of sweat. Shumsky had come to these events to dance with other women, but also to meet and talk to other lesbians. Yet the loft was kept dark, except for disorienting bursts of strobe lights, and the music was so loud there was no hope for conversation. "Women were lost to each other," Shumsky reported at the time, "in a sea of spaced-out men." The women listened in rage to the music's often brazenly sexist lyrics, watching as their new partners in gay liberation kissed and groped partner after partner on the dance floor. "The oppressive ambiance of a stimulated gay men's bar," a group of GLF women said in one leaflet, as it grimly described evenings in an "overcrowded, dimly lit room, where, packed together subway-rush-hour style, most human contact was limited to groping and dry-fucking."

Women needed an alternative to the bars as much as men; the women's bars in New York were possibly even more dreary than the men's bars. Places like Kooky's on West Fourteenth Street charged $3 just to walk in the door, the price for entrance to a bar with watered-down drinks, a mandatory 25-cent coat-check fee—even for women not wearing one—and a dank postage stamp of a dance floor. Bouncers—heterosexual men—kept an eye on the patrons to make sure they kept buying drinks, and there were "Mafia guardsmen at the door," one lesbian in the Gay Liberation Front reported in the newspaper *Come Out!* "Straight bars do not exist in this web of social harassment."

The GLF dances that meant so much to the men had, for the women, become as unsatisfying as a night at Kooky's. And the logistics of the Saturday night dance became the source that began to divide the men from the women of the GLF: What songs should be played? How loud should the music be? How dark should the room be? Women's leaders, like Ellen Shumsky and Martha Shelley, complained that men dominated the room, and women felt unwelcome. "That's because you don't come," Jerry Hoose responded, wagging a finger. "If you came, the percentages would change. If you were there, it would be more women. If you don't come, you can't complain about it." Shumsky countered that the music was too loud, and the loft too dark and sweaty. "That's what's bringing the people," Hoose answered. "That's why we have thousands and thousands of dollars in the treasury." These seemingly trivial disputes were, really, a metaphor for the increasing alienation between two halves of what had been an improbable political alliance from the start.

There would be no resolution so, finally, the women staged their own dance—and they kept the men out. Martha Shelley shed her shirt (she would not do it with men in the room), and the lesbians enjoyed an "environment of women rapping, drinking, dancing . . . relating with fluidity and grace—it's beautiful," Ellen Shumsky reported at the time. This venture into independence began to influence the way women dealt with, or did not deal with, men in other areas. They staked off a women's-only space at Alternate U. They began skipping the Sunday night GLF meetings, organizing gatherings open only to lesbians. And then, the women demanded half the revenue from the dances they had stopped attending—which precipitated a final split. "We're fighting with the women about everything," Hoose thought. Hoose quit the organization he had helped create, not that any of the women noticed or particularly cared.

The tensions in evidence at Alternate U. defined the way the homosexual rights movement developed for the first two years of the 1970s, and affected the movement throughout the decade. Relations between gay men and lesbians were turning out to be even more difficult than relations between straight men and women. The lack of sexual attraction between gay men and lesbians hadn't eased tensions at all; it might have accomplished the opposite. Gay men and lesbians did not have the same motivation as straight men and women to negotiate a peace since, as a rule, they had no desire to sleep together. And there were, for lesbians, regular reminders of the hostility that some gay men felt toward women. Gay men's bars, like the Lost & Found in Washington, D.C.'s Southeast warehouse district, explicitly barred women— "Come on," said Donn Culver, an owner. "Give us at least one place we can have for ourselves"—or demanded three pieces of identification in an effort to keep females (and for that matter, blacks) from entering. In Boston, Elaine Noble and Ann Maguire went to join the Homophile Union of Boston in late 1969 and were told that while they would be welcome on the board, they couldn't vote. "What the hell do you think we are—the brownie-baking gay women's auxiliary of the gay men's movement?" demanded Maguire, a bulky, blunt-talking woman, before leaving with Noble. The atmosphere at the meetings of the Gay Liberation Front in Washington, D.C., so swam with testosterone that its women members quit in disgust. Finally, only Nancy Tucker, one of the city's first lesbian activists, was left, and even she had had it with men who spoke philosophically of "sisters" but casually of "girls." One Tuesday night in the parish hall at St. James, she stood up, feeling like the last lesbian left in Washington's gay rights movement, and in a barely controlled fury, read aloud the first line of the goodbye statement she had written. "Fuck you, *'Brothers'!*" she yelled. Having got their attention, she read them the rest of her statement, an indictment of their casual, continuing, indifferent sexism. And then she walked out. The lesbian members of the Gay Liberation Front in Atlanta also split off, founding new households of women in a spreading pattern of houses with funny, domestic, sensual names. They created the Lavender Coven, Satin Sheets, and Ruby Fruit Jungle.

Many lesbians were convinced that gay men were misogynist (as Dick Leitsch's crude remarks about women's odors had demonstrated to Martha Shelley). Rita Mae Brown, a handsome and charismatic young writer from Fort Lauderdale who had moved from the feminist movement to become one of the most influential lesbians at the GLF meetings in New York, began arguing that gay men were *less* sensitive to women than straight men. Jeanne Cordova, working with the Los Angeles chapter of the Daughters of Bilitis, reached the same conclusion: "Gender is a stronger behavior determination than sexual orientation," she wrote. "Most gay men don't understand lesbian women any better than most husbands really understand their wives. Gay men get busted when they make sexual overtures to the vice squad in gay bars; and gay women get busted in the courts when a judge takes their children away. Most gay men do not have children; most lesbians don't make sexual passes in parks and bars. When a lesbian wants a sexual relationship, she gets to know the other woman and then has sex. When a gay man wants a sexual relationship, he wants to know where his partner lives; later he asks his name.

"All said and done," Cordova wrote, "many gay men and lesbians are coming to understand that we have little in common but the society which mislabeled us."

The very culture of male homosexuality was perplexing, if not offensive to the women. Many gay men called male friends by a woman's name, or referred to other men as "girl" or "she." This was sometimes part camp ritual, but calling another man "she" was usually meant as a put-down, as in "What's with her?" Men would find it hard to understand why women like Cora Perotta, hanging around the bays of the Gay Activists Alliance Firehouse, would bristle after hearing men refer sneeringly to another man as "she." Rita Mae Brown compared men calling each other Mary to whites looking for laughs by putting on blackface. Even more an outrage to many women were the transvestites, the men who draped themselves in the very clothing—high heels, girdles, bras—that straight and lesbian feminists had discarded as a symbol of male domination. For the women, many of whom had been forced growing up to wear uncomfortable clothing designed to make them more alluring to men, transvestitism represented an insult of the highest order.

Some of the men tried to accommodate the anger. "I am, without doubt, an oppressor," Bob Kohler of New York's Gay Liberation Front wrote in early 1970. "I have been programmed to think of women as secondary beings. My mind has been warped by family structure, controlled by the media and fucked by John Wayne." Another group of men, first in New York and then in Los Angeles, called themselves effeminists, an affirmation, they said, of feminist values. They preached against cruising, arguing, as one of them put it, that the sexual mating practice was "one of the great male chauvinist games," a celebration of male power and virility. But this did little to counter the women's growing disenchantment. They came to resent the way a man's deep voice filled a room, as the women struggled just to make themselves heard. They hated how easily high-paying jobs, college degrees and influence seemed to come to men, and they resented the way men assumed, every time they walked through a door, that they were in charge.

Rules were changing so fast it was hard for anyone to keep up. Bob Kohler, older and courteous, was chastised for holding the door open for a woman at a GLF meeting. He submitted an article to *Come Out!* in which he used the phrase "no man is free until every man is free." When he picked up the newspaper, Kohler found the line had been amended by Lois Hart to read, "no man is free until every man is free (*looking for male chauvinism, Bob?*)." Jeanne Cordova would interrupt Morris Kight whenever he used the word "chairman"—"it's chair-*person*, Morris"—or referred to women as "girls." And men were not alone in having trouble adjusting to the new rules. "Our home means different things to each *girl*," the Los Angeles Daughters of Bilitis, under the leadership of the same Jeanne Cordova, said in a January 1971 newsletter to its members. It went on to advise members to "Stand TALL and PROUD, *girls.*"

The lesbians at GLF were not only being stirred by the gay liberation movement; they were just as surely—indeed, more decisively—being influenced by the feminist movement, a formative influence on New York's Gay Liberation. Rita Mae Brown had come from the National Organization for Women, leaving after a short and noisy stint working on its newsletter. She had concluded that there was no place in the feminist movement for someone who was so young, poor and southern ("a dumb redneck," as Brown colorfully put it years later). And never mind that she was a homosexual, a fact that she did not keep particularly secret. "I'm your token lesbian," Brown announced at her first NOW meeting, charging through the door in a white gauzy blouse with frills, a mini-skirt, stockings and a Phi Beta Kappa key around her neck. It was Rita Mae Brown who brought consciousness raising, a staple of NOW, to the GLF. Brown called the exercises "dreary until death," but nonetheless maintained that by sharing stories of oppression, homosexuals would be able to adjust to their treatment by society, and women would appreciate their systematic discrimination by men.

The encounter groups, which were segregated by sex at Brown's instruction, certainly helped members understand society's hostility toward homosexuals. But they also served to fan outrage among women at their treatment at the hands of all men—gay or straight. "Once a woman becomes clued in how she is made an object to be pushed around in this culture," Rita Mae Brown said in 1974, as she recalled those early years, "those little differences you notice become infuriating." As these lesbians drifted away from the GLF they began meeting at Brown's apartment. They felt slighted not only by gay men but also, they realized as Brown told of the hostility toward lesbians among many of the leaders of NOW, by feminists. The men, many of the women concluded, were a lost cause. But, perhaps, the feminists were not.

It was May Day 1970, and four hundred women had just sat down in an intermediate school auditorium on New York's West Side when the room went dark. The Second Congress to Unite Women was scheduled to start at 7:15 p.m., with opening remarks by Kate Millett, the education chairwoman for the New York chapter of NOW. But Millett had learned a few days earlier that her speech was not to be. She had stopped by the lower Fifth Avenue apartment of Barbara Love and Sidney Abbott, where about forty women had gathered: lesbians from the women's movement and feminists from the GLF. Millett was late, and when she apologized by saying that she was preparing her speech for the women's congress, the room rolled with laughter. "You're not going to deliver any speech," Barbara Love said. The Second Congress to Unite Women was not going to be the weekend of discussions about child care, the Equal Rights Amendment and abortion rights that its feminist organizers had intended. The lesbians gathered at Love's apartment were plotting to take it over. They would talk about lesbians and the feminist movement, and try to convince the mostly straight women that demonizing lesbians played into the hands of their mutual enemies.

These women blended easily into the audience that Friday night. A rebel's whoop went up from the back of the auditorium when the lights went out, and then the padding of running feet was heard. The lights came back on, and seventeen women were standing in a line in front of the stage, each wearing a lavender-dyed T-shirt stenciled with the slogan "LAVENDER MENACE," the phrase Betty Friedan, the founder of the modern-day women's movement and the leader of NOW, was using to describe the threat which she said lesbianism posed to her movement. There was an intentional lightheartedness to this occupation; they did not wish to frighten the audience out of the hall. Rita Mae Brown considered humor a potent political weapon. "Funny people are dangerous," she said. "It's hard to hate people when they're funny." From the stage, Martha Shelley took the microphone, and invited all lesbians and their supporters to come forward. Barbara Love, sitting next to a colleague from NOW who, as best she knew, had no idea she was a lesbian, felt queasy but slipped on the "LAVENDER MENACE" T-shirt she had stuffed into a pocket and walked to the front of the hall.

"We have come to tell you that we lesbians are being oppressed outside the movement and inside the movement by a sexist attitude," one of the women declared. "We want to discuss the lesbian issue with you." There were a few cries of protest. "Do you want us to go on?" one of the protesters asked, and the response was a burst of approving applause. And then Kate Millett walked shyly to the microphone, speaking so softly that her audience, aware that she had been part of the official program and eager to hear what she thought of all this, had to lean forward. "I know what these women are talking about," Millett said. "I was there. In some ways, I still am there." That was the closest Millett had come then to publicly acknowledging being a lesbian. There were discussions for the rest of the evening, then consciousness-raising groups, an all-women's dance on Saturday night, and by Sunday, the congress had adopted the resolutions that had been drafted by the "Lavender Menace," asserting that "whenever the label lesbian is used against the movement collectively or against women individually, it is to be affirmed, not denied."

The idea of staging this confrontation had taken root in Rita Mae Brown's apartment, where the women of the GLF had taken to calling themselves the Radicalesbians, to differentiate themselves from the gay men. Brown was, both in intellect and appearance, an irresistible force, with a sexual charge and abandon which heightened her power and won her a quick and devoted following. Seated in Brown's living room, away from the GLF, Martha Shelley had suggested that the women draft a paper asserting the importance of lesbians to the women's movement. Six of the group's members spent the next few months working on the document and chose the Second

Congress to present it. "The Woman-Identified-Woman," left on every seat and handed out to women at the door, was a call to arms that thrilled the lesbians who read it, many of them committing whole sections of it to memory, able to recite passages decades later. The manifesto asserted the importance of lesbians to the feminist movement. But it also spoke, at a time of exceptional turmoil and confusion, to homosexual women who felt abandoned both by the gay movement and the feminist movement. "The Woman-Identified-Woman" called on feminists to cut their ties with men and the male culture, to redefine their own role in society by bonding with women—ideally lesbians, since they best understood the oppression women suffered in a male-dominated society.

"What is a lesbian?" the manifesto demanded in its opening line. "A lesbian is the rage of all women condensed to the point of explosion."

Women would not be free as long as they saw themselves in relation to men, as wives, mothers or sexual partners. "Those sex roles dehumanize women by defining us as a supportive/serving caste *in relation* to the master caste of men," it said. Women must discard the male identity they had drawn from a society built on male values. They should avoid dealings with men and identify with women—politically, socially and even sexually. Finally, "The Woman-Identified-Woman" urged feminists to shed their fear of lesbianism, the label that for decades had been used to discredit independent women and was now being used to bludgeon the women's liberation movement. "Lesbian is the word, the label, the condition that holds women in line. When a woman hears this word tossed her way, she knows she is stepping out of line. She knows that she has crossed the terrible boundary of her sex role. She recoils, she protests, she reshapes her action to gain approval. Lesbian is a label invented by the Man to throw at any woman who dares to be equal, who dares to challenge his prerogatives.

"As long as the label 'dyke' can be used to frighten women into a less militant stand, keep her separate from her sisters, keep her from giving primacy to anything other than men and their family—then to that extent she is controlled by the male culture," the paper argued. "Until women see in each other the possibility of a primary commitment that includes sexual love, they will be denying themselves the love and value they readily accord to men, thus affirming their second-class status."

The manifesto was, in effect, a road map to a separate political movement for lesbians, but from the beginning it proved difficult to follow. The Radicalesbians were among the first women to experiment with what was called separatism, limiting their political and social universe to women only—in fact, lesbians only. But their internal politics ended up being just as tangled as they had been at the GLF. The Radicalesbians demanded of their members a level of devotion that was, ultimately, paralyzing. There were no leaders.

"We are against hierarchical structures because as women, we have experienced first-hand that hierarchy is a fixed status system (those with power and privilege, i.e. men, assume leadership)," Ellen Shumsky explained in an article in *Come Out!* in December 1970. All decisions were reached as a consensus of the women in the group, which, in the polarized world of activist politics in the 1970s, meant that often no decisions could be reached at all.

The Radicalesbians were unyielding in their insistence that women cut their ties with heterosexual society and intolerant of any who did not. Even Kate Millett was shunned, both for being married and for permitting her book *Sexual Politics* to be published by a mainstream publisher. When Millett held a book party to mark its release, she arrived to find a flier, produced by friends from the Radicalesbians she had invited to the event, attacking her for cooperating with the "pig media," for making money from the book and for marrying a man, even though she was supposed to be a lesbian. The high-minded discussions that had produced "The Woman-Identified-Woman" soon gave way to long debates over whether the Rolling Stones were a sexist band. Before long, some of the founding members, Barbara Love among them, decided to return to what was left of the GLF. Even Martha Shelley began to wonder if it had been a mistake for the women to try to separate.

Still, the seed of separatism had been planted and would, in one form or another, continue to flourish for another ten years.

Lesbians across the country, assertive and restive, were by now increasingly challenging what had emerged as one of the early organizing goals of the gay rights movement: the right to have sex, free of the shackles of law or heterosexual conventions. The focus in such one-issue groups as New York's Gay Activists Alliance, and some hundred groups that formed across the country to imitate it, was an attack on laws forbidding sodomy, or on police departments that arrested men for public cruising. These may have been the most obvious manifestations of discrimination against homosexuals—discrimination involving housing or employment was more difficult to document, since so many homosexuals were in the closet—but it meant that lesbians often found themselves defending male sexual behavior they found unsavory. Many lesbians, meeting homosexual men for the first time, came to believe that sex for gay men wasn't one compartment of their lives; it seemed to *be* their lives. They advertised it in the way they walked and dressed. The sound of a gay liberation meeting coming to order was often the noise of rustling leather jackets and chains.

The men didn't quarrel with this notion of gay men as hypersexual. Henry Wiemhoff, founder of Chicago Gay Liberation, realized just how true this characterization was when he and Susan Tosswill forced their way onto a stage at an American Medical Association convention in Chicago in 1970 to rebut Dr. Charles W. Socarides, who made a practice of treating homosexuals. When Dr. Socarides stated that the typical homosexual man had a compulsive, uncontrollable impulse to seek out sex with another man, bringing temporary satisfaction until the cycle started anew and sent him back on the hunt, Wiemhoff, nodding and saying to himself, "Well, that's kind of true," panicked as he realized the moderator might turn to him to rebut Dr. Socarides ("Don't say anything, Henry," Wiemhoff kept thinking. "Just shut up.") But Susan Tosswill spoke up: "You know," she told Dr. Socarides, "that's the most perfect description I've heard of some straight male friends of mine."

Lesbians were more likely to practice what they liked to call serial monogamy, one partner at a time. By contrast, a typical weekend night for a gay man might include a half-dozen different sexual encounters during a stop at the baths or a back-room bar. Rita Mae Brown had long been struck and repulsed by men's single-minded fascination with sex. But she was fascinated by this world and decided to see it for herself. Brown glued a mustache to her lip, slipped on a loose football jersey to hide her breasts and—like "stowing away on the *Queen Mary*"—set out to explore two bathhouses in Manhattan. It turned out not to be fun; Brown was forever struck by how anxious and driven the men looked as they hunted the hallways for sex.

The difference between men and women and their ability to enjoy recreational sex, Brown decided, was cultural: women were raised to view sex as bad. So she set out to prove that men weren't the only ones who could enjoy sex for sex's sake. Brown and Mary Spottswood Pou, Brown's apartment mate and activist friend, rented a gay bathhouse near Georgetown University Law School. They printed 120 invitations on a stock paper with an orange stripe running down the middle, bidding their lesbian friends to "Celebrate Spring With Gay Abandon." It advised that no drugs or alcohol would be allowed ("toke up before you come"). The women would trade their clothes for a towel at the door—just as the men did every weekend—and be given the run of the cubicles, steam rooms and common areas. Spottswood Pou and Brown weren't sure what their experiment might produce: a room full of uptight lesbians or a breakthrough for lesbian sexuality. But the moment the doors opened, it was clear that this was not going to be anything like a gay man's night at the baths. Several of the women, after being handed towels, stiffly pointed out that one skimpy towel might hide everything a man had to worry about, but a woman needed more. They demanded a second towel to cover their breasts. The women stayed until 2 a.m.; they talked and, naked and invisible in the clouds of the steam room, sang songs. But that made up the extent of the "action." Rita Mae Brown disappeared upstairs with someone for a short bout of necking, but the rest of the women sat around awkwardly, their eyes all locked above shoulder level.

Many of the men considered promiscuity a badge of honor and tried to integrate it into their public, and political lives, often to the dismay of lesbians, who found themselves tarnished by their male colleagues' displays, perhaps most notably at the 1971 Christopher Street West Parade in Los Angeles. The march lasted ten blocks and ninety minutes, filled with colorful banners and "Gay is Great" balloons, and a superlative float constructed by Troy Perry's Metropolitan Community Church. It was fifty-five feet long, featured a locomotive pulling two passenger cars carting the MCC choir in red robes singing gospel songs and was layered with seven thousand fresh roses. It would take a lot to obscure what was, by Perry's estimation, a $5,600-religious monument to gay liberation, but another float—a thirty-five-foot-long construction of blue-and-white striped fabric slung over wooden hoops, carried by seven men, patterned after the Chinese dragons that surged through the streets of Chinatown on the Chinese New Year—managed to do it. At the front of the tube was a pink head with two enormous eyes and black eyelashes that could be flapped by a handle on the inside, and a vertical pink slit for a mouth. At the rear was a red sack holding two large lumps.

The men insisted it was just a caterpillar. But the people on the sidewalk knew they were watching a replica of a penis make its way down Hollywood Boulevard. And just in case anyone missed the point, the seven men hoisting the dragon on their shoulders would scrunch together and then stretch apart—"Okay, explode!" Don Kilhefner ordered from under the puppet— and it would expand into a mock-erection. The men in the front rubbed the head of the "cock-a-pillar," as they were really calling it, against a Los Angeles Police Department squad car, squishing its head against the window and batting its eyes. For Kilhefner, this was a celebration of gay male sexuality. Morris Kight playfully told *The Advocate:* "As far as I know—I'm an anal-erotic, penises are not my trip—but as far as I know about penises, from observation of mine and others, very few of them have eyes and hardly any of them have huge knobs and warts on them, and things like that." But Kight spent the evening and next day fielding calls of outrage from the community, most from women. ("How would you have felt if we had sent a great vagina down the street?" one woman demanded of him.)

It was not an isolated display. In New York, *Come Out!*, the GLF newspaper, was destroyed in a clash between men and women over the glorification of sex. The newspaper printed an article, "Cock Sucking Seminar" by Steve Gavin, which discussed, in great length and detail, the act of fellatio. The next issue was printed on plain 8½-by-11 typing paper and headlined *"Come Out! Is Dead."* The women involved in the newspaper collective denounced the previous issue as an example of "male domination/intimidation," which they had not approved. "There can no longer be such a myth as gay liberation," wrote one of the two women on the six-person *Come Out!* staff. "If freedom from sexism for homosexuals is going to happen, it will have to happen through separate lesbian and effeminist movements." The fellatio article, she wrote, was "horrendous and offensive yet it appeared in a 'gay liberation' newspaper. Was it just an unfortunate mistake or a blatant example of male supremacy, i.e. what I say goes?" One of her male colleagues, writing about the collapse, said: "The time of the original concept of *Come Out!* is over because the needs and goals and identities of gay women and men are certainly no longer the same."

October 1970, San Francisco

Del Martin had never been the type of person who angered easily. Since 1955, when she and Phyllis Lyon created the Daughters of Bilitis in San Francisco, Del Martin had proved to be reserved, even deferential, especially to the women of the DOB who were not as politically assertive as she might have liked. And she had deferred to the men of the Mattachine Society, which is what women did in the 1960s, as she knew from the trucking company where she worked. It took a lot to provoke Del Martin, and that was one reason she was surviving the new gay liberationists, even as many of her colleagues were retiring into irrelevancy.

So when Del Martin, of all people, declared in an essay in *The Advocate* in October 1970 that she would deal no more with homosexual men, it could not be ignored or dismissed. This was no young Marxist from Los Angeles or militant feminist from the Redstockings in New York, with its manifesto asserting that women are "exploited as sex objects, breeders, domestic servants, and cheap labor," and stating: "We identify the agents of our oppression as man." The steady and sharp tide of animosity among lesbians directed at gay men had now been joined by a loyal soldier of the homophile movement, who had once gladly stood with men under the supposedly unifying banner of gay liberation.

"Goodbye my alienated brothers," Martin proclaimed in her *Advocate* essay. "Goodbye to the male chauvinists of the homophile movement who are so wrapped up in the 'cause' that they lose sight of the people for whom the cause came into being.

"Goodbye to the 'Police Beat'—the defense of washroom sex and pornographic movies," she wrote. "That was never my bag anyway.

"Goodbye to the male homophile community," Martin wrote. " 'Gay is good,' but not good enough—so long as it is limited to white males only. We joined with you in what we mistakenly thought was a common cause. A few of you tried, we admit. But you are still too few, and even you fall short of the mark."

Martin wrote in reaction to the North American Conference of Homophile Organizations (NACHO) gathering that summer in San Francisco. Del Martin was a veteran of these conferences of men in suits and women in skirts, but this one was different: It coincided with the fiftieth anniversary of the ratification of the Nineteenth Amendment, granting women the vote. The National Organization for Women, four years old and thriving, celebrated the day, August 26, 1970, with demonstrations and marches by almost 100,000 women and their supporters in ninety cities—50,000 marching on Fifth Avenue in New York alone. Lesbians at these conferences always seemed just tolerated, there only to run the mimeograph machines and provide, by their presence, a shield for the men against charges of sexism. The juxtaposition of the national celebration of women's rights with the static condescension of homosexual men brought Martin's rage to the surface. "Gay women today," she declared, sitting at the podium with five other lesbians and surveying an audience of twenty-five men, "are identifying more with heterosexual women than with gay men."

It was a prophetic warning, but there was no indication the men there grasped that. Arthur Warner of New York Mattachine rose to his feet, blustery and indignant: "Women most certainly are included in the homophile movement and have been from the beginning." A member of Mattachine Midwest was astonished by this "presentation by a motley crew of gay women's liberation," this stream of "anti-male hostility," as he later put it, from a group of women whose views seemed lifted out of the books of the psychiatrists who devoted their careers to "curing" homosexuals. They dutifully passed a statement that NACHO "does affirm our support of solidarity with the women's liberation movement in their struggles against our common oppressors, a male chauvinist and sexist society." The statement, boilerplate and quickly forgotten, did nothing to satisfy Del Martin, who, in her *Advocate* essay, saw it as "wasteful, meaningless verbiage" constructed by "hollow men of self-proclaimed privilege." Homosexual men did not appreciate the separate waves of discrimination lesbians endured because of both their sexuality and their sex. The men did not understand the frightening moment of realization that was unique to lesbians; the sudden understanding that their attraction to women meant, on top of everything else, that they were economically alone, no longer able to count on the support of a husband, as so many of them had been raised to expect. Martin had assumed that homosexual men would be quick to embrace the goals of women's liberation, since they, too, were discriminated against by heterosexual men. That had been a mistake, she decided.

"I will not be your 'nigger' any longer," she wrote. "Nor was I ever your mother. Those were stultifying roles you laid on me, and I shall no longer concern myself with your toilet training." Her worst scorn came in three sentences which revealed her disgust with what she had concluded was the central obsession of the gay male movement. "As I bid you adieu, I leave each of you to your own device. Take care of it, stroke it gently, mouth it, fondle it. As the center of your consciousness, it's really all you have."

Del Martin's cry was the strongest challenge yet to the tenuous new gay rights movement. It was published in the largest and most influential gay newspaper of its time, a publication whose masthead was dominated by men, as Martin and other lesbians were reminded every two weeks, when they thumbed through pages devoid of news about women, and spiced with black-and-white pictures of men's bare chests, buttocks and torsos. *The Advocate* printed Martin's valedictory in full, with an approving editors' note on the top: "Her free-swinging candid remarks about the scene will anger and dismay many male homosexuals," the editors said, adding, "There is much to think about in what she says." Yet they ran it on page 21, deep in the paper, behind the editorial page, and after the standard diet of stories about men fighting for the right to dance, or men wanting to hold hands in bars, or men being arrested for cruising, or men battling restrictions on pornography.

By 1970, Ivy Bottini already had spent four years in the movement that was drawing the attention of disaffected lesbians like Martin: the women's movement. Feminism, not gay rights, had drawn her to the demonstration lines of the late 1960s and early 1970s. And although Bottini tended to favor what she discreetly referred to as the lesbian uniform—a blue denim shirt with the collar turned up hard against the scruff of her short hair, and blue jeans bunching up at the top of her work boots—she did not talk much about her sexuality. Indeed, Bottini was known at NOW as the recently divorced working mother of two teenage daughters who had belonged to the PTA and worked in school board elections on suburban Long Island. When she became the president of NOW's New York chapter in 1968, she seemed the perfect person for this position. Bottini, a founder of the chapter in 1966, had been married to Eddie Bottini at the time, though she was finding it harder to ignore the attraction she felt for the women in her all-women's basketball league. When Bottini confided in Dolores Alexander, her friend at *Newsday*, the Long Island daily where they both worked and who had signed her up at NOW, Alexander said: "I don't care what you do. Just don't tell anyone about it!" So at the age of forty-two, Ivy Bottini left Eddie Bottini and their two daughters and quietly moved into New York City with a woman, and devoted almost all of her time to NOW.

Ivy Bottini was impossible not to like, with her warm bursts of energy and toothy smiles, and she surfed over the ideological and sexual waves that were roiling the women's movement. At NOW, she pushed the use of consciousness-raising groups, which produced, she believed, a dramatic growth in both the chapter's membership and fervor. Bottini led some of

NOW's most dramatic demonstrations, including a takeover of the Statue of Liberty in the summer of 1970. A troop of women in maternity dresses showed up at the base of the Statue of Liberty, and ignoring the kind words of a ranger—"There are a *lot* of steps here. You sure you wanna walk up?"—made their way to the top. Ivy Bottini stayed at the bottom. She was a five-foot-tall, 160-pound, squat-barrel of a woman, and, as she put it, "I don't do stairs well." From there, she made sure the newspapers and television stations were alerted to what was going on. Once at the head of the steps, the rest of the women pulled huge swatches of cloth from under their maternity dresses, and hooked them into a sixty-foot banner that they hung from the front of the statue: "WOMEN OF THE WORLD UNITE!"

Throughout these first two years of NOW's existence, Ivy Bottini had taken discreet notice of other lesbians in the room, like Barbara Love. Sometimes the lesbians would go out after the meeting to a women's bar, or they would gather for a dinner party, and talked about lesbianism. It was never discussed at NOW. Betty Friedan called lesbianism walking proof of the very stereotypes that were being used to lampoon the women's movement and suggested that some of the women portraying themselves as lesbians were CIA agitators sent in to discredit her movement, a charge she made against Elaine Noble, then a co-chair of the Women's Political Caucus in Boston. Friedan's strong feelings about lesbians filtered through NOW, as Rita Mae Brown noted in her bristling resignation letter: NOW "consciously oppresses other women on the question of sexual preference," she wrote. "Lesbian is the one word that can cause the Executive Committee a collective heart attack."

There were constant reminders of the difficulties lesbians would encounter in finding space on the women's liberation stage. On the same day that Del Martin scolded the San Francisco homophile conference, Martha Shelley had to shove her way onto the platform of a Strike for Equality women's rally at Bryant Park in New York (Ivy Bottini had led the march into the park) to make certain that at least one open lesbian spoke. "If you don't let me through, there's going to be a fistfight here and it's going to be in all of the media," Shelley warned, her eyes black with anger. "It's going to be on TV that I punched you." The guards unlocked their elbows, and Shelley jumped up on the stage and made her way to the microphone. Raising her fist in the air, she recounted a spate of incidents where police had harassed lesbians and shouted: "We're your sisters and we need your help!"

Shelley's speech won notice—an open lesbian talking publicly at a huge women's rights rally at New York's Bryant Park, no matter that she didn't give her name—but it soon was apparent that the only barrier she really broke was the one around the stage. Betty Friedan had not wavered. And in the winter of 1970, Friedan was handed a piece of evidence which supported her warnings about lesbians in the women's movement—and it came from Kate Millett.

The artist and writer had helped shape the new wave of feminism with her powerful book on sexism, *Sexual Politics,* in which she argues that men dominate the culture, religion, politics and economy of the United States. *Time* magazine seized on her as a symbol and spokeswoman for the new women's liberation movement in the heady summer of 1970. It ran a cover story framed around a sketch of Millett, headlined "The Politics of Sex." The text described her as a "brilliant misfit in a man's world" and "the Mao Tse-tung of Women's Liberation," but it did not mention her guarded acknowledgment, in May 1970, that she was a lesbian. (She had married Fumio Yoshimura, a Japanese sculptor, in 1965 when he was facing deportation.) But when Millett spoke to an assembly of feminists and lesbians at Columbia University in November, she was confronted by a radical lesbian who said, "Why don't you say you're a lesbian here openly? You've said you were a lesbian in the past." Millett hesitated for a moment, then said, "Yes, I am a lesbian."

Time magazine reported the exchange two weeks later on its "Behavior" page. The story, "Women's Lib: A Second Look," asserted that Millett had contributed to the "growing skepticism about the [feminist] movement by acknowledging at a recent meeting that she is bisexual. The disclosure is bound to discredit her as a spokesman for her cause, cast further doubt on her theories, and reinforce the views of those skeptics who routinely dismiss all liberationists as lesbians."

Barbara Love and Ivy Bottini read this and instantly realized the threat this posed to their efforts to integrate lesbians into the women's movement. Within two days they assembled a press conference in Greenwich Village, where Kate Millett sat at the center of a table filled with microphones at Washington Square Methodist Church. A group of fifty women stood behind her as she spoke, interrupting her remarks with cheers. They issued a statement in the name of thirty feminist and lesbian leaders, proclaiming their "solidarity with the struggle of homosexuals to attain their liberation in a sexist society."

"Women's Liberation and homosexual liberation are both struggling toward a common goal: A society free from defining and categorizing people by virtue of gender and/or sexual preference," it read. " 'Lesbian' is a label used as a psychic weapon to keep women locked into their male-defined 'feminine role.' " Millett was surrounded by such feminist leaders as Gloria Steinem, who would shortly go on to become the first editor of *Ms.* magazine; Flo Kennedy, the feminist lawyer, and the writers Susan Brownmiller and Sally Kempton. Aileen Hernandez, who had succeeded Betty Friedan as NOW president the previous spring, issued a statement deploring *Time*'s "sexual McCarthyism," and NOW national board chairman Wilma Scott Heidi wrote: "So all people are bisexual, so what else is new?" Bella Abzug, who had just been elected to Congress, sent a message of support. Ti-Grace Atkinson, another member of NOW, declared: "If men succeed in associating lesbianism with the women's movement, then they destroy the movement." And there were, in a church room filled with television cameras, reporters and photographers, women who described themselves as lesbian. "People must speak up as lesbians," Barbara Love said. "I am a lesbian." She had not been planning to do that, and her statement made both the network news and the *New York Times,* prompting her to use the upcoming Christmas gathering at home to inform her family of her sexuality.

But one woman who was not there—the founder of the modern-day women's movement—counted at least as much as all the ones who were. Betty Friedan, said by her office to be out of town, had, in fact, aggressively sought to discourage NOW women from attending the press conference. "It was," Friedan told the *New York Times* in 1971, "a terrible mistake. The CIA couldn't have thought of anything worse. . . . Trying to equate lesbianism with the women's liberation movement is playing into the hands of the enemy."

Ivy Bottini was resting in a friend's apartment when the telephone call came from Sidney Abbott and Barbara Love. The New York chapter of NOW was about to hold its annual meeting, and Bottini, the outgoing chapter president, had assumed she would be elected chairman of the chapter board. But Abbott and Love had heard differently: Friedan and her supporters were planning to oust all lesbians and their sympathizers from the chapter. "They're going to try to get you," Love told Bottini. Over the past few months, Bottini had aggressively pushed the mainstream issues that were at the foundation of NOW's existence—the Equal Rights Amendment, the abolition of anti-abortion laws, government-supported child care, equal treatment and pay at the workplace. And she certainly had not been open about her own lesbianism. But even before the press conference for Millett, Bottini had organized a NOW panel entitled "Is Lesbianism a Feminist Issue?" She had placed a small notice about it in the *New York Times* and it had produced the biggest turnout she had ever seen at a NOW meeting. And while the lesbians on the panel were closeted, Bottini made no secret of her belief that it was in NOW's interest to embrace the lesbianism movement. "You don't have to be a lesbian, but if you have a fear of being called a lesbian, you could never be free as a woman," Bottini said. "You will always be able to be controlled." Kate Millett, who with Barbara Love and Sidney Abbott was among the relatively private lesbians on the panel, said the women's movement had "been carried on the backs of lesbians for about five years" and that "now it's time for the movement to do something for lesbians." The panel did exactly what Betty Friedan did not want—it raised the profile of lesbians in NOW.

Ivy Bottini also had had what turned out to be a revealing encounter with Betty Friedan. There had been a march on Gracie Mansion, the New York City mayoral residence, on an icy, sleeting winter day in December, to draw attention to feminist demands for abolition of abortion laws and government support for day care centers. Bottini mounted a sound truck to introduce the speakers and, waving a fistful of lavender armbands, urged the crowd to wear one in support of Millett and lesbians in the women's movement. Betty Friedan, standing next to Bottini, pointedly used her speech to call the lesbian issue a "lavender herring" and a "diversion" from the women's movement. Afterward, Friedan cast her armband to the icy pavement as Ivy Bottini watched. The two women shared a cab home. As Bottini opened the door to leave the taxi, Friedan leaned over to warn her that the lesbian issue was "going to sink the movement."

"I'm sorry you feel that way," Bottini responded, "but you can't have the women's movement without the lesbian issue."

Friedan shook her head no, wordless as Bottini climbed out of the cab.

"I'm sorry you feel that way," Bottini repeated.

"Well, I do," Friedan responded icily.

Still, Bottini could not conceive of anyone trying to kick her out of NOW. And when Barbara Love called with the urgent advice that she round up supporters before the organizational meeting, Bottini said, "I don't think the membership will do this. I haven't done anything."

The church was unusually crowded the night of the vote. Barbara Love had been going to NOW meetings since 1967, and the fact that she recognized scarcely a face in the crowd told her all she needed to know: Friedan and her supporters had packed the house. There followed a night of clipped debate with coded comments about the "original goals of NOW" and where the word "lesbian" was apparently never mentioned. Bottini was defeated by a stranger in what should have been a routine election as chair of the New York chapter board, and instead was elected as just a member of the board itself. Another half-dozen women who were suspected of being lesbians or lesbian sympathizers were forced out of office as well, victims to what one NOW member later called "hard hats in white gloves." One NOW member, writing about the incident in an open letter to the organization a few days later, said: "The house has been cleaned. Once again. Your enemies?? Practically all gone. . . . What has happened is that NOW has one-upped *Time* magazine. *Time,* in essence, tried to purge one woman from the movement by attempting to discredit her because she had 'confessed' to being bisexual. NOW *successfully* purged people for allegedly being 'Lesbian sympathizers.' "

A few weeks later, at her first meeting as a member of the chapter board of directors, Bottini told her friends and compatriots, "I can't work with you. You helped kill me. You are no better than the patriarchy." With that, she packed up and drove cross-country to Los Angeles, arriving in mid-May, just in time for a regional NOW convention there.

The one thing she hoped, she told Barbara Love as she was leaving, was that something good might have come out of the incident: "This had to happen," she said. "I mean, this panic, this fear, this purging, vilification, all of these things had to happen before the organization could begin to deal with lesbianism. We may have won by losing." In Los Angeles, Bottini found some reason to think she might have been correct. On May 18, the West Coast Regional Membership of NOW passed a resolution which termed lesbianism a "legitimate concern of feminism" and greeted Bottini with loud applause when she walked into the room. And when NOW held its annual convention there the following September, Del Martin and Phyllis Lyon had helped prepare a formal resolution by NOW, an apology by the women's movement to lesbians and an almost unconditional endorsement of lesbian demands. This was ten months after the lesbian purge in New York. Betty Friedan was there, and Del Martin and Phyllis Lyon girded themselves for what they assumed would be another terrible fight. They did not believe the resolution would win approval from the national convention of NOW. They were wrong.

"Afraid of alienating public support, we have often treated lesbians as the step-sisters of the movement, allowed to work with us but then expected to hide in the upstairs closet when the company comes," the resolution said. NOW "has been silent on the issue of lesbianism. Yet no other woman suffers more abuse and discrimination for the right to be her own person than the lesbian.

"Be it resolved," it said, that "NOW recognizes the double oppression of women who are lesbians, and be it further resolved: that a woman's right to her own person includes the right to define and express her own sexuality and to choose her own lifestyle, and be it further resolved: that NOW acknowledges the oppression of lesbians as a legitimate concern of feminism."

May 1971, Washington, D.C.

Rita Mae Brown hadn't stayed around to watch the Radicalesbians disintegrate in New York. She was on to Washington, D.C., to watch government up close, and in the spring of 1971 she attended a D.C. Women's Liberation weekend retreat. Once again, Brown and other lesbian-feminists sought to force a women's rights group to deal with homosexuality, but this time with considerably less success. The D.C. group had been founded, and largely influenced, by women who would turn out to be lesbian, but this only became apparent at the retreat. Charlotte Bunch, married in 1968, the year she helped organize the Washington women's movement, was one of the women. By the time of the women's retreat, Bunch, a student fellow at the Institute for Policy Studies, a liberal think tank, had left her husband and moved into a lesbian commune. It was Rita Mae Brown who had first seduced her, inviting Bunch home and then into bed after a movie a few weeks before Christmas 1970. Bunch was twenty-six, a soft-spoken and dignified Methodist from Artesia, New Mexico. Brown had at first seemed interested only in an ideological seduction. Night after night, Brown challenged Bunch's decision to divide her energies among the anti-war, civil rights and women's movements; why not give herself completely to the women's movement? On Thanksgiving weekend 1970, as the Black Panthers held their Revolutionary People's Constitutional Convention in the District, Charlotte Bunch found herself driving back and forth from the convention to her commune in the Adams-Morgan section, where Rita Mae Brown was waiting to pick up their debate: Why are you wasting time with them? Don't you see that the real revolution is the women's movement? Don't you see that lesbianism is the vanguard of the real revolution? Bunch soon concluded that Brown's interest might be as sexual as it was political, not that it bothered her. Bunch's initiation by Brown was accomplished so smoothly, and so quickly, that she would later find she could never relate to the "coming out" stories she heard from men and women in the movement. She jumped from being married to sleeping with, and then moving in with, one of the movement's best-known radical lesbians. The women's movement in Washington being what it was—a small, tight-knit world—and Rita Mae Brown being who she was, it was not long before every woman in feminist and lesbian circles knew that Brown and Bunch were living together.

By the time of the feminist retreat in the spring of 1971, Charlotte Bunch was devoting most of her time to the women's movement, but she and her colleagues had become unwilling to remain silent about their sexual orientation. Bunch, Sharon Deevey and the other influential lesbians in women's liberation, prodded by Rita Mae Brown, thought the time had come for the District's feminist movement to embrace lesbianism, and were indignant, at the retreat, when they would not. Bunch could not understand the resistance—were they so afraid, she asked, about scaring away the men who oppressed them? Didn't they understand that "Heterosexuality as an institution and an ideology is a cornerstone of male supremacy," as she later argued, adding: "Women interested in destroying male supremacy, patriarchy and capitalism must equally with lesbians fight heterosexual domination—or we will never end female oppression." There was, she said, no greater threat to male domination than the one posed by lesbians, who put women first while rejecting the dominant sexual role of a male. "Male society defines lesbianism as a sexual act, which reflects men's limited view of women," she wrote. "They think of us only in terms of sex. . . . We say that a lesbian is a woman whose sense of self and energies, including sexual energies, center around women—she is women-identified. The woman-identified-woman commits herself to other women for political, emotional, physical and economic support." Bunch, Deevey and Brown decided that weekend to sever their ties with the Washington women's movement. They created a discussion group to work solely on feminist-lesbian issues and called themselves Those Women, a sardonic reference to what they were being called. Those Women had, like the Radicalesbians in New York, come to separatism, though the break in Washington was from the feminist movement, rather than the male homosexual rights groups. Charlotte Bunch concluded that there was no space in the feminist movement "to develop a lesbian feminist politics and life style without constant and non-productive conflict with heterosexual fear, antagonism and insensitivity."

In the summer of 1971, they formed a collective open to lesbians only. They clipped their hair short and moved into three communes on Capitol Hill. They would work, live and think together, and deal only with other lesbians, embracing the true spirit of "The Woman-Identified-Woman." They would call themselves The Furies—after the mythical avenging Greek goddesses, rendered as having snakes for hair, bloodshot eyes and bats' wings, and they were devoted to forging a new lesbian-feminist politics that would force the women's movement, and society, to reconsider its view of lesbians. The collective began a monthly newspaper to spread the word of its mission. "We call our paper *The Furies* because we are . . . angry," it declared in the first issue. "We are angry because we are oppressed by male supremacy. We have been fucked over all our lives by a system which is based on the domination of men over women, which defines male as good and female only as good as the man you are with. It is a system in which heterosexuality is rigidly enforced and Lesbianism rigidly suppressed."

The Furies were twelve women, aged eighteen to twenty-eight, all feminists, all lesbians, with three children among them. They were independent and intelligent, all white. They came from the lower- and upper-middle classes; some were high school dropouts, others were graduate students; they almost all came from New York, Chicago and Washington, D.C. The group was a collective and took steps to level the economic class differences of its members. Cars became community property. Members contributed a portion of their salary, ranging from 20 to 50 percent, depending on class background, "former heterosexual privilege," education and age. By group decision, the women stopped doing drugs (which meant marijuana). They started a school to teach women auto and home repair so that they would not have to rely on men. And they prepared women to battle any man who tried to abuse them: "Know that if a man attacks you, you'll first knee him in the balls, punch to his solar plexus, trip him, then stomp on his nose," *The Furies* advised. "Or first kick to the balls, punch to the stomach, elbow to the head, or karate chop his neck. Think up your own combinations as you're walking down the street."

The Furies collective was modeled after a Bolshevist cell: they shared chores and clothes, and slept on mattresses on a common floor. These were difficult times, and the collective, an assortment of strong and very difficult personalities, was soon consumed by conflict. Differences in class and intellectual interest soon disrupted any hope of collective harmony. Rita Mae Brown and Charlotte Bunch came under attack for spending so much time writing and reading, which were considered elitist. The clashes over class also revolved around Brown. Rita Mae Brown, always reminding the women about her poor background, said the collective should freely spend its treasury on entertainment. The middle-class women, who contributed a disproportionate share of the treasury, and who, Brown noted, had grown up enjoying the privilege of entertainment, wanted to be more prudent with money. Brown was relentless in her criticism of these middle-class women and would not abide any complaints or moments of depression. Brown knew that she was, as she observed, "devoid of all diplomacy," and it wasn't long before the Furies were cannibalizing each other. By the time they voted to purge Brown—literally ordering her out of the commune—she considered living with her fellow Furies to be worse than living in a "fascist state (or Stalinist, take your pick)." The Furies disbanded that summer.

Both Charlotte Bunch and Rita Mae Brown now reconsidered the notion of separatism. From the start Bunch had viewed it as a temporary strategy and was beginning to worry about whether it had ever been a good idea. Separatism had not produced a new school of political thought but only what she called "navel-gazing politics." Limiting their universe had left the Furies isolated, ungrounded and, as Bunch put it, "trying to make a revolution in a teapot."

"Our clarity of purpose frightened others," Rita Mae Brown later wrote. "Our self-righteousness exacerbated the paranoia." Bunch suggested it was time to "clarify the confusion caused by our separatist strategy. Even if we continue to work primarily with our particular group we can assert our belief that all people can participate in creating a new society." Brown went further, ridiculing the notion of "man-hating," a sentiment that was advocated by many separatists. "It is politically dangerous, individually damaging and utterly ridiculous," she said in 1972. "All you get by remaining totally separatist based on lines the oppressor set up (sex, race, class, sex preference) is trade unionism. A strong coalition can defeat impending fascism. Nothing else will."

PART TWO

A Place at the Table

7

KAMENY FOR CONGRESS

January 1971, Washington, D.C.

Paul Kuntzler stood in the parish house of St. Mark's Episcopal Church, behind the Library of Congress on Capitol Hill, looking over the crowd. It was a Saturday evening, and Kuntzler could have been at any one of the two dozen or so gay bars, clubs and restaurants that pulsed in Washington that night. But he was curious about this gay dance. It was a new event, sponsored jointly by the old Mattachine Society and the new Gay Liberation Front of Washington, and it was being held in the same liberal Episcopalian church where Kuntzler and other Mattachine members had gathered for so long on Monday nights, in a dungeon-like room they rented for $100 a year.

The Gay Liberation Front was unfamiliar to Kuntzler. Drawn to Washington by the excitement of the Kennedy inauguration, he had been one of the Washington Mattachine's inner circle almost from the time Franklin Kameny founded it in November 1961. But Kuntzler had strayed into the anti-war movement in the late '60s, when the Mattachine lost momentum. Its meetings since then had shrunk to only ten or twelve people, and Kuntzler had come back to the church because he wanted to see what the new movement looked like. He had been rewarded. The GLF dance had drawn the young men who had never been attracted to Mattachine meetings.

The Mattachine in Washington, as in New York, had always been so cautious and disciplined, almost furtive—like the polite middle-class guerrilla group it had been at its birth a decade earlier. Its members met in a narrow, low-ceilinged windowless room, in the subbasement of the church, behind the dirt-floored space where the furnace stood. It made them feel as if they had something to hide. Anyone who wanted to join had to be interviewed by Kameny and one or two other officers, and the occasional social gatherings were predictably well behaved. Frank Kameny had the manners of a military school colonel. His favorite dances were the waltz and the polka, which he performed with gusto. But the music, as Kuntzler listened to it in the church hall that Saturday night, was psychedelic and rebellious. He was watching the lean young men of the GLF jerk and sway, thinking how different this crowd was from the Mattachine members, how much more like an anti-war gathering, when a familiar voice cut through his thoughts.

"Paulie, Paulie, Paulie!" Allen Hoffard was coming toward him, his eyes gleaming with excitement behind the thick glasses he wore. He was all nerves and energy, in the grip, clearly, of one of his conceptions. Fleshy, jovial and a little foppish in a clubby kind of way, Hoffard was a bachelor from Oregon in his late thirties who had been a newspaper reporter and editor in Portland, a Washington correspondent, an assistant producer for the network TV show *Issues and Answers* and press secretary to U.S. Senator Wayne Morse of Oregon. One of those clever young men who come to Washington and end up in middle age in bureaucracies all over town, he was a senior press officer and speechwriter at the Department of Agriculture, a closeted homosexual who loved politics. He was holding up a single sheet of typed paper, nudging Kuntzler with it. "Paulie," he said, "read this!" Kuntzler eyed his friend. Hoffard had come to the dance to give him a memo? He looked at the paper, which was underlined, here and there, with the distinctive green ink Allen Hoffard favored. As he began to read it, Kuntzler realized that Hoffard had seen a political opportunity that the rest of them had missed, right under their noses. It seemed impossible and tantalizing at the same time. But if they could pull it off, it would get national attention, and mark the beginning of a new relationship between homosexuals and electoral politics.

The federal government had given them a break. That past September, President Richard M. Nixon had signed into law an act of Congress which gave legally qualified residents of the District of Columbia the right to elect someone to the newly created position of nonvoting delegate to the U.S. House of Representatives. A primary election would be held in January 1971 and a general ballot the following March. Thus, for the first time in ninety-seven years—since a brief period after the Civil War when the District had been allowed to vote as a territory—residents of the city could elect someone to speak for them in Congress. It was part of the process by which the people of Washington, D.C., were gradually acquiring the rights of citizenship, and the politics were about race.

There were no local, state or federal elections held within the sixty-eight square miles of Washington, D.C. Its citizens had no voting rights. Congress acted as its city legislature and the president of the United States as its executive. Until 1964, when the city had almost three-quarters of a million people, its residents could not even vote for candidates for president and vice president of the United States. And then gradually, grudgingly, the southern conservatives who had dominated Congress began to lose the battle to keep the mostly black District voteless. Once Lyndon B. Johnson became president, the city's black population gained a friend in power. Granting the District of Columbia self-government became part of the civil rights agenda that Johnson, year by year, began to push through Congress. By 1969, when the city was two-thirds black, residents were able to elect their first local public officials, the members of the school board. And in the fall of 1970, Richard Nixon signed into law the act which created the new office of delegate to Congress.

At first, no one saw the particular opportunity it offered homosexuals. The moribund Washington Mattachine's last dramatic move had been the picketing of the White House, the Pentagon, the State Department and Civil Service Commission beginning in 1965; these days it was more likely to sponsor a blood drive. By the time the District was given the right to vote for a congressional delegate, people like Paul Kuntzler had left Mattachine for mainstream politics. Kuntzler was working in the campaign of the liberal black, anti-war candidate, Channing Phillips, a minister and Democratic national committeeman from the District. But when the Washington Mattachine, even in its diminished state, had distributed a questionnaire to each candidate asking him to state his position on discrimination against homosexuals, Phillips refused to complete the questionnaire, and Kuntzler concluded just days before the January 12 primary, that his candidate might have been anti-war, but he also was anti-gay. Kuntzler quit the campaign in disgust. It had given him some satisfaction when Phillips and the others in the Democratic primary were defeated by another prominent black minister who had been serving as an appointed city councilman, Walter E. Fauntroy. With Democrats outnumbering Republicans in the District by something like 9 to 1, Fauntroy would certainly win in March. It was shaping up to be an unremarkable general election—or so Kuntzler thought until he ran into Hoffard and his memorandum at the dance.

The hell with Channing Phillips and Fauntroy and the rest of them, the memo said. The gay community should run its own candidate, someone willing to campaign as an open homosexual. The dominant newspaper, the *Washington Post,* might refuse to publish an advertisement or notice of a meeting if it contained the word "homosexual" or "gay." But an openly homosexual candidate for delegate could get huge exposure in the news pages. Hoffard, who had both covered Washington news as a journalist and tried to shape it as a press officer, saw just how it would work. The newspapers, television and radio stations in Washington would be forced to give time and coverage to everybody running in the first District-wide election in a century. And the national press would have to write *something* about this historic race. It was the best chance a gay candidate would have anywhere in the country to mount a significant campaign for public office. He couldn't win, but he would get attention. They had just thirty-seven days to collect enough signatures to qualify someone to run as an independent in the general election. All they needed was the right homosexual candidate and five thousand registered voters willing to sign their names to a petition asking that he or she be certified to run. They had the homosexual, Hoffard said: Dr. Franklin E. Kameny. Now, all they needed were the signatures.

There was undeniable poetic justice in Frank Kameny's running for public office in Washington, D.C., because he had been there, twenty years before, when the national witch-hunt for homosexuals had begun. A Republican-led Senate committee had galvanized the Washington police to begin arresting hundreds of men each year for alleged perversion. A Republican president, Dwight David Eisenhower, had signed the executive order in April 1953 which mandated that employees identified by the police as "sexual perverts" be fired from the federal government. It had been in Lafayette Park, directly across Pennsylvania Avenue from the White House, that Kameny had been arrested one night in the late 1950s by two plainclothes officers of the District police force morals division. There in the park, late at night, after the lights went out in the White House family quarters and Dwight and Mamie Eisenhower were asleep, men walked the paths a few hundred feet from their bedroom windows, parked in cars at the curb and approached each other for sex. Lafayette Park was one of the prime cruising spots for homosexual men in the 1950s and 1960s, and it was there, one night, after the bars closed, Franklin Kameny said afterward, that he was walking, looking around, when he saw an arrest in progress and stopped to watch. And the police, seeing him, came after him, too. He was placed under "arrest for investigation," a procedure used by the morals squad in those years to hold, question and pressure someone they suspected of homosexuality. Because the District of Columbia essentially functioned as a federal agency, the police followed the policy laid down by Congress; in 1950 a Senate subcommittee had called homosexuals a threat to national security, and had criticized the District police and courts for not being tougher on "sexual perverts," ordering them to crack down so that the Civil Service Commission could use the information to fire homosexuals from government jobs.

Frank Kameny, trained as an astronomer at Harvard, had been dismissed from his job at the U.S. Army Map Service after his 1957 arrest. The Federal Bureau of Investigation gathered such arrest and surveillance information from local police forces for use against federal civil service employees.* The police, the FBI and/or military intelligence are believed to have monitored Mattachine meetings after its 1961 founding. Thus it was the federal government which had employed Frank Kameny, spied on him, arrested him, fired him, made records of his conduct available to other federal agencies and institutions, and probably made him unemployable in his professional field.

So, after he was dismissed and discovered that he could not get a job elsewhere, and was reduced to living on 20 cents of food a day, it was the federal government that Frank Kameny had filed suit against in federal court. No homosexual had ever done that. But Kameny was by intellect, temperament and training a dogged investigator of things, a scientist and mathematician. He had a passion for logical and measurable truth, a compulsion to know cause and effect, and to assign responsibility. He was also a very formal man, so he filed for redress with the Supreme Court after he lost his job, and he picketed the White House, the Civil Service Commission and the Pentagon for discriminating against homosexuals. Those were federal institutions, but they were also the arms of his local government. The federal government turned Kameny into an activist, and he was focused and formidable. He formed the Mattachine Society of Washington shortly after the Supreme Court turned down his petition, and sent press releases announcing the new organization to members of Congress. For years he also sent the Mattachine newsletter to members of Congress, and to the president and vice president of the United States, the justices of the United States Supreme Court, members of the cabinet and J. Edgar Hoover.

Franklin Kameny had the confidence of an intellectual autocrat, the manner of a snapping turtle, a voice like a foghorn, and the habit of expressing himself in thunderous bursts of precise and formal language. He talked in italics and exclamation points, and he cultivated the self-righteous arrogance of a visionary who knew his cause was just when no one else did. He was George Patton as gay activist: a brilliant, indomitable man, a general without

* One of the chief functions of the "Sex Deviates" filing system J. Edgar Hoover created in 1951 was to furnish information about allegations of homosexuality "concerning present and past employees of any branch of the United States government" to other agencies and, in instances "where the best interests of the Bureau are served," to officials of educational and law enforcement institutions outside the federal system. Agency policy quoted in Athan Theoharis, *J. Edgar Hoover, Sex, and Crime,* pp. 103–105.

an army, alone against everyone else. "If society and I differ on something," Kameny said once, "I'm willing to give the matter a second look. If we still differ, then I am right and society is wrong; and society can go its way so long as it does not get in my way. But if it does, there's going to be a fight. And I'm not going to be the one who backs down. That has been an underlying premise of the conduct of my life." Kameny treated *everyone* with equal disdain—gay or straight, male or female—and the membership of Mattachine occasionally rebelled, but they generally put up with it. "The only mistake I ever made with the Mattachine," he once said, "was to make it a democratic organization." Besides, he was supremely competent, and he did almost all the work.

Forced into the role of crusader by circumstance, and completely devoid of any of the feminine mannerisms that the public then associated with homosexuals, Franklin Kameny was perfectly equipped to do battle with the federal establishment by speech, testimony and memoranda. Almost single-handedly, he formed and popularized the ideological foundations of the gay rights movement in the 1960s: that homosexuals constituted 10 percent of the population, that they were not mentally ill, that they didn't need to be spoken for by medical experts, and that they had a right not to be discriminated against.

So there was no question that Kuntzler and Hoffard should ask Kameny to run for Congress, and they had little doubt that he would accept. Still, few people in Washington, Kuntzler thought, would sign a public petition asking that an open homosexual be certified to run for public office. At brunch the day after the dance, Kuntzler tested his fear with two neighbors he and his lover had invited over, midlevel federal bureaucrats who lived together as a couple, but in a quiet, unobtrusive way. Kuntzler brought up Hoffard's idea of running Kameny for office as an open homosexual and asked whether it would be possible to get five thousand registered voters to sign petitions by February 23. Could they imagine anyone being willing to do that? Yes, his guests said; they would sign. Kuntzler was stunned. If they would do it, then other middle-class homosexuals might. It might be worth trying. They had just five weeks.

The size and confidence of the homosexual community in Washington had swelled in the generation since the police dragnet was first cast there. The attacks that Kameny and the Mattachine had orchestrated against the police arrests and government firings—protesting to the police chiefs, testifying before a congressional committee, soliciting the ACLU to protest police entrapments, picketing and mailing newsletters that informed gay men of their rights—had had an effect. The police pressure had begun to relax. In October 1969 the *Washington Post* published an article on the front of the Style section under the headline "Homosexual Revolution," which observed that

gays in Washington weren't as visible, influential or militant as they had become in San Francisco and New York. As opposed to the hundred bars in San
Francisco, Washington had only twenty-some gay bars, clubs and restaurants.
But here, it said, "The gay community has better relations with the police
than in those cities." There had been only sixty-nine "male homosexual arrests" in 1968, compared to 496 in 1960, the *Post* reported. District Police Inspector Walter Bishop was quoted as saying that the police hadn't raided a gay
club in two years.

By January 1971, the Washington gay community had a large new disco,
the Pier Nine, which also housed a restaurant and a balcony bar and featured,
like the Kit Kat Club in *Cabaret,* telephones at each table so that strangers
could call each other up and flirt. It also had a gay bath, the Regency; one of
the largest gay pornographic publishing houses in the country, the Guild Press
and Potomac News Company, which turned out novels and magazines; a four-
month-old congregation of Troy Perry's Metropolitan Community Church;
and a two-sheet mimeographed community paper, the monthly *Gay Blade,*
which Frank Kameny had gotten started fifteen months before by telephoning
people until he rounded up a staff who would put out a paper. The *Gay Blade*
was run by Nancy Tucker, an editorial assistant at the company which published *Army Times* and *Navy Times.* Early issues warned about military intelligence officers taking down the license plate numbers of cars parked at gay bars,
and of blackmailers doing the same thing with cars that kept driving around
Dupont Circle, where male prostitutes cruised. "Is the government running a
security check on you? Being blackmailed? Need draft counseling?" a notice at
the top of the page in its first issue, in October 1969, asked. "Call Franklin Kameny, President of the Mattachine Society of Washington at 363-3881 for help
on these and other legal complications of being gay."

Fifteen months later the *Blade* had still attracted no paid advertisers. But
anyone reading it could tell by early 1971 that there had been a change in emphasis—away from the Mattachine and toward the Washington Gay Liberation Front, which was zapping gay bars that discriminated against women and
blacks. And then suddenly, in February, there was a story that filled up two-
thirds of the front page: "KAMENY FOR CONGRESS!!!"

Kameny was not going to make it to the ballot on the basis of one story
that appeared in a thousand copies of an earnest little mimeographed paper
left for the taking in various gay bars, which carried the *Gay Blade* only because Nancy Tucker promised to put their names in it. The support which
would qualify Kameny for the ballot, and permit him to run a credible campaign, grew along more substantial lines, and it established a pattern which
would become predictable in the national gay and lesbian community, wherever political campaigns were run for and by men, for some years to come.
The main money in the gay community came from businesses peculiar to that

community. They were of three different kinds, and they all tapped into the male sex drive: the bars, the baths and the pornography industry. For the Kameny campaign to grow, with no outside support, its organization, money, equipment and materials had to come almost entirely from within the gay community. This meant that Kameny's campaign fliers and posters ended up being printed by the chief pornographer in town, who faced federal charges of mailing and transporting obscene matter. And the campaign's biggest money contributions came from the owner of the gay baths, which was frequently the object of police interest. The meetings that Paul Kuntzler had with the chief sex purveyors of the gay community—Herman Lynn Womack, the owner of the Guild Press and the Potomac News Company, and David Harris, the owner of the Regency Baths—were almost as important as the meetings that he, Hoffard, Cliff Witt, Tony Jackubosky, Lilli Vincenz and some of the other activists had with Frank Kameny himself.

And so a core formed to run a campaign for Kameny. For the first time in his life as an activist, Franklin Kameny found himself fronting an organization he did not control. He didn't know anything about creating a political campaign. He would be its personality, its face, its voice, but it would be a campaign run by a group of men (of thirty-three names on the telephone list of people coordinating the campaign, only two were women) a generation younger than he who wanted to channel the D.C. gay rights movement away from its past, and not incidentally, away from the dominance of Frank Kameny. This was a campaign that would be run—and handicapped—by a closeted strategist, and a campaign manager and an assistant campaign manager who could not afford to have their names in the paper. Not Paul Kuntzler nor any of the inner circle of men who conceived and ran the Kameny campaign were out enough to want to be out in the *Washington Post*, the *Evening Star*, or the *Daily News*.*

On Wednesday, February 3, Franklin Kameny stood in front of the District Building in downtown Washington, ready to announce his candidacy to whoever would listen. For two and a half weeks the band of plotters behind him had worked to prepare for this moment. The Mattachine Society had voted to give Kameny $125 and the use of its office telephone. Allen Hoffard had scheduled and planned the press conference carefully, giving Kuntzler a

---

* As an employee of the federal government, Allen Hoffard was barred by the Hatch Act from working in federal political campaigns, and by federal policy was still susceptible to being fired for homosexuality. And Paul Kuntzler needed to keep his job as a purchasing agent at the Serta Mattress Company in Landover, Maryland. The owners were conservative Jews who didn't know he was gay. His name was at the bottom of virtually all the Kameny literature, but all through the campaign he would implore the newspaper and television reporters writing about Kameny not to print it.

list of different news organizations that should be notified, with news releases delivered to their offices. Hoffard had typed up the news release, a short biography of Kameny and a prepared statement by the candidate. David Livingston had retyped and mimeographed those pages at night at the secretarial office he managed by day so that there would be plenty of good copies to feed the press corps in advance and to hand out at the District Building. The campaign had even bought Kameny a new, dark blue vested suit—he was always poor, and his clothes looked it.

The day before the announcement, on Tuesday morning, the *Washington Post* had made them a gift. In an editorial headlined "Fairness for Homosexuals," the *Post* declared that the "Persecution of homosexuals is as senseless as it is unjust. They may have valuable gifts and insights to bring to public service," it said, and "their private sexual behavior is their own business; it is none of the government's business as long as it does not affect their independence and reliability. Like anyone else, they have a right to privacy, a right to opportunity and a right to serve their country." It could have been a fanfare for Kameny himself. As it happened, it was not, but it was partially a fruit of his labors. The editorial was talking about Otto Ulrich, the Washington Mattachine treasurer, who had been denied an industrial security clearance by the Pentagon because he was a homosexual. Kameny and others had worked to get the ACLU to take the case, the ACLU had sued in his behalf, and the *Post* was standing up for the ACLU and Ulrich, making the same argument that Kameny had been making for years. "The man cannot conceivably be considered more subject to blackmail than other men for the simple reason that he has made no attempt to conceal his homosexuality," the editorial proclaimed. It was a good omen.

The news release Hoffard had ready for the reporters that morning laid out the campaign in a newsy form that did not avoid the central issue. "Dr. Frank Kameny, a well-known campaigner for homosexual rights, announced his candidacy for the District of Columbia Non-Voting Delegate to Congress today." Kameny, forty-five, said his broad-based campaign "will provide a forum for the firsthand presentation to the public of the feelings, problems and concerns of the sexually oppressed.

"Although I am a homosexual," he said, "and the focus of my campaign will be sexual oppression, I appeal to all minority groups and to all individuals who differ from the contrived conventions of the majority, whether by desire or by circumstance, by race or by gender or by life style." The strategy was to say straight out that he was homosexual, but to stress his traditional credentials, suggesting that he was qualified to represent minorities like blacks and women, too. The candidate was *Dr.* Kameny. "Dr. Kameny, a physicist and astronomer, received his Ph.D. from Harvard University. He has taught at Georgetown University and worked in the aerospace industry. He is a combat veteran of WWII and has resided in the District of Columbia since 1956. He is a former member of the executive board of the Civil Liberties Union of the National Capital Area, and has been renominated for that position." The candidate's statement employed his favorite statistic: "By most estimates, gay people number some 10 percent of the populace—the largest national minority group after blacks.

"Homosexuals have been shoved around for time immemorial. We are fed up with it. We are starting to shove back, and we are going to keep shoving back until we are guaranteed our rights."

As Paul Kuntzler drove to work the next morning he kept the radio on to see if Kameny made the news. He did. The voice of the rush-hour newscaster was a barrel of warm mirth as he reported the latest political news out of Washington. "A new candidate swished into the political arena yesterday," he said.

The campaign managers decided it was probably not a good idea to tell people they asked to sign Kameny's petition that he was a homosexual; it produced rude replies, confusion and interminable discussions, and they didn't have time for that—not when it took hours and hours for one person to get a few dozen signatures, and they had only three weeks—which really meant only three weekends—until February 23. Marching orders were printed for volunteers to follow:

1. Ask prospect if he or she is a registered voter.

2. If so, hand the prospect a flier and hold out a pen while politely asking for a signature "to give the voters a wider choice."

3. Explain that this does *not* commit the voter to support the candidate's platform or to vote for him in the general election.

4. Do *not* engage in lengthy discussion or argument. If voter declines, merely say "thank you," and approach another prospect.

The flier they handed to voters spoke of the candidate ("President of the Mattachine Society of Washington, and a champion of human rights"), his party (the "Personal Freedom Party") and his eleven-point platform. The platform called for "an end to employment discrimination against homosexuals, women, blacks and other minority groups," and for "respect, dignity and security for all people regardless of sexual preference." It also called for home rule for Washington, an immediate American withdrawal from Southeast Asia and "an end to government snooping into our private lives." It did not call the candidate a homosexual. That fact was reserved for fliers distributed at GLF meetings, outside gay bars, in the baths and wherever the organizers thought they might find gay men and lesbians who would be willing to offer help. "WE NEED YOU," the flier declared. "With Kameny on the ballot, the political structure will learn that the gay community is a force to be reckoned with. Getting 5,000 signatures represents a show of strength in the one commodity that no politician or public official can afford to ignore: voting power. Homosexuals will no longer be ignored!"

Kameny's inner circle knew, however, that D.C.'s barely established gay political structure could not meet the challenge that this election and this candidate posed. There were few Mattachine members, and aside from Franklin Kameny and Lilli Vincenz, they were shy about meeting the public. The GLF was by nature chaotic, impossible to organize in a reliable way. The only well-organized group founded exclusively to advance the gay rights agenda in the political arena was the Gay Activists Alliance in New York. And so a pact was made. Washington had a matchless opportunity, and New York's GAA had a few muscles to flex and a revolution to export. On each of the middle two weekends of February, scores of GAA members from New York arrived at night on chartered buses, as if for a party weekend. They were all male, they were interested in the gay men of Washington and the gay college kids from Georgetown University, and they loved going after signatures from the crowds of shoppers in the parking lots of the Safeway markets in Georgetown, Adams-Morgan and Capitol Hill. Bruce Voeller—the tall, purposeful GAA leader, with a red bandana over his thinning blond hair—worked the parking lots with Marty Robinson. Robinson and Voeller were very good at this: they were good-looking and personable, had nerve but weren't threatening.

Troy Perry arrived in Washington, too, to celebrate the birth of a new gay congregation at a Valentine's Day service at St. Stephen's and the Incarnation Episcopal Church. St. Stephen's had agreed to lend its sanctuary for Perry's services on Sunday afternoon, February 14, but when the Right Reverend William F. Creighton, bishop of Washington, heard that Perry also planned to marry a gay couple as part of the service, he ordered the church closed to them. Paul Breton, pastor of the new congregation and one of the organizers of the Kameny campaign, had planned the service and he and Hoffard immediately saw the news potential in the change of plans. They huddled with Troy Perry and the service became a Kameny press conference. With Hoffard watching from behind a tree, fearful of showing himself but unable to stay away, about forty people gathered for a protest service on the steps of St. Stephen's. "Even though [Bishop Creighton] has locked us out of this church," Perry sang out, "God hasn't locked us out of his heart." And then, with a *Washington Post* reporter who had been alerted taking notes, Perry said he had come to town to speak out in behalf of Franklin Kameny's campaign for delegate. "Kameny is not the gay candidate, he's the people's candidate," the preacher said solemnly, spreading his hands to the people before him. "Get on board, children. . . ." The *Post* reported all this the next day, and as happened every time there was a burst of publicity about the campaign's latest aggressive move, the gay community got more excited, and more people volunteered to collect signatures.

They had about three thousand signatures even before Perry's publicity. Kuntzler trusted nothing to chance and recruited the help of David Harris, the confrontational owner of the Regency Baths off New York Avenue near Fourth Street, a place frequently in trouble with the police. Pale as a ghost—he lived at the baths—but energized by the Kameny candidacy, Harris was out every weekend gathering signatures. He gave $1,000 or more to the campaign, more than any other source, and he pressured everyone who entered the dark, steamy, mildewed rooms of the Regency for a signature. Hustlers gathered signatures in the parking lots, as if Harris had made that the price of their rent.

Kuntzler had also talked to one of the candidates who had lost to Fauntroy in the Democratic primary. Kuntzler paid $400 or $500, and the workers who had collected signatures for that politician in black southeast Washington came up with another 1,500 for Kameny. As he looked at them, Kuntzler sensed from the handwriting, the names and addresses that a lot of them were fraudulent. (Kameny, years later, could not recall any such suspicion.) But by Monday, February 22, it didn't matter. Altogether, in just three weeks, they had collected almost eight thousand signatures. Allen Hoffard had spent long days in the District Building verifying signatures; the more than six thousand they had brought in on their own were solid. The purchased 1,500 went to the bottom of the stack, and Kameny marched triumphantly into the District Building. "I am here to announce the filing of a petition containing more than 7,000 signatures—well over the required 5,000—nominating me for the position of Delegate to Congress from the District of Columbia.

"This will place me on the ballot in the March 23 election, as the first publicly declared homosexual ever to run for Congress and, to my knowledge, ever to run for any public office in this country.* As such, I am not running for office; I am *being* run for office by the homosexual community and, therefore, my candidacy is a special one and will be conducted in some special ways.

"The homosexual community has been studiously ignored by those in politics and those in public office. We expect this campaign to change that not only here in Washington but elsewhere in the country. We expect to see homo-

---

* The first publicly declared homosexual to run for public office in the United States was probably José Sarria, a waiter, drag queen and early homosexual rights performer at the Black Cat bar in the North Beach area of San Francisco. Sarria became the best-known personality in the city's gay community in the 1950s, and in 1961, during a police crackdown on the gay bars, he collected enough signatures to qualify and run for city supervisor in the fall elections. Although it is not certain that the general city electorate was aware of Sarria's sexual politics, his candidacy was the sensation of the homosexual community. He didn't win, but he got six thousand votes, more than three times the number Kameny would get in Washington ten years later.

sexual candidates running for a variety of offices at all levels, federal, state, and local, throughout the nation in the near future.

"As homosexuals, we are fed up with a government which wages a relentless war against us and others of its citizens, instead of against the bigotry of our society. This is OUR country, OUR society, and OUR government—for homosexuals quite as much as for heterosexuals. We are *homosexual American citizens*. We intend to see to it that the second and third words of that phrase, 'American citizens,' are no longer ignored with regard to us. Along with other minorities—blacks, women, students, the poor—we are first-class citizens, and we intend to play a full role in our country." Kameny looked crusty and resolute, standing there in his new, dark blue vested suit, his button-down shirt and striped rep tie. This was the image that would be reproduced on his fliers and posters—Franklin Kameny, with thinning ginger hair, a flinty, determined New England look and conservative dark suit, standing with a briefcase in front of the U.S. Capitol. And these were arguments he had been making, in one form or another, for more than a decade—but now the audience was larger than ever. "You will be hearing much from us in the next thirty days," he promised, looking sternly about him as he finished his announcement in front of the District Building, "and long thereafter."

In the month that followed, Franklin Kameny maintained the most exhausting schedule of his life. Alone among all the six men on the ballot, he accepted nearly every invitation to speak and attended almost every candidate forum, in a city that was dizzy to hear and see the candidates in this race. Only in the last two days, utterly exhausted, did he cancel two appearances. Sometimes, in his set remarks, as at the elegant old Mayflower Hotel, speaking before the Metropolitan Washington Board of Trade on Consumer Protection, or at a city recreation center in a poor black part of town, speaking to the membership of the Far Southeast Civic Association, he focused on issues that concerned his audience, and said nothing about homosexuality, an omission for which Nancy Tucker, *The Advocate*'s Washington correspondent, would criticize him. But often he did speak as a homosexual, lashing out at those he considered the oppressors of gay rights in words and sentiments that were unmistakably his own. Frank Kameny, in a press conference at the Pentagon, attacked "the Neanderthals who make up the State Department who are still quivering in terror from the trauma they suffered at the hands of a psychotic senator [Joe McCarthy] two decades ago, against whom they did not have the guts to stand up then, and from whom they are still running." And he attacked the District's sodomy and solicitation laws as absurd. "First," he said, in regard to solicitation, "we see no reason why a sexual invitation should really be placed in a different class from, say, an invitation to dinner." Referring to the District's sodomy statute, Section 22-3502 of the D.C. Criminal Code, he noted that "If you follow the advice given in most marriage manuals, in the current best-seller *The Sensual Woman,* or in David Reuben's shoddy little book about all the things you didn't know about sex, you could get ten years in jail and a $1,000 fine, here in Washington."

Often enough, Kameny's comments became the lead in newspaper stories of the campaign. When he appeared with four other candidates before an audience of fifty members of Federally Employed Women, Inc., he told them that they must fight to achieve equality just as he was fighting for equal opportunities for the homosexual community. "A lot of women are discriminated against purely because of their sex," Kameny said, "but I think the formation of your body and your genital equipment is completely irrelevant. You should be considered as human beings first and as a woman second." The *Washington Post* led with Kameny and devoted almost half its story to what he had said. The day that Walter Fauntroy added something to his speech about gay rights, the Kameny campaign knew their candidate was being heard.

His fliers and signs were everywhere. Womack, the pornographer, was printing them by the tens of thousands. A doctor of philosophy from Johns Hopkins and a former college professor at George Washington University, he was a strikingly eccentric presence, an albino of pink eyes and three hundred pounds of damp pink flesh, an enduring character in the cultural shadow of Washington and an important figure in the evolution of obscenity law. His press printed the programs for the 100th Jubilee of the United Daughters of the Confederacy, as well as pornography, and Womack had bookstores, too. In terms of volume, he liked to say, he was the fourth largest pornographer in America. In trouble with the law for more than a decade, he had made some important legal history. In a precedent-setting case in 1962, the U.S. Supreme Court had overturned Womack's obscenity conviction for sending 40,000 unsolicited copies of three magazines with pictures of nude men through the mails. The post office, the Court said, could not decide what was obscene and then block those articles from the mails while waiting for the justice system to agree. But other law enforcement agencies kept up the pressure. As Kameny entered the campaign in 1971, Womack was facing charges for sending through the mail obscene matter, which federal prosecutors said included pictures of boys as young as two years old, and he was convicted of publishing, transporting and mailing obscene matter just four months later, a conviction that would finally drive him out of Washington. But he was a learned man with a sense of humor. And he was willing to print thousands of dollars worth of literature free. There were pink cards that said "What we do here on March 23 could well determine the course of harassment of homosexuals throughout the nation. It's an awesome responsibility. . . . SUPPORT YOURSELF. IF YOU DON'T, NO ONE ELSE WILL. VOTE KAMENY

ON TUESDAY THE 23RD OF MARCH." There were fliers that GAA members handed out door-to-door by the thousands; and black on orange posters put up all over town, saying "Defend Your Right to Be Different. Vote Kameny March 23rd. Personal Freedom Candidate."

In a city where the only open homosexuals were those who had been arrested, suddenly there was Dr. Franklin E. Kameny, astronomer, physicist, Harvard graduate, a homosexual who looked and talked like an important scientist. Campaign contributions mounted. In the last days, Tony Jackubosky, the treasurer, opened one envelope and, to his astonishment, found a check for $500 from Paul Newman and Joanne Woodward, the largest single check Kameny received. Kameny had attracted $7,000 in checks and cash—the equivalent of perhaps $35,000 or $40,000 today. It was more than they would spend.

On the Saturday before the election, Franklin Kameny marched in his dark suit down Pennsylvania Avenue from campaign headquarters to the White House, with fifty men and women behind him carrying the "Kameny for Congress" placards. "Two, four, six, eight, gay is just as good as straight," they chanted. "Three, five, seven, nine, lesbians are mighty fine." At the White House gate, across the street from Lafayette Park, where he had been arrested more than a decade before, he handed a letter to the guard for President Richard Nixon, "protesting unfair treatment of homosexuals," as the *Post* said the next day. And that was the photograph and description that the paper carried on the front of the Metropolitan section Sunday morning, leading the roundup story of the last major day of campaigning: "Franklin E. Kameny, an independent who is running as an avowed homosexual," handing a letter through the spikes of the White House fence for the president. On the editorial page that same morning, the *Post* said that "Dr. Franklin E. Kameny has put special emphasis on personal freedoms, running as an avowed homosexual pledged to represent all the people in the community. His contribution to discussions of civil liberties has been eloquent and erudite, and in this sense has already fulfilled his basic campaign objective."

Walter E. Fauntroy won the election and Kameny came in fourth in a field of six, ahead of the last-place Socialist Workers Party candidate and of the Reverend Douglas Moore, a black nationalist. Gay power, one national newsweekly said, had beaten black power. The numbers weren't large. Kameny received about 1,841 votes, 1.6 percent of the total cast. But the votes were not the measure of the campaign. It was the change made in public consciousness, and in the political organization of the gay community in Washington and beyond. The wards where homosexuals lived in Washington had voted at almost twice the rate of the rest of the city for Kameny. The gay-owned and -supported businesses in the city saw the effect that money, organization and publicity could have on public perception. A week after the election, Paul Kuntzler and several others used money from the campaign treasury to finance a trip to New York (and to Fire Island), where they spent some days with the leaders of the Gay Activists Alliance. There they planned the GAA chapter that they would start in Washington, which would become the city's premier gay political group.

Frank Kameny didn't go to New York. His associates from Washington didn't invite him. Kameny said he hoped his campaign would have a germinal effect on gay involvement in electoral politics. But it would be three years before another homosexual ran for public office. And Kameny himself would never lead the gay rights movement again.

8

A VOICE IN
THE STATEHOUSE

June 1972

On a Monday night in June 1972, in a room on Joy Street on Beacon Hill, a crowd of gay activists sat and talked in frustrated animation. It had been three years since the Stonewall riots in New York. In five days the people in that room would march around the Boston Common in celebration of Gay Pride, and they had reason to be proud, but also to be disappointed.

In some ways, the gay and lesbian community emerging in Boston and Cambridge seemed more advanced than any other in the country. For a year, since the city's first small Gay Pride celebration in 1971, Boston had been home to perhaps the most radical journal of sexual liberation in America—a tabloid called *Fag Rag*, which in drawings, prose and poetry celebrated the ungoverned and apparently infinite possibilities of gay male promiscuity. The magazine was born of the split between men and women in Boston's Gay Liberation Front, and its philosopher-editor was a Boston State College professor, Charley Shively, who had come to town as a student from a poor white laboring family in Hamilton, Ohio. Brilliant, eccentric, gently sweet-tempered in person and passionately anarchistic in his politics, Shively was a Harvard Ph.D. with a coal miner's taste for up-the-establishment, and a penchant for provocative prose and action. In outlining the need for a federal nondiscrimination law in testimony at Faneuil Hall three weeks before, Charley Shively had appeared before a section of the Democratic National Platform Committee in a long, flowing dress, hand-sewn for him by another member of the Fag Rag Collective, Larry Anderson, a gay former Naval Academy cadet and Black Panther activist. Shively edited *Fag Rag* in that same spirit. The journal didn't publish often, but when it did, each issue was filled with sexual imagery, stories of boyhood affairs and adult seductions, and a series of long, ruminative Shively essays whose titles were variations of the first one: "Cocksucking as an Act of Revolution."

Bridges of common cause were being built between the gay community and the city's great church and educational institutions, too. For almost two years, Boston lesbians and gay men had had their own Roman Catholic priest, Father Paul Shanley, originally appointed to minister to the alienated street youth of Boston by the late Richard Cardinal Cushing, archbishop of Boston, and reapproved to counsel sexual minorities by Cushing's successor, Humberto Cardinal Medeiros. It was not the usual kind of missionary role that Father Shanley filled. In his speeches, talks and articles, he seemed to speak more *to* the church *for* homosexuals than the other way around, and he came to be identified in lists of gay organizations and services available as the "priest in the Archdiocese of Boston who has been working, with younger gays and bisexuals, to overcome the negative conditioning of the Catholic Church."

For a year and a half the Homophile Community Health Services Center, the first legally incorporated, gay-staffed medical group in the nation created to care for the mental health needs of homosexuals, had been providing therapy for men and women who were depressed and suicidal. For the last several months, the gay community had even had its own radio show; *Gay Way* broadcast on Thursday nights, reaching beyond the city into New Hampshire and Rhode Island on the signal of WBUR, the 20,000-watt Boston University FM station. And since late winter, the Gay Speakers Bureau, the newest expression of the movement in New England, had been sending Harvard doctoral candidates, including Laura McMurry and John Boswell, to speak at churches, schools and Rotary Clubs.

But for all of that, what the gay men and lesbians of Boston were talking about on Joy Street that Monday night was "Gay People and the Law." The question was, "How can we stay out of jail?" And for two years, Boston's gay community had not come up with an answer.

From colonial times the laws which governed Massachusetts had prohibited and punished sex between men, and the statutes gave no protections against the discriminations suffered by people who were gay. The best solution for the people who were in the room that night, of course, would be to do what other movements of social reform had struggled to do—change the laws.

But they had no experience in doing that, no entree with any of the members of the Senate or House in Massachusetts, and no idea how to go about it.

And then, in the back of the room, a blowsy, overweight man in his early thirties stood up. He looked pale and damp, as if he didn't feel well. He had dark, sullen, flat hair and thick glasses, and he sounded as if he was speaking very fast from New Jersey through a filter of mashed potatoes. He was new, and his name was Barney Frank. He *was* from New Jersey, and he had a bad cold. He had come to Boston to college ten years before, in 1962. He was a Harvard College graduate. He had been Boston mayor Kevin H. White's executive assistant, then an aide to Representative Michael Harrington in Washington, and he was coming back to Boston, he told them, to run for the Massachusetts House seat from Ward 5, there on Beacon Hill. He supported gay rights, he said, just as he supported black civil rights, just as he supported women's rights and the decriminalization of marijuana. He could help them draft the legislation to change Massachusetts's colonial-era sodomy laws, he said, and he would sponsor the bills if he was elected in the fall.

For a moment, the whole roomful of people sort of gaped. They didn't know this man. He didn't look homosexual. But he seemed to know what he was talking about. No one asked Barney Frank if he was gay. But if someone that night *had* asked him that question, Frank wouldn't have told them the truth—not then.

Barney Frank's parents were first-generation American Jews living in Bayonne, New Jersey. Because his older sister, Ann, went to Radcliffe, Barney went to Harvard. Because she was political, he became political. Writing his dissertation in American politics, Barney Frank was drawn into the 1967 Boston mayoral campaign by some Harvard connections close to Kevin H. White. Kevin White was political Boston Irish to the marrow of his bones, the son, grandson and son-in-law of past presidents of the Boston City Council. But he was running as a reform mayor, talking of civil liberties, social justice and neighborhood needs. His opponent was a stridently arch-conservative Irish Roman Catholic Boston mother, Louise Day Hicks, and they clashed over the issue of busing, which divided the city. Overweight, unkempt, impatient, abrasive and intellectually arrogant, Frank was very much an ethnic outsider in a city in which politics was mainly an Irish Roman Catholic game. But he was a witty raconteur, he could think faster than almost anyone else around him, and he had great political instincts. Kevin White was a coalition politician who reached out to blacks and whose close advisers included Jews. White's campaign slogan suggested the choice was between fighting each other or working together—"He Works WITH People," it said. And when White won the election, Frank took a leave from Harvard to become the mayor's executive assistant.

In the spring of 1968, when Ann Lewis left her husband, state Representative Gerald Lewis of Miami, she went back north to Boston, where her brother Barney was, and she, too, went to work for Mayor White. In July 1971 she attended the organizing meeting of the National Women's Political Caucus at the Washington Hilton Hotel. NOW, the better-known women's organization of the time, seemed mainly about achieving a sense of identity; the Women's Political Caucus was about political effectiveness, about securing equal rights. Many of the founding spirits of the caucus—Bella Abzug, Betty Friedan, Gloria Steinem, Shirley Chisholm—were also important figures in NOW. But the caucus was a pragmatic group with a practical goal, and when Lewis got back to Boston, she and three or four other women who had been at the Washington meeting established a Massachusetts chapter of the caucus. It would have three co-chairs, and Lewis expected that one would go to some moderate-to-liberal white woman, that one would go to a black woman, and that the third might end up in the hands of some more radical grassroots element.

She wasn't expecting that members of the Boston Daughters of Bilitis would show up, or that one of them, Elaine Noble, a speech professor at Emerson College in Boston, would be elected co-chair. Noble was tall and articulate, warm, fluid and funny, with flashing eyes and dark auburn hair, an easy laugh and a way with people. She had even brought her own troops, ten or twenty women who came to vote for her. Lewis was impressed. She can count, she thought to herself.

The two had become friends by the time Barney Frank called his sister from Washington in May 1972 to say that he wanted to run that fall for the state representative's seat that was going vacant in Ward 5, a district that had always before elected Republicans. Ward 5, which ran from Beacon Hill west through Back Bay to Kenmore Square and the Fenway, was an interesting district. Its affluent Beacon Hill residents, living in historic quarters just below the State House, were highly educated, well connected and politically sophisticated. They believed in living well, but they were liberal on most social issues. A lot of homosexuals also lived among the charming old cobbled streets and brick row houses that wound beneath the State House dome. And a lot of Boston University students and staff people lived in the western part of the district around Kenmore Square. Lewis thought about her brother's idea and called her new friend Elaine Noble, a B.U. graduate, who had become the co-host of the weekly radio show *Gay Way*. In May 1972, Elaine Noble was fast becoming the best-known gay or lesbian personality in Boston.

Noble had a lot of contacts at Boston University and in the gay communities in Ward 5. And that is how Frank got to the meeting on Joy Street a month later. If he was going to run for the legislature and support gay rights,

Noble told him as she pulled him out of his sickbed, then he needed to come to this meeting and say so.

Barney Frank had always assumed that his horizons were limited because he was Jewish. He could not even begin to imagine what future a smart, driven, politically ambitious Jewish Harvard graduate who was also gay might have. But when he realized at thirteen that he was attracted to other boys, he knew it was something he had to hide. Frank had never, through all his years in public school or in college or graduate school at Harvard, been around anyone whom he knew to be homosexual other than the high school sissy. It was not until he took a leave from Harvard to work for Kevin White in 1968 that another male approached him in a way he recognized as sexual—and he came on so aggressively that even Barney Frank, with all his layers of calculated aversion and inexperience, could not mistake it. It happened at the edge of the Boston Common as he walked home from city hall one night, and it became his first sexual encounter with another man.

At the age of twenty-eight, he was just beginning to realize the possibility of a sexual life when a man came into the mayor's office in city hall to complain that the Boston police had been harassing the crowd at a gay bar downtown called The Punch Bowl, and had beat him up in the bar. Barney Frank could not remember ever hearing anyone identify himself as gay before. Listening to the man, trying to ask questions that he hoped were neutral, he was stirred by feelings of sympathy and yearning. He wanted to help him. And he wanted to know more about that bar. Frank told the man that if he came back with more specific information, he could do something about it, but the man never returned, and Frank didn't think he should try to find him. He didn't need to be told how homosexuals were regarded in the male world of Boston politics. One morning, Frank would always remember, a major Boston Irish political figure came to his office and, referring to the writer Truman Capote, asked, "Did you see that Capote on TV? He's the friend of the Kennedys. Geez, he's just *a little fag.*"

Barney Frank very much wanted to have a future. He thought he could win the seat in liberal Back Bay–Beacon Hill. But if he wanted to have a career in public life, he decided, he would simply have to sacrifice his private life. And if he was without sin in his private life, then he might be able to take a public position on gay rights. Elaine Noble would introduce him around in the gay and lesbian community. What she wanted in return was his support for a nondiscrimination bill in the legislature, and state money to support the work of the Homophile Community Health Services Center. Politically, Frank thought, taking a stand for gay rights was risky. He was thirty-two years old and visibly unmarried. If people started speculating about him, if it became an issue, he didn't know what he would say. But Back Bay–Beacon Hill was probably one place where he *could* come out for gay rights. In liberal areas like that, in cities like Boston, gay rights was becoming part of the package of issues referred to in Massachusetts as "New Politics," which bundled together opposition to the Vietnam War, support for the Equal Rights Amendment and the decriminalization of marijuana. Whatever their fears or divisions, he thought, all homosexuals should be able to support someone who stood for gay rights; there could be a lot of votes in this still largely invisible community. And so five days after the meeting on Joy Street, early one Saturday afternoon, and with a funny feeling in his stomach, he set out from Copley Square with Elaine Noble, Laura McMurry, Stan Tillotson, Frank Morgan and perhaps three hundred others, the only political candidate marching in the Gay Pride Parade.

The excitement that had been stirred at the meeting on Joy Street grew that summer into a Boston Gay Rights Alliance. With Barney Frank's help, they drafted separate bills that would repeal the criminal sodomy laws, and would protect homosexuals against discrimination in employment, housing and public accommodations. The alliance sent out questionnaires to all three hundred candidates for Massachusetts House and Senate seats that August, asking them if they would favor such legislation, and twenty candidates responded by saying yes. But that didn't mean that they expected the Gay Rights Alliance to tell anyone else they had said so. *"What do you think you're doing?"* one furious campaign manager called to ask, after the alliance had put up a poster endorsing his candidate all through his district. *"You're going to lose us the election!!"*

Barney Frank had an easier time of it in Ward 5, winning handily. Two of his three primary opponents even followed his lead and supported the nondiscrimination bill. Frank always said afterward he won because George McGovern's coattails helped him, even if they helped no one else in the nation that year. Frank was running in one of the most socially liberal wards in one of the most liberal cities in the most loyal Democratic state in the nation. George S. McGovern lost forty-nine states in the presidential election that November but carried one: Massachusetts. The Frank campaign had even plastered hundreds of posters through the district, each one showing a grinning McGovern and Frank together, that asked: "Who's That Guy with Barney Frank?"

If a homosexual vote did form for Frank, it was impossible to track. The precincts which might have been heavily gay weren't yet identified, and whatever gay vote did occur did so in an atmosphere of signals too subtle to monitor—as Ann Lewis realized on election day, when she and her daughter Linda worked as poll watchers for Barney Frank on Beacon Hill. They were standing with another poll watcher, a man Lewis didn't know. All she knew was that the man was there for Barney, too, and that he was supposedly with some gay group. Nothing about him made that evident. But every now and then, when he spotted someone coming, he'd lay a hand on her sleeve. "I'll get this one," he'd say, and move to have a quiet word with the approaching voter.

After Barney Frank was sworn in as the new state representative from Back Bay–Beacon Hill, he introduced the legislation he had promised. The first public hearing on the bills to bar discrimination on the basis of "sexual preference" in housing, employment, insurance, mortgages and public accommodations drew radio and television coverage, as well as reporters from both the *Boston Globe* and the *Herald-American,* thus becoming the biggest news event in the short history of the Boston gay movement. Frank was terrified that someone would ask him the questions he couldn't answer. But outwardly, to the gay activists who were there, who had no idea he was homosexual, he seemed fast, focused, articulate and self-assured, talking about how the experience of having gay campaign workers had educated and changed him. He gained confidence and took other stands. One of them was against the entrapment arrests by Boston police of homosexual men seeking company around the Boston Common, homosexual men like the man who had approached Frank. As she listened to her brother speaking out against those police practices on the House floor one day, Ann Lewis turned to the two women with her, Elaine Noble and Bonnie Cronin. "You know," she said, "I think this is the first time in my life I have ever heard anything about sex come out of his mouth."

9

THE FIFTH COLUMN

July 1972, Miami

Jim Foster's jacket was a patchwork of thick lines crisscrossing on light linen, and it seemed particularly garish when he finally stepped in front of the cameras to address the Democratic National Convention in Miami at five o'clock in the morning on July 12, 1972. In less than an hour the sun would come up, and in less than eighteen hours the Democrats would nominate George S. McGovern, a two-term senator from South Dakota, to challenge Richard M. Nixon in the November presidential election. Jim Foster was a McGovern delegate from California's Fifth Congressional District in San Francisco, and he had been one of McGovern's earliest and most dedicated California supporters. Foster was a homosexual, and everyone in the McGovern camp knew that. They also knew McGovern might not have won California, and thus the nomination, were it not for a midnight signature drive Foster orchestrated at gay bars in the Castro in advance of the state primary. The first candidate to file completed petitions won the first line on the ballot, and it was Foster who had helped that happen for McGovern. He and his Alice B. Toklas Memorial Democratic Club had dispatched petition-carriers into gay bars at the stroke of midnight on the day the nominating process opened. Traditionally, the candidates would have tried to keep their supporters awake with wine and cheese parties, or rouse them from bed, so that they could sign the petitions once the midnight starting gun was fired. "Nobody in their right mind is going to get out of bed at midnight to sign some goddamn petition," Foster argued to McGovern's organizers, as he suggested there might be an opportunity in the late-night ways of the men in the Castro. That small trick gave McGovern a good six-hour jump on his competitors in collecting signatures, so he was first at the secretary of state's office door with completed petitions. Capturing the top line of the primary ballot arguably contributed to McGovern's five-point edge over Hubert H. Humphrey in California, a critical victory coming just thirty-six days before this night in Miami.

Foster's mustache was neatly trimmed, his tie straight and the top of his head—which was mostly bald—reflected the television lights as he settled behind the microphone in Miami. He was a strange sight indeed to this exhausted audience. Although it was very late at night, the hall was still packed. The delegates had spent seven hours voting on the party platform, fighting back one by one the minority planks pushed by women, blacks and the other factions in the liberal Democratic coalition. McGovern's forces realized the political dangers that lurked in a platform—how one plank inserted by one of these factions might be used by Republicans to portray McGovern as an extremist—and the delegates were under instructions not to leave the hall until a platform had been drafted which would not jeopardize the candidate's chances. The platform committee, meeting in Washington two weeks earlier, had produced a draft that attempted to balance the demands of the different factions of the McGovern coalition without dooming the candidate's presidential hopes, and as part of that calculation, a gay rights plank had been defeated, by a 54–32 vote. Still, Democratic Party rules had been relaxed in the four years since Mayor Richard Daley had ruled in Chicago, so forcing a new hearing on that argument in Miami was not hard at all, requiring the signatures of just 10 percent of the platform committee. All twenty minority planks that had been defeated in Washington thus came back to life in Miami, including the gay rights plank. It was a difficult and chaotic evening, even by Democratic Party standards. At two in the morning, Shirley MacLaine, the actress, McGovern supporter and abortion rights advocate, went before the convention to tell the delegates how strongly she supported the abortion rights plank that had been defeated in Washington, D.C.—and how important it was that it be defeated again, or risk handing the election to Richard M. Nixon. Three hours later, first Jim Foster and then Madeline Davis, the vice president of the Mattachine Society of the Niagara Frontier in upstate New York, were given ten minutes to make the case for the gay rights plank. They both knew it had no chance of passing, not that it really mattered.

"We do not come to you pleading for your understanding or begging for your tolerance," Foster said, speaking in a measured baritone and squinting into the television lights, trying to ignore the chatter from the delegates who could scarcely believe that even George McGovern had allowed a proclaimed homosexual to address a Democratic National Convention. "We come to you affirming our pride in our lifestyles, affirming the validity of our right to seek and maintain meaningful emotional relationships, and affirming our right to participate in the life of the country on an equal basis with every other citizen."

"I am a woman—I am a lesbian," Madeline Davis said moments later. She described homosexuals as "the untouchables in American society. We have suffered the gamut of oppression, from being totally ignored to having our heads smashed and blood spilled in the streets. Now we are coming out of our closets and onto the convention floor to tell you, the delegates, and to tell all gay people through America, that we are here to put an end to your fears."

In one sense, the appearances of Foster and Davis were a triumph for the young homosexual liberation movement, a validation of the first journey by gay activists into presidential politics. Never before had an openly homosexual delegate, much less two, spoken to a national political convention. Never before had a major political party debated a gay rights plank. Jim Foster had even been interviewed on the NBC evening news, offering a national audience an unchallenged argument that Americans are "certainly ready to accept" gay liberation "once they understand that the principles involved in gay liberation are very basically civil rights issues." His speech to the convention was introduced on CBS by Walter Cronkite, which, even as the sun was about to rise, gave it a certain gravity. In the hall, there were a score of homosexuals—some open, some not—who would never forget the sight of Foster and Davis talking calmly and matter-of-factly about homosexual rights. Troy Perry, there as the pastor of the Metropolitan Community Church in Los Angeles, wept.

But if this was a victory for the gay rights movement, it was a tentative one indeed. Jim Foster and Madeline Davis were speaking, but it was anything but prime time, as Morris Kight, one of the three hundred homosexual protesters picketing outside the hall, reminded anyone who would listen. "It was downright patronizing," Kight said later, a "tiny, tiny, tiny footnote to a tiny, tiny, tiny chapter." And even though Kight's dismissive reaction reflected his enduring dislike of Foster's dedication to working within the system (and, no doubt, some envy over his fellow Californian's sudden national celebrity) it was not entirely unfounded. Jim Foster and Madeline Davis spoke to delegates whose reaction ranged from indifference to hostility. The audience was so inattentive, and its disrespect so bold, that even Troy Perry began to think that Foster was just talking into the wind. Foster and Davis were endorsing a gay rights plank that would go down, in a quick and undignified voice vote, despite the fact that George McGovern had explicitly endorsed the notions it articulated. And finally, whatever pride they might have salvaged from this moment had been shattered when Kathleen Wilch of Ohio, a McGovern delegate and platform committee member, was sent to the podium by the Mc-

Govern forces to urge defeat of the gay rights plank. This was not another Shirley MacLaine arguing, as was the case on abortion rights, that an otherwise meritorious plank needed to be shelved for the greater good of electing a Democrat. Wilch, reading a statement she said had been drawn up by a Democratic Party lawyer, attacked homosexuals and gay rights with words so strong that it staggered the gay delegates and activists, inside and outside the hall, who heard it.

Minority Report Number 8, Wilch said into the television cameras, would "commit the Democratic Party to seek repeal of all laws involving the protection of children from sexual approaches by adults." It would force the "repeal of all laws relating to prostitution, pandering [and] pimping." Finally, the McGovern delegate said, "It is ill-considered because it would commit this party to repeal many laws designed to protect the young, the innocent and the weak. It would be a political disaster of monumental proportions for this party to adopt such a report." Troy Perry and seven other homosexuals with him jumped to their feet, threw their fists in the air and shouted, *"No! No! No!"* At a hotel suite nearby, Ethan Geto, a top New York aide to George McGovern, who divided his time between the McGovern presidential headquarters and the Gay Activists Alliance Firehouse, put his hand to his head. As the convention adopted the final 24,000-word platform at 6:15 a.m. and then adjourned six minutes later, the verdict on homosexuality as a political issue was clear and negative. McGovern was prepared to embrace a platform that called for an immediate withdrawal of all troops from Vietnam, amnesty for draft evaders, a minimum wage of $3,900 for families on welfare, guaranteed employment as a last resort and drastic cuts in military spending. But it was political folly to support gay rights.

When the gavel came down, some of the gay activists who had been outside pushed their way into the hall. Troy Perry herded a few of them in a circle to the side of the stage where Foster, Davis and Wilch had spoken. Up above the floor, in the gallery, a young man in ragged clothes, his fly held closed by a safety pin, stood teetering on the edge of the railing. He was a gay activist whom Barbara Love remembered from upstate New York. His arms were flung apart, his legs were spread, and his mouth was open in what, from the floor at least, seemed a soundless scream of frustration. He was swaying, and Barbara Love worried that he might collapse over the railing and onto the floor below. He was an eloquent symbol of their failure, of their ultimately silenced protest. Down below, the group by the stage huddled in a circle, clasped hands and slung arms over shoulders, and embraced. They were a tiny lifeboat, thought Nath Rockhill, floating in this sea of hostility. A few began to sing softly "We Shall Overcome." Rockhill, a lesbian from upstate New York, felt very sad, but she was not surprised. As soon as she had seen all the balloons and hoopla, she did not expect much from her days in Miami. She thought back to what Arthur Evans always said at the Gay Activists Alliance meetings in New York: What's important is not winning the battle but getting heard. That had always been the point of the drive for a gay rights bill in New York, and that was the point for the drive for a gay rights plank here in Miami. Some of the delegates had stopped to watch this strange display, and a few snickered at the scene. After these humbling days of going from caucus to caucus asking for a moment to make a case for gay rights, Barbara Love felt suffocated by defeat, and she turned to the hecklers. "All we want," she said, weeping softly, "is the right to have a job." At that, a few of the delegates around them turned their eyes to the ground and walked into the morning light. "Troy," Love said, "could you lead us in prayer?" And he did.

There were a number of roads that led to Miami for gay activists who wanted a place in the presidential selection process of 1972. Jim Foster had chosen the traditional one, working through the Democratic clubs and the McGovern organization to make his way to the convention platform. Six months earlier, on a freezing, snowy winter Saturday on the South Side of Chicago, at the barely heated Armitage Avenue United Methodist Church, with icy winds whistling through broken windowpanes, nearly two hundred gay activists, dressed in heavy coats, gathered to chart a different course. They represented eighty-six homosexual rights organizations from cities including New York, Los Angeles, San Diego and Washington, D.C., from Ohio and Minnesota, and they had been called to order by the Gay Activists Alliance of New York and the Chicago Gay Alliance. "The 1972 elections have come at a time in the history of the gay movement when we can finally, by unified effort, make our voices felt," John Abney of the host Chicago Gay Alliance declared. It was unrealistic to hope that the gay rights movement—whose members would be reminded again that weekend just how fractious they were—could agree on a single presidential candidate. The goal here was more modest: to agree on a set of positions for the candidates to adopt, and to make certain that the topic of homosexual rights was discussed in a presidential race. The conference marked the closest thing to an attempt to create a national homosexual rights group since the North American Conference of Homophile Organizations (NACHO) had collapsed under assault from radicals in San Francisco in the summer of 1970. One presidential candidate, Dr. Benjamin Spock, showed up to speak, and another, Mayor John V. Lindsay of New York, sent a telegram of support.

Still, this meeting was a long way from politics as usual, and it was not the kind of meeting where a Jim Foster, burrowing into the delegate selection process in San Francisco, would feel at home. It was dominated by some of the most radical and loudest voices of gay liberation, including Morris Kight of Los Angeles and Jim Fouratt of New York. Fouratt challenged this group of mostly white men about the lack of minorities and women in the room. He hammered that point so tenaciously that for years Fouratt would be shadowed by rumors that he was an agent paid by the FBI to disrupt the gay rights movement (a charge he forever denied). The meeting deadlocked when the question turned to whether this new gay coalition should insist that presidential candidates promise to lift the ban on homosexuals in the military. This issue produced a direct clash between the homosexual rights agenda and the general radical agenda of the time, whose supporters were not about to embrace any measure that would allow people to enter the military.

Frank Kameny, who was better acquainted with mainstream politics than almost everyone else there, said the group should establish one main goal: pushing both parties to include a gay rights plank in their platforms, and that is what they did. The platform the group endorsed was built on a proclamation that almost any homosexual leader would agree upon: "We demand the repeal of all laws forbidding voluntary sex acts involving consenting persons in private," it said. A presidential candidate, the delegates agreed, must support a civil rights bill to assure fair treatment of homosexuals in hiring, housing and public accommodations. The candidate had to pledge to issue an executive order barring discrimination against the hiring of homosexuals by the federal government, and should support dropping the Immigration and Naturalization Service's ban on homosexual immigrants. What's more, 10 percent of the delegates to both conventions should be homosexual, reflecting Kameny's interpretation of the Kinsey Report that 10 percent of Americans were homosexual. Everyone there also agreed that candidates should endorse the gay plank in writing, talk about it in their speeches and literature, appoint an openly gay person on their staff and participate in gay activities, including marching in parades.

But as the discussion moved to the fringes, the group began to adopt positions that some of the more pragmatic activists in the room, men like Steve Endean from Minneapolis, who shared with Kameny a deep respect for mainstream politics, recognized as toxic. The group voted, by a 32–24 margin, to endorse the abolition of "all laws governing the age of sexual consent," even if that encouraged the perception of homosexuals as child molesters. And it demanded the lifting of laws that restricted cross-dressing. By the end of all this, Endean decided that the "lunatics" and "agent provocateurs" like Fouratt, had succeeded in turning this into a "very destructive" meeting that would only hurt the gay liberation movement. Endean's perception of the meeting's outcome would be borne out to some extent when Kathleen Wilch took the stage in Miami five months later; and even more so, almost a decade later, when opponents of the homosexual rights movement unearthed the gay rights platform, with its age of consent plank. Most of the organizers, though, left this meeting with some optimism. "I hoped for another small step in getting gay groups together and other steps specifically in terms of presidential campaigns," Rich Wandel of New York said at the time. "What we got, I think, was a large step in terms of presidential campaigns and a phenomenal step in terms of getting a national gay movement." Kameny had a more practical, but still optimistic view of the meeting. "Realistically, we probably won't have the impact that all of us would like to have, but I think we will have enough so that it will be lasting and will lay the groundwork in terms of '76." Even Kameny's take would prove to be too hopeful.

As the leaders were meeting in Chicago, reporters from gay newspapers and activists from across the country were pushing the presidential candidates to take a position on the issue. An *Advocate* reporter cornered prospective presidential candidates by the U.S. Senate chamber during the vote on the Supreme Court nomination of William H. Rehnquist, and then printed their responses to questions about gay liberation. Bruce Voeller of New York's Gay Activists Alliance sent out a questionnaire to all the candidates, and Jack Baker, now the openly gay president of the 43,000 student body of the University of Minnesota, wrote a letter to his home-state candidate, Hubert Humphrey, asking his stand on gay rights. And early on, these efforts met with considerable success: The campaigns of George McGovern, Eugene McCarthy, John Lindsay, Shirley Chisholm and Hubert Humphrey all wrote letters, or had their campaigns issue statements that endorsed, in some form, the notion of civil rights for homosexuals. "I see no reason why homosexual Americans should be excluded from equal protection under the law," Humphrey wrote Jack Baker. "I am especially against arbitrary discrimination against homosexuals, especially as it pertains to unfair occupational hiring practices. Homosexuals are citizens; let us treat them as such." Eugene McCarthy talked to gay leaders in a conference call from his headquarters in California for ten minutes. Shirley Chisholm, the black Brooklyn representative, even raised it in a campaign speech in Buffalo, to a mostly black audience of a thousand that, at first, seemed stunned to hear a presidential candidate talk about such an unusual issue, and started to titter. "This is no laughing matter," Chisholm said. "Homosexuals are individuals . . . and entitled to their rights." Of all the major Democratic candidates, only Senator Edmund Muskie of Maine, whose campaign would not last past New Hampshire, actively avoided taking a position on gay rights. President Nixon and George Wallace did not respond to the questionnaire.

In New York, the Gay Activists Alliance began to apply to the presidential campaign the same tactics that had proved so successful locally—disruption and street theater. New York was the one city where presidential candidates had to come early and often, not necessarily for votes but for money. Muskie's refusal to endorse a gay rights plank drew the GAA to one of his fundraisers, where members distributed a leaflet which declared: "Senator

Muskie is the ONLY Democratic presidential candidate who refuses to endorse civil liberties for gay people. A contribution to Muskie's campaign is a contribution to our oppression."

New York was also the home of Mayor John V. Lindsay, whose campaign for the Democratic nomination suddenly provided activists with an unexpected opportunity to win concessions not only on national gay rights issues but on city ones as well. The city's gay rights bill had been voted down by the Committee on General Welfare by 7–5 in January 1972, the month before the New Hampshire primary, after a series of public hearings so raucous—Arthur Evans and Marty Robinson screaming "shame" at council members from the front row, men in dresses running in and out of the women's rest room at city hall—that even the group's biggest boosters laid the blame at the GAA's door. But the GAA insisted the fault lay with Lindsay, who had failed to rebut the brutal campaign waged against the measure by police and fire department unions. In the days before the vote, the Gay Activists Alliance, realizing they were heading for an embarrassing defeat, launched a final effort to salvage the bill by pressuring both Lindsay the mayor and Lindsay the presidential candidate. Lindsay was forced off the stage at a $100-a-seat presidential fundraiser at Radio City Music Hall, after fifteen activists infiltrated and then shouted the event to a halt. Rich Wandel, disguised in a suit and Abraham Lincoln–like beard, set off an air horn. "Lindsay has lied to the gay community!" Morty Manford yelled from the mezzanine, whereupon he handcuffed himself to the railing. "SINCE LINDSAY HAS NOT LIVED UP to his promises," one of the leaflets said, "WE WILL DESTROY HIS POLITICAL CAREER!" The normally measured Lindsay grew angry: "I do support your bill and it will come to a vote this Thursday. If it is defeated, it will be as a result of your actions." Lindsay left without delivering his prepared remarks.

The GAA calculated it could embarrass Lindsay enough on the presidential front to force him into action at home. "We are going to trash his campaign every time he makes an appearance in California or elsewhere in the nation," the GAA president, Rich Wandel, said. "All we have to do is send a few letters or make a few phone calls." The GAA contacted gay liberation organizations in Boston, Miami, San Francisco and Los Angeles, and sent out a mailing entitled "Declaration of War by the Entire Gay Community of the United States on John V. Lindsay." Barely one week after the defeat in the council, Lindsay produced an executive order declaring that a person's "private sexual orientation" could not be used in making hiring decisions in any city agencies. And on March 2, 1972, Lindsay wrote a warm letter to Bruce Voeller at the GAA to state "emphatically" that the "discriminatory and often cruel and abusive treatment of this minority [homosexuals] is a serious problem which cries out for solutions." Even the conservative editors at *Gay*, who had regularly criticized the young activists of the GAA for harassing a mayor the newspaper considered a friend, praised the success. "No matter what the more conservative elements in the gay community may think of the militants in their midst, one fact will stand out clearly: The militants will prove themselves effective in eliciting gay rights promises from major Democratic candidates for president. The letter to the Gay Activists Alliance from Mayor John V. Lindsay proves that the Mayor, far from being angered by GAA zappers at Radio City Music Hall, City Hall and at his campaign headquarters is, in fact, anxious to stay on the good side of the gay community."

But in California, the man who was becoming known as "Mr. Gay San Francisco" was not impressed. It would be better, Jim Foster said, to negotiate with Lindsay's campaign advisers privately rather than bully the candidate on the campaign trail. Foster knew and liked the inside game. And as the gay leaders held their quarrelsome meeting in Chicago, Foster announced the creation of the Alice B. Toklas Memorial Democratic Club, a Democratic club for homosexuals.*

August 1972, New York

Months before anyone else began paying any attention to the 1972 presidential race, Ethan Geto had decided to support George S. McGovern. Geto believed that McGovern was the only Democratic candidate committed to ending the U.S. involvement in Vietnam, and the only one who had a chance to win the nomination and perhaps unseat Nixon. In late 1971, Geto made the case for endorsing McGovern to his boss, Bob Abrams, the Bronx borough president. He argued that Abrams's political fortunes could soar if he signed on with the still unknown candidate. Abrams was a senior figure among New York City's reform Democrats, and he was Jewish, and when Abrams endorsed him, McGovern promptly appointed him the chairman of his New York State primary campaign. Since Geto was Abrams's chief political adviser, he assumed the role of political operative in McGovern's New York campaign as well. By the summer, Geto had been named the New York and northeastern press secretary for the McGovern presidential campaign.

Geto was a regular around the GAA Firehouse, and a prime source of the inside-the-fortress intelligence that contributed to the GAA's well-known reputation for guile, but no one on either Abrams's or McGovern's staff knew about that side of Geto's life. All they knew was that his marriage was in trouble, and that he had left his wife in the Bronx and was living in a room at the

---

* Foster was the chairman of the political committee of the Society for Individual Rights (SIR), but its members were not all Democrats, and they certainly were not all McGovern supporters.

Plaza Hotel in midtown Manhattan, courtesy of some of McGovern's flusher supporters. They did not know why the marriage had fallen apart. And they did not know that when Geto disappeared for hours at a time at the Miami convention, it was because he was up in his hotel suite with a young man he had met at one of the secret, daily strategy sessions of gay activists which he was also attending. Geto made his way down to the lobby one afternoon and came across a prominent West Side New York assemblyman, a McGovern delegate, who greeted him with a slap on the back and an exclamation: "I know why we don't see you around here. You're locked up in the room with some broad!" Geto took a deep breath, straightened his large frame and shifted his eyes. "Well," he said, "close but no cigar." There was nothing stereotypical about Geto's mannerisms that suggested he might be homosexual; even fellow homosexuals at the Firehouse could not quite believe that Geto was one of them.

Ethan Geto had been able to balance his two worlds—the Firehouse and the McGovern for President headquarters—because of McGovern's clear support for gay rights. Geto had sent a representative to read a statement he had written in McGovern's name in favor of the New York City gay rights bill in December. Two months later McGovern's northern California office issued a seven-point statement in support of gay rights at the request of Jim Foster, who needed it to cement McGovern's support in the San Francisco gay community. The position paper was mailed out whenever McGovern was asked about gay rights. "This statement was issued on my behalf on Feb. 2, 1972, and it represents my position," McGovern wrote to Bruce Voeller at the GAA, over what appeared to be a stamped signature, on McGovern for President stationery. McGovern's seemingly straightforward endorsement of gay rights set him apart from the rest of the field. Newspapers like *Gay* endorsed him. McGovern for President advertisements appeared in the *Lesbian Tide, The Advocate,* and *Gay* in New York. There was a Gay Citizens for McGovern Committee, an assembly of two dozen of the best-known gay and lesbian leaders from across the country. And even though Ethan Geto wasn't wearing his GAA Lambda button around McGovern headquarters—and George McGovern himself had no idea that Geto was a homosexual—activists in the gay community knew that one of their own was on the inside. An *Advocate* reporter, Guy Charles, interviewing Lindsay at city hall, made an oblique reference to Geto in suggesting that the mayor might mend his relations with the homosexual community: "I believe that you should have someone on your staff, as George McGovern may do, who is gay and who knows gay issues."

Geto's balance began to slip when the McGovern forces killed the gay rights plank in June. Geto could justify that action to himself, with some effort, just as Shirley MacLaine had justified killing the abortion plank. "It is entirely possible," Jim Foster, who shared Geto's sensibilities and political acumen, told *The Advocate* after the preconvention vote on the platform, "that Sen. McGovern is remaining aloof from the more controversial issues that have been raised before the platform committee, but I do not doubt for one minute those commitments that he has made are real." For Geto, though, Kathleen Wilch's speech was something entirely different. He had watched it on television, and he could think only of the Japanese sneak attack on Pearl Harbor. By Thursday evening, Wilch had "heartily apologized" for her remarks. "I opposed the plank for reasons of political expediency," she said in a statement. "The analogies I drew in the speech were aimed to show the possible ramifications of the plank as a political document. I was not aware that the speech would imply that homosexuals are child molesters. Child molestation is largely a heterosexual, not homosexual, problem." Geto, though, had no doubt that she had said exactly what McGovern's lieutenants wanted her to say. He heard her pledge in her apology to "do all in my power to urge Senator McGovern to publicly repudiate the statement," and he observed that, in fact, the McGovern forces did little to clarify the confusion her remarks had produced. Geto understood exactly what was going on: The McGovern camp left things muddled enough that it would be impossible for Richard M. Nixon to accuse their candidate of being sympathetic to homosexuals, and impossible for homosexuals to accuse him of being hostile to gay rights. The McGovern campaign knew that in the end, most homosexual activist voters were not going to vote, or contribute, to Richard Nixon. There was no price to pay in the general election for abandoning the homosexuals who had supported McGovern in the primaries.

Still, the climate had changed when Geto returned to New York from Miami in late July, and some gay organizations were threatening to bolt the McGovern camp. "We are shocked and saddened by your association with the offensive remarks made by a McGovern delegate," the National Coalition of Gay Organizations said in a telegram to McGovern. "We have full information that this speech was written with the assistance of and cleared by members of your staff. We demand an immediate written statement from you publicly disassociating yourself from arguments which constitute grave and abusive insults to 20 million gay women and men in every community in our nation." The editors at *The Advocate,* not usually given to extreme language, wrote: "We cannot comprehend . . . the vicious, shit-slinging attack by McGovern forces on the gay rights plank. We were surprised and appalled by it—especially because it was so unnecessary. It was unnecessary to assassinate the characters of millions of fine gay Americans and to alienate them. The proposals weren't going to pass; the simplest argument on practical political grounds would have been enough." The New Jersey Gay Political Caucus withdrew its support of McGovern. "We seriously think gays have been used by McGovern only to get on in the primaries. Now [that] he has the candidacy, he's discarding us." In Minneapolis, Steve Endean showed up at the airport the first time the McGovern campaign came into town, leading a protest; he had thought McGovern was the first presidential nominee who supported gay rights and now felt betrayed. In New York, Rich Wandel of the GAA argued that McGovern should not be permitted to soft-pedal his position on gay rights for the sake of an election. "Now his staff is worried about the November election. If he is elected, they will be worried about the 1976 election. Public commitment is the only way we can be assured of an end to Federal government discrimination against gays."

But McGovern would not—indeed, he arguably could not—change his position. As the general election campaign began, he was beleaguered, portrayed as ideologically out-of-touch with an electorate that was about to draw the line on the 1960s. Vice President Spiro Agnew defined McGovern's problem when he described the Democratic Presidential nominee as the Triple A candidate: abortion, amnesty and acid. McGovern began to feel he could not make it through a single day of campaigning without some voter or reporter asking him whether he supported the legalization of marijuana or the Equal Rights Amendment or amnesty for draft evaders. For years after this campaign, McGovern would tell questioners that the issue of homosexuality simply never came up: not at press conferences, with voters or in meetings of his advisers. According to his national political director, Frank Mankiewicz, that was not completely true. During the convention in Miami, McGovern looked out his hotel window at homosexual protesters demonstrating in the street. He turned to Mankiewicz and said: "What the hell are they doing out there? They can go fuck themselves." Mankiewicz chuckled and responded: "That's exactly the point, senator."

Ethan Geto remembered McGovern once expressing sympathy to the homosexual demonstrators upset over Wilch, but other aides squashed any suggestion that McGovern do anything to rebut her. Better that homosexuals demonstrate against you in the streets, they told him. One of Geto's jobs at the New York headquarters was to provide the daily briefing for Robert Wagner, the former New York City mayor, who had been brought in to be the New York chairman for the general campaign. Wagner was a proper New York Democrat, a pillar in the church and a future U.S. special representative for Jimmy Carter to the Vatican. Geto would run through the list of issues the McGovern campaign should be addressing in New York, and he would be sure to mention "gay rights." But Wagner would just shake his head. Geto never pushed very hard—he certainly never mentioned to Wagner that he was homosexual, or even that he was close friends with a member of Wagner's family who also was homosexual. In the evening and on weekends, Geto would head down to the Firehouse, but it was no longer any kind of escape: he had become a lightning rod for gay activists enraged at McGovern's actions. Why did McGovern seem to be committed to every liberal issue except gay rights? The gay activists were unable to understand why their man on the inside couldn't do anything about it. Geto was beginning to wonder the same thing.

The George McGovern for President headquarters in New York was at 605 Fifth Avenue: three floors in a low-rise building, crammed with desks, phones, chairs, leaflets, mimeograph machines, paper, placards, posters and telephone consoles. It was a quiet August morning, an hour before lunch and less than two weeks before Labor Day, when thirty members of the Gay Activists Alliance appeared, as if out of nowhere, and quickly and precisely brought McGovern's presidential headquarters to a halt. As soon as they got off the sixth-floor elevator, Bruce Voeller and two other GAA members walked deliberately toward three 10-button phone consoles, the main switchboards for the campaign. "What's going on here?" the operator asked helplessly as two of them chained their wrists to the phones. A McGovern deputy came bolting out of one of the back offices and tried to stop them. Voeller wrestled him to the ground. At that, two men in the party announced they were newspaper reporters—Randy Wicker of *The Advocate* and Arthur Bell, the openly gay columnist at the *Village Voice*—there as witnesses to the demonstration. The activists who had chained themselves to the consoles commandeered the telephones and, consulting a list of telephone numbers, began to call every major media outlet in New York City: the *Times*, the *News*, the *Post*, the Associated Press, the United Press and all the TV stations. "I am chained to a desk in George McGovern's campaign headquarters," each of them said. Whenever the phone rang and the light lit on the console, they would pick up the phone and announce that the McGovern for President headquarters had been taken over by gay liberationists.

McGovern's New York press secretary, Ethan Geto, came lumbering out of his office, appearing surprised and concerned. He urged his fellow McGovern aides to do nothing and remain calm while "the press is here." He said there should be no forced ejection since that would be contrary to the beliefs of the presidential candidate they worked for. And when the New York City police showed up at about noon, Geto sent them away, explaining that the McGovern campaign could handle this. "It's just not McGovern's style to call in the police and remove people forcibly," Geto told a television news reporter. "We're going to let them sit here until they get tired and go away." For the next five hours, Geto negotiated patiently with the activists from the GAA: They wanted McGovern to reaffirm his commitment to gay rights and to denounce Kathleen Wilch. And finally, at mid-afternoon, with the television cameras rolling, Geto appeared, standing next to GAA member Allen Roskoff, to read a statement: "Senator George McGovern has repeatedly affirmed his commitment to civil rights and civil liberties for all Americans. He has specifically addressed himself to discrimination directed against men and women based on sexual orientation, and has pledged to alleviate such discrimination in the federal government and in other areas of public life. Sen. McGovern believes that discrimination based on sexual orientation should be eliminated." Hal Offen of the Gay Activists Alliance saw the show on the television news that evening and just started to laugh. Here were Ethan Geto, who was Offen's best friend, and Allen Roskoff, standing stiffly together as if they were political adversaries meeting in combat. Roskoff, in his nasal voice, talked about their need to stop McGovern from reneging on gay rights, followed in counterpoint by Geto explaining how the candidate welcomed this opportunity to clarify his position. This was the same Roskoff and Geto who were as inseparable at the GAA Firehouse as they were when they were off touring the city's gay bars and bathhouses on the weekends.

Geto was by now used to providing inside information to help out his friends at the Firehouse; he had left his table at the New York City press corps's annual black-tie roast to alert the Firehouse about an anti-homosexual skit onstage. (The activists came uptown to disrupt the dinner, and several were beaten up by dinner guests in tuxedos.) But this was different. The New York press secretary to the McGovern for President campaign had planned this entire demonstration, right down to the commandeering of phones. The pressure at the Firehouse had become too intense and Geto was finding it hard to tell himself that he was effective from a closet inside the campaign headquarters, particularly when he overheard some of McGovern's senior advisers joking about the "prancing" homosexuals demonstrating against their candidate.

"Okay, if we're going to do this, let's do it right," Geto said one evening at the Firehouse. He proceeded to sketch the floor plans of the headquarters, noting the location of desks, offices, doors and elevators and the absence of security at the front of the building. He set a time to assure maximum media coverage and gave them the telephone numbers of the media organizations they should call. And he even told them what to say: "I am chained to a desk in George McGovern headquarters."

Geto's statement at the end of the day, in response to the protest he helped arrange, did not satisfy some members of the GAA, who had demanded it be issued by the campaign's national headquarters in Washington because they were afraid it might get lost in New York. At 5 p.m., Geto called the police on his friends at the GAA, and six of them were arrested for criminal trespass. The takeover of the McGovern headquarters was not applauded, particularly in the more pragmatic quarters of the gay community. "GAA's zap of Senator George McGovern's headquarters here was ill-conceived, we think," the editors at *Gay* said. "It seems they're going after the wrong man. Doesn't anybody want to get rid of Richard Nixon any more?" And for Mc-

Govern's senior advisers, issuing a statement was just an easy way to quell a minor annoyance. "Say something to show we're sympathetic and get them out of the office," Frank Mankiewicz said. But Ethan Geto considered the demonstration a success. He had made a new kind of play from inside the closet, using outside demonstrators as leverage to force his candidate to issue a statement in support of gay rights.

The reality for gay activists interested in influencing the 1972 presidential campaign was that George McGovern was their only vehicle. When members of the Society for Individual Rights (SIR) in San Francisco solicited a statement from President Nixon, they were told: "Mr. Nixon has nothing to say to the homosexual community." The National Coalition of Gay Organizations returned to Miami in August to try to influence the Republican convention and found the atmosphere even more unfriendly than it had been with the Democrats. Frank Kameny testified about gay rights to the Republican Platform Committee's subcommittee on human rights and responsibilities. The subcommittee chairman, Representative Peter H.B. Frelinghuysen of Morristown, New Jersey, excused himself without explanation at the start of Kameny's fifteen-minute speech and didn't return until Kameny had left. The subcommittee did not discuss the issue before approving a platform that made no mention of gay rights. "We didn't consider it," said Rhode Island delegate Debra Anne Jackson at the time. The issue was never raised at the convention, and there were no openly gay Republican delegates. The Republican National Committee's convention publication even belittled McGovern for his support by homosexuals. Madeline Davis, the Buffalo woman who spoke at the Democratic convention, concluded that the McGovern campaign she once supported was "cunning and vicious and it eventually caused McGovern to become the desperate and vicious person who disavowed" his earlier stands. She felt betrayed. But Davis was the exception. The Reverend Troy Perry announced that he just could not oppose George McGovern. "A vote not for McGovern would be a vote for Nixon," he said. "And I don't see how I could stand to live another four years under Nixon." Jim Bradford, the Mattachine leader from Chicago, was just as pragmatic: "Who cares whether a 100 percent gay plank got into the Democrats' platform? Freedom to live your own lifestyle free from social and legal interference is a broader and in my estimation better plank than a narrowly worded 'gay' plank." *The Advocate* struck a similar note in an editorial titled "So He's Not Ideal."

Jim Foster never had any doubt. Senator McGovern's handling of gay rights, Foster said, has been "less than perfect, but I would point out that he has made statements in support of gay rights and he has made a commitment to us." Foster suggested that the New York Gay Activists Alliance might find more suitable candidates for its zaps than George McGovern—Richard

Nixon, perhaps, or George Meany, the labor leader who warned that the "Democratic Party has been taken over by people named Jack who look like Jills and smell like Johns." After he returned from Miami to San Francisco, Foster waited a few weeks for the furor to die down, and then, with little fanfare, his Alice B. Toklas Memorial Club organized a committee of Gays for George McGovern.

10

SAN FRANCISCO:
COMING TO POWER

1972

On the outside, the Ritch Street Health Club was just an old warehouse four blocks south of Market Street. But on the inside it was a vision of what life was going to be like for gay men in San Francisco in the 1970s. The main attraction—the baths themselves, mirrored and sloshing with men, surrounded by a deck strewn with plump bean bag cushions for lounging, and backed by a dark maze of architectural nooks and corners where the patrons could slip into anonymous sex—was on the third floor, along with a small theater where Rick Stokes showed top-quality pornographic films on selected nights. The floor below held an elaborate set of showers, a steam room and dry sauna, and a warren of fifty small private rooms, with doors that could be locked. Once the owners could afford to evict the Japanese Trade Association, the tenant on the first floor, the area inside was remodeled into the slickest homosexual space in San Francisco, with a cafe restaurant where men could sit at tables and be entertained by what was going on around them, or eat and drink and get in the mood before going upstairs. The scenic attraction at first appeared to be a slice of ocean life, an aquarium filled with hundreds of gallons of salt water and schools of exotic fish. The fish shimmered and darted about, floating up and down in the wall of water, which rose about four feet from the cafe floor, above the heads of the men at the tables. The men could watch the silvery ballet of the fish or peer through them at a different kind of aquarium beyond, for on the other side of the wall of fish was a giant hot tub, fifteen feet wide and twenty-five feet long, with a bronze fountain foaming in the middle, and naked young men billowing in the water.

The Ritch Street Baths, as people called it, had been a hit from the day that Rick Stokes, his lover, David Clayton, and a dozen other investors had opened it in the fall of 1965, as a place where gay men accustomed to being hounded and trapped by the police could go and be themselves. The original partners were a mixed lot—a dentist who owned the building, an architect, a lawyer, an interior designer and some public school teachers like Stokes. But they were all men who liked going to baths, and who were tired of the dirty old commercial baths which then operated in San Francisco, with their inconvenient hours and their clientele of fat or gaunt and wrinkled, old heterosexual men. Their idea was to create the ideal baths for a young gay male. And so from the beginning the Ritch Street Baths was open twenty-four hours a day, seven days a week. It closed only four hours a year, between noon and 4 p.m. on New Year's Eve, and its reputation was such that by the time it opened again at four o'clock that afternoon, a line of hundreds of men had formed, snaking all the way from the front door down the Ritch Street alley and around the corner onto Brannon Street, waiting to get in. It was, as its happy owners liked to say, the premier gay baths in the world—and the best investment any of them would ever make in his life.

As the business grew and profited through the last half of the decade, Rick Stokes had quit his job teaching black and Asian students in the seventh and eighth grades of a junior high school in Sacramento, and entered law school at the University of California at Davis. His previous existence in Oklahoma—his dirt-poor family background, his marriage to a Southern Baptist woman, his forced confinement by his in-laws to a private mental asylum where he was repeatedly subjected to electroshock treatment to try to change his sexual orientation—had all made him determined to create a life of his own, and to find the right man to share it with. In 1960 he had met and fallen in love with David Clayton, and they had settled down. Rick Stokes had grown and changed in the decade since, and had been inordinately happy—protected, he knew, by the job security that Clayton enjoyed as a lawyer. David Clayton had been in private practice and then had worked as an attorney for the federal legal assistance program, which was administered in San Francisco by another gay lawyer, Herbert Donaldson. The arrangement had the feeling of the beginning of a network. Rick Stokes decided to become an attorney, too, so that he could do what he wanted to without worrying, as teachers did, about being fired from his job.

Part of what he wanted was to take on the system that consigned homosexuals to hospitals, jails and the margins of the culture, and since moving to Sacramento thirteen years before, and then to San Francisco, Stokes had been at or near the center of all the important events that had shaped the city's gay community and its growing political influence. He was lean and angular and sandy-haired, blue-eyed and rawboned in an urban cowboy sort of way, and his manner was earnest and quiet. But he was aggressive in his new life and organized about it. He had helped paint the rooms of the old union hall on Sixth Street when the new organization called the Society for Individual Rights (SIR) moved into its new home. He had been in the pews when the Reverend John Moore preached one of his famous "Gay is Good" sermons at Glide Church. Donaldson and his lover had introduced Stokes and Clayton to the liberal, gay-friendly church. It was a bastion of independence, thanks to its endowment by the late Lizzie Glide, and the sermon that day was the first time that Stokes had ever heard a preacher say that the destruction of Sodom and Gomorrah was God's punishment for inhospitality, not for homosexuality. Three or four old-line members of the church had walked out that morning, but afterward homosexuals came flooding in. The ministers of Glide Church and of the other liberal pulpits in the city had become important allies to the homophile movement, and Stokes had been at the New Year's Day ball the ministers had helped sponsor for homosexuals in 1965 when the police swept in, arresting Donaldson and others. Stokes had become chairman of the Glide Foundation afterward, and then president of the Council on Religion and the Homosexual, the coalition of ministers and gays which had finally pressured the police to suspend their indiscriminate attacks on the city's gay bars.

Gay politics in San Francisco, as in L.A. and New York, had been formed almost entirely in reaction to the continuing crackdown by authorities on gay bars and gay male sexuality, and in 1970, Rick Stokes had begun a law practice that was largely shaped by those issues. From the very beginning, he also represented divorcing lesbians terrified of losing custody of their children to their husbands. But his days were spent mainly in counseling and defending frightened men who had been arrested on morals charges for solicitation and sex crimes in the public toilets and bushes of places like Golden Gate Park. At night, after law office hours and on weekends, he and Clayton managed the Ritch Street Baths, where men could have sex without fear of arrest. It was an adroit balance, and one which perfectly reflected the compulsions and stresses of the culture in which Stokes lived.

As a criminal lawyer, a civil rights advocate, a businessman and civic leader in the emerging gay community, Rick Stokes was becoming very well connected, and he discovered in dealing with the police that they would rather that gay men have sex with each other in the privacy of the Ritch Street Baths than in places like the city's parks. That suited Stokes and his partners fine. The gay culture and its place in the political system of San Francisco was evolving, and Stokes's personal and professional life represented its highest state of evolution. His law practice, his business, civic, religious and political involvements all fed each other—and they were all a reflection of the fact that he was homosexual. By 1972, the expanding number of gay businesses in the city—chiefly its bars and restaurants, 110 of which were organized as the Tavern Guild—had become an important source of funding to local politicians. And the city's gay membership organizations—which meant SIR and the Daughters of Bilitis but mainly SIR—had proved their ability to deliver a gay vote. Twice, in 1969 and 1971, that vote had been decisive in electing friendly liberal politicians to important office in San Francisco. It was an achievement that no other gay community in the country could even begin to match, and by 1972, it seemed possible to Rick Stokes and his friends, the chief gay political brokers of the city, that Stokes could make a credible run for public office himself. That meant a great deal. It was something that no open homosexual had done in San Francisco since José Sarria had first dared it on his own a full ten years before. It was an important next step in a city that occupied a special place in the national homosexual experience.

There were many lesbians and gay men living in the dazzling city by the bay who believed as a matter of faith that San Francisco was *the* best place in America for a gay person to live. In one form or another, it was a sentiment repeated across the country: San Francisco was the capital and mecca of gay culture in America. When the Institute for Sex Research—the Kinsey Institute—was asked by the National Institute of Mental Health to conduct an extensive survey of what homosexual life was like in 1969, the staff had chosen San Francisco as the best place to do it, the field director of the study said, because the city had more homosexuals per capita than any other major metropolitan area in the nation. They seemed to be popping up everywhere. One man had even raised the issue of homosexuals in the culture in December 1969, in the pulpit of Grace Cathedral, where the rich and powerful of the city's social and economic establishment worshiped each Sunday. "Good morning!" said the man, an acolyte and lay reader in the church. He had shoulder-length dark hair and a mustache, and a quiet, angelic look as he stood before the congregation in his altar robes. But "instead of the appointed epistle for today," he announced, "I should like to read a public statement I have written speaking out against a great injustice perpetrated by our society." For the next five minutes, as several hundred amazed but captive Episcopalians listened, he did. Critiquing the treatment of homosexuals by law and religion, he urged the parishioners to support the legalization of homosexual relations between consenting adults and the candidacy of homosexuals for the priesthood. A few people stalked out as he spoke, and one man shouted to him to give up the pulpit. But mostly, they stayed to hear him out and even to congratulate him after Communion.

The congratulations were a departure from custom, a sign of the sympathy, if not any broad existing support, that could be won by daring. "Are we to conclude that homosexuals are socially acceptable?" the counsel for the Pacific Telephone Company had asked at a public hearing that year. "I know that I'm socially acceptable to a large number of my heterosexual friends," SIR president Larry Littlejohn had replied. "I don't think they care about what I do in the privacy of my bedroom." But Pacific Telephone did. The issue was whether the company would allow SIR to place an advertisement in the Yellow Pages. The company's answer was no. And a homosexual man still risked his life to go into a public park in the Bay Area at night, in hopes of finding another man to have sex with. The Berkeley police had killed one man that year, shooting him in the head when he allegedly solicited a young undercover officer and then tried to escape as they moved to arrest him. And a middle-aged college professor, a married man, had died of a stroke after being roughed up by Oakland police during an arrest on a morals charge in a public rest room. In all those cases, SIR had filed suit to try to change the way the local culture dealt with homosexuals. The point wasn't that men should be able to have sex in public parks and rest rooms, a SIR attorney said. The point was that young policemen shouldn't be posing as homosexuals in public places, enticing gay men into danger that they otherwise might have avoided.

The organization was beginning to get respect. The city, in recent years, had begun electing an array of young liberal politicians to office, men like George Moscone, an Italian Catholic with progressive ideas. And for the last three rounds of municipal and state elections—1965, 1967 and 1969—an increasing number of these politicians had been showing up at the candidate nights that SIR hosted in the big meeting room of its clubhouse, a former union hall on Sixth Street. Politicians began to see the city's large homosexual population as a "gay vote." No one knew the size of the homosexual population clustered around San Francisco Bay, but everyone knew it was growing, and by 1969, the estimates in political circles ranged as high as 120,000 people in the metropolitan area. Estimates of the number in San Francisco alone ranged from 50,000 to 90,000. Some officeholders—leading liberals and political allies like Phillip Burton, the representative; his brother John, the state assemblyman; Willie L. Brown Jr., the black lawyer and assemblyman whose district was heavily gay; and Jack Morrison, the city supervisor—saw gay civil rights concerns as a natural extension of their constituent base, and a big new potential vote.

The question for candidates who wanted the support of homosexuals as the 1970s began was, what could they do to get it? The answer that Jim Foster, the lean, ambitious political chairman of SIR, had ready for them, was: "Change the law. Decriminalize our behavior." Foster, who could be charming and personable while earning his living as a greeting card salesman, was aggressive when it came to Democratic Party politics. He showed up at every party gathering he could make, and his objective was to support liberal politicians who would then be obligated to help the gay community achieve its legislative goals. And the primary goal for SIR, a gay male organization, was to abolish the century-old California "crime against nature" statute, which condemned the act of homosexuality as illegal. Foster and those around him saw it as the whole basis for their mistreatment by police and government.

Willie Brown and John Burton were willing to go to bat for the sexual equality that gay men wanted before the law. Brown was a canny, fearless politician with a theatrical sense of the moment, aggressively liberal. His district ranged from Pacific Heights, the city's richest and culturally most sophisticated neighborhood, to the old hippie enclave of Haight-Ashbury, and the Polk–Van Ness Gulch. All those neighborhoods had a substantial gay presence. His district, Brown said publicly, included more homosexuals than *any* other in California, and in March 1969, he had filed a bill to legalize private sexual conduct between consenting adults, a change in the law that only Illinois had made. It was a measure of Willie Brown's self-confidence that he described his bill to the general public as a measure to end discrimination against homosexuals while characterizing it to homosexuals as a bill that would liberate heterosexuals, too. The public tends to treat homosexuals "as they do blacks and other minorities—as less than human beings," Brown told reporters when he introduced the legislation. "What I'm attempting to do is knock out the blackmail and the public condemnation, and free the cops from being peeping toms in restrooms so they can go out and do some honest criminal investigation." But there was also, he asserted, a larger issue—the issue of the right to be sexual without being intruded on by government, period. Willie Brown knew that the old state law, like most state laws against sodomy, made certain sexual acts illegal no matter *who* was committing them, so he argued that heterosexuals had an interest in changing the law, too. "My aim," he told a meeting of about two hundred SIR members a month later, "is to liberate *all* of us to engage in *any* conduct that we want, so long as we enjoy it." But Brown warned his jubilant, cheering audience in the SIR clubhouse not to kid themselves. It would be "an absolute miracle," he said, if the legislation passed that year. "The legislature has literally got to be educated, especially on sex issues," he told them. "The biggest pitch I'm making," he said, with a mischievous grin, "is to remind my colleagues that some of *them* do these things on a nightly basis, and that I want to legalize their actions." Although the City Board of Supervisors failed to endorse Brown's bill that year, four of the nine members backed it. Two years later, a majority of the board voted to endorse it, even though Joseph L. Alioto, the old-time Italian Roman Catholic who had been elected mayor in 1967 and who encouraged the police department to crack down on homosexuals, vetoed it. More and more politicians seemed to recognize that there was a growing gay constituency in the city, and that sodomy law reform was something they could promise when they

came to candidate nights at SIR. The ability of homosexuals to attract candidates and to help elect them was growing, and one of the reasons was that the
city's economy and population were changing. The old industrial and manufacturing jobs which for so long had nurtured San Francisco as a blue-collar
city of conservative ethnic neighborhoods were disappearing. Mayor Alioto, a
personable but hard-minded conservative of the old school, who had built his
political base on the Democratic vote of the old ethnic neighborhoods, made
it his policy to clear the way for developers to build the office towers that
helped reinvigorate the city as its manufacturing base collapsed. But as that
policy succeeded, it also helped erode the mayor's own constituent base.
Without jobs to pay the mortgage and feed the family in such neighborhoods
as the one around Castro Street, many of his constituents had to leave San
Francisco to find work. And the professional and clerical jobs in the new office
towers were attracting a new and culturally different urban workforce—many
of them single young gay men who came flocking from all over the country.

The city's demographic base, like its economy, was in a state of shift and
upheaval, and the resulting fissure in the city's political structure showed in the
way that different politicians treated SIR. Alioto ignored SIR's candidate
nights, its invitations to speak and its political concerns. By 1971, an average of
2,800 gay men were being arrested annually on public sex charges under
Alioto's regime, as against sixty-three such cases made in all of New York City
that year. Oral sex was a felony in California, punishable by as much as fifteen
years in prison. The police in San Francisco had made eighty-eight such arrests
in 1970 and had charged sixty men with that crime in the first six months of
1971 alone. Convictions on any kind of morals charge often carried a require-
ment that the defendant register with the police as a public sex offender. And
since applications for almost all professional occupational licenses in California at the time had to be cleared with the police—even licenses for people who
worked as hairdressers—a conviction could destroy a person's ability to work.

It was a woman running for her first public office—a wealthy, attractive
Jewish housewife from the city's richest neighborhood, Pacific Heights—who
came and listened to the men of SIR, captivated them completely by her style
and presence, and proved to the rest of San Francisco that the power of the
gay vote existed. She never seemed comfortable with the overt sexuality of the
men whose votes she wanted—she never would be—but she did see homosexuals as a legitimate political community and was happy to be a good listener to win votes. Her name was Dianne Feinstein, she was running for the
Board of Supervisors, and she was the first Board candidate ever to run campaign ads on television. Dark-haired, with pale luminous skin, a stylish
wardrobe and a confident air—moderate politics—she was glamorous and
charismatic, the most exciting new political figure in the city, and she so

charmed the men of SIR when she showed up at a candidate night in 1969
that they outdid themselves in creating a gay vote for her at the polls that fall.
They were grateful that she took them so seriously. If they could elect her, they
could prove something.

When the polls closed on election day that November, Dianne Feinstein
had won more votes citywide than any other candidate. She was a phenomenon in San Francisco politics, the first woman to succeed in a system which
had been dominated for decades by Irish and Italian Roman Catholic males.
As the top vote-getter that year, she became not just a supervisor, but president
of the board. Feinstein credited the gay vote with making the difference, and it
was she, more than anyone else, who came to personify the success—and the
risk—of the SIR policy of backing gay-friendly straight politicians. Although
she represented something new in city politics, she also represented something old in cultural relationships—the socially sophisticated, affluent, married heterosexual woman who found gay men sympathetic and agreeable,
deserving of recognition and, in this case, good political company. She
charmed and flattered them, and there were members of SIR who would do
anything for her. They made paper posies which were sold in the bars to raise
money. Some lesbians, however, had a different reaction. "Many of us quite
frankly don't trust her," said Karen Wells of the Daughters of Bilitis. "She is
more responsive to SIR than to women, and that bothers me." And there were
some men, like Rick Stokes, who saw her as a surface ally but, on a gut level,
felt she might be deeply disapproving. When Stokes and some other prominent homosexuals went to complain about police harassment and entrapment
of homosexuals in public parks and rest rooms. Feinstein's attitude, Stokes
thought afterward, was not, why are the police doing these things? It was,
"why are gay men doing these kinds of things?"

Dianne Feinstein was the trophy of Foster's hard work as political chairman of SIR, and a powerful friend. But there were limits to her sympathy and
to her tolerance, especially on the matter of sex, a fact which had become jar-
ringly clear when she made a formal speaking appearance at the SIR clubhouse on May 19, 1971. For perhaps the first hour, she was treated adoringly.
It was the first time a president of the San Francisco Board of Supervisors had
ever addressed an openly gay group. Five hundred men had packed the
second-floor corner meeting room of the clubhouse to hear her, and when she
stood before them the men hung on her every word and gesture.

"Why do so many politicians turn their backs on the gay community?"
she asked, looking out at the sea of blissful, excited faces. It was, of course, a
setup question.

"Poor judgment," she answered. The crowd loved it until she began
talking about the pornographic movie houses which were becoming a visible
sign of the growing gay male presence in the city. "What I see concerns me,"

she said, "not because of the desensitization, not only because, to some extent, some of it makes a true mockery of the very meaningful things that are provided by the gay community to this city, but partly also because we begin to see something which is having an effect on young people struggling to grow up at a time when it's hard to know what your sexual identification is." The light was dying in the eyes of the men listening to her. It sounded as if she found homosexuality threatening to young people. "We know we have a kind of hypocritical Puritan ethic on which this country was founded," she went on, "but I don't think the way this country should go is to exploit commercially those things about it which relate us more to the animals than to human beings."

The men began to boo. And although Dianne Feinstein had endorsed Willie Brown's proposal to decriminalize sexual relations between consenting adults, although she went on that summer to lead the effort to persuade the city's Board of Supervisors to outlaw discrimination on the basis of "sex or sexual orientation," and although SIR and the Tavern Guild had easily decided to support her bid to defeat Mayor Alioto in 1971, Jim Foster realized at that moment that Dianne Feinstein was never going to be a soulmate on the fundamental issue of male sexuality. Feinstein had a goody-two-shoes quality about her, and Foster knew he had to keep recruiting other politicians.

Richard Hongisto had been a maverick as a cop—a political liberal, openly friendly with blacks and gays. He hadn't always liked homosexuals. But in philosophy class at San Francisco State College in the late 1950s, Hongisto had sat next to Michael Deems and they became close friends. Several things happened to Richard Hongisto as a result of those classes. He became a philosophy major. The coursework gave a sort of formal validation to his own restless, questioning nature, and he began to examine some of his own assumptions. One of the things he decided was that his original career goal—to teach children in the public schools—had come to seem cautious and dull. Many of the students at San Francisco State, Hongisto knew, went on to become policemen, and this struck him as a much more exciting laboratory in which to experience life. When his friend Michael Deems one day confided to him his deepest secret, Hongisto discovered that he knew and liked someone who was homosexual. Deems became a public school teacher with an apartment in an old Irish and Italian working-class neighborhood of teachers, firemen and policemen around Castro Street. And Richard Hongisto became a San Francisco policeman with a friend who was gay—with, in fact, a growing number of friends who were gay, as he met more and more of Deems's friends.

It was in Hongisto's nature to be an agitator, and he became that rare sort of law enforcement officer—a cop who questioned authority. Offended by the small number of black police officers and the attitude toward blacks within the San Francisco Police Department, he helped form Officers for Justice, a new fraternal group to counter the conservative, all-white Police Officers Association. Hongisto became its only white member. His involvement caught the attention of the head of the department's new community relations division, which was supposed to establish cooperative relations between the police force and the city's minority populations. And once the department became committed to creating some liaison with the gay community, it seemed natural to Richard Hongisto that he should be part of that. Hongisto knew about SIR, and began to spend time hanging out at SIR meetings and events, serving as a buffer and liaison between the city's gay men and its black-uniformed police force.

That was where Hongisto, younger and single and interested in cultural politics, drew close to the balding, sharp-featured Jim Foster, who smoked heavily, talked a lot with his hands and arms, and was driven by his dream of building a voting bloc in the city's gay community. The more comfortable Hongisto grew with the homosexuals, blacks, hippies and other radical minorities in the city culture, the more hostile his straight white colleagues in the police department grew to him. By the time Feinstein won the presidency of the Board of Supervisors, Richard Hongisto was beginning to feel decidedly unwelcome on the San Francisco police force. "You see that guy," one detective said in a low voice to the others as a group of them stood at the elevator in the Hall of Justice, watching Hongisto pass by. "There goes a pot-smoking, homosexual, Communist Nigger-lover."

Hongisto decided he should get out of the department. He had spent ten years policing a changing city, but he couldn't stay on the police force. The Sheriff's Office, however, was a different matter. The responsibility of the sheriff, in the combined city-county government of San Francisco, was to run the jails and provide officers for the court. Sheriff Matthew Carberry, a product of the city's old Irish Catholic Democratic politics, had been in office for five terms. His incompetence and heavy drinking were widely known. He was up for reelection in November 1971, and it was only a few months before when Richard Hongisto's telephone rang. It was Foster, who had an intriguing proposition for him: Hongisto should run for sheriff. He could put together a loose coalition of gays, women, blacks, liberal Democrats and young voters—all the people who found an old-fashioned conservative autocrat like Carberry offensive. Hongisto considered the odds: it was very late to be entering the race, he had never run for political office, and Sheriff Carberry was entrenched, with the support of Mayor Alioto and the downtown establishment. But the maverick quality of the idea appealed to every part of Hongisto's nature. And he knew from Foster and other friends that the gay community was getting seriously ambitious. There was a new personality involved, a former Wall Street figure and banker, David Goodstein. Wealthy, autocratic, angry at the way he had been discriminated against as a homosexual by one of his former employers, and determined to be an influence in the city and its politics, Goodstein was in the process of establishing a new do-good political lobby in San Francisco which would pay Jim Foster a salary, freeing him to work practically full-time on organizing the gay community.

Hongisto agreed to run. And very shortly, he was standing in front of the membership of SIR at its Sixth Street clubhouse, telling them and virtually anyone else who asked in the next several months what his position was on reforming the laws on sexual conduct in California. "I don't care how a person has an orgasm as long as they don't hurt anyone else," Hongisto said. It was only one bold stand among a number that he took in running for sheriff. He proposed not only financial assistance for crime victims, but also more humane treatment of prisoners in the county jails, and his campaign quickly caught the voters' attention. The symbol on Hongisto's literature was the sheriff's badge with a peace sign in the middle. It showed a sense of humor which appealed to the young and hip, but it also conveyed a liberal message of law enforcement with a heart.

Sheriff Carberry, whose management of the jails had been criticized by a citizens' commission, sent a different message: "I wouldn't give him a job as a hairdresser in the women's jail," the sheriff said of Hongisto. It was a barroom sneer, one intended to encourage speculation that Hongisto—a thirty-five-year-old bachelor—was homosexual. Homosexuals were giving him money, printing and distributing his leaflets and posters, answering his phones, even climbing a forty-foot ladder to paint a sign high above his campaign headquarters on Market Street. Speculation about his sexuality was inevitable; Hongisto discovered that even some of the women he took out assumed he was gay. It was a more painful issue between the candidate and his parents, simple working-class people. Arguments with his father, a hard hat who had moved his family from northern Minnesota during World War II in order to work in the San Francisco shipyards, grew so violent as Hongisto grew closer to the gay community that the two sometimes almost came to blows.

But Sheriff Carberry's sneer at Richard Hongisto backfired. Gay men and lesbians, galvanized by the idea of electing a sheriff of San Francisco who actually said he liked homosexuals, embraced Hongisto with a passion. He benefited from fundraising parties at David Goodstein's mansion in Pacific Heights, where the guests ogled the Rembrandt on the wall, and at Charlotte Coleman's The Mint, a bar in the financial district where panels of silver dollars gleamed in the brick walls of the dining room. Charlotte Coleman was the leading lesbian bar owner in San Francisco. She had never held a fundraiser for a politician before, but she was friendly with Jim Foster and Rick Stokes, and involved with SIR. She had liked Richard Hongisto when someone brought him to dinner at The Mint, and she was pleased when he told her after the election that 10 percent of his campaign money had been raised at her party that night.

The gay community's drive to elect Hongisto sheriff, as well as its strong role in attempting to elect Dianne Feinstein mayor and Robert Mendelsohn president of the Board of Supervisors, became so visibly organized and intense that fall that in mid-October the *San Francisco Chronicle,* whose coverage of gay life had been confined mainly to articles about gay weddings and other such events, published an almost breathless front-page story on this emergent new political force. "San Francisco's populous homosexual community, historically non-political and inward looking, is in the midst of assembling a potentially powerful, political machine. A sustained and determined effort is underway to raise money and political consciousness, organize precinct workers, distribute campaign literature and pursue all the other avenues classically associated with the development of political muscle."

The *Chronicle* story was laced with proud, even boastful comments from gay men the paper's readers had probably never heard of before. "The stigma is gone from homosexuality," declared Robert Ross, the president of the Tavern Guild. And Bill Plath, president of SIR, sounded perfectly matter-of-fact when he stated, "We can supply a candidate with a certain number of votes, and in a close race, those votes are going to make the difference."

For Richard Hongisto, it wasn't even close. Endorsed by Representative Phillip Burton and Assemblyman Willie Brown—both liberals and allies of SIR—Hongisto came in first in a four-man race, beating Sheriff Matthew Carberry by a 4 to 3 ratio, 81,402 votes to 59,848. Dianne Feinstein did not knock Joe Alioto out of the mayor's chair, and the other candidate SIR was backing did not win enough votes to become president of the Board of Supervisors. But it was clear, in the immediate wake of the election of November 1971, that the gay vote in San Francisco had reached a critical mass. In a city where their biggest fight for two decades had been about law enforcement, the gay community had elected the sheriff. The turnabout could not have been more stunning, and the new sheriff-elect made no bones about who had put him into office. His "biggest single source of support was gay and lesbian," he told people. "Hands down." Hongisto's underdog candidacy had captured the imagination of the city's gay voters. In Sheriff Richard Hongisto they had made an ally who was not only more in tune and more indebted to them than Feinstein was, but one who would stick with them through good and bad times in years to come.

Richard Hongisto realized in 1972, as he pinned on the specially made gold sheriff's star with a peace symbol in the middle that was his campaign logo, that he could keep that star as long as he kept his base of gay votes. He knew the office of sheriff had limited powers to affect the way the police and mayor ran the city. But Hongisto also knew that Mayor Alioto and others had learned from his election that the gay community was a political force to be taken into account.

One of his signature acts as sheriff was to hire a young black man, Rudy Cox, as the first openly gay deputy sheriff. Hongisto put Cox to work in the jail, and when he began to get reports that the tough old Irish Catholic jailers were harassing him, Hongisto paid a visit. He ordered all the prisoners locked down in their cells and had the whole jail staff assembled in the front lobby. When the jailers were all lined up in their uniforms, with their creaky leather belts and jangling keys, Hongisto stood in front of them, the gold star with its peace symbol glinting on his chest, and told them he didn't want to hear any more reports about their mistreating Cox. "You fuck with him," he promised them, as he looked the line up and down, "and I will fuck with you. Your ass will be grass, and I will be the lawnmower. So I better not hear any more of this shit."

It gave Hongisto a certain thrill to imagine San Francisco as a kind of mecca for gay America. As he would later say, it pleased him to think of it as a safe harbor, a port in the cultural storms, a place where people knew they could come and be free of harassment and contempt. So long as he was sheriff.

And the great flow of homosexuals from around the nation into San Francisco began in earnest. Some of them, like Harvey Milk, a passionate and quirky New Yorker who settled in San Francisco for good late in 1972, were men in their forties who had lived more or less openly as homosexuals for years, but were still trying to fashion a life in a place that felt right to them. Some, like Harry Britt, a tall, shy, intellectual Texan who had fled marriage and the ministry of the Methodist Church in his early thirties, came in a state of confusion, hoping that they could find in the growing human potential movement in San Francisco the spiritual help they needed to unpuzzle their identities. But many more were young men in their teens and twenties like Cleve Jones, who had realized that they were gay, and who came to San Francisco, drawn by the evolving urban culture. The city had changed and these newcomers would change it again.

The three existing gay neighborhoods amidst the hills and folds of San Francisco when they arrived were the Tenderloin, a red-light district of crummy bars and cheap hotels downtown, where tall transvestite prostitutes sauntered along at night; Polk Street, a decorators' row of antique shops, furniture stores, tasteful gay bars and youthful hustlers—Harry Britt rented a room just a block off Polk his first months in the city, in such a state of numb confusion that he never noticed his gay surroundings; and the old warehouse district south of Market around Folsom Street, where SIR had its clubhouse, Rick Stokes and his partners operated the Ritch Street Baths, and a new colony of Levi's and leather bars had grown. Known respectively as the Valley of the Queens, the Valley of the Dolls and the Valley of the Kings, the three neighborhoods had been shaped by the different phases and personalities of the gay community as it had evolved.

But like Harvey Milk, and then Harry Britt and Cleve Jones, many of the new arrivals gravitated to a different part of town, flowing into spaces where the rents were cheap around the intersection of Castro and Eighteenth Streets, where Phyllis Lyon and Del Martin had started life as a couple twenty years before. There, they joined a scattering of existing lesbian and gay residents like Charlotte Coleman, the bar owner, and Michael Deems, the teacher, in a pattern of homosexual habitation which began to grow and spread. The old neighborhood, thought of by many of its Irish Catholic families simply as Most Holy Redeemer Parish, lay in an area of the city known geographically as Eureka Valley, just below Haight-Ashbury, which had become the international destination of the hippie movement of the 1960s. Some of those hippies—gay ones, in their long hair, blousy shirts and low, bell-bottomed jeans—had more recently begun drifting down into rooms and apartments in the old Victorian houses along Castro Street. Two gay bars had even sprung up.

The established gay political structure which the new immigrants to San Francisco found in place was evolving, too, but along lines already set by two decades of prior evolution, and it was a structure which already had a leadership, an overall strategy, a candidate and a plan. The strategy was to move the gay constituency to the center of Democratic Party politics, making it a power in the party and in public office. To that end, Jim Foster had, in December 1971, created a new gay Democratic political club, the country's first, and named it for Gertrude Stein's lover, Alice B. Toklas. Its membership and momentum were drawn directly from SIR and the operation of its political committee. But in contrast to SIR, which operated as a kind of educational lobby, a forum for candidates and for question-and-answer nights, the formation of a partisan club gave its gay membership an instant presence in local and state Democratic councils. Toklas could also get down and dirty: it could make political deals and give direct support to individual campaigns, as it had in its signature drive for McGovern.

For a man who had been an adopted child, who had been dishonorably discharged from the U.S. military for homosexuality, arrested by the police and accustomed to earning an anonymous, largely hand-to-mouth living as a greeting card salesman, it was enormously gratifying to Foster to be the leading gay spokesman within the Democratic Party, as he certainly was in 1972. But with the presidential race behind them, the plan that Foster and his friends David Goodstein and Rick Stokes now had in mind to advance the electoral gay presence in the city itself seemed mild in comparison. There was to be a new election that year of members to the local community college board, whose seats had previously been filled by appointment. The board wasn't a sexy or high-profile public office, but it was a sober and meaningful position, and it offered a nice quiet way for a gay candidate to campaign for votes.

If that seemed a pale ambition in contrast to the gay community's proven ability to put Dianne Feinstein and Richard Hongisto into office, it was also far from clear, in late 1972, that anyone who was openly homosexual could get elected to anything at all in San Francisco. But if anyone could, by the traditional political calculus that Jim Foster and his Toklas friends employed, it was Rick Stokes. He had the brains, the connections, the credentials, the fortitude, and—thanks to the Ritch Street Baths—enough money to feel secure. He was an attorney, a businessman and civic leader—the conscientious, responsible, dues-paying gay version of a stand-up San Francisco liberal. He had been giving speeches in public, showing audiences who had never seen one what a real, normal, unafraid homosexual looked and talked like, since his second year of law school in 1967. In 1971 he and Sally Gearhart, a former college speech and drama teacher—and an increasingly passionate public lesbian—had been named by the Family Services Agency to its board of directors, the first two acknowledged homosexuals appointed to public positions in the city. When the two were interviewed by a reporter for the *Chronicle*, neither made any bones about his or her sexual orientation. Gearhart took a radically feminist line, saying that she viewed her lesbianism as "a rejection of the oppressive role of women as barefoot pregnant helpmates chained to a kitchen stove."

But Rick Stokes took a completely different approach to the interview: what he stressed was how much he was like a married man. "I know that in the beginning, my fellow members of this board are going to regard me as just a homosexual spokesman," he said. "But I hope that early along, they'll realize that like any other family man, I have a lover and we write letters to each other and cook dinner and worry about money and have squabbles—the whole bit." The other family men on the board, obviously, didn't own and operate a gay bath where friends and strangers had sex with each other twenty-four hours a day. But nobody knew in the early 1970s what went on in gay bathhouses like the Ritch Street Health Club, and Rick Stokes didn't stress that part of his résumé. He was a lawyer, and he knew that the public value in his being on the board lay not just in being visible to the gay community, so that troubled homosexuals would feel that they could seek help from the agency, too. It also lay in his ability to educate his fellow board members by his sheer presence among them. From him, they could learn that homosexuals were ordinary, responsible people with ordinary lives—just like themselves.

Stokes had never been a radical. His approach to life had been to fight for equal treatment and opportunity, work hard, achieve and consolidate. Gay political power in San Francisco had grown in the same way: a steady accretion built through the bars, the courts, the lawyers, the liberal alliances of friends, and the votes cast and money given to win a place at the table, and to put sympathetic Democratic politicians into office. San Francisco gay politics was not about the street, as it was in New York and Los Angeles. There had not even been a significant march or celebration in San Francisco to commemorate the social revolution begun at the Stonewall Inn until 1972, three years after the riots occurred, and years after other cities were marking the occasion. Street demonstrations were just not what San Francisco's gay political establishment was about. Before the year was out, the proof of the core strategy of befriending liberal politicians would be the passage by the San Francisco Board of Supervisors of an ordinance prohibiting discrimination against gays by city contractors. It was the durable Del Martin and her partner, Phyllis Lyon, who had suggested it to Dianne Feinstein, and Feinstein had sponsored it, although her first question to Del Martin had been, "Does this mean that contractors have to hire men who wear dresses?" Their accomplishments nationally and locally were all part of the San Francisco gay political establishment's coming of age, and what it meant to Jim Foster, Rick Stokes and David Goodstein, the new financier in the city's gay politics, was that after twenty years of legal and political struggles, the groundwork was finally laid for an out gay man to run for public office in San Francisco. Rick Stokes ran as he lived: in a quiet, intent, well-organized way. Jim Foster was his strategist, David Goodstein his finance chairman. Willie Brown and Dick Hongisto made radio tapes endorsing him, and Hongisto gave him money and his list of campaign contributors. It was primarily a campaign of literature, endorsements and radio spots, not campaign speeches by the candidates. Everyone who knew Stokes knew that he was a homosexual, but he didn't trumpet that to the general public. There was no mention of his management and part ownership of the Ritch Street Baths.

Rick Stokes ran a very respectable race. He got an impressive 45,000 votes, which surprised some of the city's political analysts. But he didn't excite people. And he didn't win. The first openly gay person elected to office in San Francisco would not be anything like Stokes. He would not be someone who had been laboring in the vineyard as Stokes and his friends had been all these years, or even someone who shared their philosophy of cultivating and depending on straight liberal politicians. He would be someone, from the point of view of Foster, Stokes and Goodstein, quite different in manner and approach. They would not approve of Harvey Milk.

11

IN OUR
MOTHERS' NAMES

April 1973, Los Angeles

The West Coast Lesbian Conference had been seven months in the making, but Jeanne Cordova was nervous as she drove up Wilshire Boulevard to the UCLA campus on a warm spring day in 1973. She enjoyed these women-only conferences—the forces that were unleashed by assembling so many lesbians for a weekend of politics and culture and just plain fun. But since this wasn't the kind of conference that required preregistration forms, she had no idea how many women were going to show up. It had been organized largely by the collective which ran the *Lesbian Tide*, the "independent lesbian/feminist magazine" which Cordova had effectively annexed from the Los Angeles chapter of the Daughters of Bilitis six months earlier. The magazine had then been more innocuously known as the *LA DOB Newsletter*, but Cordova and some of the younger daughters changed the name to *Lesbian Tide*, and packed the magazine with stories about lesbian separatism and the radical gay movement. By December 1972, it was clear that the older women of DOB would be happy if the *Lesbian Tide* just closed shop and left, which it did.

The members of the *Lesbian Tide* Collective embarked on setting up this conference, and Cordova had been put in charge of publicity. She had spent much of the past five months mimeographing press releases and sending them to every gay, lesbian and women's organization she could think of, from newspapers to activist groups to lesbian coffeehouses.

As she made her way toward the campus, Cordova noticed the Volkswagen vans and paneled trucks, filled with women, rolling along the wide boulevard that cut across Los Angeles's prosperous West Side. Could these women be heading to the conference? Along Wilshire Boulevard, she pulled over to the curb and flipped open the door to let in a woman hitchhiker carrying a backpack. The woman was looking for the conference; indeed, she told Cordova, she had thumbed her way from Maine for this weekend. Cordova realized that this was shaping up into something bigger than just a West Coast regional conference of lesbians.

As it turned out, the word among lesbians across the country was that this would be, as Robin Morgan, a conference keynote speaker put it, "The Big One." By Friday night's opening ceremonies, nearly 1,500 women had made their way onto the UCLA campus, including nearly every major lesbian leader around: Rita Mae Brown, Del Martin, Phyllis Lyon, Jean O'Leary, Jo Daly and Kate Millett. The conference opened with a showcase of the folk and political music that had developed a huge underground following among lesbians. There were more than 1,300 women inside Haines Hall by the time of the show, and the room was packed and hot. The program included a performance by a folksinger named Beth Elliott, a tiny woman with a guitar slung around one shoulder, beads around her neck, wearing granny glasses and an earth-mother gown. Indeed, she might have been the only woman in the room wearing a skirt or a gown—except for the fact that Beth Elliott wasn't a woman. Beth Elliott was a preoperative transsexual, a man in the process of trying to become a woman and who, to complicate things, claimed to be a lesbian. The radical lesbians from San Francisco recognized her, or him, the moment she, or he, stepped onstage. This was the same transsexual whose demand to be admitted into the San Francisco chapter of the Daughters of Bilitis had torn the group apart. The DOB had devoted eighteen months to arguing about whether there was a place in the Daughters of Bilitis for a transsexual, before finally and bitterly voting no. "DOB has always been set up as a women's organization," Del Martin said after the 35–28 vote. The editorial staff of the DOB newspaper, *Sisters,* supported the transsexual's admission and walked out on the spot. "We are disgusted that any lesbian has the audacity to judge the sexuality of another sister. And so we resign. En masse in something akin to cold fury." In Los Angeles, Jeanne Cordova's *Tide* Collective wrote an editorial in support of Elliott and telegrammed its objections to San Francisco: "Those who vote 'no' tonight vote with our oppressors," the telegram said. "Those who vote 'yes' recognize that none of us is free unless all of us are free. Please advise our transsexual sisters that if they are not welcome in the liberal city of San Francisco, they are most welcome to the city of Los Angeles."

Jeanne Cordova was backstage, but she could hear shouts, hisses and boos as Beth Elliott began to perform. She peeked around a curtain to see a woman with a bright-red crew cut and work boots, a member of the Gutter Dykes, a radical lesbian group from San Francisco, hollering at Beth Elliott to get off and get out. Men had been explicitly barred from this conference, and for many of the women in the hall, there were few things more offensive in the gay male culture than men who mimicked the behavior of women. Cordova walked onto the stage, grabbed the microphone and asked: "What is the problem here?" The uproar was so furious she could barely be heard. As Beth Elliott sat quietly at the edge of the stage, Cordova defended the organizers' decision. Elliott is, Cordova said again and again, "a feminist and a sister." She asked for a show of hands on whether the performance should go on. The room was so divided that it took two separate counts of 1,300 hands, over the course of more than an hour, before it was apparent that a bare majority of the women favored allowing the show to continue. Some women left the hall, and others left the conference.

Robin Morgan, the feminist writer and editor, went to her room that night and rewrote her keynote address. This was, she thought, "*the* issue of the conference—one around which all hostilities and divisions magnetized." She was enraged that more than a thousand "strong, angry women could be divided by one smug male." And in her keynote address, standing atop steps overlooking the UCLA quad, she shared her anger with a huge crowd of lesbians and students.

"The organizers of the conference plead ignorance: that they didn't realize the issue would be divisive of women when they *invited* him!" Morgan said, her eyes drifting from her written text to the sea of women's faces before her. "Yet they *knew* his San Francisco history. . . . The same fine sisters who have for months worked day and night to create and organize this event have, in one stroke, inviting this man, *directly* insulted their San Francisco sisters he previously tried to destroy, and indirectly insulted every woman here."

As the crowd listened, stunned by the fierceness of her words—"Man-hating," she said at one point, "is an honorable and viable political act"—Morgan offered the strongest attack the feminist-lesbian community could muster on transvestites and transsexuals. They were, she said, men who "parody female oppression," and their behavior was not funny. "Maybe it seems that we, in our liberated combat boots and jeans, aren't being mocked," Morgan said. "No? Then is it merely our mothers and *their* mothers who had no other choice, who wore hobbling dresses and torture stiletto heels to survive, to keep jobs, or to keep husbands because *they* themselves could *get* no jobs?

"One walk down the street by a male transvestite, five minutes of his being hassled—which *he* may enjoy—and then he dares, he *dares* to think he understands our pain?" Morgan said. "In our mothers' names and in our own, we must not call him sister. We know what's at work when whites wear blackface. The same thing is at work when men wear drag.

"If transvestites or transsexual males are oppressed, then let them band together and organize against that oppression, instead of leeching off women who have spent entire lives *as women* in women's bodies."

Jeanne Cordova was dumbfounded. Why should the lesbian movement devote so much time and energy to fighting over transsexuals, considering how few of them there were? The conference never recovered, and by Sunday afternoon, it was in full mutiny. Jeanne Cordova and her colleagues from the *Lesbian Tide* retreated to a small classroom, sitting atop a few scattered desks, wondering if they should abandon the ship right then or wait until the adjournment that evening. Someone asked how conference organizers could abandon their own conference. "Well, it's easy," Cordova responded. "I think we just go to our cars and get in them and go home." The room was quiet. Cordova was heartbroken as she headed for her car.

June 1973, New York

It was late on the night before the Gay Pride Parade of 1973 in New York City, and Jean O'Leary, Ginny Vida, Nath Rockhill and the other women from a new organization called Lesbian Feminist Liberation—women who had split off from what remained of the Gay Activists Alliance in New York two months earlier—were still awake, huddled around a small manual typewriter. They were trying to finish a statement denouncing transsexuals, who were becoming such a visible part of New York's annual Stonewall celebrations, though the women were not at all sure they would be allowed to deliver their speech at the next day's rally at Washington Square Park. Jean O'Leary, an ex-nun with a short Dutch-boy haircut, had led the Lesbian Feminist Liberation group out of the Gay Activists Alliance. She had done that because, while the GAA by now had a few women in its ranks, including a vice president, Nathalie Rockhill, it remained an overwhelmingly male organization. O'Leary was reminded of that every time she walked through the Firehouse's great iron doors; it was as if she just disappeared, consumed by the mass of men there. Even with Robert's Rules of Order regulating the meetings, the women felt that they weren't being heard. And although the Gay Activists Alliance considered the municipal gay rights employment bill one of its chief goals, there was too much time devoted to stopping the police from arresting men for having sex in the open-backed trucks near the Hudson River. When the lesbians raised this concern, Bruce Voeller, the strong-willed GAA president, cut them off: How's it any different from an old-fashioned lovers' lane for teenagers? he asked. "I don't hear you raising any ruckus about lovers' lanes for heterosexuals. Hey—sauce for the goose, sauce for the gander."

The talk of separatism for lesbians had largely evaporated by now—the collapse of The Furies in Washington, D.C., had become a cautionary tale for many lesbian activists across the country—but the concerns which had prompted some women to go their own way in the early 1970s were no less intense. Everything about the gay rights movement seemed designed to render lesbians invisible, starting with the organizations' names—*Gay* Activists Alliance in New York, *Gay* Liberation in Chicago, the *Gay* Community Services Center in Los Angeles, the Minnesota Committee for *Gay* Rights. A lesbian poet in Boston named Torri described the problem in a poem called "Stalking," which was only ostensibly about bars:

> *Most women are shorter*
> *than most men*
> *It's easy to over*
> > *look us.*

The word "gay" had evolved to apply only to men, while the word for women, "lesbian," seemed clinical and clunky. It was far too often men who appeared on television and in the newspapers to discuss the homosexual rights movement. Indeed, men, and some women, were debating if there were as many lesbians as there were gay men. And whether there were or not, there clearly were fewer lesbians who were open about their sexuality. It was economically risky for a single woman, already likely to be living on the economic edge in the early 1970s, to proclaim herself a lesbian. At the same time, the thriving women's movement, less hostile to lesbians than it had been during the height of Betty Friedan's reign, became an attractive outlet for politically active, if closeted, lesbians. "You couldn't hide being a woman," Kay Tobin would say, "though you could hide being a lesbian." And that is what many lesbians did, focusing their political energies on feminism. All of this was to the great frustration of lesbians who would go to homosexual rights meetings and find a room filled with men. "Often, I have heard sisters say, 'There's no place for me there,'" Brenda Weathers wrote in a Los Angeles Gay Liberation Front newsletter, responding to complaints that Los Angeles's most influential homosexual rights group was male-dominated. "Well, that is because we haven't been there and made our presence felt and desires and talents known. GET OUT OF THE BACK SEAT, SISTERS, AS WELL AS OUT OF THE CLOSETS! Get to the general meetings and become as active in fighting heterosexual chauvinism as you are in fighting male chauvinism."

Lesbians were also less noticed and taken less seriously in the gay rights movement because women in general were less noticed and taken less seriously in society in the early 1970s. Men had more money, mobility and power. The male sex drive, some lesbian activists noted wryly, had the unexpected effect of giving a higher profile to male homosexuals, if only because their mating rituals were often so public. When it came time for the media or government (institutions both dominated by men) to seek out representatives of the homosexual rights movement, they gravitated toward the men. All of this meant that Jean O'Leary and the rest of the women found it difficult to raise much interest among the gay male activists at the time over such concerns as the struggle divorced lesbian mothers encountered trying to keep custody of their children. Some of the men dismissed the visibility complaint as trivial, but it was that grievance, more than any other, that drove O'Leary and the Lesbian Feminist Liberation out of the Gay Activists Alliance. Lesbians should be in front of microphones, they should be co-chairs at meetings, and they should have equal time in the media. "We must dedicate our energies primarily to discovering ourselves and our special causes and acting as our own spokeswomen, to promoting ourselves everywhere, at all times, as lesbian women," declared the LFL's constitution, a document that, structurally, was nearly identical to the GAA constitution. "To this end, it is crucial that we function as an organization distinct from both the gay and feminist movements."

Jean O'Leary's strength was the day-to-day grit of organizing, not political theory. She read through the dense writings on feminism and lesbianism pouring out in the radical journals and books of the time, marking passages with a yellow pen, even as she realized she couldn't quite grasp some of the theoretical arguments rolling before her eyes. And she now had an immediate concern as the 1973 Stonewall rally approached: What should be the focus of her new organization? Feminist rights? Lesbian rights? Gay rights? But there was one issue about which O'Leary knew she felt strongly: men who dressed up as women. O'Leary had attended Jeanne Cordova's West Coast Lesbian Conference, and returned to New York angrily replaying in her mind the near-riot that Beth Elliott had caused. The anniversary of Stonewall was being seized by drag queens as their holiday, a chance to celebrate their role in the original uprising at the bar. They were demanding a prominent place in the line of march, and they wanted to be the centers of attention at the rally. And they enjoyed significant support among the early male gay activists in New York. "Hey, lesbians feel no reservations or do any double takes about dressing in male clothing—some of it fairly heavy-duty, biker's male clothing," Bruce Voeller, who was known for his support of most lesbian demands, told O'Leary. "And our movements should be about people being able to be whoever they are and whatever they are." Transvestites, Voeller said, should be allowed to march in the annual parade, even if they always seem to attract the focus of the media coverage. Arthur Evans had devoted his *Advocate* column to making a case for transvestites. "Prejudice against transvestites divides us against ourselves in a way that plays into the hands of those who want to oppress ALL gays, whether transvestites or not," Evans wrote. The positions of Evans and Voeller were particularly noteworthy because both men watched New York City Council members derail the gay rights bill by warning it would allow men to wear dresses to work (the fact that some men wore dresses to the hearing, and then attempted to use the women's rest room, provided council opponents with more ammunition than they might have ever hoped). Even women who were members of the Lesbian Feminist Liberation, like Joan Nestle, now establishing a lesbian archives that would explicitly bar men, would cheerfully come to the assistance of a drag queen who had caught a heel in the webbed-iron spiral staircase of the GAA Firehouse.

But Jean O'Leary knew how she felt when she saw a man wearing women's clothing, and she knew how she had felt at the West Coast Lesbian Conference. It was a position that could unite the women of the new Lesbian Feminist Liberation, and she was intent on making her case at Washington Square Park. The women of LFL knew there would be dozens of drag queens on hand the next day. They also knew that there would be thousands of people at the rally, and as they gathered around the typewriter, they were trying to draft a statement that explained why they found cross-dressing so offensive. Robin Morgan had made it sound so easy with her speech at UCLA, but she really had been speaking only to lesbians—there were few men or mainstream media in her audience. They decided that they would narrow their objections to men who dressed as women for profit. That is what O'Leary would denounce the next day—if the organizers would let her speak.

O'Leary had spent weeks negotiating for a spot on the roster. The committee running the fourth annual Stonewall celebration included gay bar owners who were resisting political speeches; they were hoping for a boozy celebration rather than a sober rally. This was, not coincidentally, the first year that the New York march would go south into Greenwich Village, rather than north into Central Park, which meant that thousands of marchers would be deposited at the end of the day in the part of New York City with the greatest concentration of gay and lesbian bars—testimony to the commercial interests who were now helping to organize what had been intended to be a political event. "We've gone back to supporting our local syndicate bars and we've gone back to the ghetto again," Craig Rodwell, the march's originator, complained. The committee approved just two political speeches, both by out-of-towners: Morris Kight from Los Angeles and Barbara Gittings from Philadelphia. There was no place on the rostrum for Jim Owles, the former

GAA president running as the first openly gay candidate for the city council, or Bruce Voeller, the third and current president of the GAA. And there was no place for Jean O'Leary, from Lesbian Feminist Liberation, to talk about drag queens.

Barbara Gittings was exuberant as she greeted the marchers arriving in Washington Square Park on a sun-sparkled June day. She wore sunglasses, and marched back and forth across the stage, crowing to a crowd that stretched out under the trees before her. "Gay is good!" she said, leading the audience in a chant of the motto Frank Kameny had conceived. "Gay is proud. Gay is natural. Gay is normal. Everyone turn to the person next to you and say, 'You are beautiful.'" Everyone did. "So you see what a wonderful change today's show of strength signals," Gittings said, all smiles and cheer. "We meet in unity to enjoy our diversity!"

Gittings could not have been more wrong. The tussles had begun before Gittings even took the stage. Sylvia Rivera, a tall and volatile drag queen who had been at Stonewall, scuffled with parade marshals along the route as he tried to force his way to the head of the line, carrying a banner which read, "Street Transvestites Action Revolutionaries." Once at Washington Square Park, Rivera bounded onto the stage and grabbed at the microphone, but was pushed to the side. The parade organizers debated for a minute whether to let Sylvia Rivera speak as the audience roared in confusion. Realizing they had the "makings of a riot behind the platform," as parade marshal John Paul Hudson said, they gave Rivera the microphone.

"Hi, baby!" Rivera announced by way of introduction, wearing a tight pants suit, an uncombed wig—the hair was matted and streaked with blond, which heightened his bizarre presentation—and, Morris Kight noticed with a double take from the side of the stage, no shoes. Rivera's gait seemed unsteady, his words were slurred, and his voice, sometimes effeminate and soft, was a screech today, so loud and distorted through the hand-held microphone that some of what he said was lost to the crowd. "I've been trying to get up here all day for your gay brothers and your gay sisters in jail. They write me every mother-fucking day and ask for your help. And you all don't do a goddamn thing for them. Have you ever been beaten up and raped? In jail?"

Rivera confided how he had been raped and beaten "many times by men" in jail. "We've put up with enough shit. What do you people do for your brothers and sisters in jail? Nothing." The crowd had been there for fun, not politics; and there were shouts for Rivera to sit down. Vito Russo, the master of ceremonies, stood at Rivera's side, looking grim, arms folded, not daring to cut off the presentation. When Rivera was finished, Russo brought on a notorious pair of female impersonators, Billie and Tiffany, dressed in flowered dresses and broad-brimmed hats. Appearing more and more upset, Russo announced that given the unscheduled appearance of Rivera, Jean O'Leary would be allowed to give her statement on transvestites.

O'Leary took in the unruly audience as she walked to the front of the open stage. Some men were hissing and booing, drag queens were cursing at her, and she could see men and women jostling each other in the park. Russo, a slight and soft-spoken man, pleaded for calm, his voice quavering: "Listen to her!" he said. "You've listened to everyone else. That's the least we can do for her." The crowd quieted. O'Leary recounted how the Lesbian Feminist Liberation had negotiated for ten days for a chance to speak. "Because one person, a man, Sylvia, gets up here and causes a ruckus," O'Leary noted, the lesbians had finally won their spot. "I think that says something," she said. She proceeded to read the statement, attacking men who "impersonate women for reasons of entertainment and profit," saying they "insult women." There were more hisses and shouts from the audience.

Any hope that giving a moment to Jean O'Leary and Sylvia Rivera would end this squall disappeared the moment Lee Brewster took the stage. He, too, was in full drag, with thick eye makeup, a lush blond wig tumbling over his shoulders and a queen's crown resting on the wig. "I cannot sit and let my people be insulted," Brewster said. "They've accused me of reminding you too many times that today you're celebrating what was the result of what the drag queens did at the Stonewall. You go to bars because of what drag queens did for you, and *these bitches*"—he gestured to the lesbians—"tell us to quit being ourselves." Vito Russo walked over to Brewster, slipped his arm around Brewster's waist and whispered into his ear, but Brewster pushed him off.

"Gay liberation," Brewster declared, "screw you! I'm going into my closet!" With that, the queen cast his crown into the audience, which by this point was in near-brawl. Vito Russo was wiping his eyes: "Don't!" he said. "Please don't fight with each other."

Jean O'Leary and her friends from LFL gave up on the rally and walked south into Greenwich Village for a drink at Bonnie and Clyde's, a bar for lesbians. O'Leary wasn't at the rally when Bette Midler came walking under the arch at the north end of Washington Square Park and climbed onto the stage. "I just came to say congratulations on your fourth anniversary," she said, casting an eye across an audience that included many men she had normally encountered clad only in slim white towels. "I heard a little bit on the radio and it sounded like you were beating each other up out here, so I came to sing a song." With that, Midler giggled the little girl laugh the men at the Continental Baths liked so much when they saw "The Divine Miss M" perform, and sang the first line of the song "Friends": "You've got to have friends."

Midler's cheer was way too late. Some of the early leaders of gay liberation, people like Arnie Kantrowitz and Morris Kight, were despondent. The

Washington Square Park rally was supposed to be a celebration of the great advances of the homosexual rights movement since Stonewall. Instead, it had laid bare a movement that seemed both impossibly diverse and hopelessly divided.

12

NEW ORLEANS:
FIRE UPSTAIRS

June 1973

When it came his turn to speak in New York on the fourth anniversary of Stonewall, Morris Kight stood on a platform in Washington Square Park in Greenwich Village and talked about freedom, death and fire. "The only promise history has made to us is genocide," he declared. Afterward he was never sure why he chose to speak as he did, at the end of a day on which he and Morty Manford had marched from Central Park down to the Village with 17,000 other people in celebration of Gay Pride. But Kight had a sense of drama and the habit of exaggerated metaphor, and as the day ebbed and the lights of the Village began to glow in the dusk around Washington Square, he talked about the long period of darkness and fire which lay behind them, about how they had gotten the name "faggots" from the pieces of wood used by the church to burn them at the stake in the Middle Ages. He talked about the two hundred gays he said were burned as witches at Salem, Massachusetts, about the pink triangles the Nazis used to mark homosexuals in the concentration camps during the Third Reich, about the one million homosexuals who had been incinerated, he said, at Buchenwald.* "Never again," he de-

* The actual number of people classified as homosexuals who died in the Nazi concentration camps may never be known, but books of research published since 1973 mark Kight's number

clared that evening, "never again can they take our children, our lives, our houses, or deny us a job." It was a moving moment, soulful but exaggerated. The research of later years would prove Kight's estimate of the number of gay Nazi victims to be wildly inflated. And his promise of "never again" would go up in flames that very night.

On the opposite side of the nation that evening, on the beach at Santa Monica, eight hundred men and women gathered around a bonfire, a giant wiener roast organized by the Reverend Troy Perry and the Metropolitan Community Church in celebration of the day. There had been a march in the City of Angels, too, and spirits were high as the crowd looked up toward the lowering sky, their attention drawn by the thunder of a police helicopter which swept in beneath the stars and hung there, observing them. They waved gaily, defiantly, as a searchlight played over their heads and shoulders, and after what seemed a long moment, as they stared up and the police stared down, the helicopter flew on.

There had been a march in downtown Atlanta, too. Much smaller, perhaps 150 people, it had been led by, among others, the young Reverend John Gill, a graduate of the Princeton Theological Seminary who had come to Atlanta in November 1971 to form a new Metropolitan Community Church. Gill had been working in a rubber hose and coupling factory in New York when he met Troy Perry in the summer of 1971, and at dinner in Greenwich Village, accepted the mission to start a church in Atlanta, a city full of churches. He had telephoned twenty-five or thirty of those churches when he got to town—Baptist, Protestant and Roman Catholic. Only the Unitarians, the last group he called, seemed unflustered by his request. For $50, a new Unitarian church on the north side of town had provided him space to hold his first service in January 1972, and by the summer of the next year the congregation had grown enough in size to afford the rent of a vacant movie theater just off the town square in Decatur, a small city on the east side of Atlanta. Each Sunday night they rented a movie and watched it on their own big

---

of one million dead at Buchenwald as an exaggeration. *The Buchenwald Report*, trans. and ed. David A. Hackett (Boulder, Colo.: Westview, 1995), pp. 12–115, gives the total number of prisoners of all types admitted to Buchenwald from July 1937 through March 31, 1945, as 238,980. It conservatively estimates the number of deaths of all kinds at 55,000. In Leni Yahil, *The Holocaust: The Fate of European Jewry, 1932–1945* (New York: Oxford University Press, 1990), p. 536, the number of deaths of all kinds at Buchenwald is estimated as about 70,000, or 30 percent of the number admitted to the camp. Homosexuals were only one of a number of different populations marked for extinction by Nazi policy, and were probably one of the smallest in number. In *The Pink Triangle: The Nazi War Against Homosexuals*, Richard Plant, who examined the Buchenwald archives and death files, writes: "How many homosexuals were actually held in the camps remains uncertain, perhaps unknowable. One might estimate that from 1933 on, the various institutions detained at all times perhaps several hundred homosexuals. Later this increased to about one thousand. Altogether, somewhere between 5,000 and 15,000 homosexuals perished behind barbed wire."

screen, and that's what the members of the Metropolitan Community Church of Atlanta were doing on the evening of the last Sunday in June 1973 when, at about ten o'clock, an emergency call came from New Orleans for John Gill.

The news from New Orleans that night made everything else seem suddenly trivial. There had been no Gay Pride Parade that Sunday in the "City That Care Forgot." The only independent gay groups outside the city's bar culture were the Gay Students Union at Tulane University and another struggling young congregation of the Metropolitan Community Church, and neither of them was strong enough or brave enough to organize a march. There might be two dozen gay bars in the French Quarter, but homosexual life there was stealthy, and the number of people willing to join any kind of openly gay organization was small. The few members of Tulane's gay student group had dispersed for the summer, and there were only about thirty-five active members in the young congregation of the MCC.

Most of them were in the UpStairs bar in the French Quarter that last Sunday afternoon in June. There were three different bars operating in the same moldering three-story building at the corner of Chartres and Iberville Streets, and the UpStairs bar was the gay-friendly one. Up one flight of stairs from the street, it occupied three rooms on the second floor, and it was the place where the little congregation had sometimes gathered for services on Sunday mornings when the members had nowhere else to meet. On those mornings they prayed and sang in a small, theater-like room separate from the serving bar. It was the third of the bar's three rooms, a back room with a cabaret stage, more often used for drag shows than sermons. "We didn't care. If Jesus could turn water into wine, hell, we could worship in a bar," Troy Perry said. The bar became their lodge, their social hall. On Sunday afternoons, members of the congregation came back to drink and pass the time together in the barroom, or to dance together in the middle room where there was a dance floor. That's where many members of the congregation were that Sunday evening, in the UpStairs bar, lingering in the mellow afterglow of a two-hour special of free beer and all the food you could eat for $1 a head.

The free beer had been over for about an hour. The evening was slipping into night, and the lights of the French Quarter were coming on when someone entered the stairwell leading from the street to the bar's front door on the second floor, knelt and set fire to the wooden stairs. The flames gathered strength and spread, and after a moment the buzzer from downstairs rang inside the bar. The buzzer was used to signal the bartender that there was a taxicab waiting on the street below. It was just before 8 p.m. Inside the bar, a long, dim, rosy room layered in red-flocked wallpaper and carpeting and hung with old Mardi Gras decorations of paper, cloth and paint, the low, strident sound of the buzzer undercut a boozy din of talk and laughter, and the happy sound of a ragtime melody being played on a white baby grand piano in the corner.

The wallpaper, the carpet, the swagged drapes and all the propped and hanging decorations gave the bar a warm, cozy, sensual feeling. They also covered some of the windows overlooking Chartres and Iberville Streets.

Almost 125 people had jammed the UpStairs at the height of the afternoon. Two men, one who was caught stealing people's beer mugs for the deposits, and another who was drunk, hostile and trying to start a fight, had to be thrown out. There was also a hustler, angry that a customer who had agreed to pay him for sex had changed his mind, but otherwise it was a good-time crowd. When the free-beer special ended at 7 p.m., the numbers thinned, and it was a mixed group of forty to sixty people who remained. There were congregation members and other holdovers from the afternoon, and also new customers who had come up from the street. Almost all of them were men in their twenties, thirties and forties, with perhaps two women among the crowd.

There was Inez Warren, brought there by her two sons, Eddie and Jimmy Warren, of Pensacola. There was the bartender, Buddy Rasmussen, and his lover, Adam Fontenoit. There was Dr. Perry Waters, a New Orleans dentist with a large gay practice. There was the Reverend William R. Larson, the MCC interim pastor, a former Methodist lay minister who had found a home in this new church. There was the church deacon, George C. "Mitch" Mitchell, thirty-six, a divorced father of two, and his lover, Louis Broussard, twenty-six. On some weekends the men took Mitch's children, a boy and a girl close to ten years old, with them when they went to the bar, but this Sunday afternoon they had left the children at a Disney movie in a nearby theater, with instructions to wait in the lobby if they should be late. There was also Ronnie Rosenthal, a young member of the Metropolitan Community Church in Atlanta, who had come to New Orleans to see his new boyfriend that weekend. And there was David Gary, a pianist who was playing in the lounge of the huge Marriott Hotel directly across Chartres Street from the bar. David Gary wasn't a member of the church, but he liked coming across the street from the Marriott, away from the tourists, to a gay bar where he felt at home and could play what he wished. That evening he had played as the members of the MCC gathered around the piano to sing the song that had become their closing anthem each Sunday evening at the UpStairs bar. It described the way being together made them feel.

> *United we stand, divided we fall—*
> *And if our backs should ever be against the wall,*
> *We'll be together—*
> *Together—you and I.*

Arm in arm, they had rocked back and forth in lines of harmony around the piano. Rosy with alcohol and grinning in camaraderie, they belted out the words, singing again and again their song of solidarity and trust.

UNITED we stand, DIVIDED we fall—
And if our backs should ever BE against the wall,
We'll be toGE-THER—
TOGE-THER—you and I.

It had been a full day, one of the longest of the calendar year, filled with good feeling, and that was the atmosphere in the bar when the taxicab buzzer sounded from below. The New Orleans Fire Department later established the time as 7:56 p.m. Buddy Rasmussen, the bartender, raised his head at the sound and looked around. No one had phoned for a cab. He saw Jimmy Warren near the door and called over to him. "Hey, Jimmy," he said, "open the door and tell them nobody needs a cab." Warren grinned and nodded, and stepped toward the heavy steel door. He opened it—and the flames roared in.

About an hour later, in his office in the movie theater turned church in Decatur, Georgia, the Reverend John Gill listened in horror as a spent and anguished Ronnie Rosenthal described to him over the telephone the scene in New Orleans. Rosenthal had been in the bar's second room with the man he was dating, a member of the New Orleans congregation, when the flames seemed to erupt through the bar. He and his friend had barely escaped, led by the bartender through an unmarked door into another room that was like a small auditorium, with a stage at the rear and behind it, an exit that led onto an adjoining roof. He had been lucky to get out. Others had tried to jump from the windows, and some of them had died when they hit the sidewalk. Six bodies lay on the Chartres Street side of the building. Four more clustered on the Iberville side. For blocks around the intersection of Chartres and Iberville, the narrow streets of the French Quarter were a grimy, puddled, flashing tangle of fire engines, hoses, police cars and ambulances, and hundreds of tourists gazing in horrified fascination at the smoking building. Dark except for the pulsing lights of the firemen scraping and thumping inside, it gently hissed and crackled in the night air. Lifeless arms hung through the ornate iron bars of several upstairs windows. A dead man was stuck halfway through another one. He had gotten wedged in as he was trying to escape, or had been struck by something falling from above. Now he sat upright in the window like a sentry for the dead inside, lifeless, smoking, a blackened stump with a featureless face.

John Gill, the southeast coordinator for the Metropolitan Community Church, felt sick as he listened to Rosenthal. He didn't know whether Bill Larson, the pastor in New Orleans, was dead or alive. He sat for a moment after hanging up, then picked up the phone again and started trying to reach Troy Perry in Los Angeles.

• • •

In Los Angeles, Troy Perry didn't get home until well after midnight that Sunday, so it was close to dawn in Atlanta when John Gill, still calling, finally reached him as he walked in the door. In New York, Morris Kight stayed out celebrating Gay Pride Day until first light Monday morning. It was almost 6 a.m. when he got back to Morty Manford's apartment in the Village, where he was staying. Kight found Manford awake and apprehensive. People at the Gay Community Center in Los Angeles had been trying to reach him about a fire in New Orleans, Manford said.

For all of them—Gill, Perry, Kight and Manford—the word "fire" stirred a familiar dread. Two destructive fires had been set in the Metropolitan Community Church in San Francisco eleven months before, and a devastating fire had devoured the Mother Church in Los Angeles at the beginning of the year. Intended as houses of welcome, as spiritual sanctuaries and safe harbors for homosexual Christians who felt wanted nowhere else, the meeting places of the Universal Fellowship of Metropolitan Community Churches were beginning to seem like dangerous places to be. There was a dual trend developing. The Metropolitan Community Churches were emerging as the largest single membership institution in the national gay community. There were thirty-six MCC congregations scattered across the country at the time of the fire in New Orleans, and their growth demonstrated the importance of a loving church in the lives of many homosexuals. But as those houses of worship multiplied, the Roman Catholic and fundamentalist arms of the traditional Christian church were growing more and more disturbed by signs that the Word of God was being ignored, rejected or appropriated by radical forces in the culture. Their unease had been growing since the mid-1960s, and the year 1973 had begun in ways which alarmed and threatened both the vast Christian establishment in the United States and the tiny new denomination of gay- and lesbian-friendly churches.

On January 22 the U.S. Supreme Court delivered its historic opinion in the case of *Roe* v. *Wade*. Five days later, in the dark, early-morning hours of January 27, the Metropolitan Community Church of Los Angeles was destroyed by fire.

Like everything else in the gay movement, the Metropolitan Community Church arose out of personal experience, and it, too, had roots in the gay bars. It was in a gay bar called The Patch, in Wilmington, south of Los Angeles, in the summer of 1968 that Troy Perry, a previously married man and former Church of God minister, had experienced a kind of catharsis. The Patch was one of the first gay dance bars in the area, and Perry was there that night with a young married man, Tony Valdez. Before the night was out, the police had arrested Valdez and Bill Hastings because Hastings, Perry said afterward, had patted Valdez on the ass. When they had been taken to jail, Lee Glaze, the owner of The Patch, got up on the bar and yelled for the crowd's attention.

"All right, queens," he said, "I want to know—is there a florist here? C'mon, I know there's got to be more than one florist in this damned bar." Two hands went up. "I want to buy all your flowers," Glaze said. They formed a caravan of cars, drove to the station with Dick Michaels, the owner of *The Advocate,* following behind, and entered the jail decked with flowers to declare that they had come to post bail for the two arrested men. Troy Perry found his picture on the front page of the next issue of *The Advocate.* It was an exhilarating night, but also, when he brought his friend Tony Valdez home that morning, a painful one. Valdez was in agony. "We're just a bunch of dirty queers, and nobody cares about dirty queers," he said bitterly.

"God cares," Perry said, looking at him. "No, Troy," Valdez said angrily, "God doesn't care." He left to take the bus home to his wife, and Perry lay down in exhaustion to think. When Tony Valdez, at fifteen, had told his priest he thought he was homosexual, the priest would not even let him come back to Sunday school. He could not be homosexual and be a Christian, he told the boy. When Pastor Troy Perry, tired of fighting the battle within, had told his Church of God overseer that he was homosexual, the bishop had kicked him out of the church and parsonage. "I wish there were a church somewhere for all of us who are outcast," he said to God that morning after Tony Valdez left. And then the thought came to him: Why are you waiting for somebody else?

On the first Sunday in October, in the living room of the little pink house in Los Angeles that he rented with a friend, Willie Smith, Troy Perry conducted the first service of what became the Universal Fellowship of Metropolitan Community Churches. Perry had been raised a southern charismatic, among snake handlers, faith healers, shouting, perspiring preachers and people who believed that it was possible to hear the voice and know the mind of God. But because homosexuals came from families of all different faiths— and all different styles—the new church needed to be a place where people of different backgrounds could feel comfortable.

So Troy Perry, who preached a sort of passionate, street-smart, southern gay Bible-thumping sermon, wore a Roman collar and black Congregational robes. Some of the ritual and liturgy that developed as the Metropolitan Community Church grew seemed almost Episcopalian, and the rich, choral musical program Southern Baptist. But a lot of the hymns were familiar to Methodists, too, and when the congregation was called to come forward to the rail for Communion, which was basically an Anglican custom, there was an uncharacteristically charismatic, Church of God–like laying on of hands. That first congregation in Los Angeles grew so rapidly—and Troy Perry, in his clerical collar, became such a public figure as an activist for gay civil rights—that when its members bought their own place of worship, an old opera house at Twenty-second and Union Streets in which they held the first service of their new Mother Church on March 7, 1971, Governor Ronald Reagan sent a telegram of congratulations, and an astonishing crowd of 1,200 people came to witness the miracle. The Metropolitan Community Church of Los Angeles had become the first openly gay organization in the United States to purchase property of its own. But it was a church which grew nationally in the face of deep-rooted cultural and religious disapproval. And the more it grew, the more it seemed to become a target.

Troy Perry was in Denver the last week of January 1973, counseling with a rebel pastor, when a telephone call came from Los Angeles saying he had to come back. There had been a fire. He arrived to find his church collapsed, its sanctuary in ashes, the only gay-owned public institution in the nation destroyed. No one was injured. The building was empty. The authorities said the fire was of "suspicious origin." Two months later there was another telephone call. There had been a fire in the MCC meeting place in Nashville, Tennessee, destroying some holy objects on the altar. Again, the authorities suspected arson.

And then, five months later, came the call about the fire in the UpStairs bar in New Orleans—three separate fires in three separate Metropolitan Community Churches in the first six months of 1973, all of them thought to be arson.* The future held many others. There would be a total of eighteen fires in the church's first twenty-five years, and thirty-three deaths, including one MCC minister brutally murdered, stabbed thirteen times and his throat cut. But only one church fire took an historic toll of human life, and that was in

---

* From the night of the fire, when almost ninety firemen and two dozen pieces of equipment converged on the burning building, the New Orleans Police Department, the State Fire Marshall's Office and the fire department's Fire Prevention Bureau, which investigates suspicious fires, treated the blaze as a probable case of arson and repeatedly spoke of it in that vein. Major Henry Morris, the police department's chief of detectives, told reporters the next day that there were hints of firebombing, but no evidence to prove it. (Chris Segura, "Devastating French Quarter Fire Probed by 3 Agencies," *Times-Picayune*, June 26, 1973, sect. 1, p. 1.) And the head of the city's Fire Prevention Bureau, David Fontaine Jr., said four days later that he believed it was arson (Ken Weiss, "Fire Safety Check to Start in Quarter: Fontaine Believes Arson Caused Fire," *Times-Picayune*, June 30, 1973, sect. 1, p. 1). Although virtually all the contents of the UpStairs bar were flammable—some of them so much so that they would have ignited at the touch of a match—the fire clearly started on the stairs between the street door and the solid fire door at the second-floor entrance to the bar. The canvas awning over the street door was untouched. (Photograph, *Times-Picayune*, June 26, 1973, sect. 1, p. 3.) Investigators assumed that someone who had entered from the street—or exited the bar—set the fire on the stairs, pressed the buzzer and walked away. No other cause was ever identified. But no evidence remained in the charred ruins. And although an inmate of the county jail in Sacramento, California, confessed four months later to setting the fire, waived extradition and was brought to New Orleans and charged with murder by the New Orleans Police Department, the District Attorney's Office released him after twelve days of questioning, saying he hadn't done it. The man, Raymond C. Wallender, thirty-two, who identified himself as homosexual, told authorities that he had doused the stairs with gasoline purchased from a nearby station and thrown a cigarette lighter in to ignite it. No lighter or trace of gasoline was found. *The Advocate*, no. 125 (Nov. 21, 1973), and no. 126 (Dec. 5, 1973). No one else was ever charged.

New Orleans. It was the first great tragedy of the modern gay rights movement. It may also have been the last major national news event in the gay community to go almost completely unreported by the national media. In Atlanta, Los Angeles, New York and elsewhere, it was almost as if it hadn't happened.

When the fire door at the top of the stairs opened, it created a draft which sucked the flames inside, where they fed on the carpet, climbed the drapes, consumed the wallpaper, the glue and the plywood panels behind, and mushroomed out and up, devouring the decorations as they boiled through the lowered ceiling of acoustical tiles to reach the reservoir of air trapped above the tiles. Buddy Rasmussen, the bartender, yelled for people to follow him, and Ronnie Rosenthal, his boyfriend and nearly twenty other men who heard and heeded him got out through an obscure, unmarked fire exit.

But the lighting in the bar failed almost instantly as the electrical wiring burned. The darkness, the yellow-white flames and the inebriation of some patrons bred pandemonium, and the lights of Chartres and Iberville Streets drew most of the crowd in the barroom to the windows. Some of the windows were blocked by plywood panels covered with wallpaper, and most of them were caged by grilles of heavy bars. In the few short minutes before the flames exploded through the rooms—propelled, perhaps, by the alcohol behind the bar—a few people wriggled through the grilles, and some tore the plywood panels from the windows and jumped out. Linn Quintonn was standing by the piano when the flames boiled into the room. He jumped to a corner window, opened it, swung out and slid down the drainpipe. But in the darkness and confusion, most people just piled up behind the barred windows, stumbling and falling atop each other as they were pushed by a tide of flames against the grilles. The New Orleans Fire Department was very fast. The Central Fire Station in the Vieux Carré was only three blocks away, and the firemen were coupling their hoses to the hydrants in the streets as the men upstairs struggled to escape. Several men had already crashed to the pavement. Quintonn and two or three others had scrambled down signs and pipes to safety. And Rasmussen had led fifteen or so to safety through the hidden exit. Now, as they all came around to the front of the building, they, the firemen, the people in their rooms in the Marriott Hotel and the tourists in the street could hear the screams of the others trapped in the building as their hands and arms waved and groped through the window bars. One man, sweat-streaked and sooty, in a grimy green shirt, emerged halfway through a window above Chartres Street and struggled frantically to get out. It was Bill Larson, the pastor. But something held him, and as Linn Quintonn watched, the fire behind him came through the window like a torch. His clothes, his face and hair flashed and disappeared in flames, and he stopped moving.

No one else got out. To the people watching in the street, it appeared that the others didn't die of smoke inhalation. They burned to death.

Afterward the New Orleans Fire Department said the fire was under control just sixteen minutes after it had begun. Shortly before 8:15, the flames were quenched. But it took the firemen another four or five hours to remove the bodies from the UpStairs bar. Most of them had fused together in a long, low pile of blackened forms pressed up against the windowed walls inside the bar. Many were burned through to the bone. Only three or four were identifiable. It wasn't like an airplane crash where you had a passenger list to work from, Dr. Monroe Samuels, chief of pathology at Charity Hospital said, remembering an Eastern Airlines jet that crashed into Lake Pontchartrain. The bar victims could be local or from out of town. They could be anybody from anywhere. The fifteen survivors overwhelmed the burn facilities at Charity Hospital, and when the dead had been lowered by forklift and carried to the city morgue, they occupied twenty-nine long, separate metal trays.

There was one thing that the New Orleans authorities and presumably the reporters at the scene knew about the victims, which was that they died in a gay bar. But the New Orleans newspapers, like papers in most cities, did not cover news about homosexuals except as police news, which usually meant raids and arrests. The number of deaths meant that the fire in the UpStairs bar was the worst tragedy in New Orleans in almost two hundred years. But the New Orleans papers had no practice or precedent to work from in reporting, writing or putting into perspective a story which was essentially that twenty-nine homosexuals burned to death because an arsonist apparently chose to torch a gay bar. Almost two-thirds of the front page of the Monday morning *Times-Picayune* was devoted to news of the fire, as was almost all of pages 2 and 3. There was prominent mention that police were investigating reports of a firebomb, that a man who had been ejected from the bar shortly before the fire was being questioned. But the words "gay" and "homosexual" didn't appear in the *Times-Picayune* that morning. Most people in town knew that the UpStairs bar in the French Quarter was a gay bar. It didn't need to be said. But the wire service reports out of New Orleans, as out of most cities, only copied what the local papers said in their stories. So the wires out of New Orleans didn't say that someone had apparently torched a gay bar and killed twenty-nine people. The *Times-Picayune* quoted fire and police officials, but there were no statements of elected public officials and no statements from anyone who spoke for the gay community.

That was one of the first things that John Gill and Troy Perry, Morris Kight and Morty Manford noticed as they flew into New Orleans from east and west on Monday. As a man at the airport said in reply when Morty Manford mentioned that it was "because of the tragedy" that he was in New Orleans, "What tragedy? I don't know of any tragedy. Only some faggots got burned."

And when they called back later that day and the next to their homes and offices in Los Angeles, New York and Atlanta, expecting that their friends and co-workers in those places would have read and heard all about the homosexuals killed in the apparent arson of a gay bar, the people on the other end of the phone lines said no, they hadn't seen that in the paper. Troy Perry's office in Los Angeles told him that the *Los Angeles Times*, which had the advantage of being in a time zone two hours earlier than New Orleans, had a prominent story about the fire on Monday, but nothing about the bar or the victims being gay. The *New York Times* that Monday morning, in a demonstration of how much the attitude toward gays had changed in its newsroom and in Manhattan, featured a large, friendly story and photograph in its metropolitan report about the Christopher Street Liberation Day Parade from Central Park West down to Washington Square Park that had taken place on Sunday—"thousands of homosexuals" marching "past smiling policemen, wide-eyed tourists and blasé New Yorkers who passed it off with a live-and-let-live shrug." The story didn't mention the short speech Morris Kight gave at the park, but it did describe Morty Manford marching with his parents, "Dr. and Mrs. Jules Manford," who carried a sign saying, "I'm proud of my gay son." The story said nothing of New Orleans.

The New Orleans afternoon paper, the *States-Item*, quoted Major Henry Morris, the New Orleans Police Department's chief of detectives, about the difficulties of identifying these victims. "We don't even know these papers [found on the bodies of the victims] belonged to the people we found them on. Some thieves hung out there," he said, "and you know this was a queer bar." As Troy Perry would shortly discover, the only members of the city's gay community who might have been willing to speak up and rebuke Major Morris had probably died in the fire. The main gay establishment was made up of gay bar owners, and they were saying nothing.

That afternoon and evening Perry and the others began their campaign to waken New Orleans to the idea that homosexuals were people not embarrassed to stand up and speak for themselves. "I'm terribly sorry that the detective has made such a prejudicial statement at a time when gay people all over the nation are mourning over their gay brothers and sisters. And at a time when everyone needs a little more understanding," Kight told a reporter for the *Times-Picayune* by telephone before leaving New York for New Orleans.

The Reverend William Richardson, the elderly rector of St. George's Episcopal Church on St. Charles Avenue, agreed to let them hold a prayer service Monday evening after other ministers had refused. The next morning, the New Orleans newspapers quoted Troy Perry, "pastor of the national homosexual church," discussing what had happened: "Someone said it was just a bunch of faggots," Perry said.

"But we knew them as people, and as brothers and sisters, and we will never forget them." The story went on to note rather quietly, "The bar was often frequented by homosexuals," and reported that Perry and Kight were calling for a national day of mourning that next Sunday, and that Troy Perry had asked God to forgive whoever set fire to the bar on Sunday night. "The individuals who did this act, we have to pray for them, because they have to live with this," he said. "This will be on their consciences for the rest of their lives."

On Tuesday, the Episcopal bishop of New Orleans rebuked the rector of St. George's for allowing the service and forbade him to do it again. One victim, Luther Boggs, was notified while he was still in the hospital that he had been fired from his job as a schoolteacher. (He would die two weeks later.) All the rest of that week Troy Perry, John Gill and Paul Breton, another MCC minister who had joined them, worked to find some church to use for the service of mourning that Sunday, and some elected or religious official in Louisiana who would express some word of public sympathy or regret for the deaths.

On Wednesday, Troy Perry sent a telegram to the Roman Catholic Cajun governor of Louisiana, Edwin Edwards. "The tragic fire in the Upstairs Lounge on June 24 shocked and now saddens the nation. Gay, as well as non-gay, churches and organizations around the country will be observing a national day of mourning. The heartfelt sympathy of America has focused here in Louisiana at this time of need. We respectfully call upon you to join in the spirit of compassion and love by declaring Sunday, July 1, 1973, a statewide day of mourning for the victims of the New Orleans catastrophe." The telegram was hand-delivered to Governor Edwards's office, which first said, on being telephoned, that the telegram had not been received, then that no answer was yet available, and then that Governor Edwards was away for an extended time. No statement or reply was ever made.

On Thursday, Jim Hambrick, who had jumped from the building in flames, died at Charity Hospital. When gangrene set in, his hands had been amputated, but it did not save him. His was the thirtieth death. Eventually, two more victims died, a total of thirty-two people, including Inez Warren. Mrs. Warren's sons, Eddie and Jimmy, also died. So did Buddy Rasmussen's lover, Adam Fontenoit. And the pianist, David Gary. George Mitchell, who had left his children at the Disney movie, and who had escaped through the back door with Rasmussen, plunged back into the bar when he realized that his lover, Louis Broussard, had not come out. Their bodies were found lying together in the bar. The children stayed at the theater, and the manager eventually called the police to come get them. The Reverend Bill Larson's mother, who had seen her son's name published as a homosexual in the newspapers, could not bear the thought of his being buried in her hometown, in front of her neighbors and friends. Nor did she want his ashes returned. Several other families refused to claim their sons, without knowing whether they were homosexual or not. Perry, Gill, Kight, Breton and Manford made arrangements for services. They also created a national appeal for funds for the victims, the first national fundraising campaign in the gay community. It brought in about $13,000.

The only political body in Louisiana that issued a public statement of condolence for the deaths in the bar was the Young Democrats of Louisiana State University. Nor, with two exceptions, would any church official in New Orleans allow the July 1 service of mourning to be conducted in his church. The first exception—as always, no matter what city or state the issue arose in—was a Unitarian church, which volunteered its sanctuary for the service. But the church was not in the French Quarter, where Troy Perry thought the service needed to be, because the victims had died there. Roman Catholics, Lutherans, Baptists and Episcopalians all refused. Finally, someone suggested the modest St. Mark's United Methodist Church, a rare white congregation with a black minister, and the minister immediately agreed.

On Sunday morning, as the organist was playing and Troy Perry was in the back of the church putting on his robe, a woman on the church board came to tell him that the Methodist bishop of Louisiana had arrived. "Would you like to meet him?" she asked. Spurned and rejected by every reigning church official in New Orleans, Perry walked uncertainly out to see what this meant and found a small, magisterial, self-confident man in his mid-fifties, Bishop Finis Crutchfield, sitting calmly in a pew.

"Bishop, I'm just very glad you're here," Troy Perry said, as Crutchfield reached to take his hand. The bishop smiled warmly, pulled Perry down close and gave him a purposeful look. "Well, Reverend," he said, "I just wanted you to know that not everybody in Louisiana is a redneck." Perry grinned in surprise and relief, and Bishop Crutchfield continued to look at him intently. "This is not a renegade pastor in this church. He had my blessing to do this," Crutchfield said. "Some of the men who died in that fire were friends of mine."

Bishop Finis Crutchfield, a married man, father and powerful figure in the national Methodist Church, went on to become the president of the Council of Bishops and the head of the largest Methodist territory in the United States. He lived a double life all his career, and he would die of AIDS in Houston fourteen years later, at the age of seventy, as the retired bishop of the Territory of East Texas. But Troy Perry walked back up the aisle of the church that morning of July 1, 1973, with a grateful feeling. He understood what Finis Crutchfield was telling him, and he felt as if the tide had turned.

The church was full that day. At the end Perry said, "Those human beings, our friends who died so horribly, have dignity now. It doesn't matter what un-knowledgeable people have stooped to say, our friends will have respect be-cause they are forever in our hearts. I can almost feel their presence. If they could speak, they would tell us to hold our heads up high." Then the congre-gation stood and together sang the lyrics that had been printed in the memor-ial program that they held in their hands.

> *United we stand, divided we fall—*
> *And if our backs should ever be against the wall,*
> *We'll be together—*
> *Together—you and I.*

Perry told them then that there were cameras in the street outside, and if they wished to avoid being filmed and identified on television, they could leave by the back door. There was a moment of quiet, and the crowd in the pews rustled and muttered. "No!" one person said. "No!" said another.

One voice, a woman's clear, bell-like voice, picked up the lyrics again. They all began to sing:

> *United we stand, divided we fall—*
> *And if our backs should ever be against the wall,*
> *We'll be together—*
> *Together—you and I.*

And then they turned and walked out the front door. "They all filed out," the *Times-Picayune* reported the next morning. "None was seen leaving through the rear."

13

ORDINARY PEOPLE

October 1973, New York

Bruce Voeller was the third president of the Gay Activists Alliance in New York, but even with his shaggy blond hair, scraggly beard and spirited talk about gay liberation, he was quite different from the men who preceded him in the post or the activists he was leading at the GAA Firehouse. He was older than most of them, a thirty-eight-year-old divorced man whose children threw snowballs on Wooster Street in SoHo while their father, the gay liberation leader, tended to business inside the Firehouse. Voeller had lived for ten years in suburban New Jersey, and worked as an associate professor of biology at Rockefeller University. He was the type of person who, after typing his name at the bottom of a letter or the top of a press release, would always be sure to tap out the three letters "Ph.D.," which said as much about Voeller's personality as it did about his education. He would often present himself to the press and at city hall as Dr. or Professor Bruce Voeller, which was technically correct but struck some friends as a little pretentious. He had been drawn to gay liberation after he saw a David Susskind television show with gay panelists notable for being unnotable—the kind of ordinary people, he thought, with whom anyone would feel comfortable, unlike the kind of flamboyant homosexuals who Voeller believed gave gays a bad name. Voeller enjoyed dancing late into the night at the Firehouse, but he also enjoyed putting on a tie and sipping cocktails in the uptown circles of New York society.

To the rank and file of the GAA, Bruce Voeller seemed more alien the more they got to know him. Everything about Voeller suggested "privilege," Jim Fouratt said, meaning it as an insult: Voeller's middle-class background, elite education, blue eyes and blond hair, personal wealth and the fact that he was an "ex-straight man with a family." And Voeller did not hide his growing irritation with GAA members who scorned middle-class homosexuals. He scolded his fellow activists one evening for making fun of Stephen Sondheim, the composer, who turned up at the Firehouse dressed in expensive slacks, a polo shirt and a sports jacket. ("Get the faggot in the slacks," Voeller heard one man say.) Sondheim's was a brave public gesture, a furious Voeller said from the front of the Firehouse: "If this movement isn't open to all gays, there is no movement." On another evening Voeller watched in horror as an *Advocate* reporter interrupted his conversation with Betty Friedan at a fundraiser for the New Democratic Coalition. The reporter, drunk and abusive, berated Friedan for the purge of lesbians from NOW and called her a "fucking bitch," Voeller wrote in a letter to the editor of *The Advocate* expressing his "dismay and anger" at the incident.

Bruce Voeller was smart, and he didn't try to hide his disdain for people he thought were not, or his impatience with some of the strange folk who drifted in and out of the GAA orbit. He could be abrupt, condescending and pedantic. He began complaining about "blue-jean elitism," the reverse snobbery he found directed against the men like him, professional people who, he believed, were being shut out of the gay movement. He became, in short time, exceedingly unpopular, and within six months into his term as president, found himself leading an organization whose members frequently attacked him as an elitist and a betrayer of the democratic vision of the Gay Activists Alliance founders. Voeller was battling with his membership on what seemed like every front: He couldn't even convince them to pay for someone to clean up after the Saturday night dances. At meeting after meeting, Voeller complained about having to stay behind to pick up the empty beer and soda cans and bottles on Wooster Street, while everyone else had gone on to the baths or the bars or home. "You can't have it both ways," said Voeller, sounding again like the stern professor admonishing his young students. Activists like John O'Brien, who had given up on the moribund Gay Liberation Front and become a proudly disruptive force at the GAA, led the attack on Voeller's every move, suspicious of his ties to upper-class New York and what he suspected was Voeller's design to move the GAA away from its community roots. Voeller began to refer to his enemies, people like O'Brien and Morty Manford, the student leader who came down from Columbia University, as "the trolls."

In truth, the suspicions among the rank and file about Bruce Voeller were well founded. The abrasive, middle-class professor from the suburbs of New Jersey, who would speak fondly of gardening and dining by the swimming pool with his wife and children, had grown weary of the GAA. The demonstrations, the zaps, the spontaneity and the unruliness, which had seemed so fresh and liberating in the first years after Stonewall, had become stale. Voeller was, it would turn out, a transitional figure in the evolution of gay activism in the early 1970s. He stepped out of his mainstream life and into the world of street activism, and would now step back into the mainstream and attempt to bring the gay rights movement with him.

To accomplish this, Voeller initially suggested a new structure for the GAA that would give a small governing board the authority to run the organization. When word of that had reached his critics, Voeller himself became a target of protests: "STOP THE HOMOFASCISTS!!" one leaflet declared. "WHY DON'T THEY LEAVE THE ORGANIZATION TO THOSE WHO STILL HAVE FAITH IN THE DEMOCRATIC PROCESS?" The final break came when John O'Brien and his allies tried to censure Voeller for leading a spot demonstration from a police precinct in Chelsea to the Eagle's Nest, a dark and cruisy leather-and-Levi's bar on the Hudson River, where the police had been harassing patrons, handing out parking tickets and ticketing taxi drivers who stopped in front of the corner bar. Voeller's detractors argued that the GAA president had recklessly endangered its members by unilaterally authorizing the demonstration, without a vote of the membership, and they convened a meeting to discuss disciplining him. "For God's sake, don't even *go* to that," Ronald Gold, the former *Variety* reporter, told his friend Voeller. "It's going to be a zoo." Gold, too, had lost patience with what he saw as the GAA's increasingly belligerent tactics and the constant criticism from GAA members who didn't trust the older GAA leaders like himself. "Stop complaining that you don't have enough power in this organization," Gold would say at meetings, his voice pinched. "I work my ass off. If you work your ass off, you'll have power, too." But Voeller went to the meeting, while Gold stayed home and watched television. And on October 4, 1973, faced with certain censure, Bruce Voeller quit, after ten months in the job.

Quitting the Gay Activists Alliance did not, however, mean quitting gay liberation; Voeller did not even consider leaving the movement as he walked out of the Firehouse that night. He had been thinking for months about forming a gay organization ruled from the top down rather than from the bottom up—and so what if it was less democratic. It would have national ambitions, and represent his kind of gay men and lesbians. The day after his resignation Voeller was on the phone, talking to other members of the GAA who shared his disillusionment.

• • •

Bruce Voeller's home on Spring Street in SoHo, a three-minute walk from the Firehouse, had an old-fashioned kitchen, with a backyard out the window, and a fireplace. It was a comfortable room, warm with thick stone walls lined with shelves heavy with dishes and pots and pans, and it was where Voeller and his few friends from the GAA gathered for coffee a few mornings after his resignation. The evening Voeller had quit, Ronald Gold had called Nathalie Rockhill, a former GAA vice president who worked in Craig Rodwell's gay bookshop. "What are we going to do?" Gold demanded. "We must get Bruce to change his mind." Rockhill had missed the meeting at which Voeller had quit. She had been skipping more and more of the meetings; she, Gold and Voeller had been discussing their disillusionment with the GAA for months. So when Gold called her, Rockhill responded practically: "This is it," she said. "We can do it now."

Rockhill had always gotten along with Voeller; she was one of the few women who kept going to GAA meetings after Jean O'Leary led the walkout of the Lesbian Feminist Liberation. She considered herself a gay liberationist first and a feminist second. "I'm afraid I'm going to be stoned just for being gay," Rockhill would say. "I might get paid less for being a woman." Rockhill got along better with men than most of her lesbian friends. She was, more than most, uncomfortable and alarmed at the growing division between the sexes in the movement. She had never forgotten the moment at the end of one Gay Pride march where a lesbian, standing in front of Central Park, was directing all lesbians to a women-only rally on the west end of the park. Rockhill was supposed to speak at the main gay rally in the center of the park. She was heartbroken at being forced to choose between the gay struggle and the women's struggle.

Ron Gold had stood out at the GAA because of his knowledge of the New York media, an expertise that now would be critical to any kind of professional homosexual organization. Voeller also invited Gregory Dawson to his home because he had been the public relations director for Robert Moses during the 1964 World's Fair, and he moved in wealthy circles. At the GAA, Dawson and some friends in the advertising business prepared a full-page newspaper ad which depicted a despondent family over a caption that read: "Your child isn't dead, he's only a homosexual." Dawson wanted to run that ad in the *New York Times*, and he knew he could raise the money to do it, but the idea had been shouted down as elitist at a GAA meeting. With Rockhill, Gold and Dawson at this meeting in Voeller's kitchen was Tom Smith, the caretaker of the Firehouse, one of the very few blacks in the GAA.

There had already been a consensus among these five people about what was wrong with the GAA, so there was little difficulty agreeing that morning on a mission for a new organization: This would be an American Civil Liberties Union for gays, a voice for the "ordinary" homosexual. It would seek to convince mainstream Americans that most gays were not that different—they were not all mannish women or Nellie men. The new organization would seek to change the climate, to make it easier for homosexuals to come out, in the belief that the public perception of homosexuality would grow kinder as more homosexuals went public. It would join the fight to convince the American Psychiatric Association to end its designation of homosexuality as a sickness. It would seek out members of Congress to introduce a federal gay rights bill, as outlandish as that notion seemed. It would try to stop the television and movie industry from portraying stereotypical homosexuals, be they flitty hairdressers or child molesters. It would lobby U.S. corporations to adopt anti-discrimination measures for homosexuals. And it would coordinate the dozens of community gay activist groups as they fought for local anti-discrimination laws. "The whole gay movement is public relations," Ronald Gold wrote. "For me, the 'political' things we do (civil rights laws, sodomy repeal, the psychiatric changeover) are simply tools to dramatize our existence as real human beings, tired of the choice between invisibility and oppression, recognizing that invisibility is oppression—public relations tools, to create a climate in which everybody can come out."

The structure of the group was nearly as important as what it would do. It would attempt to employ a paid full-time staff to work only on gay liberation. It would have a dues-paying membership. And it would be run by a board of directors, which would be responsible for raising funds. In short, if the Gay Activists Alliance was modeled after a New England town hall, this new organization would be modeled after a corporation. It would move activism from the streets into the executive suites and government offices. It would be the first homosexual rights organization led not by the political radicals of the 1960s, but by middle-class, older, professional activists. The new organization's mission would be reflected in its name. Everyone agreed it needed to include the words "national" and "gay." Greg Dawson, noticing how popular the term "task force" had become in government, suggested it be called the National Gay Task Force. It was a clunky and corporate choice, something short of inspired. *The Advocate*, celebrating the creation of the group as "one of the most exciting developments in recent years," complained: "We don't wish to be picky right at the start, but we can't help commenting on the group's first big boo-boo—that name. It's horrible. . . . An organization such as this one urgently needs a name that attracts, that instills pride, that inspires. National Gay Task Force does none of these; it just sits there like a clunk, coined by movement people for movement people. . . . It appears there were no advertising or public relations men among the founders of NGTF (pronounced nuh-guh-tiff, perhaps?). If they have, they probably would have thrown themselves in front of a subway train at the thought of

Craig Rodwell in his Oscar Wilde Bookstore in Greenwich Village in 1971. Rodwell, who helped to organize New York's first gay pride parade in 1970, hated to read and viewed his bookshop more as a political endeavor than a literary one. *Kay Tobin Lahusen*

"ANSWER THE HOMOSEXUAL!" Arthur Evans, a founder of the Gay Activists Alliance in New York, bellows at the acting vice-chairman of the city's Board of Examiners, which in 1971 refused to issue teachers licenses to open homosexuals. *Richard C. Wandel, Lesbian and Gay Community Services Center, National Archive of Lesbian and Gay History (NALGH)*

Marty Robinson, a GAA leader, argued that the best way to get attention was to confront politicians directly, or to zap them, a tactic that he helped to develop in 1970 and that emerged again eighteen years later with ACT-UP. His target here is Nelson A. Rockefeller, the former governor of New York. Robinson would die of AIDS. *Richard C. Wandel, NALGH*

Below: The GAA drew the notice of police when in 1971 it began staging late—and loud—Saturday night dances at its headquarters, a converted firehouse in Soho. Rich Wandel, a GAA member and photographer, began snapping as officers wrote a ticket to Jim Owles, the GAA president. Vito Russo, left, and Marc Rubin and Pete Fisher, right, look on. Owles and Russo both died of AIDS. *Richard C. Wandel, NALGH*

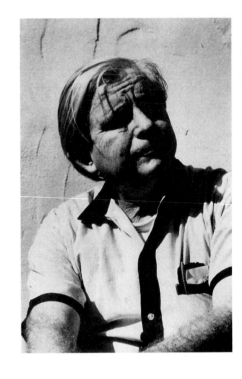

Above: Dr. Franklin Kameny at the White House gate the day before the District of Columbia's first election of its own nonvoting delegate to Congress in 1971. Fired from his government job in the 1950s for suspicion of homosexuality after being arrested one night in the park across from the White House, Kameny was running as an openly gay candidate. The photographer on the right is Kay Tobin Lahusen. The Washington Star, © The Washington Post /D.C. Public Library

Below: Elaine Noble in 1974, at the time of her election, as an open lesbian, to the lower house of the Massachusetts state legislature from Boston. *Courtesy Elaine Noble*

OPPOSITE
Top left: Michael McConnell and Jack Baker of Minnesota became the first celebrities of the young movement when they applied for a marriage license in Minneapolis in May 1970 and were featured in *Look* magazine the next January. In April 1971, Baker was elected president of the University of Minnesota student body—the first open homosexual to win any public office. *Kay Tobin Lahusen*

Top right: Morris Kight came out of the peace movement in Los Angeles to help organize that city's Gay Liberation Front in 1969 and then the Gay Community Services Center. Kight has been one of the few constant presences in the gay rights movement in America. *Richard C. Wandel, NALGH*

Bottom: Del Martin and Phyllis Lyon in 1995, forty years after founding the Daughters of Bilitis. *Clint Steib,* The Washington Blade

Barbara Gittings leads the crowd in chanting "Gay is Good!" in Washington Square Park in New York on the fourth anniversary of the Stonewall riots in June 1973. The good feeling soon dissolved in an acrimonious exchange between drag queens and lesbian feminists. © *Bettye Lane*

Above: Jeanne Cordova of Los Angeles and Charlotte Bunch of New York and Washington, D.C., appearing at the National Women's Conference in Houston, Texas, in 1977. The conference passed a resolution in support of lesbian rights, suggesting an easing of the tensions between the feminist and lesbian movements from earlier in the decade. *Courtesy of Jeanne Cordova*

Right: "I'm your token lesbian," Rita Mae Brown announced to shocked members of the National Organization for Women in 1970. Brown moved from the feminist movement to the gay rights movement to the women's separatist movement before settling on a career as a writer. Here she is in 1973 at a party marking the publication of *Rubyfruit Jungle.* © *1997 JEB (Joan E. Biren)*

The creation of the National Gay Task Force, the first national gay rights organization, was announced at a press conference in New York in 1973. The staging of the announcement by its jacket-and-tied chairman, Howard Brown, was meant to signal that the group intended to play by more traditional rules in lobbying government. Brown is seated with Bruce Voeller and Nathalie Rockhill; at rear is Frank Kameny. Voeller would die of AIDS. *Richard C. Wandel, NALGH*

Right: Steve Endean at age thirty in 1978, standing before the U.S. Capitol as the new executive director of the Gay Rights National Lobby, an organization whose office phone was disconnected for lack of payment. He would die of AIDS fifteen years later. The Washington Blade

Left: A close friend and ally of Steve Endean in Minnesota and later in Washington and California, Kerry Woodward fought the repeal of the gay rights ordinance in St. Paul, was an officer of the Gay Rights National Lobby, and was the first woman co-chair of the Human Rights Campaign Fund. © *1999* Star Tribune/*Minneapolis-St. Paul*

Jean O'Leary and Bruce Voeller, the first woman and man to share the leadership of a gay rights organization, the National Gay Task Force. *Courtesy of Jean O'Leary*

Above: Midge Costanza, assistant to President Jimmy Carter and the movement's first friend in the White House, at her new job in January 1977.
The Washington Star, © The Washington Post/D.C. Public Library

Left: The Rev. Troy Perry, founder of the Universal Fellowship of Metropolitan Community Churches, standing in the mother church in Los Angeles after it was gutted by fire in January 1973. *Courtesy of the Metropolitan Community Church, © Anthony Enton Friedkin*

Right: Gay activists in Dade County, Florida, invoked the Holocaust and the black civil rights movement in attempting to defeat Anita Bryant's campaign to overturn a county gay rights ordinance. Voters in June 1977 overwhelmingly rejected the ordinance, responding to Bryant's argument that homosexuals were a threat to children. The vote marked the start of a dark period for gay rights organizers across the nation. *Dade County Coalition for Human Rights*

Below left: By 1978, when this picture was taken, Jim Foster had worked for more than a decade in San Francisco to build a gay power base within the national Democratic Party. In Miami, he helped direct the defense against Anita Bryant but found that one of the things voters there reacted against was the image of gay sexual license in San Francisco. Foster would die of AIDS a decade later. © *Rink Foto SF '78*

Below right: When Jo Daly saw Jim Foster on television speaking about gay rights to the 1972 Democratic National Convention, she packed up her belongings and her St. Bernard and moved to San Francisco to work in Democratic politics with Foster. © *Rink Foto SF '79*

Anita Bryant singing "God Bless America" for the National Association of Religious Broadcasters in Washington, D.C., in January 1978, seven months after the repeal of the gay rights ordinance in Dade County.
The Washington Star, © The Washington Post/*D.C. Public Library*

Minnesota State Senator Allan Spear on April 25, 1978, as it was announced that voters in St. Paul that day had repealed the city's gay rights ordinance by a margin of 2 to 1. © 1999 Star Tribune/*Minneapolis-St. Paul*

Below: It was Rick Stokes (left), a gay lawyer, businessman and civic leader, whom Jim Foster and David Goodstein (right) persuaded to run for the San Francisco Board of Supervisors in 1977. Foster and Goodstein—the rich, conservative, autocratic publisher of *The Advocate,* the only national gay magazine—were determined to keep the gay street populist Harvey Milk from becoming the first public homosexual elected to office in the city. But Stokes was too quiet and traditional to appeal to the young, aggressive new male population in the Castro, and Milk won. © *Rink Foto SF '77; Avis S. Girdler, courtesy of Cornell University Library*

At the end of January 1978, his first month on the San Francisco Board of Supervisors, Harvey Milk—along with Mayor George Moscone and Supervisor Carol Ruth Silver, Milk's ally on the council—were on stage together at the annual coronation of the drag Empress of San Francisco. Moscone and Milk would be assassinated at the end of that year. © *1978 by Daniel Nicoletta*

Each time a gay rights law was repealed by voters in another part of the country in the wake of the June 1977 defeat of the Dade County ordinance, Harvey Milk led an angry rally and march out of the Castro in protest. On this night, the ordinance had been overturned in Wichita, Kansas.
© *Rink Foto SF '76*

Below left: Marion Barry and his wife, Effi, on their way to his inauguration as the new mayor of Washington, D.C., in January 1979, after he had been elected with the help of the gay vote. To attract it, he and Effi had even spent an evening over drinks at the Eagle, a gay leather bar.
The Washington Star, © The Washington Post/*D.C. Public Library*

Below right: Tom Bastow, the President of the Gertrude Stein Democratic Club of Washington, D.C., at the meeting in Mayor Marion Barry's office in February 1979 at which the newly elected mayor asked Bastow, "Well, what do you want me to do?" *JEB (Joan E. Biren)*

The National March on Washington for Lesbian and Gay Rights, the first in the nation's capital, moving up Pennsylvania Avenue toward the Mall on October 14, 1979. After Harvey Milk's assassination, the idea of the march had become irresistible.
The Washington Star, © The Washington Post/*D.C. Public Library*

Above: "The story of Shelly Andelson is the story of America at its best," Senator Edward M. Kennedy said at an American Jewish Committee awards dinner for Andelson in 1984. Andelson had asked that Kennedy speak, and when he was dying of AIDS three years later, Andelson requested that Kennedy speak at his memorial service. *Courtesy of Andelson Family*

Right: Alan Baron, the publisher of *The Baron Report* and host of Washington, D.C.'s, principal gay political salon, on the telephone in Sean Strub's apartment in New York in September 1979. *Courtesy Sean Strub*

Left: Sean Strub with Tennessee Williams, at the author's house in Key West in 1981, the year Strub persuaded Williams to sign the letter that Alan Baron had written to raise money for the nation's first gay political action committee.
Courtesy Sean Strub

Left: The gay rights movement was initially paralyzed by the emergence of AIDS and the backlash it stirred. After a messy bout of infighting, Virginia Apuzzo was named to take over the National Gay Task Force, and she immediately sought to turn its efforts to dealing with the medical and political repercussions of the epidemic. *Richard C. Wandel, NALGH*

Below: Jim Fouratt (right, wearing leather pants, at a 1983 AIDS march) has been a vocal—some of his detractors use the word abrasive—fixture of gay activism for nearly three decades. He was one of the founders of New York's Gay Liberation Front in 1969 and later was involved in ACT-UP. *Richard C. Wandel, NALGH*

Left: Larry Kramer was among the first to warn against sexual promiscuity among gay men in the late 1970s. When AIDS first appeared in the early 1980s, Kramer helped to create first the Gay Men's Health Crisis and, after a falling-out with its leaders, ACT-UP. Here, Kramer participates in a 1983 AIDS candlelight march in New York City. *Richard C. Wandel, NALGH*

Left: Jesse Jackson appeared at the 1983 black-tie dinner of the Human Rights Campaign Fund in Manhattan, an event arranged by, among others, Ethan Geto (right). The organizers had hoped that Jackson's appearance would bring political legitimacy to this political action committee and build ties between the black and gay civil rights movements. Instead, Jackson dressed down his audience as "a self-centered, narcissistic movement." © *Bettye Lane*

Right: Larry Bush was the first reporter for a gay newspaper to turn a critical eye on the leadership of the gay rights movement. Strong-minded and relentless, he himself became a power in the movement in the 1970s. © *1999 JEB (Joan E. Biren)*

Below: Virginia Apuzzo (second from left) successfully lobbied Coretta Scott King (at the microphone) to include a gay speaker at the ceremonies marking the twentieth anniversary of Martin Luther King Jr.'s 1963 march on Washington. They appear here at a 1983 press conference, with Walter E. Fauntroy on King's left. Also pictured are Gilberto Gerald, the head of the National Coalition of Black Gays, on the left, and the Rev. Cecil Williams of San Francisco. © *1999 JEB (Joan E. Biren)*

Left: Randy Shilts's detailed coverage of San Francisco's gay bathhouses and sex clubs in the *San Francisco Chronicle*—and the alarms he raised about the connection between sexual promiscuity and the AIDS epidemic—made him an extremely unpopular figure in the Castro. Shilts, too, would die of AIDS. *Rink Foto SF '80*

Below: Betty Powell and Charlotte Bunch (both on the left) at a demonstration for the Equal Rights Amendment in 1981. Powell and Bunch headed a women's caucus that sought to bring a feminist edge to the work of the National Gay Task Force in the late 1970s. Bunch came from the separatist Furies collective in Washington, D.C., while Powell was the first black woman to serve on the Task Force board. © *1999 JEB* *(Joan E. Biren)*

Below: U.S. Representative Barney Frank of Massachusetts, speaking at the annual black-tie Human Rights Campaign Fund dinner in Washington, D.C., in 1987, the year he acknowledged to a reporter that he was gay. He was first elected in 1980. © *1999 JEB (Joan E. Biren)*

Top: Michael Hardwick found himself at the center of the largest legal setback suffered by homosexuals in the 1980s: a U.S. Supreme Court decision in June 1986 upholding a Georgia law that outlawed sodomy between homosexuals. Hardwick was in bed with a man when a police officer came through the door. "What are you doing in my bedroom?" Hardwick asked. He would die of AIDS in 1991. *© 1999 JEB (Joan E. Biren)*

Center: Urvashi Vaid, the executive director of the National Gay and Lesbian Task Force, speaking outside the U.S. Supreme Court in October 1987. *© 1999 JEB (Joan E. Biren)*

Below left: Rob Eichberg was one of the middle-class gay men in Los Angeles who helped to organize the Municipal Elections Committee of Los Angeles (MECLA), the first gay political action committee in the nation, in 1977. Eichberg, a therapist, later helped David Goodstein create the Advocate Experience. He died of AIDS. The Washington Blade

Below right: Cleve Jones, who loved the baths in San Francisco as a young man, became an aide to Supervisor Harvey Milk, and after he contracted the AIDS virus, founded The AIDS Quilt, the main memorial to its victims. He was in Washington for a demonstration in June 1987. *Sean Strub*

Leonard Matlovich, the Air Force sergeant who was dishonorably discharged after declaring his homosexuality in 1975, being handcuffed by policemen wearing protective gloves during an AIDS demonstration in front of the White House in 1987. The demonstration came at a time when the AIDS movement began to eclipse the gay rights movement, and dozens of gay leaders from across the nation assembled in Washington, D.C., to protest the Reagan administration's AIDS policies. Matlovich would die the next year of AIDS. © *1999 JEB (Joan E. Biren)*

Marty Robinson (left) and Jim Foster (right) at an AIDS demonstration in Washington, D.C., in June 1987. Robinson and Foster were involved in some of the first gay organizing after Stonewall. Both died of AIDS soon after this photograph was taken. *Sean Strub*

Thomas B. Stoddard helped to accomplish in New York in 1986 what the Gay Activists Alliance began in 1970: convincing the City Council to adopt a gay rights bill. Stoddard, who served as executive director of the Lambda Legal Defense and Education Fund in New York, later unsuccessfully took up the case of gay bathhouse owners who were forced to close by the city. He would die of AIDS.

The Washington Blade

It was at the Palace Theater in Hollywood, California, in May 1992, at a fundraising event arranged by his friend David Mixner (right), that Bill Clinton made the single public appearance and speech of his campaign before an all-gay audience. The promises of support he made that night for AIDS research and for gay rights—and the attacks on gays by major Republican Party figures that summer and fall—helped produce substantial gay money and votes toward Clinton's election as president in November. © 1992 by Barry E. Levine, Inc.

making 'National Gay Task Force' a household phrase." Of course, the name *had* been conceived by a group that included public relations experts, and it conveyed exactly the image its founders had intended.

Voeller had another suggestion for the group that morning: The *New York Times* had just carried a front-page interview with Dr. Howard Brown, whom Mayor John V. Lindsay of New York had appointed in his first administration to head the huge Health Services Administration. Brown announced in the *Times* story that he was homosexual, and that he had quit the Lindsay administration abruptly after eighteen months in office because he had heard that the Washington columnist Drew Pearson was preparing a column identifying homosexuals in New York's city hall, Brown among them. Brown's disclosure had been partly orchestrated by Gold and Voeller. Voeller had met Brown about one year earlier, when the commissioner invited him to lunch at his West Village townhouse. The two discovered they had much in common. "With each fag joke my classmates told, I died a little bit," Brown confided in Voeller, and Voeller immediately thought back to his own difficult youth, growing up in the log and farming country of western Oregon. Both had spent years trying to pass as heterosexual, though the experience of being a secret homosexual had been particularly excruciating for Brown. Mayor Lindsay had no idea that Brown was gay, and Brown did everything he could to make sure things stayed that way. He brought his sister and her two children to his swearing-in at city hall, so he was seen with a woman. He greeted his lover of five years on the receiving line as if he was just another well-wisher. Brown cringed when he read a newspaper account that described him as a "forty-two-year-old bachelor who lived in Greenwich Village," since he assumed every sophisticated Manhattanite understood that coded journalistic turn of phrase. He forced his lover to move to an apartment around the corner and installed a second phone line at home for personal business, hoping anyone who thought of tapping his line would check only his main number. He closed his kitchen window shades whenever he cooked, fearful a neighbor would see him at the stove and assume that the bachelor commissioner must be homosexual. Brown had become, as he later put it, a "professional neuter."

Voeller talked to Brown about the destructive stereotypical image of gay men, the attention paid to the radical homosexual and his own encounters with the "blue-jean elitists" at the Firehouse. That was why, Voeller said as they grew closer, it was so important for ordinary people like Howard Brown to come out—to counter the stereotype, to make it easier for adolescent homosexuals to grow up, to draw more mainstream homosexuals into the movement. Brown was, in private, a man of some abandon. He ate too much and drank too much. Brown was often the oldest man on the dance floor, and he often lasted the longest, dancing wildly, his hands flinging in the air, exerting himself so much that his friends were worried that he might have another heart attack right there (he had suffered one in June 1972). Brown once told the historian Martin Duberman that he wanted to devote his life to showing that homosexuals were "jes' folks." When Duberman suggested that homosexuals had, in fact, a special perspective that should be preserved, Brown smiled and responded: "Well of course we're different—why heavens, honey, I roam around the apartment every night in high heels!—and of course we have a unique perspective, but we shouldn't stress all that just now."

At first, Brown offered Voeller and the movement everything *but* his name: his West Village townhouse, his checkbook and his network of closeted, wealthy gay men. "I knew many rich homosexuals," Brown said. So when Brown finally agreed to announce his homosexuality at a medical symposium in Belle Mead, New Jersey, Voeller and Gold were ecstatic. They suggested that he talk to the *Times* first so that the story would appear the day of the announcement speech, which Gold knew would give it instant credibility and interest, particularly if the *Times* put it on its front page, which it did. And when Brown showed up at the symposium on October 3, 1973, the forty-nine-year-old doctor, professional and quite ordinary, found dozens of reporters, photographers and television cameras waiting. "I am publicly announcing my homosexuality in the hope that it will end discrimination against homosexuals," Howard Brown said. As he spoke he realized that he could not tell through the bright television lights how his confession was being taken by his colleagues, most of whom had little idea about Brown's secret life. He pressed on, telling the other doctors that they needed to hear from him so they would reconsider their idea of the typical homosexual. "I have met more homosexual politicians than homosexual hairdressers, more homosexual lawyers than homosexual interior decorators."

At the first organizational meetings of the Task Force, Voeller proposed that Howard Brown be the group's official leader. Everyone in the room agreed, and Voeller called Brown to offer him the post of chairman of the board on the spot. "I'd love to," Brown said. On October 15, after a period of two weeks during which Voeller had quit the GAA and Brown had appeared on the front page of the *Times,* Howard Brown put on a navy blue suit, rep tie and Lambda button and walked to a microphone at a small (eighty-seat) restaurant, The Ballroom, to announce the creation of a civil rights organization for homosexual men and women. The Ballroom had opened on West Broadway, about midway between Voeller's home and the Firehouse, six months earlier, the product of a partnership of seven GAA members, including Greg Dawson and Bruce Voeller. They had opened the restaurant counting on the business of their friends at the Gay Activists Alliance. The food was good, but the prices were steep, and few GAA members spent time there. It was, though, the ideal spot for the press conference: decorated with hanging plants, globe lights that inspired its name and egalitarian rest rooms each marked "Whomsoever." Just under a dozen members of the NGTF's new board of directors, and even fewer reporters, were there to hear Howard Brown and his colleagues describe this new organization to professionalize the gay rights movement. "Gay liberation," said Ronald Gold, "has become a nine-to-five job—there's no other way to do it." This new organization, Brown said, would bring "gay liberation into the mainstream of the American civil rights movement." One of the reporters wondered if this new group might be considered elitist, and Brown did not quarrel with the perception. "Past organizations haven't provided a way for professionals to participate," Brown responded. "To go once a week and sit through a five-hour meeting with everybody talking was a most forbidding prospect. It's also been very difficult to give money to such groups. . . . I don't see us as elitist—but I do think we have opened the way for people to participate in other levels." Still, Martin Duberman, who was a charter member of the Task Force's board of directors, went home that night and noted in his diary that this new group was constructed in what he called "the liberal reform mode: 'Let us in,' rather than 'let us show you new possibilities.' Structurally, too, I can sympathize with wanting to do away with the marathon GAA membership discussions on whether to buy one or two typewriters, but decisions from the top down may carry limitations as severe (if different) from those of participatory democracy."

Once again, as with the GLF and the GAA, everything that had seemed so obvious and simple turned out to be difficult. The Task Force was blamed for the ultimate demise of the GAA: after Voeller and the others left, attendance at weekly meetings tumbled from two hundred to fewer than twenty-five, the once-rich group faced bankruptcy, and the Firehouse was gutted by arson that some GAA members thought was set to destroy financial records that would have documented embezzlement. Arthur Evans, a founder of the GAA, in a particularly harsh column in *The Advocate*, accused Voeller and the rest of the former GAA members of "aping high-class values" in search of mainstream acceptance, a strategy Evans found repugnant.

"If NGTF is going to be aimed at (and controlled by) gay professionals, then let it change its name to something like the Gay Professional Association and stop making pretenses about coordinating anybody else," Evans wrote. " . . . But if NGTF wants to be a truly national gay organization, then it had better rethink its entire structure. A national gay organization should be just that—an organization that represents ALL gays, and not just those who are famous or have titles after their names or who make a lot of money. A national gay organization must not be afraid of open and free debate and the democratic election of its officers." Voeller, furious, sent his response to *The Advocate* and a copy to Evans's home, with an angry note to his former colleague scribbled across the top: "Herewith some comments, in advance, a courtesy you did not extend me and which might have spared a considerable number of people misunderstanding. The injury you have caused could probably have been avoided had you been willing to discuss your misgivings with me." Evans responded with a note (addressed to "Bruce Voeller, Ph.D.") taking notice of Voeller's recruitment of Howard Brown. "You know damn well why he is where he now is—he's a fat-cat professional and you have him there to act as a magnet to draw in other fat-cat professionals. You want your group to be 'professional' in that you want it controlled and fed by white, upper-middle-class, well-educated rich males. In other words, by people like yourself.

"Relax a little, Bruce," Evans said, signing off. "You need your friends, even though you think them enemies."

Evans was not alone in his view. "A group of professionals—whatever that means—which removes itself from the grassroots power sources is going to create a groundswell of resentment to the gay liberation movement nationwide," Morris Kight said at the time. Kight made sure that Ronald Gold heard this when Gold flew to Los Angeles to meet with entertainment executives. Gold arranged a meeting with activists at the Los Angeles Gay Community Services Center to discuss creating a board to monitor the portrayal of homosexuals in film and on television. The room was packed with activists who jeered at every suggestion Gold made. Gold responded that he had wasted too much time in his years at the Gay Activists Alliance with "this kind of long and exhausting meeting in which everybody has his say and little is accomplished." When someone called him an elitist, Gold responded: "Yes, indeed, I'm an elitist, and the Task Force is elitist, if that's what you want to call professionals who have another style from your own."

From the side of the room, Kight piped up: "You should get to know some gay people. You might like them." Gold walked away, convinced that this encounter was not "representative of the gay community." But the Task Force encountered similar resentment all over the country. It was seen as an eastern board, dominated by middle-class people and academics. Nath Rockhill came across one letter in a gay newspaper in the Midwest that mocked the Task Force for its seemingly ostentatious choice of a stylish "Fifth Avenue" headquarters. In fact, the Task Force worked out of a dilapidated suite of offices over John's Bargain Store on the corner of Fourteenth Street and Fifth Avenue.

As the group started taking shape, Voeller realized it was one thing for civil libertarians to set up an American Civil Liberties Union, but quite another for a group of homosexuals, many of whom had lived much of their lives as renegades, to attempt the same thing. These professional homosexuals were again confronting the same difficulty—the absence of a recorded history—that confounded the Gay Liberation Front four years earlier. There was no institutional memory to draw on, no experience with organizational charts or procedures for choosing boards of directors. Voeller had envisioned the Task Force as a national board, made up of prominent activists from various communities, who had some professional expertise. Their presence, he thought, would provide the Task Force with credibility and money, and he assumed the board members themselves would keep some distance from its day-to-day affairs. But activists, by definition, had very fixed ideas and tended to be idiosyncratic, unpredictable and headstrong. The members of the first board were not going to be as pliant as Rockhill, Voeller and Gold had expected. What's more, the board members were not, with a few exceptions, experienced in the one function associated with boards of directors—raising funds. Before long, the Task Force was struggling, and Voeller wrote a plaintive letter warning board members that they were in "the midst of a financial bind that seriously threatens our future." It cost $1,000 a week to operate, including the $125 weekly salary to each of the staff of four who took care of the day-to-day administration of the NGTF, including Voeller and Rockhill. On a good day, $100 in donations might come in the mail. "We need the help of the board in every possible way," Voeller said in a politely worded letter in April 1974.

Even the most basic organizational questions seemed vexing. Everyone wanted a board of directors that represented the entire country. But with so little money—by the end of November, the NGTF had raised $13,000 of the $200,000 it said it needed to start—it was not possible to bring people to New York from much farther away than Washington, D.C. How can you call this a national organization when almost everyone is from New York, Philadelphia or Washington? asked board member Charlotte Bunch, who was from Washington. Voeller did not disagree. But assembling a national board in New York would deplete a nonexistent treasury, he said. And asking board members to pay their own way would result in a board dominated by people who could afford to come to New York.

The board, disturbed by the charges of elitism, reopened some of the basic questions that had been settled in Voeller's kitchen, including the debate over what voice the rank-and-file Task Force membership should have in running the organization. It took Franklin Kameny, another of the original twenty-two board members who had, for the most part, been selected during those early meetings in Voeller's kitchen, to put a stop to that debate. The sole function of Task Force members, Kameny said in a blunt letter to members, was to provide "an impressive statement of organizational size for publicity purposes," funds to keep the NGTF going and "warm bodies" for demonstrations. "The role of the membership in electing officers, in electing Board members, in choice of staff, in all forms of decision-making," Kameny informed his fellow board members, "should be close to, if not actually, nil. If that be 'elitist,' 'undemocratic,' or whatever, so be it."

All these disputes resulted in long, anguished and nonproductive meetings. The topics might have been more high-minded than what tied up the Gay Activists Alliance, but the resulting paralysis was the same. After one particularly grueling organizational meeting, Kameny returned to Washington and wrote a letter announcing his distress at this "morass in which we are wallowing." He spoke from experience as he predicted the inevitable expiration of "an-all-too-short-lived period of enthusiasm and good will, during which personal and ideological differences are subordinated or ignored totally and everyone works together effectively, frictionlessly, and highly productively." The board was consuming itself over questions of structure and process that should have been disposed of in the first week, he said, and was on the verge of disintegrating "into dissension-ridden nothingness.

"We are drifting and getting nowhere."

14

A QUESTION OF SANITY

December 1973, Washington, D.C.

It was ten days before Christmas 1973, and an era was ending. In Washington, D.C., the board of trustees of the American Psychiatric Association announced that it had voted, with two abstentions, to remove homosexuality from the *Diagnostic and Statistical Manual*, its official list of mental disorders, closing a battle that had been politely launched against the psychiatric community by Franklin Kameny in 1964* before erupting into a belligerent campaign by the new generation of gay activists at the end of the decade. Homosexuality might still be a sin to organized religion, and it remained a crime in most states, but with the vote of December 15, it was no longer a mental illness. It was the first great victory of the movement, and it had not come easily.

Three years before, the American Psychiatric Association had opened its annual convention in San Francisco. It was May 1970, one week after the Ohio National Guard fired on a crowd of Kent State University students protesting the U.S. invasion of Cambodia, shooting four of them to death and touching off a wave of grief and outrage, of student strikes and anti-war riots across the

---

* "I see nothing wrong with homosexuality, nothing to be ashamed of," Kameny said on television in the spring of 1964. "It is not a disease, a pathology, a sickness, a malfunction or a disorder of any sort. Underlying all these theories is the subtle suggestion that it is somehow undesirable. Psychiatrists are a biased group."

nation. San Francisco, the city where a young militant named Carl Wittman had produced *A Gay Manifesto* in the months before the riot at New York's Stonewall Inn, was pulsing with radical energy, particularly among young homosexuals. And as the radical theory of the new Gay Liberation Front formed, sweeping aside the rhetoric and remaining cautions of the old homophile movement, psychiatrists and psychologists came to be seen not just as errant figures, but as the political enemies of gay liberation. The American Psychiatric Association had placed homosexuality on its official list of mental illnesses, first published as the *Diagnostic and Statistical Manual, Mental Disorders* in 1952. Homosexuals, the *DSM* asserted, were "ill primarily in terms of society and of conformity with the prevailing social milieu." It was a definition clearly based on social rather than medical grounds. The diagnosis was that homosexuals were sick because they were not like most other people. But that classification had framed the way every psychiatrist approached his homosexual patients for a generation, and it gave medical legitimacy to the laws aimed at curtailing homosexuals.

As it happened, one of the most radical of the Gay Liberation Front groups—seething with former activists from the Student Free Speech and black power movements in Berkeley, across the Bay—had formed in San Francisco. And one of the most despised and infuriating figures in all of American psychiatry, as far as homosexual activists were concerned—the author of the 1962 study which suggested that homosexual men were the products of weak fathers and smothering mothers—was scheduled to be on a panel at the APA convention in their town. Dr. Irving Bieber, professor of psychiatry at New York Medical College, was a magnet for protesters, and the GLF decided to be there, too, not only for Bieber but for the whole convention. Konstantin Berlandt wore a bright red dress and a full beard, and he, Gary Alinder and Michael Itkin, among others, haunted the APA sessions, disrupting them with displays of guerrilla theater and angry protests from the floor. The sessions and seminars became forums in which gay men and lesbians talked about their tortured attempts to find help in psychiatric therapy. They talked about forced commitment to psychiatric hospitals, electroshock treatment and aversion therapy, in which psychiatrists "treated" homosexuals by injecting them with a nausea-inducing chemical and then forcing them to view erotic photographs of members of their own sex.

Irving Bieber, by then a pinched, aging figure with a nasal voice, appeared on a panel discussing "Transsexualism vs. Homosexuality: Distinct Entities?" It did not get very far. "You are the pigs who make it possible for the cops to beat homosexuals!" Gary Alinder yelled at the panel of doctors. "They call us queer, you—so politely—call us sick. But it's the same thing! You make possible the beatings and rapes in prisons, you are implicated in the torturous cures perpetrated on desperate homosexuals.

"I've read your book, Dr. Bieber," he shouted, "and if that book talked about black people the way it talks about homosexuals, you'd be drawn and quartered, and you'd deserve it!" For years, in obscure homophile journals that few saw, and in homosexual forums that no one else heard, the research and conclusions of Irving Bieber and another psychiatrist, Charles W. Socarides, had been criticized by homosexuals. But Bieber had never been confronted in person like this by a homosexual, much less at a session of his own professional association. He was stunned. "I never said homosexuals were sick—what I said was that they had displaced sexual adjustment," Bieber protested. His reply drew hoots and jeers of derisive laughter.

"That's the same thing, *motherfucker!*" one of the radicals shouted.

The following day a dozen or more lesbians and gay men were scattered through an audience of some three hundred psychiatrists who had gathered for a program entitled "Issues on Sexuality," when Nathaniel McConaghy, a young Australian doctor, stood at the microphone and began to read a paper written from his own research into different methods of weaning homosexual men from their attraction to other males. "With apomorphine therapy, the patient was given injections of apomorphine after which he viewed slides of [naked] males while experiencing the resultant nausea. With aversion-relief, the patient received painful electric shocks after reading aloud phrases describing aspects of homosexual behavior. Following a series of shocks, he read aloud a phrase describing an aspect of heterosexual behavior, and this was not followed by a shock. . . ."

"Where did you take your residency—*Auschwitz?*" someone screamed from the audience.

"Torture!" shouted someone else.

"Get your rocks off that way?" another voice taunted him.

McConaghy stopped, looking up from his pages. "If you'll just listen," he pleaded, "I'm sure you'll find I'm on your side." He managed to read on and finish, amid heckling, but when the program chairman announced another paper the shouting began again.

"We've listened to you, now you listen to us!" a protester demanded.

The program chairman implored them to be patient.

"We've waited five thousand years!" someone said.

"Can't you wait half an hour longer?" the chairman beseeched them.

"We've waited long enough!" the protesters began to chant. *"We've waited long enough!"*

With two papers still unread, the program was stalled. Rather than give the homosexuals the floor, the chairman made a decision. "This meeting is adjourned," he declared. The room erupted in a bedlam of strident and angry voices, some of them the voices of psychiatrists, furious at the loss of control, at the disruption and chaos, at the apparent waste of time and money.

"Maniac!" one psychiatrist screamed at a protester trying to read a list of gay demands. "Give back our airfare!" one doctor bellowed. The session ended in a heaving chaos as the San Francisco police arrived with drawn guns. And the disruptions did not end there. Psychiatrists across the nation—many of them accustomed to the therapeutic model in which they sat behind their patients—suddenly found themselves being denounced to their faces as barbarians by loud, angry, belligerent young homosexuals. Public speeches and important meetings of physicians and analysts were disrupted at least three other times that year. In Chicago, the target was Dr. Socarides, the leading psychiatric spokesman for the school of thought which held that homosexuality was a medical problem requiring a cure, as eighteen members of the Chicago Gay Liberation Front sprinkled themselves through the audience at a family medicine workshop of the American Medical Association. The protesters, by prearrangement, waited until Socarides said the word "homosexual" before they launched their disruption.

"Homosexuals are beautiful!" one yelled, as ten others bounded up to distribute a leaflet to the crowd. Socarides tried to press on, but they scattered challenges along his path. "That's a moral judgment," one yelled. "You're making things up," said another. "Do you cure your straight patients of heterosexuality?" Unlike the conference in San Francisco, the protesters this time drew enough support from doctors and psychiatrists in the audience to win seats on the panel for a gay man and a lesbian, who from the stage made the argument that was contained in the leaflets they had handed out on the floor: "We declare that we are healthy homosexuals in a sexist society, and that homosexuality is at least on a par with heterosexuality as a way for people to relate to each other." *

That leaflet echoed the declaration of sanity that Frank Kameny had persuaded his Washington Mattachine chapter to issue in 1965,† and was a reminder that the battle that these new activists were waging had begun on a bolder if quieter note, with Kameny and his colleagues of the homophile movement. But the new tactics were more disruptive and alarming to the psychiatric profession, and they were beginning to have an effect, if not obviously at first. In San Francisco, a Baltimore psychiatrist, Kent Robinson, had stayed behind in the wreckage of the APA "Issues on Sexuality" forum and fallen into conversation with Larry Littlejohn, a veteran gay activist in the city and

* In addition to the protests against psychiatrists in San Francisco and Chicago that year, on May 7, 1970, in Los Angeles, a lecture on homosexuality by a California State University psychologist at the federal building downtown was "liberated" by a GLF group who barraged the speaker with questions and comments until he yielded the floor.
† "The Mattachine Society of Washington takes the position that in the absence of valid evidence to the contrary, homosexuality is not a sickness, disturbance or other pathology in any sense, but is merely a preference, orientation or propensity on a par with, and not different in kind from, heterosexuality."

the president of SIR, the Society for Individual Rights. Robinson sympa-
thized with the protesters' feelings. The discrimination they suffered didn't
seem that different to him from the plight of blacks or women, and Robinson
thought that homosexuals were right to resent the APA's refusal to give them a
hearing on the subject of their own condition. He thought they ought to have
a panel discussion of their own at the next APA convention. Littlejohn, who
said he was there to observe (the protests were led by the younger members of
the GLF), suggested some names for the panel—Franklin Kameny, Phyllis
Lyon and Del Martin among them—and Robinson promised that he would
carry the idea to the APA leadership.

The American Psychiatric Association convened again the next spring at
the enormous old Shoreham Hotel in Washington, D.C. Robinson had succeeded, and for the first time in its history the association had agreed to include a panel of gay men and lesbians in the program. The panel, assembled
with Frank Kameny's help, included Kameny, Littlejohn, Del Martin, Lilli
Vincenz of Washington, D.C., and Jack Baker, the newly elected student body
president at the University of Minnesota. Some in the APA viewed the panel
as a safety valve, but fearing the worst, they had also hired a security consultant, in case things got out of hand.

By May 1971, D.C.'s gay activists were on a roll, and it was not the time
or the place for a calm convention. Kameny's campaign for Congress had
ended just two months before. Though the Mattachine Society now existed
mainly in name, Kameny's campaign organization had given birth to a new,
more narrowly focused group in Washington, a Gay Activists Alliance modeled on the New York example, and it was formed by a core of younger gay activists tired of Kameny's dominance. Yet Kameny and the leaders of the new
group were united by one feeling—none of them wanted to abandon the tactics of pressure and disruption aimed at the nation's psychiatrists.

For weeks, a mixed group of people—GLF types, GAAers and a piggy-
back crew of anti-war protesters who simply wanted to be part of the action—
had been meeting in Cliff Witt's cramped studio apartment on the tenth floor
of a building off Scott Circle, poring over the APA's meeting schedule and the
hand-drawn diagrams of the Shoreham Hotel's floor plan that they had made
by walking its halls, noting the location of the fire doors that opened from the
convention hall into the inviting woods of Rock Creek Park. Witt, who had
been Kameny's deputy campaign manager, was one of the founders of the
brand-new Washington GAA, and he was in the process of becoming the chief
coordinator of its zaps. He had scouted the hotel corridors leading from the
lobby to the convention hall, and also the paths through the woods that led to
the back of the hotel. The group planned to invade the convention at the
height of its largest, most ceremonial gathering—the Convocation of Fellows,

where the APA conducted its hierarchal rituals and heard its major address. Some of the protesters would come through the woods, some through the corridors. Some, dressed in coats and ties, looking as much as possible like psychiatrist-conventioneers, would enter the hall with the APA members, where they would take a seat and wait, ready to throw open the fire doors. Then they would all rush the stage, Cliff Witt would seize the microphone, and the nation's psychiatrists would find out that gays and lesbians couldn't be bought off with a panel discussion.

Former attorney general Ramsey Clark was at the podium speaking that afternoon to a crowd of about two thousand psychiatrists. In the back rows were a rank of elders of the APA, gaunt, portly, bald or silver-haired and decked in gold medals that hung on ribbons across their chests. In one front row to the side sat Kameny, Barbara Gittings, Martin and Vincenz, wearing the badges which identified them as panelists and guests. Clark was in the middle of his address when thirty or more protesters burst in from the sides and rear, and went shouting and yelling toward the stage. Cliff Witt would always remember what he saw as he ran toward the stage: a 300-pound psychiatrist, hunched up and cowering as he stood on the seat of his folding chair. In the front, Franklin Kameny had turned around, staring as if bewitched as some of the elder analysts in the rear, livid, stood and flailed away at the invaders. But Witt's glee ended with an "Oomph!" as a defensive line of angry analysts knocked him backwards against a fire door when he tried to mount the stairs to the stage. He fell against the release bar, the door opened, he tumbled backwards toward Rock Creek Park, and the door swung closed. Witt, the designated speaker, was locked out.

The convention hall had been transformed into a milling, yelling crowd. *"You Nazis!"* one psychiatrist screamed. But the energy had no focus, and as the moment drifted, in danger of dissolving, Franklin Kameny saw the gleaming microphone on the stage, saw that Cliff Witt had disappeared and knew that his moment had come once more. Ignoring the stairs, he clambered over the edge of the stage, bounced up to the podium and grabbed the microphone.

"What are you doing?" said the flustered moderator.

"I'm seizing the microphone!" Kameny said.

"Well, give me your name, and I'll introduce you," the man said.

"Psychiatry is the enemy incarnate!" Kameny thundered, as the switch was hastily thrown on the sound system, to cut him off. It made no difference. His rusty granite voice rolled across the hall.

"Psychiatry has waged a relentless war of extermination against us," he boomed. "You may take this as a declaration of war against you!"

• • •

For Dr. Richard Pillard of Boston, there was no mistaking the man shouting from the stage. Pillard was a psychiatrist, and he was gay, which made him a member of a very small class indeed. If the listing of homosexuality as a mental illness in the *Diagnostic and Statistical Manual* was a source of torture and discrimination for the average gay man or lesbian, it was a nightmare for gay psychiatrists, whom their colleagues would consider mentally ill. In 1971, Pillard, a young psychiatrist only a few years divorced, had attended his first meeting of the Student Homophile League at Boston University. It was his first encounter with a whole room full of openly gay students, and it was also the students' first encounter with an openly gay psychiatrist. That night an idea was born: gay therapy for gay patients—a mental health service in which therapists who were both trained counselors and gay could provide therapy based on the belief that homosexuality was not an illness. They would build their practice on the belief that since homosexuality was not a mental disorder, coming out was, in fact, healthy. Patients would pay what they could afford, and Richard Pillard and some others would donate their time. They would keep the service going for as long as they could. The Homophile Community Health Services Center had opened for business in Boston in January 1971, and Pillard was on his way to becoming the first psychiatrist in the nation to openly acknowledge his homosexuality.

As Pillard took in the disruption before him in Washington, he thought of the students he had met and counseled at Boston University. From some of them, he had heard about an odd authority figure, some doctor in Washington, who made the argument that there was nothing wrong with homosexuals. One of those students, Stan Tillotson, the founder of the gay student group at MIT, had heard the man talk as he lay in bed listening to a radio interview show one night in the 1960s. It was the first reassuring voice Tillotson ever heard. Another student told Pillard that there was only one person who had given him hope as a boy that he might not be abnormal—this same figure, a kind of eccentric genius, someone familiar to his family, who kept insisting that homosexuality was not a mental illness. Now, in the chaos that the convention had become in Washington, Pillard realized why the name he had just heard from the stage seemed so familiar: the man he was looking at, the balding, flinty figure booming at him from behind the dead microphone, was the man they had described—Dr. Franklin Kameny.

The agreed-upon panel of gay men and lesbians was billed as a discussion of the "Lifestyles of Non-Patient Homosexuals," and it took place at nine o'clock at night. None of the spokesmen for the disease-and-cure school—Irving Bieber, Charles Socarides or others—attended. Kameny said he had been approached by APA officials who told him that Bieber was terrified of being hurt, and would not appear unless Kameny and the other protesters guaranteed his safety, which they did. The room was set up with round discussion tables to seat perhaps 150 people for conversation in small groups after the panel. Only twenty-five to thirty psychiatrists showed up. They were silent as Kent Robinson introduced the panel of homosexuals who did not consider themselves mentally ill. Dr. Robinson spoke almost as if he were introducing specimens of a newly discovered tribe of people. "There are a number of homosexuals who have come tonight," he said. "Some are married couples, for example . . . and they would like to tell something about how they live as human beings, not as patients. So we will begin with Dr. Frank Kameny. Frank. . . ."

Kameny began formally, standing before them in a coat and tie. "I tend to feel very strongly that what we are dealing with here is not a medical problem, as again medicine and psychiatry persist in putting it, not a medical problem or emotional disorder or anything else you want to call it, but solely a sociological question in prejudice and discrimination," he said. "It has been well and truly said that there is no black problem in this country—there is a white problem—and I feel very strongly that there is no homosexual problem—there is a heterosexual problem—and many of you people here *are* that problem to a significant degree."

The care they had been given thus far, Kameny told the analysts, had been devastating. "The sickness theory itself is far more traumatic in its effects than all of the traumas I think psychiatry often attempts to cure," he said. And it was misplaced. "The person who *really* needs the psychotherapy is not the homosexual who loses his job but the employer who fires him, singularly or in the aggregate; not the homosexual who is denied a job, a civil service job, but the Chairman of the Civil Service Commission, and the President in the White House behind him who put into effect the policy denying him that job; not the homosexual who gets arrested by a police decoy, but the sick policeman, and the police chief, and the mayor behind him who put those practices into effect; not the homosexual youngster who gets *dragged* into a psychiatrist's office by his mother, but the mother, to relieve her anxieties about his homosexuality so he can live a fulfilling life as a homosexual."

Del Martin, who followed Kameny, was more pointed. Before she came to the APA convention, she said, "I was convinced that in the twentieth century, the psychiatric profession had replaced the church and the law as the most destructive force in society as far as the life of the homosexual is concerned. My experience here this week attending the various sessions has reinforced that opinion, and has radicalized me as a lesbian even more than ever before.

"You stand behind the cloak of academia and detached objectivity in providing the only valid data on homosexuality, and until tonight have ignored

the experience of the lesbian or the male homosexual as subjective and therefore invalid," she said. "You need to be aware of the many young women who
are victims of Nazi-like purges in the women's branches of the armed forces,
how so-called confessions are wrung from frightened youngsters who don't
even know the meaning of the word 'homosexual,' and of Maggie, a psychiatric social worker at a veterans hospital, who was called to the office one day
to find a tape recorder going and a federal investigator behind the desk. He
warned her that anything she said might be held against her. It seemed someone had written to a congressman saying she was a lesbian, and her interroga-
tor had been flown across the country at taxpayers' expense to determine if the
charge was true.

"You should also be aware of the custody case in Sacramento, California, where Mrs. N. was declared an unfit mother because she was an admitted
lesbian. She had been examined by a psychiatrist who had to say, in all honesty, that Mrs. N. possessed all the attributes of a good mother, but also, in all
honesty, he had to also add that all things being equal, a heterosexual adjustment would be more ideal. So the child was turned over to the father because
ideally he was heterosexual, his only recommendation, and whether or not he
possessed the attributes of an ideal father was never questioned. Furthermore,
Mrs. N., although allowed visitation rights, was never again to see her daughter alone."

Before the convention ended, Franklin Kameny and Larry Littlejohn
told Kent Robinson that they wanted to present a formal demand to the APA's
Committee on Nomenclature for the deletion of homosexuality as a mental illness from the *Diagnostic and Statistical Manual*. Robinson had them meet
with another APA official, who promised to convey their request to the hierarchy. Nothing came of it immediately. But that spring, in Washington, another
group of psychiatrists was gathering informally in the evenings, and its meetings were arguably historic in their own way. They sometimes drew fifty people
at a time on convention nights, all of them men, and they called themselves
the Gay-PA. They were homosexual psychiatrists, and they discovered, at the
Chesapeake House and at other gay bars in the city that spring of 1971, that
they had a lot to talk about.

For weeks in advance of the 1972 APA convention in Dallas, Barbara
Gittings had called around the country, trying to find some psychiatrist willing
to sit in front of his fellow analysts, tell them he was gay. That year the APA
had scheduled a panel of nonpatient homosexuals *and* psychiatrists who
agreed with them. Gittings would be one of the panelists, and one of the psychiatrists was to be Judd Marmor, a vice president of the APA, an author and a
respected figure. But when Gittings's partner, the slight, strong-minded Kay

Tobin Lahusen,* looked at those on the panel, she said, "Look, here we have two gays who aren't psychiatrists and two psychiatrists who aren't gay. And what we need is somebody who is both." But that was the problem.

Gittings had learned about the gay psychiatrists who met, very secretly, for dinner and in the bars at the annual conventions, and finally, after calling around the country, she tracked one down in Philadelphia. He agreed to do it, but only if he could disguise his face and use a microphone that would distort his voice. "Absolutely not!" Frank Kameny snapped when Gittings told him of the idea. "We are trying to overcome the need for masks. We've got to get a psychiatrist who will be himself up there." Kameny said he would find one himself, but he could not.

When the day came, the program of the Dallas convention listed the session, "Psychiatry: Friend or Foe to Homosexuals? A Dialogue," and the names on the panel included Barbara Gittings, Dr. Franklin E. Kameny, Dr. Judd Marmor and Dr. Robert Seidenberg, a professor of psychiatry at the Upstate Medical Center in Syracuse, New York. The fifth panelist was the most intriguing—"Dr. H. Anonymous." He slipped through the back corridors and then a side curtain to take his place on the panel. He was a large man in shapeless clothing, with a huge wig and an ugly, rubbery face mask. When he spoke, his voice was distorted: "I am a homosexual. I am a psychiatrist," he said. The seminar room was packed with psychiatrists looking at him intently, wondering if it was true, and if it was, who he was. There were more than two hundred homosexual psychiatrists attending the convention, he said. They even had a group of their own, the Gay-PA. "As psychiatrists who are homosexual, we must know our place and what we must do to be successful. If our goal is high academic achievement, a level of earning capacity equal to our fellows, or admission to a psychoanalytic institute, we must make sure that we behave ourselves, and that no one in a position of power is aware of our sexual preference," he said. "Much like a black man with white skin who chooses to live as a white man, we can't be seen with our real friends, our real homosexual family, lest our secret be known and our doom sealed. . . . Those who are willing to speak out openly will do so only if they have little to lose, and if you have little to lose, you won't be listened to."

He closed with an appeal: that the other psychiatrists who were gay would find the courage to press for change; and that his colleagues who were not gay would come to accept those who were. He left the room still carrying his secret. John Fryer would not formally reveal his identity until twenty-two years later, at the annual meeting in Philadelphia in 1994.

---

* Kay Lahusen used the professional pen name Tobin for writing and photography in the 1960s and 1970s. In the years since, she has added her own legal last name, becoming Kay Tobin Lahusen. All three versions appear as references in this book.

In the seminar discussions that followed, an APA convention audience for the first time heard psychiatry condemned by psychiatrists for its attitude toward homosexuals. Even as the church had grown more liberal, said Dr. Seidenberg, psychiatrists had persisted in an attitude which was rigid and hostile. Citing a "litany of atrocities" in the professional literature dealing with the treatment of homosexuals, Seidenberg concluded that "as charitable as I can possibly be towards my own discipline and profession, I cannot . . . say that psychiatry or psychoanalysis is a friend of the homosexual." Judd Marmor, the APA vice president, called a recent article by Charles Socarides in the *Journal of the American Medical Association* "a monstrous attack" on homosexuality. "The cruelty, the thoughtlessness, the lack of common humanity in the attitudes reflected by many conservative psychiatrists is, I think, a disgrace to our profession."

The tide was turning against the sickness theory. Six months before, the APA's Task Force on Social Issues had suggested that homosexual behavior in some settings—prisons, for instance—might not be pathological. Dr. Henry Brill, chairman of the Committee on Nomenclature, had written in reply that there was a substantial feeling on the committee "that homosexual behavior was not necessarily a sign of psychiatric disorder: and that the *Diagnostic Manual* should reflect that understanding."

It was in New York that fall that a crucial meeting occurred. The Association for the Advancement of Behavior Therapy—a group that made particular use of the aversion therapy technique of pornographic pictures and electric shocks—was in conference at the New York Hilton in October 1972 when the Gay Activists Alliance zapped it. Almost a hundred GAA members picketed on the sidewalk outside the hotel, and a smaller group of about a dozen got inside a crowded hotel meeting room. They handed out a flier entitled "Torture Anyone?" which demanded "an end to the use of aversion techniques to change the natural sexual orientation of human beings."

Two people in that room were new to the battle over the APA's sickness policy. One was the determined, almost manic leader of the protesters who had noisily challenged the speaker: Ronald Gold. He had a long history of psychiatric treatment and institutionalization, but he was still a relatively recent convert to the gay rights movement, and this was his first protest against psychiatry. The other person was a psychiatrist in the audience, Robert L. Spitzer. He had never thought to question the classification of homosexuality, and was furious at these homosexuals who had disrupted the presentations he had come to hear. Yet those two men began a conversation, which became a negotiation, which became a collaboration to resolve the issue.

Robert Spitzer was a married man with children. Nothing in his professional history prepared him to be sympathetic to the cause for which Ronald

Gold disrupted his meeting. A native New Yorker, Spitzer had trained at the Psychoanalytic Institute at Columbia University. Its faculty was one of the first to revise and reject Freud's view that homosexuality was not an illness after his death, and the institute had come to be one of the most severe in its view of homosexuality. Spitzer had early come under the influence of psychiatrist Edmund Bergler, the author of *Homosexuality: Disease or Way of Life?*, one of the most scornful critics of the homophile movement. And when he entered the seminar room at the New York Hilton that day in 1972, Spitzer had had only one homosexual as a patient. He had helped the man to give up having sex with other men, and the patient had gone on to date women and then to marry.

Ronald Gold had grown up in Brooklyn. Short, hyperactive, slightly effeminate; he had been sent by his family to a series of psychiatrists, because of his homosexuality, from the time he was thirteen. But when he presented himself at a New York psychiatric hospital for treatment for heroin addiction at age twenty-four, he had been turned away. Instead, he spent eighteen months as a hospital patient and then another three and a half years as an outpatient at the Menninger Clinic in Kansas, which kept him clean of heroin but failed to "cure" his homosexuality. He was thirty-nine years old by the time the Stonewall riots occurred. Now he was forty-two. The same compulsive energy that had gone into his addiction went into his work, as a reporter for *Variety*, and as the news and media chair for the New York GAA. When he shouted to the crowd at the Hilton that the GAA would not permit the aversion therapy presentation to continue, but would like to have "a dialogue" with the psychiatrists instead, a woman in the audience who had known Gold in college came over to point out Spitzer, who, as it turned out, was already making his way across the room. Spitzer was a member of the APA Committee on Nomenclature, the woman told Gold—the group responsible for updating the contents of the *Diagnostic and Statistical Manual*. Gold's eyes lit up as he looked at the stern figure approaching him. From that moment he fastened onto Robert Spitzer and never let go.

Spitzer, angry at the disruption, was heading toward Gold to tell him so, but he was curious, too, and when he reached the gay militants' spokesman, he found him passionate, articulate and respectful. When Gold argued that the members of the Committee on Nomenclature ought to give homosexuals a hearing, Spitzer promised him that he would arrange for a formal presentation before the Committee on Nomenclature, and sponsor a panel discussion at the next APA convention about whether homosexuality ought to be included in the official listing of mental disorders. It seemed the fair thing to do, but it never occurred to Spitzer that he would change his own views.

Four months later, when the Committee on Nomenclature met behind closed doors at Columbia University's Psychiatric Institute on February 8, 1973, they heard a presentation carefully prepared by Dr. Charles Silverstein, the psychotherapist who had alerted Gold and Bruce Voeller to the meeting at the New York Hilton which they had disrupted. Silverstein, in a long written survey of the research in the field, argued that the evidence supporting the idea of homosexuality as a sickness was either subjective or skewed. He pointed instead to the clinical evidence from nearly a score of medical studies, beginning with the work of Drs. Alfred Kinsey and Evelyn Hooker, a research psychologist at the University of California, who in 1957 had compared a group of male homosexuals who had not sought therapy with a group of male heterosexuals who had not, either. Supported by a grant from the National Institute of Mental Health and a list of volunteers provided by the homophile groups Mattachine Society and ONE, Inc., Hooker matched thirty homosexual men with thirty heterosexual men in terms of age, intellect and education. Then, by subjecting them all to the same inkblot and psychological tests, and by submitting the unidentified test results of all sixty men to two psychoanalysts for their judgment, she demonstrated that the therapists could not tell from the men's responses who was homosexual and who was not. It might be difficult for her colleagues to accept, Dr. Hooker concluded, but "some homosexuals may be very ordinary individuals, indistinguishable from ordinary individuals who are heterosexual."

The APA's policy was inconsistent with the evidence, Silverstein said, and he cited regulations that discriminated against homosexuals because of it: the Pentagon citing it in denying security clearances and work to homosexuals; the New York Taxi Commission requiring a homosexual driver to undergo psychiatric examination twice a year to see if he was fit to drive; a university refusing to recognize a gay liberation student group because of the harm it might do to "the normal development" of students; and a homosexual attorney denied a license to practice by the state.

"I suppose what we're saying is that you must choose between the undocumented theories that have unjustly harmed a great number of people and continue to harm them and . . . controlled scientific studies," Dr. Silverstein said as he finished his arguments to the committee that day. "It is no sin to have made an error in the past, but surely you will mock the principles of scientific research upon which the diagnostic system is based if you turn your back on the only objective evidence we have."

When the presentation was over and Silverstein, Jean O'Leary, Ron Gold and the rest of the GAA delegation filed out of the room, the eight committee members sat quietly. Then, for some time, they talked among themselves, and as the group broke up, the chairman, Dr. Henry Brill, turned to Robert Spitzer. "Okay, Bob," he said. "You got us into this mess. Now what do we do?"

To get the maximum public leverage out of the meeting, Gold had alerted a science reporter at the *New York Times* that the Nomenclature Committee was going to hear them, and the story in the next day's paper revealed how far the members of the APA committee had come in their feelings about the sickness label. "There's no doubt this label has been used in a discriminatory way," Henry Brill had told Boyce Rensberger, the *Times* reporter, after the meeting. "We were all agreed on that." The committee members had also agreed, he said, that whether someone preferred to have sexual relations with a member of the same or the opposite sex was not by itself an indication of mental disorder. "This term has been misused by the public at large," Brill said, as if the APA policy had never intended to suggest that all homosexuals were mentally ill. "The public assumes that all homosexuals are dangerous or sex fiends or untrustworthy or some other part of a stereotype. This, of course, isn't so. We know of many successful, well-adjusted people in various professions who are homosexual." On the other hand, Brill said, many homosexuals were miserable in their condition and came to psychiatrists wanting help to change. "Very often these people have very clear psychiatric problems," he said, so it wasn't a simple issue. But the committee would try to have a statement of its views ready for the APA to consider at its meeting in Honolulu in May.

May 1973, Honolulu

It would fall to Robert Spitzer to shape the committee's thinking on the issue. Because neither he nor any of the other members of the Nomenclature Committee was an expert on homosexuality, Spitzer waded into the materials that Silverstein had cited and all the other authoritative writing on both sides of the argument that he could find. As the chair of the planned symposium in Hawaii, he was determined to be informed and to make the panel truly representative. He invited Charles Socarides and Irving Bieber, as well as two critics of the policy, Judd Marmor and Ronald Gold. By the time Spitzer got to Honolulu, he had spent a concentrated period of weeks listening and talking to Gold, and once in Honolulu, he realized that the way he perceived the issue had changed in a fundamental way.

Gay activists insisted that homosexuality was not a "pathology"—a mental disorder. But Spitzer realized that no clear, common, fundamental definition of the term "mental disorder" had ever been put forward. None appeared in the *DSM-I* or the newer *DSM-II*, so one of the reasons it was difficult to agree on whether homosexuality met the criteria of a mental or psychiatric disorder was that there weren't any. Psychiatrists *assumed* it was a sexual perversion and then set about explaining it, Spitzer concluded. The real scientific question, he thought, was whether identifying homosexuality as a disorder was consistent with the way psychiatry identified other disorders. Spitzer began to think of the various kinds of behaviors that were considered disorders, and then tried to deduce from the specific what general rule bound them together.

The answer, he decided, was that all the other pathological states—schizophrenia, alcoholism—seemed necessarily incapacitating in some way, but not homosexuality. If you accept that as the criterion, he thought, then all the other diseases stay, but homosexuality has to go. Homosexual relations might not seem optimal human behavior to many psychiatrists, Spitzer decided, but psychiatrists weren't in the business of declaring what was normal and what was abnormal, and they didn't have to regard it as sick, either.

More than a thousand psychiatrists sat shoulder to shoulder, row after row, as Robert Spitzer and the six speakers took their places in the hall at nine o'clock on Wednesday morning to begin the symposium. The issue posed was simple: "Should Homosexuality Be in the APA Nomenclature?" There was a feeling in the hall of lines drawn for battle. "There is homosexual behavior; it is varied," said one speaker, Dr. Robert J. Stoller. "There is no such *thing* as homosexuality." A diagnosis, he said dryly, should be succinct, and he suggested some examples: "heterosexual, monogamous, with accompanying fantasies of being raped by a stallion; homosexual, with foreskin fetishism; heterosexual, with preference for cadavers; homosexual, with disembodied penises (tearoom promiscuity); heterosexual, voyeurism; homosexual, expressed only in fantasies during intercourse with wife." If it cannot be succinct and accurate, Stoller said, it ought to be removed. And practically none of psychiatry's disease descriptions were accurate and succinct, so probably they should junk the whole system.

Ron Gold had typed out his own speech, page after page of passionate, personal and very carefully crafted language. It was too long, Spitzer told him. He would have to cut it in half. Frantically, in the period just before the symposium began, Gold did, but he did not change the beginning: "I have come to an unshakable conclusion," he said, looking out over the sea of psychiatrists. "The illness theory of homosexuality is a pack of lies, concocted out of the myths of a patriarchal society for a political purpose. Psychiatry—dedicated to making sick people well—has been the cornerstone of a system of oppression that makes gay people sick.

"To be viewed as psychologically disturbed in our society is to be thought of and treated as a second-class citizen; being a second-class citizen is not good for mental health. But that isn't the worst thing about a psychiatric diagnosis. The worst thing is that gay people believe it."

Gold had debated how much of his personal history he should reveal, and he was worried that the psychiatrists would simply see him as crazy. But he had decided to tell them how sick and worthless, how emotionally empty he had been made to feel by psychiatrists from the age of fourteen; how he had drifted into heroin addiction, ended up in the Menninger Clinic and emerged thinking that he was still uncured because he was still homosexual. "But I soon found that all I needed for another person to love me was to like myself better," he said. "I met a young man, and we had a good, happy life for twelve years. When we broke up, our conflicts weren't out of the psychiatric literature. They were just like the tales of heterosexual divorce you read about in *Redbook*.

"The man I live with now is a warm, loving, open person," Gold said. "For the past two years we've been going through the joyful process of discovering the full repertory of mutuality—easier for two members of the same sex.

"There are advantages to being gay. I learned that in the gay movement. And I learned something else: that I was oppressed, and must make the choice to do everything I can to cease being an accomplice in my own oppression. I've had an immense sense of psychological growth through this decision. I've fought through to a sense of myself as a whole person—a good, concerned, loving, fighting-mad homosexual. I'm fighting the psychiatric profession now, but I know that a false adversary situation has been drawn between psychiatry and gay liberation," Gold said.

"I feel better since I've joined Gay Liberation. I work better, I'm happier in love. Would you rather have me the way I am?" he asked. "Or would you suggest another round of therapy? I think you really know that I'm not sick now, that my homosexuality is simply a part of me that in the past I wasn't allowed to accept. And I think you're prepared to agree that my previous illness was at least in part a direct result of the crimes perpetrated on me by a hostile society. You have been willing accomplices in such crimes. It is now time for you to prevent them. Take the damning label of sickness away from us," Ronald Gold said. "Take us out of your nomenclature."

When he had finished speaking, hundreds of psychiatrists stood and applauded. Laughter, hisses and boos greeted the now-familiar arguments of Irving Bieber and Charles Socarides when they spoke, and it seemed clear that much of the APA membership was restless for change. But the committee recommendation that Henry Brill had promised in time for consideration at the annual meeting was still unmade. Robert Spitzer seemed stalled in caution, and Ronald Gold could feel the moment passing. That night he took Spitzer to a Honolulu restaurant popular with gays called The House of Charles, to a gathering of the Gay-PA, which had invited Gold to dinner. Just as he had not met an out gay person until he met Gold, Spitzer had not yet talked with an openly gay psychiatrist. So Gold walked him unannounced into a room of about fifty of them, among them the heads of psychiatric associations, university departments and important training and research schools. Gold had warned Spitzer to keep quiet and listen. "Do not say anything!" he said. "They can make you in five seconds if you open your mouth." But Spitzer couldn't resist asking questions, and when the psychiatrists realized who he was, they were frightened and furious. "Get him out of here!" one of them rumbled. "Fuck you!" Gold hissed back. "I'm not doing anything of the kind! He's going to help us. And I want him here."

At that moment, an officer in full army uniform came through the crowd, fell on Gold and burst into tears. He was a closeted gay psychiatrist from Georgia on active duty in the military who had been so moved by Gold's speech that he went out to find a gay bar that night. The psychiatrists around them were stunned, and Spitzer returned to his hotel room that night determined to complete his task. Within a month he did.

"For a mental or psychiatric condition to be considered a psychiatric disorder, it must either regularly cause subjective distress or regularly be associated with some generalized impairment in social effectiveness or functioning," Spitzer wrote in his proposal. "Clearly, homosexuality per se does not meet the requirements . . . [but] what about those homosexuals who are troubled by or dissatisfied with their homosexual feelings or behavior? These people have a psychiatric condition by the criterion of subjective distress, whether or not they seek professional help. It is proposed that this condition be given a new diagnostic category, which will replace the current undefined category of homosexuality in subsequent printings of the *DSM,* defined as follows: *Sexual orientation disturbance. This is for people whose sexual interests are directed primarily toward people of the same sex and who are bothered by, in conflict with, or wish to change their sexual orientation. This diagnostic category is distinguished from homosexuality, which by itself does not constitute a psychiatric disorder. Homosexuality per se is a form of irregular sexual behavior and, with other forms of irregular sexual behavior that are not by themselves psychiatric disorders, are not listed in this nomenclature.*"

For six months the proposal bounced around like a pinball inside the bureaucratic committee structure of the APA. Before the final vote at the APA board meeting in December 1973, one qualifying word was added to the language about the new category of psychiatric disorder being proposed: the word "necessarily": "This diagnostic category is distinguished from homosexuality, which by itself does not *necessarily* constitute a psychiatric disorder." With that change made, the holdouts on the board were mollified. Even Franklin Kameny did not mind the creation of the new disorder, the "sexual orientation disturbance," to describe homosexuals who were unhappy with being gay. The new category made sense to him, Kameny said. Any homosexual who would rather be heterosexual would have to be crazy.

December 15, 1973, Washington, D.C.

Franklin Kameny, Barbara Gittings, Ronald Gold, Bruce Voeller and a clutch of others sat waiting nervously in the APA headquarters for the result of the board's vote. At midday, the president of the American Psychiatric Association, Dr. Alfred Freedman, announced that the board had voted to remove homosexuality from the list of mental disorders. Robert Spitzer's proposal had become policy. Furthermore, Freedman said, as television cameras, microphones and newspaper reporters recorded the event, the board of trustees had adopted a resolution which deplored "all public and private discrimination against homosexuals in such areas as employment, housing, public accommodation and licensing," and urged "that homosexuals be given all protections now guaranteed other citizens."

In the weeks that followed, there were objections to the trustees' decision and parliamentary maneuvers, primarily by Charles Socarides,* that threw the board's decision to the whole voting membership of the APA—18,000 psychiatrists—for review. But when the referendum was taken and the 10,000 ballots returned by mail were counted, in April 1974, the membership had upheld its board by almost 3 to 2.

It was probably the greatest mass cure in the history of medicine. "Doctors Rule Homosexuals Not Abnormal," the *Washington Post* headlined on December 16. "It's Official Now: We're Not Sick!" the *Gay Community News* exulted in its next edition a week later. When the APA membership held its referendum four months later, ending the formal debate once and for all, the newsletter of the National Gay Task Force capped its story with a headline shimmering in sarcasm and glee. "The Earth Is Round!" it said. One of the three great condemnations of homosexuality—as sin, crime and mental illness—had been lifted. And with its removal—and the APA's companion resolution against discrimination—the gay rights movement achieved its first great victory: social nonconformity was not the definition for mental illness. The APA's decision, and the National Gay Task Force's aggressive use of it in its lobbying efforts, would have a sweeping cumulative effect in the next few years as dozens of other national professional and church organizations voted on their own resolutions of nondiscrimination, and as gay people sought to overturn sodomy laws and legal discrimination against homosexuals.

After the vote of the board of trustees, a reporter for *The Advocate* asked Robert Spitzer whether the psychiatrists' decision meant that times had

---

* Charles Socarides's son, Richard, would turn out to be homosexual and serve as liaison to the gay community for President Bill Clinton.

changed or the APA had simply been wrong all along. Realizing that he was speaking to a gay newspaper with limited readership, Spitzer decided to be candid. "I would have to say we were wrong," he said. "Since this is not getting wide circulation, I can say that."

15

ELAINE

January 1974, Boston

Elaine Noble was just four years younger than Barney Frank, but she was a woman, which made a difference as she began thinking about her own run for public office. And unlike Frank, who had been elected to his state representative's seat in the fall of 1972, Noble was very public about her homosexuality. She was the daughter of a southern German Jewish mother and a father who was a blue-collar Democratic union hall leftist, members of the National Association for the Advancement of Colored People living in Natrona, a Pennsylvania steel-mining town. Her father was a machinist for Pittsburgh Plate Glass, and when she came to Boston University in 1963, Elaine Noble felt uncomfortable, as if it were a rich and privileged place like Harvard. In the poor black areas of Boston's South End, where the rats ran freely through the rooms at night, she found in neighborhood social activism the kind of purpose and acceptance that felt right to her. She found causes and mischief wherever she went. In New Hampshire, as a teacher at a junior college for a year after she graduated, she got tickets for her students to hear Alabama governor George Wallace, campaigning for the 1968 Democratic presidential nomination, speak at Dartmouth College, and then used them to usher a group of black student protesters into the hall. But it was not until she came back to Boston that she began to find comfort and then a political cause in her own sexuality. As a graduate student and then a teacher of voice and articulation at Emerson College, a small, liberal, independent school on the north side of the Boston Public Garden for students who aspired to careers in radio, television, theater and politics, she found other women who were lesbians to befriend and to date. She became an early member of Daughters of Bilitis, when it began meeting at the Arlington Street Church, just a few blocks from Emerson College. With her friend Ann Maguire, who taught health sciences at Northeastern University, she joined HUB, the Homophile Union of Boston. The two women did not take well to the condescending attitude that the gay men of Irish and Italian families in Boston came by so naturally. Tired of being treated like kitchen staff, they walked out one day. But they were drawn to the new mental health counseling group, the Homophile Community Health Services Center, and Noble became a member of the board.

Her increasing gay activism, Noble discovered, didn't threaten her academic career. In the loose, zany, theatrical atmosphere of Emerson College, Noble, the increasingly prominent lesbian, was just another activist. There were casually gay faculty members at Emerson, and there were openly gay students. The students thought she was hip. And when a budget crisis at WBUR, the Boston University radio station, moved the station manager to shake up the staff in the 1971–72 academic year, the new program director, Bonnie Cronin, created an opening that seemed made for her. Cronin offered time slots to the various new activist groups popping up around Boston. She was hoping to get volunteers from these groups to appear on air, and so Elaine Noble became co-host of *Gay Way* and proved to be a natural for radio—opinionated, funny, fast on her feet.

In early June 1973, David Peterson, who had founded the Gay Speakers Bureau, called a meeting at the Charles Street Meeting House to discuss another new idea. Each of the small gay organizations that had evolved in Boston—HUB, the Daughters of Bilitis, the Student Homophile League, the Gay Liberation Front, the Gay Male Liberation Front, Lesbian Liberation, the Good Gay Poets—printed its own publication, usually a newsletter, to keep members informed. The effect was chaotic, and Peterson had written out a proposal for a community-wide newsletter. Within a week a news collective was formed at the meetinghouse. The building had been left vacant by the merger of two congregations, and the departing minister had allowed it to become something of a gay community center, with office, lounge, coffeehouse, message center and weekly dance. The first issues of the newsletter were run off on a hand-cranked mimeograph machine. The staff used the pay phone on the sidewalk outside as their switchboard, and came and went through a sidewalk window they used as a door.

They called their new publication the *Gay Community News*. Some of its first stories were about the fire at the UpStairs bar in New Orleans, a memorial service for the victims in Boston, the marriage of Elaine Noble's co-host on *Gay Way*, Bob Freeman, to his lover, Harry Jones, at the Old West Church, the firing of the minister at the church by his bishop, who had been irate, and the murder of a young gay man by six men who picked him up in a bar and drowned him in a sewer.

Then, in mid-September, the *News* carried two reports about the best-known lesbian in Boston. The first, a short item, noted that Massachusetts governor Francis W. Sargent, a Republican, had appointed Elaine Noble a member of the Governor's Commission on the Status of Women; and then, on the front page, under the headline "Gay to Run," was the news that Noble was organizing a campaign to run for a seat in the legislature, in the primary election a year away, in September 1974. *GCN* would give Noble's candidacy prominent coverage, but most of the exposure she got in the coming year wouldn't come from the fledgling gay press. Most of the votes she won wouldn't come from the gay community either. Even the idea that she should run hadn't come from the Boston gay and lesbian community. Barney Frank's sister, Ann Lewis of the National Women's Political Caucus,* talked Elaine Noble into running.

Lewis and Noble met for breakfast at the Parker House, where Boston politicians loved to gossip over coffee in the morning and over whisky at night, and Lewis had brought some papers that showed the boundaries of the new legislative district that was being created, the Suffolk Sixth. The two women knew the territory of the new district very well because it had been formed by taking away half of Ward 5, the large district which Barney Frank had won in November 1972. The new Suffolk Sixth would take in practically the whole Boston University residential area, siphoning off the student votes which had been crucial to Frank. It was a poor district, jammed with students with no money, homosexuals beginning to cluster in cheap rental apartments and an even larger population of old people on small fixed incomes, the majority of them women. The issues Elaine Noble had fought for for years as a neighborhood activist—working against the wave of condominium conversions that were pushing up rents on the remaining apartments, for instance—were important to those people. "You could take it," Lewis said, tapping her finger on the irregular oval. "I'd never get elected," Noble said, shaking her head.

Noble went back to Emerson and talked to her students about it. They thought it was cool. "You ought to run," one of them said.

Ann Lewis went back to city hall, where she worked in the Mayor's Office. Sitting with Mayor Kevin White and some of his Irish Roman Catholic

---

* Ann Lewis later served as director of communications in President Bill Clinton's second-term White House.

cronies, all men, a few days later, someone brought up the new district around Boston University.

"We ought to run somebody in that," he suggested.

"I've got somebody," Ann Lewis said.

"Who?"

"Elaine Noble," she replied.

There was a moment's silence while the name registered. "Jesus Christ!" one of the city hall aides said. And that was all.

Noble did not run as a gay person. She was a woman who happened to be gay, whose sexuality wasn't an issue in a district where she was so well known from years of residency and activism. The veteran Boston consultant Van Christo printed up a sheaf of sample giveaway fliers, each with a simple message that, while never used, foretold the theme of the Noble campaign:

> The Issue Is:
> Adequate Housing for the Elderly
> Not Homosexuality.
> The Issue Is
> Better Health Services
> Not Homosexuality.

Noble was selling herself to the marginal populations of her district as someone who would take care of their problems with streetlights, potholes, rising rents, absentee landlords and Red Sox ticketholders whose parked cars jammed their streets during baseball games. It was, in a way, the same kind of troubleshooting she already did for some young gay men arrested by the Boston police for soliciting, young men of poor Irish or Italian Catholic families intolerant, to say the least, of homosexuality. She would call up the towering, gun-toting, thoroughly Irish Roman Catholic city councilman "Dapper" O'Neil, sometimes waking him up at night, using her shrewd and saucy womanly charms to get him to go downtown with her to get them out of jail. "I've got a nice Irish boy, Dap, and his mother doesn't know he's a homosexual," she'd say. "*Please,* Dap." And Dapper O'Neil would rise, dress and lumber into the jailhouse. "Take it off the roster, take it off the roster, this guy was never here," he'd say to the cop behind the desk. And then, turning to Noble, "You make sure your friends remember me at election time," he'd rumble, and head back home to bed.

Boston's biggest gay bar, the 1270 Club, was the site of Noble's big fundraising party, and on that last Saturday of January 1974, she made it clear to her audience that she would not be a gay candidate. Some three hundred people had paid $5 each to come to a party advertised as a gala to celebrate her thirtieth birthday. State Representative Barney Frank introduced her, and there was a sense of history in the air. There were now three separate gay programs airing on three different radio stations in Boston. The city's first black gay bar, The Elite, had just opened in Roxbury. There was an effort under way to begin a gay Jewish temple. And now the city's most prominent lesbian was going to run for the Massachusetts State House. There were free drinks and a live band at the 1270 that night. Frank told the crowd that as an openly gay candidate, Noble would probably draw national media attention. There were whistles and shouts, and when Noble asked if they could deal with the fact that she wouldn't be just a one-issue candidate, the crowd gave her a rousing cheer. It was an approval, as they all discovered later, that couldn't last.

The radical young lesbians flowing into the Boston chapter of Daughters of Bilitis in 1973 and 1974 from the feminist and separatist movements at colleges like Barnard, Vassar and Wellesley despised Elaine Noble from the start. It was heresy for a self-proclaimed lesbian feminist to work with men, and to seek support from so many other constituencies and groups. But the older lesbians, the ones who just a few years before had been too afraid even to join Daughters of Bilitis, were enthralled. Lois Johnson and Sheri Barden, by 1974 the two leading figures in the Boston DOB, held fundraising gatherings for Noble at their house on Warren Street, where they once were afraid for anyone to know that lesbians lived. Elaine Noble affected people that way. The *Boston Globe* might describe her as "a gay rights activist," "an avowed lesbian" or "a self-avowed homosexual." But Noble's literature stressed community issues. None mentioned the word "homosexual." And all her campaign pictures showed her talking with an old person, a student, a mother or a child. "There are times, and they are often, when I say, 'I am a lesbian,' " she told Ellen Goodman, who was interviewing her for an article in the *Boston Sunday Globe Magazine* in 1973. "Then you have to deal with me as a human being. And I have to deal with your discomfort. It's hard for both of us. But it's got to be." Goodman wrote of Noble, "The adjectives that come to mind are Strong, Open, maybe even Free."

It wasn't as wild a dream as they thought at first. Lewis's sponsorship had blocked Kevin White's organization from putting up anyone against Noble, and the apparent imprimatur of city hall generated six times as much money in contributions as any of her four primary opponents got. Elaine Noble won the primary on September 10. She carried every precinct of her district and suddenly faced a camera crew from CBS, a reporter from *Time* and a general election two months away. Her opponent, Joseph P. Cimino, was a young, dark-haired, handsome attorney and the owner of two of Boston's premier swinging singles saloons, Gatsby's and Daisy Buchanan's. The Boston Bruins liked to drink there after games. Cimino ran as an independent, not a Republican, and he used a different kind of campaign picture: it showed him standing in an expensive suit with two beautiful young women. He refused to debate Elaine Noble, but four days before the general election he released a "Dear Voter" letter which said in part:

"The fact that my Democratic opponent may become the first self-declared Lesbian-Feminist in the United States to be elected to office has attracted national attention.* I will repeat here what I have told members of the press who have attempted to reduce this campaign to a referendum on people's sexual preferences: Homosexuality is not an issue in this election. It neither qualifies nor disqualifies a person for elective office. I URGE THAT NO ONE VOTE AGAINST MY OPPONENT BECAUSE OF HER HO-MOSEXUALITY. By the same token, I would expect no one to vote for her because she is a Homosexual."

Elaine Noble carried every precinct again in the general election, November 5, 1974, an election that would be remembered as the Democratic sweep that followed the resignation and pardon of President Nixon. She became the first declared homosexual elected to state office in the nation, and her victory seemed perhaps the edge of a thin but identifiable trend. In Massachusetts, both incumbent Republican governor Sargent and Michael S. Dukakis, the Democratic challenger, had actively courted the gay vote after the primary, and Dukakis had won. In New York that week, at a panel held to mark the first anniversary of the National Gay Task Force, director Bruce Voeller talked about the "extraordinary fact of gay rights legislation in 15 cities," and noted that sodomy laws had been repealed in eight states in the five years since the Stonewall riots.

Elaine Noble asked to be assigned to the House Education Committee, and when she was sworn into office in January, the Democratic leadership gave her a desk at the back of the L-shaped Education Committee room, around the corner where she couldn't be seen, with the few Republicans then

* Cimino's letter was incorrect in one particular. In April of that year, in Ann Arbor, Michigan, Kathleen Kozachenko, a senior at the University of Michigan, a member of the radical, university-based Human Rights Party and a lesbian who had identified herself to the *Ann Arbor News* as a member of FIST (Feminists In Struggle Together) and GAWK (Gay Awareness Women's Kollective), won the Ward 2 city council seat in the city general election. Ward 2 was dominated by University of Michigan students. Kozachenko had only one opponent, a Democrat who was also a female student at UM, at the law school. Both of them favored amending the city charter to establish rent control and to make the punishment for possession of marijuana a $5 fine. The previous council member from Ward 2, Nancy Wechsler, had also been a member of the Human Rights Party, had also been a UM student and, with Jerry DeGrieck, another Human Rights Party student city councilman, had also revealed herself as homosexual—after winning office. So Kozachenko was not the first elected homosexual. But she was the first declared homosexual to win any election in the United States, and the last member of the Human Rights Party who would ever win a council seat in Ann Arbor. The power of student radicalism was fading fast, and Kozachenko won by only forty-three votes.

elected, and the black, scowling Mel King. But Noble had a mischievous sense of humor and she knew how to be one of the boys. When a colleague was condescending or grinned and told her she just hadn't met the right man yet, she would reach in her pocket and give him one of the little yellow cards she always carried. "You have just insulted a woman," it said. "In 30 seconds, your penis will fall off." House members had no personal staff assistants, but the Mayor's Office, in recognition of her singular status, assigned Elaine Noble a city hall employee to help answer phones four days a week.* There was a *Tomorrow* show producer on one line and the *Today* show on another. And calls came from San Francisco, Houston and Miami, from Mississippi, Louisiana and Illinois, from a lesbian in Boston whose estranged husband was trying to take their child away, and from homosexual men imprisoned in the South who said they were being beaten and raped. There wasn't anything she could do for any of them. It was the reality that Noble, amid the euphoria of election night, had feared. "The real horror," she said to a reporter that night, driving from one precinct to another, "will come *after winning*." Gay men and lesbians, she knew, would look to her for all the protection, comfort and representation they never had.

"I've got to say to some people, 'I'm not your Great Gay Hope,' " she had said in the car that night, staring into the future. "People are bound to be disappointed."

---

* One student, Candy Frank, persuaded Emerson to let her make working for Noble her senior field project. Noble gave her a button to wear that said "Do Not Assume I Am a Homosexual," and she and Loretta Lottman, the mayor's gift, began answering the phone.

16

MINNEAPOLIS:
THE COAT CHECK

Steve Endean checked coats each night at Sutton Place, the Twin Cities' main gay bar, and he worked the crowd there like a salesman. Winter is very long in Minnesota, and there are coats to be checked through most of the year. At a quarter a coat, it gave Endean spending money and the opportunity to get to know all the gay men who came into the bar, Democrats and Republicans alike. Endean was building a list and pitching his cause. He was the head of the Gay Rights Lobby, a one-man organization he had founded just months before. What the people who met him at Sutton Place saw was a grinning young man with pale skin, a mop of fine brown hair and the manic, challenging eyes of a terrier. And when he bit he never let go. He was from Minneapolis, from a nice, middle-class Roman Catholic family. His mother was a local television personality. His father was a businessman. He had been an altar boy, a Young Democrat and then a fraternity boy at the University of Minnesota. He was a fanatic about sports and politics. Steve Endean was obsessive about almost everything he did, and he was driven by a vision which had begun to form when he realized that he was homosexual. He had been sitting in a stall of the men's room in the West Bank Library of the University of Minnesota, studying for second-semester final exams one night three years before, when he became aware of a soft tapping beside him. He looked down to the side and saw beneath the partition, in the next stall, a foot, its toe raised and wagging slightly in the air, pointing in his direction. Furtively, terrified of discovery at any moment, Steve Endean had his first adult sexual experience in a library men's room at the University of Minnesota that spring night. For what seemed like a long time after the other man left, he stayed in the stall. Then he trudged back to his room in the Phi Gamma Delta House in a state of shame and black depression. He could find no information in the library to help him understand his feelings, but in a dirty-book store in downtown Minneapolis months later he came across a copy of Donald Webster Cory's *The Homosexual in America* and bought it. He sat down and wrote a letter, and gave his mother and father each a copy. It told them that he had always known he was different, and that now he understood why: he was a homosexual.

On the university campus that year, he discovered the new gay group, FREE, and its president, Jack Baker, and his idealistic boyfriend, Mike McConnell. Steve Endean traded his Roman Catholic guilt for a cause. In part because he was attracted to black men, he had long been emotionally involved in the civil rights movement, so, very quickly, he had come to see a connection between homosexual and racial oppression. Endean followed Baker's lead and became not just an activist but a recruiter, a fanatic early advocate of gay civil rights. Some nights he got stoned. He took to wearing a T-shirt with a gay rights slogan on it, and if people sneered, they were apt to regret it. "What the fuck do you mean by that?" he'd yell at them. It was calculated to teach them a lesson, to let *them* see how it felt to have to justify *their* behavior.

The Gay Rights Lobby was still an organization which existed mainly in Endean's head. There was no other staff, no budget and no actual office, and Endean regarded a night working the Sutton Place coat check as the place and time to let the crowd know that there was a gay political lobby group forming, and to get the names of as many men as possible on a list. Endean was funny and persistent. He had the infectious charm of a college kid with a serious cause. Men sometimes gave him 25 cents to watch their jackets and $10 to lobby the state, and sometimes they even gave up their names and addresses. On campus, Jack Baker had attracted broad student support and an aura of New Left celebrity as an openly gay law student–politician who then married his boyfriend in a real wedding with a real minister. The Minnesota Supreme Court, however, in the first such ruling by any state's highest court, had afterward declared that Minnesota law did not permit same-sex marriage, a decision which the U.S. Supreme Court let stand. And a federal appeals court had ruled against the couple, too, by upholding the University of Minnesota's action in denying a job to Michael McConnell. Baker had not let it rest. He was the president of the most populous student body on any university campus in the country, in one of the nation's most liberal states, at a time of unprecedented student activism, and when he lost in court, he became determined to force the issues into the political arena through the Democratic Party process.

Baker's first chance came in the 1972 Democratic-Farmer-Labor precinct caucuses. For the first time people at those gatherings—young men, mostly, activists from the University of Minnesota who had followed Jack Baker into the DFL Party—were openly declaring themselves gay and demanding that they be represented by a delegate at the Democratic National Convention in Miami. If women, blacks and American Indians could be represented, the homosexuals in the Minnesota party argued, why shouldn't homosexuals be represented, too? That June, at a Democratic-Farmer-Labor Party state convention enlivened by the sight of about two dozen delegates wearing lavender "DFL Gay Rights Caucus" T-shirts, a sympathetic party member gave up his place in the state delegation so that the gay caucus could send one of its own to the Democratic National Convention.

Baker and the gay caucus, with the help of liberal establishment groups like the Minnesota chapter of Americans for Democratic Action, also were able to force the adoption of a seven-point gay rights agenda as part of the state party's radical platform. It called for the legalization of marijuana, amnesty for draft resisters, the abolition of sodomy laws between consenting adults and the legalization of same-sex marriage (which was a burning issue only to Jack Baker and Mike McConnell). The party's candidates and office-holders went into shock. "There are a lot of crazy things in that platform, and I'm certainly not going to be associated with them," Hubert Humphrey, the founder of the modern DFL Party, said sternly. "I doubt many candidates can run on them." One candidate did. Balding, pudgy, intellectual, a bachelor at thirty-seven and a serious student of cultural policies and political science, Allan Spear was an associate professor at the University of Minnesota. He grew up in a Jewish family in a small town in Indiana. After earning a doctorate at Yale as a specialist in African-American history, he had become a popular figure in University of Minnesota and DFL politics, and he was running for the state Senate from a new district that included the university campus. Spear did not tell the voters what he had begun telling his friends and political allies in a series of heartfelt conversations earlier that year—that he was gay. He felt ready to come out as a homosexual or to run for public office, but not both. The DFL officials who knew him and who urged Spear to run for this new seat thought that would be just too much, even for an ultra-liberal university district. But Spear embraced the radical gay rights plank in the party's platform; he carried it into the university dormitories and student neighborhoods, and even pledged to introduce a same-sex marriage bill if elected. And like Barney Frank in Massachusetts, Allan Spear won.

That Spear could take radical positions and win 52 percent of the vote in the home district of the University of Minnesota came as no great shock. The shock was that the DFL Party and its radical gay rights stand swept the polls across Minnesota that November, capturing both houses of the legislature for the first time in its history. Steve Endean, surveying the results the next morning, realized that his skeleton of a lobbying group, which he had formally registered and renamed the Gay Rights Legislative Committee, now had the majority party as a potential new friend in power. And he had two specific goals: to repeal the state's sodomy law and to add homosexuals to the other groups protected from discrimination by Minnesota's existing human rights law.

Spring 1973

When the Minnesota legislature convened, Steve Endean had cut his hair, put on a white shirt, suit and tie, and gone to work in the labyrinth of halls and offices within the great white Beaux Arts pile of the Minnesota State House overlooking the city of St. Paul. Coached in the method and manners of legislative lobbying by Denis Wadley, the closeted gay president and chief lobbyist of the Minnesota Americans for Democratic Action, the twenty-four-year-old Endean wrote letters, handed out literature and made his case in a soft, respectful voice. His father, Robert Endean, a salesman and the owner of a vending machine business which would begin placing plastic cups sealed in cellophane in every Holiday Inn in America within a few years, watched this process in despair. "Steve, look at what you're doing: you're selling the hardest thing there is—an intangible!" his father said. "What are you going to get out of this? How are you going to make a living?" But making money was not something Steve Endean had ever cared about. What he wanted was legislation protecting homosexuals from discrimination in jobs, housing, public accommodations and public services, and the abolition of a section of law which made consenting oral and anal sex a crime. When he went to see individual legislators in the warren of offices under the capitol dome, lobbying for those causes, he sometimes provoked discomfort and open hostility. But when he saw people he had come to know at the coat check counter walking the halls of the State House, he cornered them.

Some members of that liberal legislature of 1973 were sympathetic to his goals and they weren't all Democrats. Four Republicans helped sponsor a bill to legalize sexual relations between consenting adults. And Endean also got a break that spring. Nicholas Coleman, the leader of the new DFL majority in the state Senate, represented a conservative, blue-collar, traditionally Roman Catholic section of St. Paul that also had an increasingly visible gay population. Coleman, an advertising and public relations executive, had separated from his wife and fallen in love with Deborah Howell, a reporter for the *Minneapolis Star.* Her brother, Ghent, was openly gay, and had talked to Coleman about what it was like growing up in San Antonio and how it felt now, living in a city as accepting as San Francisco. Their talks together had made a deep impression.

And so, early in the legislative session, the Irish Roman Catholic majority leader of the Minnesota Senate had introduced a bill that would protect homosexuals from certain forms of discrimination. Coleman knew that Allan Spear had made a campaign promise to do that himself, but he also knew that with a freshman senator like Spear as its sponsor, the bill—which Coleman did not expect to pass—would get no hearing at all. "They should have their rights respected like any other group," he said in the committee hearing. It was exhilarating to Endean, and a relief to Spear, who was still too nervous about his identity as a first-term, closeted gay senator to introduce a bill like that. But the bill's language grated on Jack Baker. He hated the word "homosexual." Raised as an orphan, Baker had an intense feeling and need for the traditional ties of love, commitment, family and career. Bound to Mike McConnell as he was, it offended him to be thought of simply as someone who wanted the right to have sex with men, which is what the word connoted to him. "Sex is only one aspect of our lives," he said. In a television interview two months earlier he had told David Susskind, "We're trying to legitimatize the concept of same-sex marriages, offer an alternative to the nuclear family, and educate people." Baker decided to oppose the bill. He sat at the witness table before a Senate Judiciary subcommittee in late April and told the senators that he was insulted by what they were trying to do. "The terminology is offensive. We have a right to expect our government to provide solutions to our problems in a manner that does not deprive us of our dignity as persons. . . . I consider that word [homosexual] insulting, equivalent to and on a par with the word 'cocksucker,' " Baker said.

Nick Coleman and the bill's other supporters looked grim; Endean and Spear were appalled. Endean didn't care about the bill's language. He cared about its effect, and to hurl the friendly effort of a powerful heterosexual lawmaker back in his face seemed crazy to him.

The bill passed in the subcommittee. When Coleman brought it up on the Senate floor, his proud and devoutly conservative parents happened to be in the gallery, watching their son the majority leader perform in the chamber below. But when they realized that he was proposing a bill to keep "persons of homosexual orientation" from being denied employment or fired from their jobs, their pride turned to horror and they walked out in fury.

Coleman and his measure got a more respectful treatment on the floor, though, as he expected, it did not pass. Baker's testimony had not hurt the bill, but it marked the end of his magnetic role in the gay rights movement in Minnesota. And it confirmed for Endean a private credo that would guide his life as a gay lobbyist. Trying to communicate through displays of self-righteous anger never works. It became part of his recruiting pitch to all the professional, white, mainstream gay men and lesbians whom he tried to draw into the cause. "If you want to have this movement ever become sane, you better get involved in it," he'd say, with a dead-serious glint in his eye. "Because if you don't, the crazies will run it."

Summer 1973

Steve Endean knew there was support to be had from Minnesota legislators. The DFL candidates had run away from the 1972 platform that included gay marriage, but once in office, in the off-election year, many were willing to consider other gay rights issues. The legislature's next session, in 1974, would be held in an election year, so there was no point in bringing the issue up again before 1975. But there were two other legislative bodies that Steve Endean could work on. City council elections were held in odd years. Candidates vied for their party's nominations in the spring, and then ran against each other in a general election in the fall.

Steve Endean began to talk quietly with candidates for city council seats in Minneapolis and St. Paul. He wanted Minneapolis to become the first major city in the nation to pass an ordinance forbidding discrimination against gays, and he wanted pledges of support from the candidates that they would vote for that ordinance if elected. And he had something to trade. Candidates needed willing bodies for door-to-door campaigning, and Endean could provide them his growing list of homosexuals, student activists and ADA members. Politely and persistently, he worked on the most likely candidates in the eleven Minneapolis council seat races. It was a liberal field, and some were willing to go along. Endean supplied teams of door knockers. He inspected them personally to make sure that the volunteers he drafted wore no DFL gay caucus buttons or T-shirts, or anything else that might mark them as homosexual. The candidates didn't want anyone to know that they were getting gay support. And Endean didn't want to alienate the voters by making it public.

When it came to lining up the St. Paul City Council, Endean called Allan Spear to ask him to contact friendly legislators from St. Paul. Spear called Coleman. He would do what he could, Coleman promised, and then turned the conversation around.

"By the way," he said to Spear, "I think it's time I asked you a question—are you gay yourself?"

Spear paused, then said he was.

"Are you thinking of coming out publicly?" Coleman asked.

As far as Allan Spear knew, there were no publicly elected, openly acknowledged homosexual state officials anywhere in the United States. He is the majority leader of the Senate, Allan Spear thought to himself, as he listened to Coleman. His job is to make sure he maintains his majority. What did Nick Coleman want him to say?

"I'm thinking about it. I haven't fully decided," Spear replied.

"Well, if you decide—I'm certainly not going to tell you one way or the other what you should do—but if you decide," Coleman said, "Debbie would sure like to have the story." And then, for the first time, he told Allan Spear how he'd been influenced by Debbie Howell's brother, Ghent, from San Francisco. "If you decide to do it," Coleman finished, "you'd better be in control. You better be sure who's doing the story."

For years, the Minneapolis and St. Paul city councils had been dominated by Republican majorities. But when the residents of the two cities went to the polls in November 1973 it was another Democratic sweep. The new, overwhelmingly Democratic Minneapolis City Council included five councilmen willing to sponsor an ordinance protecting homosexuals from discrimination in jobs and housing. Steve Endean did not want a repeat of Baker's performance before the Senate committee, so when the Minneapolis City Council met on March 28, 1974, the amendment it voted to adopt that day did not include the word "homosexual"; it stated that discrimination because of "affectional or sexual preference" would henceforth be unlawful in the city of Minneapolis. "Affectional or sexual preference" was defined in the amendment as "having or manifesting an emotional or physical attachment to another consenting person or persons, or having or manifesting a preference for such attachments." The wording had been suggested by a clinical psychologist Jack Baker had consulted.

The vote on the council was 10–0, with one member abstaining. The city had not been quick enough to be the first, as Endean had wanted. When Albert J. Hofstede, the new mayor, signed the bill, Minneapolis became the third major American city, after Washington, D.C. and Seattle, to provide broad protection for gays in jobs, housing and other rights. The smaller cities of Ann Arbor and East Lansing, Michigan, had also enacted ordinances. San Francisco prohibited discrimination in employment by companies doing business with the city. And in New York City, homosexuals in municipal jobs were protected by executive order. The new law had come about in Minneapolis, Mayor Hofstede said, only because of one person. "It never would have happened if it hadn't been for Stephen Endean."

The council's handling of the issue had been so calm, expeditious and unanimous—the subject was introduced, debated, voted on and signed into law in just five weeks—that it seemed almost scripted. Caught off guard perhaps, its natural opponents were not organized, and those who did appear before the council did not distinguish themselves. "This is what the

Communists want—and it has been definitely established that homosexuality is part of an international conspiracy to destroy our way of life," warned a leaflet distributed by the Reverend Joseph B. Headt. But the issue stirred no great public controversy, and the city's newspapers treated the bill's passage as something very close to routine. The *Minneapolis Star* put it in a modest story in the first section, on page 15:

"The Minneapolis City Council today amended its civil rights ordinance to protect the rights of homosexuals and selected a developer for the Lake-Nicollet Development District shopping center," the story began. It devoted four more paragraphs to the ordinance. The shopping center got seven.

The effect was immediate. In California, Minnesota and various places across the nation, AT&T and its regional Bell Telephone companies had been adamant in refusing to give work to homosexuals or to sell advertising space in the Yellow Pages to gay organizations. But within two weeks of the change in the city ordinance, the Northwestern Bell Telephone Company, which had asserted an absolute right not to employ homosexuals, quietly dropped its ban on hiring them, not only in Minneapolis, but in St. Paul, Duluth, Rochester and St. Cloud, too. "It is not entirely clear how widespread discrimination of this kind actually has been," the *Minneapolis Star* observed in an editorial, because most corporate hiring policies weren't known. But Northwestern Bell's decision to change its practice, and the new ordinance that forced it, "may be said to stem from the sexual revolution, although it also mirrors a rising demand for privacy. If nothing more, it is both humanitarian and good business, simply because it makes no sense to deny jobs to otherwise qualified people on the basis of what is now widely accepted as 'an attribute' or 'orientation.' "

Spring 1974

It was a scene of promise and contradiction. In the front of the room, at the Newman Center at the University of Minnesota, sat Steve Endean, state Senator Allan Spear and two guests flown in from different sides of the country—Dr. Howard Brown, chairman of the National Gay Task Force, and Phyllis Lyon of San Francisco. In the audience were perhaps 250 people, mostly gay men and lesbians from the Twin Cities and elsewhere in Minnesota, and one proud mother, Marilyn Endean. It was the ceremonial beginning of a new statewide organization, the Minnesota Committee for Gay Rights, formed to carry the campaign through the city of St. Paul and into the Minnesota legislature the next year, and it was meeting at the Roman Catholic student center, named for John Henry Newman, a cardinal of the church.

This was the brainstorm of McCarthy-and-McGovern-organizer-turned-gay activist Larry Bye, who had first encountered Jack Baker as a student at the University of Minnesota in 1969, and who had decided that the cause in Minnesota had now outgrown Steve Endean's Gay Rights Legislative Committee. It needed a new, bigger organization, one that could even pay Endean a salary. Spear had invited Howard Brown to come address the inaugural meeting of the new group. After Brown accepted, Bye suddenly realized that they had to have a prominent lesbian speaker as well, and he called, blind, to try to reach Phyllis Lyon and Del Martin in San Francisco. Lyon saw the invitation for the afterthought it was, but she had come, determined to make these men understand that if they wanted a natural alliance with lesbians, they had to treat them as equals.

Marilyn Endean was there because she and her son had made a deal. His sister was going to be married in a service at a Roman Catholic church, the symbol—to Steve Endean—of the guilt and repression he had felt for most of his life. His mother wanted him to be at the wedding. He wanted her to be at the Newman Center, to see what was happening in his life. His gay rights group would be the first statewide organization in the country, he told her, and the first to have a full-time, paid director. If she came to the meeting, he would go to his sister's wedding.

That the Roman Catholic Church would host both occasions was an illustration of the pervasive institutional presence of the church in the life of people in Minnesota—and also of a relationship that was being sorely tested by the burgeoning gay rights movement. The church, in the early and mid-'70s, was host to a strong, liberal social action theology. On many campuses, Newman Centers had nurtured the peace movement and other civil rights causes, and the chaplain of the center at the University of Minnesota, Father William Hunt, had engaged in friendly public dialogues about homosexuality with Jack Baker and with clerics of other faiths. Father Hunt stated at one point that homosexuality "was much more threatening to the Biblical world than to the contemporary world. In my opinion, the state could well recognize homosexual marriages without leading to the destruction of marriage, but I am not sure the Church should do the same."

Having seen how quickly the new Minneapolis City Council had moved to enact a gay rights ordinance, the archdiocese realized that the same thing could happen within sight of its own great stone cathedral at the city hall in St. Paul, and even at the Minnesota State House, before the church had made its position known. The rails, in fact, were already greased. On June 26 a bill to amend the St. Paul civil rights ordinance was introduced jointly by all seven council members, now members of the Democratic-Farmer-Labor Party. This time, vocal opposition came from businessmen's groups, the firefighters' union and the pastor of the Highland Park Baptist Church, who told council members that "a gay rights ordinance will provide moral pollution that will bury St Paul."

Six days later, on the eve of the meeting at which the council would vote, the Roman Catholic archbishop coadjutor sent a letter to St. Paul mayor Lawrence Cohen, along with an editorial from the newsletter of the Archdiocese of Philadelphia. The archbishop urged the council to vote against the gay rights amendment, "at least until further consideration can be given to this delicate issue." The editorial was more specific. It was concerned about homosexuals "obtaining sensitive positions in education or in the police." Traditional values might be undermined, it said, "if public approval were given to the profession of a deviant lifestyle." But Steve Endean had already gotten to Mayor Cohen, a liberal Jew, through Dennis Miller, who had been in charge of voter registration for McGovern in St. Paul in 1972. Miller's work had produced an influx of voters that helped Cohen win the St. Paul mayor's race the following year, and Miller, at Endean's urging, had now enlisted Cohen's support.

The archdiocese found its effort opposed by the city's main Roman Catholic politician, too. Nick Coleman appeared before the St. Paul City Council to appeal for the passage of the ordinance, dismissing the warnings about the fallout of the bill from its opponents as "utterly preposterous and largely ignorant." When the St. Paul City Council voted on July 16, 1974, the amendment passed 5–1, with one member absent.

St. Paul, the capital of Minnesota and seat of the archdiocese, had become a fortress of homosexual civil rights. The church was not pleased. The city "named for the great Apostle to the Gentiles," the archdiocesan newspaper, *The Catholic Bulletin,* lamented in an editorial, had given its "official blessing to a way of life based on abnormal, unnatural and still illegal sex acts." The result, it suggested, "may well be to encourage borderline cases of homosexuality to adopt overt lifestyles which promise only greater difficulties on the human condition."

Allan Spear called Elaine Noble in Boston in the fall of 1974, after reading of her election to the Massachusetts House of Representatives. The barrier had been broken, and it made him think some more about Nick Coleman's suggestion. That fall election in Minnesota had swept another wave of new DFL members into the state House of Representatives, where they were now a majority, and Spear dared to think that in spring 1975 it might really be possible to repeal the sodomy law and add a gay clause to the state civil rights statute. Spear went to New York City late that November, to the second conference of the Gay Academic Union, a new group of graduate students and professors formed by people like Martin Duberman and Charlotte Bunch, who had come together to lay the foundation of what would become a new field: gay studies. Spear, a university professor by training, found this concept of a new area of minority scholarship exciting, and decided he was ready to go public.

He called Deborah Howell at the *Minneapolis Star.* They met over lunch.

"When do you think this will run?" he asked as they said goodbye. Probably next week, she said.

"Where would I find it?" he asked.

She looked at him oddly. "On the front page," she replied.

On the second Monday in December, the *Minneapolis Star* carried Howell's story on page one, telling the voting public what many people in the Minnesota State House already knew. "State Sen. Allan Spear Declares He's Homosexual," the headline said. "I wanted to stop the tittering," it quoted Spear. "There's nothing I'm ashamed of. Nobody should have to talk about it on back stairways." He had been haunted by the memory of remaining silent while others in the state Senate debated the gay rights bill in 1973. And he felt an obligation to other homosexuals to go public. "It's important to gay people struggling with their own identities," he said. "They need all kinds of role models."

Allan Spear stayed at home that Monday in nervous solitude, with Steve Endean there for comfort in case he needed it. He was relieved at the number of supportive phone calls he got, from Governor Wendell Anderson on down. His own reelection was still two years away; the only thing that seemed left to do now was to change the state laws.

Spring 1975

For decades after, for the rest of some of their lives, they would remember how absolutely bright and possible the future of gay life in Minnesota looked in the spring of 1975. Public opinion polls showed broad support for protecting the basic civil rights of homosexuals. The DFL Party had developed a huge majority in the state House of Representatives, more than a hundred of its 134 members, and many of them were new, younger and more progressive than the incumbents they had replaced. The Senate majority leader, Nick Coleman, was their greatest supporter. They had learned, from Steve Endean's tactics in Minneapolis and St. Paul, the effectiveness of negotiating with politicians in private. They had the editorial backing of the major newspapers in Minneapolis and St. Paul, the support of Lutheran and other local religious leaders, the endorsement of civic leaders, of state agencies like the

Department of Corrections, and of various university offices and government boards. And they had the political example of the Twin Cities, which had adopted these very protections without any evident political trauma. Always, for the rest of his life as a lobbyist, Steve Endean would be faced with the task of convincing officeholders that they could vote for gay rights without losing the next election, and he used each victory, large or small, as a model to persuade the next set of politicians confronted by the question. As the gay rights issue loomed on the Minnesota legislative calendar, every member of the legislature received a copy of a letter that Endean had solicited, signed by eight of the Minneapolis council's eleven members.

"Despite concern expressed by some opponents at the time we passed our ordinance, we have experienced virtually no difficulty," it read. " . . . It is our belief that the deterrent effect on discrimination that our ordinance created was a positive step forward in human rights."

But for all their care, all their planning and all their good luck in being able to ride the political currents of their place and time, they did not have the support of all their own people. They did not have with them the ones whom Steve Endean called "the crazies." The difference between Jack Baker/Mike McConnell and Steve Endean, in their approach to dealing with the established political system, was the difference between purity and pragmatism. Endean was, he liked to say, "a committed incrementalist." A lobbyist "is called a lobbyist," he said, "because you have to spend a lot of time waiting out in the lobby." Baker's policy of no compromise made sense only if you had the votes. It didn't work if you were trying to *get* the votes. "While Jack has done much for the gay community in the past, his present positions and campaign are nothing more than an expensive exercise in ego-gratification that could cost the gay community," Endean had written in a letter published in *The Advocate* at the end of 1973.

But Baker and McConnell had been there first and they had their own set of demands. "As far as I'm concerned, gays have a place in party politics—but we are gays first, Republicans and Democrats thereafter," Baker declared. "When the inevitable conflict between party interests and gay interests emerges, we *must not* be willing to compromise our own interests, no matter how temporarily." That spring of 1975, Jack Baker had as allies a clutch of provocateurs who loved conflict and guerrilla theater. The bill that Nick Coleman introduced in the Senate this time was the same one passed in the Twin Cities, and within days the *Minneapolis Tribune* published an editorial urging that it be passed. But Baker's group wanted more. In subcommittee hearings on the House bill, Thomas Higgins, a Baker follower, talked passionately about the rights of gays to marry and adopt children, about how important it was that transvestites and transsexuals be protected by this legislation, and about the need for compulsory gay sex education in the schools. His testimony left the subcommittee in an uproar.

To reassure its members, some of whom were feeling constituent pressure in rural and heavily Roman Catholic districts—and some of whom were left with the impression that the bill as written would protect men who showed up for work in dresses and who used the ladies' room—Endean and the subcommittee chairman decided that they had better drop the public service and accommodations sections of the bill. When it squeaked out of the House Judiciary Committee by a vote of 12–10, another Baker ally, Tim Campbell, rose to denounce the committee for watering down the bill. He was thrown out of the room with three other protesters. Spear and Endean warned that these tactics would kill the bill; Baker rejected their caution as "a smokescreen." The position his group was taking, Baker said, "is simply a stand on equality. I agree that you should take what you can get in chunks. But we are not willing to take a step backward from what we already have in the Twin Cities."

Endean tried to make the best of it; he persuaded the *Minnesota Star* and *Minneapolis Tribune* to carry editorials suggesting that a gay rights bill so moderate that it made gay activists angry ought to be moderate enough to pass the legislature. But he could not get Jack Baker and his guerrillas to compromise. Tim Campbell chained himself to a railing at the State House and began to fast in protest. "It's a problem for a man in a dress," he said of the bill the committee had passed out. "We wanted the bill to include affectional preference in gender identity. It was meant to be broad enough to include a sissy boy, a butch girl, a cross dresser, or a transsexual." Campbell wrote a draft of the kind of bill he had in mind, and asked Allan Spear and Steve Endean if they would agree to have the bill offered. "Absolutely not," Spear said. And so Campbell, Baker and the others convinced a liberal Republican state representative, Arne Carlson (later the governor of Minnesota), to offer it as an amendment on the floor of the House.

Tim Campbell and a chorus of men in makeup and dresses poured into the halls of the Minnesota State House on the day of the House debate, invading a ladies' room, terrifying some of the women in it, and filling rows in the public gallery overlooking the House of Representatives as Representative Carlson rose to offer the Campbell legislation protecting transvestites and transsexuals. Carlson was the minority whip in the House, a man known for his sensitivity to the rights of minority groups, and he delivered a heartfelt and dignified speech urging his colleagues to support the rights of such creatures as sat in the gallery that day. He spoke of the minds of women trapped in the bodies of men, while the men in rouge and bonnets looked down from their seats above. The Democratic sponsor of the more conservative gay rights bill in the House—the one without protections for transvestites and transsexuals—had to call a vote to kill the more liberal Republican amendment in order to give the original bill a chance of passing.

Steve Endean's careful, conservative, consensus-building plan had turned into a circus. After two hours of debate that night, May 8, the House of Representatives killed the gay rights bill by a vote of 68–50. It was one of the great frustrations of Endean's life. In the months after the vote Endean thought about suicide, as he did whenever he found himself at some professional impasse. He was manically energetic and also easily depressed, and when he found himself blocked and anxious, he turned compulsively to sex. Jack Baker went home to Mike McConnell, but Steve Endean went to the baths in Minneapolis and drowned his sorrow in strange bodies.

17

ORDINARY THINGS

May 1975, Washington, D.C.

From the first time Bella Abzug ran for public office in 1970, setting her sights on a Manhattan congressional district that encompassed the liberals of Greenwich Village, the reformers of the Upper West Side and the more moderate voters of the Lower East Side, she had been a supporter of gay rights—or at least, a candidate pursuing gay votes. Her congressional campaigns brought her to the GAA Firehouse; she found herself on the stage of the Continental Baths in the winter and the dock at Fire Island Pines in the summer, stops way off the regular New York campaign circuit. And whenever anyone asked her about gay rights, Abzug would exclaim: "I have this in my platform!" She had gay people on her staff, and gay people in her life, and was the kind of New York personality—brassy and not a little campy, with her broad hats and an outlook on life which she described as figuring out every morning what she would do to "them" before they did it to her—that struck a chord among many of her new friends in New York's gay community. She was the rare politician who had fun on the job, so she laughed uproariously when her gay supporters pointed out that perhaps she should not have asserted at a press conference that homosexuals had as much right to enjoy "the fruits of society" as anyone else. "My *faygelehs!*" she'd exclaim, using a Yiddish phrase to celebrate her new army of supporters, and her *faygelehs* returned the favor, writing her checks, working the streets and, of course, remembering to vote on election day. "Bella was part of a dream," Vito Russo wrote after interviewing her for *The Advocate,* recalling the first time he saw Abzug show up at a very early GAA meeting at a church on Ninth Avenue, marching down the center aisle under the shadow of a huge purple hat. "Politicians had double-talked us for years and here was this woman coming to us!" There were not many politicians like Abzug anywhere in the early 1970s; not in New York, and most certainly not on Capitol Hill.

Abzug was drawn to what might be politely called fringe issues, though she would argue that in most cases she just had hopped on the train before everyone else. She was an early opponent of the war in Vietnam, one of the first members of Congress to call for Richard M. Nixon's impeachment and one of the first supporters of the Equal Rights Amendment. All of this just re-inforced her national image as the loud and liberal representative from Green-wich Village. Her identification with those particular subjects—the war, impeachment, abortion rights—might have seemed extreme in most of the country, but it helped her on election day in Manhattan. Still, Abzug was con-vinced that her position on one of those issues—gay rights—was dangerous. She found herself torn between the political reality of needing gay votes to win and the backlash she believed she risked—particularly in the more moderate Lower East Side patch of her district—by being seen as too closely associated with homosexual rights. And when Bella Abzug initially introduced the first gay civil rights bill in Congress in May 1974, responding to pressure from her gay constituents, she did it without a press conference, without a formal an-nouncement and without any notice to gay groups—not even the National Gay Task Force, which had listed introduction of a gay rights bill in Congress as one of its founding goals. Bruce Voeller learned of the bill from a homosex-ual on Abzug's staff, and he could barely hide his irritation. Voeller's plan had been to introduce the bill with some fanfare, a press conference that would have, not incidentally, introduced the Task Force to official Washington as well. Winning approval of a gay rights bill was, of course, out of the question, but the introduction of legislation was the kind of symbolic moment the Task Force was looking for, an affirmation of its leaders and their mainstream sensi-bilities. "Frankly," Voeller told *The Advocate,* "we were a bit upset to learn that the bill had been dropped into the hopper at a time which we feel may be pre-mature—especially since there was apparently no consultation with gay orga-nizations in advance." Publicly, Voeller was politic: he called Abzug "a good friend of gays," and suggested she might better have worked with gay activists and given them time to orchestrate a more impressive introduction. Privately, he was furious. He had asked Abzug when she was going to introduce a gay rights bill every time he had seen her in the past year. It seemed obvious now that she had slipped in the bill just so she could say she had already done it the next time she was asked.

The last thing Voeller wanted was for Abzug—the lampooned Greenwich Village liberal with the floppy hats—to be identified as the main congressional supporter of gay rights. There was no way this bill could receive significant support if it was known as an Abzug bill. And Voeller was appalled by how sloppy he found the legislation, once he read it. By Voeller's reading, it neglected to address discrimination in private employment. Voeller was convinced that Abzug neither expected nor wanted much attention paid to this bill.

Abzug shrugged off Voeller's complaints. He was naive, she said; this was always going to be a long-term project, and her critics just weren't sophisticated enough to understand that. The early versions of the legislation—what it said, how it said it, and how it was introduced—didn't much matter since it was not about to become law. Abzug considered her gay rights bill a vehicle for education, not for legislation. "I think my effort as a federal legislator should be applauded, not criticized," she said brusquely. When Voeller turned up at her office with Sidney Abbott and Nath Rockhill to discuss the next step—they wanted Abzug to draft a more complete bill and introduce it at a full-fledged press conference—Abzug cut him off: "I don't want to talk to you." Gesturing to Abbott and Rockhill, she said: "Why don't you let them do the talking here." Still, Voeller was not alone in doubting Abzug's true commitment: Charlotte Bunch, who was enjoying the relatively ordered life of a member of the Task Force board after her tumultuous months with The Furies in Washington, decided that Abzug was not really that strong a supporter of gay rights, no matter what she said. There was, for all the gumption it took to introduce a bill like this, an obvious reluctance, another reminder for Task Force members—if they needed it—of the essential unpopularity of their cause.

It would not be until March 25, 1975, ten months after Abzug quietly introduced her bill, that Voeller got what he wanted: a press conference, in the Gold Room of the Rayburn Office Building on Capitol Hill, with members of Congress, representatives of the National Gay Task Force, and leaders of the National Organization for Women, the American Civil Liberties Union, the American Psychological Association and the American Psychiatric Association. Voeller settled in behind a table filled with microphones, sitting at the left elbow of Representative Edward Koch of New York. Next to Koch was Abzug, and to her right was Nathalie Rockhill, the Task Force's legislative director. They announced that twenty-four members of Congress were sponsoring HR 5452, the "Civil Rights Amendment of 1975," which added the phrase "affectional or sexual preference" to the list of protected classes in the landmark 1964 Civil Rights Act, barring discrimination in employment, housing, public accommodations and public education. Voeller was pleased with the accomplishment, particularly considering how green he, Nathalie Rockhill and Jean O'Leary, who had joined the Task Force, had been when they started less than a year ago. They had sought help from more experienced hands at the ACLU and homosexual legislative aides on the Hill, who offered pointers, albeit on the condition that they be spared any public credit. The Task Force learned, for example, that it was easier to recruit members of Congress to support a bill if they knew they would be on a list of names. The Task Force learned to focus on the House, not the Senate, since its members represented smaller districts and were more susceptible to local pressure. And, borrowing on the lessons from Minneapolis, they, too, avoided words like "homosexual," deciding that the bill should be written to protect people based on "affectional or sexual preference." The use of the word "affectional" would, Voeller decided, make clear that "gays are whole, caring people" and dispel the notion of their " 'obsessive' hypersexuality."

Voeller was so happy at the pageantry of the Task Force's first Washington press conference, he was able to overlook the fact that the coalition of sponsors wasn't as broad as he had once hoped: seventeen of the twenty-four came from New York or California, with two from Massachusetts (including a young representative, Gerry Studds, who eight years later would acknowledge his homosexuality), and one each from Minnesota, Colorado, Washington, D.C., Maryland and Pennsylvania. Voeller was also able to overlook the fact that the one thing missing at his press conference was the press. It might have seemed like an historic event to the members of the Task Force, but it was the kind of thing that happened dozens of time each week in Washington. In this case, it amounted to little more than a show of support for a bill that had no sponsor in the Senate and was unlikely to even make it to the House floor for a vote. Most of the reporters around the Rayburn Office Building were, as Voeller later remembered it, across the hall, where Henry Kissinger had decided to hold an impromptu press conference.

Voeller remembered the empty room as just "a small regret in a day which will be remembered vividly." Still, considering the fact that the driving force behind introducing a gay rights bill had been presenting to the American public a new image of homosexual organizing—framed by the symbols of democracy—it was hard not to see the absence of mainstream press coverage as anything but disappointing.

By the time Voeller took his place next to Bella Abzug for the press conference in Washington, the National Gay Task Force had, despite the bureaucratic disputes and wrangling that shadowed its creation and would come to outlast its founders, become a dominant force in gay organizing. One reason for this was that with the Vietnam War over, activism of all sorts was at an ebb, and that included gay activism: the stage was empty. The Task Force, by design, was never meant to be a membership organization. It staged no zaps and hardly any rallies. Beyond writing a check or reading a newsletter, it demanded little of its members. The Task Force really had no choice in this regard. The emergence of the mainstream gay movement, in the form of the Task Force, had come as grassroots movements everywhere were withering. A few years before, the GAA could turn out five hundred people on a good night; the Task Force was arguably not much bigger than the list of names on its letterhead. Voeller began to see evidence of this as he tried to raise money for his new organization. He ran smack into an indifferent community that, barely five years after Stonewall, was not feeling particularly threatened. They, particularly the men, were interested less in politics and more in play. This public emergence of what had once been a decidedly renegade culture was one of the products of this new liberation, and Voeller began to view it as competition. He knew firsthand how much money homosexuals—or at least homosexual men—had to spend on having a good time: on discos, summer resorts, clothes, interior decoration, travel, alcohol and recreational drugs. That just made him all the more resentful of the rejections that greeted his requests for funds. "Where is the support for the gay movement?" Voeller wrote in an article describing his frustration in 1979. Men, he said, thought nothing of spending "an average of $6,300 apiece" for a share in a rental property on Fire Island Pines. "If we consider that there are some 900 housing units ('shares') leased to gays each summer, that's $5,700,000 on rent—a figure doubled if we include drugs, travel, liquor and entertainment." In contrast, he noted, the Task Force's annual budget barely broke $200,000. And while Voeller's numbers were exaggerated—$6,300 would buy a share in an extraordinarily opulent house—his point was not. Leonard Matlovich, an air force sergeant discharged after admitting his homosexuality, joined Voeller in throwing a champagne party on the beach at Fire Island to finance a court challenge to his dismissal. Hundreds of men showed up to drink champagne and shake hands with Matlovich. The guests were asked to make pledges and sign a mailing list. Voeller suspected something might be awry when he looked at the list and saw it included among the signatories John Maynard Keynes (who had died in 1946) and Rock Hudson (who was not there). And when the Task Force sent out the mailing, half the envelopes were returned marked address unknown: in the end, two men wrote checks, for a total of $85. Of the 120 gay bars in the New York metropolitan area, only three offered their premises for Task Force fundraisers. The owner of one of the large discotheques, which was a direct descendant of the GAA's Saturday night Firehouse dances, informed Voeller he couldn't use the club's space for a fundraiser, even on one of its dark nights, because it might tip off the public at large that this was a gay club and scare away business from closeted patrons. And when NGTF staged successful dances at the relatively small Eagle's Nest on Sunday nights, Voeller discovered that the other clubs—realizing that gay men liked to go out on Sunday nights, too—responded by opening for business, competing with the Task Force. Voeller concluded that his best sources for money were not homosexuals but sympathetic heterosexuals.

"All across the country, there are signs that the gay movement is beginning to fizzle out," Arthur Evans wrote after a gay rights bill was defeated for a fourth time in a New York City Council committee. "Average gays are bored by demonstrations and rhetoric. When I recently visited New York, an old movement friend told me, you couldn't pay people to take a leaflet on Christopher Street." He blamed it on the times. "Name any movement and you'll hear the same lament: We're slowing down and our people are growing apathetic. The United States as a whole in the 1970s has entered a period of retrenchment and reaction. . . . In the gay movement, it's now almost impossible to get large numbers of people together for a mass demonstration." Turnouts at Stonewall anniversary parades, as good a measure of gay activism as any then, dropped across the country. In New York, writer George Whitmore noted how little enthusiasm he found at the Stonewall Parade of 1975, and how divided the community still appeared. Lesbian Feminist Liberation had refused to march at all that year to protest the involvement of bar owners in organizing it. "What can you say about a crowd that can hiss Bruce Voeller as easily as it can boo the Catholic Church, for instance?" Whitmore wrote in *The Advocate*, adding: "New York has become politically vacuous, I'm afraid, and this has been accentuated by the fact that the movement has been doing a disappearing act. Groups are not simply re-forming, they're dwindling." There is a gay community in New York, he wrote, but the more he watched it, "the more I realized it has less to do with the movement per se than any other time since before Stonewall."

18

CITIZEN GOODSTEIN

January 1975, Los Angeles

The climate was changing across the country: it was, as the National Gay Task Force suggested, the middle class's turn. And though, by the start of 1975, Arthur Evans had put his protest days behind him—he had opened a Volkswagen repair shop south of Market Street in San Francisco named The Buggery—he, too, was about to fall victim to the shifting politics of gay liberation. Evans had started writing for *The Advocate* in 1972, but by 1975, he found the newspaper tedious—stories would wander on and on, and each new page presented readers with a mass of gray type. Nevertheless, *The Advocate* was still the only national gay newspaper chronicling the gay liberation movement, often in great detail.

The *Los Angeles Advocate* had been born in 1966, fittingly under the shadow of the Los Angeles police vice squad. Its first editor, Dick Michaels, then forty and a staffer at the Los Angeles Bureau of Chemical and Engineering News, was one of forty men arrested during a bar raid on lewd conduct charges. It cost him $600, and "I hadn't done a damn thing," as he later said. He joined PRIDE (Personal Rights in Defense and Education), a small gay rights organization in Los Angeles, and he and his twenty-six-year-old lover, Bill Rand, turned the organization's newsletter into a newspaper in the summer of 1967, renaming it the *Los Angeles Advocate*. (Its name was changed again at the start of 1970 to just *The Advocate,* as the publishers sought to expand the newspaper's appeal beyond California.) They typed copy in columns on a $175 IBM electric typewriter, used press type for headlines and laid out the newspaper during weekend marathons around their dining-room table. The newspaper's prospects for survival, they noted in their first editorial, "would be rated by experienced journalists at somewhere around zero." The two men kept their day jobs. The first edition, twelve pages and five hundred copies, was printed in August 1967 on a press in the basement of ABC network headquarters in Los Angeles, where Bill Rand worked.

It was for a long time a renegade operation. No newspaper distributor would circulate a newspaper like the *Los Angeles Advocate,* and the two owners managed to attract just $27 in advertising in the first edition, most of it from bar owners, and most of it billed but never paid. Dick Michaels insisted they charge 25 cents a copy for the paper because he didn't want the *Los Angeles Advocate* to get mixed in with the piles of giveaways that were stacked up on cigarette machines and ledges in gay bars. "People don't respect anything they get for free," he said. The paper was sold at bars and, eventually, from street boxes, until gradually some newspaper stands put it on their racks. By the end of 1973, *The Advocate* had an audited circulation of 37,828, a third of its readers in Los Angeles, and 97 percent of them male—typically college graduates in their mid-thirties, affluent men who lived alone and lived well. They had money, and they were not the kind of readers, an *Advocate* brochure for advertisers noted, who spent their paychecks on "diaper services, baby food, Little League uniforms, orthodontists or a wife's clothes."

The editors of *The Advocate* were more conservative than Arthur Evans, but they were producing a paper devoted to the homosexual rights movement, and they gladly printed Evans's columns, in which he relived old victories, lecturing Bruce Voeller at the National Gay Task Force, tangling with such difficult questions as the role of transvestites in the movement. He wrote exactly as he spoke—lucid, blunt, provocative and a little breathless. And he got paid for his efforts: $25 for each column published, usually twice a month. *The Advocate* was sold in November 1974 to a former Wall Street broker from New York, David B. Goodstein, who now lived in San Francisco. Evans didn't know anything about David Goodstein, but he was not unhappy at the news: Evans thought the paper was designed to appeal to closeted, and apolitical white men, and he hoped the new owner would nudge the paper in a more serious direction.

The new *Advocate* regime announced itself to Arthur Evans in the form of a thick envelope containing a stack of his unpublished articles, together with a typed letter of two sentences from John Preston, Goodstein's new editor:

"Your column duplicates material planned for future editions of the *Advocate*. I'm returning the enclosed manuscripts, which I take to be submissions under the previous editorship."

Arthur Evans sat down at his typewriter, red and angry, and pounded out a short retort to Preston, and a longer letter to the new publisher. He reminded Goodstein that he had written for *The Advocate* for two years, and expressed how "deeply offended" he was at the curt letter from Preston. "Has my column been losing the interest of readers? Is my viewpoint inconsistent with the new regime?" he asked. "I'm mature enough to be told the truth and not have my intelligence insulted."

Goodstein responded one week later:

Dear Mr. Evans,
Thank you for your letter of Jan. 16th. Do not read more into Mr. Preston's letter than necessary. Two sentences suffice. It is not even desirable, from your point of view as well as ours, that there be explanations of decisions that are made.

Arthur Evans, the philosophy graduate student and Stonewall activist, had signed his letter to Goodstein with a flame: "Yours for gay liberation." David Goodstein, the businessman, signed his to Evans with a cordial: "Very truly yours."

Evans had not noticed Goodstein's quiet but persistent emergence in San Francisco homosexual organizing over the past four years. He had not taken note of how Goodstein used his personal fortune to break into mainstream gay politics, or read the Goodstein letters and columns published in California gay newspapers through the 1970s. Evans had not even noticed the veiled warning the outgoing *Advocate* editors offered to readers in their farewell editorial: "We have been assured by the new publisher that he, too, appreciates this newspaper's place in the movement and that he will not deemphasize news coverage. . . . Remember that you are the real bosses of any newspaper. If you don't like what's going on, just yell like blazes." The concern signaled by the departing editors was grounded. David B. Goodstein was not quite like anyone the gay liberation movement had seen before. He was forty-two years old, a product not of the working class or of the middle class, but of the upper class. His tastes ran to breeding show horses, which he rode most mornings, and collecting art, including a Rembrandt hung over his bed. He enjoyed his Italian sports car and his crisp business suits, accented with ties displaying prints of galloping horses, his wrists and fingers glistening with

gold and jade. Goodstein had studied economics at Cornell and law at Columbia, and used his earnings as a criminal lawyer to co-found a wildly prof-
itable Wall Street firm called Compufund, which used a computer to manage
its portfolio of stock transactions. Goodstein moved to San Francisco in 1971
to manage the portfolio of a bank which then, he claimed, fired him upon discovering his homosexuality. Goodstein's termination set him adrift in San
Francisco, angry, rich and—since he had sold both Compufund and his New
York brownstone—with plenty of time on his hands. He turned his furies and
fortune toward becoming a gay power in an increasingly homosexual city.
Goodstein's political and newspaper career was thus launched in the spirit of
retribution. He told his friends that he lived by one credo: "Don't get mad—
get even."

Goodstein used $10,000 of his fortune to create the Whitman-Radclyffe
Foundation (named for Walt Whitman and Radclyffe Hall), working on behalf of gay legal, social and political issues. In January 1972 he formed a second organization, the Committee for Sexual Law Reform, to rally support
behind Assemblyman Willie Brown's foundering effort to repeal the state's
sodomy law. These two organizations gave him the opportunity to hire some of
San Francisco's better-known gay activists, including Jim Foster, named executive director of the Whitman-Radclyffe Foundation. That gave Foster a salary
and the time to work at his Alice B. Toklas Democratic Club. It gave Goodstein the ability to brag—which he did—that he had some of the state's most
influential gay leaders on his personal payroll. Still, David Goodstein was always restless and looking to expand his influence. "Being anonymous,"
Goodstein once said, "is like being dead." And when Bill Rand and Dick
Michaels contacted him to help find a buyer for *The Advocate* in late 1974,
Goodstein saw a way to establish himself as one of the preeminent leaders of
the homosexual movement. All it took was $300,000 in cash and long-term
notes.

Goodstein was, in many ways, not unlike the men and women who had
formed the National Gay Task Force in New York thirteen months earlier. He
shared their distaste for the radicals who had enjoyed such a public profile in
the years after Stonewall, like Morris Kight in Los Angeles and Jim Fouratt in
New York. But he was different, in a fundamental way, from Task Force leaders like Bruce Voeller, Ronald Gold and Nathalie Rockhill, who had all
started at the GAA, and for whom the pull of the street was always there.
Goodstein had no such conflicts. As far as he was concerned, homosexual
radicals were as much of a threat to gay liberation as the most conservative
heterosexuals in the nation. When his Committee for Sexual Law Reform
met for its second annual conference, in February 1973, in West Hollywood,
he faced a rebellious contingent led by Morris Kight and Jeanne Cordova,
who considered Goodstein's goal of repealing the sodomy law a waste of time

and energy. And when the organizational vote was held by Goodstein's committee, Kight and Cordova had managed to wrangle a majority of a new eight-
member interim board of directors that would be running Goodstein's
organization for the next year. It was just a paper victory: Goodstein and Jim
Foster made clear they would rather abandon the enterprise than cede control
to people like Kight. But Kight's attacks on Goodstein were brutal. He called
Whitman-Radclyffe a "basically corrupt organization" whose activities had
been directed by a "small cabal of elitists." Goodstein's lasting hatred of Morris Kight was born that night.

Four months later, in June, Goodstein and a group of other gay leaders,
including Jim Foster, Troy Perry, Jo Daly and Del Martin, were lobbying for
the California bill to legalize homosexual acts between consenting adults.
Only six of the forty senators they contacted met with them, and twenty said
outright they would never meet with homosexual lobbyists. Goodstein wrote a
report for California gay newspapers that put the blame on this debacle not on
the legislators but on homosexuals themselves. "They regard us as freaks," he
said of the lawmakers he had met. "Most of the behavior of gay liberationists
they have seen in the media confirms the stereotypes they have been taught to
perceive." Goodstein said that homosexual activists needed to change their
behavior. "Our spokesmen must be willing and able to argue intelligently, rationally and quietly. They must wear Establishment clothes. They must not
confirm stereotypes." Goodstein singled out for criticism the "radicals who affect bizarre costumes. They insist that they represent all gay people. Their behavior, their zaps, and their picket lines reinforce bigotry where it exists and
frighten already timid legislators away from our cause. I do not naively believe
that these people will desist in their behavior, but the rest of us must make
sure that they are not the only or even the most frequent spokespersons."

What is more, Goodstein said, the time had come to deal with groups in
the homosexual community that "hold back our progress": in particular, the
men who hunted for sex in public rest rooms, whose cause had been made by
many of the early gay liberation groups. "A very small minority of gay men is
permitting the police of California to run roughshod over the rights of the rest
of us. Either we as a community face up to this responsibility or the oppression will continue indefinitely." Public sex, Goodstein wrote later, was behavior that "honestly, and perhaps even rationally, disturbs many straight and gay
people. Public sexual conduct makes it more difficult for us to promote legal
changes and gives ammunition to our enemies, especially the police." These
remarks would prove to be as representative of his thinking as anything David
Goodstein would say for the rest of his life.

The new publisher of *The Advocate* was different in another way, too.
David Goodstein was ugly, or so he thought. He had a gnarled body, twisted

by scoliosis. He was paunchy, with a doughy face, which he sometimes hid with a thick, black beard, and he had slicked brown-black hair that his friends assumed came out of a bottle, though no one dared to ask. Goodstein could make for a startling first impression, his high-pitched voice barking from a five-foot-five-inch, hunched frame. He tried to compensate for his looks with, first, his money, intelligence and wit, but finally, with withering displays of temper. With little warning, Goodstein's face would twist into a black scowl, his skin would flush crimson red, his eyes would bulge, he would gather his hands into balls of rage, pounding them on the glass table in the *Advocate* conference room. He would bellow profanities as spittle foamed at the sides of his mouth. For those who got to know him and like him, this behavior became less terrifying as it became more familiar. Part of it was defensive. Goodstein saw disagreement as a personal attack. It was also the orchestrated tantrum of a man who wanted to get his way. Goodstein tended to let down his guard with people who were not afraid of him or his outbursts. He would refer to himself as a "troll." He would allow these people to be in his office at what was for him a private moment—when he was being yanked back and upside down by the humming electric gravity inversion machine in his office, physical therapy to straighten the twists out of his curved spine. He would tell these people stories about his childhood that were perhaps designed to make people forgive his outbursts. He had never fit in, he would say; he was short, chubby, effeminate and bespectacled as a boy growing up in Denver, so taunted by schoolmates that he would take a different route home each day. Things were no better at home, where he would hide under the porch. Goodstein said he was more afraid of his own family than he was of the schoolmates who taunted him.

In presenting himself to the world, as in the first issue of his *Advocate*, Goodstein focused on a different formative chapter of his life, his encounter with the bank that later fired him. It was an act of "overt discrimination," he said in an *Advocate* profile, which pictured its new publisher posing with one of his horses. His experience, Goodstein said, should put to rest the notion that "wealthy gay people are either immune to discrimination or refuse to acknowledge its presence." He would always recount that "shattering experience" when he told his life story—amazed that something like that could happen to someone of his position and intellect. "I thought, if they can do that to me," he said, "what can they do to some poor devil without any clout?"

Evans wasn't the only one who found himself out of a job when Goodstein took over. There was a sweep of the activists whose views had littered the pages of *The Advocate* and who, in Goodstein's opinion, were largely responsible for what was wrong with the gay movement in 1975. Goodstein's *Advocate* reflected and encouraged the gay rights movement's swing away from the streets and back to mainstream efforts, the focus before the riot at the Stonewall. "This issue begins a new era for gay people," proclaimed the cover of Goodstein's first issue, which featured a head shot of a gay porn star, Cal Culver. Within a few issues, there was a new front-page slogan, "Touching your lifestyle." Gone were the reports of the L.A. bar raids, the plodding accounts of the latest conference of homosexual activists. The new layout was a far cry from *The Advocate* that had come off Bill Rand and Dick Michaels's dining-room table. It emphasized celebrity interviews, vacations, fashion and fun. A rare serious note was struck with a spate of reports on the rise of venereal disease, a product of promiscuity, a topic that fascinated Goodstein. But other news was relegated to short dispatches at the front of the newspaper. "The regular media is running more gay news, so that frees us of the responsibility," said Preston, a bearded former seminary student who had founded Gay House in Minneapolis before being recruited by Goodstein. The assertion could be disproved by even a cursory glance through the major city dailies of 1975.*

There was one other new feature, "Opening Space," a column by David B. Goodstein, who wrote at first about the importance of homosexuals coming out, holding himself up as an example.† But Goodstein's columns became increasingly provocative. He complained about the bad image gay revolutionaries were giving the movement, lectured on the lessons to be drawn from Machiavelli's *The Prince*, a book that he quoted reverentially around the office, attacked the "flamboyant exhibitionists" and "media freaks" who, he said, cared only about getting their names in the newspapers and faces on television. And he chided wealthy homosexuals who did not support gay causes. "If the competent chickens of our community don't accept responsibility for its condition, they have no one but themselves to blame that their egg hatches out a vulture." The columns ended on the same, often discordant note: "Enjoy the ADVOCATE!" it said, followed by the crunched, scrawled signature, "D. B. Goodstein."

At his first staff meeting, Goodstein announced his newspaper would no longer publish the names of people he considered the enemies of the movement. Morris Kight was at the top of that list. Goodstein also included Bruce Voeller, though that was less a condemnation of Voeller's politics than a reflection of Goodstein's fear of competition with the head of the only national gay

---

* Newspapers were running comparatively more gay news than they had before, but a reading of the *New York Times, Los Angeles Times, San Francisco Chronicle* and *Minneapolis Star* shows that no newspaper, not surprisingly, was providing the coverage of gay issues that *The Advocate* had before David Goodstein purchased it.

† Despite Goodstein's urging that his readers come out, his newspaper always promised subscribers that their names would, under no circumstances, be shared with anyone else, and *The Advocate* came in a plain wrapper, with a return address of L.P. Inc.

rights organization in the country. Goodstein moved *The Advocate* to San Mateo, twenty-five miles south of San Francisco. The new office was closer to his home. But Goodstein made clear that the move was mostly intended to insulate his staff from the pressure of radicals who lived in San Francisco and L.A. "We were under a virtual state of siege by gay leaders" in southern California, he complained to the *Wall Street Journal* in 1975. Discussing the move with his staff, Goodstein said: "If the liberation fairies want to protest something we write, they'd never come down to San Mateo." He placed a sign on his desk: "Grand Fairy."

Goodstein hired a journalism graduate student from Oregon, a talented and aggressive reporter named Randy Shilts. Shilts had been openly homosexual at the University of Oregon in Eugene—his slogan when he ran for student body president was, "Come out for Shilts"—and he ignored the advice of a professor who told him that no mainstream newspaper would employ an openly gay man. Shilts had been an Eagle Scout growing up in Aurora, Illinois, a young conservative who campaigned for Goldwater as a teenager. Now, he had long bushy hair and a mustache, and divided his time in Oregon between newspaper work and gay activism. It was clear to the people at *The Advocate,* meeting Shilts for the first time, that his driving interest was not really gay liberation but proving his professor wrong and making it as a mainstream journalist. Shilts's first stories were written with the kind of distinctive voice that most journalists don't display until well into their careers, and before long Goodstein was pushing Shilts to investigate the people the publisher saw as enemies, pressing story ideas that would often lead to loud arguments. Shilts resisted Goodstein's demands for exposés, arguing for traditional newspaper standards of objectivity and fairness. As it was, Shilts was writing for a newspaper whose soft-core advertisements and explicitly sexual personals embarrassed him. This was his first full-time job after college, and he didn't dare send a copy of his newspaper to his parents in Illinois.

This conflict between Shilts and Goodstein would lead to Shilts's departure, but not before he attempted to produce what Goodstein wanted most of all: a negative story about Morris Kight. Goodstein directed Shilts to buy a six-pack of beer and bring it along for the interview of the aging activist. ("He's an alcoholic," Goodstein told Shilts of Kight, an assertion that by all accounts was completely unfounded.) Shilts did not bring beer, but Kight figured out what was going on as Shilts made his way down his long list of questions. Do you pay taxes? How do you support yourself? Do you consider yourself a socialist? Shilts left feeling slightly soiled, he later said, and convinced that there was no story here. No Kight "exposé" ever appeared in *The Advocate,* but Kight never forgave either Shilts or Goodstein. Kight considered Goodstein a homophobe and elitist, and would, even twenty years later, derisively mangle his name as "GOOZ-steen."

September 1975, Seattle

Charles F. Brydon had not considered the television cameras when he invited David Goodstein to speak before the Dorian Group in Seattle, an organization of professional homosexuals—lawyers, insurance brokers, clerks, midlevel government bureaucrats—that Brydon, an insurance executive, had put together as a luncheon group just before Christmas 1974. It was sort of a Rotary Club for homosexuals. In just nine months it had become the largest homosexual group in the Pacific Northwest, dining with the mayor one week and a candidate for governor the next. Brydon saw Goodstein as an intriguing character with an irresistible story—the former Wall Street executive with the conservative notions about gay liberation—which is why he invited him to come speak. But Brydon was unprepared for the call from a television station which wanted to send over a news crew. Brydon, the highest-profile gay leader in Seattle, had an arrangement with the local reporters then that he be identified only as a "Seattle insurance executive." And Brydon was bolder than most Dorian Group members, many of whom almost revolted the first time Brydon turned up at one of their private luncheons with a city hall commissioner. The Dorian Group was nonthreatening and nonconfrontational, designed to help its participants slip "over the sill of the closet," as Brydon put it.

So Brydon negotiated a deal: the television crew could not enter until everyone was inside and seated. Shortly after 7 p.m., as the television crew came down the back steps of the restaurant and the room turned tense, Brydon took the microphone. "If anyone objects to the presence of the [television cameras]," he said, "then they will leave." The crew, he said, would aim their cameras at the podium and David Goodstein, showing the audience from behind. "Does anybody, anybody whatsoever object?" Brydon asked. Not a voice was raised. Brydon then introduced Goodstein.

Something about the speech Goodstein proceeded to deliver moved Brydon in an unexpected way. We have moved quite a distance, Brydon thought as Goodstein offered encouragement to the aspirations of this new organization. And that night Charles Brydon allowed his face to appear on a Seattle television station.

By day, Brydon was the thirty-six-year-old field office manager for an insurance consortium, and he looked the part: conservative in dress and spirit, quiet-spoken and earnest, the kind of man who might use the word "dialogue" as a verb. His thick black mustache, which filled his upper lip and curled down around the sides of his mouth, was his only discreet nod to the style becoming popular in San Francisco's Castro district. Brydon and David Goodstein had similar views of the world, and Randy Shilts was assigned in

1975 to produce a long and admiring story which held Brydon and the Dorian Group up as the future of gay organizing in America. Brydon had put together the Dorian Group as an alternative to the bars and to the radical gay activism that existed in Seattle when he moved there from San Francisco in 1974. It started small, with twelve people, but by the time Brydon convinced Mayor Wes Uhlman to come to lunch nearly eighty people filled every seat at Hounds and Foxes. Flattered by the simple fact that the mayor had agreed to visit them, they tossed him the gentlest of questions, and followed up the meal with contributions and work on his successful campaign. The lunches fit neatly into Charlie Brydon's view of homosexual politicking. The best way to promote acceptance of homosexuals was to have society meet people like himself, a homosexual who would sooner put on a suit and sell insurance policies. Brydon had grown up in the suburbs of New Jersey, attended a military prep school and, after college, served twenty months as a captain with the First Cavalry Division in Vietnam. He saw his constituency as the "non-radical, conservative, establishment people who have never felt represented by any gay organization." And he was proud of his background. "I am incredibly middle-class," Brydon explained to *The Advocate* in 1978. "I find nothing wrong with that. The term is viewed as sort of an epithet by some gay people, but I think the majority of gay people are out of the middle class, and they have the right to have their perspective articulated." The Dorian Group never staged demonstrations, and it never took over buildings; it was in many ways a Mattachine Society for the 1970s, if slightly more aggressive and high-profile. It sought to work with and inside the establishment. Dick Leitsch had loved the way he could write letters to Mayor Lindsay; now in Seattle, Charlie Brydon took it a step further, referring to the mayor as Wes. He loved to tell the story of the afternoon he was talking with Wes in his top-floor office as a gay demonstration was proceeding in full fury on the street. Their business concluded, the mayor and Brydon walked onto the porch outside the mayor's office to look at the demonstrators below. The protesters, catching sight of Brydon and the mayor, responded with a roar of anger. Brydon never cared what other homosexual activists thought of him. Like Bruce Voeller's National Gay Task Force, the Dorian Group was not intended to be democratic, or even a participatory organization.

March 1976, Chicago

David Goodstein celebrated the anniversary of his first year at *The Advocate* by devoting an entire page of the January 14, 1976, issue to his "Opening Space" column. He recounted how the "movement people" had responded to the changes he brought to *The Advocate* with a "barrage of adverse criticism." His critics, Goodstein said, "never asked us whether we had a reason for making the changes we made. They didn't give us a chance." *The Advocate*, which in its anniversary edition devoted ten pages to discussing winter vacation spots and another seven pages to an interview with Lily Tomlin, had become, Goodstein asserted, *"the* place to find well-written news and features about gay people. We believe our first editorial judgments have been vindicated. . . ."

If Goodstein had made a calculated attempt to tone down his rhetoric—and by all indications, he at least attempted that in his first year—then that ended with this "Opening Space" column. "One must be deaf and blind not to notice that most gay people actively dislike most of the people speaking publicly on their behalf," Goodstein declared. "They are fearful of the image being portrayed." The majority of gay organizations, Goodstein said, are "dominated by people who took them over from more responsible persons through hysterical attacks on their integrity. These are the spokespeople whom our majority shuns. The straight media pay attention to them because they confirm the stereotypes they're looking for. Our people resent them for the same reason. They appear unemployable, unkempt and neurotic to the point of megalomania." The silent gay majority, Goodstein said, rejects lesbian separatism. Its members feel no kinship with Marxism or socialism. They see the constant infighting more as "signs of egomania than anything else." The state of the homosexual rights movement, Goodstein proclaimed, was such that whenever a respectable group of homosexuals attempted to forge a serious organization, "the neurotic types take the floor to harangue about oppression, persecution, personal hurt, fascism, sexism, or whatever.

"Our people are hiding in anger and distress from their alleged leaders," Goodstein declared. "It is up to anyone purporting to lead to pay attention to his or her followers. As it is, it's damned lonely on the front lines!" With that, Goodstein ended with his cheerful signature sign-off: "Enjoy the ADVOCATE!"

The column was so abrasive and confrontational, even for David Goodstein, that six published *Advocate* writers wrote a letter of protest.* "It is Goodstein himself who actively dislikes gay people. He seems to have raised a number of complex questions that do deserve examination in order merely to offer his own biased prescription for what the movement should be—strictly reformist civil rights efforts under the leadership of an 'enlightened' few." Goodstein shrugged off their criticism in a published response: "Love the fact

---

* They were David Brill, Arnie Kantrowitz, Vito Russo, George Whitmore, Allen Young and Dave Aikens. They were all well known as either activists or writers; Russo, for example, was building a following for his intelligent film reviews and celebrity interviews, and Kantrowitz for his candid if seamy views of New York's underground gay life.

my comments stirred you up. Love the fact that you all are writing for the *Advocate*. Sorry you missed my point. I must be a worse writer than any of you."

As it turned out, Goodstein was not looking for another sparring match. He had bigger plans. Goodstein still did not like the direction the gay movement was heading, and he would use the power of *The Advocate*—the most influential gay newspaper in America—to change it. Three weeks after that "Opening Space" column, Goodstein announced that there would be an Advocate conference to discuss the future of the homosexual rights movement. The goal would be to create "a new organization . . . to lobby Congress for full civil rights for gay people in these United States," and ways, clearly, to replace the radicals—the "spoilers"—with responsible activists who reflected Goodstein's views.

The Advocate Invitational Conference was held on the last Saturday of March 1976. The name of the conference and its location spoke volumes. This was, first and foremost, an *invitational* conference, and Goodstein's guests were mostly activists who shared his vision of working in the system. Goodstein had learned a lesson from his confrontation with Kight and Cordova in Los Angeles. Goodstein was paying for this conference, down to the airfare and hotel rooms for many of the guests. "Because we are intent on accomplishing the narrowly defined goal of this conference," Goodstein said, "we have invited gay people who, we believe, agree with the basic objectives and who can help raise the money to make them a reality." To make sure he did not lose control of this conference, Goodstein refused to provide the list of invitees in advance, protecting his guests from pressure or harassment from the militants who were not invited, and held the conference in a city with a comparatively small gay activist community, Chicago, to make it that much more difficult for the militants from New York, Los Angeles and San Francisco to attend. As an extra precaution, Goodstein put the convention at a hotel at O'Hare Airport, fifteen miles northwest of Chicago's downtown. And finally, Goodstein posted uniformed guards at the door, who were instructed to allow in only those people wearing the mandatory blue name tags.

Since it was David Goodstein's conference, he established the ground rules, and for Goodstein, Robert's Rules of Order would not be enough. Each of the sixty-two participants, representing almost two dozen organizations from fourteen states, were issued in advance a document headlined "Complete Text of the Agenda, Position Papers and Ground Rules for *The Advocate* Invitational Conference."

"There is a lot of work to accomplish in one day," the document said. "We simply have to move along." All meetings would "begin on time," reflecting Goodstein's complaint that homosexuals thought nothing of being tardy when dealing with other homosexuals. The *Advocate* staff would take phone messages for participants and distribute them at one of the two scheduled ten-minute breaks or at lunch. The agenda would be "strictly adhered to"; there would be "no binding votes on matters" not on the agenda, and the only arguments that would be entertained would be those that had been submitted in advance and in writing. Talking with seatmates would be "vigorously discouraged." Participants would be permitted to speak only when recognized by the chair—Goodstein—and remarks would be limited to two minutes. "It is our experience," Goodstein wrote, "that everything worth saying can be stated in two minutes or less."

Even those familiar with Goodstein's career were appalled. "The autocratic San Mateo millionaire has gone too far," wrote *Newswest,* a Los Angeles gay weekly that was founded, in part, to protest Goodstein's purchase of *The Advocate.* "He has cooked up a dangerously vicious plan, which if successful, would silence any gay person whose ideas differ from his own." The uproar gave some of the community's most respected leaders pause. Troy Perry of the Metropolitan Community Church issued a press release defending his decision to attend. But the church, Perry promised, would "not be a party to any move that will seek to keep any gay person from exercising their constitutional rights as to seeking redress to their grievances from public officials, their right to speak to the press or their right to seek change in this country." The furor seemed to please Goodstein. The publisher announced in a column on the eve of the conference that he would henceforth refer to all his opponents as obstructionists. Writing in the style of a dictionary entry (a device he used frequently, in everything from his columns to his holiday greeting cards),* Goodstein continued: "My definition of gay obstructionist is: Noun. A rare breed of homosexual of either sex who talks a lot about many things but accomplishes nothing. It fails at every endeavor it attempts, always blaming someone else for its failure and its state of being ostracized. Its plumage run the gamut from funky drab through business gray and clerical black to outrageous drag so visual identification is impossible. . . . Syn.: Spoiler, pain in the ass."

Barbara Gittings had never been to a place like the Hyatt Regency O'Hare, where the rooms opened out onto balconies that hugged the inside walls of a towering atrium. *The Advocate* Invitational Conference convened in the Philippine Air Line Room in the morning and the Air France Room in the afternoon. They were sharing the hall with the regional midwest competition of the Sweet Adelines, women barbershop ensembles there with their husbands and children. The sweet harmonic tones of women singing together

---

* For example, his 1979 greeting card had this message: "I cannot imagine a greater privilege than the one you have given me in 1979 by allowing me to have a relationship with you. May 1980 see each of us expand knowing who we are out of our relationships." It was followed by the dictionary entries for the words "imagine," "privilege," "relationship," "know," and "love."

drifted above the droning speeches in conference, and Gittings would leave the room to listen, tickled by the contrast between her crowd and these women. She loved coming around a corner and encountering groups of women in matching outfits—Swiss Alps yodelers on one corridor, waitresses on another. The Adelines apparently took note of their fellow conventioneers as well.

"Who are those people with the blue name tags?" one of the Sweet Adelines inquired of a friend as the elevator whooshed up the atrium.

"They're here for some kind of homosexual meeting."

"See," the first woman said. "I told you this is a classy hotel."

Everyone loved that story, and it provided some welcome relief to a weekend that certainly needed it. Goodstein had prepared fifteen separate resolutions for approval, and printed them with supporting arguments, dissenting arguments and alternative amendments sent to him in advance. ("We realize the people we invited are busy," Goodstein said. "We want the meeting to run smoothly and be free of unnecessary debate.") The call to order was at 9:30 a.m. Saturday and Goodstein intended to have all the work done by mid-afternoon. The room was cramped and stuffy, an environment that seemed designed to encourage people to hurry up. Goodstein opened by acknowledging that he had provoked anger. But he said he was not there to oversee another gay liberation conference which degenerated into squabbles and accomplished nothing. "I don't intend to say much today, If I can help it," he said that morning, a promise he would not keep.

Goodstein's proposal for a new Washington-based lobbying organization enjoyed nominal support, though it was an unstated attack on the National Gay Task Force, whose executive director, Bruce Voeller, was in attendance. Voeller knew the conference was aimed at knocking out the Task Force, which in its first twenty-nine months had been successful at winning mainstream press attention, and enjoyed a higher profile than Goodstein did. Goodstein, who had left New York for California six years before, did not believe that a national gay rights group could work out of Manhattan—a point that was not hard to dispute, given that Voeller and other Task Force members had to borrow the desks of the Metropolitan Community Church lobbying offices across the street from the Capitol whenever they wanted to lobby Congress. The Task Force, Goodstein said, was too spread out; better that it cede the responsibility of lobbying Congress to this new group than seek to open up a Washington branch. Voeller, realizing that he'd been outmaneuvered, made a preemptive bid to protect turf and dignity by conceding the need for a new organization. "We've got plenty on our plate; it's damn foolish to sit around quarreling," he said. "Go ahead, do it."

The creation of the new group—at Frank Kameny's suggestion, it would be called the Gay Rights National Lobby—turned out to be Goodstein's only clear victory that weekend. He had packed the meeting and was running it from the podium with a script he had written, but in the end Goodstein still couldn't have his way. Gary Aldridge, an openly gay administrative assistant to Senator Alan Cranston, offered a keynote speech laced with attacks on his host. He paid tribute to the people "who took to the streets" to launch the modern gay rights movement, most of whom had not made Goodstein's guest list, and suggested that any movement would die "at the first breath of autocracy." When Goodstein invited the editor of *Oui* magazine to be the last-minute luncheon speaker to discuss gay newspapers, most of the women walked out, enraged that he would give a platform to a man they considered a pornographer. Goodstein openly expressed his disgust at the walkout: "Women lost a golden opportunity to confront someone they allege is a male chauvinist pig. Maybe they both would have learned something."

The conference supported Goodstein's idea for a new organization, but by a narrow margin of only 33–26. He lost on most of the votes having to do with the details. Goodstein wanted it known by an "innocuous" title so that wealthy homosexuals would feel comfortable writing checks to support it. "Particularly," he wrote, "the name should not include the word 'gay' or 'homosexual' in it." To homosexual liberationists who had spent much of their adult lives fighting for openness, Goodstein's notion seemed almost insulting. "We just simply cannot afford to be doing our lobbying in a closety fashion," said Frank Kameny. The conference then required that the new group's name include the word "gay" or "homosexual." Goodstein wanted it run by a seven-member board of directors. By a lopsided 49–6 vote, the conference took Bruce Voeller's suggestion that it be run by a thirty-member board; a board, as Voeller knew from his own constant squabbles with his own thirty-member National Gay Task Force board, that would be resistant to manipulation by Goodstein. Voeller also suggested that the board be half male, half female, and that the organization have two executive directors, one man and one woman. Arthur Warner, the veteran homophile leader, complained that efficiency was being sacrificed on the altar of women's rights, which drew a rebuke from Jean O'Leary, who was now co-director with Voeller of the Task Force. "You cannot separate the issue of sexism from gay rights," she said. "Sexism is at the root of gay oppression." The conference supported that idea, too. Goodstein wanted the board selected only by those who paid $50 or more in dues. A representative from NOW called this "elitist," and the conference overruled Goodstein again, lowering the membership cost to $15 and allowing any member to vote. Goodstein's most complete repudiation came when he tried to formalize his exclusion of "radicals." The new organization, he argued, must "disassociate itself from groups or individuals unwilling or uninterested in working" with the present government. "The nature of a lobbying office is law reform, not revolution." It was essential to aggressively cut off the revolutionaries, he said, or "we are at the mercy of our most fringe spoilers." That idea was tabled. Goodstein also proposed establishing teams of gay activists in every community to "make certain that gay spoilers cannot dominate the media and create a one-sided image of gay people" back home. "Sometimes your cost need only be for some clothes and grooming aids to find an upfront spokesperson who behaves responsibly and deals with the concerns of civil rights instead of spouting jargon and anger," he asserted. That idea was killed outright.

The meeting ended with Goodstein under attack. One member of the National Organization for Women said Goodstein's sentiments "border on the hysterical and seem irresponsible," adding: "I resent this kind of attitude, even when it is not directed at me." In the audience, Adam DeBaugh, the lobbyist for the Metropolitan Community Church in Washington, concluded that Goodstein's weekend had highlighted the very characteristics of the gay political community that Goodstein had intended to avoid: rancor, bitterness and clumsy power struggles. It fell to DeBaugh to write a candid account of the weekend's events, in a press release MCC put out that week. "*The Advocate*'s publisher, David B. Goodstein, was forced by his invited conferees to open up the process of creating a national gay civil rights lobbying effort." Taking note of Goodstein's attacks on gay leaders in *The Advocate,* DeBaugh reported that conference attendees "openly condemned this approach and urged that all people in all segments of the movements" be allowed to join the projected civil rights lobbying organization.

David Goodstein's verdict on his own conference came a month later, and he delivered it not in the pages of *The Advocate* but in an "exclusive interview" with the *Gay Community News,* the Boston newspaper controlled by the "radical" men and women Goodstein despised. The conference had neglected to deal with a most important problem, Goodstein said. "It's evident to me that closeted people are not going to be part of the movement as long as they feel that spoilers are playing a major role. It's absolutely clear that that is their perception. We have to find a way to make them feel secure." Then Goodstein announced he would not provide financial support to the new organization he had conceived if he deemed it to be "irresponsible." And when the five people designated at the conference, all men and all from Washington, D.C., returned home to begin incorporating the Gay Rights National Lobby, it turned out to be the start of an extraordinarily difficult and lean three years. David Goodstein had returned to San Mateo, turning his attention and wallet back to his newspaper.

19

BROTHERS
AND SISTERS

June 1976, New York

By the time Bruce Voeller and Jean O'Leary of the National Gay Task Force attended the Advocate Invitational Conference in Chicago, they had shared a small office for seven months and discovered that they got along quite well. That came as a surprise to more than a few people, starting with Bruce Voeller and Jean O'Leary. Three years earlier O'Leary had led women out of New York's Gay Activists Alliance in a display of separatism that Voeller never understood or accepted. Their easy working relationship now stood out at the Chicago conference—indeed, it stood out in a movement notable for the continuing friction between men and women. It was Voeller and O'Leary who convinced the conference that the new D.C. organization founded in Chicago should have a board of directors made up of an equal number of men and women, and be run by two executive directors, one male and one female. The Task Force already had a co-sexual board, as it was called in those days. But it had just one executive director—Bruce Voeller. O'Leary was second in command. "Are we going to practice what we preach?" O'Leary asked Voeller as they flew back to New York. It was an obvious question, and when the Task Force board met that June, two weeks before the seventh annual Gay Pride Parade, Voeller moved that O'Leary be named co-executive director.

The story of Bruce Voeller and Jean O'Leary was, perhaps, inspiring, but it was not particularly representative of the gay rights movement in the mid-1970s, or even of the Task Force itself. The changing composition of the movement had, in some cases, slapped a polite veneer on relations between gay men and lesbians. But the sores were far from healed. The Gay Academic Union in New York, for example, was wracked by divisions between men and women from its very first meeting in 1973. Women, who did not have an equal number of members, demanded equal voice in governing the organization, insisting that the first goal of the group, which had been founded to deal with gay issues in an academic setting, should be to "combat oppression against women." Arnie Kantrowitz, the Staten Island English professor and former GAA member, argued, "There are organizations in this country for equality of women. There are no organizations for the equality of gay people in academia. Gay people should be at the top of the list." When women suggested that his perspective was skewed because he was middle-class, white and male, Kantrowitz responded by noting that he had declared himself homosexual at work in 1970, to his obvious disadvantage. "I do not get a promotion at work because I am openly gay. I don't consider that privilege. I consider that I have chosen to join the ranks of the oppressed." He was booed.

Discrimination against women in men's bars remained as widespread as ever: from Los Angeles to Washington to New York, club bar owners barred entry to anyone wearing open-toed shoes, which in practice meant anyone who was a woman. The hostility often went both ways. In the 1976 New York gay parade, one woman carried a placard that proclaimed, "Cocksucking causes cancer," which struck some men as insulting. Lesbian bars also barred men, gay or straight, from coming in the door. When some men complained about that, one lesbian activist, Renee Hanover, a lawyer in Chicago, explained that it was acceptable for lesbian bars to be exclusive because there were so many more gay male bars. "Men ought to imagine how they would feel if women had 92 places to choose from, but men only had four or five," Hanover said.

In truth, the peace that O'Leary and Voeller found did not extend much beyond their own friendship. But O'Leary's official position as Voeller's equal at the Task Force, following the vote in Chicago, was evidence that institutionally, at least, women were being incorporated into the gay rights movement as never before.

The executive board of the Task Force met on weekends, so out-of-town members could enjoy a few free days in New York City, courtesy of the organization. For the men, this was the gay male equivalent of Spring Break: New York's gay nightlife in the mid-1970s had a variety unsurpassed anywhere else in the United States. The bars were humming, and so were the sex clubs and baths. The Continental Baths gave free admission and a locker to anyone with a valid NGTF membership card.

But the women board members did not go out on Friday nights. They went to Brooklyn, to the home of Betty Powell, a Task Force co-chair and a black lesbian, a rare breed in the almost all-white homosexual organizing world, and her lover, Virginia Apuzzo. There, over a roasted chicken cooked by Apuzzo, followed by mugs of steaming tea, they discussed feminism and lesbianism, and scripted the weekend's meetings, right down to which woman would make which resolution.

The Women's Caucus of the National Gay Task Force had been created at one of the Task Force's first meetings, after Sidney Abbott's proposal that the board be comprised equally of men and women—the same issue that had created such dissension at the Gay Academic Union—was attacked by men who brought with them traditional views on the relations of the sexes and on quotas. Why should the board impose a quota on itself? Frank Kameny asked. Why draw another distinction between men and women? Why are we confusing the gay rights movement with feminism? Abbott explained again and again how the homosexual rights movement was white and male, and hostile to anyone who was not. "Bullshit it is," Ronald Gold responded: The door was open to women and minorities, and they had just chosen not to walk through it. (Jean O'Leary came to consider Gold perhaps the single most sexist gay man she had ever encountered.) Bruce Voeller supported the idea of equal representation, in no small part because he had watched male-female divisions roil the Gay Academic Union and the Gay Activists Alliance, and did not want the same thing to happen again. When the board approved the plan, Gold quit the board in protest.

Over the intervening two years, the issue of how women fit in at the Task Force was never fully settled. Many men on the board—from parts of the country where the lesbian-feminist movement was largely unfamiliar—dismissed the women's demands for representation as tokenism, and they could not understand what Jean O'Leary meant when she described the absence of "lesbian visibility." "Why not just let whoever's best take it, and if it's a man or woman what difference does it make?" asked Gary Van Ooteghem, the former county treasurer from Houston. Charlie Brydon, the Dorian Group founder from Seattle, suggested that there just weren't that many women interested in the homosexual rights movement, and they shouldn't try to force it.

The Women's Caucus was a success, in no small part because of those Friday evening dinners at Betty Powell's house. At its instigation, the Task Force recruited women at feminist gatherings across the country, and began to lobby for the Equal Rights Amendment and the legalization of abortion with the vigor that had been reserved for passing gay rights laws and repealing sodomy legislation. It worked to assure lesbian influence on women's organizations, particularly NOW.

The Women's Caucus also fought what it considered destructive forces within the homosexual rights movement. And one of its first targets was David Goodstein's *Advocate,* which was frequently the subject of complaint at Betty Powell's home. It ignored lesbian news, the women said, and they found themselves constantly embarrassed by a newspaper that Powell reminded her colleagues was, for better or worse, the paper of record for the homosexual community. "It doesn't represent me as a lesbian," Powell complained as she thumbed through a copy, scrunching up her face at the stories and pictures about men and sex. (The women felt *The Advocate* fed the worst public images of homosexuality, which was precisely the criticism Goodstein had leveled against the newspaper before he bought it.) But Goodstein was a businessman, *The Advocate*'s readership was overwhelmingly male, and everything about the newspaper reflected that. The newspaper conducted a readers' poll after Goodstein took over in 1975. Of two thousand questionnaires collected, only six were signed by women.

The Women's Caucus met with Goodstein to discuss its objections, and at first it seemed to have some influence. Goodstein wrote sympathetic columns about the political difficulties lesbians faced, and he publicly wrestled with how his newspaper should cover that community. "My observations during years of experience in the gay movement are that gay women are even more closeted than gay men," he said. "They circulate in very small groups; women's bars are far fewer in number and size." Goodstein began to talk about the need to expand coverage of lesbian and women's issues. He hired Jeanne Cordova to write an opinion column, despite their past differences. There was a noticeable increase in stories on lesbian issues, enough so a few men wrote to complain, letters which Goodstein published as testimony to the changes he had made: "I've just about had it with the *Advocate,*" one man from Tuscaloosa, Alabama, wrote. "What's wrong with your news anyway? All I ever see is photos and stories about women. Who cares about them anyway?"

Still, Goodstein would go only so far, and the line he drew was a reminder of the basic division that had emerged back when the Gay Liberation Front was debating the volume of music at its dances in New York City in 1969 and 1970. Goodstein might devote more space to lesbian issues, but he wasn't about to cut back on the pictures of nude men, or the articles about men and sex—which was, in the end, what sold newspapers. Sex ads were the margin of profit for an *Advocate* almost completely devoid of mainstream advertising. It was a matter of money, but it was also a matter of politics. Goodstein would always remember what Jim Foster once told him: "David, never forget one thing: What this movement is about is fucking." It was a remark Goodstein repeated throughout his life, as uncomfortable as he sometimes seemed with its manifestation.

Goodstein tried to appease his women critics by moving the explicit personal and sex service ads in his newspaper to a separate removable section which, as he told his readers, "allows you to keep all or part of the *Advocate* on your coffee table." But that was all he would do. He finally made clear to Betty Powell that he thought the women were behaving prudishly: that they didn't understand male sexuality, and they were demanding lesbian freedom while "stepping on our necks." Rita Mae Brown, who by this time was spending most of her time writing, away from the gay rights and feminist movement, described Goodstein as one of her closest friends, yet she became convinced that he loathed women.

The question of language went to the heart of the division between men and women. The battle over basic descriptive phrases—was it "sexual *orientation*" or "sexual *preference*"?—had first been joined on the psychiatric front, but now came to highlight the different way men and women viewed homosexuality in the mid-1970s. The dispute was sometimes lightly referred to as the "Chorientation Debate" (a combination of the words "choice" and "orientation"), but it proved to be as divisive an issue as any that came between the sexes. The women of the Task Force favored "sexual preference," believing that in the press and with political leaders, this terminology served to play down the biological aspect of sexuality. From this point of view, sexual relations were voluntary, an affirmative decision, and not a reaction to an instinctual surge. This was particularly the case for a number of women who came to lesbianism through feminism; they were often called political lesbians, women who had left relationships with men for women, arguably as much a political statement as a sexual one.

The men on the board believed that "sexual *orientation*" more accurately indicated their view that homosexuality was not a matter of choice, and that homosexuals had as little say over their sexuality as black people had about their color. The women were largely uncomfortable with this view of homosexuality because it was reduced to its most physical level, but the men argued that it was politically the smarter way to go. If homosexuality was a choice, then opponents of gay rights had a powerful argument: Just choose to be heterosexual, the assertion gays had been fighting for years. This was a regular subject for discussion at the dinners at the home of Betty Powell and Virginia Apuzzo, but it was much more than an academic debate. In Washington, Bella Abzug awaited a Task Force decision on wording for the latest version of her gay rights bill. The men lost the argument; Abzug's legislation in 1975 used the phrase "affectional or sexual preference" for the first time. The bill read that way each time it was introduced until February 8, 1979, when the phrase, in deference to the men's argument, was changed to "affectional or sexual orientation."

Each success of the Women's Caucus stirred resentment among the men, some of whom privately derided the women as "The Brooklyn Mafia."

After Task Force meetings adjourned, men and women would often break up into two groups—men in one, women in the other—and head out to dinner. The women enjoyed each other's company. But some of the men came to see those dinners as proof of the irreconcilable rupture between the sexes. Gary Van Ooteghem considered many of the women on the board "hateful" and complained of "their bitterness." Van Ooteghem could not tolerate, for example, the way the women cut him off when he said "men" instead of people.

Before long, even Bruce Voeller became a lightning rod for resentment among the women on the board. He could be high-handed and authoritarian with everyone, regardless of gender. Although that was understandable for an executive director dealing with a contentious board of directors, many of the women, who tended to be deliberative, saw it as an example of male domination. Voeller was an impatient man, and often made decisions before reviewing them with the board. "If we came to you first," he'd say, sounding vaguely condescending, "it would be too late." Of course, he had never intended the group to be particularly democratic at all. Still, the women felt that he was trying to manipulate them, and his encounters with them became increasingly surly. Betty Powell felt that the board should be honored to have an activist of her stature on the board; she felt taken for granted by Voeller, whom she considered devious and untrustworthy. Her opinion gained currency among the other women on the board. Voeller found the women on the board increasingly argumentative and abrasive. It would lead him to resign.

PART THREE
The Backlash

20

THE GOVERNOR
OF GEORGIA

In the fall of 1974, Jimmy Carter, the outgoing governor of Georgia, was using his position as chairman of the Democratic National Campaign Committee to build a network of support across the country, campaigning for promising young Democrats who were locked in close races for the election in November. In the Northeast, one of those Democrats—who would play a crucial role in shaping the relationship of the Carter White House to both the growing gay rights and evangelical Christian movements—was the passionate, funny and fiercely liberal vice mayor of Rochester, New York, Midge Costanza.

Her name was Margaret, but everybody, including the local newspapers, called her Midge. Tiny and intense, with huge soulful eyes, she was an Italian Roman Catholic with a high school education, the secretary to the owner of a large construction company—and his longtime lover. He was a power in the Democratic Party, and she had become active in local politics. Elected the year before as the first woman on the city council—and with more votes than any of the men—Costanza had been persuaded to run for Congress in 1974 against an entrenched Republican incumbent. She was sitting in her campaign office on the ground floor of a building in downtown Rochester one day when her campaign manager yelled to her that Jimmy Carter, the governor of Georgia, was on the line.

Midge Costanza gave him an incredulous look. "What does he want?" she said.

"He wants to come and campaign for you," her manager said.

"This has got to be a nut," Costanza muttered, reaching for the telephone. And then she listened as Carter's soft, thin voice came over the line, telling her that he wanted to come up to Rochester and help her.

Costanza was stunned. This is the governor of Georgia and he wants to campaign for *me*? she thought to herself. She was an ethnic New Yorker, an urban liberal populist, an environmentalist, a full-blown supporter of the ERA and the first major Roman Catholic politician in Rochester to be pro-choice on abortion. She was probably *for* all the things that the governor of Georgia was against, she thought.

"Can I call you back?" she said brightly.

But she soon discovered that Jimmy Carter had a reputation as a new kind of southern politician, a big supporter of human rights, and from the first moment she saw the slight figure step off the plane at the Rochester airport, carrying his coat slung over his shoulder the way Jack Kennedy had, she loved him. He seemed so sure of himself, of who he was. They were opposites: the cool, toothy, grinning Carter, always in control; and the birdlike, big-eyed Midge Costanza, animated and irreverent. She narrowly lost the race for Congress, but they took to each other personally, and when Jimmy Carter announced his campaign for president that December, he asked her to be his New York State campaign coordinator, in charge of the upper half of the state. She pushed him on issues important to women, like abortion rights and the ERA. And she assumed that because of his emphasis on equal rights, he shared her feelings about other matters, including gay rights. It hadn't been a central issue in her congressional campaign or, for that matter, in her life. But when she had run for city council in 1973, Midge Costanza had been contacted by some members of the gay student group at the University of Rochester, who wanted to know where she stood. "I don't even know what a gay right is," she said. "I can't tell you what my position is." The students were so new at approaching politicians—and so fearful of the process—that they arranged to pick her up on a street corner at night and drive her to an undisclosed location for an interview, insisting that she keep her eyes shut as they bounced along in a Volkswagen to their destination. Her heart went out to them, and as a result, she had ended up campaigning that fall in the city's gay bars. Homosexuals just wanted the same rights that other people had, she decided.

In the wake of Senator George McGovern's overwhelming loss in 1972, Jimmy Carter was running as a political centrist. He had no wish to repeat the McGovern debacle. And in the aftermath of the Watergate scandal and Richard Nixon's resignation in August 1974, Carter's strategy was to appeal to the electorate as a moral man and a competent leader. Those were the themes he stressed. "I will never tell you a lie," he said, again and again. The issue, he told audiences, was faith. Carter's honesty, his openness and sureness about things appealed to Midge Costanza. But she was also drawn to him as a civil libertarian, a champion of human rights. She campaigned for him in upstate New York all through 1975, assuring her friends—most of them liberals more inclined to support the campaign of Representative Morris K. "Mo" Udall—that they should take Carter seriously. As the winter of 1975 rolled into the spring of 1976, and the Carter campaign survived and grew, Jimmy Carter spoke out about discrimination against homosexuals in a way which made it seem to Midge Costanza that he felt as she did—in principle, at least—on that issue, too.

Thus, when she received a letter signed by Jean O'Leary and Bruce Voeller of the National Gay Task Force, asking to meet with her to talk about gay rights and the Democratic Party platform, Costanza didn't say no. She was now the co-chair of the New York State Democratic platform committee, and the question of whether the party should include a gay rights plank in its platform had come up at virtually all of the state committee hearings she had held in New York City. Costanza had listened to the testimony of the activists, and as a member of the national committee which would hammer the party platform together in advance of the Democratic National Convention, she took their views seriously. By late spring, it was clear that Jimmy Carter was going to be the Democratic nominee. So Costanza, after carrying the Task Force letter around unanswered for a while in her bag—along with pleas from environmentalists, ERA supporters, abortion rights activists and other groups—had scrawled her usual warm, personal response, and sent it off, handwritten, to Voeller and O'Leary. Certainly she would meet with them, it said.

March 1976, Los Angeles

For months, quietly working through a network of family members, friends and preachers, Jimmy Carter had been trying to stir the nation's 13 million Southern Baptists to his candidacy, and in North Carolina, one night in March, he talked to reporters about the importance of religion in his life. He called himself "a born-again Christian." It was a phrase which quickly boiled to the surface of the presidential campaign, changing Carter's image. But few of the evangelical Christians who began to identify with him after that declaration heard what the former Georgia governor had to say that month in Los Angeles about the subject of gay rights. Discrimination against homosexuals was not an issue that had ever come up in gubernatorial politics in Georgia, and Carter didn't bring it up during the southern primaries. As he campaigned in places like California, New York and Pennsylvania that spring, however, it began to be a question for Jimmy Carter, and the answer he gave, when asked, left the gay activists who heard him surprised—and as excited by his apparent support as Christian fundamentalists were to know that Carter was "born again."

In March, in Los Angeles, the Reverend Troy Perry joined a small crowd of local Democrats invited by Los Angeles County supervisor Ed Edelson to meet Carter. Edelson was a co-chairman of the Carter campaign in California, and Troy Perry was curious what his fellow southerner and fundamentalist would have to say. Finding himself one of about eighty people in a small banquet room, he listened while Carter talked about himself, and when he called for questions Troy Perry raised his hand. "I have one for you, Governor. Are you willing to sign an executive order banning discrimination against gays and lesbians in America?" Perry asked. Then, in his breathless, rapid-fire way, he listed the categories to which he thought the order should apply.

"I'm sorry," Carter said, looking at the big, bearded minister in his black coat and clerical collar. "Would you name those four areas again? You talk sort of fast." And so, without much hope, Perry spelled out once more the areas in which he was asking if Carter would ban discrimination against homosexuals: in the military, in housing, in immigration and in civilian contract positions which needed Pentagon security clearances.

"I only have a problem with one of those," Carter began, as Perry, surprised, thought to himself that the former commander of nuclear submarines was going to say that homosexuals didn't belong in the military, "and that's only in the area of having security clearances where the person's not out and open."

Troy Perry was dumbfounded by what Carter had just said. If a person wasn't openly homosexual, he *could* be subject to blackmail, so he probably shouldn't have a security clearance. But banning discrimination in the other areas was apparently fine with Carter. Perry, whose Metropolitan Community Churches were now the largest gay and lesbian organization in the country, happily stood to have his picture taken afterward with Rosalynn Carter. Jimmy Carter was smart enough not to appear in a picture with the founder of a church for homosexuals, just as he had been smart enough not to actually say that he would sign an executive order. But he had given the impression that he would, and Troy Perry was a Carter man from that moment on. "He's going to be the next president," Troy Perry said in his emphatic way, when people asked him if he was sure he knew what he was doing.

It was not the only time that Jimmy Carter pledged to oppose discrimination against homosexuals. He made the commitment several times that spring, orally and in writing, as he campaigned in states on the East and West Coasts where there were large gay communities. "I oppose all forms of discrimination on the basis of sexual orientation," he wrote in April to a gay group in Philadelphia, in a letter published in a local paper there before the

Pennsylvania primary. "As president, I can assure you that all policies of the federal government would reflect this commitment." In May, back in California, at a press conference in San Francisco, Carter stated clearly that he would sign the bill introduced in the House by Bella Abzug. "I will certainly sign it, because I don't think it's right to single out homosexuals for special abuse or special harassment," he said.

In one sense, Carter's promise was a safe pledge to make. No one expected the gay rights bill to pass anytime in the foreseeable future. Carter didn't expect to win the California Democratic primary, either. Jerry Brown, the popular governor of the state, was running against Carter there, and California was the one state in the country where Carter's polls showed that the voters would not accept a southerner for president. But the homosexual community in San Francisco represented probably the largest, best-organized single bloc of gay votes anywhere in the nation. The Carter campaign made a practice of appealing to every group of voters it could, and the California primary was only two weeks away.

Jimmy Carter didn't limit his statements on the subject to local or gay events in Los Angeles, San Francisco and Philadelphia, however. Questioned about his views on *The Tomorrow Show* by host Tom Snyder, who had interviewed Air Force Sergeant Leonard Matlovich not long before, Carter had gone on record as opposed to discrimination against homosexuals in March. "I think my position is fairly advanced on that subject," Carter said with apparent pride, when Snyder asked him about Matlovich three weeks before the New York primary. "I favor the end of harassment or abuse or discrimination against homosexuals."

Compared to his opponents, Jimmy Carter *was* advanced on the subject of gay rights. Jerry Brown then regarded the issue of gay rights as politically "threatening." President Ford, questioned as he was campaigning for reelection in Peoria, Illinois, two weeks before Carter's comments on *The Tomorrow Show,* told a crowd of eight thousand university students that the issue of gay civil rights was "a new and serious problem" for which he had no "pat answers." But "I always try to be an understanding person as far as people are concerned who are different from myself," he added. Weeks later Ford still hadn't formed an answer. After Mark Segal, the head of the Philadelphia Gay Raiders, had twice written to the president's Pennsylvania campaign headquarters asking for Ford's position on gay rights, he finally got a candid response: "Rather than insult your intelligence with a phrase such as 'a person should be judged by a prospective employer on the basis of his or her qualifications,' we would like to state the absolute truth, which is that President Ford has not taken any position on gay activity at the present time," his state headquarters said.

Senator Henry M. "Scoop" Jackson of Washington, who was campaigning for the Democratic nomination, made no effort to seem sympathetic when he was confronted by a small group of demonstrators at a rally in Queens in New York City on April 3. Jackson—accompanied by Connecticut governor Ella T. Grasso and Daniel Patrick Moynihan, who was running for the U.S. Senate—was talking about how to increase employment when he began to be heckled for once describing homosexuality as "bad" and "wrong." Suddenly he turned on the protesters. "Go on and have your own rally!" Jackson told them. "Our people want work. We don't want gay jobs. You have your gay jobs. You just do your own thing and stay away." Though gay rights wasn't a major issue in the campaign, even in New York, Jackson's remarks still seemed "rather extreme" for somebody who wanted to be president, *New York Times* columnist Tom Wicker wrote two days later. And Jackson had apparently been even more caustic in Colorado, Wicker reported, declaring to a newspaper there that "I am not about to give in to the gay liberation and codify into law the practice of homosexuality . . . it is the first beginning of a breakdown of a society."

But as Jimmy Carter's reliance on his Southern Baptist faith became better known, he found himself needing to try to reassure groups who felt threatened by the cultural implications of his beliefs. "When Gov. Carter was asked how he could reconcile his religious faith with his support for Gay peoples' rights," a press release issued in his name in California in late May stated, Carter replied, "I don't consider myself one iota better than anyone else because I happen to be a Christian, and I have never done anything other than keep strictly separated my political life from my religious life. There would be no conflict in my life as President having my own personal, deeply felt beliefs." As reassurances go, the one offered in Carter's name seemed somehow thin, as if what he really might be saying was that he didn't like homosexuals but was capable of containing the feeling. It was the same kind of reassurance that Carter was trying at the time to give to Jewish voters, many of whom were spooked by his southern fundamentalism. "There has been a great deal of concern expressed to me by Jewish leaders about my beliefs," Carter said to a Jewish group at the Beverly Wilshire Hotel in Los Angeles at the end of May. "I'm a devoted Baptist. . . . I ask you to learn about my faith before you permit it to cause you any concern. . . . There is no conflict between us [concerning] the separation of church and state. . . . I worship the same God you worship," he told them. It was the same reassurance about his ability to separate church and state that John F. Kennedy had felt compelled to give as a Roman Catholic in 1960.

As the summer began, Midge Costanza and the other members of the Democratic National Platform Committee were to gather in Washington. Neither Jean O'Leary nor Bruce Voeller, the two directors of the National Gay Task Force who had asked to see Costanza, had ever met her before. They did have a connection through Virginia Apuzzo, who had been in charge of the Task Force's effort to organize support for a gay rights plank at the platform hearings in New York and across the country. But O'Leary was surprised by Costanza's handwritten letter saying that she would be glad to meet with them and would call when she was coming to the city. As Jean O'Leary was only beginning to realize, the gay rights movement was in luck. It had found an advocate.

That summer was probably the height of Jimmy Carter's popularity, the crest of good feeling that existed between a man still mainly unknown and the various constituencies he was wooing and who were trying to know him. Christian fundamentalists had taken him up like a long-lost cousin, and the tribal excitement sweeping evangelical circles had made a big difference in states like Texas. By the time of the Baptists' annual meeting that month in Norfolk, Virginia, political passion for Carter was spreading through the Southern Baptist Convention like a fever. One of the convention's main speakers was Bailey Smith, pastor of a big church in suburban Oklahoma City and a future president of the convention. Jimmy Carter had visited Smith, had gotten down on his knees and prayed with him—fervently—before going out to speak to Smith's congregation. Now Bailey Smith returned the favor, stirring 15,000 pastors and laypeople to cheers and laughter when he told them that America needed "a born-again man in the White House—and his initials are the same as our Lord's: *J. C.!*" But Bailey Smith was a conservative preacher, alert to moral threats to the American culture, and one of the trends that disturbed increasingly restive Baptists like him was the rising profile of homosexuality in parts of the nation. At the same meeting that hailed Carter, the conservatives led the assembly to pass its first resolution on the subject. Noting that homosexuality "has become an open life style," the assembly condemned it as contrary to "Biblical truth regarding the practice of homosexuality as sin," and resolved that overt homosexuals should not be hired or ordained as preachers.

The gay rights movement was warming to Jimmy Carter, too, but two events soon made it clear that there were limits to what Carter was and wasn't willing to do for homosexuals. As the Stonewall anniversary neared, Carter decided to send his son Chip, who had been his emissary to the Southern Baptists in Texas during the Democratic primary, to San Francisco. Chip Carter rode in the much-hyped Great Tricycle Race, a gay event then usually held on Memorial Day weekend. His picture, sitting grinning on a tricycle, appeared in papers around the country. But the closest he got to endorsing gay rights was to say he was there to show his support for the "gay peoples' political situation."

In Washington, when the Democratic platform committee met to work out the party's official positions, Carter's political aides sent a much more definitive message: he would not risk alienating the general public over the issue of gay rights. No matter what Midge Costanza, Jean O'Leary, Bruce Voeller and Ginny Apuzzo had been led to believe by his earlier words, the statements of support he had made during the primaries were not something he was willing to include in the party platform. As Chip Carter had also said in San Francisco, his father "doesn't think homosexuality is right, but he doesn't want to inflict his morals on other people." Jimmy Carter didn't sound in June and July the way he had in March, April and May.

Jean O'Leary and Midge Costanza liked each other enormously, forming a personal and political bond that would last for years to come. O'Leary was a forceful personality, magnetic and seductive, and the tiny Costanza, with her big eyes, passionate intensity and flip wit, melted the reserve of almost everyone she met. After the struggles of the early '70s over the role of lesbianism in feminist theology, both the National Organization for Women and the National Women's Political Caucus had settled into agreement on the basic package of causes shared by feminist groups: passage of the Equal Rights Amendment, and support for abortion rights, day care and lesbian rights.

As feminists, O'Leary and Costanza agreed on the issues that the lobbyists for NOW and the National Women's Political Caucus had been pressing in the platform committee draft sessions. Ginny Apuzzo had been pushing those lobbyists not to forget the part about lesbian and gay rights, and if it seemed a long freight train of issues that faced the platform committee, it was a train in which lesbian rights was the caboose. Abortion rights was the consuming issue that year. But Midge Costanza pledged to Jean O'Leary that gay and lesbian rights would be addressed.

Without Costanza, O'Leary and Apuzzo really had no leverage. There were only four openly gay delegates to the 1976 Democratic National Convention: O'Leary from New York; Josephine Daly and Jim Foster, who had addressed the 1972 convention, both from San Francisco; and Clayton Wells, from Los Angeles, who became visible only at the end of the convention. None of them could claim to have made a difference for Jimmy Carter in one of the primary state contests the way that Jim Foster had for George McGovern in California in 1972. This was Jimmy Carter's convention, and the platform committee was packed with his people and run by his issues manager, Stuart Eizenstat, and his deputy, Joseph Duffey. What the Carter forces didn't want wasn't going to get in. "Your issue is not a priority," Duffey told Ginny Apuzzo. But Jean O'Leary had Midge Costanza's promise. O'Leary was a pusher, and one day she walked out of a meeting in the Task Force office, went to her desk and called Costanza, who was still in Rochester. "Midge, listen."

The gay rights issue might come up tomorrow at the platform committee in Washington, she said. "Let's go down a day early and go tackle it."

O'Leary and Ginny Apuzzo drove that night from New York in Apuzzo's yellow Volkswagen bug. They were blocked from speaking before the committee, but the next afternoon O'Leary slipped into the room where Costanza and more than twenty other delegates sat working their way down an agenda around a huge long table. She knelt down by Costanza and hissed in her ear, "Now. You've got to bring it up *now.*" And Costanza, knowing that it wasn't on the agenda, and that this would be regarded as a move by those crazy liberals from New York, did.

They could no longer disregard the issue of gay rights, she told the other delegates around the table. It had been raised at numerous draft committee hearings, and the one thing that needed to be done at this convention could be done through the platform. They should at least include the words "sexual orientation" in the anti-discrimination civil rights language in the platform, Costanza said. That was all the gay rights movement was asking for at that juncture, and that would satisfy that constituency of the Democratic Party. The reaction of many of the delegates at the table was hostile, as if this was an inappropriate and threatening idea. But there were also liberal delegates who had been pledged to Udall or Frank Church in the room who were sympathetic. The discussion was lively. The Carter forces also did not want to be seen as steamrolling or insensitive to the interests of different elements within the party, so late that night Midge Costanza found herself alone with Stu Eizenstat, Carter's pale, brainy issues chief.

A lawyer from Atlanta—one of three Jews in the Carter inner circle—Eizenstat didn't upbraid her or belittle the issue, but he was serious about keeping it out of the platform. "Midge," he pleaded, "let's do what we have to do for the gay rights movement—but let's do it after we get to the White House. For God's sakes, don't let us carry this albatross going into the campaign. We have to win this election."

Eizenstat was determined to keep all extreme and provocative positions out of the platform, and every special interest group in the party had been bending over backwards to be agreeable, passing up all kinds of opportunities to pick fights that the Republicans could make use of. Delegates from heavily Roman Catholic states had voted not to try to include a constitutional amendment against abortion. Labor leaders were allowing a weaker national health insurance plan than they had supported in years. Delegates from Alabama and Mississippi even let a vote to put the party on record against busing for desegregation fail for lack of support. But Midge Costanza had given her commitment to Jean O'Leary, so the motion to add the gay rights language went to a vote of the full committee. It was tabled, 57–27.

• • •

This was a very different convention, they all realized, from 1972, and Jim Foster, Jean O'Leary and Jo Daly—the three gay delegates with the most experience in Democratic Party politics—decided to put the best face on it when the Democratic National Convention got under way in New York City's Madison Square Garden in mid-July. "We've made significant gains," Jo Daly told the editor of Boston's *Gay Community News*, as she reminded him how long it had taken the black civil rights movement to gain support within the party. "It was in 1940 that the first black person took part in a Democratic Convention. It wasn't until 24 years later that the civil rights act was passed. This year's platform was built around the candidate," she said. "The Democratic Party is not hostile. We've got to work within it."

Not everyone felt that way. Paul Kuntzler, who had orchestrated the founding of the Gertrude Stein Democratic Club in Washington, was impatient for the movement—and the Stein Club—to make its mark. The platform committee decision not to mention sexual orientation, and the fact that gay rights was nowhere on the agenda of the convention itself, had left him dismayed. "They produced a document which did not even recognize our existence," he fumed in a letter sent to one hundred gay activists around the country. "Thus we are faced not only with being left behind, but having the tiny gains we realized four years ago wiped away." To recoup the lost opportunity, Kuntzler urged that they nominate a gay candidate for vice president from the convention floor. But Foster, O'Leary and Daly opposed him and prevailed. "The convention is so tightly controlled this year that it would have been impossible," Jean O'Leary told the *Gay Community News* near the convention's end. "It's vital that we don't set ourselves up for failure, and that is exactly what we would have been doing." Like the other—and more powerful—elements of the Democratic Party, the handful of gay and lesbian activists inside the convention hall had decided to cast their lot with Jimmy Carter. Helping him get elected, they figured, was their best chance for progress after the election.

So the achievements at the convention itself, such as they were, were small. Inside the hall, some eight hundred signatures were collected on a petition supporting gay civil rights and the repeal of state sodomy laws. Outside the hall, gay groups managed one sizable march by about seven hundred people, from Washington Square in the Village to Madison Square Garden. For the first time, the gay Democratic clubs won the party's approval of a gay caucus, but its first meeting was a bare event: two women and two men sitting at a table on a stage in a room with seating for three hundred, far off in an inconvenient part of the convention hall. The convention management had not even listed them on the day's calendar of events. For the two dozen reporters who managed to find it, to see what a gay caucus was all about, Jim Foster put on a brave front, touting it as progress. "We're building within the Democratic party for 1980 by encouraging gay persons all over the country to participate in party activities," he said. "There's no reason for the party to pay much attention to our issues until we move more into Democratic politics as gays. By 1980, this party will understand that our issues are not regional issues, but issues that affect 20 million gay people all over the country."

Evangelical Christians, on the other hand, were approaching a state of political ecstasy. The Reverend Bob Maddox, pastor to Jimmy Carter's son Jack and daughter-in-law Judy at the First Baptist Church of Calhoun, Georgia, was almost beside himself the night he sat in a box in Madison Square Garden, listening to Midge Costanza give Jimmy Carter's second nominating speech, and then watching as the nominating vote totals for Carter rose state by state. He had flown up only that day on a twin-engine plane lent by Bert Lance, Carter's close friend and fellow evangelical, the head of the National Bank of Georgia. His friendship with Jack and Judy Carter had led Bob Maddox to the center of American politics. The whole experience gave Maddox such a rush that after seeing Jimmy Carter nominated, and talking with him later in the Carters' suite at the Sheraton Century Hotel, he lay in bed, unable to sleep, his mind racing through the night.

That July a full-page advertisement placed by a group called Citizens for Carter appeared in the magazine *Christianity Today*. Founded twenty years earlier by Dr. Billy Graham, *Christianity Today* had become the main publication of American evangelism, and the question the ad posed, in large letters, was this: "Does a Dedicated Evangelical Belong in the White House?" Yes, the ad said, because "in this post-Watergate era, people throughout the country are disillusioned with the moral corruption and incompetent leadership they see in the political arena." The excitement about Carter in evangelical ranks was becoming a contagion, and as the summer wore on, Representative John Conlan of Arizona, a right-wing Republican with extensive contacts among Christian evangelical and business groups, made a worried telephone call to another friend on the Republican right in Washington to say that he was seeing Jimmy Carter mentioned repeatedly in all manner of Christian papers and newsletters. "They are really taken with Carter," Conlan said. "I'm afraid he may end up getting elected." Paul Weyrich, listening to Conlan as he sat in his office in an old carriage house behind the Library of Congress in the nation's capital, thought to himself that Jimmy Carter getting elected might not be such a bad thing, and told Conlan so. Weyrich, the head of the right wing's principal grassroots lobby, didn't know much about Southern Baptists and other evangelical Christians. When one of his young assistants that summer, a college student from Virginia Beach, had tried to persuade Weyrich that he needed to meet Pat Robertson, the television evangelist and founder of the Christian Broadcasting Network, which had its studios in Virginia Beach, Weyrich hadn't been interested. He didn't know anything about Robertson and had never seen his show, *The 700 Club*, a sort of faith-healing Christian commentary and entertainment magazine, and although his young intern had some connection to Robertson, and said he could arrange an introduction, Weyrich didn't take him up on the offer.

He depended on people like John Conlan to tell him what he needed to know about the world of evangelical Christians, and for the moment, that was good enough. Paul Weyrich was German Roman Catholic, an arch-conservative who cared mainly about economic, not social issues, and for the last five or six years, with money from Colorado beer magnate Joseph Coors and others, he had been building new think tanks and grassroots lobbying organizations to push the right-wing agenda in Washington. The organization that he had founded two years before and that he ran from his carriage house office, the Committee for the Survival of a Free Congress, tried to train and elect conservatives to the House and Senate from across the country. But Gerald Ford seemed insufficiently ideological to Paul Weyrich in a lot of ways, a man with no conservative agenda, and Betty Ford was far too liberal on a lot of cultural and family issues for Weyrich's strict Roman Catholic tastes.

Maybe if Jimmy Carter was elected, he would appoint some other born-again Christians like himself to office, Weyrich told Conlan. Maybe he'd be a better conservative in some ways than Ford. The thought stayed in Weyrich's head, and in Dallas a few weeks later, he gave a speech in which he told a group of conservatives that he might not be unhappy to see Jimmy Carter win this election. He just might turn out to be a conservative president, Weyrich told them. Weyrich found himself warming to the idea. And then the November issue of *Playboy* magazine came out, in mid-September, and he discovered, to his astonishment, along with much of the rest of adult America, that the "*Playboy* interview" was with Jimmy Carter.

The idea had been to show Carter as a regular guy, perhaps to damp down some of the concern about his being a straitlaced evangelical, and Carter, in three long interviews with Robert Scheer, had tried to explain how the Bible led him to deal with contemporary issues of human sexuality. Scheer was a probing, pushy interviewer. Jimmy Carter was trying to be understood. The result was some remarkably candid language from someone who wanted to be president. It was Jimmy Carter being decent and thoughtful, but the interview ranged over some very tricky ground, in ways that were personal and revealing. And the result was that Carter's views, or at least his expression of them, as he strained to make himself understood, sounded strange and disquieting to almost everyone he was trying to reassure.

The part of the long interview article that made the news in mid-

September, just before Carter's first debate with President Ford, was what Carter had said to Scheer at the end of their last interview, as Carter had tried one last time to explain what he had learned from Christ's teachings about pride, and why he didn't feel he was better than anyone else. "I try not to commit a deliberate sin. I recognize that I'm going to do it anyhow, because I'm human and I'm tempted. And Christ set some almost impossible standards for us. Christ said, 'I tell you that anyone who looks on a woman with lust has in his heart already committed adultery.'

"I've looked on a lot of women with lust. I've committed adultery in my heart many times," Carter said. "This is something that God recognized I will do—and I have done it—and God forgives me for it. But that doesn't mean that I condemn someone who not only looks on a woman with lust but who leaves his wife and shacks up with somebody out of wedlock. Christ says, 'Don't consider yourself better than someone else because one guy screws a whole bunch of women while the other guy is loyal to his wife.' "

Carter's ruminations about heterosexual lust and sin and pride were what bounced around the nation's news and editorial pages. The comments seemed crude and oddly tortured, making many people wonder about his point of view.

But much of the interview was also about homosexuals and the issues they posed for American law and politics. To homosexuals who read what Jimmy Carter had to say about *that*—and who took Carter at his word—his sincerity in trying to come to grips with their condition was evident. But his thoughts were far from reassuring. In the month of June alone, two more states, West Virginia and Iowa, had repealed their sodomy laws. One-third of the United States had now decriminalized sex between people of the same gender. But the U.S. Supreme Court, in a 6–3 decision at the end of March, had upheld the state of Virginia's right to make such acts a felony by law.

"Do you think such laws should be on the books at all?" Scheer had asked Carter.

"That's a judgment for the individual states to make. I think the laws are on the books quite often because of their relationship to the Bible. Early in the nation's development, the Judeo-Christian moral standards were accepted as a basis for civil law," Jimmy Carter said. "But I don't think it hurts to have this kind of standard maintained as a goal. I also think it's an area that's been interpreted by the Supreme Court as one that can rightfully be retained by the individual states."

Scheer had pressed him. "What we're getting at is how much you'd tolerate behavior that your religion considers wrong. For instance, in San Francisco, you said you considered homosexuality as sin. What does that mean in political terms?"

"The issue of homosexuality always makes me nervous," Carter had admitted. "It's obviously one of the major issues in San Francisco. I don't have any, you know, personal knowledge about homosexuality and I guess being a Baptist, that would contribute to my sense of being uneasy."

Scheer: "Does it make you uneasy to discuss it simply as a political question?"

Carter: "No, it's more complicated than that. It's political, it's moral, and it's strange territory for me. At home in Plains, we've had homosexuals in our community, our church. There's never been any sort of discrimination— some embarrassment, but no animosity, no harassment. But to inject it into a public discussion on politics and how it conflicts with morality is a new experience for me. I've thought about it a lot, but I don't see how to handle it differently from the way I look on other sexual acts outside marriage."

As Scheer continued to push Carter to explain how a biblical view of morality would guide him in dealing with contemporary sexual and social issues, Carter had grown frustrated and then exasperated. *"I can't change the teachings of Christ,"* he snapped at Scheer. "I can't change the teachings of Christ! I believe in them, and a lot of people in this country do, as well."

It was the outburst of a man who felt both blessed and bound by rules he didn't make. Even granted that the feeling was genuine, it was troubling to homosexuals.

But to evangelical Christians, whose perspective Jimmy Carter was trying to honor and explain, the very idea that he would pour his heart out in a magazine dedicated to sexual abandon—and filled with naked women—was shocking in itself. To hear that he had actually talked about "screwing" and "shacking up" was beyond the pale. "We're totally against pornography," said the troubled Bailey Smith, who just months before had urged Baptists to rally behind this politician with the same initials as Jesus Christ. " 'Screw,' " he said, "is just not a good Baptist word."

Within days the building wave of Christian support began to break. The Reverend Jerry Falwell, pastor of Thomas Road Baptist Church in Lynchburg, Virginia, and host of *The Old Time Gospel Hour* on television on Sunday mornings, was quick to jump on Carter. Falwell, who had never liked what he sensed about Jimmy Carter's politics, spoke in mock sorrow and secret satisfaction. "Like many others, I am quite disillusioned," he said. "Four months ago the majority of the people I knew were pro-Carter. Today that has totally reversed."

The Reverend W. A. Criswell of Dallas, granddaddy of the archconservative movement within the Southern Baptist Church and pastor of its largest congregation, pronounced himself "highly offended" and endorsed Gerald Ford right on the front steps of the First Baptist Church. The Ford campaign began running a television ad in which, with President Ford and his wife, Betty, sitting in the congregation, Criswell said from the pulpit that the president had confided to him that he, too, had been asked by *Playboy* to grant an interview. But Jerry Ford, Criswell declared, had said "*No!*" News of the *Playboy* interview very nearly cost Jimmy Carter the election. His ten-point lead over Ford evaporated overnight. But it could not turn back the whole swell of cousinly feeling for Carter among evangelicals and in the South, and on election day in November, the momentum narrowly carried him through. Jimmy Carter won with 50.1 percent of the popular vote, mainly by sweeping eleven of the thirteen southern states—all except for Virginia and Oklahoma. The Reverend Bob Maddox and his wife spent that election night in the Omni Hotel in Atlanta with the Carters, sharing a suite with Jack and Judy Carter. Maddox had caught the fever, and when they all got back to Calhoun, he sat down and put the idea which had been racing through his mind into words. He wrote a proposal for an office of religious liaison for the president, gave the memorandum to Jack Carter to give to his father, and waited to hear.

Over the next few weeks in Washington, Paul Weyrich analyzed the election results, saw how Jimmy Carter had carried the conservative Christians and the South away from the Republicans, and decided that he ought to go down to Virginia Beach to meet Pat Robertson after all. Weyrich flew to Virginia Beach in February 1977, only to discover that Jimmy Carter had beat him there by more than a year. Carter had courted Robertson, as he had other prominent preachers, and Robertson had been impressed. He had taken to speaking well of him on television, and Carter had appeared as his guest on *The 700 Club*. But Robertson, a lawyer and the son of a U.S. senator from Virginia, was no innocent, and he felt he had cut a deal: in exchange for his support in building an evangelical Christian vote, Jimmy Carter would appoint evangelical Christians to cabinet positions and other offices if he won. The election should have made him a happy man, but Pat Robertson did not seem that way when Weyrich met him. Instead, he wore the flinty, injured look of someone who was beginning to think that he'd been had. Robertson and his staff had taken the trouble to consult the "Plum Book," the fat directory of appointive positions in the federal government, and had sent Jimmy Carter a long list of hundreds of names of evangelical Christians who could be appointed to fill this post or that. He had heard nothing in response, not even a thank-you from Carter or his staff for the effort. Nor had any of the people whose names he had sent in heard anything. Pat Robertson never would hear anything in return, and his anger would grow and harden against Jimmy Carter and his White House. One of the things that Bert Lance, director of the Office of Management and Budget, did not long after he arrived in Washington as the closest friend of the president of the United States was to appear on *The 700 Club*, to try to mollify the offended Robertson. Lance was a guest several times on Robertson's show. His wife, LaBelle, appeared even more. Pat Robertson never was appeased. And he never heard from Jimmy Carter.

But Bob Maddox did hear back. The word was that Jimmy Carter didn't intend to set up any special listening post for evangelicals in his White House. He didn't think he needed any help relating to them. After all, he was one. Besides, he had made them no promises.

In the days after the election, he had instructed Stu Eizenstat to draw up a list of all the promises he had made during the campaign, in speeches or public statements, to any group. Eizenstat had compiled the list, a document of more than a hundred pages, and had given it to Carter on November 30. Entitled "Compilation of Campaign Promises," it had three categories: promises to consider, promises to support and promises to take some kind of action. There were many groups of various kinds listed to whom promises had been made: senior citizens, mineworkers, women, Hispanics, the disabled, maritime workers, Italian Americans, and even Southern and Eastern European Americans. Nowhere were gays or Christians listed.

21

A VOICE IN
THE WHITE HOUSE

In December 1976, President-elect Jimmy Carter announced that Margaret Costanza would be his assistant to the president for public liaison. Over the next six weeks the White House mailroom was deluged with letters addressed to this woman from Rochester, New York—ten thousand in a single week, so many that news photographers took pictures of the presidential assistant now known as Midge plopped on the floor of her new West Wing office, knee-deep in envelopes. There had never been a woman named as an assistant to the president before. There were only nine people in the world who could claim the title of assistant to the president, and when White House operators placed Costanza's calls, as was customary for someone in her position, they announced who was on the line by saying, "The White House is calling." Midge Costanza's appointment was novel in every way. She was, in many ways, something short of a typical politician: She was candid to the point of impertinence, and not particularly impressed with the pomp and ritual of her new station. Costanza was also a liberal Democrat, and the only person from the Northeast in the new president's inner circle. Most of all—and this explained much of her celebrity—she was a woman who had succeeded in what had always been the most male of worlds, the White House. Midge Costanza became recognizable in a way that assistants to the president usually are not, with her short hair, oversized hexagonal black-rimmed glasses and apparent determination to say whatever was on her mind. Her official title was public liaison, but Costanza called her job the "window for the nation to the president" and invited anyone who had anything to say to the White House to contact her. She pledged an "open door policy" and an answer to every letter, and said she wanted people to think of Jimmy Carter as *their* president. Even Costanza was surprised by how many people took her up on the invitation.

The public liaison title was also a polite way of saying that Costanza's job included responding to what were known as special interests, groups with particular problems or special demands. There were many of them, and they had grown restless after eight years of Republican administrations. They wanted to get messages to the new president and to meet him, and they wanted him to come speak to them. And if President Carter couldn't do it, they often wanted Midge Costanza. She tried to respond to the letters, since she had said she would, and stayed up late dictating replies. Many of the phone calls went unanswered.

But Jean O'Leary's phone calls were always returned. The two women had become increasingly close since they met during the campaign, and now O'Leary visited Costanza at the White House so often that she joked that the Secret Service had issued her a permanent White House pass. She was on the preapproved list of regular visitors kept by the guards at the White House gate. For Midge Costanza, overwhelmed with attention and demands for her time, O'Leary was her Seeing Eye dog for this patch of political terrain, the organized homosexual movement, just as Gloria Steinem and Bella Abzug helped her navigate through the organized women's movement. Thus, when calls started coming in from people wanting to meet with Costanza about gay rights—names like David Goodstein and Elaine Noble—Costanza turned to O'Leary for guidance. "Jean," Costanza said, "who is David Goodstein?" Goodstein certainly knew who Costanza was, and he believed that homosexual activists now had a supporter in the White House. But *The Advocate* had not endorsed Jimmy Carter in 1976, advising its readers that it saw no difference between Carter and Gerald Ford. Goodstein had met Carter and found his commitment to gay rights tepid. "In good conscience we cannot recommend that gay people vote for him," *The Advocate* said; Goodstein now had his work cut out for him in his quest for influence, and he called Costanza within two weeks of President Carter's inauguration. He also used his newspaper's pages to lavish praise on Costanza and the new president. But Goodstein had probably not considered the prospect that Costanza would check his request with his old foe at the Task Force. "Whoa, whoa—wait a minute, what are you *talking* about?" O'Leary told Costanza upon hearing Goodstein's name. "No way."

O'Leary now sought a reward for her early support of the new president. She thought the administration should receive a delegation of homosexual leaders publicly at the White House. "It's time, Midge," O'Leary told her friend. "We've got to discuss the issues of gay rights and discrimination against gays in this country—we've got to do it now."

"Now?" Costanza asked, and O'Leary nodded. O'Leary was not looking for a quiet half hour in the shadows to push her agenda, or even an invitation for lunch in the White House mess. She wanted an official meeting, an event that would amount to an affirmation of the gay rights movement by the White House. Costanza told O'Leary that she and Voeller should begin assembling a list of invitees.

The meeting at the White House would be held at 1 p.m. on Saturday, March 26, 1977. President Carter, off to Camp David, would not be there, and Midge Costanza had not told him what she was doing. She did not clear her meetings with the president, but she did list them on her own schedule, which was sent to the chief of staff. Costanza later said she had never given any thought to whether the president would be around. If she had, she might have realized that this was the first weekend of spring, and that it was likely that almost everyone, starting with the president and his senior staff, would be away from the White House. Costanza had chosen a Saturday, she explained, because she wanted this meeting to be held in the Roosevelt Room, the conference room with the long table across from the president's office, a room as rich in history as any in the White House. She could more easily have reserved a room in the Executive Office Building, across the drive from the White House, a fine old building filled with the second tier of White House officials. But that was not the White House.

Costanza and Voeller chose fourteen people for the delegation, seven men and seven women, four more than Costanza had originally agreed to, but that was the best Voeller and O'Leary could do after fielding requests from gay activists clamoring for a chair in the Roosevelt Room. The men were in ties, the women in skirts, and they were—as the National Gay Task Force press release distributed that day made clear—a group of respectable, professional, working men and women. There were Charlie Brydon, Charlotte Bunch, Los Angeles attorney Ray Hartman, Elaine Noble, Troy Perry, Betty Powell and, of course, Franklin Kameny. Jack Campbell wasn't there. He was one of the Task Force's main benefactors, but he was also the founder and owner of the nation's largest chain of gay male bathhouses, and O'Leary and Voeller agreed that this was not the kind of person they should be bringing into the White House. David Goodstein was, of course, not there either, and the Task Force soon all but vanished from the pages of *The Advocate*.

The delegation spent Friday evening rehearsing their presentations in the Capitol Hill office of Senator Alan Cranston, the California Democrat with the openly gay assistant, who provided the office. It was a tense and nervous night, filled with awkward fumblings that left Bruce Voeller cross and fearing disaster. None of them had ever played on this kind of stage before. The next day Midge Costanza met them at the White House front gates. Frank Kameny, who had never heard from President Kennedy when he asked for his own meeting fifteen years before, suddenly found himself cleared by the Secret Service and walking the White House grounds. Costanza, who had an uncommon ability to put people at ease, displayed that skill as Voeller and O'Leary began introducing the delegation in her office. When they reached Frank Kameny, Costanza cut them short: "Oh, I know all about Dr. Kameny. I have an entire dossier on him," she said soberly. "But we decided to let him in anyway." Kameny blanched, until Costanza threw her arms around him. "Frank, of all the wonderful people here, I'm the most deeply moved to meet you. Welcome inside." In truth, Costanza had no dossier on Kameny, and she knew nothing about his arrest in Lafayette Park by Washington, D.C., vice police.

Costanza took the group down a narrow hall with a low ceiling, even more hushed than usual because it was a weekend, and stopped at the Oval Office. There was a guard in front, and it was roped off, as it always was when the president was out of the West Wing. From there, they walked across the narrow hall and into the Roosevelt Room. Troy Perry found himself thinking of his civics class back in Mobile, Alabama. It was just as he remembered it from his book, right down to the bronze of Teddy Roosevelt perched against the wall. Midge Costanza sat at the head of the table, flanked by her deputy, Marilyn Haft, and Robert Malson, a civil rights specialist with the Office of Domestic Affairs. Everyone had his or her assigned presentations: Charlotte Bunch talked about immigration laws that prohibited homosexuals from entering the United States as a visitor or an immigrant. Charlie Brydon, the Vietnam veteran, discussed the ban on homosexuals in the military and argued for changing the policy of giving less than honorable discharges to gay men and lesbians. Kameny recounted the problems homosexuals had in winning security clearances. Kameny and Bill Kelley of Chicago explained the problems the IRS posed to homosexual groups seeking nonprofit tax status that would allow donors to make tax-deductible contributions. (Kameny, for instance, had been struggling for fifteen years to persuade the IRS to designate the Mattachine Society a nonprofit educational group.) The final topic was "Oppression, Discrimination and the Need for National Leadership and National Legislation," as Costanza had put it in her letter to O'Leary and Voeller laying out the agenda of the meeting. There were a few awkward moments, since in the rush to provide representation to different racial and geographic constituencies, the Task Force had recruited people to speak on subjects that were out of their expertise. George Raya, an investigator in the San Francisco District Attorney's Office and a former Chicano activist, as the Task Force described him in its official press release, spoke on health care, and he took to talking about anal warts and tertiary syphilis, to the discomfort of some of the people in the room.

No one could rise to the performance of Troy Perry. "Rather than read my prepared statement," he said, "I just want to share from my gut for one moment." He then shared the story of the 1973 fire at the UpStairs bar in New Orleans, of the victims who had never been identified, since no family would claim them, and of how local churches refused to honor their memories with services. He spoke about how many of his churches had been gutted by fires, and how the congregations kept coming back to raise money and rebuild them, again and again. Midge Costanza did not know any of this, and her face went flush and her eyes teared. The room was silent, and Costanza thought that Perry was the kind of preacher she had met from time to time who made her want to forget everything, drop to her knees and pledge devotion. "Thank you, Reverend Perry," she said. "I had no idea."

The meeting lasted almost three hours. As they walked outside the front door of the West Wing onto the rain-soaked lawn in front of the White House, they found reporters waiting. The White House press corps was there that Saturday, and since President Carter was not, they had found themselves with little to do until word got out about what was happening in the Roosevelt Room. The very first question was whether the president knew that this meeting was going on. Costanza gave the answer that popped into her head: "No," she said. "We were all hiding in the bathroom. As soon as he left, we came out." She then turned serious, explaining that this meeting was the first of what she hoped would be a series of sessions involving senior administration officials and gay activists. "The issue of human rights has become a very important one in this administration," she said. "It is my interpretation that the discrimination against gay people and the oppression that results certainly is an element of human rights." The meeting received fairly extensive and generally uncritical coverage, and Costanza was heard that evening on the network news, including on CBS: "I wish that the citizens of this nation could have joined me in that room to listen to the examples of oppression I heard today. Perhaps the issue of homosexuality would be better understood and perhaps more widely accepted if they could hear what I heard."

The Task Force received more attention that afternoon than it had received since its founding in Bruce Voeller's kitchen. After the cameras had gone, and Midge Costanza had headed back to her office, Voeller, O'Leary and Perry walked down the driveway to the gate. They paused for a moment before leaving. "Can you believe what just happened?" Bruce Voeller said.

There were some accomplishments that arose from that afternoon, and it was not an exaggeration to term the meeting historic, notwithstanding the fact that *The Advocate* relegated the event to page 35, where it shared space with an advertisement for Colt's latest male skin magazine. Over the next two months, the Task Force met with senior officials from the Department of Justice, the Federal Bureau of Prisons, Housing and Urban Development, and the Immigration and Naturalization Service. Costanza would meet with Voeller and O'Leary beforehand to help them plan what to say. If it appeared that a department was not assigning a senior enough person to tend to the Task Force requests, Costanza announced that she would attend the meeting, which ensured that the department head would also attend. "The power of the White House," Costanza said. Often, Costanza would show up just long enough to make sure the department head was there and then leave. In time, many of the critics of the Task Force concluded that the White House meeting and the meetings that followed were more a display of style than of substance—of generally meaningless access, press releases and tinkering with federal regulations. There certainly were no grand shifts in federal policy, but this was one case where appearance may have counted more than substance. "Thrilled to death," was how Troy Perry termed his reaction, and the White House visit became a regular part of his sermons. Jean O'Leary remembered the meeting as the high point of her years at the Task Force. That was the day, Midge Costanza would say, when gay rights became a national issue. President Carter never mentioned it to her, even after she sent him a memo recounting her three hours in the Roosevelt Room. But her stacks of mail began to include letters of thanks from homosexuals and the parents of homosexuals.

Costanza received other reaction as well: livid calls and letters of protest from Christian fundamentalists who had helped elect this Southern Baptist president. She found her desk covered with citations of Leviticus, with its admonition against men lying with men. And as it turned out, the single most significant response to what happened at the White House that day—one that would ultimately dwarf the incremental policy gains of the meeting—came from one of those fundamentalists, 929 miles away, in Dade County, Florida.

22

MIAMI:
THE FUNDAMENTALISTS
AWAKE

March 1977

It was such an exhilarating moment, standing in the White House driveway, talking into the microphones of network correspondents, that no one
paid much attention to the questions about Anita Bryant. After three hours in
the Roosevelt Room, her campaign to repeal a Dade County homosexual
rights ordinance seemed distant and inconsequential. Troy Perry felt a little
annoyed when a reporter asked him what Bryant would think of fourteen
homosexual leaders being granted an audience in the White House: Why
should Anita Bryant care about what was going on in Washington? And why
should they care what she thought?

By the next afternoon, the reporter's question was answered. From Villa
Verde, the thirty-three-room Spanish stucco mansion on Biscayne Bay where
Bryant lived with her husband and four children, the woman known for her
Florida orange juice commercials issued a statement demanding to know why
the White House was "dignifying these activists for special privilege with a serious discussion on their alleged 'human rights,'" and permitting them to
"pressure President Carter into endorsement of a lifestyle that is an abomination under the laws of God and man.

"What these people really want, hidden behind obscure legal phrases, is the legal right to propose to our children that there is an acceptable alternate way of life," Anita Bryant declared after services at Northwest Baptist Church in Miami, where she taught Sunday school. "No one has a human right to corrupt our children. Prostitutes, pimps and drug pushers, like homosexuals, have civil rights, too, but they do not have the right to influence our children to choose their way of life. Before I yield to this insidious attack on God and his laws, and on parents and their rights to protect their children, I will lead such a crusade to stop it as this country has not seen before."

That statement displayed for the nation a political force that had been quietly gathering in the four months since a gay rights ordinance had appeared on the calendar of the Dade County Metro Commission. Anita Bryant had made a career of singing at conventions and selling orange juice, and she had never before shown any interest in politics. But in those four months, she had become the symbol for a political crusade, fired by religious passion and single-minded intensity. Bruce Voeller did not even recognize Bryant's name when he first read that she had forced the Dade County Metro Commission to submit the new gay rights ordinance to public referendum. But that said more about the head of the Task Force and New York than it did about Bryant and Florida. In the South, across the Bible Belt, and among the 13 million Southern Baptists who shared Anita Bryant's faith and celebrated her emerging leadership, she was nearly universally admired. Each time she closed her eyes and threw her head back to sing a hymn or a patriotic anthem—her face scrubbed, red and glowing; her black-red hair shining; her high, handsome cheekbones a reminder of the beauty queen she had once been—Bryant embodied an idealized vision of American motherhood. She was the kind of woman whose 1959 official biography reported that the nineteen-year-old Miss Oklahoma and Miss America second runner-up "eventually hopes to marry and have a family of six children." Anita Bryant was a local treasure in Miami: The premature birth of her twins was a running story in the newspapers. At Christmas, the newspapers ran a photograph of the Anita Bryant family, posed in front of the Christmas tree.

She was born in Barnsdall, Oklahoma, the daughter of an oilfield worker, and she decided to become a performer after she "met the creator of Stars, Jesus Christ Our Lord," at age eight, and He told her to become a singer. Arthur Godfrey made her famous, after his talent scouts discovered her singing on the Tulsa television stations and invited her to perform in New York. By her mid-twenties, Anita Bryant had three gold records, but even then she was more than just another popular performer. Bryant toured seven times with Bob Hope and the USO, entertaining troops at Christmas, and appeared at Billy Graham rallies in Madison Square Garden. Bryant sang at the Super Bowl, and was part of the team of network commentators at eight Orange

Bowls. President Lyndon B. Johnson had her to the White House fourteen times during his five years in office. He led a standing ovation to her after she dedicated an emotional "Battle Hymn of the Republic" to the troops in Vietnam during a 1966 state dinner honoring the United States ambassador to Vietnam, Henry Cabot Lodge. *Variety* said it was the first time in memory a performer in the White House had been given a standing ovation. Anita Bryant returned the favor; she was unstinting in her support of the president's Vietnam policy, likening it, not surprisingly, to a crusade. "I feel very strongly that this is a war between atheism and God," she declared, and when Johnson died she sang "Battle Hymn of the Republic" one more time for her friend the president, at his graveside.

Anita Bryant was a registered Democrat, but both parties embraced her. In 1968 she sang "Battle Hymn of the Republic" at the Democratic convention in Chicago, and "The Star-Spangled Banner" at the Republican convention in Miami. By 1977, she was best known for her employment by the Florida Citrus Commission, which pressed her smile and voice into the service of selling Florida orange juice. "Come to the Florida sunshine tree! Florida sunshine naturally!" she'd sing, proclaiming, "A day without orange juice is like a day without sunshine." The citrus commission paid her $100,000 a year. Her total annual income was four times that, from appearances at religious conferences and corporate conventions. She was paid $7,500 a night at the conventions, and had made $700,000 in 1976, the Bicentennial year, because, according to her agent, Dick Shack, Bob Green had encouraged his popular wife to accept every one of those $7,500 invitations.

There had not been much interest in politics among Miami's sizable homosexual community, either, at least until the summer of 1976, when Jack Campbell, forty-five years old, assembled a group of gay men and lesbians in his home in Coconut Grove to talk about creating a gay rights lobbying organization. Campbell, a former president of the University of Michigan Young Democrats, joined the Cleveland Mattachine Society in the mid-1960s, and soon put his own singular stamp on the movement. In 1965 he and a group of investors paid $15,000 for an out-of-business sauna in downtown Cleveland. He turned it into a homosexual bathhouse, and business was so good he opened up a second one within the year. The Club Baths were a source of an enormous personal fortune but, Campbell argued, they were also an expression of gay and sexual liberation. His sizable contributions earned him a seat on the National Gay Task Force board, where Campbell would make a point of sitting next to Troy Perry at its meetings. Perry would introduce himself as the founder of the Metropolitan Community Church, where "we have a hundred churches and a total of 30,000 members." And Jack Campbell would always follow the same way: "Well, although we only have thirty churches, we have *300,000* members."

The Club Miami, which he opened in 1970, was the twentieth in what would become a forty-two-bathhouse empire. Campbell was openly gay in everything he did, which was unusual in Miami then. He ran for Miami City Commission in 1975, and he campaigned against vestigial laws that prohibited homosexuals from working in or owning bars. In the midst of the race, the city commission abolished the ordinance, leaving Campbell without an issue, and he finished a distant second in a field of four. The next year he donated $1,800 to the Carter campaign and was rewarded with an invitation to the inauguration. He placed the souvenirs from that trip—a silver-plated peanut and a 1977 inaugural booklet—on display at his home.

The other key person at Jack Campbell's home that day was Robert Kunst, a slick, bearded product of the anti-war and civil rights movements, a chatty bantam rooster with brown eyes. Kunst, thirty-four, had sold encyclopedias door-to-door in Brooklyn and Queens and then in Boston, before fleeing the northeast winters for Florida. He sold program ads for the Miami Toros, a soccer team, and campaigned for Benjamin Spock's presidential campaign of 1972. Kunst was the kind of person who enjoyed seeing his name in the newspapers, and he had become known in Miami for founding the Transperience Center, four rooms over a marine supply shop in Coconut Grove that offered workshops on bisexuality. Kunst believed everyone was a bisexual, and those workshops involved small groups of men and women who stripped and spent three hours, eyes shut, touching their partners' bodies, from head to genitalia to toes. By the end, Kunst reported, no one could tell the difference between the touch of a male or female hand, and the resulting high was "better than a quaalude."

Campbell called the meeting at his concrete-block house, a low-slung bachelor pad behind a green hedge in the flowering, garden-like checkerboard of Coconut Grove, a liberal, bohemian collection of cottages and old estates, pastel-colored homes with pools and a discreet colony of well-to-do homosexuals, like Campbell. The assembly at Campbell's house was an unlikely mix, including members of a gay motorcycle group, the Thebans, Gay Catholics and the lesbian caucus of the Miami chapter of NOW. An election was coming up, and the organization formed at Campbell's house that day— the Dade County Coalition for the Humanistic Rights of Gays—decided to support candidates who supported gay rights. It mailed two hundred questionnaires; sixty-five candidates responded, and forty-nine provided answers that earned the new group's endorsement. The coalition's resulting support—it distributed leaflets to gay bars and baths, and provided donations and volunteers—was discreet, designed to win attention among homosexuals without alerting the community at large. On election day, forty-four of its candidates won.

Within weeks of the elections, the coalition asked one of those candidates, Ruth Shack, to introduce at the Dade County Metro Commission an amendment to the civil rights ordinance to bar discrimination based on "affectional or sexual preference" in housing, public accommodations and employment. Shack was a school board administrator making her first run for public office. She had worked in the civil rights movement, and then the women's rights movement, so the gay rights movement seemed a natural next step. She could not imagine how anyone could quarrel with the notion that homosexuals had the same right to a job or a home as anyone else. In December, the Metro Commission took the first step toward adopting Shack's ordinance, voting 9–0 to schedule a public hearing the following month. Barring any unexpected complications, it would become law upon second reading and passage.

Robert Brake, a fifty-one-year-old lawyer, read about the Shack ordinance in local newspapers at the end of 1976. Brake, a Roman Catholic who went to church every Sunday and sent his children to Catholic schools, never wavered in his devotion, so when his Protestant friends related their "born-again" experiences to him, Brake would look at them quizzically: Why would anyone need to be born again? Brake, a conservative Democrat, had been among the first to enlist in the fight against abortion rights, even before *Roe* v. *Wade*. Homosexual rights was an issue he had never really considered. When he served in the Judge Advocate's Office in the air force during the Korean War, Brake had encountered a few soldiers who disclosed to him they were homosexual, and he always responded with the same advice: "Don't tell anybody. You don't know my sexual tastes and I don't know yours." He didn't want to know what they did in their off-hours. That always struck him as the way homosexuality should be handled—by "indirect social control," as he liked to put it.

Brake had spent two years on the Dade County Metro Commission, so he understood its procedures, and kept close track of everything it did. Shack's ordinance would, he determined, apply to parochial schools in Dade County, and it could force schools like St. Theresa's, where two of his four children studied, to hire open homosexuals. Everything about the law bothered Brake: the way he thought it threatened his family, its explicit endorsement of a practice he found immoral, the way he believed it would force him to associate with people he did not wish to know. The bill had passed its first hurdle by a 9–0 vote; clearly, homosexuals had become a force to contend with. But this was not a lost cause: Brake knew the county charter, and he knew there was a way to force the commissioners to submit their vote to the electorate. It was a matter of gathering names on petitions.

Anita Bryant learned of the proposed ordinance from her pastor, the Reverend William F. Chapman of the Northwest Baptist Church, who came to her home one afternoon to talk about this worrisome development. Chapman said the bill would force parochial schools to hire practicing homosexuals—schools like the Northwest Christian Academy in North Miami, which all four of Bryant's children attended. Bryant had never taken too much of an interest in local elections, but had made a small exception in one race that year: The wife of her talent agent had been a candidate for the Metro Commission, and Bryant had recorded a radio commercial on her behalf and contributed $1,000 to her campaign. Bryant's agent was Dick Shack and his wife was Ruth Shack, and Anita Bryant realized that afternoon that she had lent her name and money to the woman who was leading the fight for gay rights in Dade County. Chapman wanted the religious community to rise against the bill and told Bryant she was the person to lead the crusade. You have a "mother's heart," Chapman said, as a warm breeze blew in off the bay, "and it takes a mother to do this."

At first, Anita Bryant wrote a letter. "If this ordinance amendment is allowed to become law," Bryant argued to the Metro Commission, "you will in fact be infringing upon my rights or rather discriminating against me as a citizen and a mother to teach my children and set examples and to point to others as examples of God's moral codes as stated in the Holy Scriptures." She called Ruth Shack, imploring her to withdraw her bill, which she said had embarrassed her at Northwest Baptist. Shack told her husband's client that the ordinance was nothing more than an attempt to guarantee equal rights for all people, adding: "The first thing any politician does upon getting into office is disappoint." Bryant ended the conversation by saying she was praying for Ruth Shack, and warned that she was condemning herself to damnation with this bill. Bryant had intended to keep her involvement low-profile. But she changed her mind before the hearing and decided to become a leader of the campaign. The conversion came, Bryant later explained, as she was driving in Miami with her nine-year-old daughter and they came upon a three-car accident at 136th Street. Had they been there moments earlier, Bryant said, they might have perished, and she thanked God for sparing them. It was then, Anita Bryant said, that her daughter asked: "Mommy, if God can help you like this, can't he help you in the Metro Commission?" Anita Bryant said she burst into tears. "Yes, Barbara, he can," she said, and decided to accept the Reverend Chapman's calling. That story was embraced by Anita Bryant's supporters as nothing short of a message from God, proof that their campaign was divinely inspired. Bryant's opponents saw her entry into the fight as part of a calculated plan by the singer and her husband to promote her career, inspired by a quest for more bookings rather than by a vision taken from a chance car wreck. Whatever her motivation, by the time the Metro

Commission gathered for its public hearing at the Dade County Courthouse on January 18, 1977, Bryant was in the audience with a Bible and a speech. The hearing room was filled to capacity a half hour before the commissioners took their seats; people, bused in by their local parishes, were three and four deep against the wall. There were a hundred people outside, waving placards:

"God says NO: Who are you to say Different?"

"Protect our Children: Don't Legislate Morality in Dade County."

Bob Kunst was completely unprepared for this show of force. The front row of the courthouse was the only place to sit and he found himself seated at Anita Bryant's elbow. When Ruth Shack arrived, walking up the steps to the 1920s-style courthouse, she heard curses and hoots from the churchgoers assembled outside in the unseasonably cold air. Each side was limited to forty-five minutes of debate. During those ninety minutes eight different books of the Bible were quoted on both sides of the argument. "As an entertainer, I have worked with homosexuals all my life, and my attitude has been live and let live," Bryant said. "But now I believe it's time to recognize the rights of the overwhelming number of Dade County constituents." There were shouts of "Amen!" from the audience. The gay rights ordinance had passed unanimously on first reading in December. It passed again the second time, but by a 5–3 margin. The fundamentalists had changed a few votes, but not enough to overturn the decision. "We are not going to take this sitting down," Bryant declared as the commissioners hurried from the room. "The ordinance condones immorality and discriminates against my children's rights to grow up in a healthy, decent community."

Even before the vote, Robert Brake had been prepared to gather the ten thousand signatures needed to force a referendum. He had expected to do it alone, but after hearing Bryant speak, he knew he wouldn't have to. He walked across the room, introduced himself to Bryant and asked if she would head his petition drive. She looked at her husband, Bob Green, and then at her pastor, Bill Chapman. Both nodded yes.

Villa Verde had its own waterfall and fountains, and a private altar on the second floor of the mansion where Anita Bryant went to pray. It also had a pool, a sunken heart-shaped double Jacuzzi, a tropical garden with banyan trees, a goldfish pond and a dock for the family boat, *Sea Sharp,* as well as a replica of the Anita Bryant bust that was in the Oklahoma Hall of Fame. Most of the dozen people who showed up for the first organizing meeting of Save Our Children, Inc., had never experienced such opulence before, save for the glimpses of the celebrity mansions on Key Biscayne that could be caught from the road across the bay. Robert Brake came expecting nothing more from Bryant than the use of her name, and was immediately struck by her devotion to the fight. Bob Green cut a less impressive figure that day. Green and Bryant had met when she came to perform in 1959 in Miami Beach, where he was a disc jockey, one of the first to play the new rock and roll format. She was taken with this man who drove a white Thunderbird with his name painted on the side, who wore silk suits and always seemed to have a pretty woman on his arm. Anita Bryant was certain of her attraction to him—he looked like Robert Redford, she later said—and he was the first man she went to bed with, by her account. But she worried he was not devout enough. The night before their wedding in Oklahoma in 1960, Bryant insisted that her fiancé stay up to pray for salvation. Green began to describe himself as born-again after that night, and he converted from Lutheran to Baptist. Still, it was his interest in Miss Oklahoma that led him to prayer rather than any newfound spirituality, and now, seventeen years later, as he surveyed the religious leaders in their home, Green knew that he was out of place in this room. Some of the people there that day were suspicious of Green, noting that the publicity from a referendum would surely help them win religious bookings. Bob Green later said he had some doubts about the very cause that supposedly united them: He agreed that homosexuality was immoral, but not any more or less immoral than, say, adultery. He said none of that then, though. Anita Bryant was like a freight train once she set her mind on an issue, he liked to say: single-minded and obsessed. When she told him that "God spoke to my heart," Green knew there was nothing that would stop her.

It would prove to be a remarkable assembly: clerics and professional conservative political operatives, joined by their shared opposition to homosexual rights. There were representatives from major religious denominations in Dade County: Catholics, Baptists, Orthodox Jews, Spanish Presbyterians and the Greek Orthodox Church. And there were political professionals like Mike Thompson, a thirty-seven-year-old advertising executive and Republican state committeeman. Thompson was chairman of the Florida Conservative Union, and had been a GOP convention delegate for Richard Nixon in 1972 and Ronald Reagan in 1976. He lived next door to Robert Brake, and Brake had decided that the religious devotion of the fundamentalists and Anita Bryant would get them only so far. Thompson knew how to handle reporters, how to construct a campaign message, how to make an advertisement, and Brake had invited him to join the campaign. A campaign like this, Thompson thought, would surely fail if its leaders did not take direction from someone with his experience. As the group quibbled line by line over the statement Anita Bryant would make announcing the petition drive, Thompson suggested that he be allowed to write it alone. He quickly scribbled a few paragraphs and handed them to Bryant, who read them with a burst of emotion that left no doubt in Thompson's mind about the talent of the Save Our Children spokeswoman. Afterward Bryant said to Thompson: "Stand up. I want to hug you." She went over, embraced him and kissed him on the cheek.

"You kiss real good for a girl!" Thompson said. Anita Bryant froze for a minute, then realized it was a joke. Everyone laughed.

Save Our Children needed a campaign that, as Thompson and Brake described it that day, was honest but brutal. It would, Brake said, be a "dignified campaign," that did not engage in name-calling, but that would address the issues forcefully. There was no time for subtlety. So when Bryant appeared before the press a few days later to read the words Thompson had written for her, there was a new crispness to the group's attacks. Bryant, surrounded by clerical leaders, stood under a banner that read, "Save our Children from Homosexuals," inviting people to "sign petitions here to repeal Metro's Gay Blunder."

"The homosexual recruiters of Dade County already have begun their campaign," she said, displaying a piece of literature she claimed had been recovered from one of the local high schools. Homosexuals, she said, are "trying to recruit our children to homosexuality."

Six weeks later Save Our Children submitted its petitions to the Dade County Elections Department. Ten thousand names were needed. By their count, the coalition forces had gathered 64,304, so many signatures that county officials stopped counting at number 13,457. The Metro Commission, in a 6–3 vote, put the referendum on the ballot in a special election called for June 7, 1977.* "By its action today, the commission, for better or worse, has made Dade County a national battleground in the fight for civil rights of parents and their children," Bryant said. "Homosexual acts are not only illegal, they are immoral. And through the power of the ballot box, I believe the parents and the straight-thinking normal majority will soundly reject the attempt to legitimize homosexuals and their recruitment plans for our children.

"We shall not let the nation down."

Jack Campbell liked to boast that Miami Beach was a gay playground—"beaches, bushes, fun, sand, sex" and, of course, his own very popular gay bathhouse. But for all Miami's gay pleasures, there wasn't much in the way of gay politics. Ruth Shack realized that at the public hearing for her ordinance in January. As she watched preacher after preacher denounce the bill, she couldn't understand why the local gay community hadn't found its own cleric or local civil rights leaders to speak for the bill. There was little choice but to turn outside for help now. The National Gay Task Force seemed the obvious place, but its leaders were not inclined to make this fight; that, Ron Gold ar-

---

* The referendum was worded: "Shall Dade County Ordinance No. 77-4, which prohibits discrimination in areas of housing, public accommodations and employment against persons based on their affectional or sexual preference be repealed?"

gued, could elevate a passing local storm into a national referendum on gay rights. The Task Force was sanguine in its assessment of the Dade County referendum and scornful of its spokeswoman. "Bryant is really the perfect opponent," it said in an April 1977 mailing to its members. "Her national prominence . . . insures national news coverage for developments in the Dade County struggle, while the feebleness of her arguments and the embarrassing backwardness of her stance both makes her attacks easier to counteract and tends to generate 'liberal' backlash in our favor. Her 'Save our Children' campaign vividly demonstrates just why gay rights laws are needed—in order to protect our people against the sort of ignorant, irrational, unjustifiable prejudice typified by Anita Bryant. We can make her rantings work *for* us just as Sheriff Bull Connor's cattle prods and police dogs ultimately aided desegregation in the South."

But in California, an alarmed David Goodstein had a different view. Like it or not, this was a national battle, he said, and Anita Bryant was anything but "the perfect opponent" the Task Force perceived. The homosexual community needed to dispatch all of its resources to help the besieged leaders of Dade County. "Save Us from the Anita Nightmare" read the cover of the April 20 *Advocate*. "If the orange juice cow and her bigoted cohorts have their way in Dade County," Goodstein wrote, "you can rest assured they'll bring their hate crusade to your front door in Los Angeles, New York, San Francisco, Chicago or wherever you think you're living in relative safety." He added: "If Hitler had been stopped in Czechoslovakia, World War II would not have occurred. The analogy is exact.

"At best, her campaign is a publicity stunt for her . . . sagging career," Goodstein said. "At worst, it is the beginning of an organized conspiracy to turn us into America's scapegoats. Some of you may think you're safe in your closets. You are not." Goodstein and Jack Campbell agreed there was a need to import professional political consultants into Dade County, ideally campaign operatives who were openly homosexual. In the spring of 1977, there were probably just two people in the country who fit that description: Ethan Geto of New York, now open about his homosexuality, and Jim Foster, now one of the most powerful political organizers in San Francisco, gay or straight.

Geto and Foster arrived in Florida seven weeks before the vote. The Dade County referendum was not without precedent: In May 1974 voters in Boulder, Colorado, had overturned a gay rights ordinance 13,107 to 7,438, and recalled the councilman who had sponsored it. But that vote had been barely noticed outside the West. By contrast, the Dade County referendum was exploding into a national story. "Anita Bryant is a fine Christian lady," Senator Jesse Helms of North Carolina said as Geto and Foster arrived in Florida. "She is fighting for decency and morality." A confident Bryant was already talking about bringing her crusade to Congress and to other states. If

Anita Bryant wins, Elaine Noble said, "it will not be long before they turn up in California, New York and Massachusetts trying to do similar things."

The stakes could hardly have been higher, and the situation that Geto and Foster found in Florida could hardly have been bleaker. Save Our Children, Inc. had evolved into a political juggernaut, with its emotional rallying cry and a network of churches and synagogues that could rival any party machine in the country. By contrast, Miami's homosexual community was unsophisticated and fragmented. There was no campaign plan, no organization, no strategy. The Dade County Coalition for the Humanistic Rights of Gays had been paralyzed by a dispute over whether it should align itself with the national orange juice boycott that had been launched to punish Anita Bryant. For homosexuals outside Florida, this was an obvious tactic. But a boycott was certain to provoke a backlash in Florida, and Campbell opposed it. Bob Kunst had broken off from the coalition and was now promoting the boycott on his own. But it was Kunst, as much a sexual liberationist as a gay liberationist, to whom newspaper reporters turned when they needed a quote, as Geto and Foster soon realized—to their dismay. Geto would talk about human rights, while Kunst would talk provocatively about oral and anal sex, activities he suggested were enjoyed equally by heterosexuals and homosexuals. Gay people were much more psychologically healthy than heterosexuals, Kunst proclaimed in one interview. The gay rights activists were only trying to "put the community on the couch" and force it to deal with its sexual hang-ups. "Am I a role model?" Kunst said to a reporter during the campaign. "Sure. I'm an absolutely positive role model." Geto tried to tone Kunst down. "Bob, this is counterproductive," Geto told him. "People can't process this, people can't understand it, it's too confrontational, it's scaring them, it's easy for Anita Bryant to say gays are militant." Kunst ignored him, as Geto discovered when Governor Reubin Askew, a Democrat, announced his support for Bryant. "If I were in Miami," the governor said from Tallahassee, "I would have no difficulty in voting to repeal that ordinance. I would not want a known homosexual teaching my children." Geto offered reporters a carefully considered response to Askew, asserting it was dangerous when "someone in your position arbitrarily decides who in this society should have their human rights and who in the country should be the victims of bigotry." Bob Kunst simply blasted the governor of Florida as "sexually insecure," which was the quote that made it into the newspapers the next day.

Geto and Foster had twenty-five years of professional political experience between them. Jim Foster had worked in the presidential campaigns of George McGovern and Jimmy Carter, and the San Francisco campaigns of George Moscone, Dianne Feinstein and Richard Hongisto. Geto had worked for some of the best-known liberal Democrats of the 1970s: McGovern, Hubert Humphrey and Birch Bayh. Foster and Geto had seven weeks to design, finance and launch a campaign against an opposition which seemed to have the winds of victory at its back. To complicate matters, the idea of bringing in two out-of-towners was stirring new tensions among the activists already there, and provided ammunition to the opponents, who began referring to them as carpetbaggers. Geto made no effort to smooth over bruised feelings. He pushed people he considered incompetent off the coalition's executive board and forced the Floridians to change the name of the organization, the Dade County Coalition for the Humanistic Rights of Gays, to the Dade County Coalition for Human Rights. The word "humanistic" was pretentious, the New York consultant said, and better that the word "gay" not be in the name. Geto could not have been more culturally different from his new political associates. Everything about him shouted New York—his Bronx accent, his rough sense of humor, his close-cropped gray beard and intense, deep-set eyes, accented by dark circles that suggested Geto preferred long hours of work and play to sleep. People mistook Geto for Italian because his name ended with a vowel, but Geto was a Russian Jew. He was a strange match with the activists in Dade County. When a woman showed up at one meeting carrying a gun, saying she needed it for self-protection, Geto decreed that no guns would be allowed in the offices of the Dade County coalition. Geto could barely hide his disdain for the Florida activists.

What Geto found at the Dade County coalition in mid-May was not that different from what Mike Thompson had found at that first meeting of Save Our Children. In both cases, men who made their living at politics were working with people unfamiliar with the mechanics of running a campaign. The first thing both Geto and Thompson did was order a poll to determine the best way to proceed. The two polls reached similar conclusions about the Dade County electorate and this issue. Voters supported the ordinance, albeit without enthusiasm. Jewish voters in particular, who made up 20 percent of the electorate, rallied behind a measure that was presented as a law to protect a class of citizens from discrimination. The main difference between the two polls was that Thompson got his results in early March, giving him a two-month head start over Geto. The poll finding that struck Thompson—and guided everything Save Our Children did from that day on—was how overwhelmingly women voters supported gay rights: by a 2–1 margin, more than enough to counterbalance the opposition to the measure among men. He had some theories for why Dade County women held homosexuals in high regard. The homosexuals whom most women encountered, he said, were hairdressers, dress designers or dog groomers. "They love their dogs," Thompson would say of women with pets, "and they love the people who love their dogs." There were also women who enjoyed the social company of gay men, for dinner or a movie. Thompson learned that these women were known as "fag-hags"—they sought out the company of male homosexuals, he explained to his associates at Save Our Children, because they were charming and expected nothing at the end of the night. The key to winning was forcing women to reconsider their notion of homosexuals as harmless. Thompson suggested, half jokingly, that they change public opinion by filming the sexual activity that went on in Campbell's bathhouses. But Save Our Children did not have to sneak a camera into a bathhouse to suggest there was, as Thompson put it, more to homosexuality than poodle-grooming and hairdressing. All it had to do was show an event that homosexuals themselves viewed as a celebration of their lives: Gay Freedom Day in San Francisco. The resulting television commercial turned up on Dade County airwaves in late spring. It began with a clip of the Orange Bowl Parade, high-school marching bands and apple-cheeked youngsters. "Miami's gift to the nation," the announcer said. "Wholesome entertainment." The image was replaced by a videotape of a San Francisco Freedom Day Parade. Instead of majorettes, viewers saw men wearing skimpy leather outfits and snapping whips, topless women on motorcycles, men in dresses and the most bizarre forms of drag. The camera lingered on that picture as the announcer underscored the contrast: "In San Francisco, when they take to the streets, it's a parade of homosexuals. Men hugging other men. Cavorting with little boys. Wearing dresses and makeup. The same people who turned San Francisco into a hotbed of homosexuality . . . want to do the same thing to Dade." The advertisement was devastating. "That commercial," Thompson boasted then, "is just driving them nuts!"

The other way to force women to reconsider their view of homosexuals was to present gay men as a threat to children. Since homosexuals don't procreate, Anita Bryant said, the only way to increase their numbers was to recruit, and what better place to do this than in the schools? "Some of the stories I could tell you of child recruitment and child abuse by homosexuals would turn your stomach," Bryant told reporters. The newspaper advertisements were equally direct. "This recruitment of our children is absolutely necessary for the survival and growth of homosexuality—for since homosexuals cannot reproduce, they must recruit, must freshen their ranks," read one. "And who qualifies as a likely recruit: a 35-year-old father or mother of two . . . or a teenage boy or girl who is surging with sexual awareness?"

The Save Our Children forces stumbled across a powerful weapon to underscore this attack, courtesy of the gay movement itself. The afternoon mail brought a copy of the gay rights platform homosexual leaders had adopted in Chicago in 1972, including the plank calling for the abolition of age of consent laws. Steve Endean had presciently warned that the plank would one day be used against the movement. Now it was reprinted under a line saying "What the homosexuals want," part of a full-page advertisement in the *Miami Herald* headlined, "THERE IS NO 'HUMAN RIGHT' TO CORRUPT OUR CHILDREN," which included a montage of newspaper headlines, such as "Teacher Accused of Sex Acts with Boy Students." The ad copy underscored the point: "Many parents are confused, and don't know the real dangers posed by many homosexuals—and perceive them as all being gentle, non-aggressive types. THE OTHER SIDE OF THE HOMOSEXUAL COIN IS A HAIR-RAISING PATTERN OF RECRUITMENT AND OUTRIGHT SEDUCTION AND MOLESTATION, A GROWING PATTERN THAT PREDICTABLY WILL INTENSIFY IF SOCIETY APPROVES LAWS GRANTING LEGITIMACY TO THE SEXUALLY PERVERTED."

In the midst of this barrage, Geto and the coalition decided on a more subtle campaign, a decision made in part because a May poll showed them winning, with voters supporting the ordinance by as much as a 62–38 margin. But the poll also showed that while Bryant's supporters would surely turn out on election day, only 15 percent of the ordinance supporters were likely to vote. Most voters, it appeared, had no problem with the ordinance, but had difficulty seeing homosexuals—with their fancy clothes and homes and cars—as victims. Geto and Foster designed a campaign to alarm their supporters into turning out. Their supporters, the poll found, tended to be older, from New York, people who considered themselves liberal and tolerant. And many of them were Jewish, who had fled to the United States to escape Nazi Germany. "By making the campaign a human rights issue, it was something all people could identify with," Foster explained then. All they needed to do was "hit people with the fact that if the rights of one minority are threatened or taken away, their rights are also jeopardized." The only problem with that approach was that Mike Thompson had made the same discovery about Jewish voters two months before. He had already recruited one of Dade County's most prominent rabbis—Phineas Weberman, secretary to the Orthodox Rabbinical Council—to head a council of Jewish leaders opposed to the gay rights ordinance. And as soon as the first ads appeared comparing the gay rights plank to the discrimination Jews had suffered, Jewish leaders at Thompson's side were ready with a rebuttal: "Tell *us* about human rights?" they demanded indignantly. "What right is there to corrupt our children?"

Ethan Geto began to wonder if they were going to lose, and quietly made a few decisions that reflected his concern. He took to spending as much time talking to reporters from outside Miami—from the *New York Times*, the newsmagazines, the networks, even from Europe—as with reporters from Dade County. It was not what he had been hired to do, but Geto decided that even if they lost the vote in Miami, they could still sway opinions elsewhere. He was also concerned about turning the campaign into a daily debate that associated homosexuals with child molesters. Geto, thinking as much about how the campaign was playing outside Florida as he was about the contest at hand, took the opportunity to offer a sober and academic rebuttal to the notion that homosexuals were predators on children. He flew in experts to hold press conferences discussing the issue. John Spiegel, the former president of the American Psychiatric Association, for example, asserted that sexual orientation was established at a young age, by three or four, before children entered school. But the coalition ran no television advertising engaging the attacks by Save Our Children. A week before the election, Geto told a Miami reporter: "I could easily put together newspaper clips of heterosexuals molesting children. And I'd have 10 times as many clips." But he never did it.

As election day approached, Bryant posted guards around her home, and Campbell wore a bulletproof vest. Jim Foster told Geto that one night, after he stopped his car at a red light, a group of men pulled up in a car next to him, pointed a shotgun out the window at his car and said: "We're gonna blow your fuckin' brains out." They sped off into the night when the light turned green. One afternoon a suspicious two-inch-thick manila envelope with a Manhattan postmark arrived in the mail at Bryant headquarters. The bomb squad blew it up, and everyone looked a little sheepish as gay rights leaflets came raining down. The newspapers and television stations ran so many stories on homosexual child molestation cases that Geto became convinced the local media were out to inflame the electorate. "This is really a sewer," Geto thought of Miami. "They're against us." (It was not a groundless concern: The Sunday before election day, the *Miami Herald* ran a United Press International story headlined "Homosexual Ring's Ad Lured Boys: 17 to Face Charges in New Orleans," about a two-year-old scandal in New Orleans with no obvious news hook.) When the coalition tried launching its own barrage of newspaper advertisements, the *Herald* and *News* refused to run many of them. They would not print a swastika as part of an advertisement aimed at the county's sizable Jewish population which reprinted this 1936 decree from Heinrich Himmler, the head of Hitler's Gestapo: "Just as we today have gone back to the ancient German view on the question of marriages mixing different races, so too in our judgment of homosexuality—a symptom of degeneracy which could destroy our race—we must return to the guiding Nordic principle, extermination of degenerates." Foster discovered a series of three pictures of Anita Bryant wearing a skimpy, fringed, cowgirl outfit while performing what appeared to be a sexually provocative number at the 1971 Ozark Empire Fair in Springfield, Missouri. The cutline on the photos, discovered in a Chicago trade newspaper that year, was: "Strip Tease? Not Quite." Foster did not use them because, he said later, "We didn't want to get down in the gutter with them."

For all the problems in Florida, homosexuals across the country were rallying to the cause of gay rights in a way they never had before. "Every gay bar in town has agreed to stop serving orange juice altogether, or squeeze their own California oranges," said Lenny Mollet, president of the San Francisco Tavern Guild. The Florida Citrus Commission wavered over whether it wanted to keep Anita Bryant on (until an uproar from her supporters forced it to back off). Homosexuals disrupted Bryant's performances. In Washington, D.C., activists staged a Bryant roast at the Pier Nine disco. And in San Francisco, the writer and columnist Armistead Maupin noted the sight of homosexuals climbing into cars and driving to Miami with a "campy defiance" he had never seen before. "There was never anything for them to identify with before," he said. "Who wanted to get on a flatbed truck with a bunch of drag queens?" Indeed, Jack Campbell found that most of the money the coalition collected came out of San Francisco, where men walked down the Castro wearing T-shirts proclaiming, "Squeeze a Fruit for Anita." "Nothing has ever grabbed the gay community like this one," said Chris Perry, president of the San Francisco Gay Democratic Club. Campbell encountered Bryant at a commission meeting in Miami toward the end of the campaign and went over to thank her for unifying the nation's homosexual community. Bryant looked bewildered, until Bob Green rushed over: "Don't you know who that is?" Green demanded, and pulled her away.

In the final weeks, Bryant's speeches became increasingly emphatic. She proclaimed that God had inflicted a drought on California because the state was tolerant of gays. She referred to homosexuals as "human garbage," and said the Dade County ordinance would protect the right to have "intercourse with beasts." She cheered when the Reverend Jerry Falwell of the Thomas Road Baptist Church of Lynchburg, Virginia, a fellow Southern Baptist beginning to tie together his church and his conservative politics, proclaimed at a Save Our Children rally at the Miami Convention Center: "So-called gay folks [would] just as soon kill you as look at you." Bryant rejected the idea that homosexuals deserved sympathy or dispensation because they were born that way. "Homosexuality is a conduct, a choice, a way of life. And if you choose to have a lifestyle as such, then you are going to have to live with the consequences. It's not a sickness, but a sin." When a reporter asked her if she would also like to see other morality laws enforced, including ones that forbid out-of-wedlock fornication, adultery and cohabitation by unmarried couples, Anita Bryant responded: "I would, yes." Bryant was a singer, not a politician, Mike Thompson realized; she worked best when reading from a script, and he tried to avoid spontaneous engagements in the daily campaign. Bob Green considered his wife sincere but politically naive. He told her to tone down the rhetoric; he was getting uncomfortable complaints from religious friends who found her extreme.

Even so, by the beginning of June, Anita Bryant and Save Our Children were steamrolling the opposition. Their polls attested to the success of their strategy: women had decisively swung against the ordinance. Ruth Shack found a wholesale defection by Dade County's liberal community—people she had worked with for years on civil rights and women's rights—over this issue. And Bryant herself was an elusive target. She was a woman, she was devout, and she was almost impossible to attack.* At one memorable campaign face-off at a Kiwanis Club luncheon, Bryant and Bob Kunst were each given twelve minutes to speak. Bryant spoke for six of them, and then threw her head back and burst into song: "Mine eyes have seen the glory of the coming of the Lord," the start of six minutes of "Battle Hymn of the Republic." The performance left even Kunst applauding—what else could he do?—and nearly speechless. In one last indignity for the Dade County Coalition for Human Rights, Bryant's campaign turned the main source of coalition support—the city of San Francisco—into an argument against gay rights. Sheriff Richard Hongisto, who spent a week in Miami campaigning against repeal, tried to explain to Dade County voters why homosexuals were such an asset to San Francisco. "They seem to work," Hongisto said, refurbishing "drab" houses and raising property values. Mike Thompson called a press conference to rebut Hongisto and present his own picture of San Francisco as a "cesspool of sexual perversion gone rampant. We cannot believe that the people of Dade County want to pattern our community after the debased standards of that city." Added Green: "San Francisco may be completely gone. There may be no saving it. They even have a gay sheriff there." Hongisto, who was heterosexual, returned home to report that the vote had turned into a referendum on San Francisco itself.

The high-minded campaign envisioned by Geto and Foster was collapsing, and the two out-of-towners found themselves under attack. Jack Campbell told Geto he could not understand why things had gone so wrong. "You showed me a poll that said we could win," Campbell said to Geto in one angry exchange before the two men ceased talking to each other completely. Steve Endean thought Campbell and Geto were naive, taking the high road while the other side effectively played to voters' fears. Kay Tobin and Barbara Gittings had questioned why they were sending down a New York ideologue like Ethan Geto to do battle with Anita Bryant. Why not send Troy Perry, the

---

* Bruce Voeller, among others, made this argument; Morris Kight argued the opposite was true: that men were harsher to her because she was a woman. If this was true, it was in private; she was barely attacked during the campaign itself.

minister who grew up in Florida, and fight "fire with fire?" said Tobin, imagining how Troy Perry would match Anita Bryant, Bible quote for Bible quote.

On the last Sunday before election day, religious leaders across Dade County devoted their sermons to attacking the gay rights ordinance—"This is the Lord's Battle and it will be the Lord's Victory," the Reverend William Chapman declared from the pulpit of Bryant's church—while the *Miami Herald* devoted five news stories to it, including an editorial that called for repeal. "We believe that the ordinance, while well-intentioned, is unnecessary to the protection of human rights and undesirable as an expression of public policy," the *Herald* editorial said, in an about-face from the previous January, when it commended the Metro Commission and Ruth Shack for "mustering courage to hold fast to the principle of non-discrimination" in approving the ordinance. The mood among gay activists was grim as voting day approached, and the leaders of the gay coalition decided to use their fundraising surplus to assure their election night festivities were as grand as possible. They rented the biggest ballroom at the Fontainebleau Hotel and played host to almost one thousand people, including as large a national press corps as anyone had seen at that hotel since George McGovern stayed there in 1972. It turned out to be a very short night. The first returns showed the ordinance losing by 2 to 1, and the margin never narrowed. Dade County was united in its opposition: 45 percent of the electorate had turned out, and the ordinance was defeated in virtually every neighborhood (Jack Campbell's Coconut Grove being one exception) and every ethnic group (including Jewish voters). The final vote was 202,319 in favor of repeal to 89,562 against; almost 70 percent of the voters had voted against gay rights. Leonard Matlovich, the air force sergeant discharged in 1975 for being homosexual, reminded the Fontainebleau crowd of Bryant's promise to take this campaign across the country. "But when she gets there, she's going to find us waiting for her. We shall overcome." With that, the thousand people at the Fontainebleau started to sing "We Shall Overcome," adding a stanza to the civil rights anthem: "Gays and straights together, we shall overcome, someday."

Anita Bryant embraced her victory at the Zodiac Room in the Holiday Inn on Collins Avenue. She was dressed in powder blue, glistening and happy as she emerged to read her written victory statement to her audience of reporters and supporters. "Tonight the laws of God and the cultural values of man have been vindicated. I thank God for the strength he has given me and I thank my fellow citizens who joined me in what at first was a walk through the wilderness. The people of Dade County—the normal majority—have said, 'Enough! Enough! Enough!' They have voted to repeal an obnoxious assault on our moral values ... despite our community's reputation as one of the most liberal areas in the country.

"All America and the world have heard the people of Miami," she said. "We will now carry our fight against similar laws throughout the nation that attempt to legitimize a lifestyle that is both perverse and dangerous to the sanctity of the family, dangerous to our children, dangerous to our freedom of religion and freedom of choice, dangerous to our survival as a nation."

The next morning Jean O'Leary, who had come down to Miami in the final days of the campaign, boarded a plane for New York, escaping a city which had offered her "all the evidence anyone could need of the extent and virulence of prejudice against lesbians and gay men." Once aloft, she opened the *Miami Herald*: There on page one, was a quarter-page head shot of Anita Bryant and Bob Green, kissing. "This is what heterosexuals do, fellows," Green said. O'Leary felt suffocated by the defeat.

Gay leaders tried to throw the best light on the disheartening results. "We've taken one step backward and two steps forward," said Campbell. "It did bring the entire gay community together." David Goodstein said that the election had trained homosexuals in how to deal with this kind of public referendum. "We had an army of recruits," Goodstein wrote. "Now we will have an army of veterans." In defeat, Ethan Geto agreed that they might have made some mistakes. Should they have rebutted the child molestation advertisements on television? Had he paid too much attention to the out-of-state media? "While we might have done some things differently or better," Geto wrote Shack three weeks after the vote, explaining the strategy he and Foster had employed, "with hindsight I feel the campaign was not winnable—with more time and a slightly different strategy, we might have done better, but we doubt the outcome would have been very different." He noted the "very little spade work done in Dade County by the gay community prior to the final, active phase of the election campaign," and concluded, "We are not ashamed of the campaign that was waged in Dade County."

Shack didn't even try to sugarcoat the debacle; it was, she said, "three times worse than I ever expected. They came out of the woodwork. It was a huge step back nationally. We even lost among Jewish liberals in Miami Beach." Indeed, it seemed that Anita Bryant could not have hoped for anything more. There was a new movement afoot, of fundamentalist conservatives, and it had found a rallying point, a cause that seemed likely to stir more passions than the fight against abortion rights or for prayer in schools. The vote seemed to be a repudiation of homosexuals by the American public. And the Dade County results revealed that the movement remained painfully unsophisticated, divided and dominated by extreme personalities, and apparently unprepared for the fights that lay ahead.

• • •

Bella Abzug was asleep in her townhouse on Bank Street in New York's Greenwich Village. It was nearly two o'clock in the morning, four and a half hours after Anita Bryant had read her victory statement, when Abzug awoke to noise outside her window. "Martin," she said, to her husband sleeping next to her, "I hear someone calling my name."

"Go back to bed," he said. "You're dreaming."

But the chants from outside on Bank Street grew louder: "Bel-LAH! Bel-LAH! Bel-LAH!" The former representative, rousted from bed, opened the second-floor window to the street outside. More than three hundred gay men and lesbians had made their way to the doorstep of the woman who had introduced the first gay civil rights bill in Congress. Abzug put on a nightdress and went outside. It was hard not to feel sad for this crowd, and Bella Abzug cast about for some encouraging words. This will end up being a good thing, Abzug said, grabbing the outstretched hands, her loud voice booming up Bank Street. It will create more determination and a more mature political movement among homosexuals. "And now it's time to go to bed," she said, bidding them good night.

In one way, Abzug was right. The results in Dade County that night roused many homosexuals, and the gay movement, as nothing had before. It was a turning point for gay men and lesbians who years later would trace their own coming out or interest in gay politics to the Anita Bryant victory. In the days after the repeal, there were marches in cities large and small, from Los Angeles to Indianapolis; from San Francisco, where thousands of people marched through to Union Square chanting "Out of the bars and into the streets," to New Orleans; from Boston to Houston. Gay Pride marches that month saw record turnouts. Jeanne Cordova always marked the vote as the beginning of a migration of lesbians back into the gay rights movement. Gay organizations popped up all over the country; existing ones saw their membership rolls swell. The National Gay Task Force saw its membership double in just four months.

Indeed, it soon became clear the referendum had not quite inspired the national reevaluation of homosexuality that either Ethan Geto or Anita Bryant had expected. There were limits on how far the gay rights movement could go, but there were also limits on how far the emerging religious right could take its campaign to restrict homosexuals. "Let Miss Bryant and her own militant crusaders not misinterpret their victory: No mandate has been given to put the gays on the run, or to repress their right of free expression," wrote William Safire, the conservative *New York Times* columnist. "She has turned back a danger posed by wrongheaded gay activists, and deserves credit for that; she does not deserve to be matriarch of a new movement that would pose a new danger to those homosexuals who want to be left alone." Safire drew an important distinction in how society should deal with homosexuals. The gay activists in Dade County wanted "the seal on their housekeeping to say 'good.' That is a moral judgment they have the right to make, but not to insist upon from the rest of society."

Still, it was a tense and gloomy atmosphere, and the gay rights movement turned on itself and its more visible members. "Democratic issues are won and lost on simple public relations and ours is shameful!" complained a letter-writer to *The Advocate.* "How easily the Save Our Children could get footage of 'Cockapillars' and queens for their emotional television attack." When the black movement got "hot and heavy," the writer said, "you did *not* see Uncle Toms and Stepin Fetchits" showing up with watermelons to push for black civil rights. "Why do *we* let them? . . . Think about the next time a 'friend' starts a comment with, 'Listen, Mary.' Mary isn't listening. Anita is!"

The political professionals drew a less emotional lesson: Homosexuals should avoid taking their case to the public. "In 1965, if the federal civil rights act was voted on in Selma, Alabama, what would have happened?" Ethan Geto said, in a round of sometimes defensive interviews after the vote. "Of course they would have taken away blacks' civil rights. A referendum is a lousy vehicle to extend or expand the rights of a minority."

23

A VERY BAD YEAR

June 1977, Boston

On a Saturday afternoon, eleven days after the vote in Dade County, the Boston Gay Pride parade wound through the streets of the old city and onto the Boston Common, pooling into a crowd of several thousand in front of the bandstand, not far from the spot where a Quaker named Mary Dyer had been hung as a witch by Puritans three centuries before. There was a tension in the air as the red-robed figure of Professor Charley Shively, a teacher of history at Boston State College, stepped to the microphone. He and Ann Maguire, the big, athletic lesbian who had managed Elaine Noble's successful campaign for state representative three years before, were the two keynote speakers for the celebration that day, and Shively looked out at a crowd sprinkled with familiar faces, people who had helped shape the movement in Boston over the last decade. It was, he knew, not so much a movement in flow as it was a family at war, as fractious and conflicted as the politics of Boston itself. Its elements ranged from Roman Catholic conservatives on the right to the sexual liberationists of the left—a group more enduringly radical, probably, than in any other city but San Francisco. It was Shively himself who anchored the far left end of the gay political spectrum in Boston, but it was the absent Anita Bryant who charged the larger than usual crowd on the Boston Common that day. It was the kind of moment Charley Shively savored, and he and his band of supporters had marched to the Common prepared to do battle, holding aloft a banner which they had hidden until the parade began. "Christianity Is The Enemy!" it said. He was about to give an incendiary speech.

When Shively had left his family roots in the rigid, religious, poor white Appalachian mountain culture of West Virginia, Kentucky and Ohio to come to college in 1955, he had been warned that Harvard would turn him into an atheist, a Communist and a homosexual. He liked to joke that it had all come true. He had a doctorate in American history from Harvard, and he had become the purest kind of sexual liberationist, an anarchist and provocateur opposed to any law or institution or person that sought to restrict his freedom. *Fag Rag,* the journal that he published, offered an unending serialization of male sexual fantasies, many of them centered on young teenage boys. It was a paper, Shively liked to remind people, in his mild, deadpan way, which had been denounced on the floor of the United States Congress as "the most loathsome publication in the English language." Lesbians and many gay men found it enormously offensive.

If gay activists thought Charley Shively was extreme, his atheism, his social communism and his literary celebration of sex with children made him the bogeyman of Anita Bryant's worst nightmare. But she was also his worst nightmare, and Shively had come to the Boston Common that day draped in his faded, crimson Harvard doctoral robe, with his thick, shiny black hair flowing in the breeze, and a Chinese wok, a book and a clutch of papers in his hands. He had scripted a performance and, in experimenting with a friend and fellow *Fag Rag* writer the night before, had found that cigarette lighter fluid worked best. Now he squirted some fluid in the bottom of the wok, lit it and held up what looked like a certificate to the crowd. "I have here my Harvard diploma," he declared in his thin, twangy mountain voice. Shively's radical thoughts and the voice and manner of the person uttering them often seemed almost a parody of each other. "They're only worth burning," he added. There were gasps and whoops as he dropped the paper into the flames. Then Shively held up the next document, and the next. In succession—as symbols of one sort of oppression or another—he burned a U.S. dollar bill, his insurance policy, a letter from Boston State College denying his request to teach a course in gay studies, and a copy of the commonwealth of Massachusetts's 300-year-old statute against sodomy. He first read it aloud, then threw it into the fire.

There were howls, cheers and cries of "Burn it! Burn it!" And then Shively held up the book he had brought with him. It was the Holy Bible. He opened it to Leviticus, to the passage on which the Massachusetts statute and so many other laws against sodomy had been based through the centuries. In his slow, deliberate voice, he read from chapter 20, verse 13: "If a man also lie with mankind, as he lieth with a woman, both of them have committed an abomination: they shall surely be put to death; their blood shall be upon them." And then, as the crowd realized what was coming—and some people began shouting *"No! No!"*—Shively dropped the whole Bible into the burning wok and watched in satisfaction as the pages began to curl in flame.

The crowd, which to that point had treated Shively's performance as a kind of carnival satire, erupted in a pandemonium of conflicted feelings, much of it rage. However much the people watching Charley Shively might have been united in despising Anita Bryant for her judgment of them, they certainly didn't believe that she spoke for God, or that God was necessarily their enemy, or that Christianity was the enemy's religion, or that the Bible was the enemy's book. Much of the important early support for the gay rights movement in Boston, as in other cities, had come from churches and ministers—Unitarian-Universalist, United Methodist, American Baptist, even Roman Catholic. Under Cardinals Cushing and Medeiros, a Roman Catholic priest in Boston had ministered openly to homosexuals, and scores of people watching Charley Shively that day—people now screaming at him in anger— were members of Dignity, the national organization which had been founded in 1973 to give comfort and voice to gay Roman Catholics. Others belonged to Integrity, the Episcopalian gay group, and still others were members of the Metropolitan Community Church in Boston.

One of the members of Dignity stunned by Shively's act was a lean, dark-haired, angelic-looking young man named Brian R. McNaught. A former altar boy, a devout Roman Catholic, he had been fired in 1974 as a columnist and writer for the *Michigan Catholic,* the diocesan newspaper in Detroit, when he revealed that he was gay. Some years earlier, as a guilt-ridden young homosexual, he had attempted suicide, and failing, had decided to live as who he was. The rejection of the Detroit Archdiocese had turned him into a Roman Catholic dissenter and activist. He fasted. He wrote articles. He appeared on television. He made speeches to bishops and to high school groups.

By the time he moved to Boston, he had become director of social action for Dignity, and part of what that meant was trying to get Roman Catholic homosexuals involved in the movement. McNaught was politically attuned, and he had thought that inviting Charley Shively to speak at Gay Pride, less than two weeks after Anita Bryant had defeated the Dade County gay rights ordinance by casting homosexuals as godless libertines, was asking for trouble. Now, watching Shively drop the Bible into the flaming wok, McNaught was beside himself. People around him were going crazy, and he could see the television news cameras cranking away. The tall, freckled, auburn-haired figure of state Representative Elaine Noble loomed nearby, and McNaught made a grab for her.

"You've got to go up there and do something!" he pleaded. "This is insane! This is going to be on the five o'clock news!"

Noble was almost halfway through her second—and last—term in the state legislature (she would be squeezed out by a redrawing of the district lines the following year, a change which would force her to compete against Barney Frank or withdraw. She would withdraw). Still the most prominent homosexual elected official in the nation, she had been the first to speak from the bandstand when the parade had wound its way onto the Common, and she and then Ann Maguire and Barney Frank had all stirred the crowd to cheers of good feeling. But she instantly understood the political damage of Shively's actions, and she also thought it possible, as she moved through the crowd toward the red-robed figure behind the wok, that someone might try to kill him for what he had just done. "Go to Hell!" people were screaming at him. "Get off the stage!" "Burn him!"

A man had vaulted up onstage, grabbed the wok away from Shively and dumped its smoldering contents on the bandstand floor. He was stamping on the Bible, trying to put out the fire as a television cameraman locked his lens on the frenzied, smoking scene. Noble reached Shively and pulled him close to deliver a message: the members of Dignity were threatening to kill him for burning the Bible if Brian McNaught was not allowed to speak, she said. That may have been hyperbole, but Elaine Noble's argument won the microphone for McNaught.

Brian McNaught had a mop of dark hair, big soulful eyes and a boyish passion, and he pleaded with the crowd—and the television cameras—to realize that Charley Shively wasn't speaking for all gay people, that he and most others didn't feel that way about religion, and that it was the Bible which had inspired him and many other homosexuals to accept themselves as they were ("To thine own self be true"). The last society that burned books, he reminded the crowd, was Nazi Germany.

McNaught's words seemed to dissipate the anger around the bandstand, and people began to drift away. At Elaine Noble's insistence, Charley Shively stayed behind, until the camera crews and the crowd had gone. And then, feeling suddenly very much alone, he folded up his Harvard robe, put it and the wok under his arm and began walking home, thinking to himself that it had been a satisfying, if surreal, day.

In homes across New England that night, especially in the heavy Roman Catholic populations of Rhode Island, Massachusetts and New Hampshire, not a few viewers of the television news went to bed angry, convinced that gay militants had burned the Bible on the Boston Common and then stomped on it. Emotions were running high. They seemed to be turning violent. And Anita Bryant herself had yet to come to Boston.

In Boston and other cities across the country, the battle lines were being drawn. The repeal of the Dade County gay rights ordinance unleashed a flood of feelings, public and private, within the homosexual rights movement and among conservative Christians who had never organized politically around a social issue before. For the gay rights movement, it would prove to be a very bleak year.

June 1977, Minneapolis-St. Paul

In Minneapolis–St. Paul, where each of the Twin Cities had its own gay rights ordinance, the newspapers reported that a jubilant Anita Bryant had promised to bring her crusade to other places which had enacted gay rights laws, starting with Minnesota. In fact, the forces that lifted Bryant to victory in Florida had already begun to be felt. Three weeks before the Dade County vote, the Archdiocese of St. Paul and Minneapolis had engineered the defeat of legislation which would have made it illegal to discriminate on the basis of "affectional or sexual preference" in the state of Minnesota. The archdiocese was moved by the same fear that had motivated Roman Catholics and Southern Baptists in Dade: that a gay rights law would force church schools to hire homosexuals as teachers. Across Minnesota, bishops and priests spoke out against the proposed law, and the lobbyist for the archdiocese testified against it in legislative hearings.

The church's active opposition had caught Steve Endean by surprise. He thought that his arguments to the church hierarchy had persuaded Archbishop John R. Roach, a moderate churchman, to stay neutral, but they had not. The Twin Cities ordinances were three years old. The bill in the legislature was the third attempt to enact a state gay rights law, and it was the missing piece in the legally tolerant culture that had long been Endean's dream for Minnesota. He and state Senator Allan Spear had gotten virtually the whole liberal political establishment of the state to endorse the proposed new law: the governor, the attorney general, the secretary of state, the Senate majority leader, the speaker of the House, the League of Women Voters, the National Council of Churches, the National Education Association and the major daily newspapers.

Archbishop Roach was perceived as a progressive, caring prelate, and his decision to oppose the law had given many hesitant legislators the reason they needed to vote no. Late on a Wednesday night, in the vaulted and muraled Senate chamber, across from the great stone bulk of the Roman Catholic cathedral on its hill, the gay rights bill died a few votes short of passage. Standing on the Senate floor afterward, a bitter Allan Spear denounced the vote as a victory for "bigots." The bill had been killed, he said, by "a campaign of vilification led by people who call themselves Christians." A mild, owlish man, an academic by profession, Spear was barely in control of his emotions, and when he had finished speaking, Steve Endean led him from the chamber into a private room, where he broke down and wept.

For Endean and the other Roman Catholics in the gay rights coalition who had lobbied so hard for passage (Spear was Jewish), the archdiocese's opposition was especially bitter. Dennis Miller, one of the lobbyists who had worked the State House, was a member of the Dignity chapter which met at the Newman Center at the University of Minnesota. The night of the defeat, he sought the comfort of a friend, George P. Casey, a Jesuit priest who had been chaplain of the Dignity group. Father Casey was as angry with his church as Dennis Miller was, and the object of his wrath was Archbishop Roach. He should be made to understand what he'd done, Casey kept saying. The conversation with the priest fed Miller's resentment all the more, and later, he told Patrick Schwartz, an attendant at The Locker Room, a gay bath in Minneapolis, what George Casey had said. Schwartz, a Roman Catholic, wasn't particularly religious, and he hadn't been much involved in the gay rights cause. But he was drawn to the sort of anarchistic, theatrical politics that Robert Kunst practiced in Miami, that Charley Shively practiced in New England, and that Jack Baker and Mike McConnell increasingly personified in Minnesota. And he had an idea.

The following week Archbishop Roach was to receive the National Brotherhood Award from the National Conference of Christians and Jews. There would be hundreds of people at the dinner—the religious, business and political establishment of Minneapolis–St. Paul. When the archbishop rose to speak, Patrick Schwartz, posing as a press photographer, was hunched down with a camera and briefcase between two tables in front of the podium of the hotel banquet hall, staring up at Roach. In the briefcase was a rapidly liquefying chocolate cream cheese pie. Schwartz and Miller had bought it at a market on their way downtown, with the $20 that Father George Casey had contributed to the plot. They would need money for the pie, Casey had said excitedly, and for cab fare after throwing it, if they got away.

A wave of applause rose to greet the graying, bespectacled archbishop when he stepped to the microphone, and as he began to speak Schwartz opened his bag, scooped out the pie, leaped toward the incredulous churchman and heaved it straight at him, glopping his nose, chin, neck and left shoulder with a gooey spread of chocolate cream cheese. The room erupted in pandemonium, and Schwartz and Miller turned and hightailed it for the door.

They didn't get away. The Minneapolis police chief and an impressive array of law enforcement officers were at the banquet, too, and a ring of policemen and hotel security guards surrounded Schwartz and Miller as a sea of angry dinner guests heaved and cursed beyond the cordon. Newspaper photographers and reporters were also there, and when they asked Patrick Schwartz why he had done it, he said it was because of the archbishop's opposition to the gay rights bill. It was hypocritical of him to accept a brotherhood award after refusing to recognize the brotherhood of another part of the human family, he said.

Schwartz was arrested. Jack Baker, now a lawyer, represented him before a municipal judge in St. Paul, where Schwartz pleaded guilty to disorderly conduct and was sentenced to do eighty hours of community service. George Casey, the Jesuit priest, fared worse. His role in the pie plot was leaked to the *Minneapolis Tribune* by a renegade activist, Thom Higgins, one of the loose group of theatrical gay radicals who clustered around Jack Baker. The Roman Catholic Church was not amused to learn that a Jesuit priest had been part of the plot to throw a pie at the archbishop. Father Casey disappeared from the Archdiocese of St. Paul and Minneapolis. Exiled to a distant state, he never came back to live in Minnesota. He died in the mid-90's of AIDS, and some who heard from him in later years said he felt the incident had destroyed his life.

It was in this atmosphere that two state senators who had been among the strongest opponents of Spear's anti-discrimination bill learned of Anita Bryant's offer to help in Minnesota. They announced the establishment of a Minnesota branch of Save Our Children, Inc., with the goal of overturning the St. Paul gay rights ordinance by a voter referendum. (The Minneapolis law didn't permit voter repeal.) Robert Brake, the secretary of Save Our Children in Miami, promised that Anita Bryant would make an appearance if the local group thought it was necessary, and predicted that Save Our Children would win in Minnesota, too. Dade County is "probably as liberal, if not more so, as Minneapolis," Brake said. "Basic morality is still the will of the people. This is the land of liberty, not libertines."

Jack Baker laughed at the threat. He had formed a new group called Target City Coalition, a band of mischief-makers that included Schwartz and Higgins. The coalition bought advertisements in the *Miami Herald* and the *Miami News* urging "gay refugees" to leave Dade County and come live in Minneapolis–St. Paul, with the goal of doubling the Twin Cities population of lesbians and gays in the next year. Coalition members began ambushing local public figures, twice throwing pies at a state senator who had prominently allied himself with Anita Bryant. "We welcome the challenge," Baker said of Bryant's intention to campaign against the law in St. Paul. "We think the people will side with us if it comes to a showdown."

He was wrong.

June 1977

In San Francisco, a murder two weeks after the Dade County vote so shocked the city that Mayor George Moscone ordered the flags at city hall lowered to half staff, and a solemn crowd of 200,000 marchers, gay and also straight, flowed in a massive demonstration of somber emotion on the Sunday of Gay Freedom Day. Four days earlier, thirty-three-year-old Robert Hillsborough, a city gardener, had been attacked by four young men outside his apartment in the Mission district. One of them had stabbed him in the face and chest fifteen times with a knife, yelling "Faggot! Faggot!" witnesses said, as Hillsborough died. Many of the marchers that Sunday carried flowers for Hillsborough, which they laid at the steps of city hall. Many of the speakers blamed Anita Bryant for stirring hatred of homosexuals.

"My son's blood is on her hands," said Helen Hillsborough, as three thousand people filled Grace Cathedral to mourn him on Monday. Three days later Mrs. Hillsborough filed a $5-million civil suit in U.S. district court against Anita Bryant, her husband Bob Green, California state Senator John Briggs and the officers of Save Our Children, Inc., charging that they had precipitated the murder by mounting "a campaign of hate, bigotry, ignorance, fear, intimidation and prejudice" against him and other homosexuals. Hillsborough's attackers, the suit alleged, had yelled "Here's one for Anita" as they killed him.

But as a place where sympathy for the gay condition seemed to have grown in the wake of the Miami vote, San Francisco appeared once again to be a special case. Across the rest of the country in the months after Dade County, the public and political attitude toward gay rights seemed more often cold, wary, resentful or alarmed. After weeks of pressure Mayor Maynard Jackson of Atlanta met privately with twenty local ministers, a group dominated by the kind of large fundamentalist and evangelical churches that had been roused to politics by Jimmy Carter's 1976 campaign. The preachers were upset that Jackson had proclaimed a Gay Pride Day in the city the previous year. Some of them, like the Reverend William L. Self, pastor of the huge, suburban Wieuca Road Baptist Church, had also been leaders of Citizens for a Decent Atlanta, the group which had attacked the mayor with full-page newspaper advertisements, accusing him of "taking pride in perverted sex." The ministers warned the mayor that there would be hell to pay if he did it again. He did not. Instead, Maynard Jackson proclaimed, more blandly, the commencement of Civil Liberties Days.

When it became clear that Maynard Jackson, the black mayor of the civil rights capital of the South, was going to turn away from the city's gay civil rights coalition in order to accommodate the newly risen and mainly white force of charismatic and fundamentalist Christian preachers, about 1,200 people turned out for the Gay Pride Parade on Saturday, three or four times the number in 1976, and their signs showed their displeasure. "Democracy, Not Theocracy," one read. "Jesus Died for My Sins, Not My Sexuality," another declared. One speaker at the rally that followed in Piedmont Park referred to Anita as a "vicious bigot," and when a TV reporter started interviewing one of several men in drag, some other marchers became upset. "That's a stereotype," they shouted. "We're not all like that."

The policies of the Atlanta government were turning against homosexuals. A political columnist for the *Atlanta Constitution*, alerted to the fact that the police department had quietly stopped trying to screen out homosexuals, mentioned it in a column. Atlanta's new black public safety commissioner, Reginald Eaves, an old friend of Maynard Jackson's, had been brought by the mayor from Boston, where he had been director of the Office of Human Rights for Mayor Kevin White. "I have no problem with" hiring gays on the police force, Eaves had said after taking over the department in 1976. But one month after the Dade County vote, Reginald Eaves changed his mind. "I don't think I need that additional problem," he explained, as he announced that the department would resume using lie detectors and asking the question it had dropped before: "Have you or have you not had sexual relations with a member of the same sex?"

On June 27, the eighth anniversary of the Stonewall riots, the U.S. House of Representatives voted 230–133 to amend the Legal Assistance Act so that no federal money could be spent to provide legal help "in any proceeding or litigation arising out of disputes or controversies on the issue of homosexuality or so-called gay rights." The ban was one of the first instances of federal legislation written specifically to deny help to homosexuals that was available to others. Although the bill would die for lack of a companion measure in the Senate, it was an early strike by the emerging forces of what would come to be called the religious right. Its author was U.S. Representative Larry P. McDonald, a Democrat, active John Bircher and fervent Christian who represented Georgia's Seventh Congressional District, which stretched from Marietta, on the northwestern shoulder of Atlanta, to the Tennessee line. And from Washington, U.S. Senator Jesse Helms wrote to his constituents in North Carolina that he had had a number of telephone conversations in the last few weeks with Anita Bryant, "a fine, Christian lady whose face and voice are familiar to most Americans." She was concerned about a bill that U.S. Representative Edward I. Koch of New York had introduced into Congress to amend "the so-called Civil Rights Act of 1964," Helms said, so that "employers would be required by federal law to seek out and hire homosexuals on a quota basis." He had pledged Bryant his full support in her fight against homosexuals, Helms told his constituents, and he promised that he would fight the Koch bill, "with every means at my command, with every bit of strength I can muster." Helms did not have to muster much. Koch, tipping his hat to the changing political winds, offered an amendment to make clear his bill did not allow for quotas involving homosexuals. "One of the reasons for the [Dade County] repeal was the scare tactics used by the opposition in insisting that the legislation required employers to engage in affirmative action, which would result in the compulsory hiring of homosexuals to make up for prior years of discrimination," Koch said, explaining the change in his bill.

The national culture's gradual acquiescence to gay rights was slowing, and in some cases turning around. Under the boldface headline "Enough! Enough! TV Is Killing Us with Gays," the *Atlanta Constitution*'s Sunday magazine published a prominent opinion piece by Amy Larkin, its former "Dear Amy" advice columnist, railing against the gay invasion of the private lives and home spaces of decent people. "I don't hate homosexuals, or think their sex life is my business," Larkin began, "but I'm tired of their coming out of the closet into my living room." That month, in Houston and Pasadena, Ku Klux Klan bookstores began running tape-recorded telephone messages stating, "The Ku Klux Klan is not embarrassed to admit that we endorse and seek the execution of all homosexuals." The message cited Leviticus as its justifying authority.

Even the word "gay" seemed to have become an irritant. "Gay used to be one of the most agreeable words in the language," the historian Arthur Schlesinger Jr. observed. "Its appropriation by a notably morose group is an act of piracy." In New England, the Adam Smith Fish Company, owners of the vessel *Gay Wind,* filed notice with the U.S. Coast Guard that they wanted to rename it. A group of citizens in Knoxville, Tennessee, petitioned the city to change the name of its main thoroughfare, Gay Street. If that was unsuccessful, said the group, it would try to persuade homosexuals to give up describing themselves as "gay." After reading an editorial on the Knoxville street question in the *Montgomery Advertiser,* Benjamin Smith Gay sat down and penned a letter to the editor. "Having lived more than 73 years, bearing my family name 'GAY,' I am deeply wounded by the fact that a group of divergents now call themselves Gays," he wrote. "I have not been one to institute litigation, but when such groups defile one's name, it is justified."

There were a few signs of advancement for gay rights, the biggest, not surprisingly, in San Francisco. There, a brash, pushy, opera-loving camera store owner named Harvey Milk, a transplanted New Yorker who had become the most prominent neighborhood activist in the Castro district, was elected to the city Board of Supervisors on his fourth try for public office. He was the first openly gay candidate to attain elected office in the city. He was only the second acknowledged homosexual in the nation, after Elaine Noble, to be elected to any prominent public office. Allan Spear was already a state senator when he came out in Minnesota, and won reelection. Milk's victory was not just historic; it signaled a change in the rules. He had beaten Rick Stokes, the lawyer and former bathhouse owner running as "The Respectable Candidate," endorsed by *The Advocate* and backed by the gay political establishment. The vote was thus a repudiation of the strategy the organized gay political community had followed for a decade in San Francisco, a strategy of supporting gay-friendly mainstream candidates, or establishment gays like Rick Stokes who had mainstream ties. Milk's election—and the previous election of Mayor George Moscone, who had openly sought gay votes—represented a quantum leap in the political pride and clout of the city's gay community. The same election which swept Harvey Milk into office, setting off a huge, jubilant demonstration of gays, also elevated a former policeman, a conservative Irish Catholic husband and father named Dan White, to the Board of Supervisors. It was men like Dan White, and families like his—Irish or Italian Roman Catholic—who had lived in the Castro before homosexuals like Milk began to take it over. When White looked at Milk and all he represented, he did not see progress.

But progress for the gay rights movement did occur in other places in 1977. In small, liberal university cities like Wichita, Kansas (in September), and Eugene, Oregon (in October), and in Champaign-Urbana, Illinois, Iowa City and Aspen, Colorado, city councils stood against the tide and enacted strong new ordinances making it illegal to discriminate against homosexuals in such areas as employment, housing and public accommodations. The ordinances passed some of the city councils by the barest of margins, in Wichita by a single vote. In Eugene, home of the University of Oregon, a city of 100,000 and a place so mellow that the Grateful Dead hung out there in the summertime, the city council vote was 5–3. It came after years of being lunched and lobbied by gay activists—and after an election campaign in which some council members had accepted significant amounts of gay money. In forty or more municipalities, as winter began, gay rights had become a matter of law.*

In both Eugene and Wichita, the new ordinances produced a quick reaction. "Well, we have a lot of happy homosexuals in Wichita today and a majority of other people who are awfully unhappy," said the Reverend Ronald Adrian, head of Concerned Citizens for Community Decency in Wichita. The

---

* The exact number of towns and cities which had enacted gay rights ordinances by the fall of 1977 is difficult to determine, but various news accounts make it clear that the total hovered at forty or more by the end of the year.

Roman Catholic bishop of Wichita, David Maloney, a prelate who rarely involved himself in public issues, declared that his diocese would defy the ordinance. He urged all Catholics to join him in "prayers and in active works" toward its repeal. The Reverend Adrian said that Concerned Citizens would begin a petition drive to collect the signatures necessary to demand a referendum. "I have no doubt that we'll have enough signatures to force the referendum and I have no doubt that the law will be defeated at the polls."

In Eugene, Terry Bean, a gay businessman who had helped persuade the council to pass the ordinance, found himself talking in the council chambers with the leader of the opposition, an attractive, dark-haired young housewife named Lynn Greene. She was demure and well-spoken, and dead-set against the ordinance. It was not a civil rights issue, she said, because gays had all the protection they needed under existing law. There was no need for special legislation. This startled Bean; it was a much more sophisticated argument than the one that had been made by Anita Bryant: intellectual rather than biblical, political instead of personal—and years ahead of its time.

December 1977, St. Paul

Craig Anderson was home in his apartment in St. Paul when he got a call from Steve Endean asking him to go to church. "We've heard they're passing a petition around at Temple Baptist Church," Endean told Anderson. "We need to know what's going on." Anderson was an Episcopalian, red-haired, freckled and wholesome-looking. Part of the second wave of Minnesota activists, he had come to Macalester College in St. Paul from Dallas in 1971, in large part because his parents, affluent Republicans, had refused to send him to any of the schools they thought of as breeding grounds for radical students, like Columbia University in New York. But Macalester turned out to be the most radical of the five private church colleges in the Twin Cities, and in his senior year, Anderson helped form the Gay Students Collective. When he graduated, in 1975, he began working for Steve Endean and others in the Gay Rights Caucus of the Minnesota Democratic-Farmer-Labor Party. By the winter of 1977, Anderson was as close to being a veteran gay rights activist as there was in St. Paul.

Anderson called the office at Temple Baptist Church and told the woman who answered that he wanted to help the petition drive. Could he come by? Temple was an independent Baptist church in a working-class section of St. Paul. Its pastor, Richard A. Angwin, a handsome, thirty-three-year-old fundamentalist from Kansas, was directing a petition drive to place a referendum on the ballot in the municipal spring election. Angwin was determined to repeal the three-year-old gay rights language of the city's nondis-

crimination law, and he had 150 volunteers marching door-to-door, sometimes wearing ski masks against the bitter cold of air twenty degrees below
zero, collecting signatures to force a referendum.

Craig Anderson took some forms home, and told Endean, Kerry Woodward, Larry Bye and some others what he had learned about Angwin and his
mission. The Dade County vote, the emerging repeal efforts in Wichita and
Eugene, and the obvious ability of the fundamentalists to build an opposition
movement from scratch in the middle of a Minnesota winter filled them with
dread. On January 17, Angwin and his group, Citizens' Alert for Morality, delivered 7,151 signatures to city hall. The pastor's position was simple. I "don't
want to live in a community that gives respect to homosexuals," he said.

Minnesota was a long, cold way from Miami. There were no Southern
Baptist churches by the Great Lakes, and Christian fundamentalists had never
been a political force in the region. Roman Catholics and Lutherans were the
strong influence. But all the respect for gay rights that Steve Endean and Allan
Spear had worked to gain through most of the 1970s now seemed in peril,
and they raced to rally the whole progressive political establishment of the
state behind the St. Paul ordinance. They announced a defense committee,
St. Paul Citizens for Human Rights. The words "gay" and "homosexual"
were nowhere in the title—just as they were nowhere in the ordinance in
question—and Steve Endean, the driving force behind the new committee,
was not even its titular head. St. Paul was a city of 280,000 people, many of
them Roman Catholic and working class, and more conservative on average
than the residents of Minneapolis. It had been hard to find any gay men or
lesbians in St. Paul willing to testify in favor of the ordinance at the time of the
city council's vote, and it was important now that St. Paul Citizens for Human
Rights not be seen as an organization run by professional gays from Minneapolis.

"I can't do this—I don't know what to do," Kerry Woodward said when
Endean asked her to chair the group. She was a lesbian long active in the
cause, attractive, and a resident of St. Paul.

"That's okay," he said. "I'll tell you."

Lobbying, cajoling, pleading the civil rights case in a state famous for its
commitment to civil rights, Steve Endean worked in private to line up the
public endorsements of scores of Minnesota's leading political and cultural
figures. Both U.S. senators—Muriel Humphrey, Hubert's widow, and Wendell Anderson—supported the city's ordinance. Even the Right Reverend
John Roach, to Endean's astonishment, came out on their side. That Roman
Catholics would feel pained and aggrieved enough to attack him with a chocolate cream cheese pie—and that a Jesuit priest had been part of the plot—had
troubled Roach deeply. He had thought about it, prayed over it and decided
that he had been wrong. Just two weeks after the pastor of Temple Baptist

Church marched his petitions into the city clerk's office, the archbishop issued a statement for the guidance of the 500,000 Roman Catholics in Minneapolis and St. Paul. It was his own statement, and it sounded almost as if he was preaching a sermon to Pastor Angwin.

"Both the Christian tradition and our American nation are committed to the inviolable dignity of the human person. Some persons find themselves to be homosexual in orientation, through no fault of their own," Roach said. "Like all persons, they have a right to human respect, stable friendships, economic security and social equality. Social isolation, ridicule and economic deprivation of homosexual behavior is not compatible with basic human justice. Consequently, both religious and civil leaders must seek ways to assure homosexuals every human and civil right which is their due as persons, without, however, neglecting the rights of the larger community.

"Although sexual expression between two members of the same sex cannot be condoned or regarded as of authentic human value," the archbishop cautioned, "nevertheless, the churches and society must carefully avoid passing judgment on the inner moral state of any individual."

The traditional elements of church and state seemed lined up in support of keeping the ordinance. And Steve Endean had even found a new way to raise money, by taking advantage of the fact that gay activists were battling three repeal movements at once. In Eugene, Terry Bean had proposed forming a Tri-Cities Fund to help pay to defend the ordinances in St. Paul, Wichita and Eugene. Endean was friendly with Jack Campbell, owner of the Club Baths chain and treasurer of the Dade County defense effort, and from Campbell he got a list of people who had sent money to fight Anita Bryant in Miami. There were almost seven thousand names, the first semblance of a national gay donors' list, and Terry Bean and Endean used it to send out an appeal for help across the country. Within two or three months they had raised $55,000, which they divided 40-40-20, after expenses, between St. Paul, Eugene and Wichita.

A random poll of the public's attitude about homosexuality commissioned by the *Minneapolis Star* in November, before Pastor Angwin filed his petitions, had shown that 67 percent of the residents of the Minneapolis–St. Paul metropolitan area thought that it was wrong for two adults of the same gender to have sexual relations. But the *Star* poll found far less hostility to homosexuals locally than two earlier national polls had found in the country at large. According to a 1970 survey by the Institute for Sex Research, formerly the Kinsey Institute, 74 percent of respondents agreed that gays were "dangerous as teachers or youth leaders because they try to get sexually involved with children." That was Anita Bryant's argument, but only 40 percent of those polled by the *Star* thought that was the case.

The *Star* poll made no attempt to test the difference in attitudes between the population of Minneapolis, on one side of the Mississippi, and St. Paul, on the other. Anyone in Minnesota who was politically aware knew that the demographics of the two cities were different. And Pastor Richard Angwin had some outside help to draw on. He consulted by telephone with Anita Bryant, and the Reverend William F. Chapman, her pastor at Northwest Baptist Church in Miami, flew up to St. Paul on what he described as a five-day "fact-finding mission." Chapman preached at Temple Baptist Church one Sunday and said afterward that he would give Anita Bryant "a very positive report" on Angwin's efforts.*

Endean and his defense team worked long hours, raising and spending more than $70,000, a figure comparable to the money Angwin's group was said to have. They recruited ministers in mainstream churches to speak for the ordinance. They got strong editorial support from the newspapers. The Reverend Troy Perry, the founder of the Metropolitan Community Churches, flew in. St. Paul mayor George Latimer, who was running for reelection, campaigned door-to-door with them. Yet with all the planning, help, canvassing and money they had, they could feel the advantage slipping away. As Endean grimly observed afterward, they had let homosexuality become the issue. Nor did it help that Jack Baker—now always the spoiler—attacked the effort that Endean and Woodward were making to reassure the mainstream, and instead brought in Bob Kunst, who had proved himself such a loose cannon in Miami, to conduct a "media blitz" about what the gay lifestyle was; or that Anita Bryant, less than three weeks before the vote, announced that she would come to St. Paul. Steve Endean, compulsive in planning, in worrying, in everything, reacted as he always did to stress and uncertainty. On the way home from the office where he kept everyone working late each night—and with the whole leadership of St. Paul Citizens for Human Rights in the car—Endean stopped at an adult bookstore at Dale and University Streets and told the others to wait while he went in. Time crept by. For an hour or more, Kerry Woodward, Dennis Miller and the rest of them sat by the curb with mounting anxiety, seething and praying that Endean wouldn't torpedo the defense of gay rights in St. Paul by getting arrested in a dirty-book store in the middle of the night. Meanwhile, Endean prowled the interior of the store and its darkened little booths, seeking comfort in the compulsive and anonymous sex to which he was always driven in times of stress.

---

* There was talk within Pastor Angwin's group that Bryant's organization in Miami had contributed $10,000 to the crusade to repeal the St. Paul ordinance. There was no way to know. Worried that contributors to either side might face reprisals, the city had waived the terms of its financial disclosure law, which would have required the contributions to be public record.

Spring 1978, St. Paul, Wichita and Eugene

The elected officials of Dade County, St. Paul, Wichita and Eugene had, over the years, become comfortable with gay rights activists and with the issues they raised. Because of the private discussions held with people like Allan Spear, and all the votes gathered for them by Steve Endean—and all the contributions from people like Jack Campbell and Terry Bean—politicians in those places had come to accept homosexuals as a legitimate part of the process. Many of them had also come to agree that homosexuals did not have equal protection under the law, that gay men and lesbians were sometimes fired, evicted or refused service for being who they were. So they had voted to expand the laws to protect homosexuals from discrimination. But only after the anti-discrimination ordinances were passed did many residents of those cities wake up to the fact that there were communities of gay people in their midst, and that these homosexuals had apparently been organizing for years. Pastor Richard Angwin, living and preaching in the Twin Cities, didn't notice at first when Minneapolis and then St. Paul added the words "affectional or sexual preference" to the language of their existing human rights ordinances. But when he did notice, it came as a shock, and he felt called to political action. "I felt that as a father—a Christian—I just couldn't let something like that go unchallenged," he said. "Homosexuality is a murderous, horrendous, twisted act. It is a sin and a powerful, addictive lust."

In St. Paul on April 25, in Wichita on May 9 and in Eugene on May 23, 1978, concerned and angry voters like Angwin repealed each city's gay rights ordinance. It didn't matter what the traditional mainstream church clergy said, or how supportive the political establishment was, or how much money the defense committees raised, or how much Troy Perry flew around from place to place, trying to counter the same biblical morality which had driven him from the southern church years before. The risen energy of outraged conservative Christians—and of newly aware and disapproving voters—prevailed. The margin of defeat was 2 to 1 in St. Paul, 4 to 1 in Wichita and 2 to 1 in Eugene.

Pastor Angwin's congregation in Temple Baptist Church greeted the joyful news with shouts of "Hallelujah" and "Praise the Lord!" But to people like Steve Endean, Allan Spear, Dennis Miller, Larry Bye, Kerry Woodward and Terry Bean, the results were devastating. It seemed that the acceptance and understanding they had worked most of their adult lives to build was being destroyed by a narrow Christianity which many of them remembered from childhood all too well. The St. Paul Repeal was the death knell for the Minnesota Committee for Gay Rights, which expired within a couple of years, its membership dispirited, its faith in mainstream politics gone. The mood in the state legislature changed. The two houses, which in 1975 and 1977 had seemed so close to passing an anti-discrimination bill, would not be receptive to Allan Spear's arguments again for fifteen years.

Steve Endean, in a few short months, would move to Washington, D.C. Woodward and Bye would leave for California. Jack Baker, increasingly bitter and unfulfilled as he became less influential in politics and less successful in law than he had hoped, would become more distant from the gay community. In a few years, in a conscious decision to try to earn money and enjoy life, he and Mike McConnell would pack up their papers, the archives of a decade of pioneering legal and political activism, and vow never to speak about the gay rights movement again, in public or between themselves.

Anita Bryant had not been welcome in Eugene, although she had offered to appear. Lynn Greene and others fighting for repeal made it clear that they were contesting the issue on different terms. And Bryant had not returned to St. Paul. She had promised to appear with the Reverend Jerry Falwell at a "God and Decency" rally there a week before the vote, but after being met by a wave of protesters on a trip to the Twin Cities the previous spring, she let her husband, Bob Green, speak for her at the rally, bringing word to the crowd of ten thousand that she was ill.

As the gay rights movement seemed to veer toward eclipse, so did Anita Bryant's own credibility and appeal, and it happened even as the political force she had gathered continued to gain power. Bryant became a magnet for feeling on all sides, and everywhere she went, emotions and gay activists rose to meet her. Homosexuals "are haunting us wherever we go," Green said. "They won't let her alone." When she received keys to the city in Des Moines, Thom Higgins and Patrick Schwartz, members of Jack Baker's pie-throwing guerrilla brigade from Minneapolis, were waiting in ambush. Hit with a strawberry rhubarb pie, Bryant dropped to her knees to pray, and to weep. In New York, where she had gone to appear live on the *Today* show, NBC decided to tape her appearance in advance after receiving three threatening telephone calls. More than 150 people marched outside the NBC studios as her interview with Tom Brokaw aired. The network was so concerned about her safety that it provided her with a security guard, and spirited her out a side entrance back to her hotel.

A woman who wept easily, in place after place, she was reduced to tears. "I am clearly a victim of religious persecution," Bryant said when the Florida Citrus Commission again considered replacing her. "There are those forces in this country who through boycotts and influencing some of the staff of the Department of Citrus want me fired only because I took a stand as a concerned citizen and for the protection of my four children." Her bookings had fallen by 70 percent, and even at religious and political rallies she was not the draw she had once been. Only half the expected crowd of ten thousand showed up to see her at a "Rally for Decency," held to "reinstate sodomy as a felony in the state of Indiana," and 650 protesters marched against her outside. When Bryant agreed to come sing at a "pro-life, pro-family" rally for Howard Phillips, a member of the Republican New Right and former Nixon appointee who had changed parties to run as a Democrat for the U.S. Senate from Massachusetts, Phillips booked her into the Hynes War Memorial Auditorium, a hall which could seat five thousand people. Only seventy-eight tickets were sold. The rally was canceled, and Anita Bryant left town. The biggest public event of her visit ended up being the demonstration against her.

From an all-American figure, a patriotic performer welcome at both Democratic and Republican events, Anita Bryant had been reduced to an almost farcical symbol of bigotry. She could see this herself by turning on Johnny Carson where, on almost any night, he would receive huge laughs at her expense. "Was the New York blackout an act of God?" Carson asked in July 1977. No, "because Anita Bryant would never have given him time off." Soon after, eight hundred high school students surveyed by *Ladies' Home Journal* chose Anita Bryant as the woman who has "done the most damage to the world." The man was Adolf Hitler. Even her personal life was unraveling. Bryant's marriage, always strained, was now collapsing. Financial losses and constant quarrels with her husband over her performance schedule would lead them to divorce in two years.

Support came from unlikely sources. "She has been threatened with violence, hit in the face with a pie, and called unprintable names. Her views, we think, are benighted," the *New York Times* said in an editorial, "but she has a right to express them without suffering abuse." Even old-line liberals came to her defense. "This is exactly what happened during the McCarthy years," Ira Glasser, the executive director of the New York Civil Liberties Union, told Nat Hentoff, the *Village Voice* columnist. Hentoff agreed. "This time," he wrote, "the victim is Anita Bryant."

Anita Bryant was sinking fast, but she had shown the way, and those who would follow her in the religious right would be more savvy and more successful. Her last big event came in June 1978, at the Southern Baptist Convention in Atlanta. It included many of the stars of the fundamentalist Christian world, including James Robison, a Texas-born evangelist who announced that he planned to create a multi-million-dollar pulpit on national television from which he would condemn homosexuality and other sins in prime time. The era of big-time television evangelism, with stars like Jerry Falwell and Pat Robertson, was dawning, and the threat posed by militant homosexuals was one of the themes that would sustain it.

The Anita Bryant who attended this convention was more a martyr than a star. She made her entrance before 24,000 pastors and their wives singing "I'll Be a Friend to You." They gave her three standing ovations, and she left the hall damp-eyed and exhilarated. But a year after Dade County, her secular bookings had dwindled "to what you could count on one hand," she said. She was singing mainly "for God's people," having to work twice as hard because it didn't pay nearly as well. She spent her time in Atlanta in a guarded hotel room, and she entered and left the Georgia World Congress Center by a side door. That way she was able to avoid the two thousand or so gay rights demonstrators waiting for her outside.

24

AN UNEASY VICTORY IN SAN FRANCISCO

June 1977

When Jim Gordon finally got home to his apartment on Sanchez Street the night of June 7, he was exhausted and apprehensive, but excited, too. It was almost 2 a.m. in San Francisco. The sun would soon be rising from the Atlantic east of Miami, turning the dark sky pink and the beaches gold, but Miami didn't seem so much a paradise anymore. It had been an extraordinary day, and although he had to be at work in just a few hours in the fish department of the California Academy of Sciences, Gordon made some notes in his small, neat hand for the detailed entry he would write in his journal when he had time.

"Orange Tuesday," he wrote. "Gay rights ordinance repealed in Dade County, Florida by a vote of 202,319 to 89,562." News of the overwhelmingly negative vote had hit this gayest of all American cities like a shock wave, and word spread by mid-evening that a crowd was forming at Market and Castro Streets for a candlelight vigil. Jim Gordon was in the middle of "Gay Rap" when he heard about it, which was as good a place as any to process the revelation of what voters in Miami thought of men like him. His rap group, thirty or forty men in their twenties, thirties and forties, came each week to the Congregational Church, at the intersection of Post and Mason Streets in the Tenderloin, to talk about being gay, the life which was still unfolding for them all.

They met together at first and then split into smaller groups, and the subject for discussion in Gordon's group that Tuesday night was "forming honest relationships in the New Age."

There were no rules in place to govern the new lives and relationships that were being built in San Francisco, and Gordon's wasn't the only group meeting that night. There were dozens and dozens of classes, courses, discussion and therapy groups organized as part of "Lavender U.," a freestanding institute begun in 1974. Its classes, in every subject from duplicate bridge to overcoming shyness to Gestalt therapy workshops to garden design, met in apartments and homes in different neighborhoods. There was a gay mental health group in Berkeley, a gay band, and the next year there would be a gay chorus—all part of a growing network of support and interest groups in which hundreds of homosexuals might sit in conversation with each other on any given night in various rooms around the city, sorting out the daily issues of the identity they had accepted, and the lives they had chosen to create in the beautiful city on the bay. Perhaps 100,000 homosexuals had settled in San Francisco in the last five years to become part of the new ethos growing there. No one knew the real number. There was no way to count it. But it was a visible phenomenon which set San Francisco apart. Other major cities across the country had lost blue-collar families along with blue-collar industrial jobs. Other cities had seen white middle-class families flee to the suburbs. In many of those cities, homosexuals from small towns and rural areas had begun to fill in those emptied spaces. But it was to San Francisco—far smaller than Los Angeles, Chicago and New York—that a disproportionate number moved, and in which a noticeable and aggressive new gay population grew. There had never before been a distinguishable gay colony, rural or urban, in which the dominant population and manners were openly homosexual anywhere in the United States. But a gay village—a gay male village, to be precise—is what had begun to form along the linear spine of Castro Street in the years since 1972.

Its new inhabitants—people like Jim Gordon, Harry Britt, Claude Wynne and Cleve Jones—were different in attitude from Jim Foster, Rick Stokes and the other members of the city's gay political establishment. The new generation of gay men coming of age in San Francisco in the late 1970s were living lives which were increasingly, if not exclusively, homosexual. They were building a separate culture, and one of their number, the mouthy, gregarious New Yorker named Harvey Milk, had achieved such prominence as a leader of the gay population in the Castro that he was a character of interest in the city at large. But wherever they came from, whatever traits they brought with them, what these men had in common by the time they met each other in San Francisco was how new they were to the lives they led—and how different those lives were from their old ones. Jim Gordon, short, quick and eager to please by nature, was a trained zoologist, detailed and precise. The only child of a Polish-American Roman Catholic family, he had been such a devout son of the church that in 1962, as a twenty-four-year-old graduate student in philosophy at the University of Chicago, he had dutifully written to the archbishop to ask formal permission to study works then banned by the church in its Index of Forbidden Books. The vicar general, responding for Albert Cardinal Meyer of Chicago, had written back promptly to deny the young man's polite request, suggesting instead that he be guided in his coursework by a priest he named in the letter. Gordon began to turn away from the church, but he remained so subservient to its teachings that by the summer of 1972, a decade later, he still had not had sex with anyone at all. Then, late one afternoon, he came upon a writhing knot of men on the nude beach at Devil's Slide, a stretch of shore south of San Francisco where he had begun to take long, inquiring walks. It seemed as if he could join them in sex, and after a long, longing moment, standing there, he did, and his chastity came to an end. He was thirty-four years old.

Harry Britt's awakening came in 1973. Through boyhood, college, graduate school, marriage and a career as a Methodist minister, Britt had held to the cultural values he was raised by in southeast Texas. Then, overweight and exhausted in early middle age, he had left his wife and pulpit behind in Dallas and moved to San Francisco. Despite the gregarious profession he had worked in so long, he was by nature an introvert, a man who loved books and solitude.

He had always found the quiet world of libraries and graduate studies sheltering and safe, and in his numb, dispirited state, he had chosen San Francisco over Boston because he had noticed, as he researched a list of cities in the library, that San Francisco had more bookstores. A year after arriving, Harry Britt had found work as a mailman in the Castro. He was living in a rented room, seeing a gay psychiatrist, doing his best to figure out who he was, when he answered a personal ad in the *Berkeley Barb* and went out on his first date with another man. He was thirty-five years old.

Claude Wynne, who came to town in the late summer of 1974, was part of the younger generation of new arrivals. A black orphan, born addicted to the heroin that his mother took, he had been placed with a sternly religious foster mother—a woman old enough to be his grandmother—who raised him in various rented rooms in Queens and Brooklyn. A rebel and a runaway by the age of thirteen, he left home for good at fifteen. In Greenwich Village, he discovered gay feminist radical hippies and leftist politics. Drawn by the excitement and kinship of Vietnam protests, gay liberation demonstrations and GAA meetings at the Firehouse, he had ended up at a national conference of the Socialist Workers Party at Oberlin College in Ohio in the summer of 1974, as a member of the Young Socialists' Alliance. There he had met Howard Wallace, a party member and career leftist, a veteran of the civil rights and anti-war movements who had become a Teamsters union organizer in San Francisco, a heavily unionized town. Wallace was white, square-jawed, bigger and almost twenty years older, but Claude Wynne had more experience with men. The two spent several nights talking and sleeping together, and when Wynne got back to New York, he packed his few things and left for San Francisco, where he moved in with Howard Wallace and two other men, living in a crowded apartment on Fourteenth Street. He was eighteen years old.

The new immigrants to San Francisco all felt they had a lot of catching up to do. For the next three years, as his inhibitions yielded to innumerable sessions of bioenergetic therapy, hours with a psychiatrist and long meetings with his own Gay Rap group, Harry Britt did nothing with his spare time but shoot pool and chase other men who were dressed as he now was, usually in snug soft blue jeans, boots and a T-shirt and flannel overshirt, bought for a few dollars at the J. C. Funky secondhand clothing store. He had shed more than eighty pounds of tired ministerial flab. He wore his hair close-cropped. He had become a fixture at the gay bars and pool halls along Castro Street, marveling and grateful that at 3 a.m., an hour after closing time, there were still twenty other men like him, standing under the streetlights, waiting to take someone home.

The androgynous Castro hippie look was passing from the scene. The new style, as Britt, Gordon, Wallace and Wynne settled into their lives, was more aggressive and masculine, and one of the social and recreational centers for the new Castro crowd was the Ritch Street Health Club baths started by Rick Stokes and his partners a decade before. It was an increasingly confident male culture, one with a growing swagger and a swelling sense of its own separate identity, and it was ill-prepared to hear the results of the Dade County referendum that Tuesday night.

The epicenter of the Castro lies at the intersection of Castro and Market Streets, and it was there that the men who had transformed the neighborhood began to gather in the wake of the news. The election had been on the other side of America, but the men of the Castro knew that the vote was about them. They were not, most of the time, a politically attuned population. The Castro was a community based on pleasure, not politics. Few of its residents, probably, had heard Jim Foster's speech to the Democratic convention in 1972. Some didn't identify with what he said. Many of the new residents were too young to be paying attention then, and Foster now—with his coat and tie, his conservative manners and assimilationist point of view—simply did not appeal to the Castro men. But they had all read the *San Francisco Chronicle* that morning.

"S. F. Is the Issue in Miami," the headline on the front page said.

For six months, the story reported, San Francisco had been denounced from pulpits and depicted in televised ads in Miami as a modern-day Sodom and Gomorrah, an example of what Miami would become if its gay rights ordinance was allowed to stand. The filmed footage of San Francisco's raunchy, theatrical Gay Freedom Day Parade, shown over and over again, had made its point.

In truth, the street behavior of the gay male village in the Castro *was* beginning to repel some people, a fact which had become bruisingly apparent in the last two or three years—first when the police began attacking and arresting gay men along Castro Street late in 1974, and again in 1976, when suburban teenagers had begun harassing and assaulting men they took to be homosexual on the streets late at night. As in the past, the assaults had prompted the organization of new groups. One of them, which drew on community anger stirred by police beatings, and by the arrests of gay men in a nearby playground and on Castro Street "for blocking the sidewalk" at 2 a.m., was founded early in 1975 by a mixed group of leftists from San Francisco and Berkeley led in part by Howard Wallace and Claude Wynne. In keeping with the radical politics of the group—and in purposeful contrast to the traditional Democratic Party politics of Jim Foster's Alice B. Toklas Club—they had christened it Bay Area Gay Liberation. Everyone called the Toklas Club "Alice" for short. And at the suggestion of Jim Gordon, who realized that the acronym of the new Bay Area Gay Liberation almost spelled his favorite doughy bread, the group promptly adopted the nickname "Bagel." The first meetings attracted hundreds of men. At one Bagel gathering early in 1975, more than three hundred men and a few women crowded into the First United Methodist Church across the street from Howard Wallace's apartment, as Jim Foster, silent and envious, stood watching at the back of the hall. In November 1976, after young suburban toughs attacked gay men on the street with lead pipes and other weapons, Wallace and Wynne formed the Richard Heakin Memorial Butterfly Brigade, a neighborhood patrol named in memory of a gay activist from Lincoln, Nebraska, who had been beaten to death in front of a homosexual bar in Tucson, Arizona, in June 1976. It was a killing for which a judge had given four teenagers suspended sentences.

That Tuesday, as the judgment of the voters in Dade County was delivered, the public reaction from San Francisco's gay community fell into two different camps. At the Ramrod Bar on Folsom Street in the early afternoon, Sheriff Richard Hongisto, receiving a hero's welcome from a crowd of a hundred gay bar and restaurant owners, reported on the week he had just spent in Miami campaigning for the gay rights ordinance and trying to stand up for San Francisco's reputation. The Tavern Guild, composed of the city's leading gay businessmen, had helped finance his two elections, and they cheered as he told them he had been "very pleased to have used a week of my vacation to go to Miami and campaign against lies." The bar owners, the oldest organized group in the city's traditional gay political structure, gave Hongisto a case of California oranges in thanks. But in the Castro, as Jim Gordon and the other members of his Gay Rap group made their way down from the Tenderloin, thousands of the bar owners' patrons took to the streets. For the first time in the short, pleasure-loving gay history of the Castro, many of its new residents massed in anger and marched through the night.

Because a letter opposing the gay rights ordinance had been read in the pulpits of Roman Catholic churches in Miami two days before the vote, much of the anger in San Francisco focused on the Catholic Church. At the Gay Center on Grove Street, amid the glum remains of what was to have been a victory potluck supper, the idea was born to gather at the crossroads of Castro and Market, and march in candlelit protest on the Church of the Most Holy Redeemer, the parish church and traditional cultural anchor of the old Castro neighborhood—and a center of resentment among conservative Catholic families engulfed by the gay migration.

The word went out through the city's bars and clubs, and by ten-thirty, the intersection of Market and Castro was jammed with 1,500 people, almost all of them men in their twenties and thirties. Bearded, mustached, dressed in denim and flannel shirts or old military fatigues, they were holding up lighted candles, roaring with emotion as they began to move. Chanting *"Out of the bars—into the streets!"* they headed toward Most Holy Redeemer, drawing more and more marchers as they went. But the volume and energy were too great to be satisfied with a rally at a neighborhood church, and the crowd surged on—up Market Street, shouting "Two, four, six, eight, Gay is just as good as Straight!" Scouts ran ahead, calling men in bars and restaurants to join the throng as it swept north on Polk Street, up and over Nob Hill, east, and then back south. As they approached each intersection, for more than three miles, the marchers wondered whether the police might block their progress. The officers ahead called in reinforcements, but they turned traffic aside and let the marchers pass, as white-banded members of the Butterfly Brigade stood vigil at the corners, watching and holding their walkie-talkies. By the time the crowd pooled into Union Square for a midnight rally, it numbered more than five thousand. Holding candles, they listened as a few speakers shouted themselves hoarse over a ten-watt bullhorn, and then, with feeling, sang "We Shall Overcome."

It was a defining night. The Tavern Guild, the group that Sheriff Dick Hongisto had reported to earlier in the day, was the city's old gay political establishment. But the midnight march was wholly a product of the city's new gay population, one angry and aroused, with its own neighborhood, its own distinct cultural values, its own community organizations and leaders, and its own way of reacting to events. Anita Bryant's victory had helped bring them into focus. As a large red banner emblazoned with the words "Gay Revolution" was run up the flagpole on Union Square that night, there was a new reality emerging in San Francisco, and it was emerging in the middle of a crucial political campaign.

When the crowd that poured out of the Castro reached Union Square, the main speaker they heard, as the red flag flapped above them, was Harvey Milk. Dark-eyed, passionate and voluble, he was a theatrical, even outrageous personality. He had become the voice of the Castro in the years since 1972, and the midnight march and rally—with thousands of people swarming up a hill, cheering as a determined lesbian climbed up a pole to untangle the red flag of revolution—was his kind of event.

Rick Stokes, the quiet candidate of the old gay establishment, was nowhere to be seen. It was not his thing. Stokes was not a street person. He was a lawyer and businessman, a man who spoke softly and seriously, as careful and thorough in his politics and investments as he was in his personal life. He had recently sold his interest in the Ritch Street Health Club baths because his partners couldn't understand the need to invest more money in order to revive the club and regain its edge. But Stokes and his allies, Jim Foster and David Goodstein, were not oblivious to what was going on in the Castro. It was a neighborhood that Rick Stokes knew well. He and his lover, David Clayton, lived just four blocks off Castro, and he walked the streets every morning, watching as the city's growing reputation as the mecca of gay America drew more and more young men to spend their leisure hours hanging around the bars and restaurants and other new gay businesses that began proliferating along Castro Street.

One of them was Harvey Milk's. He had opened a camera shop in a vacant Victorian storefront on Castro Street in March 1973, a few months after Rick Stokes's unsuccessful run for the community college board. Pushy, engaging, hard to label and not the least concerned about it, Milk was a New Yorker, but he had the long, wavy, shoulder-length beard and hair, the personal habits and the anti-establishment attitudes of a middle-aged Hippie. He was forty-three when he and his thin, blondish, much younger boyfriend, Scott Smith, rented the space with the bay window on the sidewalk, and moved into the apartment above. Milk didn't seem to care much about selling cameras and processing film. But he spent endless hours schmoozing, and gradually, the Castro Camera shop had become the general store and center of political life for the gay neighborhood growing around the two-block business strip of Castro Street. Some of the Irish Catholic neighbors and shopkeepers, people like the crusty old couple who ran Andy's Donuts, seemed resistant, even hostile, to the endless number of gay young men, and put up signs about how customers should dress and behave if they wanted to be served. But they could not hold the line. They represented a conservative cultural tradition that was passing. Rick Stokes, in his suit and quiet, serious, professional manner, was being passed by, too.

Harvey Milk had been many things before—schoolteacher, insurance company actuary, financial clerk and analyst on Wall Street, and even, as his younger and more hip boyfriends had led him into radical culture, a co-producer of the rock musical *Hair,* and later of *Jesus Christ Superstar.* He had come to town with the road production of *Hair* several years before. But when he left New York for good and returned to San Francisco, bored with the world of finance and radicalized by the anti-war culture, he had no clear idea what he would do. For long weeks, even months, he and Smith had passed the time working at giant jigsaw puzzles. But gradually, Milk began to focus on the neighborhood around him, and as time passed it was Harvey Milk, newly settled in town, filling in the blank space of his own middle age, who began to embody the spirit of the Castro.

He and Rick Stokes were the same generation, almost the same age. Stokes was actually younger by five years, and in many ways they cared about the same things. But they were planets apart in where they were born, in how they lived, and what they wanted to do. Their lives had begun so differently. Stokes was a poor farm boy, on the dusty plains of central Oklahoma, where the Southern Baptist Church was the chief cultural institution; Harvey Milk was a New York Jew from the middle-class suburbs of Long Island, but still close enough to Manhattan to discover the music of the Metropolitan Opera and to be groped by the men in the standing room at the back. When Stokes was married, to the daughter of the wealthiest man in Shawnee, Oklahoma, Milk was getting out of the Navy. When Stokes fell apart emotionally after an automobile accident and his wife and in-laws committed him to a hospital in Oklahoma City where the doctor used electroshock to try to destroy his homosexual urges, Harvey Milk was teaching math and history at a high school on Long Island, spending weekends in the gay section of Riis Park Beach in Queens. And when Rick Stokes broke free and moved west to California, to find the man he would spend his life with, and a career in law and business, Harvey Milk was wandering through a series of jobs in New York by day, engaged at night in a series of romances with the curly-haired young men who would always be the passion of his life.

By 1973, they both were living in the area of what was coming to be called the Castro. Many of the old residents had sold out and left when the first two gay hippie bars had opened in the late '60s. The exodus had continued, accelerating the neighborhood's state of decay and apprehension, and Harvey Milk made it his mission to befriend the old neighbors and business owners near his camera shop, introducing himself at each door. But when the established business group, the Eureka Valley Merchants Association, turned hostile and tried to block the license two gay men needed to open an antique

shop, Milk called the other gay small-business owners together. In the back of
a pizza parlor they created a new, rival merchants' group, the Castro Village
Association. It put on a street festival which drew five thousand people. Business boomed along Castro Street that day, and the old merchants, impressed,
began to join the new association. Local politicians took notice and began to
come to CVA meetings, and Harvey Milk began a campaign to persuade the
Castro's new residents to register to vote.

Harvey Milk first ran for office himself in 1973, only months after taking
up residence on Castro Street. When he decided, in his impulsive, unilateral
way, that he was going to run for the San Francisco Board of Supervisors, he
went to see Jim Foster. Milk was going to run as an openly gay candidate, and
he wanted the Alice Club's endorsement—or at least Foster's agreement not
to support someone against him. But there could hardly have been a meeting
of two more different men. They were fated to be enemies. A Milk candidacy
wasn't what Jim Foster had been working for all those years, and when Milk
turned up at his doorstep, Foster's reaction was annoyance and distaste. He
told Harvey Milk he had paid no dues. The Democratic Party, said Foster—
who had changed his own registration from Republican a decade before—
was "like the Catholic Church. We take converts, but we don't make them
Pope the same day."

Besides, he said, "It's not time yet for a gay supervisor." Harvey Milk
went away seething at Foster's arrogance. "When is it ever going to be time?"
he fumed, and Foster was enraged at Milk's gall. The Alice Club's endorsement went not to Milk, but to a straight liberal politician who had been a
friend in the past. Harvey Milk ran anyway, arguing that the liberals would
never give up power to gays—"You have to take it," he said. He didn't win.
Council members were then elected at-large, by a city-wide vote. Harvey Milk
had come to the city as a nobody just months before, and he refused to cut his
hair or change his hippie clothes for the campaign, even after he realized he
would need to, to have any chance to win. But he was provocative and entertaining, a neighborhood populist, a sharp critic of the city's inefficiencies and
of the Alioto administration's developer-friendly policies—and ingenious at
getting publicity from the city's two daily newspapers. Better than any other
candidate, Harvey Milk understood that politics was theater, and he was always good for a quote. On election day, he surprised people, just as José Sarria, the famous drag performer at the old Black Cat, had surprised people
when he ran for supervisor more than a decade before. Sarria voted for Milk,
and so did about 17,000 other people. The newcomer drew about 10,000
more votes than Sarria had, and came in tenth in a field of thirty-two.

He had beaten the rest of the field in the districts that were heavily gay, in
the precincts around San Francisco State University and in the hippie neigh-

borhoods of the city. It was the first time Harvey Milk had ever run for anything, and it whetted his appetite for more. He *loved* campaigning. In 1975 he ran again, wearing an old coat and tie, and shorter hair. Like Foster's, Milk's background was Republican, and he ran as an economic conservative and social liberal, appearing everywhere in search of votes. At a benefit dinner in October 1975, a juggler, a gay balladeer, a blues singer and a country-and-western guitarist all performed, and Sheriff Dick Hongisto, Allan Baird, the Teamsters representative, and Oliver Sipple, the gay ex-marine who had saved President Gerald Ford from an assassin's bullet in San Francisco just two weeks before, all turned out. It was Allan Baird and Milk, together with Howard Wallace and the membership of Bagel, who had brought the union and the gay bars together that year in a boycott of Coors Beer, protesting the company's attitudes toward minorities and the right-wing politics of its president, Joseph Coors. It was a good way to demonstrate the economic power of the city's gay colony, and Coors was feeling the pinch as the boycott was spreading. (Within two years, Coors chairman William Coors would be publicly declaring his support for gay rights in *The Advocate*.)

The politics of San Francisco were unique, as a tenth anniversary celebration of the Reverend Cecil Williams's pastorship of Glide Memorial Church demonstrated on November 30. Gay American Indians, members of Friends of the Earth, Black Muslims and "Moscone for Mayor" volunteers all came together to drink apple juice, munch on bagels and hear speeches by an assortment of city lights: the black radical Angela Davis; Assemblyman Willie Brown; Senate majority leader George Moscone, who was running for mayor; the Reverend Jim Jones, leader of a mysterious, cultlike group called People's Temple, which could turn out whole troops of regimented volunteers for political campaigns; and a prostitute-rights activist named Margo St. James, who had started a legal reform group she called Coyote, an acronym for Cast Off Your Old, Tired Ethics. By then, with the help of Bagel and large support in the Castro—and despite the fact that Alice had endorsed someone else again—Harvey Milk had done even better at the polls in his second run for supervisor. No one considered him a fluke anymore. He was part of a phenomenon, the sheer accumulation of gay influence in the city; the gay vote was, Dianne Feinstein's campaign manager told the *Los Angeles Times*, "probably the largest liberal voting bloc in the city." The result, the *Times* story said, was that the city's "politicians are rushing virtually en masse toward what they see as a rich new source of campaign strength." The boldest, most visible new element of that voting population was in the Castro, and by the end of 1975, Harvey Milk was clearly its voice—and the most public gay figure in the city.

He loved being the center of it. But politics aside, Castro Street in the middle '70s was a conveyor belt of the lean young men whom Milk loved to flirt with and romance. To some of the younger ones, the ones still in or barely out of their teens, who had come for the endless good times and sexual opportunities they had discovered in San Francisco, Harvey Milk's obsession with running for public office, and his interest in getting them to register to vote and work as volunteers in the gay politics of the Castro, made him seem an old, egocentric bore. When Milk had stopped a tall, skinny, baby-faced kid named Cleve Jones at the corner of Castro and Eighteenth Street one day in 1973 and begun to make his usual pass, the boy just blew him off.

Cleve Jones loved life in the Castro as much as Harvey Milk did, but his priorities were different. The son of Quaker parents who were teachers in Arizona, Jones had come to San Francisco as a high school senior for the annual Pacific Meeting of Friends in the summer of 1972. The city was then still a center of the radical student movement, and as Jones discovered, there was a large, active subset of gay and lesbian Quakers at the meeting, and a notice posted about a gathering of them in the city. He went, met gay men from San Francisco, and heard about Phyllis Lyon and Del Martin, and Jim Foster, who was already being spoken of, among more radical gays, as an elitist. Cleve Jones had a secret Quaker boyfriend back in Arizona, but he found the city— and the radical gay strain within the Quakers—exhilarating. Within a year, he had told his parents he was homosexual, joined the Gay Liberation Front, dropped out of the freshman class at Arizona State University and left home to become one of the young gay men adrift in San Francisco. That first night he slept in a cheap room at the Leland Hotel on Polk Street in the Tenderloin, befriended by a teenage pimp and five Mexican and Filipino kids working as hustlers on the street. Jones soon did the same, peddling his body, pedaling a bike as a messenger boy, peddling his body again as a houseboy for two fat old men in an apartment overlooking the Castro. After a while he found a job and settled into the Castro himself, and when Harvey Milk the first-term candidate tried to pick him up, Jones the young radical was unimpressed.

"No," he said. "I don't like your politics."

"Aw, c'mon, why don't you come help?" Milk grinned.

"Electoral politics is a bourgeois affectation," Jones told him, and sauntered off. It was the scene on Castro Street that interested Cleve Jones, and the baths, and Golden Gate Park. When he first tried the baths, he was terrified, afraid of rejection. Before long, he loved them. His best friends all became hot-tub buddies. They all had sex with each other. If Harvey Milk, with his scruffy jeans and shirts and long, dark hippie hair, seemed too establishment to the nineteen-year-old Cleve Jones, then Rick Stokes was hopelessly over the hill. Jones knew Stokes as one of the middle-aged establishment gays who clustered around Jim Foster, and to Jones, their pursuit of civil rights through traditional party politics seemed hopelessly elitist, irrelevant and dull.

• • •

Not everyone new to San Francisco felt that way. Jo Daly had come to town because of Jim Foster and the politics he represented. She was working six days a week selling cars in Manassas, Virginia, doing well at it, wearing $300 suits and living in a log cabin on a lake when she stayed up to watch the coverage of the tumultuous Democratic National Convention in Miami in 1972, and saw Jim Foster and Madeline Davis speak from the podium. Maybe it really could be done that way, she thought, listening to Foster talk about the need for a gay rights plank in the platform. Daly was ready for a change, and after some days of reflection, alone in her cabin with Michelle, her shaggy, drooling, orange and white St. Bernard, she made a decision. She quit her job, packed up her things and drove with Michelle to San Francisco.

Josephine Daly was short, a little on the heavy side, with a bowl of cropped black hair, an infectious grin, and boundless energy for politics and business deals. She found Jim Foster at an Alice meeting soon after she arrived in town, and almost immediately became one of the few important lesbian political activists in San Francisco. There had never been many. Del Martin and Phyllis Lyon had been the two dominant lesbian personalities in town for almost twenty years. Their ideas and energy were important to every evolving phase of the movement. Charlotte Coleman, the owner of The Mint, was the leading lesbian bar owner in the city, an active member of SIR and an important fundraiser in Richard Hongisto's campaign for sheriff. But just as Coleman was notable in part because she owned one of the few lesbian bars— there were from three to five at any time, compared to the hundred or more gay male bars by the mid-'70s—the absence of any significant number of women in the gay politics of San Francisco had always been striking. Whether in old organizations like the Tavern Guild, the Council on Religion and the Homosexual and SIR—or in newer ones like the Alice B. Toklas Club, which Jo Daly began to help Foster build in 1972, and later in Bagel—there had always been few women. Partly that was because there were fewer openly gay women than men. Partly it was because they had their own separatist organization in the Daughters of Bilitis. But it was also true that gay men didn't really want them as equals, a fact they had demonstrated time and again. The main gay political issue, when Jo Daly arrived in town as Rick Stokes was running for the community college board in 1972, was the effort to repeal the sodomy law. It was a law of concern to some lesbians, particularly those who were mothers. In custody cases, if their lesbianism was known, they could be considered "unapprehended felons" by the courts and lose their children. Rick Stokes was one of the lawyers who represented lesbian mothers in such cases.

But it was men who got *arrested* for sex offenses. The politicians on whom Jim Foster and the others in SIR and Alice relied to repeal that law were men—the straight, liberal politicians that Foster worked so hard to make indebted to the gay community. But it might have been natural that the political figure Jo Daly drew closest to in San Francisco was a woman, Dianne Feinstein, the president of the Board of Supervisors, a moderate who made plain her deep misgivings about the rampant sexuality in San Francisco's gay male community.

The friendship between the poised, elegant, married Feinstein and the chunky, kinetic, blue-denimed Daly became a measure of what was different about San Francisco's politics. Feinstein was not, by San Francisco standards, a liberal. But she stayed close to the political leadership of the gay male community, which had provided the margin of her election victory as supervisor and president of the board in 1969, and which again in 1973 returned her to the president's office, an office she had lost in 1971. Jo Daly soon became Jim Foster's closest female ally in Alice, and by 1975, had become vice-chair of the club. She made history in the city that year—and probably in the nation: she became the Human Rights Commission's first full-time, paid liaison to the gay community, an appointment engineered by Phyllis Lyon and Del Martin. Jo Daly was now a notable figure in the political culture of San Francisco. She had also met and fallen in love with an older, well-to-do woman named Nancy Achilles, who had become a supporter and substantial financial backer of Dianne Feinstein.

The three women were close, but when Jo Daly and Nancy Achilles told Feinstein one day in 1975 that they had decided to marry and wanted her to be there for the wedding ceremony on a rented boat in the bay, they were not prepared for her reaction. Feinstein immediately said no.

"No," she said, "why don't you do it in my garden? *I'll* perform the service."

And so they did. On a mild, sunny afternoon, in the privacy of the garden behind Feinstein's house in Pacific Heights, with the president of the San Francisco Board of Supervisors in a long cotton dress, all the other women in pants, Del Martin and Phyllis Lyon standing up with the wedding couple, and thirty or more friends in attendance, Dianne Feinstein led Jo Daly and Nancy Achilles through a service she had helped to write. Everyone except Feinstein seemed to be struck dumb by the event. Afterward, as Dianne Feinstein's husband, Bert, tended bar, Jim Foster, David Goodstein and the others in the garden grinned at each other, amazed and gratified by the symbolism of the day.

Feinstein's relationship with the Alice Club, and with Daly, posed a wrenching choice for Foster and the rest of the club as the 1975 city election approached. Gay power in city politics had become not only undeniable, but celebrated. "I rode in the Gay Freedom Parade and am *proud* of it," one candidate told a crowd assembled by the Gay Voters League at Bo-Jangles, a dimly lit gay bar in the Tenderloin that September. The candidate so pleased to be there was running for sheriff against the incumbent, Hongisto; some of the crowd were dressed in drag. "The gay vote is a key element for any elected official in San Francisco," Supervisor John L. Molinari explained to a reporter for the *Los Angeles Times* that fall. And the endorsement that virtually every candidate wanted was the one from the Alice B. Toklas Club. Feinstein was running for mayor in 1975, and her loyalty to her gay constituency was undiminished. At the fourth annual Police vs. Gays softball game that summer, she had stood before a crowd of five thousand people and led one of the gay cheers *against* the police. "Peaches, peaches, fuzz, fuzz, fuzz," she sang out, waving her hands. "If you don't win, you're the team that wuz."

But state Senator George Moscone was running for mayor, too, and needed the city's gay vote to win. Although he had never been a particular crony of the Alice Club—there were people who couldn't remember his ever appearing at a meeting—that year he had finally pushed the Senate into passing what had become known as the Brown bill, the bill introduced by Assemblyman Willie Brown in 1969 and every year since which legalized sex in private between consenting adults. That had always been the fundamental goal and ambition of the gay male culture of San Francisco, the political litmus test that Jim Foster demanded of candidates who wanted gay support, and its passage that year had been especially dramatic. The liberal Moscone, the majority leader of the Senate, had called in every important political chip. The Senate had deadlocked in a tie, 20–20, and Moscone had literally held it there by locking the doors of the chamber until the lieutenant governor could fly back from Denver and arrive to break the tie by voting with Moscone.

Feinstein's own sympathy and support for the gay male community had always been the weakest when it came to sex, and although Daly tried to win the Alice endorsement for Feinstein—or, failing that, keep it from going to Moscone—she could not prevail. Jim Foster and the members of Alice joined virtually every other gay organization in the city in backing Moscone. The Alice endorsement brought with it not just the votes of those influenced by the club's position, but hordes of Alice volunteers to man Moscone's main phone bank and hand out leaflets door-to-door.

The liberal and moderate votes of gay support helped push Moscone past Feinstein in the election that November, and into a runoff with conservative Italian city superintendent John Barbagelata, who treated gay leaders who interviewed him with such obvious discomfort and distaste—"You people," he kept saying, in a breakfast meeting with twenty-five of them—that it helped consolidate the gay vote for Moscone. No liberal candidate had ever been able to put together a coalition of minorities large enough to win the city's mayoralty. The December runoff was thus a test of the power of black, Latino, gay and white liberal votes against the city's old conservative ethnic Roman Catholic base. Moscone beat Barbagelata by 4,400 votes, a margin he could not have had without gay support.

For the first time, the city had a mayor publicly indebted and friendly to the gay community. But the gay leader to whom George Moscone first looked was not Jim Foster. It was Harvey Milk, who had very nearly won his second race for supervisor, coming in seventh in the citywide voting for all candidates for a six-person board. A study of the voting pattern showed that he had deep support in one-ninth of the city's precincts, ranging from gay and hippie neighborhoods to the wealthy, liberal enclave of Pacific Heights. If Harvey Milk could ever run for office in the precincts where he was strong, and not the rest of the city, he could win. But for the moment, he was clearly the city's principal—if not yet elected—gay politician. Moscone, in thanks and tribute to him and the vote he represented, appointed Milk a member of the city's powerful Board of Permit Appeals, the court of last resort for any question involving a city permit. On a crisp January morning, Harvey Milk climbed the broad sweep of marble steps in city hall to the mayor's office. There he joined Moscone's other appointees—a black woman, a neighborhood activist and a Filipino—and was sworn in as the first openly gay board commissioner in the city's history.

It was a political gesture intended to hold him until the next supervisory election, in 1977. Within weeks, however, Milk, who was always unsatisfied with the standard way of doing things, found himself unsatisfied again. He looked at the map with the precincts colored in where he had done so well, and decided that he could run and win a state legislative seat in the district being vacated by the assemblyman seeking Moscone's old Senate seat. It did not matter that the city's entire political establishment was already committed to supporting Art Agnos, the chief aide to the speaker of the state Assembly, or that some of Milk's friends feared he would alienate the voters if he ignored his prized appointment and ran again so soon. He ran, gleefully trumpeting the race as a contest between "Harvey Milk and the Machine," which became his campaign slogan. To be accused of machine politics was embarrassing to the coalition of liberals now dominating many of the city's major offices. It was the kind of accusation that Jim Foster and Rick Stokes would never have made, particularly since they were also committed to supporting Agnos, as part of their allegiance to the politicians who supported them. But Milk, a maverick, loved flying in the face of convention. It was part of his charm, one of the reasons the voters found him so entertaining—and other politicians found him so aggravating. And Mayor Moscone, who had warned Milk that he would kick him off the Board of Permit Appeals if he ran, did so. In his place he appointed Rick Stokes.

To anyone paying close attention to the shape of gay influence in the city, it was clear that in growing and maturing, it had developed two heads. It was also clear, when the election was held in November 1976, that a contest was looming which only one of them could survive. In his race against Agnos for the Assembly seat, Harvey Milk had been beaten—narrowly—again. But a measure he had campaigned for each election since 1973 had finally been approved. The voters had decided to give up at-large elections and elect their city supervisors by districts. It seemed clear that if Harvey Milk ran for the supervisor's seat from the Castro, he would win. *Some* gay candidate would win. But only one—from that one district. There was no other in which enough gay votes existed to make it happen.

It was inconceivable to anyone that Harvey Milk wouldn't run. So Jim Foster and David Goodstein, confronted with the inevitability of their worst nightmare—the election of Harvey Milk as the city's first major gay officeholder—decided that they had to head him off. They had to run a candidate of their own for the Castro seat. When Rick Stokes, who customarily kept his head deep in his law practice and business affairs, sat down with Foster and Goodstein to discuss the lessons of the recent election, he thought afterward that they must have rehearsed what they had proceeded to tell him: why he had to run against Harvey Milk. Rick Stokes wasn't voluble or funny or passionate like Milk. He didn't enjoy campaigning. In fact, he hated the slipperiness of politics, the inability to trust people to really feel the way they said they did or do what they said they would do. He didn't particularly relate to the men of the Castro, either, except as a businessman who had owned the baths, and as a lawyer who defended them in court, and who worked to reform the sex crime laws. But Stokes was smart. He was honest. He was able. He was the only gay candidate the Alice Club had ever tried to run for public office. He was the best candidate Alice could offer. And he lived in the Castro. It was his neighborhood.

The trouble was that it was not really his neighborhood anymore. The men of the Castro were on the march. Again and again those nights in June, after Dade County, hundreds or thousands of men took off through the city, demonstrating to themselves, to their fellow San Franciscans, to the world around them, that they had an identity, and a community, worth fighting for. The vote in Dade County had been a call to arms, but distant. Robert Hillsborough's murder had united the city and its newly assertive gay neighborhoods; three thousand mourners filled Grace Cathedral for a memorial service on the Monday after that year's Gay Freedom Day Parade, a march that had been swollen to an enormous number, 200,000 or more, by the change in feeling, and transformed in character from celebratory to solemn. There were fewer drag queens, no nudity, many more women marching, a multitude of black armbands, an effigy of Anita Bryant that was burned in the Civic Center, and a huge banner in the march front saying " 'Human Rights Are Absolute.'—Jimmy Carter."

It was a community aroused and militant. Men like Cleve Jones, who had come to the city for sexual pursuit and pleasure, were feeling a different sense of identity. Within a year, as voters overturned gay rights ordinances in Eugene, St. Paul and Wichita, it would be Harvey Milk leading the marches out of the Castro, Cleve Jones at his side. Politics within the Castro community were evolving, boiling with the times. The Bagel Club had split in two. The more conservative leftists, a minority led by Howard Wallace and Claude Wynne, broke off in November 1976 to form the Gay Action Caucus and its Butterfly Brigade. The more radical majority captured the group, and in December, led by Jim Gordon, Chris Perry, Hank Wilson and David Goldman, formed a new club that was designed to have the street legs of Bagel, but the more sophisticated political acumen of Alice. They called it the San Francisco Gay Democratic Club. Frustration with the leftist rhetoric and lack of real political traction at Bagel meetings had led Jim Gordon and Harry Britt, among others, to begin attending Alice meetings. The traditionalism there felt stifling to them, but it also gave them an idea. Alice had traditionally welcomed all comers; numerous members weren't homosexual, and straight politicians had long since delegated their wives to represent them at meetings.

It was part of what made Alice feel so old-fashioned to the more radical men of the Castro, but it also helped to make Alice relevant—and its endorsements influential—in the rest of the city. Regardless of what the real gay population of San Francisco was, whether it was 75,000 or 150,000, only a tiny portion of it was active in street or Democratic Party politics. The rest of the population took its political cues from those more in the know, and the most influential recommendations in the city's gay community and in the liberal community beyond were the endorsements that came from Alice. It was Rick Stokes's most potent asset. No matter how dull and old-fashioned he might seem to the young men of the Castro, there were still plenty of other gay and nongay votes that would be influenced by the endorsement of Alice.

That endorsement would certainly go to Stokes unless—unless it could somehow be prevented. Harry Britt had had five years to recover from the burnout of his old life as a minister and married man. His new, free, more virile existence in the Castro—he lived in an apartment at No. 2 Castro Street and wished only that it were No. 1 Castro Street—had restored his energies. He knew Rick Stokes from the Methodist church that Stokes attended every Sunday. But Harvey Milk posed a more visceral attraction. Britt, stopping by Castro Camera one day, had found himself lusting for Milk's blond, curly-headed boyfriend, Scott Smith, who had the soft eyes and slow drawl of his Mississippi roots. From that day in 1975, Britt had taken a more and more active interest in Harvey Milk's campaigns, and the political skills which had served him well as a minister and black civil rights organizer in Chicago in earlier years now made him realize that there was an opportunity for Milk in the Alice Club. He could never get the club's endorsement. But there were a number of younger members of Alice who, like Britt and Gordon, had recently joined. And there was Rita George, a feminist and president of the local national women's political caucus chapter, who was seeking the supervisor's seat, too. If she could be encouraged to stay in the running for the club's endorsement rather than drop out and give her votes to Stokes, and if they could swell the ranks of the meeting on endorsement night with as many Milk supporters as possible, they might be able to split the vote enough to deny Rick Stokes the two-thirds he needed and expected as his natural due.

On the night of September 12, Britt sat at the Alice meeting with Milk and Claude Wynne beside him, afraid that at any moment Milk would say or do something so typically intemperate that he would offend the room and blow their chance at a strategic coup. The things he had said in public about Rick Stokes, Jim Foster and the rest of them were rough enough. "A handful of self-serving people who are utilizing the movement for their own advantage," Milk had described them once. "These people have to be weeded out for the sake of their community," he had said. And Milk had not liked the idea of trying to block Stokes's endorsement by Alice. The stealth of it, and the notion of going himself to seek favor in the enemy's den, went against his grain. But Harvey Milk could be pragmatic. He held his tongue that night, and in the first round of voting for Assembly District 5, with Wynne and others speaking up for Milk, the club's ballots split, and Stokes failed to carry the endorsement by two votes.

The room was stunned. Balloting continued on the other races and then came back to District 5. Harry Britt held his breath. Would the other votes stay firm or dissolve and flow toward Stokes? They held. Rick Stokes failed to win the endorsement of the Alice Club by a single vote.

Stokes was staggered. The hurt in his eyes was plain to see. It was a club he had helped build. It was *merit* that mattered to him, and loyalty. He would never understand the quicksilver turns and betrayals of politics. Milk was an entertainer, spontaneous and winning, but Stokes was not. He needed the Alice endorsement that would have marked him as *the* gay candidate of choice, and its denial left him stranded. Jim Foster knew what the blocked vote meant, and he was seething. "I've *never* liked you!" he shouted at Claude Wynne as the meeting broke up that night.

Milk's victory in the District 5 race was ordained from that night forward, but the actual vote, when it came in early November, was stunning to the city, elating to a movement which had come under assault from the newly gathered fundamentalists, and sweet for a man who had whiled away his time at jigsaw puzzles only five years before. It was historic—the first time an openly gay candidate had been elected an officer of any major city in the nation.

It was an extraordinary victory, but there was tension, too. From an adjacent district, the voters had elected a representative of the old ethnic San Francisco, a son of the culture that had been displaced in the Castro by gays. His name was Dan White, a former city policeman, an Irish Roman Catholic, the sort of man from the sort of family that had found gay men in the Castro so offensive.

"As the years pass, the guy can be educated," Milk reassured a friend who worried about Dan White. "Everyone can be reached. Everyone can be educated and helped. *You* think some people are hopeless—not me."

Others, later, would have cause to remember what Rick Stokes had said in a bitter, prescient moment in the 1977 campaign. "Harvey," he said, "was born to be a martyr."

25

MONEY IN THE
HILLS OF BEL AIR

June 1977, Los Angeles

The pool deck at Sheldon Andelson's home at 900 Stradella Drive in the hills of Bel Air offered one of the best views in town: a long and winding strip of Santa Monica Boulevard, cutting a swath through Beverly Hills and West Hollywood. To the east were the skyscrapers of downtown Los Angeles, and to the west, the hazy Pacific Ocean. Down the hill that dropped off the edge of Andelson's pool was Beverly Hills, where Andelson kept his law office on Sunset Boulevard, and West Hollywood itself, with its concentration of gay men and lesbians, many living in the bungalows and apartment houses Andelson started buying up in 1951. Andelson's grandmother had told Sheldon, when he was growing up on the South Side of Los Angeles, to do as she did: buy land, the best investment of all, since people always need a place to live. Andelson had listened to his grandmother. His real estate investments were shrewd, and by the 1970s, his spins around the real-life Monopoly board, as he liked to call it, were turning him into a millionaire. He had invested some of that money into a state-of-the-art gay bathhouse at 8709 West Third Street—a sprawling sex warehouse, with a discriminating door policy that admitted only the most handsome men. That enterprise produced so much cash that the Saturday night take often had to be stuffed into big plastic garbage bags. Those Saturday nights were one of the reasons he could afford to build his own house in the hills of Bel Air, and why he could give his lover, Waldo Fernandez, one of Hollywood's most sought-after designers, a free hand in designing it, as he had designed the bathhouse. The result was a villa in the hills designed first and foremost for entertainment. It had a great hall for a living room, forty feet by twenty feet, with sand-toned walls that stretched up thirty-two feet to a ceiling crisscrossed with beams made from bleached telephone polls. There was no art on these walls, and little furniture on the floor. The room was a cold, elongated cube that was big enough to hold three hundred people standing, or seventy people for sit-down dinners around the tables that were folded up and stored in the garage. It was, as Andelson once remarked, not the kind of place that suggested snuggling up with a cup of coffee. When the *Los Angeles Times* society writer, Marylouise Oates, came upon his mirror-covered dining room while touring the villa, and asked if this was where Sheldon Andelson took his morning breakfast, Andelson recoiled. *"Here?"* he responded in mock horror. Andelson lived upstairs, in one of the two bedroom suites on the closed-off second floor, with sliding glass doors that opened up to a deck overlooking his pool and his city.

Most people in Los Angeles's homosexual community knew Shelly Andelson, or at least knew of him. He was a wealthy lawyer and landlord; they called him the Godfather of West Hollywood, and it was not meant as an insult. Andelson, in fact, lived parallel lives in two Los Angeles societies—gay society and straight society—and he was an intriguing if enigmatic character in both worlds. He was on the founding board of the Los Angeles Gay Community Services Center, and he was one of the American Jewish Committee's best fundraisers. He broke bread with governors like Jerry Brown and with street activists like Morris Kight. Andelson was a society lawyer who helped Hollywood's elite beat traffic tickets and minor drug raps; and he was the discreet vice lawyer who had helped hundreds of homosexuals escape the embarrassing consequences of a 647(a) lewd conduct arrest. Almost everyone in both of Shelly Andelson's worlds knew of the gay San Simeon he had commissioned in Bel Air, and almost everyone wanted to see it. And on June 5, 1977, two days before Anita Bryant registered her victory over gay rights in Dade County, the deck around Sheldon Andelson's pool was packed with people, mostly gay men. They were celebrating. There had never been so many people at Andelson's house before, as he had repeatedly warned his friend Rob Eichberg, a therapist on the staff of UCLA as they planned the event. "Where are we going to put three hundred people? I don't think we can hold more than a hundred people. Do we need valet parking? I think we need valet parking." There was no need to worry. There was valet parking, and there were buckets of champagne, pitchers of Bloody Marys and trays of canapes rolling out of the kitchen that had been designed for use by a caterer.

The defeat that was unfolding in Dade County didn't matter on this beautiful Sunday in the hills of Los Angeles. Here, for gays in Los Angeles—or, more precisely, for wealthy gay men on the West Side of Los Angeles—there was cause for celebration. The municipal elections, the April 5 primary and May 31 runoff, had marked a political coming of age for them and a new form of gay political activism in the nation—a gay political action committee, the Municipal Elections Committee of Los Angeles, or MECLA. Ten of the eleven candidates MECLA supported—in the form of $19,450 in contributions—had won. The people who were enjoying Andelson's hospitality had, in truth, purchased the honor, by contributing a minimum of $50 to this new gay political action committee. The crowd did not include any of the familiar faces of gay activism in Los Angeles—there was no Jeanne Cordova or Jim Kepner or Don Kilhefner walking around the pool deck. These were wealthy and professionally successful gay men, who had raised the money swiftly and efficiently, with a series of small dinners and cocktail parties at homes like this one in Bel Air. They called themselves A-Gays, borrowing the term from Armistead Maupin's *Tales of the City* series in the *San Francisco Chronicle*. Like Sheldon Andelson, they could afford to live in the snug estates that clung to the hills on the West Side of Los Angeles.

Anita Bryant deserved some credit for the turnout at Sheldon Andelson's party. Her growing influence at the start of 1977—and her promise that a victory in Florida would inspire similar campaigns in places like Minnesota, Washington, D.C., and California—had finally convinced a closeted homosexual, David Mixner, who was the manager of Mayor Tom Bradley's reelection campaign in 1977, to accept an invitation to talk politics before a small group of professional gay men, a session that would lead to the celebration at Andelson's home. Mixner had met with an assembly of twenty men—all white, all middle-class, all from the West Side of Los Angeles: lawyers, therapists, accountants, screenwriters, music executives and film executives—who would, after hearing Mixner, formally transform themselves into the organization that would be known as MECLA. Rob Eichberg had gathered them at his home after a fiasco of a fundraiser that a few West Side gay men had organized for a friend running for the school board. It raised $900. "People spend more money to give a party than we just raised," Eichberg remarked to his friend Peter Scott, a corporate lawyer from Dallas, as they shared a drink at the Paradise Ballroom afterward. The men who came for brunch at Eichberg's also couldn't understand why a constituency so sophisticated and wealthy had so little influence in Los Angeles. They were alienated by what there was of a gay movement in their city, and embarrassed by the people they saw quoted as their representatives. Why had the media decided that Morris Kight—a disheveled, old man with thick glasses who boasted of taking a "vow of poverty," a man most of them would not even invite to their homes for a cocktail—was *their* leader? The answer, of course, was that none of these men had devoted a moment to homosexual activism and Kight had, as Eichberg reminded them over quiche and champagne. "Don't ask Morris Kight to look like you," Eichberg said.

The atmosphere for homosexuals in Los Angeles that day was certainly better than it had been six years earlier, when unyielding police raids of bars and bathhouses led to the founding of a Gay Liberation Front and the Gay Community Services Center. Mayor Bradley had appointed a liaison to the gay community, Bill Carey. City officials, including city attorney Burt Pines, campaigned openly for gay votes. Pines had been elected on a promise to end prosecutions of men for such technical violations as trying to pick up a man in a bar, and he had honored his promise. Still, there were daily reminders of just how little power the gay community had. When Pines issued his order to stop prosecuting gay men for morals violations, the assistant police chief, Daryl Gates, defied him: "We don't take instructions from the city attorney." The Los Angeles Police Department deployed a hundred police officers with guns and two helicopters to raid a Los Angeles Gay Community Services Center fundraiser at the Mark IV bathhouse. The fundraiser was, to put it charitably, bizarre: it was a slave auction, where audience members bid for the services of men onstage dressed in leather sado-masochistic outfits. But the LAPD's response, arresting forty men on violation of the "involuntary servitude" law and displaying for the media the sexual paraphernalia they confiscated from the raid, created such a furor that charges were dropped against all but four of the men.

The men at Eichberg's house set two goals after brunch. The first was to raise money from the historically ungenerous gay, white, male middle class of Los Angeles—to "shake money out of the Hills," as Eichberg said. The second was to determine how to use that money to increase its influence, and that was why they had asked Mixner to come speak to them.

Mixner was thirty years old and resolutely closeted, but had been tentatively looking for ways to get involved in the city's gay political and social community. He had stumbled into a meeting of the Stonewall Democratic Club, which Morris Kight had founded in 1975, a gay Democratic club patterned after the Alice B. Toklas Club in San Francisco. Mixner made the mistake of wearing a jacket and tie to this event, and everyone either looked at him suspiciously, as if he were a police agent, or just ignored him. "This is the gay political movement and there is no place for me," Mixner said to himself, and left depressed. By contrast, the men he met at Eichberg's home were very much like himself, professional and politically ambitious, monied and middle-class. To this audience, Mixner was not an object of suspicion, but a celebrity, a proven and experienced political professional. Mixner had been one of the co-chairs of the Vietnam Moratorium Committee, which had organized the successful October 15, 1969, strike to protest the Vietnam War, and worked his way west in campaigns to Los Angeles.

There was, in truth, much about Mixner's life then that was either secret or manufactured. He sought sexual release at bathhouses and public cruising spots, where he would give a fake name and telephone number to men who asked. For his heterosexual friends, Mixner made up whole chapters of his life—about romances with women who never existed—or altered details of episodes that he described as formative. He spoke, for example, of falling in love with an eighteen-year-old at Arizona State University who, he later said, was killed in a car accident which Mixner reported witnessing from the front porch of their home. To his few gay friends, he would relate the story in full detail, including the fact that the student was male, and the details of a funeral that was all the more excruciating because he felt he had to hide his real grief. Years later, when friends and colleagues working for Eugene McCarthy's campaign in 1968 asked him if he was dating anyone, he told them this sad story, but said the student was a woman—his fiancée—and the experience had been so upsetting that he could never bring himself to date again. Years later, when Mixner told Bill Clinton that he was homosexual, the future president was shocked and perplexed. He had always been moved by the distressing story of his friend who told of seeing his fiancée die in the flames of a car wreck.

Although Mixner agreed to speak to an audience of men who knew he was gay at Eichberg's brunch, he certainly wasn't about to lend his name to the organization they wanted to form. But he was focused and clearheaded about what they should do: You can be a force in Los Angeles, he told them, and it would not cost more than $20,000 in strategically chosen contributions to candidates for the city council. Six members of the fifteen-member council were already sympathetic to a gay rights bill, by Mixner's calculation. The gay community could shift the balance of power in Los Angeles by winning just two seats—and $20,000 was more than enough to do that.

Mixner's presentation that day was remembered, even twenty-five years later, as a turning point for Los Angeles gay political organizing. But the brunch turned out to be unexpectedly disturbing for Mixner. He left feeling despondent at what he had seen: a room full of men like himself in every way, except they had friends and lovers and their lives, mostly, were not a secret. Mixner returned to his anonymous world of running Bradley's campaign on weekdays, waiting for the weekends to escape into his world of heavy drinking and LSD—narcotics he needed to seek the sexual company of other men.

Bill Carey, the mayor's gay liaison, had a few ideas about how the group could raise the $20,000: a barbecue, perhaps, or even a bake sale, charging

$10 a head. But Steve Lachs and Rob Eichberg had grander plans. Lachs was from Brooklyn, the son of a clothing store owner, a lawyer who worked in the Los Angeles Public Defender's Office and wanted to become a judge. He was earnest, smart and likable, and entirely ordinary. If he were straight, Lachs would say, he'd be living in the San Fernando Valley and be president of the men's club at the local synagogue. Eichberg, by contrast, was from L.A. He was boyishly handsome, with blue eyes and a flashy smile. His interest in therapy colored everything about him: He was sensitive and tended to be emotionally intimate, even on first meeting. He loved the social circuit, but had never really found politics that interesting, and in truth found the notion of meddling in city council races a little boring. Eichberg wanted the organization, which they were calling Orion, to be high-profile and splashy, a presence in the media, rather than the city council chambers.

Eichberg and Lachs were different in many ways, but they were both Jewish and saw no reasons the fundraising formula that had worked so effectively among wealthy Jews couldn't work among wealthy homosexuals. Eichberg and Lachs both knew firsthand—Eichberg from watching his father work on the board of the Jewish Federal Council, Lachs as the president of his own small B'nai B'rith chapter—that there were more effective ways to raise money than charging people $10 for a cook-out. Why devote weeks to planning an afternoon fundraiser which might raise $1,000, Lachs said, when a single lunch with a rich benefactor could yield the same result? "That's the way you raise money," Lachs told Carey. "Spend one hour with a person who can write out a check for $1,000."

What was different here was the Los Angeles gay social circuit. Eichberg recalled a very unusual party that had been thrown a year earlier by Michael Nicola, a Hollywood dress designer, and his lover, Stephen Smith. Nicola, like Eichberg, loved the exclusive gay parties that welcomed only men who were very rich, very famous or very attractive. He adored the theme parties—with names like "Pretty Me, Pretty You!"—where everyone dressed in white or black, smoked marijuana and angel dust, and more often than not ended up in a huddle of bodies somewhere down a hall or up a stairway. Nicola and Smith, a Dallas man with a soft southern accent who had made his money from real estate and film distribution, had organized a fundraiser on behalf of Senator John V. Tunney, a Democrat who was preparing to run for a second term, at their English Tudor home in Beverly Hills. It was the usual gay party, except that people had to donate money to Tunney's campaign in order to attend. Nicola took care of the cooking and the decorations. And he used his Hollywood connections to produce a guest, the actress Bette Davis. When Davis showed up, on the landing of the staircase that led down into the two-story living room, 125 men fell silent at once. "Well," Davis said as she surveyed the scene below her, "it would seem there are no more young ladies in Hollywood." The men burst into delighted applause, and everyone in West Hollywood soon heard of this very successful fundraiser.

There was a lesson here. Why not combine the political and the social? Why not, Eichberg and Lachs thought, make it glamorous to give money to politics, to integrate political activism into the "A-Gay" culture? They knew that in the world of Jewish fundraising, social status was measured by the amount of money one returned to the community. Why not create an ethos in Los Angeles's gay world where a man's social standing—they were thinking now only about men—was measured not only by his clothes, his home and his physique, but also by how much he contributed to politics? As for the gay men who were not part of their world, well, would they not gladly pay some money for the privilege of entree, to attend a private dinner party at the home of, say, a Sheldon Andelson? It might finally "shake money out of the Hills."

The first fundraiser for MECLA was held in the back room of the Carriage Trade restaurant on Beverly Boulevard in early 1977. Nineteen men were invited. The goal was $20,000 in pledges, and the planners chose people of roughly equal means to attend. Rob Eichberg made the introductions, laying out the plan to elect a sympathetic city council along the lines suggested by David Mixner. "Now, this is what it's going to take to do this," Eichberg said, throwing out the $20,000 figure. At that point, by prearrangement, one of the men in the room rose to his feet. He was a shill whose role was to set a floor on the contributions before anyone else could. "I've just got to do this," he said. "This is so important. I'm going to give you a check for $1,000." Eichberg nodded in choreographed acknowledgment. "I want to see us go around the room and everybody to match that," he said. By the end of the evening, they had obtained their pledges.

That evening provided the formula for thirty fundraisers before the runoff election in June 1977. The MECLA executive committee prepared a master list of five hundred potential donors, and rated each person's contributory worthiness based on his income, spending patterns, donation history and social and political involvement. "That sounds elitist, I know," Eichberg acknowledged to a reporter at the time. "But it is also practical. We only had so much time and so much energy." From this list, MECLA assembled groups made up of people roughly of the same income level. Someone would always rise first to set the floor on contributions. The dinners were intimate and elegant, at the homes of the organization's wealthier members. Business attire was encouraged after Eichberg observed that men in suits gave more money than men in jeans. And Eichberg set the standard for how to get people to open their wallets. He would walk up close to his target, eye to eye, making him feel ill at ease. "Now, what about you?" he'd say loudly in a room filled with the man's friends. "How much are you going to contribute?"

"I'm aware that many of us experience a great deal of difficulty and resistance to asking people for money," Eichberg wrote to other MECLA members in a primer on fundraising. "The only way to overcome this is to ASK. It is important not to expect to be successful every time, we are bound to be turned down by some people. It is okay to be turned down."

It was only after the first Carriage Trade dinner that Lachs, Eichberg and Scott got around to considering a name for this new political action committee for homosexuals. The word "gay" or "lesbian" would not appear; no one should have to worry about what he wrote on a check, they decided, adopting the policy David Goodstein had unsuccessfully pushed in Chicago two years earlier. So with little debate, it was decided that this new group would be known as the Municipal Elections Committee of Los Angeles, or MECLA (pronounced MECK-lah), as unrevealing a title as anything since the Mattachine Society. The initial plea for funds that went out under MECLA's letterhead and over Peter Scott's signature was marked in big capital letters: "PERSONAL AND CONFIDENTIAL."

There was little ideology here, other than the ideology of power and influence. These were people who enjoyed the glamour of politics, the social standing that came with touching elbows with the people who ran Los Angeles and California, of being able to call the mayor "Tom," even if that didn't translate into winning the immediate goals of gay liberation. "We don't demand instant acceptance of our total program," explained Richard Kaplan, another of the early members. "That wouldn't be realistic. We prefer a favorably inclined but cautious friend to an avowed enemy." The new organization reflected the place where it was born: a city where social status was often measured in money, where one lived, and what parties one attended. Street demonstrations and sit-ins might work in a city like San Francisco, with its concentrated and generally more radical gay population. But that would never work in a city as geographically and culturally dispersed as Los Angeles, with homosexuals clustered in communities spreading out from Santa Monica to Silverlake, with a downtown abandoned on weekends and week nights, and where there were no obvious central places to stage demonstrations. San Francisco had people but Los Angeles had money, and politicians in Los Angeles would listen to money before they responded to a street demonstration. "Politics runs on money," Peter Scott said. "And that's why MECLA was born." As MECLA's founders wrote in what was apparently its first letter to supporters: "The time has come for the hundreds of thousands of gay men and women in Los Angeles to be heard in the political arena, and to speak with the voice that politicians understand best—MONEY."

• • •

Sheldon Andelson came to personify MECLA, even though he had not been one of its founders, and even though he really hadn't thought much of the idea Eichberg first described to him over lunch at Hamburger Hamlet on Sunset Boulevard. This kind of forceful lobbying for a gay rights bill could create a backlash that would set back the gay rights movement in Los Angeles, Andelson warned Eichberg.

"Sheldon, we're not here to ask for your permission," Eichberg responded. "This is what we're doing. We're asking you to be a part of it."

Andelson was forty-six years old in 1977, ten years older, and ten years more cautious, than most of the men who created MECLA, and Eichberg took that to be why Andelson was worried about a backlash. In fact, Andelson was probably more concerned about competition than any kind of backlash. The Beverly Hills lawyer had spent the past five years making himself into a one-man political action committee, with his own contributions to politicians, and had nothing to gain by encouraging a group of gay men to do the same thing. But once Eichberg made clear that MECLA was happening, Andelson lent his name to the organization's masthead as chair of the advisory council, made it a regular beneficiary of his contributions, and opened his home to its fundraisers, large and small, even as he continued writing his own separate checks to politicians.

By spring 1977, Andelson was as well established and secure as any gay man or woman in Los Angeles, conspicuous in his success. He was coming to the end of what he later described as an eight-year coming-out process, which would culminate, fittingly, at a $150-a-plate black-tie roast of himself in October 1979 at an evening to raise money for the Gay Community Services Center. President Carter's mother, Lillian, Governor Jerry Brown and Andelson's family—including his father, whom Andelson flew in from Chicago—all heard Andelson talk publicly about what by then was quite obvious. "I would be fooling you if I said this was easy," he said that night, his eyes moist behind his yellow-tinted glasses as he peered over the 850 people in the Beverly-Wilshire Hotel ballroom. "It's not easy. But it is right. It is right to be who you are. That gives others around you the right to be honest back.

"If I am any sort of role model at all," he continued, "it is to prove that being an open gay person is not inconsistent with financial success, personal happiness and family love." Most people who knew Andelson had long before that night realized he was gay, and as he acknowledged, there were no signs that it had hurt him professionally or socially on either side of the line that Andelson crossed so effortlessly.

He had come a long way from his days as a young man, starting a law practice in L.A. in the mid-1950s after graduating from the University of Southern California Law School. The school was less than twenty blocks

away from his childhood home at the corner of Fifty-second Street and Vermont Avenue, a blue-collar Jewish neighborhood named Boyle Heights,
where he grew up with his mother and her second husband, Billy Andelson,
whose name Sheldon Horwitz took after Sheldon's mother divorced his father, Al Horwitz, in Chicago and took her young son to the West Coast. Sheldon Andelson came of age in L.A. when Joseph McCarthy was at the peak of
his power in Washington, and the stories of homosexuals being purged filled
the local newspapers. Andelson constructed his career accordingly, as his
friend Rand Schrader, the judge and lawyer, later observed. He built his
"early professional career," Schrader said, "using the gay skill of being straight
with straight people and gay only with us." As it turned out, to be "gay only
with us" applied not only to Sheldon Andelson's social life, but to a large part
of his legal practice as well. Through the 1960s he was one of the few L.A.
lawyers defending 647(a) lewd conduct arrests—a small enough group that
the attorneys met each morning to divide the cases by jurisdiction.

This was how Morris Kight came to meet Andelson. Kight suspected
Andelson was "a brother"—why else would he be defending all these homosexual men busted in sex cases?—but needed to know for sure. So when a
young man arrested for soliciting sex at a public park bathroom came to the
Gay Liberation Front for advice, Kight sent him to Andelson, with instructions to report back everything that happened. The man called back to describe the exchange, particularly the way it ended: Andelson had walked
around the desk, leaned over the young man and said: "Sweetie, don't you
worry, we're going to take care of this." Kight was elated and called Andelson
directly for a meeting. Kight informed Andelson that the Gay Liberation Front
was on the lookout for good lawyers to handle lewd conduct arrests, and the
two men struck an arrangement: Kight would funnel cases to Andelson, providing he handle some of them at a reduced fee and others pro bono. They
kept a log: of every ten cases, four would pay the full fee of $1,500.

Kight was charmed. He had never encountered anyone quite like Andelson: genteel, cultured, wealthy, with expensive tastes in clothes and food.
Kight's delight grew after Andelson won acquittal for the young man Kight
had sent over, who was, as Kight put it, "guilty as hell." Andelson was perhaps
the best vice lawyer Kight had met, charismatic, gregarious and aggressive,
with a network of courthouse contacts and an uncanny ability to work the system to his client's advantage. Kight and Don Kilhefner began to refer all the
647(a) arrests that came to Andelson. "Send them over," Andelson would say.
There was a measure of altruism to Andelson's behavior—his aggressive
lawyering was on behalf of fellow homosexuals in trouble—but there was
profit in his charity.

When Kight and Kilhefner went on to form the Gay Community Services
Center, Andelson wrote the occasional check to keep the lights on or the rent

paid at Wilshire Boulevard. But Kight and Kilhefner thought of another way for Andelson to show his gratitude. He would be on the center's first board of directors. Kight turned up at Andelson's office one day with a copy of the center's articles of incorporation, and told him he wanted Andelson to serve as a member of the founding board. Andelson skimmed it, nodding his head. "Fine, fine," Andelson said, apparently not taking the request seriously or thinking through its implications. With that name in place, Kight and Kilhefner and stationery printed up—blue ink on heavy stock paper—with the board of directors printed on the top, listed in alphabetical order. Sheldon Andelson's name came first, just to the side of the words "Gay Community Services Center." And that was the heading on the letter of introduction Kilhefner sent to the city's judges, requesting they consider the social services the center was offering when they came across down-and-out homosexual defendants. Andelson learned of the letterhead when a judge summoned him to the bench to express interest in Andelson's decision to publicly announce his homosexuality. Andelson was dumbfounded: "How does he know I'm gay?" he wondered. Andelson's name had begun appearing in the *Los Angeles Advocate* in May 1968 in cases involving lewd conduct arrests, but he was barely out in the homosexual community, and certainly was not public about his sexuality in the legal community. He left the courtroom and called Morris Kight at home.

"You didn't tell me my name would be on a letterhead," Andelson said.

"Sheldon," Kight responded, "it goes with the ball game."

If Andelson was upset at this gambit, he kept it to himself. For years Andelson would credit Morris Kight with tricking him out of the closet, describing himself in an interview almost fifteen years later as "ripe to be used by the movement." Kight waited another six months after their initial conversation before raising the subject. "I think," Kight said to Andelson, "we've not harmed you. I think we've helped you." Andelson was happy to be out, he told Kight. It had brought him status, notoriety—and clients.

The relationship that evolved was a curious one. Andelson was one of a handful of people with whom Morris Kight shared one of the best-kept secrets of his early life: that he had been married, at the age of thirty-one, from 1950 to 1955, and fathered two children, who gave him two grandchildren. Kight never mentioned this in his many newspaper interviews and rarely confided it to any of his friends, as if worried that a heterosexual involvement might undercut his credentials as a gay leader. Kight and Andelson clearly liked each other; that said, they used each other without apology. Kight bragged that he made Andelson rich. Andelson boasted that he helped Kight out with his rent, slipping him a few hundred dollars here and there in unspoken remuneration for the cases Kight sent him, since rewarding Kight outright for the legal referrals would be illegal. "I keep Morris off my back," Andelson said with a friendly laugh as he described to David Mixner how he bought himself some peace. Thus, when Morris Kight soured on MECLA, he never attacked Andelson. The founders of MECLA, Kight observed caustically, cared only about their social status and not about gay rights. "Manipulators," Kight called them, "jacket-and-tied, coiffed and perfumed, and teeth adjusted every six months, with credit cards." Kight, who never had a problem finding an unkind word to say about a rival, praised Andelson as a dedicated and a civilized man. Andelson returned the favor in his public remarks about Kight. He always mentioned him in newspaper interviews, and at a 1979 testimonial dinner for Kight, Andelson purchased a full page in the dinner program:

> *Thank you Morris.*
> *for enriching my life*
> *by being the one*
> *who opened my closet door*
> *and began my involvement*
> *with our wonderful community.*
>
> *SHELLY ANDELSON*

There were limits on how public Andelson was prepared to be about his personal life. When Sheldon's sister-in-law Michelle called each year to invite him for the family's Passover seder, he would typically accept and say, "Will you call Waldo and invite him?" Andelson never said why he wanted Fernandez there, suggesting that he was just a particularly close friend, though members of the family understood it was more than that. Andelson and Fernandez had been lovers since 1962; they had met nine months after Waldo Fernandez left his homeland, Cuba. He was fifteen and Andelson was thirty-one. They were introduced by Andelson's Cuban hairstylist. Fernandez took an instant liking to this bright and successful lawyer, and invited Andelson to attend his sixteenth birthday party. That Andelson was so private about his life reflected in part his discomfort with intimacy, as he confided to friends. He considered it a shortcoming, a regrettable contrast with his confident and engaging public manner. Arlen Andelson found that his older brother was delighted to talk anytime about politics or law, but he was silent if the discussion turned personal. He felt more comfortable at work than at play; at family functions, he'd be forever getting up to take and make phone calls, leaving early for the next social engagement. He was an enigma to his brothers and their wives—an "intimate mystery" as his oldest brother, Sherman, said when he later summed up Sheldon's life. For a long time Arlen wondered if his brother even had a sexual or romantic life. Arlen was wrong, of course. His brother was simply meticulous about shielding the details of his gay life. Indeed, his sexual indulgences were well known by the other gay men in his circles, people like Duke

Comegys, who knew Sheldon Andelson because they were in the same therapy group, an assembly of rich and powerful upper-middle-class gay men. Comegys loved to tell the story of the afternoon that he and a boyfriend rented a helicopter so Comegys could spot his mansion from the air. Comegys ordered the pilot to fly over Andelson's villa, six houses up the road from his own home. There, Comegys looked down to discover Andelson in his hot tub with two very handsome, very young, very muscular and (as best as he could tell) very naked men. Comegys instructed the helicopter to circle lower and lower until the young men fled the hot tub, in search of towels, and Comegys, laughing, ordered his pilot to fly on. And although Andelson's home was most publicly known for its elegant society parties, it was also the location of some fairly notorious weekend parties, when the big living room and pool deck were filled not with men in ties and women in dresses, but handsome, young men. There would be drugs and sex. In short, Sheldon Andelson's home provided the venue for a fairly typical gay Los Angeles party.

Andelson himself was a strange sight indeed, showing up at the Los Angeles Gay Community Services Center, with its radicals and out-of-luck street hustlers. He would typically pull up in front of the headquarters in his Jaguar, dressed in a cashmere sweater, following the tug of his pair of elegant short-haired whippets, Pussy and Willie. By the time MECLA was founded, Andelson seemed quite comfortable moving between his two worlds, upsetting the presumptions about homosexuality in both of them. Steve Lachs learned that when he first ran for municipal court judge, and Andelson insisted that he campaign at Andelson's bathhouse. It was like Bella Abzug at the Continental: Steve Lachs was wearing a suit and everyone else wore a towel (if anything). The sounds and smells of sex enveloped him, and Andelson tugged Lachs through the hallways, shouting out: "Everybody, I want you to meet the candidate for judge, Steve Lachs!"

No one expected MECLA to do so well so fast, and a few weeks after the June reception at Andelson's home, Rob Eichberg, Steve Lachs and a few of the other founders slipped into Lachs's hot tub to consider whether it was already time to broaden their mission. They had helped elect a city council decisively sympathetic to gay rights. And there was now an astonishing degree of interest in this new organization, from politicians who saw it as a source for money, and from gay men—and some women—intrigued by this new political party circuit. There was even competition for the seats on MECLA's board, and members of Los Angeles's gay community fought over them as if they were invitations to an exclusive party. By midsummer, contributions had reached $40,000, most of it collected from four hundred people.

They decided that the group would involve itself in *any* election in which a resident of Los Angeles was able to vote. That meant that MECLA would make contributions to candidates for the state legislature, for governor, for the county Board of Supervisors, for the House of Representatives, for the U.S. Senate and for president. This new organization would no longer settle for just being a power in L.A.; it would seek to become a power in the state of California.

The sudden interest in winning seats on MECLA's board was one indication of its newfound success. Another was that MECLA was suddenly swept up in the same fight that engulfed all major gay organizations in the mid-1970s: the battle over whether its governing board should consist equally of men and women.

MECLA had been founded as an all-male organization. Two women wanted to change that: Roberta Bennett and Diane Abbitt, law partners and lovers, who had become friends and dinner partners with Peter Scott, David Mixner and Steve Lachs. These were two influential and articulate women, and they were as different from the better-known lesbian leaders in the city, like Jeanne Cordova, as Rob Eichberg was from Morris Kight. Bennett and Abbitt had both once been married, and used to vacation together with their husbands and children. Abbitt had two sons, and Bennett two daughters, who came to live with them when they divorced their husbands and moved in together. Bennett and Abbitt had felt isolated in Los Angeles, two lesbian mothers who belonged to the homeowners association, and owned two station wagons. They felt no kinship with the city's lesbian groups, which Abbitt would note, with acerbic humor, believed "in anarchy and drowning baby boys."

They were interested in politics, though, particularly after Abbitt's husband, upon learning of his wife's lesbianism, threatened to challenge her for custody of the children. Abbitt then discovered how vulnerable a lesbian mother was and how few, if any, people in the gay movement had even considered it an issue. Abbitt called the Los Angeles Gay Community Services Center asking for the name of a lawyer who specialized in lesbian custody issues. No one could help her. She tracked down the San Francisco phone number of Del Martin and Phyllis Lyon, after finding their book on lesbianism on a supermarket shelf in 1973. "I'm a lesbian mother," she said. "I'm facing a custody battle. I don't know what to do." Lyon and Martin had no advice. Abbitt's husband eventually backed down, but that experience prompted both Abbitt and Bennett to go to law school and to help create the Lesbian Rights Task Force of the National Organization for Women.

Abbitt and Bennett believed there should be women in MECLA and Peter Scott agreed with them. With the city elections behind them, Scott and Abbitt suggested that the board work toward becoming evenly divided between men and women. Eichberg led the fight against an idea he dismissed as a silly, knee-jerk proposal. Women did not raise money anywhere nearly as well as men did, he said: Why should they be awarded half the seats if they were raising only one-fifth of the money? he asked. MECLA's appeal, he said, was based on convincing men to pay money to dress up in black tie and go to events where they would meet other men who had paid a lot of money to dress up in black tie. The truth was that gay men didn't like spending time with lesbians. "Yes, I agree—we need to include women more," Eichberg said. "But now, how do we do that and not lose the social desirability for the men?"

Scott, the first MECLA chairman, was a soft-spoken southerner, who was a Republican in Texas and had become a Democrat here in California. He didn't speak often, so when he did people tended to listen. "Either you believe that women are equal or you don't," he said. "If you believe that women are equal and you understand that they have suffered oppression, then you also understand that it's your duty to bootstrap them up. If we really believe that all people deserve recognition, then we should be co-sexual." The board agreed with Scott, and in a secret ballot a month after the Andelson reception, in July 1977, expanded the board from nine men to fifteen people— five women and ten men. But the same secret ballot replaced Scott with Eichberg as the chairman, an obvious punishment to Scott by the original nine members for having pushed for equal representation of women on the board.

MECLA's coming-of-age struggles include an odd twist: whether heterosexuals should be allowed on the board. Eichberg wanted MECLA to incorporate the straight West Side society people he considered his friends. He liked the company of heterosexuals and he didn't like the ghettoization of gay life. In fact, he considered himself bisexual, though he didn't advertise it, and had deliberately not dated women as he got involved with Los Angeles's gay world because he was afraid it would isolate him. Abbitt and Mixner fought Eichberg's idea, asserting that it demeaned homosexuals to bring heterosexuals onto the board, as if homosexuals weren't sophisticated enough to fight their own battles. The pride of battle was as important as the pride in victory, Mixner said. "There's a difference in self-esteem if you're in the field picking cotton and the master invites you into the house because you've been good, and you walk into the house and sit at the table. It's just a different feeling to get about yourself." Beyond that, the environment would change if heterosexuals were allowed in the door, Mixner added. He liked to say that he tried not to see straight people after seven o'clock at night, and he was only half joking. Abbitt and Mixner taunted Eichberg, saying he was a closet heterosexual. It was meant to be funny, but it was also meant to be mean, and Eichberg said he took it so seriously that he broke out sobbing while driving on the freeway. But when the vote came on the new board, Eichberg won: Five of the fifteen new board members would be straight. One of them, a fundraiser and political veteran, Bev Thomas, would become the MECLA co-chair within a year.

• • •

California state Senator John V. Briggs was in Dade County the night Anita Bryant won her referendum. Briggs, a Republican from Fullerton, in Orange County, California, had been a state senator for two years and an assemblyman for ten years before that. Now, he was standing at the back of the Zodiac Room at the Holiday Inn in Miami Beach, exulting with a reporter he knew from California, explaining why it would help his own challenge to Governor Jerry Brown. The reporter was Randy Shilts, the correspondent for KQED, the public television station in San Francisco. Briggs did not know that Shilts, a freelancer who had paid his way to Miami, used to work for *The Advocate*, or that Shilts himself—bearded, intense and engaging—was gay. "We won! We won!" Briggs exclaimed to Shilts as Anita Bryant came into the room. He explained why he was so happy: In the last gubernatorial election, only half the voters had gone to the polls to elect Jerry Brown. "And today, you got half the voters of Dade County at the polls just to vote for this," Briggs told Shilts. California, he said, was not that different from Florida, with its large populations of fundamentalists and homosexuals. A public referendum on homosexuality would create a furor in California, Briggs believed, and would turn him from a long-shot conservative candidate for the Republican gubernatorial nomination to a crusader against homosexual rights. Since California didn't have a statewide gay rights bill that could be put before voters, he would return to Sacramento to introduce a state law barring homosexuals from teaching in public schools. And if the California legislature refused to adopt that bill—which, of course, it would—he would gather signatures to put it on the ballot.

When Briggs returned home, he went not to the state Capitol in Sacramento, but to the granite steps of city hall on Polk Street in San Francisco, right "into the lion's den," as his associate, Orange County Reverend Lou Sheldon, thought as he saw the "screaming, shouting mess" that greeted Briggs. It was just two weeks after the Dade County vote, and Briggs and his supporters had exactly the backdrop they wanted: a strange and hostile crowd of jeering and jostling homosexuals, shouting Briggs down as he described his idea to protect the children of the "normal people of the majority" from homosexuals. The Associated Press distributed a picture of Briggs nose to nose with a presumably gay male heckler wearing an earring. "I think the rights of the majority of people of California need to be heard," Briggs said. The *Los Angeles Times* described the politics of the appearance in a particularly critical editorial on June 17: "Who is John V. Briggs and why was he yelling at homosexuals from the steps of San Francisco City Hall the other day? John V. Briggs is a state senator from Fullerton who wants to be the Republican nominee for governor next year. He was yelling at the homosexuals because he knows that most Californians have never heard of John V. Briggs and that a confrontation with San Francisco's large and militant gay community might just improve his name recognition."

It would be more than a year before Briggs's initiative went to the voters. But California was not Florida. The members of MECLA had been considering this threat from the day Mixner first spoke to Orion. Briggs's city hall announcement was less than a week after Sheldon Andelson's reception. The members of California's gay community had seen the mistakes in Dade County. They would be ready.

26

A BLACK-TIE AFFAIR

August 1977, Los Angeles

Stephen Smith was on a mission when he showed up at David Mixner's West Hollywood apartment in late summer 1977. Smith was a real estate broker and a film distributor, but his love was politics. He had been president of his high school Republican club in Dallas and chairman of his Youth for Goldwater chapter, but by college, he had found his way over to the Democratic Club at Vanderbilt University. When David Goodstein asked him if he had any interest in serving as the *Advocate* publisher's unpaid southern California political operative, Smith jumped at the offer. One of Smith's first assignments was to present David Mixner with a list of personal questions Goodstein wanted answered. The *Advocate* publisher had noted Mixner's rising profile in gay politics in California and was giving serious consideration to, as he told Smith, "blowing Mixner out of the water."

Mixner had just begun working as a paid consultant to New AGE, or New Alliance for Gay Equality, an organization that had been hastily created in southern California after Anita Bryant won in Dade County and state Senator John V. Briggs presented his proposal to bar homosexuals from teaching in public schools in California. New AGE was noteworthy in that it was made up of both middle-class professionals, through MECLA, and the street activists who had previously dominated the scene. The two groups didn't like or trust each other, and the fact that they were seated around the same large table in a conference room at Sheldon Andelson's law office one day after Briggs's combative press conference suggested how concerned they were. They were feeling confident after their success in the L.A. municipal races, but Briggs was threatening a whole new league of campaign—a statewide referendum around an issue. And they were determined to head off the kind of public bickering and drift which had splintered the gay leadership in Dade. New AGE would combine the fundraising and professional skills of MECLA with the organizing and street power of grassroots leaders like Troy Perry and Jeanne Cordova. "Los Angeles will be ready for Bryant and her friends," Rob Eichberg, the MECLA chairman, proclaimed in an article published in Cordova's *Lesbian Tide*.

To this end, New AGE hired a political consulting firm to prepare an electoral profile of Los Angeles: Mixner-Scott Associates, for $2,000 a month. The new firm had two partners, David Mixner and his best friend, Peter Scott, the first MECLA chair. They had decided that Mixner's political connections and Scott's legal and corporate expertise—and the fact that they were openly gay professionals—might prove to be a lucrative combination. Hiring them raised Goodstein's ire. David Goodstein had been traumatized by the loss in Dade. He was certain that gays would lose again in California, and that the political repercussions of a defeat in California would be enormous. Goodstein wanted New AGE to meet Briggs in the courts rather than at the ballot box. Tie him up with lawsuits, Goodstein said at New AGE's first meeting. "If we fight this, we're dead," Goodstein argued. Taking on Briggs would turn this into a "life and death issue."

"But it is a life or death issue," Troy Perry responded. "If we don't win California, we're dead."

The group was going ahead without him, and Goodstein, realizing that he was not going to get his way, angrily rose to his feet and turned toward the door. "I've got a newspaper to run," he said. Troy Perry had come to both dislike and distrust this egotistical publisher of *The Advocate*.* But Perry knew the danger of letting the publisher storm out of the room today, and he stopped him at the door. "Promise me one thing," Perry said. "Promise me you're not going to be divisive in this." Perry did not want to spend the next year responding to attacks on the anti-Briggs campaign in *The Advocate*.

---

* Perry had, as part of the preparations for the fight against Briggs, conducted another fast, this one for sixteen days at the Los Angeles County Courthouse, with a goal of raising $100,000. Goodstein called Perry and asked him to hold off the fast so it could coincide with the next deadline of *The Advocate*. The publisher wanted to devote his "Opening Space" column to Perry and announce to his readers that he was pledging $5,000 to Perry's effort. "Can't you wait for my newspaper?" Goodstein said. Perry refused. "David," Perry replied, "The Lord has spoken to me."

"I promise you that," Goodstein said, and he left.

Goodstein kept that promise in the pages of his newspaper. But he didn't refrain from meddling with the organization itself, particularly when he learned about its decision to hire Mixner's new firm. Mixner had come out of the closet in a way that telegraphed both his sexuality and his intention to bring his mainstream political talents to the gay political world, sending a form letter to a hundred of his friends and associates (including Bill and Hillary Rodham Clinton) that disclosed his sexuality in one paragraph and requested contributions to fight Briggs in the next. Mixner was on his way to becoming a major player in the gay community, raising for Goodstein, once again, the specter of competition.

The second, and more pressing, reason for Goodstein's reservations had to do with an episode involving Mixner that spring which had raised, even among Mixner's friends, questions about his character and stability. In the weeks after Bradley's primary victory, Mixner, who was thirty, had begun confiding to his friends and associates a tragic turn in his life: he had terminal cancer and was going to die. He had become an invaluable adviser to members of MECLA, and its members were proud that one of their own—even if he was still in the closet—was so prominent and successful. And they liked him. Mixner was witty and fun, extraordinarily knowledgeable about politics and able to drop the names of a long list of powerful politicians he had encountered in his career. When Steve Lachs learned that Mixner had terminal cancer, he couldn't stop weeping. This was 1977, and gay men were not accustomed to watching contemporaries die.

But there was one problem with Mixner's story. David Mixner did not have cancer. He had made it up. Mixner was in the midst of a nervous breakdown, one so severe that he disappeared for a month to the Malibu beachfront home of his friend Shirley MacLaine, whom he had met during the peace movement. The strained balance between his public political life and his personal sexual life that Mixner had tried to maintain with alcohol and drugs had begun to fall apart after the meeting at Eichberg's house, where he saw professional gay men who welcomed him so warmly and "made a lie" of his own existence. When Mixner attempted to inform his parents that he was a homosexual, the episode proved traumatic, and they told him he was not welcome in the home where he grew up. Mixner could not turn to his new friends for help, since he was sure a confession of his own emotional turmoil would disillusion them. He became convinced that his homosexuality would become known to the entire city, and his career as a political consultant would end. He would go home at night and cry uncontrollably. Rob Eichberg, the therapist whom he met through Orion, the group of Los Angeles men who had taken an interest in politics, drove up to visit Mixner in Malibu almost every day, and they would take long walks by the Pacific surf. Eichberg suggested that Mixner view his breakdown as a symptom of his inability to deal with his homosexuality, and of the need to integrate the separate compartments of his life. Within the month, Mixner left MacLaine's home, shattered but calm with the help of anti-depressants, and prepared to announce both his true sexuality and his true health.

The news that Mixner did not have cancer was almost as difficult to take as the news of his imminent death. Steve Lachs was so angry and humiliated that he could never bring himself to raise the subject with Mixner. Mixner personally told Tom Bradley he had fabricated the story, and even though Bradley was cordial Mixner still felt mortified. The Mixner incident was as embarrassing for MECLA as it was for him: its most prestigious member appeared, by all accounts, to be at least crazy.

David Goodstein couldn't understand how Mixner had survived this episode, how he had gone in a matter of months from a high-profile nervous breakdown to a premier job in gay politics (though Mixner's career would be filled with a series of dramatic stumbles and equally dramatic recoveries). Why was someone who presumably needed the cushion of a low-stress environment, Goodstein asked Steve Smith, being hired for such a high-pressure public role? Smith went to Mixner's apartment house—on the corner of San Vincente in West Hollywood, where Sheldon Andelson had lived until he built the home in Bel Air—and launched into his interrogation.

Did you really have cancer, as you told Mayor Bradley and everyone else, or did you make it up?

"It was a lie," Mixner said, locking his gaze on Smith's eyes.

Did you suffer a nervous breakdown?

Yes, I did, Mixner responded.

Do you have a drug problem that led to the breakdown?

"Acid," Mixner said, responding affirmatively, though Smith, whose vices did not include recreational drugs, did not understand the reference.

And did your therapist advise you not to subject yourself to unnecessary stress for six months?

Yes, Mixner responded.

Steve Smith did not know that Mixner had a history of fabricating stories. Smith did not know about the death of the phony fiancée, or the heart condition Mixner told associates he suffered while running the Vietnam Moratorium Committee. Still, he realized as he headed to his car that Mixner had just confirmed for him a huge amount of public lying. Indeed, the stories that Mixner told of himself that enhanced his standing—some true, some not—from going to Woodstock ("Didn't everybody?") to being asked to the White House to meet Richard Nixon and Henry Kissinger while working in the peace movement, either confirmed his stature as someone who moved in high and powerful circles or fueled the suspicion that he was a self-promoting impresario. California's gay community was breaking into two camps when it came to Mixner. Goodstein was not alone in his distaste. Mike Nicola, Steve Smith's lover, detested Mixner from the first time they met at the John Tunney fundraiser. Mixner is a "phony" and a "snake," Nicola told Smith as Mixner left their house: "I don't trust that man as far as I can throw him." Mixner was a polarizing figure; for every Mike Nicola, there was a Peter Scott or Diane Abbitt who intensely admired him.

Mixner, a political professional, knew why Smith had come to see him; it seemed logical, Mixner thought, that Goodstein in defeat would turn his guns on him, for Mixner had assumed that his nervous breakdown would be used against him. But Smith had not anticipated Mixner's honesty, and when he called Goodstein, he offered a favorable report: "I don't think he's the right guy to be doing this right now," Smith said of Mixner and the anti-Briggs effort. "But I don't think it's so clearly a black-on-white case." Goodstein dropped his opposition to David Mixner, but Smith's recommendation was only one of the reasons. Goodstein was now distracted: something that had nothing to do with Briggs or Mixner had captured his attention.

September 1977, San Francisco

On the weekend of September 16, 1977, a group of sixteen wealthy gay men from the San Francisco Bay Area, chosen by Goodstein and his friend, the attorney Jerry Berg, gathered at a complex called Pajaro Dunes on the Monterey peninsula, between Santa Cruz and Monterey. Since 1974, Goodstein had been fascinated with what was known as the human potential movement, the est workshops created by Werner Erhard, which used intimate and psychologically brutal exercises to give people a higher sense of self-esteem, and a sense of greater control over their lives. Goodstein had undergone est training, and had come to consider Erhard "a friend and a mentor." On the Friday after Anita Bryant's victory in Miami, the publisher, dispirited and listless, had gone to Erhard's home for dinner. When Goodstein arrived at Erhard's door, the est founder looked at his dinner guest and said: "Hello, Goodstein! You obviously think that lady in Florida canceled your vote, don't you?" using est jargon to mean that Bryant had killed him, or ended his life. "Yes, I do," Goodstein responded. "Well, asshole, you're wrong! She hasn't canceled your vote. Can't you see that you're having dinner with me?" It was an inspiring moment for Goodstein, who then decided that the correct response to Anita Bryant was not political organizing but raising the esteem of the gay community. Dade County had revealed that the real problem with homosexuals was that so many were in the closet and self-hating. Goodstein decided the time had come to design an esteem training program for gays so other homosexuals could, like David Goodstein, "be proud of themselves."

The weekend at Pajaro Dunes would be led—or "facilitated"—by Eichberg, the MECLA chair. He designed it, borrowing liberally from Erhard, who had declined Goodstein's invitation to do it himself. Goodstein not only wanted to develop a human potential workshop designed specifically for homosexuals. He was hoping that a weekend at the Pajaro Dunes involving powerful gay men from San Francisco might have a political result as well: the creation of a northern equivalent to MECLA.

A northern California MECLA did not emerge from the meeting. But two 12-hour days produced the outline of a gay self-esteem program so successful that the sixteen men came to be known as pioneers, called the Dunesmen, or Dunies, who gathered with Eichberg eleven times over the next nine years to repeat the workshop. Goodstein left the weekend ecstatic. "All of us, including those who had been active in the gay movement, held our gayness differently," Goodstein reported. "We were a lot clearer about it, a lot prouder and a lot more willing to deal with being gay." Eichberg and Goodstein left for an L.A. fundraiser featuring Bette Midler to raise money for the anti-Briggs campaign. As the car left the condominium resort, Goodstein leaned across to the man who designed this program: "Eichberg," he said, "you've got to take this on the road."

Goodstein followed up his challenge to Eichberg with a lunch invitation within the month. They should create a self-discovery program, to help gay men explore self-hatred and problems in the gay community, and determine how to take control of their own lives and come out of the closet—the enduring theme of Goodstein's life since being fired from his bank job. Goodstein presented Eichberg with a marketing plan that would lead to Advocate Experience workshops held all over the country. *The Advocate* would, of course, publicize the project, and Goodstein told Eichberg he would put up $150,000 to make it work. "You need to decide whether you want to do this with me," Goodstein told him. "Be forewarned. If you don't, I will find someone who will and I'm going to do it anyway."

The result, unveiled at the start of 1978 in an "Opening Space" column by Goodstein titled "Enriching the Gay Experience," was layered with the language of self-awareness familiar to anyone who had experienced est. "In this issue, we announce the Advocate Experience," Goodstein wrote. ". . . The objective of this undertaking, the logistics of which remind us of the Normandy Invasion, is to begin a process whereby the totality of people's gay experience, which can only be described accurately as 'scanty,' will be enriched. The specific purpose of the Advocate Experience is *'to transform the participants' experiences of being gay or homosexual into a richer context wherein their individual lives can be lived in ways that are truly self-enhancing and contribute to all society.'* We are determined that Advocate Experience participants always get in touch with their [our] own magnificence. We know that means we and they have to be willing to confront and go through personal barriers to self-esteem. For that we need safe spaces. The Advocate Experience creates those safe spaces."

This program, Goodstein explained, was designed to confront what Goodstein defined "as 'toilet mentality,' that is, a willingness to accept a second-rate status as human beings, expecting to lose rather than win, and constant involvement in petty, right-wrong games" that affected everything from dating to politics. This gay "human potential program" was designed, he said, to "get large numbers of gay people to feel good about who they are," and then from there, for many of them to enlist in the liberation movement, and fight the threat posed by people like Anita Bryant and John Briggs. There would be a hundred people per session, at $150 per person, and it would start in San Francisco and L.A. The Advocate Experience phones would be staffed twenty-four hours a day.

The first Advocate Experience was invitation-only, at the Jack Tar Hotel in San Francisco. There were nearly eighty people there, among them Randy Shilts and Armistead Maupin. The session began at 9 a.m., or "9 a.m. sharp," as the official report in *The Advocate* put it, reflecting Goodstein's familiar impatience with tardiness in the gay community and est's emphasis on the importance of doing what you say you are going to do. So at 9 a.m. sharp, a man walked to the podium of the hotel ballroom: "I am Rob Eichberg. I am your facilitator for this morning's session. This is the Advocate Experience. It is your experience." For the next two days, twelve hours each day, Eichberg ran the crowd through the Pajaro Dunes workshops. Friday night was reserved for small group sessions to discuss what they *liked* about being gay. On Saturday evening, the participants were given sheets of paper and instructed to write a letter disclosing, in detail, their homosexuality to the person closest to them—usually a parent—still unaware of their sexuality. It was a safe if not easy exercise, an emotional trial run, until the end, when Eichberg distributed stamped envelopes and challenged everyone to address the envelope and return it to Eichberg, who would then mail the letter. And Eichberg would badger participants: "Honey, aren't you going to mail this? How full of shit are you? How much are you going to continue to lie to the people closest to you in your life? And if you're lying to your parents, I bet you you're lying to yourself, aren't you?" It was so traumatizing that organizers joked about bringing along a carton of tissues for that one night, so many participants broke down.

The other memorable exercise came on Sunday, the last day, and it went to the heart of Goodstein's complaint about the physical caste system among homosexual men. The participants were arranged in concentric circles, one circle face in and the other circle face out, rotating person to person, rating each person's physical appearance on a scale of one to 10 before moving to the next step. It was so unsettling that the men at the inaugural session mutinied and refused to carry it out until Eichberg and Goodstein explained its purpose: to make people focus on the shallow and degrading rating system that dominated the male homosexual social world.

Goodstein believed the Advocate Experience had an immediate and profound influence on the gay movement, producing new gay leaders and training the ones already involved, particularly on the West Coast. There is little evidence that these workshops affected the course or personality of the movement itself; it remained as rancorous as ever. But it did produce some changes in Goodstein. The man who had spent the better part of a decade battling his enemies suddenly found a need to make peace. Bruce Voeller learned this when Goodstein invited him to dinner in the Castro. Goodstein, Voeller once said, was the one person whose "mere name could cause me to have headaches and a sleepless night." But over dinner, Goodstein confided to Voeller his difficult childhood, growing up as the fat outcast, hiding under his porch from his father and schoolmates. Voeller was touched and shared his own turmoil, of having to fight his wife for the right to visit their three children once he became a gay activist. It was cathartic. "If we can pick up from here, having left the past behind, let's see what we can do together," Voeller told Goodstein, who invited Voeller to bring his lover to the next Advocate Experience, which he did.

David Goodstein even called on Morris Kight, but befriending him proved more difficult. Kight had never forgiven Goodstein for barring his name from *The Advocate* or for assigning Randy Shilts to investigate his personal behavior. He was intrigued by Goodstein's invitation, though, and he went to the Advocate Experience offices on Wilshire Boulevard. The session itself, as described by Kight, was almost identical to Goodstein's meeting with Voeller, though the result was not the same. Once again, Goodstein shared the painful formative experiences of growing up. He then asked Kight what he thought of *The Advocate* and the movement. Kight told Goodstein he considered the paper "warmed-over pap." Goodstein also asked Kight if he would undergo an Advocate Experience weekend. Kight had viewed the Advocate Experience as the latest attempt by Goodstein to control the gay movement— "ill-conceived brainwashing"—and he declined Goodstein's invitation. "I don't think I'd care to join a cult," Kight responded.

March 1978, Los Angeles

MECLA's first anniversary dinner, a black-tie affair that cost $100 a plate, was held at the Grand Ballroom of the Beverly-Wilshire Hotel in Beverly Hills. There were less expensive hotels in Los Angeles, but in spring 1978, as John Briggs's supporters were gathering signatures for his teacher initiative, MECLA wanted to communicate its influence and stature. The Grand Ballroom of the Beverly-Wilshire Hotel was where the state and city Democratic and Republican Parties held their fundraisers. Presidents, governors, senators, congressional members, mayors and state party leaders had stood at its podium.

There had been some debate about whether this should be a black-tie dinner, since that might confirm the perception that MECLA was elitist. But Rob Eichberg had decided he didn't care what other gay activists, like Morris Kight, thought of the group. He had given up arguing that MECLA was not elitist after attending monthly meetings of gay community leaders at Kight's home. Anyone who signed in at the door could talk on any subject, at any length, so First Tuesday evenings often turned into First Wednesday mornings. It was, in short, everything Rob Eichberg hated about street politics, and he was boiling by the time his name rose to the top of the speakers' list. "Well," Eichberg said, "I came here to tell all of you that MECLA was not an elitist organization. But now I'm convinced that perhaps it is and it ought to stay that way."

The dinner was a blue-chip event, lush and glamorous, from the moment the 443 guests left their cars with the parking attendants outside, to the floral centerpiece on every table in the ballroom, to the meal itself, to the speeches by known politicians, to the entertainment by a disco performer of the moment named Patti Brooks. The dinner, which would, without exaggeration, be described as unprecedented, raised $40,000. No gay organization had ever attempted a formal political fundraiser for a gay cause, hosted by homosexual activists, seated side by side with elected Los Angeles public officials, including the city controller and the city attorney, as well as members of the city council, the state Assembly and the state Senate. Art Agnos, the California state Assemblyman, flew down from San Francisco to speak. The guests were welcomed by Peggy Stevenson, the city council member who, like all the public officials there, was listed in the program as "the honorable," the compromise struck after the men and women of the MECLA board devoted a few unexpectedly rancorous evenings quarreling over whether she should be called councilman, councilwoman or council person. ("This is great," said Eichberg, still irritated that the board had voted over his objections to be co-sexual. "We're raising consciousness, but we're not going to solve all the problems here. We've got a dinner to produce—let's get this done.") All that was forgotten when the Honorable Peggy Stevenson said, "I am surprised how important you have become in such a short time. As someone who has been involved in gay affairs"—the audience tittered as Stevenson blushed at her choice of words—"and gay politics, I'm happy to see so many new faces are coming into the struggle."

It fell to Eichberg, as the chair, to provide what was in effect a summing-up of the movement in 1978, what it was that led to this evening. It was a long list of names, from Morris Kight to David Mixner. Eichberg considered mentioning David Goodstein, who was seated at a table near the back, but thought better of it. Goodstein was extraordinarily unpopular by the spring of 1978, and crediting his partner on the Advocate Experience might be unseemly. When Eichberg finished listing the names of the state's gay pioneers, he saw the *Advocate* publisher stand up, gather his things, his shoulders stooped, and scurry angrily out the door.

27

CALIFORNIA: THE MAIN EVENT

May 1978

John V. Briggs had been cocky and confident when he confided in Randy Shilts his plan to introduce a voter referendum compelling the removal of homosexual teachers from public schools in California. But it had taken eleven months from that night in Miami until he filed the 500,000 signatures needed to qualify the ballot initiative. His first attempt at filing petitions was ruled invalid by the state Attorney General's Office because of a clerk's typing error on the petition sheets, a setback as damaging to Briggs's gubernatorial ambitions as it was to the gay teachers' initiative. Briggs had wanted the initiative vote to coincide with the June 1978 Republican gubernatorial primary, assuming that people drawn to the polls by the referendum would support the man who came up with the idea. But the clerical error meant that his initiative would be delayed until the general election ballot that November.

Briggs had hoped that the teachers' initiative, a second initiative he was advocating that would expand the use of the death penalty, and his own public identification with Anita Bryant—which Briggs promoted with a statewide mailing of a picture of himself and Bryant, inscribed by Bryant, "God bless you for coming to Miami"—would establish him as a leading candidate for governor. But now, as he filed his signatures for the teachers' initiative for a second time, it was becoming clear that Briggs had miscalculated. Conservative leaders were more interested in the initiative than in seeing Briggs elected governor. The Reverend Louis P. Sheldon, an Orange County cleric who took a leave from his ministry to work on behalf of the Briggs initiative—at the suggestion of Anita Bryant, whom he met at a Christian rally after her Florida victory—had all but dismissed Briggs, after deciding the state senator was only using the initiative to further his political career. By the time Briggs embarked on a May 1 three-county swing to file signatures, he was bombarded with reminders of his own political misfortunes. Why, a reporter asked Briggs at the Los Angeles Courthouse, were polls showing him running fifth in a five-person field? "It's important to provide leadership," Briggs responded obliquely, trying to deflect the question. In fact, his gubernatorial campaign was collapsing, and he would drop out in less than three weeks.

Still, Briggs had collected the needed signatures this time: 500,000 by his count, comfortably above the 312,404 valid signatures that were required. He might not get to be governor of California, but Briggs was now certain that California, like Dade County, would come down against homosexuality. Dade County, St. Paul, Wichita and Eugene had been the preliminaries, he said. "We're going to have the main event right here in California."

California was by any measure the "main event," the most important of the voter-initiated challenges to gay rights. It was the most populous state, largely tolerant and extremely diverse, with a polarity of constituencies: from the established communities of homosexuals in San Francisco and Los Angeles to the conservative suburbanites in Orange County. It was politically unpredictable, able to elect both Ronald Reagan and Jerry Brown as its governors. The Briggs vote would be the best measure yet of the sentiment against homosexuals. And it would test what, if anything, gay activists had learned from the past year's defeats.

But there were other differences between the upcoming Briggs fights and the previous initiatives. For one, Anita Bryant's victory had itself changed the political dynamic, inspiring middle-class and mainstream homosexuals to go public and take an interest in politics. There was money, connections and professional expertise waiting to be tapped. In Dade County, the issue was a law which extended to homosexuals the same civil rights guarantees offered to blacks and other minorities. It offered up a huge target for opponents who questioned why homosexuals should be considered the same as blacks, or why homosexuals should be given preference over Anita Bryant's "normal majority." Briggs's initiative was simpler: It stated that a school board "shall refuse to hire as an employee any person who has engaged in public homosexual activity or public homosexual conduct, should the board determine that said activity or conduct renders the person unfit for service." Briggs wanted the debate to be about one question: Should California tolerate homosexuals teaching its children? "Believe it or not," Briggs asserted, "right now in California, a teacher can stand up in the classroom and say he is homosexual and introduce his wife, Harry, and not a single thing can be done about it. The bottom line in the initiative, if it passes, is that if you lead a homosexual life style—preaching it, practicing it or showing up in drag at gay bars—and your students find out about it, a school board may conduct hearings to consider your dismissal. At present, it can't." But in Briggs's attempt at simplicity, he had drafted legislation that was unexpectedly far-reaching. Its wording meant it could be used to bring charges against any school employee, homosexual or not, who publicly supported homosexual rights. It defined the offense of "public homosexuality" as "advocating, soliciting, imposing, encouraging or promoting private or public homosexual activity directed at, or likely to come to the attention of school children and/or other employees." As it turned out, Briggs's narrow focus would provide a wide target for the forces lining up to defeat it.

The California referendum was different for one final, important reason: John Briggs. An insurance broker by trade, he cut a very different figure from Anita Bryant. She was devout and delicate, not at all like a politician. Briggs was blustery and ambitious, combative and calculating. Bryant's opponents disliked her, but no one doubted her convictions, or her passion when it came to homosexuality. Starting at least with his conversation with Randy Shilts in Dade County, Briggs never tried to hide that the initiative was, at least in part, a means to a different end: higher office. And in the course of the campaign, there was no better witness to the depth of Briggs's commitment to the anti-gay cause, or lack thereof, than Randy Shilts. The more time Shilts spent with Briggs—his assignment for KQED after his return from Miami—the more he became convinced that Briggs did not believe his own anti-homosexual rhetoric. Improbably, the two men forged a friendship that Shilts thought remarkable enough to describe in a lengthy feature he wrote for the *San Francisco Chronicle* near the end of the campaign. Shilts had not at first told Briggs he was gay, and when Shilts covered a Briggs speech to a fundamentalist gathering in San Jose, the state senator pulled him aside with a friendly warning.

"You know there are homosexuals in there," Briggs said to Shilts.

"How do you know that?" Shilts asked.

"You can tell by looking at them," Briggs responded "mischievously," as Shilts recounted in the *Chronicle*.

"How's that?"

"Ahh—you can tell by the whites of their eyes." The two men then "chuckled," Shilts wrote. Shilts shared the encounter with the *San Francisco Chronicle* columnist Herb Caen, who suggested in print that the Orange

County state senator take a closer look at the whites of the eyes of his favorite reporter. Briggs called Shilts the next day to register his surprise, adding: "I never would have known. You just don't look like one."

Shilts's homosexuality apparently never bothered Briggs; when a questioner once asked if he knew any homosexuals, Briggs responded of course: he knew Randy Shilts. There was the wink and quick smile directed at Shilts that often came after his most bruising remarks about homosexuality. There were the private jokes he made at Anita Bryant's expense; Briggs repeated the line he had heard homosexuals were saying about Bryant and her good-looking husband in Miami: "We don't want your children, Anita. We want your husband." Briggs once even seemed to apologize to his reporter-friend for the whole campaign, explaining, "It's just politics."

Similarly, Briggs's public displays of anti-homosexuality did not bother the openly gay young journalist. "I simply knew a different John Briggs—a privately charming fellow who changes dramatically in public debate," Shilts wrote in the *Chronicle* about his friendship with Briggs. "Then his wide grin becomes a tight-lipped Puritan grimace. His expansive gestures turn stiff, short and controlled. . . . Yet I sensed there was a more profound reason why we could smile pleasantly at each other while the senator would recite his anti-gay catechism. Increasingly, I suspected that John Briggs does not really believe what he says about gays.

"His easy acceptance of a gay reporter was no less surprising than my acceptance of him. Just as Briggs never seemed at all personally threatened by working closely with me, I never felt personally threatened by his rhetoric. Instinctively—for reasons I would not understand until later in the campaign—I never took his protestation against homosexuality seriously."

The Shilts-Briggs friendship, not incidentally, gave birth to a permanent mistrust of Randy Shilts among many gay activists. Arthur Evans, now living in Haight-Ashbury, drafted a parody of Shilts's friendship piece, and plastered it to telephone poles, mailboxes and garbage cans across the Castro. He headlined it "The Human Side of Hitler," and featured an interview with a reporter named "Randy Shits" who had written a sympathetic story for *Die Berlinische Chronik* about his relationship with Adolf Hitler. When the interviewer asks "Shits" if he has come to know Hitler personally, the journalist responds: "Oh yes. Al—we're on a first name basis—and I got along famously. As his favorite gay reporter, I've gotten to know the private Al Hitler, a man who casts a far different profile than the public crusader. . . . He's actually quite charming when he's off stage. When he's on-stage, we smile pleasantly at each other whenever he calls for the annihilation of gays and Jews. The truth is, he's not really a bigot at all. He doesn't actually believe what he says publicly." When the interviewer says, "Some gay activists have criticized your friendship with him as traitorous," Shits replies: "Well, look at it this way: I'm an up-and-coming aggressive journalist who happens to be gay. If I don't suck up to straight bigots in the straight media, what kind of career am I going to have?"

June 1978, San Francisco

Harvey Milk, elected in November 1977 to the San Francisco Board of Supervisors, had as keen a sense of politics in California as anyone. He was convinced that a Briggs victory was inevitable, particularly as he watched the senator adopt Anita Bryant's playbook. Briggs named his committee California Defend Our Children. In places like Balboa Park in San Diego, Briggs supporters would campaign by asking strangers: "Do you want to protect your children against molesters?" Briggs, like Anita Bryant, distributed literature displaying headlines about homosexual child molestation cases. He also printed leaflets which linked his death penalty and teacher initiatives, showing a teenage boy lying in a pool of blood and stating: "You can act right now to help protect your family from vicious killers and defend your children from homosexual teachers." Briggs's speeches were also often indistinguishable from Bryant's in Miami. "We can't accept you as normal people because you are not normal people," he said. "The only way they can get children is to recruit our children. I can't think of a better setting than the classrooms."

In "Deviants Threaten the American Family," a column for the *Los Angeles Times,* Briggs wrote: "Children in this country spend more than 1,200 hours a year in classrooms. A teacher who is a known homosexual will automatically represent that way of life to young, impressionable students at a time when they are struggling with their own critical choice of sexual orientation. When children are constantly exposed to such homosexual role models, they may well be inclined to experiment with a life-style that could lead to disaster for themselves and ultimately, for society as a whole."

The one thing worse than Briggs winning the state of California would be Briggs winning the city of San Francisco, and Harvey Milk decided that, at the very least, he would try to stop that from happening. Milk accepted nearly every invitation that came to speak against the initiative, or to debate Briggs, and he delivered memorable attacks on Briggs at both the Los Angeles and San Francisco Gay Pride Parades that June. Almost 350,000 people marched in San Francisco, the turnout swollen by Briggs and Bryant. The marchers walked behind a banner that read "Human Rights Are Absolute."

"My name is Harvey Milk—and I want to recruit you," Milk announced to the crowd after riding the parade route in an open-topped car, wearing a white T-shirt and flowered lei. "I want to recruit you for the fight to preserve democracy from the John Briggs and Anita Bryants who are trying to constitutionalize bigotry. We are not going to allow that to happen. We are not going to sit back in silence as 300,000 of our gay sisters and brothers did in Nazi Germany."

Milk was not alone in his pessimism. David Goodstein had considered this a losing cause from the start and became more convinced he was right as the summer approached. There was no reason to believe that California voters would defy a clear national trend. Even in Seattle, a comparatively liberal community, a police officer had easily gathered the signatures needed to put that city's gay rights ordinance before voters in November. And a New AGE poll seemed to confirm Goodstein's fears. Only one-third of voters questioned thought homosexuals should be allowed to work as teachers, school principals or scout leaders. Seventy-three percent agreed it was important to protect impressionable children from gay people.

"This is one of those times when the truth we have to report is very unpleasant," Goodstein told his readers on June 14. "The bottom line is that it is most unlikely that the Briggs initiative can be defeated in the November election. . . . We may lose even in San Francisco. We can expect a multi-million-dollar media campaign of lies and hate directed at us. Some gay people probably will commit suicide under this onslaught of hate." Goodstein proceeded to offer his by now familiar prescription to minimize the damage. The "gay extremists" and "hedonists"—the drag queens, the advocates of man-boy sex, the feminist-separatists, the leather enthusiasts, the sexual liberationists, the Marxists—must keep out of sight and leave it to the professionals to try to salvage the campaign. Straight people are put off by homosexuals, Goodstein said, so "almost all gay people could help best by maintaining very low profiles." The gay community needed to recruit heterosexuals to speak on its behalf, Goodstein said. The "gay media freaks" had to "get off the television and let our friends and allies speak to the non-gay issues.

"Constructively, we should assist in registering gay voters, stuffing envelopes in the headquarters, and keeping out of sight of non-gay voters, except persuading straight friends and relatives. Destructively, we can do a lot to assist John Briggs by being visible and in any way stereotypical. I know this sounds awful; this is an awful situation." Goodstein had been pushing a nearly opposite line in urging homosexuals to live their lives openly in his Advocate Experience, which underscored the gloom with which he viewed the situation.

New AGE had by now expanded into a new statewide organization called Concerned Voters of California, a coalition of anti-Briggs activists from Los Angeles and San Francisco. It was run by an old-line, San Francisco-based consultant, Don Bradley—fifty-eight, balding, with thick jowls and heavy bags under his eyes, who had run the northern California presidential campaign of Adlai Stevenson, and the California campaigns of Kennedy and Johnson, as well as the races of Governor Pat Brown and Mayor George Moscone. Nearly thirty years in the business had given him lines into most of the state's Democratic organizations, and a measure of authority that none of the new gay activists could match. Troy Perry warned some lesbian activists to give Bradley some slack. "Sisters, I hear he's a crusty old man and has no consciousness around—let's start with this right now and get it over with—over feminist issues. We will not get into a fight with that. We will educate him as we go along." New AGE got a taste of Bradley's style at their first meeting. Jerry Berg, the Palo Alto lawyer working with David Goodstein on the Advo-cate Experience, said by way of introduction: "Well, Mr. Bradley, we under-stand we can't win this." Bradley picked up his hat off the table and started to rise: "I don't need to talk to you then," he replied. Perry had to stop him from leaving the room.

Don Bradley was a heterosexual, and neither Morris Kight nor David Mixner liked that a gay rights group had turned to a heterosexual for help.* But Goodstein was one of the main financial backers of the anti-Briggs effort, and his opinion, expressed in meetings and in his column, carried a lot of sway. For his part, Bradley showed no concern about lending his reputation to a gay organization, which was remarkable in 1978. "I wasn't concerned about my own sexuality," he told a reporter after the campaign, "so I didn't see what the problem was." One of the first things he did was suggest that Mixner-Scott Associates be hired by the statewide group as the deputy managers of the campaign.

The strategists in the anti-Briggs campaign were worried, but they did not believe that it was a lost fight. The same poll that convinced David Good-stein of the futility of fighting was, for a more experienced political operative like Mixner, a road map to potential victory. Voters in California respected public school teachers and were worried that innocent school employees might be hounded out of work should this initiative become law. Californians also were concerned about their own privacy. There was, finally, evidence in the poll that people thought that adequate protections were already in place to deal with teachers who behaved improperly with students. There were clear signs that voters had hesitations about this initiative, and there were five months to go.

The privacy issue was particularly intriguing. The theme used unsuc-cessfully by gay activists in Miami, St. Paul, Eugene and Wichita had been human rights. But it was clear, after a year of defeats, that it simply wasn't working. Heterosexuals were apparently not moved by the argument that ho-

---

* It was unusual, but it had happened before. The Mattachine Society of New York's executive director in the late 1960s and early 1970 was Madolin Cervantes, a straight woman.

mosexuals are entitled to the same human rights as everyone else. But they surely understood privacy. In Seattle, where a similar referendum was now on the ballot, gay rights advocates had prepared what appeared to be two particularly effective television advertisements: one showing a family living in a fishbowl, with faces peering in from the outside, and the other depicting a huge keyhole lock with an eye staring through it.

The error on Briggs's petitions had given his opponents a long time to prepare, and by midsummer the campaign against him in California had taken off. Anita Bryant had pushed professionals like David Mixner out of the closet; this was the first time people like Mixner had so completely dominated a gay political battle. Unlike Dade County, where Geto and Foster encountered daily resistance from other activists who questioned their tactics, the mainstream homosexual leaders essentially ran the race against the Briggs campaign: from the fundraising to television commercials to the coordinated speakers' bureau, to attempts to win newspaper publicity and sympathetic editorials. They had a state press officer, Sallie Fiske, who had worked in public relations in New York City and had hosted a public affairs talk show in Los Angeles. She had devoted one of the shows to gay rights and the Briggs initiative, and introduced the show by describing an L.A. march by gays protesting Anita Bryant. "For years many of us have marched for many causes, and we have sung 'We Shall Overcome' for many people," she said. "This week for the first time I among hundreds sang it for myself." She lost her job three months later, and signed on what was now being called "No on 6," named for the number that had been assigned to the Briggs initiative.

To raise money, No on 6 organized clip-ins with hairstylists in Hollywood nightclubs. David Mixner used the MECLA network. Bob Hattoy, a closeted young aide to the California Democratic Party, attended a fundraiser at Laguna Beach where Mixner, wearing jeans and a shirt, walked out on a diving board to appeal for funds to the tanned and fit men crowded around the pool. "I know you spent $100 to come here today," Mixner said. "But I want you all to give more, give much more. Reach into your pockets and give much more." Everyone laughed, since most of them were wearing bathing suits. But Hattoy noticed that the men found more money to contribute before they left. Women in the community—whose fundraising abilities had been disparaged by the founders of MECLA—did at least as well as men. Gayle Wilson, a real estate broker, arranged a Beverly Hilton fundraiser that drew 256 people, almost all women, to hear Midge Costanza, in her first speech in private life—she had left the White House in August 1978— denounce the Briggs initiative as a "witch-hunt."

The frictions between grassroots and middle-class activists seemed forgotten. The deputy campaign director for southern California, Ivy Bottini, who had been purged from NOW in New York seven years before, was in charge of the traditionally grassroots efforts: registering voters, making phone calls, painting picket signs, driving people to the polls. "Money has its limitations," Peter Scott said. "It can give you access to a leader—you can even develop a fine personal relationship with a leader. But that politician's perception of your grassroots power will determine how much they'll go out on a limb for you." Bottini was the link between the "money people," as she called them, and the volunteers. The hiring of Bottini bought peace with the street activists, though David Mixner insisted that was not his intention. Bottini recalls that Morris Kight, however, was livid that she had joined Mixner's organization, rather than work with him on his own No on Briggs Initiative Committee; which sponsored a 1,203-mile walk by opponents of Briggs from San Ysidro, at the Mexican border, to the Oregon border of California. Kight later boasted that this was what turned around the campaign; in fact, though, the effort received little notice.

There were problems. Fundraising was hampered by a California law requiring the campaign committee to report the names of anyone who contributed $50 or more. Thus they collected a fistful of $49 checks, including, Mixner later reported, one from Rock Hudson. "They're afraid they'll get put on a list," Mixner said of the $49 contributors. "Who knows where those lists will end up?" And in the midst of the campaign, Jack Campbell, the bathhouse owner, head of the Dade County campaign against Anita Bryant and a member of the National Gay Task Force board of directors, was arrested in San Francisco after an undercover police officer responded to an ad Campbell put in the *Bay Area Reporter* looking for young men to work as "escorts." "Sometimes it includes dinner and seeing the city," Campbell reportedly told the officer on a tape recording of the meeting, "but mostly it's strictly sex." Campbell was paying the men $30 an hour and operating out of a house in Pacific Heights up the street from the home of San Francisco supervisor Dianne Feinstein, who tipped police to her suspicion that her neighbor was running a call-boy operation. Campbell was arrested for felony pandering. "The damage done by Campbell's arrest in this year of the Briggs Initiative is incalculable," *The Advocate* editorialized. "We can only shudder to contemplate what our enemies will make of this matter in the forthcoming campaign." The fear was misplaced. The incident was never effectively used by Briggs.

But one incident impressed Ivy Bottini more than anything else that happened during the campaign. And it is what won the election.

By 1978, everyone knew Ronald Reagan was going to run for president. He had come close to winning the Republican presidential nomination in

1976, and he was a leading contender for the 1980 nomination. When he showed up for civic events, the band would strike up "Hail to the Chief." David Mixner, Peter Scott, Diane Abbitt and Roberta Bennett found themselves talking about Reagan during one of their frequent dinners. The campaign's outcome was at best in doubt. The first statewide poll by Mervin D. Field for the *San Francisco Chronicle* in September showed the Briggs initiative leading, 61 percent to 31 percent. But if Ronald Reagan were somehow to come out in opposition to Briggs, the four of them said that night, it would sink the initiative. They could think of nothing else that could so certainly affect the outcome.

Recruiting Ronald Reagan wasn't such an outlandish proposition, Mixner argued. This was not a gay rights bill; it was a question of government meddling in private life. A student faced with a failing grade could blackmail a teacher under this law; it could create chaos in the public school system. If the argument could be framed that way, Mixner said, Reagan might accept it. Ronald and Nancy Reagan moved in the same circles as many homosexuals—Rock Hudson being the obvious example—so this was not as alien a subject to them as it might be to, say, John Briggs. "If we could get that message to Reagan, he would understand that," Mixner said.

Getting a message to Reagan turned out not to be so difficult. Mixner and Scott knew a leading Reagan adviser, Don Livingston, the vice president of Carter Hawley Hale Stores. He was particularly discreet about his homosexuality, and invited Scott and Mixner over for drinks only when his wife was out of town. And as they hoped, Livingston was intrigued by the argument. Another man, an even more senior Reagan adviser, also married, also homosexual, might also be sympathetic. Livingston agreed to make inquiries with this Reagan aide, and called back shortly to say that the aide was willing to meet with Mixner and Scott to consider arranging a meeting with Reagan. His identity, though, had to be strictly protected—no one could know who he was, no one in No on 6, no one in MECLA, none of their friends.

Just being seen having coffee with Mixner and Scott could compromise the aide's anonymity. He suggested they meet at a Denny's in East Los Angeles, where nobody would spot them. Again and again, the man—who is still married and in the closet—sought reassurances from Mixner and Scott that he could trust them. We don't want you to lobby Reagan on the Briggs initiative, Mixner said. All they wanted was a chance to make their case to Reagan. The Reagan adviser agreed to go back to the former governor, but again with conditions: No one could know the story of this extraordinary meeting. And they would have to review with the adviser in advance the arguments they planned to make. If they agreed to that, he would get them fifteen minutes.

• • •

Mixner bought a new suit for the meeting, a blue one. Don Bradley told them that Reagan could win or lose this election, but winning Reagan's tacit support would not be enough. The governor would have to issue a statement that the campaign could use in its newspaper and television advertising.

As soon as Mixner and Scott arrived at Reagan's office, it was clear that Reagan had been briefed on the topic and was curious to hear what they had to say. The meeting dragged on beyond the scheduled fifteen minutes to more than an hour. Mixner and Scott made all the points that they had discussed at dinner with Bennett and Abbitt: the bill would allow students to blackmail teachers, it would destroy school discipline, and it would waste taxpayer money in pointless litigation. As Mixner recounted it, Reagan stirred in his chair when they talked about school discipline. He and Peter Scott exchanged glances, so they returned to the point, again and then again. The meeting ended cordially, and when Mixner and Scott returned to their headquarters on Wilshire Boulevard, the Reagan political adviser telephoned to say the governor had been impressed with the presentation. He was certain the governor would not endorse the Briggs initiative, though he could not promise that Reagan would come out against it. The Reagan aide asked Mixner and Scott to draft a statement for Reagan's consideration, which they did. They heard nothing again until August 20, when Citizens for Reagan, the future presidential candidate's political committee, released a statement in Reagan's name. It was as much of a shock to Scott and Mixner as it was to Briggs. The Briggs initiative, Reagan said, "has the potential for real mischief . . ." and "the potential of infringing on basic rights of privacy and perhaps even constitutional rights.

"What if an overwrought youngster disappointed by bad grades imagined it was the teacher's fault and struck out by accusing the teacher of advocating homosexuality?" Reagan's statement asked. "Innocent lives could be ruined. . . . Prop. 6 is not needed to protect our children. We have that legal protection now. It could be very costly to implement and has the potential for causing undue harm to people." The former governor doesn't "approve of teaching a so-called gay life-style in our schools," the statement said, but "there is already adequate legal machinery to deal with such problems." Mixner and Scott had the bullet they were looking for. It took a few days to turn it into a television commercial. And Ronald Reagan's name, with excerpts from his statement, was put at the top of newspaper ads signed by people opposing Proposition 6. The election turned almost overnight. At the beginning of September, a poll by Mervin Field found voters favored the Briggs initiative by 61 to 31; by the end of the month, they favored it by a statistically insignificant 45 to 43, with 12 percent undecided. The reason, the California pollster said, was the "increasing number of influential voices now being raised against the measure," an obvious reference to Reagan. Bottini, tracking the election through her volunteers, had the same sense. Before Reagan's announcement, she was resigned to defeat; now she was sure they would win. She had learned a lesson from Mixner and Scott: they had used the establishment to turn the campaign on its head. In October, Briggs himself told a reporter: "That one single endorsement—Ronald Reagan's—turned the polls around." But, he asserted, "For Ronald Reagan to march to the drums of homosexuality has irrevocably damaged him nationally."

In the final days, Briggs grew increasingly strident as his proposal drew national attention. Homosexuality, Briggs began to argue in the face of declining polls, "is a more insidious threat" than Communism: "It is like a creeping disease, where it just continues to spread like a cancer throughout the body." He asserted that one-third of San Francisco's public teachers and 20 percent of the teachers in Los Angeles were "practicing homosexuals." He gave a long interview to the *Los Angeles Times* which seemed to confirm his opponents' criticism of the initiative: A homosexual school employee, he said, should be dismissed, even absent a physical or verbal threat to a student, because "he's a threat to children. We already know that homosexuals are attracted to children. If you look like a duck and you walk like a duck, in my opinion, my friend, you are a duck. If you have a proclivity for having sex with young boys or people of your own gender, then you ought not be put in a position where you are going to be tempted." When the reporter asked Briggs if that meant that Midge Costanza, who had advocated the rights of homosexuals, would face dismissal if she worked as a teacher in California and this bill was passed, Briggs responded: "Yes, she probably would." Briggs's opponents could scarcely believe their good fortune. Briggs and Milk debated the initiative before any audience that had two microphones, a stage and a spare two hours, each reciting a script they knew by heart. By the end, Briggs was warning about the number of homosexuals in public schools, and Milk was comparing Briggs to Joe McCarthy.

Briggs grew increasingly isolated, until some of his principal supporters were the American Nazi Party, the Ku Klux Klan and Jerry Falwell, the director of the television program *Old Time Gospel Hour.* Virtually everybody else opposed him. The board of education in Los Angeles endorsed a resolution against the initiative, as did the city council. Politicians from Governor Brown to George Deukmejian, a conservative Republican running for attorney general, to Bradley, who invoked Adolf Hitler and Joseph McCarthy, all opposed it. Archbishop John Quinn of San Francisco, head of the National Conference of Catholic Bishops, called the initiative "perilously vague" and said it would "wrongly limit the civil rights of homosexual persons if it passed." Even President Carter came out against Briggs, though indirectly. Campaigning for Jerry Brown's reelection, Carter had finished his speech, when Brown told him to announce his opposition to the Briggs initiative: "You'll get your loudest applause," Brown told the president. "Ford and Reagan have both come out against it. So I think it's pretty safe." Carter returned to the lectern: "I ask everybody to vote no on Proposition 6." (A television microphone picked up the private exchange.) Even Briggs's rivals for the GOP gubernatorial nomination opposed the initiative—among them Edward Davis, the former Los Angeles police chief who had made a career attacking homosexuals and had never expressed any second thoughts about his own department's aggressive arrests of them. The initiative allowed the ex-chief to recast his own history. "I've never had anything against homosexuals," he said. "I figure this means more girls for the rest of us."

Even Anita Bryant disappointed Briggs. Bryant, struggling with a loss of bookings, demonstrations at every turn and her deteriorating marriage, said that a trip to California to help Briggs would mean spreading herself thin. Bryant could not even muster any long-distance enthusiasm for Briggs or his initiative. When California reporters pressed her on whether she owed Briggs anything for the help he gave her in Dade County, she responded: "Senator Briggs asked if he could come help us. We said it was a local issue—we did not want outside help and if he wanted to come, it would be his own decision."

The Briggs initiative dominated the news through the fall, and newspapers polled voters almost up until the last day. The outcome—defeat by more than one million votes—was not a surprise: 3.9 million to 2.8 million, or a margin of 58 percent to 42 percent. It even lost in Orange County, Briggs's home seat. On the same night, November 7, 1978, voters in Seattle defeated an initiative to repeal its gay rights law, 63 percent to 37 percent. At the Beverly-Wilshire Hotel news of the victory came at 8 p.m. Nearly 2,500 people were crammed into the ballroom—people were turned away at the door—and they screamed their approval, dancing and cheering with delight. "How sweet it is," Mayor Tom Bradley told the celebrants. "Proposition 6 was an evil, pernicious, dangerous measure."

It was appropriate that Bradley was the main speaker at the victory rally that night. It was a reminder that even in the end, the campaign had succeeded by putting a straight face on the issue. "We've been trying to stay away from the homosexual identification," Don Bradley told the *Los Angeles Times*. "If it gets down to a plebiscite on homosexuality, we'd lose."

Still, when it became clear how big the margin was, Troy Perry felt relief. They had shown they could do this; they had raised $800,000, developed an effective campaign theme, and produced television commercials and endorsements. As the vote had neared, Harvey Milk, who once feared that the Briggs initiative might win in San Francisco, instead became worried about complacency among his friends and followers. (It lost in San Francisco by a 75 to 25 percent margin.) "You've heard of sore losers," Milk said that evening, delivering a victory speech in the Castro. "Well, I'm a sore winner.

"This is only the first step," he said. "The next step, the more important one, is for all those gays who did not come out for whatever reason to do so now. . . . Every gay person *MUST* come out."

28

A FRIEND IN CITY HALL

September 1978, Washington, D.C.

On a muggy Saturday evening at the end of summer, as the crowd began to thicken in the front room of a downtown bar and restaurant called the Eagle, a black man and a light-skinned woman strolled through the door, settled at the long counter and ordered drinks. Every eye in the place turned toward them. The Eagle was a gay bar, the city's premier Levi's and leather bar for men. City Councilman Marion Barry and his tall, lean new wife, Effi, were the only heterosexual couple there. They were very cool about it, as if they hadn't noticed—or if they had, thought nothing of it, or as if it suited them, and that's why they had decided to come. Barry's big expansive face was all smiles and warm expressions, and he drank, talked and laughed with Don Bruce, the owner, and the others around them as if he were not so much campaigning for votes as taking a break from the campaign to be with friends.

Marion Barry was tending to business. The city's primary election was on Tuesday, September 12, three days away, and Barry was running for mayor.* A renegade politician and canny strategist from his earliest days as the leader of SNCC in Washington in the mid-1960s, he was challenging the older black political establishment for the reins of the city, trying to take the

---

* The offices of city council chairman and six of the council seats were also being contested.

Mayor's Office away from Walter E. Washington, who had held it since 1967. A *Washington Post* poll taken two weeks earlier showed Barry trailing both Mayor Washington and his principal other challenger, city council chairman Sterling Tucker, by seven points. To come from behind, Marion Barry had to be different from the mayor with the same name as the city. He had to build a different coalition. He had to zig instead of zag.

The votes on the Briggs initiative in California, and on the attempt to repeal the gay rights ordinance in Seattle, were still more than two months away. In all the popular referenda held around the nation thus far, gay rights had gone down to defeat. Across the country, politicians wanted nothing to do with gay issues or gay support, and in a majority black city like the District of Columbia, traditional sexual attitudes were strongly intolerant of homosexuality. But Barry was betting against the tide. He had no fear of being seen in a gay bar. The conservative black church vote, he knew, would go to the older, more conservative Washington anyway, or to Tucker, supported by many preachers. Barry was gambling that a show of friendship to the gay community would help him, and as he and Effi lingered at the bar, the charmed, magnetic center of a clubful of two hundred or more curious men in denim jeans and T-shirts, leather boots and vests, the buzz stirred by their visit moved out the door and down the street. Effi, men repeated to each other, as the story traveled across the city, even had on *leather* pants.

By noon Sunday, the word had spread through the gay bars, churches and brunch haunts of Washington. In neighborhoods like Capitol Hill, Dupont Circle, Adams-Morgan and Georgetown, the Barrys' visit to the Eagle was the talk of the day. As political theater, played to an audience hungry for respect, it was, at most, a small masterstroke. But it was only the final visible piece of a strategy that Marion Barry and the white political leadership of the city's gay community had come to share. They needed each other: he to get elected, they to gain a friend in power. They had been cultivating each other for years.

Sterling Tucker, the other councilman challenging Mayor Washington, had begun to court the gay vote, too, and so had some other black candidates for office, but not as early, not as hard and not as often as Marion Barry had. So, while Tucker had been endorsed by the D.C. Coalition of Black Gay Women and Men—a new group of doubtful size and influence—Barry had won the endorsement of the white, male Gertrude Stein Democratic Club, support which meant real money, real leaflets, real phone bank workers and poll watchers, and real votes. The Stein Club, in fact, had given Barry the first endorsement of any major political group in the city, and when Richard Maulsby, the Gertrude Stein president, announced it and presented the Barry campaign with a check for $1,000, Barry proclaimed it "the New Hampshire" of his campaign. It meant that his years of increasingly close alliance with the gay cause in Washington were going to pay off. In an interview with reporter Larry Bush in a special preelection supplement published by the city's reigning gay newspaper, *The Blade*—a supplement whose pages, story by story, drilled home the importance of a gay vote in this election—Barry ticked off the long record of his support for gay rights. It had begun when he was president of the D.C. school board and pushed it to declare, in 1972, that it would not fire, or refuse to hire, teachers for being homosexual. When he ran and won a seat on D.C.'s first elected city council two years later, he had voted for Title 34, the city's sweeping human rights ordinance, which had been passed the year before by the appointed council, and had to be reenacted by the elected board, to protect homosexuals along with others. Barry had helped stop the worst of the police harassment, too. "I worked on dismantling the perversion branch of the police department," Barry said. "I've been there when the need was there. I was there for Gay Pride week. I've taken a lot of hell over that." It was all true. Marion Barry had early on equated the gay movement with the black civil rights movement, and he touted his close alliance with the city's gay community not only in the pages of *The Blade*—a paper he knew would go unread by the vast heterosexual majority of the District's voting population—but also volunteered it, unbidden, in a television interview for a general audience. Marion Barry figured he had little to lose and everything to gain.

But no one knew what that gain might be. The size of the gay vote was an unknown, even if the figures that were known were tantalizing. From 1970 to 1976 the number of unmarried residents fourteen or more years old in the District of Columbia had risen from 190,000 to 310,000, a number which represented 55 percent of the city's population, and both the U.S. Census and the District's Office of Vital Statistics calculated that the lion's share of the increase had come from unmarried adults moving to Washington. People like Paul Kuntzler, who had been laboring for years to build a gay-conscious electorate in the District, operated on the theory that a large, perhaps disproportionate share of that number was composed of young homosexual men. With more than 500,000 residents of voting age in the District but less than 250,000 of them registered, the election on Tuesday might draw fewer than 150,000 voters. If homosexuals could be encouraged to vote as a bloc, it could make the difference. To that end, the Gay Activists Alliance claimed to have distributed 20,000 or more campaign leaflets, and the Gertrude Stein Club provided most of the Barry campaign's core staff of volunteers. Some days, three of every four people calling registered voters for Barry were gay men. To keep them working, Don Bruce sent over sandwiches from the Eagle kitchen, and he sent money, too. Bruce was an unusual political backer. He didn't look the part of the white, urban business leader drawn into Democratic Party fundraising. Dressed in jeans and a cowboy shirt, with a close-cropped beard, a paunch and baggy eyes, he looked more like a dissipated roughneck. His father had been a policeman, and he had opened the Eagle, he told people, because he couldn't stand the girly manners of the gay bars of his youth. An Eagle fundraiser, a jacket-and-tie dinner of beef Wellington and French-style green beans, together with another affair that Bruce and the owners of the gay disco Pier Nine held, had raised nearly $10,000 for Barry. All told, the Stein Club and its allies in the gay community may have funneled $22,000 into the mayoral and council campaigns, and most of it went to Barry.

But the effort which may have had the largest direct effect on the gay electorate was one which was never publicized and had nothing to do with the gay Democrats who worked with Barry's campaign. Robert S. Carter, a Washington resident and one of the highest-ranking officials in the national Republican Party, was gay, and for twenty-five years had lived with Leonard Haft, an architect and member of the city's wealthy Haft family, owners of the Dart Drug chain. Carter had been state chairman of the Republican Committee for the District of Columbia. He had been co-chairman of the Republican National Convention which nominated Gerald Ford in Kansas City in 1976, and would be chairman of the Republican National Convention which would nominate Ronald Reagan in Detroit in 1980. But Carter and his lover Haft led an entirely separate existence among a huge number of gay friends and acquaintances in Washington and in Rehoboth Beach, Delaware, where they kept a house. And that late winter and early spring of 1978, some of those friends prevailed on Haft to get Carter to help energize a gay vote for Barry in the District elections. It would mean helping a black Democrat, they knew, but no Republican was going to be elected to any local office in the overwhelmingly black and Democratic city of Washington.

Carter and Haft held a series of small cocktail parties, with fifteen or twenty handsome, socially ambitious young men recruited from the bars, at their penthouse apartment and terrace in a building that Haft had designed at Sixth Street and I Southwest. The guests were flattered to be invited into the realm of men so wealthy and powerful, and all of them, after a drink or two, were quietly lectured by Bob Carter about the opportunity to make a difference in the election this year. "I want all of you to take fifteen voter registration cards, and go out and have a party for fifteen friends and sign them up," he'd say. And when one of the young men—to be sure that he understood what Carter was telling them—asked if he meant, of course, that they should register Republican, Carter would shake his head, smile a little and say, "Well, I'm a Republican. But in this city, if you want your vote to count, you have to register as a Democrat." The leaders of the Gertrude Stein Democratic Club later estimated that Carter and Haft's campaign was probably responsible for registering a thousand young gay men—more, it seemed, than the GAA or Stein Club efforts had.

And that proved to be the margin by which Marion Barry won an upset victory in the Democratic primary race for mayor on September 12. He beat Sterling Tucker by just 1,356 votes, with Walter Washington trailing not far behind.* The rank and file of the Stein Club, even the gay men manning the phones in Barry headquarters, hadn't really thought he could pull it off. It had been too much to hope for, and all the negative votes across the nation in the previous fifteen months had left them glum. But he had won, and it looked as if the gay vote had provided the edge.

Steve Endean stood dazed in a roomful of jubilant people the night after the election. He was holding a glass of cheap champagne. The people around him were euphoric. He felt disoriented. In the wake of the St. Paul Repeal, after much agonizing, he had finally decided to leave Minnesota and its frustrations behind for good, and come to Washington. He had arrived just that day, and he felt a little like Alice, as if he had fallen through a hole into Wonderland. Here, in the Way Off Broadway Theater, in the alley behind the Lost and Found Bar, was a roomful of gay men convinced that *they* were the new power in Washington's municipal politics. Not only had Marion Barry won, but they had helped another councilman, Arrington Dixon, trounce the gay-baiting Reverend Douglas Moore for the council president's seat—and they had helped elect four other council members. Endean listened as Paul Kuntzler, the Gertrude Stein Club's intense, dark-haired strategist, analyzed the election for the men in the room. He had a precinct map and a clutch of papers in his hands. He had identified twenty-one precincts in heavily gay neighborhoods like Dupont Circle, Adams-Morgan, Georgetown and Capitol Hill. Altogether, Kuntzler calculated, those precincts represented 15 percent of the city's total electorate, and on Tuesday, he told the grinning crowd of Gertrude Stein members, those precincts had given 56 percent of their vote to Barry, just 28 percent to Tucker and only 16 percent to Washington. In the rest of the city, he said, Barry had averaged only 30 percent of the vote, running behind both Washington and Tucker.

"We believe that the gay community was the only voting bloc that did not split its vote," Kuntzler said, his eyes glittering and triumphant, his square jaw raised high, as he looked around the room. "It's my conservative estimate that we cast about 5,000 votes, and that Marion Barry carried some 80 per cent of those votes." *The Blade,* in its next edition, published an electoral map of the District of Columbia, with the precincts Kuntzler had identified shaded in.

* The totals were Barry, 31,265; Tucker, 29,909; and Washington, 28,286.

Two months later, after the general election in November, which Barry carried handily, the mayor-elect held first one, then another, then a third meeting with the gay leaders who had supported him. "Well," the new mayor-elect said, looking at Tom Bastow, the new president of the Stein Club, and the others, "what do you want me to do?"

The power of the gay vote quickly became part of the new political wisdom of the city. It was confirmed by the appointments Marion Barry began to make and, six months after the general election, by a page one story in the *Washington Post*, which printed its own version of Paul Kuntzler's precinct map as an illustration of the new reality. "Through hard work, their ability to raise campaign contributions, assemble platoons of volunteers and deliver votes, homosexuals have established themselves as a highly respected and eagerly sought-after political constituency," the *Post* reported. "They are now ranked by city politicians with such traditional power blocs as organized labor, the black church and business community." In a city where the right to vote had come so late, a city dominated by minorities, homosexuals had now joined blacks at the table. That did not make everyone happy. The gay clout was so obvious—and its complexion so white—that there was grousing in political meetings about Marion Barry being in the pocket of these mainly white gay men, and public grumbling in the black community about the Barry administration's "Gay Agenda." Barry did not budge.

"I will not allow anyone to attack gay rights," Barry said when he came to the Gay Activists Alliance inaugural ball at The Pier, a gay disco the night of his inauguration. "I don't care if 2,000 or 10,000 gays voted for me. My commitment to gays is one of a basic human rights issue."

November 1978, Washington, D.C.

In the nation's capital, the political position of gay men and lesbians was now secure. But in the nation at large, despite the victories in California and Seattle, which seemed to have slowed the momentum of the Christian backlash, their position was far from secure. The places where they were protected were few and far between, and the only way that homosexuals could gain the same broad civil rights protections that other minorities enjoyed nationally was if Congress voted them. Congress was a different world—almost a different galaxy—from the District of Columbia City Council. But the string of municipal defeats over the last year and a half had spread the feeling within the movement that the cause could not be won if it remained subject to a popular vote at the local and state level. It had to be won in Congress, and Steve Endean's new job was to carry the gay rights cause up Capitol Hill.

Endean had come to Washington to run the Gay Rights National Lobby, the group that David Goodstein had created in Chicago to compete with the National Gay Task Force, and which he had abandoned at its very inception. Intended as the primary means of lobbying Congress for homosexual civil rights, GRNL was the only national gay political lobby in Washington, but Goodstein's withdrawal had left it with no real financial base, no independent ability of its own and no presence on Capitol Hill. In the last few months, with its treasury empty, its office manager given up and gone, and most of the seats on its national board vacant for lack of money to hold new elections, GRNL had been in a kind of organizational coma. Endean had left home two months before, in the grim and dispiriting aftermath of the repeal of the St. Paul ordinance in April, convinced the fight was over in Minnesota. "We're not going to win in the state," one of his gay financial backers said. "I think maybe you ought to go to Washington." Endean should transfer his obsession about passing a gay rights bill to the federal level, and work for GRNL.

"There's no money," Endean said.

"I'll give you $25,000 to get it off the ground," said the man, whom Endean would never identify, even years later. Endean could take $18,000 for salary and the balance for expenses the first year. Endean was torn. Staying in Minnesota had become a torture to him. But this angel was a man who drank, and who had made good on some pledges of support and not on others. When Los Angeles attorney Ray Hartman, co-chair of GRNL's executive committee, and Franklin Kameny and Paul Kuntzler, the lobby's two most prominent board members in Washington, heard that Endean might be interested, they jumped, promising that he could function as a strong executive director, with the freedom and authority he needed to build an effective national lobby. Endean's benefactor put up $2,000 in cash, and on the day after the D.C. primary Endean arrived, to find the office telephone disconnected, the mail unopened for months and $9 in the bank.

He posed for a photograph in front of the Capitol: a pale, chunky, square-cut young man with short dark hair, neatly dressed in a jacket, button-down shirt and striped tie, the picture—he hoped—of a serious political professional. He was thirty years old, with an organization all his own to revive and run in the most political city in the world. He had high hopes. With the promised $25,000 in seed money from Minnesota as a start, Endean said, he thought GRNL could raise $50,000 or $60,000 in the next year by expanding the membership, holding benefits and bringing in pledges. But in an interview in *The Blade*, he warned that building support for gay rights in the Congress was going to take a long time. "I don't want people joining GRNL thinking we can get legislation passed in two, three or four years. We can't," he said. "It's going to be a long, hard fight. I'm prepared to be here for as long as it takes."

He was, as he liked to say, a committed incrementalist. He took the long-term view, but he wasn't going to have a long time to work uninterrupted, and one of the first things Endean discovered, as he began to assemble a new board of directors filled with people whom he liked—people he trusted to support him, like the preacher Troy Perry, the bathhouse baron Jack Campbell, and Kerry Woodward and Larry Bye from Minnesota—was that he could get no more money out of his angel. The $2,000 in cash was it. The money he had counted on to pay his salary and expenses until he could begin to bring in more had to be replaced. He put out notes and literature and phone calls. And then one day, in the mail, came an envelope with no return address. In it were a note, written in a crabbed, tortured-looking hand, and a postal money order for $700. "I just sold my furs and my jewels," the note said. In a few days, there was another envelope, with $1,000 in it. "I sold some more," she wrote. Then came another one. Steve Endean called her "Crazy Alice Jackson." He never knew where she lived, or how to reach her, or what moved her to do it. In between the Alice Jackson letters came an envelope from a man who had picked up one of the brochures Endean had strategically left in a dirty-books store. The man had read it, and he enclosed a short, supportive, sincere note, and a check for $2,000. It began to look to Steve Endean as if he would survive, if he could just build some momentum.

One last grand scheme had emerged from the smoke of defeat of St. Paul's ordinance, and it was now absorbing Endean's colleagues back in Minneapolis: a national lesbian and gay rights march on Washington, patterned after the black civil rights and anti-war marches of the 1960s and early 1970s. The idea had surfaced with a splash at a lesbian-feminist fundraiser held at the University of Minnesota in spring 1978. "What are you planning to do if you lose?" demanded Robin Tyler, the lesbian-feminist comedienne from Los Angeles who was the main entertainment. She was referring to the imminent repeal of the city's gay rights law. They had to fight back, she told the audience. "We ought to have a march on Washington. We could all sleep in tents on the Mall. You know how gay men love to camp." It was a pun, a joke on gay male sensibilities. But when the women started roaring again, Robin Tyler realized that they liked the idea.

Tyler returned to Los Angeles after her show, but in Minnesota, in the grim aftermath of the St. Paul Repeal, the idea of a march caught fire, and a committee was formed. There was something particularly lovely, in such a glum period, about the image of a vast, mighty gay throng advancing down Pennsylvania Avenue toward the Capitol. But short on money and rent by tensions between women and men, the Committee for a March on Washington collapsed by the end of October. There was little support for the idea in Washington, or even in California, where Harvey Milk, in the midst of the Briggs fight, was dismissive of this idea from Minnesota.

But with the Briggs initiative defeated, Milk embraced the concept. Robin Tyler had spread the seeds in stage appearances in California, too, some of which she shared with Milk, and Milk was now arguing that the march be held on July 4, 1979, because it would have "great symbolic impact, reminding people of the Declaration of Independence, in which gay people were left out." Endean, who made no secret of his dislike for Milk, was appalled. "Do you know what Harvey Milk's talking about?" Endean fumed on the telephone to Kerry Woodward. What a numbskull idea, Endean thought. Congress would be in recess for the summer. The city would be an oven. If the march failed to attract big numbers, it would be devastating to a movement whose sense of siege had just been lifted by the electoral victories in Washington, D.C., California and Seattle. It would make his job at GRNL even more difficult. And if the march succeeded in exciting gay activists across the country, it would be hard to compete for resources against it, when his own organizational goal seemed such a distant glimmer.

Either way—succeed or fail—Endean couldn't see a national march on Washington helping. The other movement people in Washington, as well as the leadership of the National Gay Task Force in New York, the Metropolitan Community Church, and the groups Dignity and Integrity, all felt the same way. The march wasn't their project, and it made them nervous. But the whole equation changed when Harvey Milk and Mayor George Moscone were assassinated in San Francisco.

November 1978, San Francisco

From the very first day they held office together, there had been a tension, a cultural conflict between Harvey Milk and his fellow new councilman, the Irish Catholic former policeman Daniel James White. They were the cultural extremes of a diverse new membership on the Board of Supervisors—a Chinese American, a Latino, a black woman, an unwed mother (Milk's friend and ally, Carol Ruth Silver), and Dan White and Harvey Milk. Harvey Milk was forty-seven. An unexpected success in middle age, he had been a politician for less than five years of his life. But he had not become the first elected gay official of any major American city by being quiet and conciliatory. On the day of his installation, grinning and triumphant, Milk dressed in a suit and tie. Then he set off to walk the fifteen blocks from Castro Camera to city hall hand in hand with his new young Mexican lover, Jack Lira, at the head of a noisy throng of 150 supporters—and recording crews for six television and radio stations. "This is not my swearing-in, this is *your* swearing-in," he told the joyful crowd, after insisting that the ceremony be held outside the city hall rotunda to accommodate them all. "You can stand around and throw bricks at Silly Hall"—his name for city hall during the campaign—"or you can take it over. Well, here we are."

His first official act that day—after refusing to vote aye to make Dianne Feinstein's election as president of the Board of Supervisors unanimous—had been to introduce a bill amending the city's human rights ordinance to ban discrimination against homosexuals in employment, housing and public accommodations. The proposed ordinance upset Dan White and seemed to make Dianne Feinstein nervous, too. But before it came time to discuss and vote on it, Carol Ruth Silver proposed that they vote a certificate of honor in recognition of the twenty-fifth anniversary of Phyllis Lyon and Del Martin, the founders of Daughters of Bilitis, who had each served on important city boards. "Twenty-fifth anniversary of *what?*" snapped the conservative Quentin Kopp. Harvey Milk stood up to answer him. "Twenty-five years of working together, living together, loving each other—working together to put together a movement," he said.

"You shouldn't be rubbing people's noses in it," another council member grumbled. The resolution passed nonetheless, by a vote of 8–2.

When the gay rights bill came up, Jim Gordon recalled that Feinstein wanted to know if landlords would have to rent to sadists and masochists. Tenants could only be rejected or evicted for illegal behavior, the city attorney replied. Dan White questioned whether Roman Catholic schools would have to hire gay teachers and counselors. They could not discriminate, the attorney said. But when the vote came, it showed the new realities of city politics. Dianne Feinstein was indebted to the gay political community for each of her elections to the board. Dan White was not, and in the end, he was alone in voting no. When Mayor Moscone signed the sweeping new city ordinance in April, in a ceremony under the crystal chandelier in the mayor's office, he did it with a flourish—and then handed the pen to Harvey Milk. Gay political power—and the power of the new coalition of urban minorities that Moscone's mayoralty represented—was rising. The influence of the city's old conservative ethnic minorities—which Dan White, alone among the new council members, represented—was in decline.

It seemed a golden, ascendant time for the brash new spirit of the Castro men. From the night of Milk's election, when Sheriff Dick Hongisto gave him a personal motorcycle escort to his victory party, Harvey Milk was on a roll. Mayor George Moscone had made it plain that he regarded Milk, and not Jim Foster, as the leader and representative of the city's gays. And in a city with a long history of police attempts to suppress gay life, the new police chief appointed by Moscone when he took office, Charles R. Gain, had an empathy for gay men. Gain's parents were poor white farmers, migrants who blew west from Texas and Oklahoma to California when he was seven, in the middle of the Great Depression. They were Okies, traveling in a caravan of old cars like

John Steinbeck's characters in *The Grapes of Wrath*. In Oakland, where his family landed, Gain was made fun of as a boy—for his freckles, his red hair and twangy southern tongue, and he never forgot being treated cruelly for being different. It made him a different kind of police chief—a reformer, but a disciplinarian with no tolerance for abuse—when he became police chief in Oakland and then in St. Petersburg, Florida. His first radical pronouncement, after being named by Moscone as the first San Francisco chief from outside the department in sixty years, came when he spoke to a gay Democratic club in the city. Gays on the San Francisco police force should "come out of the closet" and demonstrate that they could be good police officers, Gain said. "We will hire gays the same as we hire anyone else." His pledge was a direct reflection of Moscone's wish, and an unmistakable signal of the new chief's intent to shake up and modernize a department that he regarded as one of the most insular in the nation—a closed system impervious to the modern influences that had changed other big city forces. It was an inbred culture, awash with alcohol and dominated by an Irish Mafia of conservative Catholic San Francisco natives like Dan White. Gain warned Moscone that changing it to reflect a more diverse and sophisticated city would take years, longer than they both would be around.

Gain's speech that day identified him instantly as an enemy to the old-line cops. Inside the department, as the new chief changed recruitment procedures, his office decor, even the color of the squad cars—to a kind of powder blue—the hostility was intense. Gain kept an open line to Harvey Milk. He had lunch often with Jim Foster. The cops nicknamed him "Gloria." Leaving the building at the end of the day, Gain frequently found graffiti about him scrawled in the department elevators and the windshield of his police car encrusted with spit. He ordered the elevators cleaned and the car washed, and sometimes, after dinner at night, he and his wife, Florence, would go to a gay bar. He found the company relaxing.

The city seemed on the path of a new, more liberal cultural politics. For a time, in the wake of the municipal election, there was a certain spirit of being new together. Paired as natural opponents by the local media, Harvey Milk and Dan White at first made several cheerful, mutually congratulatory appearances together. White sat congenially the night after their swearing-in at a fundraising dinner held to pay off Milk's campaign debts—an event filled with liberal politicians. But the new coalition of good feeling in the city didn't really include Dan White. As the vote on the gay rights ordinance and the resolution celebrating Phyllis Lyon and Del Martin's relationship made plain, it was an era in San Francisco politics that favored newer minorities, and board politics seemed hard on White. He wasn't built to be flexible, and he didn't seem to learn. In the council chamber and on the field at the supervisors' annual softball game with the mayor's office, he played hard. He always thought he was right. He always wanted to win. Feinstein tried to shelter and prompt White, and make him an ally. But he remained prickly and stubborn on issues, and turned silent and angry when he lost. Without a career or real work besides the part-time supervisor's job, White also felt pinched and poor, unable to provide properly for himself, his wife and baby.

Harvey Milk, on the other hand, was having a grand time. He, too, was often on the minority end of votes, sometimes just he and Carol Ruth Silver standing against the rest of the board. But Milk rejoiced in the drama of being outside the fold. "What do you think of my new theater?" he liked to ask, leading friends through the soaring marble spaces of San Francisco's grand city hall. He used the role to make himself an agent of change. Briefly serving as acting mayor once, when Moscone was away—a temporary courtesy—Milk arrived at city hall in the mayor's limousine and summoned the press to point out that this was history: he was the first openly gay mayor of a major U.S. city. At a state meeting of Democratic clubs in San Diego, he went further. He had been acting mayor of San Francisco the day before, he said, but he could still be rejected for a job at Macy's because he was gay. Milk began to enjoy the politics of negotiation from a position of power. He spent late nights in the apartment above the camera store studying the details of city government. And if he took pleasure in holding loud, profane, phony telephone conversations whenever he knew that the prudish Feinstein was passing his door, he also supplied his colleagues on the board with a steady stream of jokes and jelly beans, and began to impress them with his preparation.

The city's political community was beginning to respect him. The gay community took comfort in his rhetoric—and pleasure in its own emergence. Good humor ran high. On Easter Sunday 1978, drag queens paraded in Easter bonnets on Castro Street, along with a man dressed in leather, with black bunny ears and a cottontail, and a large rabbit in black tails and a top hat, handing out plastic eggs filled with jelly beans, and buttons that said, "How dare you presume I'm heterosexual!" But those were backdrop events. Most of Harvey Milk and Dan White's first year in office was a time of conflict and drama, centered on the issue of homosexual civil rights. Each time there was a setback for gay rights elsewhere in the nation, the Castro was the staging area for gay reaction, the march downtown was its expression, and Harvey Milk was its leader and voice.

The first march had occurred spontaneously the night of the Dade County vote, in June 1977. Harvey Milk's election as supervisor that fall shattered the gloom which followed Anita Bryant's victory. But when the defeats resumed, as voters rejected gay rights ordinances in St. Paul, Wichita and Eugene that spring, it was in San Francisco that gay crowds took to the streets and marched. Time and again, Milk and the cadre of men who had matured around him: Harry Britt, who had become president of the San Francisco Gay Democratic Club; Jim Gordon, the club secretary, who recorded every event in his journal; Cleve Jones, who became the choreographer and drum major of the marches; Howard Wallace, Claude Wynne—they and thousands of others all marched out of the Castro, up to Union Square. Each time gay rights was rejected somewhere else, the rhetoric of the marchers grew a little hotter.

"Gay rights now. Gay riots now!" they chanted when the ordinance fell in St. Paul.

"Civil rights or Civil War!" they chanted when the ordinance lost in Eugene.

With each march, there was more emphasis on the looming battle against the Briggs initiative. Organizing against it, speaking against it, debating Briggs around the state took more and more of Milk's time, the time of the Alice Club, and all the other parts and personalities of the gay movement. The issue naturally came to dominate politics in San Francisco.

The decisive defeat of the Briggs initiative on November 7 was the greatest electoral victory the gay rights movement in the United States had known. It conferred a particular aura of historical celebrity on Harvey Milk, and at the victory party in San Francisco that night, he called for a gay march on Washington in 1979. Three days later, frustrated and angry with politics and public office, Dan White resigned his seat on the Board of Supervisors. He almost immediately changed his mind and asked Mayor Moscone to reinstate him, a request Harvey Milk opposed. With a different, more liberal supervisor in White's place, Milk could envision a progressive majority on the council. He gave Moscone an ultimatum: if he appointed Dan White he could forget the gay vote.

Moscone decided not to reappoint White. It was a decision the former supervisor learned from a reporter. He didn't sleep that night. The next morning, November 27, the day Moscone was to announce his decision about White's seat, Dan White climbed into a side window of city hall, avoiding the metal detectors at the main doors. Carrying his .38-caliber police revolver in its holster, he went to see the mayor. When the two were alone in the mayor's private inner office, he drew the gun and shot Moscone twice in the chest and twice in the head. Then he moved quickly across the hall, closeted himself in a room with Harvey Milk and shot the man he so despised five times in all, twice in the head, with exploding, hollow-point bullets. He then walked down the hallway past the horrified Dianne Feinstein's open office door, and left city hall. From a pay phone, he called his wife to meet him at St. Mary's Cathedral. As Chief Charles Gain raced to city hall, to find the mayor and Harvey Milk dead, Dan White drove to turn himself in at the Northern Police Station. There he was taken into custody and questioned by some officers he knew.

• • •

Turning on the radio at his desk at the California Academy of Sciences that morning to find out whom Moscone had appointed, Jim Gordon heard the news. It left him blank and dazed. He had not felt that way in fifteen years, since Kennedy had been killed in Dallas. He walked away from his desk and drove to Harry Britt's apartment, and at 6 p.m. that evening, he, Britt, Cleve Jones and others, planned what they thought would be a last march for Harvey Milk. At eight-thirty, thousands of people gathered along both sides of Castro Street, holding lighted candles in little foil bases. At the head of the line, someone held up a sign. "Two Shall Become Ten Thousand," it said. Cleve Jones read a testament Harvey Milk had taped two weeks after his election a year before. Milk had always had a fatalistic—some thought theatrical—sense of martyrdom, as his opponent Rick Stokes had complained during their campaign. But he had also received death threats. If he should be assassinated, Milk said, as Jones quoted him aloud, he hoped that people would turn their frustration and anger into something positive. He hoped that gay people would come out in the open.

The long mass began to move silently toward city hall. At each intersection, people raised their candles high, so that the broad line up Castro became an undulating river of glittering light. It moved in rustling silence except for the beat of a drum, a lone harmonica that played "Battle Hymn of the Republic" and a horn that slowly moaned the cadence of "We Shall Overcome." Between 25,000 and 40,000 people pressed in at the Polk Street side of city hall, holding candles aloft as the trumpet played "Taps" and Joan Baez sang "Kum Ba Yah." Then she sang "Ain't Going to Let Nobody Turn Me Around," and someone played a tape of Harvey Milk speaking at the "No on 6" victory party election night, urging people to come out of the closet and march on Washington.

The people in the crowd listened. Then they placed their candles and flowers at the base of city hall and around its statue of Abraham Lincoln, and melted sadly away into the night.

The political effect of Milk's killing was immediate. When the San Francisco Gay Democratic Club met in angry, solemn haste after the murders, the membership voted to rename itself the Harvey Milk Gay Democratic Club and began talking about the march. When the telephone rang in the office of the Coalition for Lesbian and Gay Rights in New York City the day that Milk was murdered, the caller said that "the community" in San Francisco wanted to go ahead with the march. The New York coalition's main purpose was to get a gay rights ordinance passed by the New York City Council, but the phone call, and the idea of the march as Harvey Milk's legacy, changed the chemistry in the group that night. Steve Ault and Joyce Hunter, two of the people in the coalition office on lower Fifth Avenue when the phone rang, would work on almost nothing else but the march for the next year.

The news did not turn Steve Endean's head. He had despised Milk. "They got to him just before I did," he liked to say. Milk's manner—his ego, his abrasiveness, his insistence on doing things his way—ground on Endean's midwestern sensibilities, and also probably on his insecurities. But practical politics came first, and Endean did not trumpet his personal feelings about Harvey Milk in the aftermath of the killings. Instead, he used revulsion at the murders of Milk and Moscone to gain additional co-sponsors for a congressional gay rights bill. In Minnesota, Endean had been able to buttonhole individual legislators, and he could tell whether he was making any progress changing their minds. In Washington, it was almost impossible to see members of Congress themselves. Instead, he had to persuade some staff assistant—whose job it was to protect the congressman—that supporting gay rights was the right thing to do, and that it wouldn't destroy the congressman at the polls.

It was a hard argument to make, and Endean began looking for some way to document his contention that the voters were *not* hostile to politicians who supported gay rights. Eventually, he found the person he needed, a member of the Congressional Research Office in the Library of Congress, and persuaded him—the LOC didn't allow moonlighting—to make a study proving that supporting gay rights was not political suicide.* But he could find no United States senator willing to introduce a gay rights measure as a companion to Bella Abzug's bill in the House. Within the House, however, there were liberal Democrats from urban districts which were heavily gay, and support for Abzug's bill was growing—modestly. Henry A. Waxman, representing Hollywood and the West Side of Los Angeles, was willing to introduce the bill that session. Then Representative Ted Weiss, D-New York, who represented the West Side of Manhattan and had once sponsored a gay rights ordinance as a New York City councilman, surprised Endean by dropping a bill with broader protections into the hopper. Weiss did not seem to know that GRNL and Steve Endean even existed, but suddenly Endean had the happy problem of more sponsors than he had imagined. As he worked with the two congressional offices and canvassed others, it began to seem that a consolidated bill might attract as many as forty-six co-sponsors in the Ninety-sixth Congress, half again as many as had signed on before.

* The result, sponsored by GRNL and the National Gay Task Force and first issued in the spring of 1980, was called *Does Support for Gay Rights Spell Political Suicide?: A Close Look at Some Long-Held Myths.*

But Carter administration support for gay rights was eroding. The meeting in the Roosevelt Room had turned out to be the high point. To Carter's inner circle, Midge Costanza's outspokenness on gay rights and other issues—the Equal Rights Amendment, abortion and the need to get rid of Bert Lance—had branded her as a loose cannon on the left, a threat to Carter's support among Christian conservatives. Costanza's star steadily dimmed from that point on. She was replaced as assistant to the president for public liaison by Anne Wexler, a liberal New Yorker who returned the Office of Public Liaison to currying support for the president's positions with key groups, rather than carrying the concerns of special constituencies to him.

In August 1978, her authority reduced, her staff shrunken, her office relocated to the basement room where President Nixon had stored his tapes, Midge Costanza had resigned. She wrote in her letter to President Carter that they had shared the same concerns, but "it is clear that our approaches to fulfilling them are different.

"My own approach has been one largely of advocacy," she told Carter. "There are those who suggest that I should have simply carried out your policies and not voiced my own opinions and ideas openly. But that was not my style." The Carter White House continued to receive *The Advocate*. It assured leaders of the Task Force that the administration would work behind the scenes for the reforms Costanza had initiated. And Carter family members were occasionally visible at gay events. But with Costanza gone, the movement no longer had a voice in the White House. Gay rights had never attracted Jimmy Carter's particular sympathy or personal interest. "The President doesn't understand the gay issue," Costanza told a reporter for the *San Francisco Chronicle* who asked if Carter would agree to demands that he come out strongly for gay rights. "He has trouble with it. He's a wonderful guy and supports human rights, but personally, I just think he's uncomfortable on the issue."

It might have surprised the gay activists to know it, but they had something in common with Anita Bryant, Jerry Falwell, Pat Robertson and the rumbling legions of conservative Christians. Perhaps the only large group which felt more shut out of Jimmy Carter's White House than homosexuals did were the evangelical Christians who thought their votes had put him there. Jimmy Carter had never responded to appeals from Harvey Milk or other gay leaders for some action or statement in support for gay rights. He had also never responded to the appeals of Anita Bryant and the religious right for some statement of support for their crusade *against* gay rights. Each group had expected more—the evangelical Christians because Jimmy Carter was born-again, and the homosexuals because of Jimmy Carter's reputation as a supporter of human rights. As the spring of 1979 turned toward summer, neither group was happy.

October 1979

By the second week in October, when the "Gay Freedom Train" pulled away from San Francisco Bay and headed toward Lake Tahoe, Denver, Lincoln and Chicago—on a three-day run across the continent that would bring its load of homosexuals to Washington, D.C., for the first National March on Washington for Lesbian and Gay Rights—all the main national groups in the movement had come to accept that the march was going to happen. Just as the train's crew of traditional black conductors, stewards and dining car waiters gradually got accustomed to a hundred homosexuals yelling out "Avenge Harvey Milk!" the establishment gay rights groups had eventually grown resigned to the idea of the march, and, belatedly, had given the event their blessings and endorsements. A second planning conference in Houston in July showed that the national march committee was organized enough to make it happen, and also that the march organizers had toned down the most radical of their demands. In particular, the demands of a group newly formed from the old *Fag Rag* sexual liberationist left in Boston—the North American Man-Boy Love Association—had disappeared. The lesbians in the planning sessions, who were sensitive to the issue of sexual domination by men, had taken offense at the idea that homosexual men should be able legally to have sex with young boys, and believed that lowering the age of consent would also make young girls prey to sexually aggressive heterosexual men. They had fought the issue and won, and in the place of the age of consent demand was a call to "protect lesbian and gay youth from any laws which are used to discriminate against, oppress and/or harass them in their homes, schools, jobs and social environments." People like Kerry Woodward, who was monitoring the Houston meeting as a board member of the National Gay Task Force, reported back to their organizations that the march was going to happen, that they ought to go ahead and endorse it.

By late summer, the early opponents had come around, and march organizers had the endorsements they needed. Steve Endean had figured out his own ways to use the march to GRNL's benefit, by lobbying for a gay rights bill. Robin Tyler had cornered Troy Perry over lunch one day in Los Angeles and turned him on to the whole idea.

Together, Tyler and Perry rode the train from Los Angeles to San Francisco and eastward, alighting at the head of the band of activists at each station stop to make a speech and say a prayer, and show the spirit to whatever newspaper, radio and television reporters the local activists in each city had been able to drum up—no matter what hour the train arrived. Sometimes there was only one lonely lesbian or gay man waiting on the platform when the train came in. Sometimes there were a dozen or so. The idea that groups of homosexuals would openly cross the country to march in Washington was a radical notion in much of the cultural territory the train traversed. As it moved from California, where the movement had developed a huge political presence, to Washington, where it had become a power in city government, the train cars crossed great expanses in which homosexuals were still regarded as freaks. At the Nevada line, state troopers climbed aboard and stayed aboard until the train hit Utah. In Ogden, Utah, the Reverend Robert L. Harris lay down on the tracks to protest the train. "Gay people have no rights," he said. Troy Perry got off the train, walked up the tracks to where he lay, and the two of them dueled with Bible verses.

The train rolled on, and when it reached the capital and all the other people who had come in by bus, car and train—there was another trainload from New York City—they all assembled on Sunday morning and marched up Pennsylvania Avenue, past the White House and down the Mall to the Washington Monument, perhaps 75,000 strong.* When a reporter for *The Blade* had tried to gauge the size of the crowd in advance by checking travel reservations in San Francisco, Chicago, Denver, Philadelphia and Miami, he found them slim. But it was in the smaller cities of the South and Midwest that the idea of the march had seemed daring and exciting, and many of the people came from those places. They filed past the White House, where President and Mrs. Carter had just filled the North and South Lawns with receptions for Pope John Paul II, inviting evangelists like Jerry Falwell and others who were nursing grudges. Some, like Pat Robertson, declined.

The pope's visit had brought a tidal wave of media attention. But for the first National March on Washington for Lesbian and Gay Rights, there was only token interest. A twenty-person delegation from the march met at the White House with Jane Wales, a holdover from Midge Costanza's staff who had become a low-level aide to Anne Wexler, Costanza's replacement. The *New York Times* and *Washington Post* gave the march prominent—though modest—front-page coverage. There were brief television network reports. *Time* and *Newsweek* ignored the event totally.

It was the people who marched to whom it was so extraordinary. Enough of them had been sufficiently excited and organized beforehand to work with GRNL, making appointments to see their senators or representatives or aides on Monday. They visited 160 different congressional offices, and persuaded three Democratic representatives to become co-sponsors of the gay rights bill. One was Robert Duncan of Oregon, and the other two were James Corman and Leon Panetta of California. "Until now," said Representative Henry Waxman, the chief sponsor of the gay rights bill, "many members of Congress may

---

* The Parks Service estimated 25,000. The District of Columbia police put it at 75,000. Some march enthusiasts used the number 250,000.

have not been aware that there's a homosexual constituency willing to make it-self heard. They haven't understood that there are sizable numbers of such voters to be taken into consideration—not just the fundamentalist Christian constituency that wants to deny rights to homosexuals."

"The events of that weekend," as David Goodstein wrote in his column in *The Advocate,* were in every way "dignified, impressive, moving and impor-tant." The Reverend Jerry Falwell stood to one side with Gary Jarmin of Christian Voice in Washington on that Sunday, October 14, declaring as the marchers passed by, "God did not create Adam and Steve." But his presence did not diminish the experience of the March on Washington for many who were there.

They flowed past Falwell to assemble on the Mall. And it was there, sit-ting on the grass with his lover, two of many thousands, all of them singing out "We Are Everywhere. We Will Be Free!," that Jok Church felt the meaning of the words they were singing. He had come all the way from Sacramento on the "Gay Freedom Train." Through town after town, they had looked through the train windows at every station stop for other homosexuals on the platform. Sometimes they spied some; sometimes they did not. Now on the Mall, among so many others like himself, from so many places, all chanting that verse, the meaning of the song suddenly became very clear.

"We *are* everywhere. We *will* be free."

29

COLLIDING FORCES

October 1979, Los Angeles

Governor Edmund G. Brown Jr.'s challenge to Jimmy Carter for the 1980 Democratic presidential nomination had seemed unlikely from the start, and by the time Brown arrived at Sheldon Andelson's home in Bel Air for dinner in September 1979, his campaign was nearly broke and not a vote had been cast. Brown's presidential committee had $90,410 on hand as of September 30, 1979, which was not a lot of money, considering it was four months until the New Hampshire primary, and Senator Edward M. Kennedy of Massachusetts was about to join the race. A Gallup poll of Democratic voters found Jerry Brown trailing far behind the unpopular Jimmy Carter, by a 48 percent to 34 percent margin, while Kennedy beat the president, by 62 to 24 percent. Those kinds of poll numbers only made it more difficult for Brown to raise money, particularly to finance a challenge to an incumbent president, and especially with Ted Kennedy on the horizon. And the thin bottom line on Brown's presidential bank account did not even convey the extent of his financial difficulties. In order to qualify for federal campaign subsidies, a candidate was required to raise $5,000 in twenty states, in individual contributions no larger than $250. Jerry Brown had met that qualification in only two states—California and Florida. Notwithstanding the fact that he was governor of California, and one of the nation's most recognizable politicians,

Brown was, in the fall of 1979, the longest of long shots for the Democratic presidential nomination.

All of that explained why Brown was at Andelson's home for dinner: he needed money. Brown had found his way to the wealthy Los Angeles lawyer through the consulting firm David Mixner and Peter Scott created in 1977, which Brown's presidential exploratory committee had hired at $1,000 a month. Mixner and Scott suggested that Brown attempt nationally what the organization they had helped found, MECLA, had done in California—tap contributions from gay men and women, a source ignored by presidential candidates. Mixner and Scott could provide Brown with contacts and political advice, but Sheldon Andelson could provide him with money, which is what he needed most. Andelson had learned that access was the reward for a contribution to a state or city candidate, and the presidential race was the obvious next step. Sheldon Andelson liked to say that his goal in life was to be chief of protocol at the White House (he also wanted to become a member of the California Board of Regents), and signing on early with a presidential candidate was one way to achieve that ambition. So he immediately agreed to host a Brown fundraiser. If Brown had any doubts about the fundraising potential of the gay community, he lost them that night: he left Andelson's home with $30,000 in campaign contributions, one-third of his entire campaign bank account.

Brown's willingness to attend a gay fundraising dinner was the first sign that the 1980 presidential campaign was emerging as a new kind of opportunity for gay activists. Four years ago, Virginia Apuzzo and Jean O'Leary had been barred from even arguing for a gay rights plank in the Democratic Party platform. Now, a candidate for the Democratic presidential nomination—albeit, a long-shot one—was actively and openly seeking gay support. The governor's twin beacons of political pragmatism and curiosity in the offbeat had drawn him to the gay community, and would help transform the presidential race that was about to unfold.

The Jerry Brown presidential campaign was arguably not the ideal platform upon which to launch this new era of gay activism. He was a comical figure in many parts of the country, the living symbol of the state of "fruits and nuts," the target of comic strips and television humorists. Brown had also been slow to oppose the Briggs initiative. Gay rights, Brown thought when Briggs began his campaign, was a treacherous issue. When a reporter asked the governor that summer if homosexuals should be allowed to teach, he bobbed: Each case should be decided "individually." And when asked if he considered homosexuality immoral, Brown demurred again: "I'm not going to offer my judgment on individual behavior." Brown had appointed no openly gay people during his first term; his record on the issue was so suspect that some gay groups considered not supporting him when he ran for reelection in 1978.

But by 1979, the start of his second term, and with a presidential campaign in the offing, Brown seemed to shed his misgivings. His inaugural address called for adding "sexual preference" to the anti-discrimination provisions of the state's Fair Employment Act, and he issued an executive order prohibiting discrimination in the hiring of homosexuals in state government. He attended the MECLA fundraising dinner that spring.* And two weeks before his dinner at Andelson's house, Brown appointed Stephen Lachs, one of the founders of MECLA, to the Superior Court of Los Angeles, making him the first openly gay judge in the country and fulfilling one of the most urgent demands from Los Angeles's rising political establishment. "The Democratic candidate who has done the most for gay people in California is Jerry Brown," David Goodstein, the *Advocate* publisher, wrote in an early assessment of the presidential race. Brown even went so far that year as to invite two *Advocate* writers to his home in Laurel Canyon for an interview. He told them that gay rights had been advanced by the Briggs initiative in 1978 because it had forced debate about a taboo subject, and that it would be advanced again by him in the presidential campaign. "What may seem to be a risk in 1980 will be recognized over time as part of the evolution of our society," he said. For their part, the interviewers were as struck by the substance of the interview as by seeing the inside of the home of a candidate for president, which they described with a combination of slack-jawed awe and bemusement. "Above the sooty fireplace was a large, round, convex mirror—the kind that are suspended in stores to discourage shoplifting. A desk consisted of metal sawhorses with a board laid on top. There were two beige sofas separated by a large, sickly-looking palm, and a huge gold-brown pillow next to the fireplace. A bead curtain—vintage Cost Plus—hung between the living room and the entryway."

"Well, he can't be gay," the writer Lenny Giteck remarked to his partner, Scott Anderson, *The Advocate*'s news editor, referring to the rumors—by all accounts, unfounded—that inevitably attached themselves to the unmarried governor. "Just look at his taste."

As it happened, the gay fundraisers that Mixner and Scott set up for Brown often, at the governor's request, did not find their way to the public schedule handed out to the reporters traveling with him. When Brown spoke to a gay organization in Portland, Oregon, his aides specifically told reporters to take the night off, assuring them he had only a private fundraiser. Brown felt that any time he spoke to a gay group, the story would be that the governor of

---

* He went over the advice of some aides, who thought it was risky, in no small part given his unmarried status and recurrent rumors about his own sexuality.

California had appeared before an audience of homosexuals—no matter what he said in his speech. Even for a campaign like his, scrapping for money and publicity, there was no gain in a story like that.

Still, the Andelson dinner set a pattern for similar fundraisers in Chicago, Los Angeles, Boston and New York. "The view in the camp is that there is a lot of gay voters and a lot of gay money," Peter Scott told the *San Francisco Chronicle.* Two weeks after Brown left Andelson's home, the directors of the National Gay Task Force held a press conference to announce that Jerry Brown had sent them a telegram conveying his "wholehearted support" for an end to discrimination against homosexuals in the federal government and the military, and for a federal gay civil rights law. What was more, he was outlining that position to voters in a speech that day in Manchester, New Hampshire.

November 1979, Washington, D.C.

The red, white and blue banner was stretched tight across the foot of the stage at one end of The Pier disco in Washington's Southwest section. It read, "Gay Vote USA" and framed the newspaper photographs of Brown's appearance at the kickoff of what gay groups were calling the National Convention Project. This was a drive to elect gays as convention delegates, pressure presidential candidates to discuss homosexual issues and ultimately convince the parties to include a gay rights plank in their platforms. Brown was seeking out the gay vote in California, but in Washington, D.C., gay activists were seeking out the presidential candidates.

Brown's appearance at The Pier was an enormous coup. Initially planned as a modest effort to raise money, stir excitement and recruit delegate candidates, the rally was transformed by Brown's appearance into a national event, spotlighting the guiding premise of the convention project: that there was a "gay vote" to be had, made up of a class of people whose political definition of themselves included their sexual orientation. It did not matter that Jerry Brown would never win the Democratic presidential nomination. He was a serious candidate for president, and he was going to speak in front of a gay audience, with reporters in the room. Brown had agreed to this for the same reason that he had agreed to go to Sheldon Andelson's home in Bel Air two months earlier. He needed money, and David Mixner and Peter Scott told him this was one very good way to raise it. If Brown would speak at the rally, Washington gay leaders pledged to raise $5,000 in the District of Columbia for him, bringing him one state closer to qualifying for federal matching funds.

• • •

The National Convention Project unveiled that night had been conceived by two political forces that were maturing side by side in the charged political atmosphere of Washington, D.C., in 1979: Steve Endean and the Gay Rights National Lobby, on the one hand; and the city's established gay political organizations, on the other. Endean believed in the political system, and even in party platforms, which, as a rule, were mainly a way to appease constituencies and were forgotten after election day. Endean had been a page at the 1972 Democratic-Farmer-Labor state convention when the Minnesota political party adopted a gay rights plank, and he saw a difference in the way he was treated in the State House once gay rights was given the imprint of legitimacy that came with a plank: It was like "night and day," he said. Endean, after a year in Washington, believed the dynamic there was the same as in the state where he began: "Until at least one party has a platform supporting gay rights, there's little chance of passing pro-gay legislation at the federal level." It almost didn't matter if the plank was never passed, he said, so long as it was debated.

The second force behind the National Convention Project was the group of Washington, D.C., gay leaders—Paul Kuntzler, Richard Maulsby and Tom Bastow, among them—who had supported Marion Barry's election. Their influence over the new municipal government was so great that the battle for gay rights had lost its urgency in Washington; indeed, it had almost been won. So they had set their sights on larger battles, starting in the summer of 1979, when Kuntzler and Endean invited Bastow, who was president of the Gertrude Stein Club, to lunch. Bastow was bright, quick and compulsively well organized, a hardworking and self-effacing former naval officer and a University of Michigan graduate with a Harvard law degree. Kuntzler and Endean wanted him to head the new gay rights project. It was the kind of prestigious political position that would transform his career, Kuntzler said.

For the second leader, Endean and Kuntzler turned to Mary Spottswood Pou, called "Spotts," a well-known Washington feminist who had organized many of the women's music festivals which were part of the 1970s underground lesbian culture, and was now involved in governmental public relations and lobbying. She would take the job, but insisted on a few conditions. One was that her male counterpart, Bastow, read every back issue of *Quest: A Feminist Quarterly*, Charlotte Bunch's magazine devoted to feminism and lesbian issues. And Spottswood Pou said she would not take the job if Jean O'Leary was involved. O'Leary was abrasive, she said, and had made too many enemies among some of the Democratic leaders who would be as key in this election as they were in 1976, when O'Leary had been involved.

The 1979 March on Washington, one month before the National Convention Project's kickoff, had brought to Washington almost every major gay activist in the country, giving Bastow and Spottswood Pou the opportunity to recruit candidates for delegates. The march participants arrived to read about the National Convention Project in a front-page story in the *Washington Blade,* accompanied by side-by-side profiles of Spottswood Pou and Bastow. The story irritated Charlie Brydon, now the co-director of the National Gay Task Force, because it looked as if his organization was being shut out of the 1980 election. Brydon protectively suggested the project be run by a governing board made up of two members each from the Task Force and GRNL, and Endean agreed. "It made no sense whatsoever for both organizations to have separate projects which would in any way compete," Endean told members of his board in describing what was a highly unusual attempt at cooperation among two different gay rights organizations at the time.

Endean had helped Bastow and Spottswood Pou lay the groundwork for the kickoff, introducing them to well-placed officials in the Democratic National Committee and staffers at other lobby groups, such as Common Cause, who provided the fledgling project with tactical guidance. Endean proved himself invaluable, so when a few weeks into the project he turned bright yellow and collapsed into bed, there was reason for alarm. Endean had contracted a severe case of hepatitis, one of the serious contagions plaguing sexually promiscuous men in the late 1970s, and it left him unable to oversee the project he helped conceive. Bastow and Spottswood Pou were suddenly running what was the most ambitiously mainstream political project ever launched by a homosexual group, with little idea of how to proceed.

There were over five hundred people at The Pier the night Jerry Brown appeared, according to newspaper reports, based on the organizers' slightly exaggerated accounts. Frank Kameny introduced Brown, who had spent the past three days in New Hampshire, Massachusetts and Vermont. "Frankly, you know you have arrived, you know you have reached the inner sanctum," said Kameny, "when a major candidate for the presidency comes here." Paul Kuntzler, Tom Bastow and Richard Maulsby stood on the stage next to Brown, trying to pick out national political correspondents they recognized from the network news, standing in a gay bar.

Brown hadn't known any open homosexuals before he met Mixner and Andelson. And although he later said he had felt slightly uncomfortable in the setting, he was nonetheless fiery and authoritative, talking for nearly ten minutes, promising an executive order to bar discrimination in the federal government and pledging to make gay rights central to the Democratic Party. "I've sent neither a letter nor a representative, but have come here to be your comrade-in-arms," Brown proclaimed. "There is a great opportunity to overcome past struggles. There should be no discrimination on the basis of age, race, sex or sexual preference—that's the movement and I join you in it." Brown said he supported the gay rights plank and intended "to debate it." As his audience cheered, Brown added: "Any president should make that pledge." President Carter had not, instead sending a deputy assistant, Michael Chanin, as his proxy. Chanin was jeered when he took the microphone—"Where's Midge?" someone yelled, referring to Midge Costanza—as he tried to defend the administration's record for having "made a start." The evening's importance was captured later that week, in a column in the *Washington Star* by Jack Germond and Jules Witcover. "Such has been the growth in the influence of homosexuals in politics," they wrote, "that a presidential candidate, and official representatives from the president himself and a third candidate, Edward M. Kennedy, had all attended a public fundraiser for a gay cause. "Only a few years ago," the journalists wrote, "such an undertaking would have been snickered away."

June 1980, New York

The gay rights plank drafted by Tom Bastow and Mary Spottswood Pou, and pressed from the first Iowa caucus in January to the last platform committee hearing in Washington in June, was as mainstream as the project that created it. Two sentences long, it put the party on record against discrimination, in favor of a gay civil rights law and a presidential order barring bias in hiring, and for repeal of laws used against homosexuals, including the bar on immigration by homosexuals. It did not call, for example, for an end to the military's ban against homosexuals because Bastow and the other leaders thought the country just wasn't ready for that. And it ignored the contentious issues that had rumbled through the first gay rights presidential campaign platform, adopted by a more radical assembly of gay leaders in Chicago in 1972. There was no talk here of abolishing age-of-consent laws, or lifting restrictions on cross-dressing. Bastow and Spottswood Pou had put nearly a year into writing and lobbying for the platform, and they were not about to let it dissolve into an ideological exercise.

By the end of the primary season in June, the National Convention Project had, as an organization, essentially collapsed. Initial financing by Jack Campbell was followed by other checks from other bathhouse owners. That proved to be a mixed blessing. Mary Spottswood Pou could not hide her unhappiness that the gay male sex industry was financing the homosexual movement's debut on the national presidential scene. And sex industry money was not enough to finance the project alone, especially once Brown was out of the race and the California money had dried up. The evidence of the National Convention Project's financial straits was apparent in stacks of unsent fundraising appeals piled in the office, signed by Mayors Marion Barry of Washington and Dianne Feinstein of San Francisco (as president of the Board of

Supervisors she had become mayor after Moscone's assassination). The letter, which called for a "new national coalition to support the civil rights for gay people," was almost certainly the first major direct fundraising appeal for a gay cause signed by two major politicians, and was distributed only when local political and religious homosexual organizations came up with the money to pay the postage. The National Convention Project raised barely $40,000.

Bastow had promised from the start to lobby both the Democratic and the Republican Parties, if only to make sure that Republican homosexual voters would feel comfortable contributing to the project. The Republican effort turned out to be as difficult as he expected. When Convention Project officials had written for information on platform procedures, Roger Semerad, executive director of the platform committee, wrote back: "To suggest that the gay lifestyle is compatible with a conservative philosophy is unrealistic," and refused to provide it. A project volunteer had to go to the Republican National Committee office posing as a senatorial aide in order to obtain a list of committees and a description of procedures.

But the project itself was enjoying some success. Ted Kennedy had become unhesitating in his support for gay rights, echoing Jimmy Carter's early and abandoned tentative statements of 1976. Kennedy sent representatives to all the forums that Bastow and other activists arranged. A month before the California primary, Kennedy had made a personal pilgrimage for gay votes and money to the home of Clyde Cairns, a member of the MECLA board. Another board member, Steve Smith, had donated $1,000 to the Kennedy campaign before there even was an official Kennedy campaign. "I stand for gay rights and lesbian rights as a United States Senator and will as president of the United States," Kennedy said. Kennedy's campaign had debated how aggressively the candidate should push a gay rights plank in the party platform. Kennedy had watched his standing slip as the public focused on his personal behavior. "I'm going to do it," Kennedy finally informed his divided staff. "Look at it this way. It's the upside of my downside," he said. "No one will think I have a self-interest."

But as the New York convention neared, Kennedy was becoming increasingly irrelevant. And President Carter, assured of the nomination, was thinking about Ronald Reagan and noting, with alarm, that the religious right, so critical to his 1976 victory, was drifting away. Carter's perceived attitude toward homosexuals—the Costanza meeting was a particular irritant—accounted for much of the erosion. In that context, even Bastow and Spottswood Pou's mild gay rights plank was too strong. At the end of June, when the platform committee gathered in Washington, gay leaders learned from the White House how homosexual rights would be addressed: The platform would suggest that "sexual orientation" would be added to the list of traits "protected from discrimination," along with race, color, religion, national origin, language, age and sex. The platform would stipulate that "appropriate legislative and administrative actions to achieve these goals should be undertaken." The words "gay" and "lesbian" would appear nowhere in the document, and the platform would not endorse a gay rights bill.

The evening of the meeting, the six gay members of the platform committee and the leaders of the National Convention Project gathered in Jack Campbell's suite to discuss how to respond. Should they accept the amendment, stripped of the word "gay" and explicit endorsement of gay rights? Should they take their fight to the floor, in hopes of winning attention to their cause? Paul Kuntzler and Bill Kraus, a Kennedy delegate who was president of the Harvey Milk Gay Democratic Club in San Francisco, argued that the plank was a sellout. Kraus, his voice quivering, asked why they should settle for this. Kuntzler said they should try to force a debate before a national television audience, and did not care whether they won the vote or not.

But a more pragmatic view won out that evening. "I'd rather get my foot in the door and wedge it open," said Steve Endean, now recovered from his illness. If the group took the fight to the floor it would lose, Endean said, and the story would then be that even the Democrats had repudiated homosexuals. Bastow argued that Carter was trying to "present the smallest target he could" to gay rights opponents. If Carter lost that November, the National Convention Project might well find itself taking the blame. Apuzzo told a reporter that even a diminished platform proved that they had arrived in the Democratic Party. "We are no longer an embarrassing issue to this party, and the same people who would have nothing to do with us four years ago are now courting us. They must have learned how to count." Indeed, on the same day that the Democratic Platform Committee accepted the modified sexual orientation plank, Carter endorsed a measure proposed by Senator Alan Cranston which would end the restriction on gay immigrants. And the party's rules committee banned discrimination against homosexuals in party activities. Still, it would prove to be the last time in that election that Carter made any serious gesture for support from homosexual voters.

In 1976, the gay caucus to the Democratic convention would have fit around a small table in a crowded coffee shop. In August 1980, as Democrats gathered in New York, it filled the Georgia Room of the Statler Hilton— seventy-seven delegates, alternates and committee members, larger than twenty-five state delegations and nearly twenty times the representation of four years ago. Most of the critical work had been done. The platform had been negotiated, and Carter was assured the nomination. But from the first meeting of the caucus on Sunday night, there was a clear desire to do something— to turn this show of force into a display of power. And an idea Paul Kuntzler had pushed without success at the 1976 convention, to nominate a vice presidential candidate, suddenly seemed to make a lot of sense. This time, though, he thought, the candidate should not be Frank Kameny, but Melvin Boozer.

Few people outside Washington, D.C., had heard of Mel Boozer. A thirty-five-year-old sociology professor at the University of Maryland, he had been elected president of Washington's Gay Activists Alliance the year before. He was popular and charismatic, reserved and dignified, but was not part of the group that had established a gay rights movement in the District. Because he was black, he was an unusual figure in the mostly white delegation and, indeed, in the movement itself. It took an extra measure of courage, Boozer said, for a black gay person—and a D.C. native—to be openly homosexual in Washington. Most Washington activists were people who moved there for a job. But Boozer grew up in the city, as he pointedly noted after his election as the GAA president. "It's a lot easier to come out and be politically active in the gay community when you don't live near your family than when you do," he said.

It would take 334 signatures, or 10 percent of the delegates, to nominate Boozer and win him a spot to speak. It seemed impossible. Delegates would not want to sign a petition forcing Walter Mondale into a purely symbolic battle for the vice presidential nomination. The fact that the petitions were for a homosexual candidate, an explicit effort to win a lectern speech about gay rights, made it even more difficult. Although some gay delegates said the honor should go to a woman, or someone with a name that would not suggest demeaning jokes, or a caucus member with a more established record in the movement, Kuntzler argued that delegates who might not be inclined to give a gay man a spot might be more reluctant to oppose a black speaker, whatever his sexual orientation.

For three days members of the gay caucus canvassed the floor and the conference rooms of Madison Square Garden, encountering hostility many found startling, a reminder that advances for the gay movement were confined to the nation's larger cities. "Why don't you just shut up?" one man said to Boozer. "You wouldn't get fired from your jobs if you just shut up." "Go back to California," someone yelled at Jeanne Cordova, who wore a "Lesbian for Kennedy" sandwich board. Another delegate called her a "screwball." But they got nearly four hundred signatures, and early Thursday evening, Boozer made his way to the lectern to present his case for the vice presidential nomination. The scheduling of his remarks made certain that they would not be carried on television. Boozer glanced across a two-thirds empty floor; most delegates were out to dinner before the evening session. There were a few boos, but the gay delegation was out there, small but determined, holding its signs aloft. "Lesbians for Boozer" read one; "Carter and Boozer—a ticket for the '80s." Boozer's speech wasn't typed, so he had to keep a finger on the page of his handwritten text, which had been rewritten a dozen times by members of the delegation. His throat was parched, and he couldn't wait to finish, since he was sure his voice would give out.

"I rise in anguished recognition of more than 20 million Americans who love this country and who long to serve this country in the same freedom that others take for granted. Twenty million lesbian and gay Americans whose lives are blighted by a veil of ignorance and misunderstanding.

"Mr. Chairman, we come from towns and cities where our friends are jailed and beaten on the slightest pretext. We come from churches which have been burned to the ground because they admit us to worship. We come from families which have been torn apart because our jobs have been lost and our names have been slandered by false accusations, myths and lies." As Boozer finished, he drew a link between the discrimination he had suffered as a black man and the discrimination he suffered as a homosexual. "Would you ask me how I dare to compare the civil rights struggle with the struggle for lesbian and gay rights? I can compare them and I do compare them, because I know what it means to be called a nigger and I know what it means to be called a faggot, and I understand the difference, in the marrow of my bones. And I can sum up that difference in one word: None. Bigotry is bigotry, Discrimination is discrimination. It hurts just as much. It dishonors our way of life just as much. And it betrays a common lack of understanding, fairness and compassion just as much."

On the floor, Tom Bastow found himself unexpectedly moved. There had been some doubt about whether Mel Boozer had been up to this. No one had been prepared for his eloquence and quiet dignity. It may have gone unnoticed, a provocative and moving speech in a mostly empty hall, but that didn't matter to the gay delegates on the floor. Boozer gathered forty-nine votes that evening, before Speaker of the House Thomas P. O'Neill declared the voting over and Mondale the choice by acclamation.

September 1980, Washington, D.C.

Gay activists had lost their battle for meaningful inclusion in the Democratic Party platform. And they faded more as the president moved to stop the flow of right-wing Christians toward Ronald Reagan. Through the spring of 1980, Jerry Falwell had given the Carter White House a lesson in just how far apart the religious right and this president had grown—and how far Falwell and allies like Paul Weyrich of the Free Congress Foundation were willing to go to defeat him in November. He was by then deep into a schedule of speeches and appearances for the Moral Majority, a plan worked out with Weyrich, that would take him hundreds of thousands of miles back and forth across the country before the year was out, preaching the nation's need for "spiritual rebirth" and attacking Jimmy Carter's "lack of moral leadership." He was doing that at a flag-bedecked "I Love America" rally in Anchorage, Alaska, in March when he began to tell the crowd about his confrontation with Carter at a White House breakfast in January, when a group of hostile preachers invited by the Rev. Bob Maddox, Carter's newly appointed minister-in-residence, sat down with the President.

"Sir," Falwell said he had asked the president, "why do you have known practicing homosexuals on your senior staff here in the White House?"

"Well, I am President of all the American people and I believe I should represent everyone," Falwell said that Carter had replied.

"I said, 'Why don't you have some murderers and bank robbers and so forth to represent?' " Falwell shouted. At that, the crowd broke into cheers and applause. But the transcript of the meeting contains no such exchange, and when the Carter White House heard about Falwell's speech and called him on it, Falwell issued a statement saying that the fictitious conversation was just "an anecdote intended to dramatically get the attention of the audience." It was, however, Falwell insisted, "an absolutely accurate statement of the President's record and position on gay rights."

It was not. But Falwell's effort to tag Carter as a friend to the gay rights movement was part of an evolving strategy by a group of fundamentalist religious leaders including Pat Robertson to defeat Carter in November. The preachers had been put off, initially, by Ronald Reagan, who was divorced, and had strained and distant relations with some of his children. But soon Reagan began making more explicitly conservative statements. Reagan, who had never taken explicitly anti-homosexual positions in previous campaigns, still enjoyed a huge reservoir of goodwill among gays for his 1978 statement against the Briggs initiative in California. "Since many people believe his was the most influential statement in the campaign," David Goodstein wrote at the start of the year, in a column urging gay voters to play some role in Republican presidential candidacies, "it is entirely appropriate that we reward him by becoming actively involved in his campaign." But as the religious right began to consolidate around him, Reagan's position hardened; he did not respond to a National Gay Task Force questionnaire on gay issues. Then in March, the same month that Falwell made the statement about Carter defending the employment of homosexuals, Reagan told the *Los Angeles Times* that the gay rights movement was seeking "a recognition and acceptance of an alternative lifestyle which I do not believe society can condone, nor can I." When the reporter asked why not, he said: "Well, you could find that in the Bible. It says that in the eyes of the Lord, it is an abomination."

Carter had used the themes of family and religious values with considerable success against Gerald Ford in 1976, and he had promised in an address to the National Conference on Catholic Charities that his administration would sponsor a White House Conference on the American Family. But by the time the White House conference was finally mounted, in an attempt to draw conservatives back to his campaign, the Carter administration was in such internal disagreement about the contemporary definition and needs of "the family" that the conference had become simply a series of meetings around the country, none of which came closer to the White House than Baltimore. The umbrella name for the serial event—suggesting that the American family assumed many forms—had become the White House Conference *on Families.* Never has a plural cost a president so much: religious right leaders seized on the name change as evidence of what they saw as the administration's anti-family attitude, and began to argue that the conference was just a smoke screen to legitimize the homosexual lifestyle.

The National Gay Task Force, backed by a liberal coalition of other cultural groups ranging from the American Red Cross to Catholic charity organizations, had sought to be included on the conference's national advisory committee. It had been rejected by the Carter administration, which also blocked the coalition's recommendation that gays be specifically listed as a "diverse" family form. But Jim Guy Tucker, the former Democratic representative from Arkansas who was chairman of the conference, had deflected the issue with a more general ruling that potential delegate candidates couldn't be discriminated against on the basis of their sexual orientation. In other words, homosexuals could be delegates, and when he went to explain the conference's objectives to Paul Weyrich's Library Court Group, a coalition of leaders and financiers of the religious right, that spring, Tucker found he had walked into a lion's den. The carriage house meeting room was crowded, and Connie Marshner, a Weyrich ally, asked Tucker what his definition of family was.

"What do you mean?" he replied.

"I want your definition of family," she said flatly. Was it the traditional one of people related by blood, marriage or adoption?

When Tucker said no, family structures were more varied than that, and suggested that a better description might be any two or more people living together with a commitment to each other's welfare, the meeting erupted. There was more trouble in store. In July, at the final session of the Conference on Families held in the Los Angeles Hilton Hotel ballroom, six hundred delegates voted to endorse the Equal Rights Amendment, the right to government-funded abortions and nondiscrimination against homosexuals in housing—an almost surreal ratification of the religious right's most extreme prophecies.

At a counterconference organized in Long Beach by the Moral Majority, seven thousand fervent Christians gathered at the Long Beach Arena to listen to such speakers as Republican Senator Jesse Helms of North Carolina, Phyllis Schlafly and Tim LaHaye, a strong Reagan supporter who had become president of Californians for Biblical Morality. LaHaye charged that "Jimmy Carter has falsely used his born-again image to hoodwink people into thinking he is one of us. The White House Conference in Los Angeles does not represent the more traditionalist viewpoint of the family, but instead favors the feminist and pro-homosexual viewpoints espoused by the liberal establishment." The conference delegates approved resolutions against the ERA and abortion and in favor of voluntary prayer in the schools, almost exactly as the Republican Platform Committee, pressured by Reagan supporters, had done the week before.

Carter's position grew more complicated as the general election progressed because of John B. Anderson, a ten-term Republican representative from Rockford, Illinois, who had failed to win the Republican nomination and was running as an independent. Liberal on cultural issues, Anderson was attractive to the young, and to people who found Carter's leadership dispiriting and Reagan too right-wing. Polls taken through the summer showed Anderson getting more than 20 percent of the vote. In April, Anderson had signed on as a co-sponsor of the gay rights bill in the U.S. House of Representatives. "If freedom under our Constitution is to have real meaning," he said, "this legislation is a natural extension of one's individual rights." Anderson, who was also a born-again Christian, came under considerable criticism from conservative Christians for his regular statements in support of gay rights, but he did not back off. "We believe that discrimination due to sexual orientation should not be tolerated by the federal government," he wrote in a letter to gay organizations. Endorsing the Cranston measure just as Carter had, he said, "An Anderson administration would work to repeal the section of the Naturalization and Immigration Laws which excludes individuals from immigrating solely on the grounds of sexual orientation." William Schneider, a Harvard professor and international affairs fellow at the Council on Foreign Relations, noted in a lengthy *Los Angeles Times* article on the rise of urban gay political power that Anderson "has sometimes been described as appealing to the 'new class' of young, upwardly mobile, well-educated professionals who are liberal on social issues but moderate to conservative on economic issues. If so, then gays may turn out to be a core constituency for him."

By contrast, the Republican platform had endorsed the anti-gay Family Protection Act introduced in Congress by Reagan's campaign director, Senator Paul Laxalt of Nevada. There were, for the first time, two openly gay delegates to the Republican National Convention, but there had been no testimony on the subject of gay rights before the GOP platform committee. Bastow considered the GOP platform, with its repeated references to the "sanctity of family," a disaster: "This is both a hopeful and dangerous time to be gay in America," he said at a dinner of the Association of Suburban People, a gay group. "There is a real danger of the Republican Party being taken over by people who don't think very much of our rights as gay people."

In the months until November, Jerry Falwell's Moral Majority and Gary Jarmin's Christian Voice printed and distributed to fundamentalist Christians a blizzard of leaflets and scorecards comparing the Democratic and Republican Party platform positions on homosexuality and other issues. And on the first Tuesday of November, Jimmy Carter, who had won the southern born-again vote and the South itself in 1976, lost all but Georgia and West Virginia to Ronald Reagan. Reagan got 51 percent of the national vote; Carter got 41 percent and Anderson 7 percent. Ginny Apuzzo, Tom Bastow and other gay leaders now saw that their attempt to make gays and lesbians a force in national politics had done something else: it had fed the conservative Christian movement that helped elect Ronald Reagan.

30

THE PINK INVITATION

December 1980, Washington, D.C.

Weeks before the inauguration of Ronald Reagan as president of the United States, an invitation went out to several hundred men in the District of Columbia and across the country. On it were scenes from old Reagan movies, one with the president-elect in football uniform as a lean young George Gipp ("The Gipper") of Notre Dame, another of him modeling a bathing suit and a third of Reagan at a close angle through a window, his face romantically framed, in the Hollywood style of the '40s, by the turned-up collar of his overcoat. The invitation was printed on pink paper, and it asked those who received it to a "Pre-Inaugural Ball," on Saturday, January 17, 1981, at the home of one of the most unusual figures in the political life of the nation's capital, Alan Baron. He was the only person in Washington who could have thrown such a party.

To many in Washington, the invitation might have seemed odd. Baron was one of the most famous liberal spirits in the Democratic Party. Why was he inviting a horde of men to commemorate the success of the Reagan Revolution? The 1980 election had ended not just Jimmy Carter's presidency but also the political careers of some of the most powerful liberal Democrats in the Senate—towering figures from the Midwest and West like George McGovern of South Dakota, Birch Bayh of Indiana, Frank Church of Idaho and Warren

Magnuson of Washington State, supporters of the ERA and of abortion rights, men to whom Steve Endean had looked as co-sponsors of the anti-discrimination bill that Paul Tsongas of Massachusetts had introduced in the Senate. Now they were gone: targeted with deadly precision by NCPAC, the New Right political action committee run by the gay, closeted Terry Dolan, and also by the populist lobbies of the religious right—Jerry Falwell's Moral Majority and the Christian Voice of Gary Jarmin. The Republicans had won back control not just of the White House but of the United States Senate for the first time in twenty-six years. The election had been a disaster for Democrats, but particularly so for the liberal wing of the Democratic Party, and Alan Baron was a fanatically liberal Democrat, a Jew from Sioux City, Iowa. He was also astute, and he had seen it coming: he had predicted that the Republicans might sweep the Senate.

A political prodigy from childhood—he had refused to go back to summer camp at age thirteen because the camp had no television, and he didn't want to miss seeing his hero, Adlai Stevenson, at the 1956 Democratic National Convention—Baron had grown into a short, pale, dumpy adult, a pudgy dervish with thick glasses, a mass of unruly hair—and an irrepressible personality. Manic, messy, spewing ideas and energy (and food, when eating) in all directions, Alan Baron was funny, endearing and ingenious at intuiting and dissecting the trend lines and folkways of politics. He had been a McGovern Democrat and the executive secretary of the Democratic National Committee in 1972, and he felt that Jimmy Carter was so phony—neither a true liberal nor a true Democrat—that he had led the "Anybody But Carter" movement within the party in 1976, even after it seemed evident that nobody but Carter would get the nomination, and even George McGovern had endorsed him. Baron's was a renegade movement and a stealthy one, as McGovern had discovered when he called his own Senate office late one night and heard Baron, his legislative assistant, answer the phone, "Anybody But Carter."

Fired by the embarrassed McGovern, Alan Baron started a political newsletter. Fed by his own obsessive curiosity, his sense of humor and an endless chain of telephone conversations, it was called *The Baron Report,* and by 1980 it was being widely read in the White House, in Congress, and throughout both the Democratic and Republican Parties. Alan Baron had become the capital's prime purveyor of political analysis and inside information, and something of an institution. Even his arrest for possession of cocaine in August 1979—a charge which the *Washington Post* treated as front-page news, and which was later dropped—did not interrupt his growing stature. Terrified that the arrest might destroy his career, Baron instead found a way to turn it to his advantage. The *Post* story had described him as the owner of "a monthly newsletter which is considered essential reading by both liberals and conservatives in Washington," and Baron simply put out a new brochure which quoted the paper.

He was a man with a wide range of close friends and admirers—from Senator Edward Kennedy of Massachusetts and the actor Warren Beatty on the Democratic left to the direct-mail wizard Richard Viguerie (an ally of Terry Dolan, Paul Weyrich and Jerry Falwell) on the New Right. The political columnists David Broder of the *Washington Post* and Al Hunt of the *Wall Street Journal* were friends. James Baker, the Reagan White House chief of staff, would become a regular poker-playing buddy in the years of the Reagan administration, along with Viguerie, the Republican consultant Roger Stone and Ken Bode, the television network political correspondent.

Brilliant, witty, loyal as a dog and physically unattractive, Baron was loved by his friends. Most of them knew that he used cocaine. Gossip about it was widespread, particularly after his arrest, and some people realized that his use was heavy. He snorted the powder regularly while writing his newsletter, and when his computer keys began to skip erratically and to jam in the early 1980s, a repairman was called to the townhouse on Independence Avenue that Baron used as office and home. He lifted the facing off the keyboard and found the cause of the problem. "There's something stuck in here," he said. "It's all—it's like some white powder."

But in those years cocaine was a staple drug on the disco scene and had become fashionable in circles of influence, too. There were plenty of other prominent Democrats and Republicans in town who used it—some of them with Baron—and Baron's abilities hadn't yet been noticeably affected by his habit. Ted Kennedy, whom Baron had advised in his 1980 campaign for the Democratic nomination, thought so highly of Baron that he asked him to take his nephew John F. Kennedy Jr. on as an intern. For a period of months one summer, the son of the late president worked as Baron's assistant in the townhouse on Independence Avenue, answering the phone, performing office chores, ordering out for pizza and Chinese, and clerking for *The Baron Report*.

Teddy Kennedy might have thought it odd to receive one of the pink Reaganesque invitations to Baron's "Pre-Inaugural Ball." But he wasn't on the list. Neither was Richard Viguerie, who would have found both the invitation and the crowd of hundreds of men jamming the halls, rooms and poolside of the townhouse that night a little strange. It was a roaring party—the kind where the kitchen floor and downstairs halls went muddy with spilled beer and melted ice, the bathrooms ran out of tissue paper, the air grew pungent with the scent of marijuana, and repeated runs had to be made to Schneider's, the liquor store on Capitol Hill. It was nonpartisan, with key Reagan advisers, other Republicans who would be working in the White House and administration, and more Democrats—members of Congress, congressional staffers, and political operatives, the same sort of people as the Republican guests.

As the invitation had hinted, it was a particular kind of crowd. The hosts were Alan Baron and Drew Breen—a name that meant nothing to Baron's political friends. But Breen was well known to Baron's gay friends as the lean, blondish, handsome young waiter who lived with him. And the striking thing about the party was the number of handsome young men circulating, a number of whom ended up late that night having sex in the upper rooms and a loft space at the top of the house.

Steve Endean was there, too. He had been determined in his pursuit of Alan Baron from the first time he saw him in a gay bar and realized who he was.* Endean wanted Baron for his access and his skills, and the director of the Gay Rights National Lobby had done his best to make Baron a friend of the cause. Baron, always receptive to new discoveries, found Endean and the movement fascinating. He was personally thrilled by it. He was also intensely nervous about being around someone so publicly homosexual, but the two men had begun to talk back and forth in the last months of 1980. Baron began to advise Endean. He included him in some of the small casual evenings of pizza and political talk that he held at his townhouse—the gay ones—and Baron had decided to invite Endean to the pre-inaugural party, even though he worried that his presence might scare off some of his closeted gay friends who were in Congress and other important positions around town.

Baron worried about what his traditional friends and colleagues would think if they knew he was gay, and made efforts to keep the different spheres of his life apart. His standing with his peers meant everything to him, so he had been tremendously touched and proud to be asked to take the martyred president's son as a temporary intern. He took the responsibility seriously and made sure that Ted Kennedy knew that. But the twenty-year-old John-John was as Hollywood handsome as Alan Baron was homely, and the compulsive Baron, tantalized by him, grew obsessed with finding out how big the young man's penis was. He eyed him when Kennedy came in from the rain or emerged from the townhouse pool in his underwear, but even with John Jr.'s casual ways, the sight eluded him.

The party was a kind of breakthrough, the first time so many politically involved gay men—young or old, Republican or Democrat, established and powerful or new in town—had all come together in one Washington salon, mixed together with a sprinkling of hip, mostly younger non-gay friends. It marked the emergence of Alan Baron's house as the center of gay political and intellectual life in the nation's capital as the Reagan years began—a place

* Alan Baron could not recall how he and Endean met, but said he did frequent Washington's gay bars. It seemed likely to friends of the two men that Baron and Endean had met that way.

where men who were gay and politically talented could meet each other and also politically prominent men who weren't gay, and where they could gossip and talk seriously to each other about politics, public policy and cultural issues. It was a salon and a kind of casual think tank.

When Steve Endean decided, in the wake of the 1980 election, that homosexuals needed to have their own national political action committee to give money to congressional candidates if they were to have any clout in Congress, he knew there was only one man in Washington who could help him. Endean decided to make a formal business appointment with Alan Baron at his townhouse.

As dark as the 1980 election results seemed for the cause of gay rights, it was a cloud with silver linings, too, and Steve Endean had only to look over the gay bar scene in Washington at night to find signs of progress in who was there and who was not. One face that had become a shadowy staple on the bar scene—the tense, tortured features of U.S. Representative Robert Bauman of Maryland, a leader of the right wing of the Republican Party—was gone. An arch-conservative, a self-righteous man, a devout Roman Catholic husband and father, and a bulldog combatant on the floor of the House, Bauman had been a founder of Young Americans for Freedom, chairman of the American Conservative Union and a champion of the pro-family rhetoric of the New Right. To be returned to office that November, as part of the vote which elected Ronald Reagan, would have been to share in the victory of an ideology he had helped to shape and nurture. But Bauman was also a man consumed by alcoholism and his own homosexual desires, and he had become a frequent presence at night at The Chesapeake House, a gay bar where lonely unattached or married men like Alan Baron and others went to watch the go-go boys take their clothes off. The dancers were usually available for hire, and young hustlers lined the bar. Starting in 1979, Bob Bauman had been buying sex from teenage male prostitutes, and a month before the general election in 1980 his furtive life collapsed on him. Bauman had been charged by the U.S. Attorney's Office in the District of Columbia with a criminal misdemeanor, soliciting for sexual purposes, and he pleaded guilty rather than face felony indictments. In a tense, painful news conference, the representative announced that he suffered from severe alcoholism and was receiving treatment, but that effort didn't begin to answer all the public questions raised by the charges. Much of the vote in his district—48 percent—stood by him in the election which followed. Some politicians, public figures and members of the press were charitable. Richard Nixon sent a private handwritten note of support. On television, Jerry Falwell spoke of "prayer and forgiveness." But Bauman's fellow Roman Catholics William Buckley Jr. and Paul Weyrich declared that he should resign his seat and positions in the conservative movement. The representative had "ordained standards of conduct which he himself transgressed," Buckley wrote sternly in his column. "It's not that I don't forgive him," Weyrich insisted to reporters at the National Press Club in Washington. "It's that he has brought dishonor to the movement in which he has been involved." Condemned as well by the *Salisbury Daily Times*, the main paper in his district, Bauman lost his seat, his career and his marriage.

But if the voters of Maryland had removed one kind of homosexual from the U.S. House, the voters of Massachusetts had added another, and on a night not long after Alan Baron's pre-inaugural party, Steve Endean took his friend Barney Frank, the newly minted—and at that moment, rather nervous—representative from the Fourth District of Massachusetts to the Lost and Found, the gay bar, for a drink. Frank had come to Congress in a roundabout way, courtesy of the Vatican, which had forced U.S. Representative Robert Drinan, Democrat of Massachusetts, to retire. Father Drinan, the liberal dean of Boston College Law School who had become well known as an anti–Vietnam War activist and as the first Roman Catholic priest ever elected to the U.S. House, had bowed the year before to the church's rule that its priests not run for elective office. Barney Frank had won his seat.

Frank, still closeted, came to Washington determined not to lead the kind of suffocating private life that he had imposed on himself as a state representative in Boston. Although a champion of gay rights in the Massachusetts legislature, he had hidden his own homosexuality from almost everyone. It left him feeling bottled up, and when Endean had made a trip to Boston for the Gay Rights National Lobby, Barney Frank had been so glad to meet an openly gay man involved in politics that he had confided to him in a men's room one day that he was, too. Endean, who had assumed that Frank was simply a northern Jewish liberal sponsoring the gay rights bill in Massachusetts out of principle, was astonished. It had never occurred to him that the fat, blowsy, brusque Barney Frank might be homosexual.

Frank's first deliberate act, between his election and swearing-in, was to have a candid conversation with the other closeted homosexual member of the Massachusetts congressional delegation. Gerry Studds, the hardworking bachelor representative from what was then the Twelfth District, which ranged from New Bedford through Martha's Vineyard, Nantucket and Cape Cod to Boston's suburbs on the south shore, had been elected in 1972, the same year that Frank had won a seat in the legislature. A liberal passionately opposed to the Vietnam War and a former prep school teacher, Studds had been pragmatic enough to learn Portuguese in order to campaign among the district's large population of fishermen. Once elected, he paid close attention to local maritime interests, even persuading Congress in his first term to pass a bill extending the U.S. territorial waters two hundred miles offshore. That kind of constituent service won him the deep loyalty of the working-class voters in his district. It also allowed him to take stands on political issues which seemed more distant and exotic—like co-sponsoring the gay rights bill in the House. Except for the pulsing gay presence in Provincetown, at the tip of Cape Cod, Studds's district was geographically removed from the fractious politics of gay life in Boston. He had no role in it, and it had none in his campaigns. Like Barney Frank, Studds permitted himself almost no gay life. Both men were intellectual, driven, socially awkward and defined by their work. Neither one knew how to relax. Neither of them really dated nor allowed himself the prospect of romance, and both of them had sex lives which were either austere or furtive, and bound to get them into trouble.

It was the kind of straitjacket existence from which each man would injure himself trying to escape in coming years. But in early 1981, Barney Frank and Gerry Studds still led lives constrained by what they thought were the rules required for political success. Each of them viewed gay life as a kind of minefield—dangerous, off limits and strange. Barney Frank, as the chief elected political supporter of gay rights at the State House, had the radar and gossip of the Boston gay community at his disposal, which was how he heard that Gerry Studds was gay.

It was some comfort to them to be honest with each other, but they each wanted more, and it was to Steve Endean—a role model, as far as Barney Frank was concerned—that the new representative from Massachusetts turned when he came to town. "I want to start living a life with other gay people. I can't be this totally repressed anymore," Frank said. Through Endean, he began to discover the hidden gay social life of Washington. It was a life in which Democrats and Republicans alike came together, to drink, to talk, to dance, to find out what they had in common and perhaps go home together. The next person at the bar might be a junior bureaucrat at the Commerce Department, an officer at the Pentagon, a Democratic representative or Robert Carter, the chairman of the Republican National Convention. It could be Dan Bradley, the Democratic head of the Legal Services Corporation. Or Terry Dolan, the right-wing Republican head of the National Conservative Political Action Committee. Or Dallas Coors.

To Barney Frank, who was discovering it for the first time at age forty—his birthday was that March—it seemed the kind of society he understood that Switzerland had been during the Second World War: where the opposing spies all recognized each other across the bars and tables of the clubs they all frequented at night, but treated each other neutrally, knowing that they all had to drink and eat, and get through the war. That first night with Endean, the new representative from Massachusetts met someone at the Lost and Found who was attuned to every nuance of the political moment. Steve Endean introduced them, and the overweight, unkempt Barney Frank found himself talking to the other sloppiest person at the bar, a pale, fast-talking, politically obsessed, partially closeted figure like himself, with his shirt blousing out of baggy pants, and a million stories to tell. It was Alan Baron.

Each knew immediately who the other one was. They had read and heard about each other, and been around each other at Democratic Party conferences. They were tickled to actually meet in the dim, fraternal, cloistered light of a gay bar. But Alan Baron was also appalled. "What are you taking him *there* for?" Baron demanded of Endean on the telephone later. "He's important to us and you'll get him in trouble. Don't *do* that!"

Jesus. He was just doing what Barney Frank had asked him to do, Endean replied. But he was glad to hear Alan Baron use the word "us." Steve Endean had an idea in mind, something that had been discussed in gay rights circles for a year or more, and Alan Baron could be important to it. The movement had been successful, through the Campaign Project, in electing enough delegates to the Democratic convention to get a gay rights plank in the Democratic Party platform. But the Republican Right had organized national and local political action committees to knock off gay-friendly Democratic officeholders before the party's newly stated policy could begin to do the movement any good. Clearly, gays and lesbians needed to learn and copy Republican campaign techniques, and Endean had asked Larry Bye, his old friend from Minnesota and an experienced political organizer, to work up a plan for a new organization.

Endean wanted a national political committee that could be as effective for the cause in Washington as MECLA had been in Los Angeles and California. By law and structure, the Gay Rights National Lobby could raise money from its own membership for the purpose of lobbying and educating politicians, but it couldn't raise or spend money on political campaigns.

Endean wanted something modeled on MECLA, but he wasn't comfortable in Los Angeles. The gay scene there, and in particular the MECLA crowd, was too monied, slick and glamorous for his midwestern ways. With his lusterless brown hair, pale skin and increasingly blocky body, Endean found the lean, tan, beautiful men of Los Angeles intimidating. They made him feel like a bowling pin, he would say. As much as he had despised the late Harvey Milk, Endean was much more at home with the gritty style and populist street politics of San Francisco, and with the scale of the city itself. Even his dislike of Jim Foster, the reigning gay political power broker there, and Foster's closeness to David Goodstein couldn't sour him on San Francisco. Besides, he would need the support of both of those men for his plan. Larry Bye had come to know them well, and Kerry Woodward, who had moved from Minnesota to Oakland, across the bay. Like Endean and Bye, she had fled Minnesota after the St. Paul Repeal. She could be useful, too.

• • •

Endean flew out to San Francisco several times after the 1980 election. Larry Bye had proposed a new group to be called the Human Rights Campaign Fund, which would be built in two ways: by using targeted mass-mail techniques to create a national list of donors; and by holding a series of black-tie fundraising dinners in key cities across the country, to raise money for the congressional campaigns of 1982. If the New Right had shown what it could do in 1980, the gay rights movement would try to strut its stuff in the next go-around. There wasn't much time, and money was crucial. In the 1970s, money and other substantial campaign support had come mainly from the gay male sex industry, from men like Herman L. Womack, the porno publisher; Jack Campbell, the bath baron, and Sheldon Andelson. But there were other wealthy gay men in San Francisco. Many of them, Endean knew, clustered in a kind of small galaxy around *Advocate* publisher David Goodstein, who had drawn them in through the Advocate Experience. But one person who found Goodstein as arrogant and abrasive as Endean did was a man of inherited wealth, who might be willing to contribute to a cause that gay men from wealthy families had always been afraid to claim.

James C. Hormel was from Minnesota originally, from the Hormel meat-packing family. Like Dallas Coors, he was a man whose grandfather had created a family fortune, and he had grown up on a 200-acre estate, closely shielded by chauffeurs and bodyguards for years after the kidnapping of the Lindbergh baby. He had become a Republican, a married man with five children, a graduate of Swarthmore College and the University of Chicago Law School. He was the youngest dean of students in the law school's history, hired by Edward H. Levi, the law school dean and later attorney general of the United States. But Jim Hormel had left his wife and his traditional life at the end of the 1960s, moving first to New York and then to Hawaii, sorting out his life. In 1976 he had come back to the mainland and settled in San Francisco with a young artist who was his lover, and had begun to get involved in gay causes.

Tall, thoughtful and quietly aristocratic, he had class, brains and money. He might lead them to more of the same. At a meeting in Jim Foster's roomy big Victorian flat in San Francisco, Endean, Bye and Foster showed Hormel the analysis Larry Bye had done of other PACs, and described the one they had in mind. The seed money for the new organization would come from just a handful of angels, each of whom would give an initial $5,000. One was Jim Hormel. One was David Goodstein. And one—the lone Republican—was the conservative Dallas Coors.

Endean had met Coors, who lived in Washington with his lover, at the Lost and Found, and had actively courted him, inviting him to the tiny office of the Gay Rights National Lobby. Coors was no rebel. He was a banker, with a banker's personality, a man of inherited wealth from a family of notoriously conservative politics, a traditionalist and a bit of a snob. But he had money, a name famously synonymous with resistance to gay rights, and he was Republican—all of which appealed enormously to Steve Endean's sense of strategy and humor. He did what he could to flatter and soften Coors up, and then left it to that other gay millionaire, David Goodstein, to put the arm on him. Endean knew he would need Goodstein's personal and editorial support, and Coors was one of Goodstein's first conquests. The publisher flew into Washington and took Coors to lunch at the Eagle one day, and persuaded him to join the new PAC. Coors became the token Republican on the board—proof of the Campaign Fund's claim that it was not a partisan organization.

The new group's fundraising strategy, its officers and board of directors were all approved at a meeting in Washington that summer, by Goodstein, Hormel, Endean, Bye, Jim Foster, Jack Campbell and others. Kerry Woodward and Jerry Berg, an activist San Francisco lawyer close to both Hormel and Goodstein, would be the co-chairs of the board. Endean would be the executive director. He would still run GRNL as well, and it was clear that this new PAC was not a group in which membership would have a voice. Endean packed the board of directors with his friends and supporters, some of whom—like Jack Campbell and Ginny Apuzzo—were also on the board of GRNL. Having drawn David Goodstein into the core of the group—but not onto its board—Endean had done his best to insulate himself from Goodstein's urge to control whatever he touched.

At the PAC's first meeting, they had agreed to do the direct mailing and to mount the black-tie dinners. Jim Foster was hired as a consultant, under contract to organize the dinners and make the ticket sales a success. Having the tall, charming Foster, the best-known gay personality in the Democratic Party, in charge of the highly visible social end of the project pleased Goodstein—and Endean, too, because he thought it would keep him and Foster apart.

The first order of business was the mailing. Only two substantial lists of contributors had ever been compiled, and Endean had worked on each: those who gave to the fight against Anita Bryant in Dade County in 1977, and those who donated to the Tri-City Defense Fund for St. Paul, Wichita and Eugene in 1978. But there was no standing national list of political givers. And no one had ever sent a letter nationwide to people who might be moved to give. No one had any idea how to write such a letter or who might sign it.

Alan Baron, Steve Endean thought, would know how to do those things.

Baron's tutor in the evolving art of direct mail was his close friend Roger Craver, head of the preeminent Democratic consulting firm of Craver, Matthews, Smith. Craver often passed on work to Baron, who wrote direct-mail letters for some of Craver's top clients. Although Baron had never done anything professionally for the cause of gay rights, his interest in the movement had grown. He had gone to see the March on Washington in 1979, watching excitedly as thousands of lesbians and gay men from around the country had passed by the White House. In the drift of the crowd afterward, a friend had hailed him and introduced him to a pert, ginger-haired former Eagle Scout, a young lobbyist for the Kellogg cereals company in town for the weekend named Gregory King. They met again at dinner at someone's house a few months later, and Baron encouraged him to move to Washington from Battle Creek, Michigan. They could find him a job, Baron said.

When Gregory King moved in 1981, he became one of a network of politically interested young men whom Alan Baron helped to train and employ in the nation's capital. A series of them—usually handsome, talented and gay—he employed or mentored in his office, a pattern that some of Baron's other friends had noticed. Alan Baron helped some of his assistants build careers in politics, but some of those relationships were also at least casually sexual.

One was with Sean Strub, a lean Irish Roman Catholic youth from Iowa, with dark, beguiling eyes and the face of a fawn. The son of a prominent merchandising family in Iowa City, Strub was smart, driven and politically ambitious, and he had persuaded Senator Dick Clark of Iowa to get him a job as an elevator operator in the Capitol, and had wangled the number one car on the Senate side, which stopped closest to the Senate chamber, the majority leader's office and the Senate dining room. By day he took senators like Gary Hart, Ted Kennedy, John Glenn and Edmund Muskie up and down, trading pleasantries and jokes and even books to read, and one night, out browsing the bars, he had met Alan Baron in the Lost and Found. Baron took Sean Strub to the Democratic midterm convention in Memphis in 1978, and one evening, to dinner with a group that included David Broder of the *Washington Post*. Baron, self-conscious about his relationship with Strub, knew that a Democratic Party boss would also be at the table with an attractive young man he had brought with him. Baron worried that the straitlaced Broder would notice a pattern, and wonder why he was traveling around with a young man who looked like Donny Osmond. But Strub was eager to meet David Broder, and nervous or not, Baron took him to dinner.

Alan Baron worried when the segregated parts of his life overlapped in that way. But his subsequent arrest—and all the attention paid to it—had left him feeling somewhat liberated, perhaps even immunized. By the spring of 1981, he had become a germinal influence in American politics and in the Washington gay community. And if he had never used his political expertise or party contacts to do anything for gay rights, it was at least in part because no one had ever asked him to. When Steve Endean came to see him, to ask that he create the fundraising letter and mailing list for a new national gay PAC, Baron, intrigued, agreed. He even agreed to raise the money to fund the mailing, about $10,000. It was a challenge. It was also anonymous work. Alan Baron's name would be nowhere on it.

But it was a dicey proposition. The letter would go out to people who weren't expecting it, who might have given nothing to gay rights before, who knew nothing about this new group called the Human Rights Campaign Fund and yet would be asked to give money to it. The psychology was crucial. Nothing about the project should scare off potential donors. Endean wanted the broadest possible base of support, which was why once again the word "gay" wasn't even in the organizational name. But Alan Baron, who understood the manipulative craft of direct mail and the broader lessons of the election just held, thought the name Human Rights Campaign Fund was a dud. In the mind of the electorate, he knew, "human rights" was a liberal theme associated with Jimmy Carter, a failed and rejected president. It was a conservative tide that had swept through the 1980 election, and its lesson, Baron thought, was that people weren't worried about the rights of others. So, as Baron began to phrase the letter, with some help from Strub and Roger Craver, he didn't speak at first of "human rights." Instead, he talked about "the *threat to our personal rights* posed by the Religious New Right and the moral majoritarians.

"I'm writing to seek your help for **PRIVACY RIGHTS '82**, a new political action project designed to *protect your rights* from invasion by the self-righteous moralists," he wrote.

"Not since the blacklisting in the entertainment industry in the 1950's has there been as potent a threat to individual rights as exists in America today." He went on for five pages, choosing his phrases and underlinings with great care. He did not mention the word "homosexual" until page 2, or the name Human Rights Campaign Fund until page 4 of the text.

He hinted at a war for survival, in which the enemy was an ancient religious intolerance newly empowered by modern technology: "our enemies—*I don't think enemy is too strong a word for people who advocate the death penalty for homosexuals*—have powers their predecessors could not imagine. Today's New Right leaders *reach* tens of millions of people via electronic broadcasting . . . *raise* hundreds of millions of dollars through computerized fund-raising techniques . . . and *recruit* high-caliber, highly paid pollsters and public relations experts to shape their messages and images."

It was an intimidating force he described, yet one which could be faced down and even beaten if people would back decent public servants willing to make a stand. Baron told the story of U.S. Representative James Weaver of Eugene, Oregon, a state that had turned Republican in recent years. Even in liberal Eugene, the home of the University of Oregon, the voters had overturned a gay rights ordinance by a margin of 61 to 39 percent in May 1978.

When Representative Weaver agreed, despite that vote, to co-sponsor the national gay rights bill in the U.S. House of Representatives in 1979, Baron wrote, "Weaver was targeted for defeat." He was outspent by $133,000, denounced in churches on Sunday mornings as "anti-Christian" and "anti-family."

"If anybody should have gone down to defeat with Jimmy Carter in 1980, it was Weaver," Baron quoted an unnamed Democratic Party strategist as saying.

"But Weaver didn't lose." He was helped by environmentalists, who appreciated his standing up to the timber industry, but he was also helped with money and hundreds of volunteers by a new group, *something called the Human Rights Campaign Fund,*" and he won by as big a margin as in 1978.

The lesson was that homosexuals could help politicians who helped them, and that politicians who stood up for gay rights could win—even against a force as frightening as the religious right. To Steve Endean, the Weaver case was a very personal issue. It was Endean who had talked Jim Weaver into signing on as a co-sponsor of the gay rights bill in 1979, as part of an effort to demonstrate that politicians in the cities that had overturned gay rights ordinances were still willing to support the movement. But only Weaver and Representative William Lehman of Miami had been willing to do that, and when Weaver was attacked for it in his reelection campaign, Endean had steered as much money as he could to him, mainly through individual donations, perhaps $10,000 in all.

The task in 1982 would be to do for gay-friendly candidates across the country what gay money and support had done for Jim Weaver in Eugene. Politicians willing to be supportive had to know that meaningful support existed for them, too. "To build an effective political action committee," Baron wrote, "we need to raise $500,000 during the next twelve months."

And here he had to make the pitch. Endean believed in the power of endorsements, and he had gotten a scattering of political and cultural leaders across the country to lend their names. "I hope you will join me—and such other Americans as Joel Wachs, the Republican President of the Los Angeles City Council; Donald Fraser, the Democratic Mayor of Minneapolis; Otis Charles, the Episcopal Bishop of Utah; Dr. John Spiegel, the former President of the American Psychiatric Association; Julian Bond, the Georgia State Senator and black leader; and Gloria Steinem, the Publisher of *Ms.* and leading feminist—in our effort to stop the threat to our individual rights posed by the militant moralists," the letter concluded.

"The stakes are simply too high for all of us—indeed for any of us—to delay.

"Please take this courageous step and let me hear from you today."

"Sincerely yours,"

The signature line was blank.

Who should sign it? Who *would* sign it? Not Alan Baron. Not Steve Endean, Baron said. If the letter was to have any impact, it needed to come from someone famous, someone admired, some public figure who would be taking a risk by signing it. Someone gay—but not threatening to heterosexual liberals who might be willing to contribute.

They could think of no one famous, no one admired in the whole broad American culture who admitted to being gay.

As they wrestled with the question of who should sign the letter—and who might be willing to—Baron and Endean cobbled together a list of people to receive it. David Goodstein would not share or sell *The Advocate*'s national subscriber list—arguably the best list in the country of people interested in gay issues and events—but Endean still had access to the two contributor lists he had helped create. To those names, he and Baron added others they got from some straight liberal donor lists, from gay papers in some of the major cities, and they bought lists from publishers of some of the gay porno magazines. All combined, it made a motley and uneven collection of thousands of names, but it was a start.

Over Chinese dinners at the kitchen table downstairs in Alan Baron's house one night, as Baron and Steve Endean and a group of others sat trying to figure out whose name should be on the letter, Gregory King said they ought to ask Gore Vidal. He was toweringly famous and politically well connected. He had written one of the first novels with a frankly homosexual theme to be printed by a major American publisher. He wrote extensively about American cultural politics. And everyone assumed he was gay. But none of them knew Vidal. And then Sean Strub had an idea. "Well, what about Tennessee Williams?" he said. Like Gore Vidal, Williams was legendary, lionized and widely assumed to be gay. But he had never done anything publicly for gay rights that anyone knew of. He was also infamously alcoholic and unreliable. But Strub was insistent. "Let me see if I can get Tennessee Williams," he said.

Strub had met the playwright at a party in Washington, and Williams, who had been a college student in Iowa City, where Sean Strub's grandfather had owned Strub's Department Store, recognized the name. "I'm going to have to buy you a drink sometime, baby," he said. "I left town owing your grandfather's store some money."

Strub smiled and batted his long lashes. "Well," he said, "sometime when I'm down in Key West, I'll come collect it."

"Sure—you call me, baby," Williams told him. The memories of Iowa City seemed to warm him. He had lost his virginity there, on North Dubuque Street, he said. Like Alan Baron and innumerable others, Tennessee Williams was taken with Sean Strub. And Strub, Alan Baron knew, was good at getting what he wanted. He had charmed United States senators and captivated Baron. He had sat for hours with the Democratic direct-mail wizard, Roger Craver, at Alan Baron's house one night, making notes on napkins as he got Craver to explain how direct mail worked. He was full of energy, and he wanted to be involved.

Strub, Alan Baron thought, could talk his way into anything. He was cute enough to get Tennessee Williams's time and attention. And he might be willing to go to bed with Williams to get him to sign the letter. If Strub could get Tennessee Williams to sign the letter, Alan Baron said, he would buy the young man's plane ticket to Key West.

Since the first time he made love—with someone who caught his eye walking in Georgetown one night—sex for Sean Strub had been a bowl of candies. He went to bed with cute boys he met in bars. He went to bed with cute hustlers he met in bars or on the street. He went to bed with middle-aged men—married and unmarried—whom he met at bars or at Democratic Party conferences or dinners or anywhere else. He went to bed in Washington and New York, Kentucky, Iowa, anywhere he found pleasure and opportunity. He considered himself a late bloomer. He had been active for only five years, since 1976, but they had been the most sexually charged five years of gay male life in American history.

He was just twenty-three years old, and he was ambitious, talented and entrepreneurial, a self-starter, a boy who had always had big dreams and projects. He had long wanted to run for public office. He thought someday he might be president, so when he had met Steve Endean, part of Strub's reaction, in addition to awe, was fear and also pity at being around someone who was ruining whatever political future he might have had by being so publicly involved in gay rights.

Yet even if the public nature of the gay rights movement scared Sean Strub, it fascinated and thrilled him, too. And the letter had given him a part to play, a role that would matter to history in a way that getting close to Democratic Party officials or consultants in New York or Washington never would. If he could get Tennessee Williams to sign the letter, Steve Endean told him, it would bring in money to influence Congress. Williams became Strub's goal. He wrote once, twice, to the elusive playwright, and in the early summer of 1981, Strub, by now working at the state Democratic headquarters in Kentucky, met Tennessee Williams in New York, at Williams's suite at the Elysée Hotel. He had the letter Alan Baron had written in his pocket, ready for Williams's signature. It was two o'clock, late enough in the day so that he could be reasonably sure that Williams would be drinking, but early enough,

Strub hoped, that he wouldn't be drunk yet—and that Williams wouldn't expect him to stay the night. He didn't want to have to go to bed with Tennessee Williams, but if that's what it took, he thought, he might.

The door opened, and Williams stood looking at him with a grizzled smile. He had three or four days' growth of beard, and a glass in his hand.

They kissed, a casual hello, and settled themselves and began to chat, and after a bit Strub told him why he had come. He showed Williams the letter and explained that he thought bringing it to him was the most important thing he had ever done in his life. Williams put on his glasses to read it, and they talked about Endean and this new PAC. Sitting at the bar in his room, refilling his glass from a thermos, his round, worn, flushed face tilted down toward the letter in his hand, Williams seemed interested, and when Sean Strub told him how much his signature might be worth—a quarter of a million dollars, he said, just making it up—the playwright seemed amused.

"What would you do for it?" he asked, his eyes glinting at Strub. He was joking, Sean Strub thought, but only on the surface. "Almost anything, but I hope I don't have to," he said quietly, looking back at the decaying playwright.

In a moment, Williams laid the letter aside and started talking about his new work, *Clothes for a Summer Hotel,* and the director. Sean Strub knew nothing about New York theater or about this play, but he had a small black feeling inside that grew and spread as half an hour, and then an hour, and then an hour and a half slipped by, and Williams said nothing more about the letter. Strub kept smiling and laughing as Williams talked, but he knew an important moment had passed, and after two and a half hours it was time to go. Williams had an engagement, and Strub rose and turned leadenly toward the door. He had never felt worse.

Tennessee Williams picked up the letter and waved it at him. "Baby," he said, "don't you want your signature?"

His first signature was so sloppy that Sean Strub turned the letter over and got him to sign it again. "The lawyers are going to kill me," Williams said, as he wrote in a big, careful slant. "The lawyers are going to kill me."

From a telephone booth on the street Strub called Alan Baron. "I got it," he said. "I got it." He realized he was crying. The letter, with its call to arms against the fundamentalists, could go out. The gay rights movement and the religious right were joined now in a battle for understanding and public support that would continue through the 1980s and beyond.

31

UNTIL
THE PARTY ENDED

September 1980, New York

By the start of September 1980, with opening night just three Saturdays away, Bruce Mailman was still worrying about how much his gay discotheque in New York's East Village was really going to cost. Here he was, constructing what would almost certainly be the most technologically extravagant and costly dance club anywhere, and he was looking for any way he could to save a dollar. Even as Mailman was signing off on his designer's request for 1,500 spotlights, and for dramatic sloped runways so the men who would flock there could make a grand entrance up onto the second-level dance floor, he searched the country for secondhand air-conditioning units that might cool this huge shell of a theater. All of this was perfectly in character for Bruce Mailman, a man barely five feet five inches, balding and thin as a pencil. He was now involved in the most extravagant project in a life of extravagant projects. Since arriving in New York from Chester, Pennsylvania, in 1961, Mailman had bought and designed a half-dozen small theaters, produced five Off-Broadway shows, made a small fortune on real estate investments and sold contemporary art. Mailman's most recent project had been to renovate the New St. Marks Baths, a gay bathhouse also in the East Village that was unlike any in New York, or most of the country: five stories of cubicles and steam rooms and hot tubs, well lit and sparkling clean, with a restaurant and a video lounge, and unlimited supplies of clean towels, combs and razors. Its design was an argument that even a sex club could be fashionable. Still, there was no question what the New St. Marks Baths was about: Mailman liked to call it a sex factory. It was designed to keep men walking in a constant flow, from floor to floor, from stairway to stairway, from cubicle to cubicle, stopping for sex along the way—a carnal conveyor belt. There weren't many rules at the New St. Marks Baths, but one of them was that no music could be played on the top three floors, where the cubicles were. The only music Mailman wanted was the sound of men having sex.

The New St. Marks Baths had been expensive and ambitious, but it was dwarfed by what Mailman was now building in the abandoned theater at 105 Second Avenue at Sixth Street. The building had been home to a Yiddish theater troupe, then the Loews Commodore and finally Bill Graham's Fillmore East. Now, as the building once again changed with the times, it was about to become a discotheque for homosexual men, and Mailman had named it The Saint.

From the moment Mailman decided to build a gay dance palace, he had searched for a way to combine the secret and thriving, late-night primitive ecstasy of the male gay dance clubs—places like Flamingo and 12 West—with the drama and flash-bulb glamour of the grand theatrical dance clubs, like Studio 54. His solution was a dance floor built under a hemispheric dome, reflecting constellations and lighting effects beamed from below—like the Hayden Planetarium, only bigger. Much bigger. For this to work, the dance floor would have to be huge—an 80-foot circle, he calculated. The abandoned Fillmore East was the only place Mailman saw that could contain his idea. The renovation had taken nearly a year, and as opening night approached it was the talk in the circles Mailman wanted it to be the talk in, the wealthy gay men of New York who summered in Fire Island and enjoyed nothing so much as having fun, no matter what the cost. Their interest was piqued by Mailman's decision to establish The Saint as a private membership club, whose announcement took the form not of an advertisement but of a personalized invitation, made of the folded architectural plans of the dome and the building, describing the gay dance experience in mystical terms: *"Since the beginning of recorded history the male members of the species have joined together in ritual dance. Adorned, semi-naked with rhythm instruments, they used this tribal rite to celebrate their Gods and themselves. The Saint has been created to perform the mystery—to continue the rite."* It was mailed only to Mailman's friends and their friends, a self-selected group that formed the base of The Saint's membership of three thousand. Anyone who wanted to join had to be referred by a member to the membership office for screening. The clientele reflected the screening process: nearly all white, professionals in their twenties and thirties, mostly good-looking and muscled, with the mustaches and short hair that were the style of the time. By appearance, Mailman did not qualify for membership in this group. He knew this, or if he didn't, he would be reminded of it during his occasional waits at the ropes of Studio 54. Mailman was not the kind of man these clubs tended to welcome: He was too old, too small, too ethnic. And even though he tried to distinguish himself—he dyed his hair and mustache blond, or shaved his head—he was still a forty-one-year-old Jewish businessman from the East Village. Jack Stoddard, the day manager of the New St. Marks Baths and then a manager at The Saint, came to believe that one of the reasons Mailman built his own disco was because of his nights at the ropes of Studio 54. The ropes at The Saint were its membership list, which Bruce Mailman had approved.

Mailman had told his financial backers that the entire project would cost $2 million. In the end, as Mailman learned on opening night, the cost had come to $4.6 million. It was a lot of money to spend on a party, but Mailman and his backers had a lot of money, as did the nearly four thousand men who showed up on opening night, September 20, 1980, in blue jeans, T-shirts and leather bomber jackets, forming a line that by 3 a.m. curled north up Second Avenue, west one block over on Seventh Street and then south again on the other side of the block. They had paid up to $150 to join the club (the fee was higher for those who rented a locker) and would pay up to $30 for an evening's admission. The Saint didn't even have a bar since the people who went there weren't particularly interested in drinking alcohol.

From the first night, there was no argument that Bruce Mailman and his backers had gotten their money's worth. The dome was as breathtaking as Mailman had hoped. It was seventy-six feet across, constructed of perforated aluminum, a theatrical scrim that was opaque to reflect the lights aimed at it from underneath and transparent when the lights dimmed, allowing the dancers to make out the black walls of the theater that surrounded them, while the viewers in the balcony could watch the silhouettes of dancers below them. The dance floor was 4,800 square feet, oak laid atop rubber insulation pads for comfort, designed without pillars, walls or any other obstructions or any points of reference. At the center was a platform mounted on a double-hydraulic lift, which held the star field projector. The star machine alone cost $96,000; it was usually not powered up, from a switch in the control booth on one side of the floor, until well after 4 a.m., when the dancers would cheer the spinning constellations that floated above their heads. There was a trapdoor at the top of the dome, which opened to allow a three-foot mirrored ball to drop slowly down, reflecting the 1,500 colored spotlights riveted to the platform below and embedded behind sliding panels across the curvature of the dome. The sound system was no less elaborate: 500 speakers, powered by 630 drivers and 32 amplifiers, 26,000 watts in all. "The outcome is not unlike the fantasy of space travel," The Saint declared in a brochure boasting of its accomplishments. "It takes thousands of dancers into a new dimension of sound and light . . . leaving the imagination in charge of the physical being. To the reader, this might appear mere rhetoric; to the dancer, this is serious business." Indeed, The Saint's producers were quite serious about their creation; they searched through years of history to find an edifice with which to compare it in their advertisement, settling finally on the Pantheon, the circular Roman temple constructed about 2,007 years before The Saint opened its doors.

For Mailman and the thousands of people who came that first Saturday night, and kept coming until the club closed for the summer and the patrons moved the party to Fire Island, The Saint was not just another gay disco. This was a temple, a "religious experience," as Mailman said. It was also a place that celebrated—and, in fact, quickly came to epitomize—the tribal culture of dance, sex and drugs that was defining much of gay male life in New York, San Francisco and Los Angeles as the 1980s began. Mailman stayed until closing on opening night, which didn't come until noon on Sunday—"Go until the party ended" was The Saint creed—and as night turned into morning, the patrons, dazed and bleary-eyed, pulled him aside to thank him. But Mailman wasn't happy. He couldn't help thinking about the money that had been spent on all this technology, light and sound, and even felt vaguely embarrassed at the excess of it. But Mailman was there every weekend, one of close to five thousand gay men in New York—Saint members and their guests—who would awaken from a nap every Sunday at 2 a.m. and head for the unmarked entrance on Second Avenue—a door slightly ajar, lit by a single bulb, with no sign. It was hidden, by design, to protect the secret world beyond, up the grand flight of steps at the end of the half-block-long lobby.

December 1980, San Francisco

Arthur Evans's mood turned dark as he watched the men of the Castro welcome in the 1980s with what seemed to be their own unending party. The streets of San Francisco offered, in theory at least, a cross section of America's male homosexual community, but, Evans thought, one would never know it to walk down Castro Street. All these men looked identical, with their short haircuts, clipped mustaches and muscular bodies, turned out in standard-issue uniforms of tight, faded blue jeans and polo shirts. The image was one part military, one part cowboy, one part 1950s suburbia and conformity, and they swaggered down the street, many aloof and unfriendly, as if their affected distance enhanced their masculinity. These were not the gay men Arthur Evans had encountered in San Francisco in the early 1970s. They certainly were not the gay men he had met at his first Gay Liberation Front meeting in a church in New York in 1969, or at the Gay Activists Alliance. These men had no inkling of gay liberation, he thought; and, by all appearances, very little notion of oppression, at least now that they had escaped their hometowns for the gay life of San Francisco. Gay liberation had somehow evolved into the right to have a good time—the right to enjoy bars, discos, drugs and frequent impersonal sex. A whole industry was sprouting from and glorifying this male culture, with clothing stores like All American Boy on Castro Street, a gym called Body Works, and dozens of sex clubs and baths, with names like Animals. The sex clubs catered to every imaginable sexual taste: the leather set; men who enjoyed being tied up; men who wished to be urinated on. The bathhouses had once been seen as an expression of gay liberation, at least among those who equated gay liberation with sexual abandon. Now, they were celebrating and enforcing the values that Evans saw parading down the Castro every day: The premium was put on physical appearance and conformity. Indeed, proof of that came from a spat between the manager of Club San Francisco Baths and his lover, who stole a copy of the baths' "86" list—a file with written documentation of those barred from entry and why. There was the "fat queen," the "nasty queen," the "very fat toad," not to mention the man who was "chubby" and the one who was "not well-built"; there was the black man described as having a bushy Afro. Evans's days of political activism were largely behind him, but the list inspired him to picket briefly in front of the baths at Eighth and Howard, until the club's management terminated its door policy. In truth, these standards were clearly in play at all the big bathhouses, from Sheldon Andelson's 8709 bathhouses in L.A. to Bruce Mailman's New St. Marks bathhouse in New York. The sex clubs catered to their clientele, even if that meant that gay men were now discriminating against gay men.

San Francisco did not have a Saint, but the West Coast version of the patrons was catered to by promoters who arranged one-night parties in different venues that were just as elaborate. They rented huge spaces, malls and open-aired piers, and spent up to $25,000 to produce one-night parties with names like The Mothership Arrives, during which the forty-foot skylight at the top of the five-level Galleria design center opened in the middle of the night to reveal a giant spaceship, with landing lights, descending over the audience below. Another of these parties was called Let It Snow, and the dancers were sprinkled with artificial snow strewn from the balconies above. It was a not very inside joke about what was going on in virtually every dark corner of the place, as even *The Advocate* noted when it printed a picture of the party: "Artificial snowflakes weren't the only white stuff dropped." Indeed, this crowd was able to keep going all night and into the morning—and to "lose themselves" in the music and the men, as Bruce Mailman had said of his Saint patrons—in large part because they consumed a medicine chest worth of drugs: cocaine, quaaludes, speed, MDA, angel dust, poppers, marijuana and LSD. Sex was just as plentiful. Randy Shilts, who had left *The Advocate* and was writing a biography of Harvey Milk, adored these parties, but even he was taken aback at the public displays of sexual intercourse. There would be thousands of men dancing, and next to them, in the plain light, clusters of men engaged openly in sex. It reminded Shilts of a Fellini movie.

Some thought that the excesses were evidence of the vitality of a coalescing gay colony. For Randy Shilts, who considered the Castro particularly inspiring, it set the standard for gay liberation. Arthur Evans saw not style or ideology, however, but a complete absence of political awareness for which, he concluded, he deserved some blame. The GAA and the hundreds of gay organizations it had inspired had changed the way homosexuals lived in parts of America—openly, in self-sufficient gay ghettos. Gay night life was no longer defined by the Mafia and overpriced drinks, but it was just as maddeningly centered around the bars and the baths, at least for men. The early gay activists could certainly claim much of the credit for the new openness. But Evans saw the real beneficiaries of this change as the baths, clothing stores, discos and bars. For Evans, as morose as at any time since he came out, the Castro was a depressing wasteland, and gay liberation a testosterone cult. He turned again to posting leaflets around the Castro. "Afraid You're Not Butch Enough?" Evans scrawled across the top of the first one. He advised readers to bulk up at the "Zombie Works" (as opposed to Body Works) and to buy their uniforms at "All American Clone" (as opposed to All American Boy). "After just a few weeks at the Zombie Works, you'll look just like everyone else on Castro Street. No more anxiety over being an individual! Now you'll blend in and look like you came from the same mold as everybody else." Evans made hundreds of fliers, sticking them to poles and signs with a powerful glue made from condensed milk and wheat powder. And when gay men tore them down after seeing themselves mocked as "clones," Evans just slapped up more.

There was a new confidence among the men under the dome of The Saint and in the streets of the Castro. Anita Bryant had won in Dade County, but gay organizers in California had defeated Briggs, and many homosexuals had come out in the past few years, to no obvious ill effect, a vindication of the contention of New York activists at the start of the 1970s—and David Goodstein's Advocate Experience—that coming out was the key to power. But with the new confidence came complacency, and the energy that had once gone into marches and organizing was now being channeled into pure pleasure. Where lesbian separatists had founded a political movement, the men of the Castro were largely avoiding any organizing, at least beyond sex parties and dances. There was no gay political organization in the country that could match the Saturday-night turnout at The Saint. There were waiting lists of men wishing to purchase a $150-a-year Saint membership, while in Washington the Gay Rights National Lobby was struggling to pay its postage. In the Castro, Harvey Milk's murder had not unified the gay men whose political energy he had represented; instead, it had created a vacuum with ramifications for at least a decade. The closest The Saint came to being political then was Bruce Mailman's refusal to allow entry to heterosexual couples. He would discriminate against heterosexuals, Mailman vowed, as long as New York City refused to bar discrimination against homosexuals. But The Saint also included in its official membership rules severe restrictions on the admission of women—straight or lesbian. "THE SAINT is a private club for men. . . . Male members wishing to bring women guests must receive permission from the Membership Office prior to any given event at THE SAINT. *Under no circumstances will women guests of male members be permitted in the club on Saturday nights.* In addition, female guests should be reminded that high heels are inappropriate and that pants and T-shirts are in keeping with the style of the club." There was no equivalent written rule when it came to blacks, but considering that the only way to get a membership was through a referral by another member, there was no need for one, and the white faces on the dance floor were testimony to the result.

Evans was not alone in his misgivings. Bruce Voeller had left the National Gay Task Force, complaining, among other things, about the lack of support, financial or otherwise, from the men he was working to help. David Goodstein scolded *Advocate* readers for their behavior, even as his newspaper harvested profits with editions dedicated to "The Gay Pursuit of Muscle" and advertisements for places like New York's East Side Sauna. The publisher took despondent note of the "headlong pursuit of anonymous sex by gay men in the great gay centers," and the economically thriving "badly lit, crowded back rooms," clubs which accommodated public sex. A woman of his acquaintance, Goodstein reported in early 1980, had toured the Castro and found it "highly depressing. 'Everyone seemed so serious, so intent, so heavily into sex,' she reflected. 'Nobody was laughing and they all looked alike. It was like visiting a communist country.'

"Sex is wonderful, but it is not all there is in being alive," Goodstein wrote. "The time has come when gay men must validate more than the piece of meat between our legs. We have much more to offer than sleaze. It's time we contribute more than our sexuality to each other and the rest of society." This was what had driven Del Martin away a decade earlier, with her "Goodbye my alienated brothers" letter. Now, lesbian activists such as Sally Gearhart, a communications professor from San Francisco, were concerned that lesbians would be identified with a culture she found reprehensible. Gearhart hated the pornography, the advertisements in the San Francisco gay press for clubs with "glory holes," and the "cock-centered" gay literature which talked "about the penis, the cock, the phallus, the prick, as being supreme and [which] is worshiped in a way that straight literature never has." Lesbians, she said, are "tired of explaining to Middle Americans that we do not seduce young boys, that we do not have sex in public bathrooms, that we are not going to go to the barricades to lower the age of consent and [of having] to spend so much time and energy defending those issues, which are the issues of my gay brothers."

At first, the only glimpse the world at large had of this gay male culture was during such extravagances as the Gay Freedom Day Parades in San Francisco, broadcast to such devastating effect in Dade County. But now, as gay male life thrived, accounts were showing up in mainstream books, movies and even on television. In 1978, Hollywood screenwriter Larry Kramer published his first novel, *Faggots*, which he presented as a satirical look at New York's gay male world, an attempt to address the question of why he, and therefore, he suggested, most gay men, were unable to form lasting romantic attachments. Kramer offered his readers detailed descriptions of some of the sexual habits and drug use among some homosexuals in New York, played out by a cast of callow and unlikable gay men, interested in the most extreme sexual practices and disdainful of emotional intimacy. It was a startling, sometimes repulsive, glimpse at gay male life—for many homosexual men and women, certainly, and probably even more so for any straight people who might have read it. The book was disturbing in its frankness and its broad sweep, and many saw it as an insidious attack coming from within. Martin Duberman, the gay historian and a member of the first National Gay Task Force board, thought the novel was explicitly anti-sex, a "foolish, even stupid book." He expressed those sentiments in a withering review in *The New Republic*, earning Kramer's lifelong enmity. "The book fails," Duberman wrote, "because it has nothing of discernment to say about that scene nor, in place of insight, any compensating literary distinction. Announced as a searing indictment of the giddy Fire Island set, *Faggots* merely exemplifies it. And often cannot manage that. The book's wooden dialogue, strained humor and smug disdain are no match for the inventive flamboyance of Fire Island hedonism when viewed from an angle wider than primitive moralizing."

Faggots might have been impolitic, and Kramer did project his own sexual and emotional struggles on the entire male gay community, which put a premium on appearance, and thus put Kramer at a disadvantage. Still, the more disquieting chapters of gay sex life that he presented were based on his own observation and, sometimes, personal experience. Kramer was shocked by the outrage against *Faggots*—he had "meant it to be funny"—and an *Advocate* reporter arrived to find the writer swaying nervously back and forth in a rocking chair. "Because this kind of gay lifestyle is so visible, it's what other people judge us by," Kramer said, when asked why he had focused only on this part of gay life. "Why do we have so much sex without tenderness? Why do we perform such extreme sex acts? Why do we take so many drugs? Why do we vacation on Fire Island so voraciously? I think the basic thing underlying a lot of this has to do with ghettoizing ourselves and having a poor self-image. When you have a bad image of yourself, it's very hard to fall in love. If you don't love yourself, how are you going to let anyone else love?'"

Kramer found that many men he counted as friends stopped speaking to him, ignoring him at parties, at the beach and in discos. Craig Rodwell would not display *Faggots* on the shelves of his Oscar Wilde Bookshop in Greenwich Village, keeping copies stacked under the counter only for patrons who knew to request one. Kramer stopped by the store one day to curtly inform Rodwell that if he was only going to sell *Faggots* from under the counter, to please not sell it at all.

"Done," Rodwell responded.

The director William Friedkin, who had made *Boys in the Band,* wrote and directed a 1980 movie based on gay life, *Cruising,* about a sado-masochistic serial killer. The movie, starring Al Pacino, depicted much of the world that Larry Kramer had brought to light, and for an even larger audience. It was the work of a heterosexual, based on a novel by a heterosexual, and it was seen as such a threat that many New York gay activists attempted to halt its filming in the streets of Greenwich Village, and protesters picketed the premiere in several cities. Arthur Bell, formerly of the GAA and now a *Village Voice* columnist, described it as the "most oppressive, ugly, bigoted look at homosexuality ever presented on the screen." That spring CBS News produced an hour-long report from San Francisco called "Gay Power, Gay Politics," filled with grainy video of men cruising and coupling in city parks. "There is a consequence to the homosexual lifestyle here. Traditional values are under attack," said CBS reporter George Crile in the narration.

"CBS displayed enough footage of cavorting gays and public displays of male homosexual sex to make a heterosexual viewer reluctant to walk the streets of San Francisco without wearing a suit of armor," wrote Howard Rosenberg, the television critic for the *Los Angeles Times*. Mayor Dianne Feinstein compared it to "doing a documentary on Italians and only showing the Mafia." Five years later, a group in Houston successfully used clips from the CBS documentary in their television commercials aimed at nullifying that city's gay rights ordinance.

Cruising and "Gay Power, Gay Politics" were distortive but, like *Faggots,* had more than a few kernels of truth, and together helped feed anti-homosexual sentiment. Six weeks after "Gay Power, Gay Politics" was broadcast, voters in San Jose, California, rejected, by nearly 3 to 1, city and county gay rights ordinances that barred discrimination against homosexuals in employment and housing. "Our whole theme was, 'Don't let it spread,' " said Dean Wycoff, executive director of the local Moral Majority. "We don't want the cancer of homosexuality spreading from San Francisco down to Santa Clara County." In Peoria, Illinois, the editorialists of the *Journal-Star,* after reading that the San Francisco city coroner was holding classes to teach homosexuals how to engage in sado-masochist sex acts without killing or injuring each other, suggested that "Frisco Needs Another Quake."

"There is no doubt that San Francisco is the most bizarre city in the U.S.," the editorialists wrote, "where the local government is holding classes to instruct homosexuals in how to engage in sadistic perversion without killing each other. . . . Scientists assure us that the time is not far off when the Big Earthquake will split California from north to south and send it tumbling into the Pacific Ocean. That isn't exactly what happened to Sodom and Gomorrah, but it sounds good enough."

May 1981, New York

Larry Mass, the son of a physician from Macon, Georgia, was a physician as well, an anesthesiologist by training, who worked in drug addiction programs in New York City. He enjoyed New York's gay sex scene. He was a regular at the baths and had met his lover, Arnie Kantrowitz, an early member of the GAA, at the Everard. Over coffee afterward, Kantrowitz told Mass that the two had actually had sex at the baths once before. Mass's firsthand knowledge of the sexual habits of New York's gay community informed his professional work, and since 1979 he had written about health for gay newspapers across the country. Mass was the only gay man with an "M.D." after his byline writing about gay issues—in *The Advocate, Gay Community News, Christopher Street* and later a New York paper, the *Native*—so before long he found himself writing about a new health issue that appeared to involve homosexuality.

In 1979 the spread of sexually transmitted disease in the male gay community had been a recurring story. The story of VD in the gay community was not new. Randy Shilts had written for *The Advocate* in 1977 about contracting hepatitis B. The disease, he reported, made him feel like "a record player from which the plug had been pulled," and was, he argued then, "the decade's best-kept medical secret." By the end of the 1970s, two-thirds of the gay men in San Francisco had been exposed to chronic hepatitis, and it was a subject *The Advocate* regularly returned to, reflecting Goodstein's fascination with venereal diseases. But by the start of the 1980s, the diseases were approaching epidemic proportions. The reason for this was obvious to Mass and anyone else who ever toured a gay bathhouse or sex club on a Saturday night, where one man might have multiple sex partners in a single night, and where anonymity was key. Mass found himself writing about surges in gonorrhea, syphilis and chronic hepatitis. He was also writing about comparatively unfamiliar diseases, such as amebiasis, a parasite spread mostly through anal-oral contact. It was extraordinarily contagious and resistant to treatment, so men kept reinfecting each other. Its incidence was also a good gauge of all sexually transmitted diseases, and thus, presumably, the increase in sexual promiscuity. There had been just 17 cases of amebiasis reported in San Francisco in 1959. By 1975, there were 78 cases. By 1978, there were 144 cases, and for the first six months of 1979, the health department had reported 128 cases. By the start of 1980, amebiasis had reached near-epidemic proportions.

When the first reports of a new sexual disease surfaced anecdotally in the gay community in the spring of 1981, people naturally turned to Larry Mass, who began to hear jumbled and ominous accounts of gay men in intensive care units suffering from what seemed to be a new and deadly form of pneumonia. After a few phone calls, Mass determined there was more here than alarmist rumors. He wrote a story that appeared on May 18, 1981, in the *New York Native,* the article based more on word of mouth than solid reporting or hard facts. "Disease Rumors Largely Unfounded," said the headline in the bottom left corner of page 7, offering its readers an assurance that Mass felt did not reflect his story. "Last week, there were rumors that an exotic new disease had hit the gay community in New York," the story began. A city health department official reported that a pneumonia (Pneumocystis carinii), normally found only in extremely debilitated patients whose natural ability to ward off infection had been compromised, had been diagnosed in eleven men, most of them gay, who appeared by all indications to be otherwise healthy. The previous week, Mass reported, one of them had died. It was the first story reporting on what would come to be known as AIDS. That edition of the *Native* listed twenty-two separate gay male sex clubs, pornographic movie theaters and back room bars open that week in Manhattan.

Six weeks later, on July 3, 1981, the Centers for Disease Control's weekly newsletter, the *Morbidity and Mortality Weekly Report,* ran an item entitled "Kaposi's Sarcoma and *Pneumocystis* Pneumonia Among Homosexual Men—New York City and California." KS was a disease that, until then, had been associated with elderly Jewish men. It had now been discovered in twenty-six gay men—twenty in New York City and six in California. Six of them also had pneumonia. "The occurrence of this number of KS cases during a 30-month period among young, homosexual men is considered highly unusual. No previous association between KS and sexual preference has been reported." The story was reported on page 20 of the *New York Times* under the headline "Rare Cancer Seen in 41 Homosexuals," the larger figure based not on government reporting but on reports of physicians. It said the cancer was often rapidly fatal, and that eight of the men had died within twenty-four months of diagnosis. Dr. Alvin Friedman-Kien of New York University Medical Center reported that at least nine of the forty-one had "severe defects in their immunological systems."

Mass returned to the subject with a four-page feature that started on the front page of the *New York Native* in the middle of July. This one was headlined "Cancer in the Gay Community." Mass was familiar enough with the highly sexualized gay male community to understand the medical implications of a fatal disease that was transmitted by sexual contact. But Mass knew much less about politics, and he had no way of knowing just how unprepared the gay rights movement was for what now lay ahead.

PART FOUR

Out of Anger

32

AFTER DISCO

July 1981, New York

Charles Brydon hadn't noticed the articles about the outbreaks of cancer and pneumonia in New York and Los Angeles. It was the summer of 1981, and Brydon, one of the two executive directors of the National Gay Task Force, was too busy fighting to hold on to his job. Brydon had come to New York to replace Bruce Voeller as executive director in January 1979, when Lucia Valeska, a feminist, sociologist and instructor in women's studies at the University of New Mexico, had replaced Jean O'Leary as co-executive director. Brydon had been the founder of the Dorian Group in Seattle, but by contrast, Valeska was barely known among national gay political leaders. Unlike Brydon, Valeska was charismatic, ideological, energetic and articulate. And also unlike Brydon, she had no experience running a large organization, and little knowledge of the "mixed gay movement," as she put it, a remark that suggested her feminist, separatist grounding.

In truth, few people were paying much attention to what the National Gay Task Force was doing in New York at the start of the 1980s. After the defeats of anti-gay initiatives in Seattle and California, the gay movement, or what there was of one at the start of 1980, had turned to investing its energies in passing local gay rights ordinances or electing open homosexuals to public office in places like San Francisco. The gay rights bill introduced in Congress had no chance of passing and, in any case, Capitol Hill came under the purview of the Gay Rights National Lobby. With the Task Force, Brydon and Valeska had taken over an organization whose profile was dissolving, and whose responsibilities and goals were not at all apparent.

From that uncertain foundation, the two new executive directors proceeded to lead the Task Force through a series of missteps which pushed it nearly completely out of existence. For two years, under their leadership, it seemed to position itself on the wrong side of nearly every major issue. Valeska and Brydon initially opposed the 1979 gay march on Washington. Brydon criticized homosexuals in San Francisco for rioting after the Dan White verdict. But the Task Force tried to stay out of the dispute over the filming and marketing of the movie *Cruising*. And when the North American Man/Boy Love Association advocated the legalization of sex between men and boys as a gay rights issue, to the particular distress of feminists—"There is a new threat to the Lesbian and Gay Rights movement which comes not from our traditional enemies but from within," the Lesbian Feminist Liberation of New York asserted—Brydon tried to laugh it away with a joke. "I don't care what they do, as long as they don't frighten the horses," he said, a clumsy statement that seemed to align the Task Force with NAMBLA. On the eve of the California primary between Jimmy Carter and Edward Kennedy, Brydon graded Carter's performance C-minus when it came to homosexual rights, a remark that the gay journalist who interviewed him, Larry Bush, publicly characterized as a "calculated insult."

The choice of Brydon and Valeska had seemed, at worst, harmless when it was announced in 1979. But that was no longer the case after Ronald Reagan's victory. Conservatives were turning back the small advances gay advocates had made with the Carter administration, and bringing before Congress explicitly anti-gay legislation, such as the Family Protection Act, which would cut off federal funds to any group or individual who advocated or supported homosexuality. The number of sponsors of the gay rights bill in Congress dropped from fifty-six to forty-seven. The Reagan White House sent a letter to *The Advocate* requesting that it be removed from its complimentary mailing list. The change of climate, and its political implications, seemed obvious, yet the leaders of the Task Force appeared ill prepared to respond to it. "Now that the national power is in the hands of those who willfully misunderstand us and want the nation to believe that our goals are threatening, we can no longer afford to be ambiguous or ambivalent about those goals and how they are achieved," Virginia Apuzzo said in a speech at the Kennedy Institute for Politics at Harvard University in December 1980, in a harsh assessment of the national movement. "We can no longer patronize the shortcomings of our national organizations as though they are beloved children who are incapable of reaching maturity."

• • •

As the task force struggled, its rival, the Gay Rights National Lobby, thrived. It was fighting the Family Protection Act in Congress one day, and efforts by the House of Representatives to prohibit the Legal Services Corporation from actions to "promote, defend or protect homosexuality" the next. Steve Endean, characteristically trying to turn events to his advantage, spiked his direct-mail appeals with warnings about the conservative resurgence. The Task Force did not try to conceal its contempt for its rival. Lucia Valeska, in a speech to NOW, dismissively contrasted the Task Force, with a staff of eight people, fifty volunteers and an annual budget of $350,000, with the Gay Rights National Lobby, "a one-person operation with a board of directors that hasn't met in two years and [has] an annual budget of $50,000." Brydon and Valeska also decided that they would lobby Congress on any issue that they chose to, effectively abrogating a turf-sharing agreement that had been informally worked out when GRNL had been formed at David Goodstein's conference in Chicago. It made for some messy politics.

When Lucia Valeska learned in the spring of 1981 that the moderate California Republican representative Pete McCloskey was about to introduce legislation to end the military's ban on homosexuals, she asked him to shelve it, warning that raising the issue now would inflame the religious right. "The climate in the present Congress is one of great caution when it comes to dealing with the emotionally charged issues for which the members lack a clear constituent attitude," Valeska wrote him. "Gay rights is one of those issues." Endean had asked McCloskey to introduce the bill, so Valeska's letter meant that the Task Force was now lobbying against the National Lobby. "I am once again writing regarding developments which I fear not only exacerbate the tensions between NGTF and GRNL, but potentially harm the struggle for equal justice and civil rights for lesbians and gay men," Endean wrote Valeska in a tense note of complaint. "The language used in this letter, were it to be widely known on Capitol Hill, is precisely the type of justification for opposing gay rights on a daily basis." It quickly became a very public feud over turf. "There tends to be a view on some people's part that they [the Task Force] are the grand masters and if you don't have their imprimatur then you can't go forward," Endean complained to the *Gay Community News* of Boston. The Task Force returned the volley. "I think the relationship between us and GRNL is unhealthy and ultimately will harm movement goals, if it hasn't already," Valeska said. "Steve Endean still uses words like *turf.*" The exchange confused the organizations' friends in Congress—"You can understand our bewilderment," an unnamed McCloskey aide told *The Advocate*—and left established gay leaders despondent. "We might revel in all the differences between NGTF and GRNL," said Frank Kameny, who was a member of the boards of both groups. "But to the people on the outside being lobbied, it's all the gays are queers and all the differences mean nothing and we're left with zero and they do what they want with us."

The image of the Task Force warning a member of Congress away from a gay rights issue proved to be devastating. In San Francisco, where memories of Brydon's criticism of the Dan White demonstrations were still fresh, three gay Democratic political clubs passed resolutions condemning the Task Force. Assemblyman Art Agnos of San Francisco, a reliable supporter of gay initiatives in that city, wrote the Task Force in complaint: "I feel very strongly that it is precisely because of that increased pressure from the New Right that such legislation must be fought for even though the chances for passage are slim." And Larry Bush wrote in *The Native*: Battling discrimination against gays "was once a major purpose of NGTF, but it argues today that this approach merely stirs the Christian crazies." Indeed, Bush, as was becoming clear during this period, was no ordinary reporter: Uncommonly skilled at gathering information, he had strong and informed opinions, and was not hesitant about sharing them with his readers and gay leaders, particularly his friend Ginny Apuzzo. His shifting role, between chronicler of the movement and behind-the-scenes activist, perplexed Brydon and Valeska, particularly as Bush's coverage of them grew more critical to the point where he wrote one story, in the *Native*, in which Apuzzo advocated their ouster. "I think the current leadership of NGTF must resign," Apuzzo told Bush. "I think that will allow us to roll up our sleeves and get to work."

There was another battle occurring within the offices of the Task Force itself. Charlie Brydon and Lucia Valeska were two strong-minded and prickly leaders, and they found themselves at war. Valeska made no secret of her scorn for the public behavior of many gay men, particularly those who had sexual liaisons in parks and toilets. Public sex was "obnoxious" to society, Valeska said, adding in her speech to NOW: "Gay public sex hurts all gay people. . . . If gay culture is reduced in the minds of the nation to what is visible in the gay ghettos, we won't get our civil rights. If men would just put their clothes on and come in from the bushes, we could get on with the real job." Her feminist background was alert to ingrained patterns of prejudice against women, and she reported having discovered them at the Task Force. Men, Valeska reported, tended to hold the "heavier positions," including handling money. Brydon had expected, given his work at the Dorian Group in Seattle, that he would be in charge of the Task Force lobbying. He was startled to learn that Valeska did not agree with that division of labor. The Task Force became so paralyzed that no letter or statement, however minor, could go out before both Brydon and Valeska had approved and signed it.

According to Larry Bush, Valeska began to speak off the record with him, and her complaints about Brydon produced a new round of critical stories. "Crisis at the Gay Task Force: Demands for Resignation Increase" read the block-type headline on the front page of the *New York Native*. The Task Force sent out a letter to gay newspapers, complaining that Bush's articles had "at times been inaccurate in their depiction and description of NGTF's activities," and were brimming with unfair editorializing and commentary. "NGTF requests editors to exercise caution in printing or reprinting stories concerning NGTF written by Larry Bush." The effort made the Task Force seem amateurish. Brett Averill, editor of the *New York Native*, wrote: "The co-directors have chosen instead to attack—not the homophobic Right, nor the critics in gay political circles, but the movement's premier independent journalist. . . . A number of adjectives come to mind to describe these latest antics of Brydon and Valeska. *Brazen. Petty. Vicious.* . . . We hope they quickly dab their eyes and overcome petulance; we encourage them to stop their sniveling and get to their jobs—i.e., do a little work for the cause of gay rights."

Charlie Brydon quit the Task Force in August 1981, leaving Valeska the sole executive director. His departure was more than a story of an individual failure or petty infighting. The National Gay Task Force was arguably the nation's most established gay organization, and now its competence and relevance were in doubt.

There was an unusual drawing on the contents page of the July 23, 1981, issue of *The Advocate* that reported Charlie Brydon's departure from the Task Force. It was a sketch of a man with a mustache, a receding hairline, and sunken eyes and cheeks. His name was T. Brent Harris, and a notice announced that the 322nd issue of *The Advocate* was dedicated to his memory. Harris, an *Advocate* associate editor for arts and entertainment, had worked at the newspaper since 1978. He was forty-two when he died. There was a story of Harris's final days, of how he was kept in isolation to protect him from infection, of how in the end he lived in what the *Advocate* editor, Robert McQueen, called a "disease-ravaged body that neither of us recognized any more." He had fallen victim, McQueen wrote, to "a rare and insidious form of cancer." McQueen spared his readers the details of Harris's last months, and just as well. It had been something out of a horror movie: Harris's limbs were bloated to twice their normal size, and his skin would burst open, exploding pus, at the slightest touch. There was one other item of note in the same edition of *The Advocate*. Three paragraphs in the "For the record: A concise review of Gay News" column. " 'Gay Pneumonia?' " asked the headline. " 'Not really,' says researcher."

August 1981, New York

Most of the eighty gay men who gathered in the third-floor apartment overlooking Washington Square Park did not know who Charlie Brydon was. They knew little about the National Gay Task Force, and what they did know they had learned from the stories in the *New York Native* about the infighting and upheaval, which only reinforced their contempt for people who made a career of gay activism.

If anyone wanted to determine why the modern gay rights movement seemed stalled in the city of the Stonewall riots—as their host on this hot August evening had attempted to do eighteen months earlier, in a column on the *New York Times* op-ed page—he could probably have started and ended the inquiry right in that book-lined living room. These were men who, for the most part, enjoyed New York's gay life to its fullest. Most of them were good-looking professionals, who could afford to spend summers on Fire Island Pines, and their Saturday nights and Sunday mornings at The Saint. They were not the kind of people who returned to New York on the last Sunday of June for the Gay Rights Parade, or who shared their income with the few gay rights organizations that were struggling along in 1981, or did anything to push along the gay rights bill at city hall, which had not advanced in the eleven years since the GAA first proposed it. Some homosexuals might have considered themselves oppressed in 1981, but that would have been difficult to prove from the group assembled in the well-appointed Fifth Avenue apartment of Larry Kramer.

It was more than a little ironic that these of all men were in this of all places, the home of the author of *Faggots,* to discuss the outbreak of what was being called the "gay cancer." The book had established Larry Kramer as one of the homosexual community's most relentless inside critics. Its satire had opened him to criticism that he was, in effect, providing aid to the enemy. "I'm asked to sign petitions to help people who have been nabbed by policemen for sucking off guys in the toilet of the IRT," he said in one interview, referring to a New York City subway line. "*I won't!* They shouldn't fucking well be sucking off people in the IRT. You want to see your mother or father or your brother and sister sucking off people in the IRT? *They* don't do it, why should we? . . . I think it's shameful and shocking, the lives that we do lead and the way we do treat ourselves. And if it [*Faggots*] is ammunition for 'them,' then maybe they'll make us change if we won't do it ourselves." Kramer had written an op-ed piece in the *New York Times* critical of the gay rights movement in New York City, after returning from a book promotion tour that brought him to San Francisco during the funeral for Harvey Milk. "I am not a crying man but I had tears in my eyes, as well as shivers of pride, while I was in San Francisco that week, all for a man I had never known and only vaguely heard about," he wrote on December 13, 1978. He reported that the mayor, Dianne Feinstein, had paid tribute to Harvey Milk, that 30,000 people had filled the streets carrying candles in the deceased supervisor's memory. Kramer had returned to New York to read that the gay rights bill had failed for an eighth time in the city council. "I am back in New York, missing, very much, the sense of community I felt in San Francisco," Kramer wrote. "I call several of my friends, but no one is home. I know that most of my friends are at the bars or the baths or the discos, tripping out on trivia. We haven't had an acknowledged homosexual member of the City Council representing our constituency. But, gruesomely, I wonder if what happened there should happen here, would Governor Hugh Carey be in the front row? . . . Would our one million homosexuals march with lit candles?

"The City Council was right," he wrote. "We are not ready for our rights in New York. We have not earned them. We have not fought for them."

In truth, Larry Kramer was as distant from the gay political movement as the homosexual men he was attacking. In 1969, the year of the riots at Stonewall, Kramer was in England, writing and producing the movie *Women in Love.* By his own account, he spent most of the next ten years living the typical life of the New York gay man. The gay movement was alien to him, represented by "straggling, pitiful marches" of "loudmouths, the unkempt, the dirty and unwashed, men in leather or dresses, fat women with greasy, slicked-back ducktail hairdos." Kramer believed there was a divide between the "politically correct" gay leadership which detested *Faggots* and the general gay audience which, he said, responded to his work with letters of praise. And now, as Kramer pushed for a new organization to fill a political void made evident by illness, he belittled whatever political structure there was in the gay movement. "I see no one leading us in an organized plan to gain our civil rights in New York," he declared at the start of 1982. "I see no one making our annual march up Fifth Avenue to Central Park anything other than the messy, scraggly, un-coordinated, unconvincing mess it is."

Accordingly, Kramer was well known and not particularly well liked by the people he had invited to his apartment. They were there because they had read the *New York Native* articles by Larry Mass, and the July story in the *New York Times* about what was still known only as gay cancer. Kramer had been shaken by the *Times* report that the typical victims of the disease had up to forty different sexual encounters a week, used recreational drugs to enhance their sexual pleasure and had a history of venereal diseases. Kramer felt as if he was reading his own medical chart. He went to New York University Medical Center to meet with Dr. Alvin Friedman-Kien, the dermatologist who had reported the first cases of Kaposi's sarcoma in gay men in New York, and Friedman-Kien agreed to speak at the meeting at Kramer's apartment.

"This is the tip of the iceberg," Friedman-Kien told the men. But there were not many questions he could answer that night. Was this transmitted by sexual contact? Could it be caused by drugs? Was it some toxic substance in the walls of the popular sex clubs, scattered through a West Greenwich Village neighborhood that stank at night of the rotting blood and beef left over after the area's meat markets closed? Were there treatments? A cure? Could it be spread by casual contact? And when someone asked him how they could avoid getting sick—the most pressing question—Friedman-Kien responded with the worst possible answer: stop having sex. "Each man swallowed their panic," recounted Nathan Fain, a writer who chronicled the early years of the epidemic "and—if you were there, you remember the exact moment—found himself shocked into action." They raised $6,635 that night to fund what would be a new organization.

By their very presence in Kramer's apartment, these men were, consciously or not, passing judgment on the state of the gay rights movement. They were not building on history but discarding it, and thus were acting out what had been, and what would continue to be, the recurring theme of the gay movement in New York and across the country. The men in Kramer's apartment were doing what the men and women of the Gay Liberation Front had done to the Mattachine Society and the Daughters of Bilitis twelve years earlier, almost precisely to the night. Faced with a threat more insidious than Anita Bryant, the men in Kramer's apartment did not turn to the Gay Rights National Lobby in Washington or to the National Gay Task Force, whose headquarters was a six-block walk north from where they were meeting. They formed an entirely new organization, what would be the Gay Men's Health Crisis, or GMHC, to respond to the emergency.

Inevitably, given this latest break with the past, everything about creating a new organization—its function, its relationship to government, what it should say to homosexual men, even what it should be called—was in dispute from the start. And the single largest reason for that was Larry Kramer himself. From the first meeting, Kramer was a polarizing figure: confrontational, bitter, brooding, strident, given to exaggeration and personal attack. He seemed to be always angry, and it was difficult to tell how much of his rage reflected his sour judgment of gay male culture and how much resulted from his resentment at the way it had treated him. Kramer had always been all sharp edges; middle age had done nothing to soften his personality. He had always complained that the gay world was superficial, fixated on bodies, drugs, disco and promiscuity. Writing *Faggots* had not let any steam out of Kramer's kettle.

And Kramer had strong notions about what this new organization should be doing: It should be confrontational and aggressive, alerting men to the hazards of sex and aggressively demanding attention and money from the government. "It's difficult to write this without sounding alarmist or too emotional or just plain scared," Kramer had explained in a paid announcement, "A Personal Appeal from Larry Kramer," published in the *Native* in the summer of 1981. One hundred and twenty men, mostly in New York, Kramer wrote, are suffering from "an often lethal form of cancer called Kaposi's sarcoma or from a virulent form of pneumonia. It's easy to become frightened that one of the many things we've done or taken over the years may be all that it takes for a cancer to grow from a tiny something or other that got in there who knows when from doing who knows what." But when Kramer and the other men left his apartment and headed to Fire Island for Labor Day weekend, the reception they got ranged somewhere between hostile and indifferent. Volunteers handed out 1,500 copies of Mass's article "Cancer in the Gay Community." Kramer and Paul Popham, a poised vice president of Irving Trust and a fixture of the island's social scene, sat outside the Ice Palace, a Cherry Grove disco, from midnight to dawn. That Saturday night they raised a total of $126—the equivalent of twelve admissions to the disco—at a club which easily held a thousand people. The entire take for Labor Day weekend, one of the busiest weekends of the season, was $769.55.

Kramer's warnings were, in effect, being overshadowed by his reputation. And the fact that this new disease might somehow absolve Kramer for his previous writings—a medical exoneration for the presumed sins enumerated in *Faggots*—made people only more mistrustful. Kramer's "personal appeal" in the *Native* drew retorts from men suspicious of more doomsaying from the author of *Faggots*. "Basically Kramer *is* telling us that something we gay men are doing (drugs? kinky sex?) is causing Kaposi's sarcoma," playwright Robert Chesley wrote in the *Native* in October. "At the beginning of his appeal, he states that it is difficult for him not to sound alarmist on this issue—but I don't think he tried *not* to be alarmist. . . . I think the concealed meaning in Kramer's emotionalism is the triumph of guilt: that gay men *deserve* to die of their promiscuity. In his novel *Faggots*, Kramer told us that sex is dirty and we ought not be doing what we're doing. Now with Kaposi's sarcoma attacking gay men, Kramer assumes he knows the cause (maybe it's on page 37 of *Faggots*? Or page 237), and—well, let's say that it's easy to become frightened that Kramer's *real* emotion is a sense of having been vindicated, though tragically: he told us so, but we didn't listen to him; nooo —we had to learn the hard way, and now we're dying.

"Read anything by Kramer closely," Chesley concluded. "I think you'll find that the subtext is always: the wages of gay sin are death. . . . I am not downplaying the seriousness of Kaposi's sarcoma. But something else is happening here, which is also serious: gay homophobia and anti-eroticism."

Kramer responded in the *Native* with a front-page attack on Chesley, questioning his motives by asserting that "we have made love in the past" and portraying the playwright as a wounded ex-lover. "This is outright savagery," Kramer wrote in a muscular verbal display that hinted at what his critics faced if they took him on. Kramer said his appeal was meant to be "stirring and emotional and scary. I didn't, and don't think that anything less than scary was, and is, occurring.

"*Something* we are doing *is* ticking off the time bomb that is causing the breakdown of immunity in certain bodies," he said. ". . . Isn't it better to be cautious until various suspected causes have been discounted, rather than reckless?

"I am not glorying in death. I am overwhelmed by it. The death of my friends. The death of whatever community there is here in New York."

The central question of whether GMHC would be a hard-edged, confrontational political organization, as Larry Kramer wanted, or devoted to helping the gay men of New York cope with a health crisis, as most everyone else wanted, was resolved within a week after the organization was formally created, in January 1982, again at Kramer's apartment. Kramer had been instrumental in bringing GMHC together and considered himself the obvious choice for leader. But the men selected Paul Popham as its first president—a distressing choice to Kramer, but hardly a surprise to anyone who had lived through the turbulent six months since the first meeting. Most of the men who turned up at the January meeting had been brought into the organization by Popham, a businessman and former Green Beret, easygoing and likable, who always seemed to be followed by a flock of handsome young men. Popham was unusually attractive—trim, masculine, with square-jaw good looks and a mustache—and the gay movement had always tended to reward its best-looking members with leadership posts. Popham did not share Kramer's confrontational views; he was conservative by nature, a registered Republican who grew up in Oregon and once confided to Kramer that he had never met a Jew until college. He was also someone who always kept one foot in the closet. He would ask that his name not be used in mainstream articles about the Gay Men's Health Crisis during the four years he directed what would become one of the largest gay organizations in the country.

The relations between Kramer and the rest of the founders dissolved quickly, as they battled over the basic question of what this organization should be saying to gay men. Kramer wanted the warnings to be direct and alarming: Gay men had to be told that sex could kill them. But Kramer was making the argument during what was turning out to be a particularly difficult time for the homosexual rights movement. Reagan was president, and the religious right was seizing on homosexuality as an issue around which to rally support and raise money. "Homosexuals on the march!" read a typical fundraising appeal from the Moral Majority, with a picture of men in embrace contained in a sealed envelope marked "Caution: this material may be harmful to minors!" The House of Representatives voted 281–119 to nullify legislation passed by the Washington, D.C., City Council that abolished the city's homosexual sodomy statute. The House was responding to a personal appeal by Jerry Falwell, who branded the law a "perverted act about perverted acts" that would turn the nation's capital into "the gay capital of the world . . . another Sodom and Gomorrah." The D.C. sodomy statute forced the first direct confrontation between the Moral Majority and homosexual activists, and Larry Bush described it as homosexuals' "biggest and most conclusive defeat to date." (Steve Endean tried to put it in perspective with some tart humor: "Not only will two-thirds of the members of this body violate the laws they just put back on the books, but half of them will do it by midnight tonight," he told reporters.)

In an April 1981 op-ed piece in the *New York Times,* Bush wrote, "The Christian right's attack on gay civil rights is taking on a new life and intensity. The outcome is uncertain, but two things are clear: The Moral Majority will stop at nothing to make scapegoats of gay people and the gay community is becoming more united as a result." David Goodstein inaugurated 1982 with a gloomy "Opening Space" column. His despair was not based on this new disease—which, by all indications, had not yet tripped his radar—but on the rising religious right and the prospects of an economic recession. The coming year, he wrote, was "going to be a crossroad for us. The worst fears of many of you may be realized. . . . There is a real possibility that we shall become the scapegoats of the United States, just as Jews (and gay people) were the scapegoats of Nazi Germany."

The new disease seemed certain to offer fuel to the attack by the religious right on homosexuality. It appeared to be explicitly linked to homosexuality; it was even called gay cancer, then, GRID, or Gay-Related Immune Deficiency, both in the gay press and by federal health officials. This was the politically threatening atmosphere in which members of the Gay Men's Health Crisis listened to Kramer publicly chastising gay men for "fucking their brains out." They worried that such public statements would now be used against them by their new political enemies. "We won't need to criticize each other once the Moral Majority gets wind of this," Arnie Kantrowitz wrote in the *Native*. "They even blamed us for blizzards and droughts." Kramer lost his battle on how GMHC should proceed. "The current opinion," read one of the GMHC early-warning brochures, adopting language written by Larry Mass, "points to something like a virus that **may be** transmitted sexually." Mass had insisted that the words "may be" be set in bold type. **"Therefore until we know better, it makes sense that the fewer different people you come**

**in sexual contact with lessens the chance that this possibly con-
tagious bug has to travel around. Have as much sex as you want
but with fewer people and with healthy people."**

The editors of *The Advocate* knew why their associate T. Brent Harris
died, even if they hadn't explained it in the tribute or the obituary, and even
though he was the first man most of them knew to have succumbed to this disease they had read about, not in *The Advocate,* but in the *New York Times* and
the *New York Native. The Advocate*'s most influential figures, publisher David
Goodstein and editor Robert McQueen, subscribed to the notion of recreational sex as an integral part of male homosexuality. Goodstein still believed
what Jim Foster had told him long ago: "Never forget one thing: What this
movement is about is fucking." McQueen once calculated he had had sex
with 15,000 different men. *The Advocate* essentially ignored the story of the
"gay cancer" until the spring of 1982. McQueen and Goodstein were disapproving of what to them was the irresponsible and sensationalistic torrent of
stories in the upstart *Native.* McQueen and Goodstein—confident that this
would turn out to be a gay equivalent of Legionnaires' Disease, with a quick
scare, some deaths, followed by a cause and a cure—did not want to frighten
their readers (or, no doubt, their advertisers). The different approaches of the
two major gay newspapers of the time could be seen in the space of a single
month: In October 1981 the *New York Native* featured the "personal appeal"
from Kramer and a disturbingly candid interview by Mass of an anonymous
person with gay cancer (Donald Krintzman, a founder of GMHC). That
month *The Advocate* ran a lengthy, illustrated feature entitled "Breaking the
Taboos on Anal Pleasure." Writing later about this period, Goodstein said:
"As I encountered each new revelation, I kept expecting the clouds to open,
organ music to boom a Bach requiem and an outraged Jehovah to order me to
stop fucking forthwith." The editors of *The Advocate* were no different from
many gay men at the time, who believed and lived the sexual revolution, and
who decided, at least tacitly, to try to ride it out. But *The Advocate's* caution
meant that for ten months, the subject of the epidemic was largely ignored in
the nation's most widely read gay newspaper. For years, the editors of the *The
Advocate* would struggle with whether they allowed their allegiance to sexual
freedom to interfere with their news judgment. Even as late as early 1983,
Goodstein would write: "I am really proud of our careful coverage of these
health problems in 1982 and before."

By the spring of 1982, GMHC was in full operation in New York, and
Representative Henry Waxman of Los Angeles, who was chairman of the
Subcommittee on Health and the Environment, held a day-long hearing on
the disease at the Los Angeles Gay and Lesbian Community Services Center.

"I want to be especially blunt about the political aspects of Kaposi's Sarcoma," Waxman said on April 13. "This horrible disease afflicts members of one of the nation's most stigmatized and discriminated-against minorities. The victims are not typical, Main Street Americans. They are gays, mainly from New York, Los Angeles and San Francisco. There is no doubt in my mind that if the same disease had appeared among Americans of Norwegian descent, or among tennis players, rather than among gay males, the response of both the government and the medical community would have been different." At the *Advocate* offices, Bruce Voeller, who had left the National Gay Task Force to found the Mariposa Education and Research Foundation to study human sexuality, warned Goodstein that the threat was real and deadly. "Look at the epidemiologic data," Voeller said. "This is very frightening. Everyone in this room may be dead in two or three years and there may be nothing we can do about it." It was impossible for *The Advocate* to ignore the disease any longer. Nathan Fain, a founder of GMHC, joined *The Advocate* as a correspondent, and he wrote a two-part article entitled "Is Our Lifestyle Hazardous to our Health?" Goodstein's "Opening Space" dropped its ambivalence in the issue of March 18, 1982. "Whether we like it or not, the fact is that aspects of the urban gay lifestyle we have created in the last decade are hazardous to our health," Goodstein told his readers.

"The evidence is overwhelming," Goodstein acknowledged. "The most prevalent sexual pattern among those who died was one of promiscuity: men who spend several nights a week having many sexual encounters take risks with their health that men with fewer encounters don't. Likewise, the anonymous sex in back rooms and sex places is riskier than sex in bedrooms with friends. It could be that sex palaces, which encourage orgies and lack adequate shower facilities, are public health hazards. And I shudder at the political implications of this notion." Even with that, at the end of 1982, Goodstein would list AIDS as ninth among the top ten stories affecting homosexuals that year.

August 1982, Dallas, Texas

Lucia Valeska survived the year as the sole executive director of the National Gay Task Force, though barely, and she was in Dallas on the third weekend of August 1982, to speak at a national conference called by the Dallas Gay Alliance. Its theme was "Celebrating the Movement: Planning for the Future," and its weekend agenda was made up of workshops on police relations, legal rights, the gay press, racism, sexism, lobbying and fundraising. There was also a new forum devoted to the subject of Acquired Immune Deficiency Syndrome, as it had just been named. (At the urging of Bruce Voeller and Virginia Apuzzo, the federal government would drop GRID—Gay-Related

Immune Deficiency—and designate the disease Acquired Immune Deficiency Syndrome, or AIDS, in July 1982.) The forum was sponsored by the
National Gay Task Force, and it was, effectively, the established movement's
first acknowledgment that there were political implications to the disease. The
halls and lobbies of the Dallas hotel were filled with the familiar faces of gay
liberation—Troy Perry, Jean O'Leary, Bruce Voeller, Charlotte Bunch and
Jim Foster—brushing shoulders with the new class of activists, among them
Larry Kramer, Paul Popham, Nathan Fain and Larry Mass.

By now, GMHC was by far the most organized response to the disease in
the country, and its representatives seemed cocky, insistent and pushy, particularly to people from outside New York. GMHC had expanded rapidly since
January. It had held its first fundraising event in April, "a benefit to aid gay
men with Kaposi's Sarcoma and other gay-related immunodeficiencies."
They called it Showers (as in April showers) and took over the Paradise
Garage disco. The poster for Showers and full-page ads on the back of the
New York Native featured a drawing of a muscular man's torso, in a bulging
pair of briefs, with a hose in one hand and a hook in the other. Kramer complained that the sexually charged image seemed to celebrate the very behavior
that had caused the problem in the first place. By the afternoon of the April 8
benefit, a disappointing nine hundred tickets at $20 apiece had been sold.
"We had told ourselves that if Showers did not work, if the community did
not support us, we'd stop after tonight," Nathan Fain later wrote. But the
night of the party, 2,500 men turned out, lining up as they had at The Saint
and other nights at the Paradise Garage. A jubilant Paul Popham reported
from the stage that night that $52,000 worth of tickets had been sold, for a net
of $32,086. Things were going so well for the organization—GMHC was
planning to open an office that fall—that the conflict between Kramer and
Popham had been put aside momentarily.

As far as the new leaders of the GMHC were concerned, they could make
it without any help from the federal government, a boast that did not immediately endear them to some of the more experienced people attending the conference in Dallas, one of whom was Tim Westmoreland, the counsel to Henry
Waxman, who had organized the congressional hearing at the Los Angeles
Gay and Lesbian Community Services Center. Westmoreland's area of expertise was public health, and as soon as he learned about the outbreak of a sexual epidemic among gay men in Los Angeles, he went to see Waxman. "I need
to talk to you about my private life," Westmoreland told the representative,
"because this disease we're talking about is affecting gay people and I'm more
familiar with this community than just professionally. And people may see a
conflict of interest here. I do not." Waxman asked if Westmoreland thought he
could handle the work in an evenhanded way, Westmoreland said yes, and that
was the end of the discussion. The result was that by complete coincidence,

the chief aide to the House subcommittee that would deal with AIDS, and thus the congressional staff member who had about the best command of the details of the federal response to the new epidemic, was openly gay.

Westmoreland couldn't help smiling when Kramer, Popham and Fain, in a brash display of self-confidence, boasted to him of the money they had raised at Showers. Westmoreland knew the kind of money it would take to launch the emergency research program that seemed necessary, and it was nowhere near what these men had raised at the Paradise Garage. "It won't keep you in rhesus monkeys for a year," Westmoreland told them. "You need the federal government involved in this."

Lucia Valeska was to give the keynote address in Dallas, and her audience was particularly curious to hear what she had to say. She and the National Gay Task Force had managed to stay out of the spotlight for most of the year after Charlie Brydon's departure. She had asked for a "honeymoon" from the gay press—in other words, from Larry Bush—which had been granted.

Valeska opened her speech with a joke.

"What's the difference between love and herpes?" she asked, addressing a dining room filled with gay leaders. "Herpes lasts forever." There was little laughter. Valeska then launched into a speech that left her audience sitting in embarrassed silence. She stopped and started, thoughts and sentences drifting off into the air. Even her friends cringed with every awkward pause and stumble. At a few tables, people quietly gathered their belongings and left. At first, Valeska's audience thought she had taken too many glasses of wine with dinner. But in the end, the reason for her performance hardly mattered. What should have been a showcase speech for the National Gay Task Force had turned into a debacle. The next day, the members of the Task Force board gathered with other gay leaders to discuss the catastrophe. People in the room kept returning to the same question: "What are we going to do about Lucia?" Bruce Voeller, worried that the organization he had founded was in danger of collapsing, told the board to dump Valeska and replace her with his friend Virginia Apuzzo, who had shared a table with Goodstein and Larry Bush during the Valeska speech.

Two weeks later, at an emergency Labor Day meeting in New York, a majority of the board of the National Gay Task Force decided to fire Valeska. The board, however, was so polarized it could not even accomplish that. The women were distressed by Valeska's performance, but were even more unhappy with what they saw as a power play by men. They forced the board to adjourn without taking a vote. Valeska told a reporter she had no plans to resign.

Any possibility that Valeska might survive ended a week after the Labor Day meeting, when Larry Bush published his toughest attack yet on Valeska.

"Terminal Illness at NGTF: Valeska to Gay Community: Drop Dead," read the *Native* headline, echoing to potent effect the famous *New York Daily News* headline about Gerald Ford and New York City. Bush had a new disclosure for his readers: Lucia Valeska was not the real name of the executive director of the National Gay Task Force. She was "a former suburban Chicago house-wife who had tossed aside her identity as Maggie Murphy to become a sage-brush feminist from New Mexico." He presented Valeska's name change as a deception, suggesting that the leader of the nation's leading gay rights organi-zation was shielding her true identity from even her fellow gay activists.

In truth, women had changed their names, discarding the names of their fathers, or former husbands, to establish their own identities and shake off the reign of what they called the patriarchy. Charlotte Bunch called Bush's article a sexist smear, and Bush's attack drove the wedge deeper between men and women on the board. But Valeska could not survive such a public as-sault, and by the end of September, a deal had been struck for her departure. On September 20, the same day that Valeska's resignation was accepted by the board, the Gay Men's Health Crisis celebrated the opening of its first of-fice, on the second floor of a building on West Twenty-second Street in Chelsea. For the second time in a year, the survival of the Task Force was in doubt.

What ultimately led to Lucia Valeska's resignation—that she had once been Maggie Murphy of Chicago—was something Valeska, or Murphy, had shared with Virginia Apuzzo, with whom she had had a brief affair, and who later mentioned the fact to Larry Bush, according to his later recollection of events. Apuzzo would now replace Lucia Valeska as the executive director of the National Gay Task Force.

Nathan Fain of the Gay Men's Health Crisis in New York wrote a letter to Tim Westmoreland the day after he and the other GMHC founders returned from the Dallas conference. Fain was, in a sense, apologizing for their disrup-tive behavior that weekend, but then again he was not.

> *Dear Tim:*
> *How can you STAND politics? I feel as though I've contracted a new opportunistic infection. But I suppose that's insulting. I must say you do what you do very well and with style.*
> *I don't know how this idea got started that we were all fascists and control freaks, but we aren't. We don't want to be controlled ourselves, that's all. But please be frank with us, always. If you don't like the sound or look of something, say so. We all feel a certain trust has been put into our hands by a lot of very cynical people and if we make one false move-*

ment, all that will evaporate. You can appreciate how vital keeping that trust is right now; a lot of guys in New York are so frightened that, for better or worse, we're all they believe in at the moment.

I've been wondering what would come along after disco and late nights in the back rooms. And now I think I know.

33

SWEPT AWAY

October 1982, New York

"Your purpose tonight is to participate in and influence the 1982 campaign. That is my purpose, too." The speaker, Walter F. Mondale, the former vice president and a leading contender for the 1984 Democratic presidential nomination, was standing at the front of the Grand Ballroom of the Waldorf-Astoria Hotel in New York. There were a thousand people seated at the tables assembled before him at this political dinner, or three times what had been projected by the organizers, the new Human Rights Campaign Fund. The black-tie audience was made up almost exclusively of gay men and lesbians, who had paid $150 to hear the former vice president address the first national political action committee dedicated to advocating homosexual rights, the organization that had been born from Tennessee Williams's signature and Alan Baron's counsel. Mondale's appearance trumped even Ted Kennedy's speech the previous spring at the annual MECLA dinner in Los Angeles, and it confirmed the arrival of the Human Rights Campaign Fund, or the HRCF, as a gay rights organization whose influence stretched from coast to coast.

The dinner was viewed as a triumph, even before the final tally showed it had netted just over $50,000. "Upscale, Upbeat, Uptown: Making History at the Campaign Fund Dinner," read the *New York Native* headline. Colman McCarthy, a *Washington Post* columnist, wrote: "Today it can be a political death wish *not* to be for gay rights. Mondale, who had previously stayed in the closet by avoiding public involvement with the issue, is now racing to catch up with the 1980 Democratic Party platform, the National Council of Churches, Ted Kennedy, Jerry Brown and nearly 60 members of the House who are cosponsors of a gay civil rights bill."

And the dinner almost never happened. That it did was due largely to the work of Mondale's fellow Minnesotan Steve Endean, who was by the end of 1982 Washington's most visible gay lobbyist (and who was quietly enjoying the troubles of his counterparts at the National Gay Task Force). Mondale's previous encounter with a group of homosexuals had been a disastrous appearance at the Hall of Flowers at Golden Gate Park in San Francisco in June 1977, three weeks after the Anita Bryant vote. "When are you going to speak up for gay rights?" yelled Arthur Evans. Mondale looked nervous as a chorus of boos swelled from the audience, and he tried to appease the crowd with a general statement about human rights. Finally, a little flushed and more than a little humiliated, the vice president said, "Thank you very much," to his audience, and "I'm not speaking anymore," to the other Democrats onstage. He cut his visit short by nearly an hour. "As Mondale concedes," the *Washington Post* political columnist David Broder wrote a few days later, "he was unprepared, politically or personally, to deal with the homosexuals' protest. It made him distinctly uncomfortable, just as another 'lifestyle' issue, that of abortion and women's rights, proved so vexatious to Carter in the 1976 campaign."

Not surprisingly, when the delegation from the Human Rights Campaign Fund, led by Endean, Kerry Woodward and Jim Hormel, met with the former vice president at his Washington office in early June 1982 to discuss the HRCF dinner, Mondale had immediately telegraphed to them his apprehensions. "You should realize that I'm very uncomfortable" talking about homosexuality, he said. But the meeting lasted two hours and Mondale's candor, and his decision to see them, led his guests to assume he wished to repair the damage from the San Francisco debacle. Endean knew there was no chance that the socially conservative Mondale would ever "approve or understand" gay people. But the group appealed to his Democratic political instincts, arguing that the time had come to support civil rights for a disenfranchised group of Americans—and, not incidentally, to take note of a "hidden vote," as Hormel put it. And when Mondale nodded in agreement, Endean moved in and asked if he would be their keynote speaker. Such a daring gesture would enhance his image in the liberal community, Endean said, at the expense of Ted Kennedy, a rival for the nomination. To Endean's surprise, Mondale said yes.

Ten thousand invitations were mailed out for the dinner, and a slightly suggestive full-page ad—"Put your money where your mouth is"—appeared in the gay press. The honorary committee was testimony to the growing main-stream standing of the HRCF: Senators Edward Kennedy of Massachusetts, Daniel Patrick Moynihan of New York and Alan Cranston of California, and the mayors of San Francisco, Minneapolis, Boston and Atlanta. Mondale's agreement to appear merited a story in the *New York Times* three weeks before the dinner. Until the day of the fundraiser, HRCF leaders worried that the former vice president would cancel. And when he did appear and began to speak, Steve Endean could hear the words the vice president was *not* saying that night—"gay," "lesbian" and "homosexual"—and he began to worry that the audience might jeer him. Mondale's language was cloaked, but he explicitly endorsed his party's 1980 platform language opposing discrimination based upon sexual orientation or, as he put it, "irrational discrimination."

"Tonight I pledge to you to continue the fight against all forms of irra-tional discrimination—wherever it occurs, whatever the reason, whoever the target," Mondale told the excited crowd. "Let us hold fast to the most basic American principles: In our form of government, questions of personal con-duct that do not threaten the peace and order of society cannot rightfully be decided and enforced by the government, or by any self-appointed private group. In all matters that do not affect the rights of others, every citizen must be left alone by his government." Endean leaned back into the waves of ap-plause around him as Mondale concluded and appreciated the accomplish-ment—their accomplishment—that night.

Steve Endean had by now heard about the so-called gay cancer, or AIDS, but he did not appear even slightly worried about it. It did not prompt him to reconsider the missions of the Gay Rights National Lobby or its politi-cal arm, the Human Rights Campaign Fund, even when his associates began pressing him to shift gears. "You're going to be swept away if you don't pay at-tention to this," said Tim Westmoreland. "This is going to overcome civil rights." But Endean had no patience for dealing with complicated budget procedures, meeting new members of Congress or being measured against the yearly votes of a congressional budget committee, certainly not on behalf of a disease which, he was certain, would not be a problem for long. The Gay Rights National Lobby had set up an AIDS unit after the conference in Dal-las, and Endean was careful to mention GRNL's concern about the disease in his mailings, but he made no secret that his interest in AIDS was as a fundraising tool. "The one thing AIDS [was] good for is giving people you need a guilt trip," Endean later said. The health scare seemed to have little ef-fect on Endean's after-work activities as well. He boasted of evenings at the baths when he had sexual relations with fifteen or twenty men a night, and how on slow days in the office on Capitol Hill, he'd hop a bus for a few hours at the baths across town. His friends and associates would later wonder whether Endean had let his sexual urgings cloud what had seemed, until then, to be an unfailing sense for politics.

December 1982, Washington, D.C.

Steve Endean viewed Virginia Apuzzo, the new executive director of the National Gay Task Force, with awe and more than a little jealousy. He did not like her, but she was the kind of person, he would say, who could inspire even her enemies—a group that would come to include Endean—to walk barefoot on hot coals. There had never been anyone quite like Ginny Apuzzo in the gay rights movement. Apuzzo grew up in the Pelham Bay neighborhood of the Bronx, in a world built around the family and the Catholic Church. As a teenager, Apuzzo struggled with the realization that she might be, by the teachings of her Catholic Church, barred from salvation because of desires she could not understand. These conflicts took her into a convent at the age of twenty-six. "Sister Virginia," as they called her, concluded after three years of prayer and study that she could be happy living as both a lesbian and a Catholic, but not as a nun, so she left the convent.

As a political organizer, Apuzzo had her detractors—activists put off by the politicking that she had, at the very least, countenanced to oust Lucia Valeska—but even they admired her command of politics and government, and most of all, her public presence. Apuzzo was magnetic: She was the best speaker the gay movement had produced, whether debating Jerry Falwell on the Phil Donahue show or lecturing on political theory at the Kennedy School of Government. She spoke in rising, clipped sentences, delivered with the swagger of the Bronx. Her speeches blended emotion and logic, inspirational one moment, badgering the next. Gay men and lesbians lived every day "on parole," Apuzzo would declare. One wrong step would leave them without a job, without a family or in jail. Her ability to turn a compelling phrase left her gay audiences nodding in comprehension.

Apuzzo knew her talents and ambitions, and it was clear from the start that she intended to be remembered as more than the leader of the gay rights movement. She wanted to run for Congress. "I have Potomac Fever," Apuzzo told an *Advocate* reporter soon after arriving at the Task Force. It was typically direct, and it was the way Apuzzo handled her personal and professional affairs, as Betty Powell had discovered at the start of what would be a ten-year romance between them. They met at Cathedral High School in Manhattan, where Powell was head of the French department and Apuzzo was teaching black studies. Powell would go on to become the first black woman on the board of the National Gay Task Force, but in 1972 she was just coming to terms with the fact she might be a lesbian. When the women returned to

Powell's apartment after their first night out, Powell confided that she thought she was gay, and that she thought she was in love with Apuzzo. Apuzzo bounced off the couch and grabbed onto a lamp for support. "Are you crazy?" Apuzzo said. "You're black, you're a woman, and now you want to be a lesbian?"

Apuzzo seemed to have the organizational strengths of Charlie Brydon, the feminist credentials of Lucia Valeska and the political soul of Steve Endean rolled into one compact frame, along with an extra splash of personality that propelled her to the front of the small class of gay leaders. "The strongest negative I've heard about Ginny is by people who describe her as hard and tough," Endean told *The Advocate* at the news of her selection. "I've seen the side of Ginny where she's warm and sensitive and a loving human but she is hard and tough in a lot of ways. And boy, we need people who can make tough decisions, who are willing to be tenacious and bulldogging in their approach."

It was hard to imagine a person better suited for the moment than Apuzzo: She was a former assistant commissioner for operations in the New York City Health Department, where she studied the rise of amebiasis among gay men. She understood mainstream politics, and although she had lost her one race for office—for the New York State Assembly from Brooklyn in 1978—there were few people who didn't believe she might well be the first open lesbian in Congress. Apuzzo had been on the periphery of the gay movement for nearly a decade, close enough to know what was going on, but far enough away so that she had never been burned. She was also skilled at winning favorable press, whether to advance herself or the organization that was paying her salary. And she counted as her confidants the most influential gay journalists of the time, Larry Bush and David Goodstein.

In ways that Endean did not understand at first, the ascension of Ginny Apuzzo to the Task Force was a dark turn for his own career. For one thing Apuzzo was already worrying about the epidemic. A member of the AIDS Network, a group of New York political activists and health professionals who met once a week at 8 a.m. to review the latest developments, Apuzzo was already considering the implications of the health emergency in ways that never occurred to Endean. She understood that it was a medical and political catastrophe that threatened the lives, and the *way* of life, of many of the gay men she knew in New York. And that, as Tim Westmoreland had warned Endean, it threatened to subsume everything the gay movement had worked on for the past decade. The new executive director of the National Gay Task Force thus had an exact idea of what the gay rights movement should be doing in the fall of 1982, and rallying members of Congress behind Steve Endean's quixotic gay rights bill was not part of it. The main issue was AIDS. The Task Force's Washington lobbyist was Melvin Boozer, the gay speaker at the 1980 Democratic convention. Boozer was working from his apartment, but as far as Apuzzo was concerned, he wasn't doing very much at all. She fired him and replaced him with Jeff Levi, the son of religious German Jews who had emigrated in 1939 to New York's Lower East Side. Levi, conservative in temperament and tactic, was president of Washington's Gay Activists Alliance, the post Boozer had also once held. Apuzzo gave him an office, a computer and a mandate: "We need to take over the AIDS issue in Washington," she said. Apuzzo told him not to worry about turf or Steve Endean. The gay community was "being bombed," adding: "Go wherever the issue takes you."

December 1982, New York

By the winter of 1982, one battle was being joined in Washington, where established gay leaders like Apuzzo were preparing to appeal to Congress and the Reagan administration for help. But a second and equally tangled battle was being fought within the homosexual community, and each new bit of information about AIDS—about the death count, about the apparently inevitable fatality of the immune system breakdown and, most of all, about the route by which this disease spread—polarized gay men and women a little more. The tensions had started with Larry Kramer's first articles and were now in full bloom across much of the country. And the issues of contention were as old and entrenched as the modern gay liberation movement itself.

The official announcement that this disease—a breakdown of the immune system which led to the appearance of a series of often fatal opportunistic infections—was caused by a virus still was a year and a half away. But by the end of 1982, it seemed increasingly clear that its principal method of transmission was through sexual intercourse, principally anal intercourse between men, through the use of shared needles and through blood transfusions. Homosexuals, drug addicts and recipients of transfusions were at immediate risk. And one fact was also clear: the incidence of disease among gay men was directly related to a life built around promiscuous sex and heavy drug use. In November, a group of affluent Los Angeles homosexuals who called themselves the Probettes—they built their weekends around a club called The Probe, a smaller, Los Angeles version of The Saint—created a local counterpart of the Gay Men's Health Crisis, called AIDS Project Los Angeles (APLA). None of the Probettes was ill, but they had spent part of the summer of 1982 at Fire Island Pines, and they knew founders of the Gay Men's Health Crisis from the beach and the Pavilion, the all-night disco there. The Los Angeles group was made up of men like Matt Redman, a designer who often spent four nights a week dancing at The Probe, and its heart came from Nancy Cole, a wealthy, heterosexual costumer and makeup artist. Cole, a fixture on Los Angeles's gay social scene, was a full-fledged Probette, who kept pace with everything the men did, starting at the disco and ending with early-morning group sex-and-drug sessions. The founders of APLA saw what was happening in New York and assumed, correctly, that they, too, would be touched by this, since all of them, including Nancy Cole, had danced, slept and partied with the men from New York who were now becoming ill.

The realization that this was a disease spread by sex was political and cultural dynamite. In 1981, when the first cases were being reported, it seemed a question only for gay men to argue among themselves about how they conducted their private lives. But now, with gay leaders like Apuzzo turning to Washington for help, it was obvious the debate could not be confined to homosexuals. New and difficult questions were beginning to arise at the end of 1982 that would swell over the next three years, engulfing the gay community and much of society. Should bathhouses and sex clubs be closed or policed? If so, should the gay community crack down on its own or should government be allowed into what had for so long been a secret world? Should men infected with the virus—if that was, indeed, what it was—be segregated or even quarantined?

Most fundamentally, was fighting for the rights of people to have sex what the gay liberation movement was about? Here were the same questions first posed by separatist lesbians a decade before, and they now presented themselves with a new urgency. The gay male sexual liberationists after Stonewall had hijacked the movement, Larry Kramer declared, and homosexual men had constructed their culture on a corrupt foundation. They had made a "virtue of fucking," glorifying sex above all else. As more men fell ill, Kramer's views attracted more adherents. Michael Callen and Richard Berkowitz, both twenty-seven years old, gay and sick, wrote an article for the *New York Native* in November 1982 that laid out the case against male sexuality. It was perhaps the most revealing essay on gay urban life since *Faggots*. "We know who we are," announced its headline; "Two gay men declare war on promiscuity." Callen and Berkowitz had been proud frequenters of the baths, sex clubs and Greenwich Village piers. Facing death, they blamed themselves and "those of us who have lived a life of excessive promiscuity." The Centers for Disease Control had reported that the median number of lifetime sexual partners among AIDS patients was 1,160, a statistic that Callen and Berkowitz asserted had been ignored by the gay and mainstream press.

"Our lifestyle has created the present epidemic of AIDS among gay men," they wrote. ". . . We have remained silent because we have been unable or unwilling to accept responsibility for the role that our own excessiveness has played in our present health crisis. But deep down, we know who we are and we know why we're sick." The reaction was fierce and predictable: Once again, it was clear that to expose the issue of gay male sexuality was to attack it. "What is 'excessive' to some may be prim to others," Nathan Fain, a Gay Men's Health Crisis founder, wrote in *The Advocate* of the Callen-Berkowitz confessional, "but by advertising their guilt so candidly, these men detonated the issue of promiscuity as dangerously as they knew how."

The pursuit of sex was, to many gay men, as honorable and legitimate as a traditional heterosexual marriage with children; it was as fundamental to "gay liberation" as enacting gay rights bills or electing an open homosexual to the city council. Significantly, some of the founders of the nation's first Gay Activists Alliance, including Marty Robinson and Jim Owles, were not involved in the early response to the AIDS epidemic. They resisted the suggestion that this disease was a price of their political victories of ten years before. And they were not alone. Frank Kameny announced that he was proud to have devoted his career to promoting "the concept of recreational sex," adding: "I have never looked upon promiscuity as a dirty word. It is a natural and normal style of living, while monogamy is a deeply entrenched cultural overlay." In Los Angeles, Morris Kight simply refused to consider the notion that the disease had anything to do with homosexual intercourse. He kept a piece of yellow paper on which he scribbled each new rumor about the cause of this disease—monkeys, cats, hepatitis B—and he told Ivy Bottini, "This is a plot to control gay sex." As late as 1984, Kight would insist, "The correlation in this case does not specifically link anal intercourse to the route for AIDS," though a just-published UCLA report suggested the exact opposite. "If somebody can tell me what AIDS is and how it's transmitted, I'll call a press conference and say, let's not do that anymore." Bottini found Kight's position so disturbing that she stopped dealing with him for nearly three years.

Many of the men who found themselves drawn into this latest debate had never considered their sexual lives in public terms, and the attacks forced them to articulate a response. "During the last sixteen months, American gay men have suffered their roughest communal turbulence since the Anita Bryant assaults of 1977," Michael Lynch wrote in November 1982 in *Body Politic*, a gay newspaper in Toronto known for its frank coverage of sexuality. Reviewing the community debate, including David Goodstein's comments that gay male life had become an "elaborate suicide ritual," and Larry Mass's sober chronicling of the epidemic in the *Native*, Lynch wrote that many homosexuals "seek to rip apart the very promiscuous fabric that knits the gay male community together and that, in its democratic anarchism, defies state regulation of our sexuality. Just as disturbingly, gays are once again allowing the medical profession to define, restrict, pathologize us." The gay response to this "health crisis"—Lynch put the phrase in quotes, as if to suggest that it might not even exist—represented a "communal self-betrayal of gargantuan proportions and historical significance. Have we wielded, ourselves upon ourselves, a major setback in the cause of what we used to call gay liberation?"

Lynch's article equated promiscuity with political freedom, and it was the leading edge of a growing backlash among many gay men, who continued to resist controls on sexual behavior. Larry Mass was attacked and ostracized by men who had once been his friends. And when Nathan Fain wrote his two-part *Advocate* article that asked the question, "Is Our Lifestyle Hazardous to Our Health?" a letter writer from San Francisco responded: "Two hundred cases of a deadly disease among 20 million gay people in this country is hardly something to write a series about, unless you're a doctor who needs business or someone who has a morbid imagination." In New York, one *Native* writer said the Callen-Berkowitz article "borders on the hysterical." The writer posited a hypothetical gay man in his thirties who was "ragingly promiscuous," consumed "lots of recreational drugs" and kept a weekend house three hours north of New York City, in Woodstock. "In the coming year, that man is more likely to be injured or killed in his car on the way to or from Woodstock than he is to develop AIDS."

March 1983, San Francisco

The article "1,112 and Counting," written by Larry Kramer, appeared first in the March 14–27, 1983, issue of the *New York Native,* and was then reprinted in gay newspapers across the country, although *The Advocate* remained the noteworthy exception. It was a milestone, like Stonewall, Anita Bryant's campaign in Dade County, or Harvey Milk's murder.

"If this article doesn't scare the shit out of you, we're in real trouble," it began. "If this article doesn't rouse you to anger, fury, rage and action, gay men have no future on this earth. Our continued existence depends on just how angry you can get." Kramer reviewed the acceleration of AIDS diagnoses, the scant coverage by the gay press, the failure of government to respond and the lack of alarm in the gay community. There were now 1,112 cases; there had been forty-one known when the first *New York Times* story appeared twenty months before. "Unless we fight for our lives, we shall die," Kramer wrote. "In the history of homosexuality we have never been so close to death and extinction before."

Kramer was being forced out of the GMHC because his co-founders were more annoyed than ever by the style and tactics on display in this article, his rage and what they saw as his alarmism, and his confrontation of public figures, notably the mayor of New York, Edward I. Koch. When Koch first encountered Kramer at a going-away party for the city cultural affairs commissioner, Kramer, in a one-man zap, surged past the mayor's police detail, yelling: "My friends have died! Eighteen of my friends have died and you're not doing anything!"* Kramer was constantly threatening to assert on television that Mayor Koch was afraid to respond to the epidemic because he was a closeted homosexual. Though gossip about Koch's supposed homosexuality had been common in New York gay circles since he was elected to Congress— Koch had, at different times in his political career, either denied it or refused to discuss it—Kramer's insistence on using it as a political weapon offended closeted homosexuals like Paul Popham.† The differences between Kramer and Popham over whether the organization should focus on health or political activism, which had divided the two men since the founding of GMHC, were proving irreconcilable. "I am sick of everyone in this community who tells me to stop creating a panic," Kramer wrote in "1,112 and Counting," referring as much to people inside GMHC as without. He complained to his friends that an organization that needed to scare men into curbing their sexual behavior and prodding the government to action had instead been taken over by social workers "helping people die." The final break came after Koch agreed to meet with AIDS activists on April 20, 1983, responding to a letter Kramer helped write. Kramer was not included on the list of ten activists who would meet with the mayor. "Larry, you can't have it both ways," Jim Fouratt, one of the remaining Stonewall-era activists, told him. "You can't call someone a murderer and then expect him to meet with you." When Kramer announced he would quit the Gay Men's Health Crisis, Popham replied that the board would do nothing to dissuade him. Larry Kramer was out of favor with the most influential AIDS organization in New York and, most distressingly for him, without an organizational platform.

But the Kramer article set off the first national tremors of AIDS activism. There were candlelight marches in Los Angeles, San Francisco, Chicago, Houston and Manhattan by grim gay men and their supporters demanding help from the federal government. Gay newspapers outside New York, which relied heavily on the advertising revenues of baths and sex clubs, now began to respond, if hesitantly. "I and the editors of the *Advocate* do not

---

* Koch later said that he was intrigued by meeting Kramer, and after reading one of his articles in the *Native*, wrote him a letter inviting him to come in for a meeting. Koch said an adviser urged him not to send the letter because Kramer was too controversial in the gay community. The New York mayor said he always regretted following that advice.
† Koch has at times said he is not homosexual, and at other times, including an interview for this book, declined to comment on the question. The New York mayor's sexuality has been the subject of speculation since his days as a congressman, if only because he never married and lives in Greenwich Village. There have been repeated attempts by gay activists and journalists to corroborate this assertion, without success. Regardless, virtually every major gay activist in New York, starting with the Gay Activists Alliance in the early 1970s and continuing with Kramer and the AIDS activists in the 1980s, simply assumed that he was, and dealt with him accordingly.

agree with Kramer that panic or hysteria will help solve the AIDS problem," David Goodstein wrote in the *Advocate.* "There is already too much panic in the gay community. Being horny is bad for one's health, too. Sex is not bad, even now."

One of the people who noticed Kramer's essay was Randy Shilts, now working at the *San Francisco Chronicle.* He had played a small role in his paper's notably extensive coverage of the epidemic. He sent Kramer a note the day after he read the essay: "Thank God you had the guts to say what needed to be said—keep stirring the shit—thanks for the common sense." And almost overnight, Shilts turned himself into a full-time AIDS reporter, and a singularly effective one. Shilts knew firsthand the world of San Francisco bars and baths, and thought the role they must be playing in the transmission of the disease was obvious. They were too serious a threat, he argued, to justify the cautious response of the city's homosexual leaders. Sixteen days after "1,112 and Counting" was printed in New York, Shilts published a story which reported the results of an unreleased study by two researchers at the University of California at San Francisco, who found that one in every 350 single men in the city's gay neighborhoods had been diagnosed with AIDS. The study had been provided to Shilts by a senior official in the health department, upset that the city was sitting on it in deference to gay Democratic club leaders. "Startling Finding on 'Gay Disease' " announced the headline on page one, and it was published with a chart tracking AIDS diagnoses, the line of infections shooting straight up and out the top of the chart. Shilts published his story over the objections of Randy Stallings, president of the Alice B. Toklas Memorial Democratic Club. "They'll put barbed wire up around the Castro," Stallings told Shilts. "It will create panic. People won't go to gay businesses in the Castro. It will be used to defeat the gay rights bill in Sacramento." Shilts, who thrived on the attention that came with criticism, shrugged off the callers who urged him to hold the story. "I don't get paid to not write stories," he told them.

Shilts later remembered the spring of 1983 as the season when the gay community snapped to attention. He could see it where he lived: The crowds were thinning in the Castro and attendance was down in the baths, bars and sex clubs. "I'd estimate that business in bars is off 25 percent and business in baths is down 50 percent," Karl Stewart, who covered the leather scene for the gay *Bay Area Reporter,* told Shilts for a May 2, 1983, piece in the *San Francisco Chronicle.* The Castro, which Shilts had once found so inspiring, now seemed dark and under siege. "Isn't it something," Shilts told a *Newsweek* reporter that spring, "that what brought most of us here now leaves tens of thousands of us wondering whether that celebration ends in death." The same thing was happening in other communities. Bathhouses printed half-price admission coupons in local newspapers. "Like heterosexuals who have to contend with unexpected pregnancy, we are learning that sex has its consequences," Arnie Kantrowitz wrote in *The Advocate* in March, just before Kramer's "1,112 and Counting." Another New York writer, George Whitmore, found a city "obsessed with AIDS," adding: "We've finally come down off the psychosexual binge of the 1970s."

May 1983

At first glance, the report in the *Journal of the American Medical Association* seemed as if it might actually help. The single biggest obstacle gay leaders had found in dealings with government was lack of interest: AIDS was a problem for people on the edges of society. No matter what advances gay leaders believed they had made in the past ten years, the slow response from local and federal governments, and the disinterest shown by most of the country's major newspapers, notably the *New York Times,* were reminders of their impotence. "Why are health officials so inexplicably hesitant to investigate AIDS when afflicted Americans are dying by the dozens?" Gerry Studds, the Massachusetts Democrat, asked in a speech on the House floor in May 1983, three months before his homosexuality and his affair with a congressional page were revealed. "The principal reason is that most AIDS victims—at least so far— have been homosexuals," he told his fellow House members, who would censure him for the affair. Studds's somewhat subtle "at least so far" was framed more emphatically by Kramer, who said flat out that he had always presumed nothing would happen until the first child became infected.

The report in the *Journal of the American Medical Association,* then, seemed almost propitious. A pediatrician in New Jersey, James Oleske, had discovered eight unexplained cases of AIDS among children in Newark, four of whom had died. They were born into homes where family members had or were at risk for AIDS, but none of the infants had been exposed to blood transfusions, sexual intercourse or intravenous needles. "Our experience suggests that children living in high-risk households are susceptible to AIDS and that sexual contact, drug abuse or exposure to blood products is not necessary for disease transmission," Oleske reported. Anthony Fauci, the director of AIDS research at the National Institute for Allergy and Infectious Diseases, wrote an editorial for the *Journal* that put the study in alarming perspective: "If routine close contact can spread the disease, AIDS takes on an entirely new dimension." Oleske had failed to mention a fourth possibility: that the children had been infected in the womb, which is what turned out to be the case. The study set off a furor. "Evidence Suggests Household Contact May Transmit AIDS," an AMA press release announced. "Routine Contact May Spread AIDS," said the two-column headline in *USA Today.* The *New York*

Times headline in its first edition, based on an Associated Press story, said: "Mere Contact May Spread AIDS." (The headline was changed in subsequent editions to read: "Family Contact Studied in Transmitting AIDS.") Nathan Fain reviewed the newspaper coverage inspired by the *Journal* story in his column the next month. "The result?" Fain wrote. "Planting the idea in the general population that [members of] AIDS risk groups are like walking Three Mile Islands."

Any hope that a perceived outbreak of AIDS in the general population would turn society's sympathy and attention to this emerging epidemic turned out to be a miscalculation of the highest order. Homosexual men found themselves under a whole new kind of siege, the objects of a backlash of fear and hate. "The sexual revolution has begun to devour its children," Patrick Buchanan, a former Nixon speechwriter and now a syndicated conservative newspaper columnist and television commentator, wrote in the *New York Post* in May 1983. "And among the revolutionary vanguard, Gay Rights activists, the mortality rate is highest and climbing." Sexually active homosexuals were a threat to society, Buchanan warned, members of "a community that is a common carrier of dangerous, communicable and sometimes fatal diseases," who had no place in the company of children or handling food. "The poor homosexuals," Buchanan wrote. "They have declared war upon nature, and now nature is exacting an awful retribution."

Buchanan articulated a growing fear. The backlash hit first and hardest in San Francisco. The city issued masks and vinyl gloves to 250 firefighters and police officers worried about close contact with homosexuals in emergency situations, and the moment was captured in pictures distributed to newspapers across the country. San Francisco's bathhouses began to receive unwanted attention. The *Chronicle* columnist Herb Caen reported that a gay doctor he knew had run into three of his AIDS patients in the baths. The city's public health director, Mervyn Silverman, contemplating the dangers posed by the annual arrival of probably uninformed out-of-town gay guests for the Gay Pride celebrations in June, asked bathhouses to post signs alerting patrons to the disease risks. "There's the potential that AIDS will spread from here around the country," Silverman said.

The backlash was not confined to cities with such visible homosexual populations. In Houston, fundamentalist preachers urged city officials to close gay bars as a health hazard. A city pool in Tulsa, Oklahoma, was drained by recreation officials after word leaked out to a terrified public that the local gay rights group, Oklahomans for Human Rights, held its third anniversary party there. The *Tulsa World* chastised the city for overreacting, but added that in light of recent events, "it might be a good idea to find a better name than 'gay' for these distressed and now fear-haunted people." Virginia Apuzzo discovered that the 800 hotline number she had set up at the Task Force to provide information to scared homosexual men had unexpectedly become a reliable measure of anti-gay sentiment. "Get AIDS and die!" was a typical message. The mail was equally hostile, and Apuzzo grimly dropped each new hate letter into a folder on her desk.

The fear in the general public was reflected, and nurtured, by much of the media. One 1987 study would find that major news organizations collectively published five times more stories on AIDS in the immediate aftermath of the *Journal* study than during the entire first two years of the epidemic. While some stories were emotional accounts of young men confronting early death, many were unsympathetic reports that presented homosexuals more concerned about their sexual gratification than public health. "WHITE-WASH," read the white type headline splashed across the red cover of *California* magazine that summer. "While the number of AIDS victims doubles every six months, gay leaders in California have obscured vital information about how the deadly disease is spread, endangering thousands of lives." The story opened with a steamy description from inside the Liberty Baths in San Francisco, with the "muffled sounds of ecstasy" coming from inside closed cubicles. The story recounted a conversation the authors—Peter Collier and David Horowitz, well-regarded biographers of the Rockefeller, Kennedy and Roosevelt families—reported overhearing a conversation at the bathhouse lunch counter between two naked and unidentified men.

" 'We're just little time bombs, aren't we?' " one says. The report continued: "Then, he stands, stretches, and wipes his mouth with a napkin. 'Well, I don't know about you, but I'm going to have some fun while I *tick*.' " In *Screw* magazine, Al Goldstein, the sexually libertine publisher who had made a career of being offensive, jokingly hailed AIDS as a disease that transforms its victims from "fruits to vegetables."

"We are speechless," wrote Nathan Fain, who rarely was.

"All we can do is keep repeating the facts," Dr. Selma Dritz, the San Francisco Health Department's specialist in disease control, said at each new report of a fearful reaction to AIDS and homosexuals. But the "facts"—that AIDS appeared to be transmitted only by sexual intercourse and needles—did little to calm a population alarmed by the AMA *Journal* report. The general public's first questions about AIDS, then, were not how can we help, but just how contagious is this disease? What about mosquitoes? A kiss on the lips? Sweat? Through the air? Could a homosexual waiter spread it by plate to a restaurant patron? Could a dentist pass it on with his instruments? How about a doctor who had just completed a physical examination of a homosexual patient? What if the doctor or dentist was a homosexual?

Homosexuals were struggling with the same issues. Vin McCarthy, a Boston lawyer, and a member of the Human Rights Campaign Fund board, felt guilty as he found himself nodding when a heterosexual friend remarked that she would not now go to Provincetown and risk being bitten by a mosquito swollen with blood drawn from an infected homosexual. In Los Angeles, when the father of a close friend of David Mixner's, Marylouise Oates, the society columnist for the *Los Angeles Times,* went into Cedar-Sinai Medical Center for quadruple-bypass heart surgery, Mixner insisted that she round up friends to donate blood before her father's operation. "Marylouise," Mixner said, "get people you know who are *non-gay.*" Bruce Voeller noticed that gay friends who used to greet each other with a full kiss on the lips now kept their greetings to a dry and presumably safe peck on the cheek.

A public which was beginning to associate homosexuals with an epidemic learned about places like the Hothouse, a San Francisco sex emporium, with hot oil rooms, slings and mirrors. It closed down, after business dropped 50 percent, with what Randy Shilts in the *Chronicle* described as the "kinkiest garage sale" in city history. "The various restraining devices would easily have filled the demands of several medieval dungeons," Shilts reported, in a story rich with the kind of detail which reflected the author's familiarity with his subject. The closing of the Hothouse was the opening anecdote to a nine-page *Newsweek* cover story that summer entitled "Gay America in Transition," which announced that "AIDS may mean the party is over."

"For Gay America, a decade of carefree sexual adventure, a headlong gambol on the far side of the human libido, has all but come to a close," *Newsweek* wrote. "The flag of sexual liberation that had flown as the symbol of the gay movement has been lowered. Caution and responsibility—to oneself, to one's friends, to the larger and still pressing concerns of gay life in America—are now the watchwords of gay liberation, and many homosexuals do not regret it."

In *The New Republic,* Charles Krauthammer wrote: "Now—just as homosexuality was prepared to take the last step and free itself from the medical mantle which at first protected it and now confines it—comes the 'gay plague.' Just as society was ready to grant that homosexuality is not illness, it is seized with the idea that homosexuality breeds illness." A Gallup poll that summer underscored the point: 25 percent of respondents believed they could contract AIDS by "casual contact," and 21 percent said they now felt "less comfortable with friends and acquaintances who are homosexual." Fifty-eight percent of respondents said homosexuality should not be considered an acceptable alternative lifestyle, up from 51 percent a year before. Those kinds of sentiments reverberated in places like Sacramento, where Senator H. L. Richardson, an established opponent of gay rights, cited the AIDS epidemic as one more reason for California not to approve a gay rights bill. "Because of the very real medical problems currently plaguing the homosexual community, our decision may also be one of life and death," he said.

• • •

By early summer of 1983, the gay community in San Francisco, the most influential in the nation, was divided over what, if any, obligation the city had in curbing sexual behavior that was spreading the disease. AIDS is the "most political disease I've ever seen," Mervyn Silverman told Randy Shilts, after the health commissioner came under fire for his request that bathhouse owners post simple warning notices. The Alice B. Toklas Club had termed the order a "direct attack on the social and economic viability of our community. There is no evidence that the bathhouses or private clubs are the cause of this illness. To single out one type of gay business as somehow 'responsible' for this epidemic is to begin the process of destroying our community." When Supervisor Carol Ruth Silver, one of the gay community's strongest supporters, asked if the city should consider closing the baths until the AIDS epidemic was contained, she was met with a loud chorus of hisses.

Even the elemental task of preparing a health department brochure on AIDS was jammed in the political machinery, as the city's major gay political clubs, rather than the health department, battled over what it should say. The more progressive Harvey Milk Gay Democratic Club pushed for explicit leaflets. But the more conservative Alice B. Toklas Club chastised the Milk Club for advocating something which it feared would be a public relations disaster. The Milk Club, led by Bill Kraus and Cleve Jones, responded by printing a manifesto in the *Bay Area Reporter*:

"What a peculiar perversion it is of gay liberation to ignore the overwhelming scientific evidence, to keep quiet, to deny the obvious—when the lives of gay men are at stake. What a strange concept of our gay movement it is to care more about what they may do to us than about the need to spread the news about this disease to our people so that we can protect each other." To that, the Alice Club responded: "There is a trend among some elements of our community to be anti-sexual and panic prone at a time when we should be banding together to defend a way of life that is precious and hard-won." The dispute stalled the Feinstein administration, since the mayor could not very well ignore the wishes of the Alice Club, which had helped her survive a recall election earlier that year. The Harvey Milk Club did what Bill Kraus termed "an end run around" the city: the club itself began to prepare and distribute the brochures that the health department would not.

On July 4, 1983, Jerry Falwell took the stage at a rally of the Moral Majority in Cincinnati. The religious right was locking onto a new issue: the "plague of the century," as Falwell called it. "If the Reagan Administration does not put its full weight against this, what is now a gay plague in this country, I feel that a year from now, President Ronald Reagan, personally, will be blamed for allowing this awful disease to break out among the innocent Amer-

ican public," Falwell told the cheering crowd. He called for the government to
shut down gay bathhouses and to prohibit homosexuals from donating blood.
Falwell said he had nothing against homosexuals themselves—only their "perverted lifestyle." AIDS was "the judgment of God," Falwell said. "You can't
fly into the laws of God and God's nature without paying the price."

For homosexuals, the specter of a populist backlash fanned by the religious right was nearly as alarming as the disease itself. Gay leaders began to
worry about whether quarantine for men with AIDS, or all homosexuals,
might be over the horizon. "It's happened before," warned a full-page ad
placed in the *New York Native* by the Human Rights Campaign Fund in June
1983. "It happened in America, where for the 'common good,' Japanese-
Americans were stigmatized and then quarantined. . . .

"We don't know the cause of AIDS. . . . We do know that *fear* of AIDS
and its identification with the gay community may be the next epidemic. An
epidemic of fear on the part of Americans threatens all of us in the gay community, *regardless* of our health or lifestyle."

August 1983, Washington, D.C.

By the August morning when Virginia Apuzzo led a handful of homosexual lobbyists to Room 2154 of the Rayburn House Office Building in Washington, D.C., for the first of two days of congressional hearings on the federal
government's response to AIDS, it was clear that the gay movement now
started and ended with this new epidemic. The words "gay" and "disease"
were linked everywhere. The Task Force had been resurrected in the ten
months since Apuzzo became its executive director, and AIDS, more than
anything else besides the director herself, accounted for its rebirth. The Task
Force was the only organization equipped to deal with AIDS as a national
problem; groups, such as Gay Men's Health Crisis, AIDS Project Los Angeles, and the Kaposi's Sarcoma Research and Education Foundation Inc. and
the Shanti Project in San Francisco had enough to do locally. It was left to the
Task Force to gather itself on each new unexpected battlefront about AIDS.

Thus, when the National Hemophilia Foundation, reacting to the news
that eight hemophiliacs had contracted AIDS, demanded "serious efforts" to
exclude blood "donors that might transmit AIDS"—by questioning potential
donors to determine if they were, among other things, homosexual—the Task
Force opposed it as a "political solution to a medical problem," which would
stigmatize a group of citizens. "I don't have to tell you what gay blood, bad
blood could mean to a community that has historically been discriminated
against, particularly in employment," Apuzzo said at a press conference in
Manhattan. When medical leaders suggested the gay movement was putting

civil rights ahead of the nation's safety—"People are dying. The medical problem is more important than the civil rights issue," said Dr. James Curran, the head of the Centers for Disease Control Task Force on AIDS—Apuzzo dispatched Bruce Voeller to respond. He was a biologist, and, as he brusquely reminded scientists who challenged his motivations, "I have three children. I have two elderly parents. I have two sisters and their families. . . . I'm as committed to a clean blood supply, if not more so, than you are." And now, on the first day of August 1983, Apuzzo was going before Representative Ted Weiss's Intergovernmental Relations and Human Resources Subcommittee to attack the government's response to AIDS and tangle with Republicans wondering why Washington should rescue gays from a plague they had seemed to bring upon themselves. "The government's policy is one of gestures, not actions," Apuzzo said, seated at the table in the center of the hearing room, her glasses slid down to the tip of her nose. "The government's timetable is unacceptable. We count not in hours, days or weeks—we count in lives."

That Virginia Apuzzo was speaking before Congress was a sign of how much Steve Endean's power had ebbed over the past ten months. There were a tangle of explanations for his now tenuous position. Largely because of Endean's hesitant response to the AIDS epidemic, he was at war with Larry Bush, and, for that and other reasons, with David Goodstein. Even as Apuzzo brought the Task Force back to prominence with the AIDS issue, Endean resisted changing course. Endean's Gay Rights National Lobby had advised the U.S. Conference of Mayors in Denver to pass a resolution urging Congress to spend $50 million on AIDS in fiscal 1984; Apuzzo and the Task Force had wanted twice that much. Apuzzo and Bruce Voeller, now the Task Force's adviser on AIDS, were flabbergasted at Endean's more modest demand. A gay man had undercut a lesbian on AIDS, Apuzzo thought. And when they confronted Endean, he replied not with a scientific argument, but a political one: their request for $100 million was unrealistic. At first, Endean had seemed unable to shift his political focus on AIDS, and at that, he was not much different from many gay men. But by the summer of 1983, the epidemic had become serious enough to warrant two days of congressional hearings, and Endean seemed overwhelmed and outmatched, particularly when sharing a stage with Apuzzo.

Endean's problems had begun after the November 1982 elections. The Human Rights Campaign Fund had raised $588,000 by election day—more than twice what anyone expected—funding contributions in 118 House and Senate campaigns. It had chosen well: 81 percent of the candidates it backed won. With the election over, Endean wanted to put the Human Rights Campaign Fund in hibernation until the 1984 elections and shift its fundraising apparatus to his financially beleaguered Gay Rights National Lobby. Endean shared this scenario over dinner in California with David Goodstein and Bruce Voeller. Goodstein was enraged. He had devoted the past six months to the HRCF, traveling the country and using his column to beat wealthy homosexuals into contributing, and was pleased at his success. "I don't care how much they support the opera, the symphony or other bastions of respectability, or even how great their parties are," he wrote one week. "Not until they support the communities of which they themselves are members will they deserve any respect." Goodstein believed it was a mistake to abandon the donors. "We will need a huge war chest for the 1984 election," he said, "and two years is not a long time to raise it." His rage swelled as Endean shrugged off his advice. "I just want you to be clear, Steve," Goodstein finally told Endean. "If you don't do what I say, what you do will be in the news." Endean ignored Goodstein's threat; he assumed he was now too established to be hurt by anyone.

It is difficult to reckon how much the subsequent attacks on Endean were the price of his defiance, and how much they reflected the considered conclusions of Goodstein and Larry Bush that Endean was failing in Washington. Until now, Bush had been praiseworthy of Endean and his Gay Rights National Lobby. "Even with the glacial attitude in Congress toward gay rights this past session, GRNL has succeeded marvelously," Bush wrote at the end of the 1982 congressional session, and he listed Steve Endean second, behind only Virginia Apuzzo, in his list of "Ten People Who Made the Most Difference This Year." Endean, Bush said then, had been a key player in moving homosexuals "out of the fringe and into the mainstream in political circles." Now, less than a year later, Bush went to Endean to warn he was failing. Bush suggested that, among other things, Endean immediately turn his attention to the AIDS epidemic. Endean nodded in agreement, but Bush thought Endean was only trying to divert him from writing more critical stories. Endean was an obstacle, Larry Bush concluded, and his personal limitations had become limitations on the movement. He shared his views with David Goodstein, and with members of Endean's boards of directors at GRNL and HRCF. "Why are you guys not asking questions of your director?" Bush demanded. "This is unacceptable."

Endean began making mistakes under pressure. At a Human Rights Campaign Fund meeting in Miami, he announced the fund was out of money and asked board members to write checks on the spot. When the *Washington Blade* wrote about this stormy meeting, Endean denied the account and promised to produce tapes that would "exonerate" him. He then withdrew that offer. Bush wrote a sarcastic column in *The Advocate* suggesting Endean was playing an elaborate game of "hide and seek" with the press to mask the severity of his mismanagement. The Human Rights Campaign Fund had less than $2,000 left out of what had been a total budget of nearly $600,000. The purpose of a political action committee was to raise and contribute money to sympathetic politicians, so the depleted bank account was arguably a sign of the Campaign Fund's success. But both Voeller and Goodstein pronounced themselves startled at HRCF's financial plight. "The gay community raised the largest amount of money in the history of the movement," Voeller told a reporter. "Then, out of the blue, they gave out a cry that they can't pay their rent and payroll. How can that possibly happen?" In March, Endean wrote a private "Dear David" letter to Goodstein, "responding to a number of the concerns you have raised at various points." The act of conciliation struck Goodstein as a sign of weakness. Finally, in a phone conversation that was one part a newspaper interview and one part job evaluation, Larry Bush informed Endean that many in the gay political community considered him impossible to work with and overextended. Bush said it was time for Endean to step aside from one of his jobs, as executive director of the Human Rights Campaign Fund. Under siege, Endean heeded the advice of "journalist" Larry Bush, as he sarcastically called him, and resigned in the spring of 1983 the executive director's post, holding onto his job at the Gay Rights National Lobby.

That wasn't enough. Endean was having continuing financial problems at the GRNL, and even supporters who described him as visionary concluded he couldn't manage. "GRNL's current financial plight includes a massive shortfall of income and an excess of expenses over budget," Bruce Voeller had written in a February 1983 letter to the organization's board members. "Lack of a cash plan in 1982 was unprofessional and disastrous." Bush and Goodstein argued that this demonstrated that Endean should not be on the payroll of any major Washington gay organization. "Even though it pains me to say so," Goodstein wrote in a particularly brutal "Opening Space" column in June 1983, "I believe we have boys and girls doing men's and women's jobs at the Gay Rights National Lobby (GRNL) and the Human Rights Campaign Fund (HRCF). More accurately, the job has outgrown the people there. . . . Events have moved faster than their ability to handle them. . . . Whether Endean's failures are the result of his own incompetence or his soft heart is irrelevant."

Endean tried to dismiss this as a class issue. "David has a Hollywood picture of what a lobbyist is," Endean said. "That's not the only model." Endean sent letters to gay newspapers, urging his critics to "stop demanding immediate perfection." And other gay leaders came to his defense. Mel Boozer, himself pushed out of a job by Virginia Apuzzo, said the problem lay not with Endean but with Bush and Goodstein, and he observed that "a few powerful people were using the media and money unfairly" to criticize Endean. "No medieval scene would be complete without a bishop," he wrote in the *Washington Blade.* "Thus far there has been only one reporter, Larry Bush, who has aspired to such an exalted status." He said the incident demonstrated that the gay movement had become too vulnerable to the whims of one newspaper. "I object to the *Advocate,* its owner, and its Washington editor practicing intimidation politics," Boozer said. Bush replied that as the gay movement had evolved, the role of the gay press had graduated from being the "movement's propaganda arm, reprinting organizational press releases almost verbatim, to a watchdog role, questioning mainstream politicians and gay politicians who speak on behalf of lesbians and gay men." And when it came to Steve Endean, Bush was indeed much more than a journalistic watchdog. He had gone from a reporter to a player, as powerful as anyone on the payrolls of the nation's gay organizations.

David Goodstein almost always got his way, and when it seemed as if Endean was holding on, Goodstein launched his ultimate weapon. He announced that he would withhold contributions from gay organizations that employed Steve Endean, and advised his readers to do the same. "You can be very certain that if I had had the power, the board of GRNL would have fired Stephen Endean, their chief honcho, last February for what I perceive to be dereliction of duty, incompetence and mismanagement of funds and staff," Goodstein wrote in October. "That Endean still has a job in the gay community is a testimonial not only to the incompetence of the board of that organization but also to my own lack of power. Perhaps you will choose to join me in refusing to donate one red cent to GRNL until Endean leaves, which is the only way to insist that the organization acts competently and urgently." A report on GRNL's fundraising activity a month later attested to the power of Goodstein's column and pocketbook. An appeal for funds had brought in $11,000, less than a quarter of what Endean had projected. On Saturday, October 15, 1983, as the Gay Rights National Lobby executive committee met in a basement dining room of a Chicago church, Endean, citing a "poisoned atmosphere" created by "half-truths, distortions and factual inaccuracies," resigned. "I believe the attacks on me during the past nine months can largely be attributed to a political vendetta combined with a quest for power and control of our movement," Endean wrote in his letter of resignation. Without naming names—it wasn't necessary—Endean said: "They describe my unwillingness to take their marching orders as incompetence."

There was a backlash to this latest episode of muscle-flexing by David Goodstein. "We are uncomfortable with the Great White Father image that the *Advocate* publisher and his supporters are cultivating," the *Philadelphia Gay News* wrote in an editorial. "Social status, wealth and power are emerging as the main criteria by which members of the gay community should be judged. Image is becoming more important than substance. We see an increased exclusion of minorities, women and middle-class blue-collar gays from the decision-making process." Frank Kameny called Goodstein's coverage a "vendetta waged mercilessly with all the power of the press gone wrong."

Charles Stewart, a Los Angeles black activist, a co-chairman of the national Black and White Men Together organization, and also a friend of Endean's, posed one final question in a letter to *The Advocate*: "Goodstein and Bush do agree on one thing about Endean: He has consistently failed to heed their advice. Well, so much for Endean. Now, who's next?" The answer came soon: The *Washington Blade* joined a chorus calling for the creation of one organization to handle gay issues. There was no debate about who should lead the unified gay movement. "The Gay Movement in the nearly 15 years since Stonewall has not produced an abundance of national leaders," the *Blade* editorialists said. "Indeed, one might well argue that it has produced none. Until Apuzzo."

Endean could not comprehend how quickly his world had collapsed. He was very close to suicide, struggling, he later said, with a nervous breakdown. Kameny, who was untroubled by the insecurities, compulsions and self-recriminations that raged within Endean, was surprised by how traumatized his thirty-five-year-old friend seemed by all this. After twenty years Kameny had come to expect this kind of battering at the hands of other homosexuals. It proved again the truth of what Donald Webster Cory of the Mattachine Society had told Dick Leitsch after Cory was voted out of the Mattachine Society in New York in the mid-1960s: "They call me the father of 'the homophile movement,' and homosexuals always turn on their fathers," Cory said, "so I should have expected this."

34

LITTLE TO CELEBRATE

October 1983, New York

Jesse Jackson was the keynote speaker at the Human Rights Campaign Fund's second fundraiser in the Grand Ballroom of the Waldorf-Astoria in New York, and his presence was testimony to the success this kind of big-ticket, black-tie gay activism had attained. Jackson, like Walter Mondale, the speaker in 1982, was running for president, but his visit was notable for reasons which had little to do with Jackson's political ambitions. Never before had a major black leader spoken before a homosexual gathering like this. There was an estrangement between many blacks and many white homosexuals, and that was clear from a glance across the white faces in the Grand Ballroom, and from an inspection of the leadership and membership rosters of the major gay organizations of the previous ten years. There was not, and there had never been, any alliances between gay and black civil rights activists during their struggles of the past fifteen years, even after Mel Boozer, who was both black and homosexual, sought to connect the two movements from the stage of the 1980 Democratic convention. ("Bigotry is bigotry, discrimination is discrimination. It hurts just as much.")

The explanations for this reflected both the forces at work in the society at large and the particular tensions that emerged between black and gay rights activists. Examples of discrimination practiced by gay white men against blacks were frequent and notorious. Studio One, the West Hollywood night-club, demanded triple identification as proof of age from blacks, but never whites, or refused admission to people in broad-brimmed hats, which were in style with some blacks. In the case of Studio One, blacks who talked their way past the door would find themselves treated rudely inside. Bobby Smith, a black gay activist, would remember spending ten minutes waving for the bartender's attention as the white men around him collected their drinks. It was not unusual. Less than twenty blocks from where Jackson was speaking that night in New York, a chrome-and-neon basement dance club called the Ice Palace 57 had been picketed for nearly a year by Black and White Men Together, a gay political and social organization that sought to deal with racism among homosexual men, and whose organizers included Henry Wiemhoff, the white University of Chicago dropout who had founded Chicago Gay Liberation in 1969. Black and White Men Together devised a sting to document discrimination at the Ice Palace, borrowing its strategy from the NAACP's campaigns to illustrate racial discrimination in the South. Ten volunteers were sent to the door to judge whether blacks and whites were treated differently. The white couples and a racially mixed couple were welcomed. But four black men were told to show multiple forms of identification, and two were turned away. The New York Division of Human Rights found this display convincing enough to order the Ice Palace to pay $6,000 in punitive damage to the four black men.

For bar owners, discrimination was good business. "Let's face it," said Scott Forbes, the owner of Studio One. "Every club has a door policy and a different way of catering to the kind of crowd it wants. Customers don't come just for the drinks or the decor. They come for the clientele. It's like casting." That meant keeping the crowd as male, white and handsome as possible. Blacks were sent away—but so were women and, at Sheldon Andelson's bathhouse in Los Angeles, older, heavier or unattractive men. And for the most part, the white clients didn't mind. When Black and White Men Together distributed leaflets urging patrons to dance someplace else besides Ice Palace 57, citing the discrimination it had found there, the men on the way for a night of dancing took a pamphlet and continued down the steps into the club. "There's a complacency that seems to be setting in, as well as just inherent racism," said one of the leaders of the Ice Palace campaign.

And it didn't end with the bars. There was hardly a black face in the leadership ranks of any of the major gay organizations in 1983. The best-known national black gay activist, Mel Boozer, had been replaced as the National Gay Task Force's Washington representative by Ginny Apuzzo. The net effect was to leave the nation's oldest gay organization even whiter. Betty Powell, Apuzzo's lover, who was black, never forgot how alone she felt when she joined the Task Force board; looking around, she knew exactly why she was there. The composition of these organizations often reflected a pragmatic if cold calculation by gay white leaders, which Charles Stewart, a black activist from Los Angeles, discovered as he tried to find a place in the white gay circles of power. As an eleven-year-old boy visiting his great-grandfather in Birmingham, Stewart was instructed to drink only from the fountain marked "Colored," and to step into the gutter for white people coming up the street. As a young man in Los Angeles, Stewart had been barred at the door of Studio One. Stewart was one of the first leaders of the national Black and White Men Together, and he appealed for a seat on the board of the Human Rights Campaign Fund or the National Gay Task Force. But Steve Endean—who would go on to become one of Stewart's closest friends—turned him down. Blacks, Endean told Stewart, had no track record when it came to raising money— and Endean considered fundraising more important than racial equity. "The only thing on this planet I love more than black men is the gay movement," Endean told Stewart, referring to his sexual tastes, "and I will not allow anything to dilute it. Nothing." Stewart was silenced by his candor. In Los Angeles, Stewart was rebuffed again by the leaders of MECLA, which also had an all-white board of directors. "It's not about race prejudice," Roberta Bennett, one of MECLA's leaders told Stewart. "It's about money prejudice." It was the same argument that had been used by men to keep women off the board in its early years.

It flowed both ways. Black leaders had, with the notable exception of Huey P. Newton of the Black Panthers in 1970, never welcomed homosexuals or their leaders into their midst. The black civil rights movement had sprung largely from the pulpits of the churches of the South, where preachers taught that homosexuality was sinful. Betty Powell found anti-homosexual sentiment in the black movement overwhelming after she disclosed her lesbianism by running a conference of the Gay Academic Union in New York, she resigned her membership in the Association of Afro-American Teachers, chilled by her treatment by colleagues she considered friends. Many blacks resented the argument that there was any equivalence between the plight of blacks and homosexuals. On the contrary, many black leaders believed that blacks undercut their political influence by allowing themselves to be associated with the homosexual movement. The Leadership Conference on Civil Rights, a coalition of black, Hispanic and women advocacy groups, refused to admit the National Gay Task Force in 1977, and did not relent until 1982. And in 1983 homosexual leaders were first rejected when they sought a place in a demonstration marking the twentieth anniversary of Martin Luther King's March on Washington, sponsored by an alliance of civil rights, women's rights, labor, youth, religious, environmental and peace organizations (just as Bayard Rustin, a homosexual, was barred from a public role at the 1963 civil rights march, which he had helped to organize). The twentieth anniversary march director, Representative Walter Fauntroy of Washington, D.C., who had defeated Franklin Kameny in the race to be the District's nonvoting delegate in the House in 1971, said the presence of homosexuals would be "divisive," and that allowing gay leaders to share a stage with blacks and other leaders of progressive causes "might be interpreted as advocacy of a gay way of life." Only after a two-and-a-half-hour telephone conference call among a half-dozen black and gay leaders, including Virginia Apuzzo and Coretta Scott King, did the organizers relent. Apuzzo, who had taught black studies at Cathedral High School in New York, reminded Coretta Scott King of Martin Luther King's "Letter from a Birmingham Jail," written in 1963 to liberal white clergymen who attacked him for persisting in his demonstrations against segregated Birmingham. "Mrs. King," Apuzzo said as the clock ticked past midnight, "your husband wasn't speaking to conservatives, he was speaking to his liberal friends. I'm speaking to my liberal friends. If not now, when? Just go back and read 'Letter from a Birmingham Jail.' " Mrs. King finally murmured her agreement, and homosexuals were given their moment on the podium, if a short one. Audre Lorde, the black feminist-lesbian writer and poet, spoke for three minutes, though five minutes was allocated for the other speakers. Still, she said afterward, it was "the first time that the black civil rights movement and the gay civil rights movement joined hands and acknowledged each other." Apuzzo determined from this experience that the case for gay rights, which she already believed had not been embraced by the general public, was even less compelling for blacks. For many blacks, discrimination based on skin color was a more urgent concern than the arguably more avoidable bias based on sexual orientation.

So the atmosphere was tense and expectant when Jesse Jackson rose to speak at the Waldorf-Astoria. He began by endorsing civil rights for gays and then reading the names of members of the Congressional Black Caucus who supported the federal gay rights bill (each name was greeted by waves of appreciative applause). He proclaimed homosexuals to be part of his "rainbow coalition of the rejected." But Jackson's speech soon turned into something else: a dressing down of his audience. There would be no rapprochement between blacks and homosexuals here. For forty minutes Jackson lectured his predominantly white, male, middle-class audience, questioning the cause which had inspired them to pay $150 for dinner. "You must grow beyond a self-centered, narcissistic movement," he said, standing stiff in his tuxedo, his voice echoing off the tiers of the Grand Ballroom. He criticized homosexuals for being "historically a part of the white economic and political establishments," which had "tended to represent a small circle of middle-class men and women who frequently consolidate rather than share their power and positions." There were few blacks in the gay rights movement, Jackson noted disdainfully. He urged his audience to think "beyond yourself" on such issues as health care. "AIDS is not the only disease in the nation tonight. Be concerned about AIDS, but also sickle cell, bubonic disease, and pneumonia. Be concerned about the human rights of gays, but also Native Americans trapped on reservations and blacks in ghettos.

"Ours is a challenge to search for common ground," Jackson said. "We must move from the sexual battleground to the economic common ground. We must get bigger than ourselves." And finally, leaving no question of his own view of the gay rights movement, Jackson declared: "Sex is a thrill, but so is getting the Voting Rights Act. Sex is a thrill but so is getting ERA [passed]. Sex is a thrill, but so is unscrewing those nuclear warheads that could destroy the human race."

Harvey Fierstein, the playwright and master of ceremonies, seated at Jackson's right elbow, stared coldly through his wire-rimmed glasses at the audience, his chin nestled in his clenched-up right fist, his face set in stone. "I don't like this," Fierstein whispered to Ethan Geto, who now worked as a political consultant and who had orchestrated Jackson's appearance. Geto did not want to see this groundbreaking moment for blacks and homosexuals spoiled by an angered Fierstein. "Harvey, look," Geto pleaded behind his hand, "this is very important. Don't say anything."

"No one can stop me," Fierstein said. And the moment Jackson finished, the master of ceremonies rose to the microphone to rebuke the evening's honored guest.

"Sex is a thrill," Fierstein said, his gravelly voice familiar to this crowd from his starring role in his play *Torch Song Trilogy,* "but homosexuality is not just about sex." That remark won the biggest cheer of the night. Glancing at Jackson, Fierstein challenged the assertion that sexual orientation was a "personal and private" matter. "I'm tired," Fierstein said. "I want to be able to kiss my lover on the street just the way you kiss your wife in public."

Jackson's speech was sobering, and not only for its racial implications. Jackson had no chance of winning the Democratic nomination, but he would influence the Democratic Party and its candidate, and he had the luxury of expression that comes with being a candidate who does not expect to win. Jackson's speech was a reminder of how even the most liberal Americans had come to see gay rights: It was about sex and nothing else. Public laws were needed only to protect carnal passions that should be kept private. Homosexuals should turn their attention to more serious issues confronting the country. This perception—that the gay rights movement was only about sex—had grown with the stories about the AIDS epidemic. The disease had put homosexuals on display as never before but, as Jackson's speech made clear, only one sliver of the spectrum: sexually active gay men. There were people in Jackson's audience who did not share the sexual concerns of these men—lesbian mothers who were losing their children in custody fights, activists documenting incidents of anti-gay violence, homosexuals who had lost jobs or apartments or the loyalty of their families—but they were missed by Jackson that night, as they were missed in the portraits of homosexuality that were becoming common in newspapers and on television.

July 1984, San Francisco

The Democratic National Convention came to San Francisco in the summer of 1984, and with it, a week of media expeditions into the fabric, fringes and all, of what had come to be viewed as the nation's homosexual capital. This was an obvious story by now, and while it was unsettling to the city's homosexual leaders, who found the attention unwanted and inflammatory, it was not unfamiliar. For the past year, out-of-town reporters had been coming to San Francisco to report on AIDS and the increasingly depressed way of life of homosexual men. Even the convention issue of *The Advocate* played the theme: it displayed a photograph of a despondent, bearded man, slumped and covered in speckle, under the headline: "Is the *Party* OVER?" The coverage presented the city's homosexual community as at once sad and sordid. Still, the stories that appeared about San Francisco outside the city were, if embarrassing to the city's image, ultimately of little consequence.

But the coverage of AIDS and homosexuality by a San Francisco journalist who was, by now, well known in the city—Randy Shilts—could not be ignored. His explicit reporting for the *Chronicle* had become largely responsible for the city health director's move to crack down on bathhouses and sex clubs, a battle that gripped and threatened to embarrass the city just as the convention began. Shilts was one of only two openly gay reporters working for mainstream newspapers in the country,* and he might have been more unpopular in the Castro than Jerry Falwell himself by the summer of 1984.

Shilts had long been an enigma to homosexuals in San Francisco. On first inspection, he seemed to be just another gay man of the Castro: a familiar bearded face in the crowded bars on Saturday night, a wiry, trim figure often spotted tunneling through the shadowy, red-lit corridors of places like the Hothouse. The gay men of San Francisco, Shilts would say, rebutted the sissified, desperate and lonely stereotype that had defined homosexuality for him as he grew up in Aurora, a suburb of Chicago. The men of the Castro—because that was really about whom Shilts was talking—were proud, assertive and masculine, whether they were strutting down the street for a night out, pushing their way into the city's political world, or chasing out gay-bashers

* The other was Joe Nicholson of the *New York Post*.

who ventured through the neighborhood. Shilts's pride in the Castro was well known, so people had assumed that in print, he would be as much a booster of the Castro as any of the neighborhood's business, civic or political leaders.

That assumption was incorrect. Shilts's homosexuality and his allegiance to the Castro complicated his life as a newspaper reporter as the health crisis unfolded. But no matter how much he admired the Castro, he was not a partisan. He considered himself an exceptional reporter—he *was* an exceptional reporter—and no one would ever accuse him of putting the interests of the Castro ahead of his professionalism. Shilts's homosexuality turned out to count in only one way: It qualified him as an expert on the subject he was covering. He had traveled this terrain since college, when he worked as a towel boy in a gay bathhouse in Portland, Oregon, earning money to put himself through two years of community college. Shilts knew about the sexual underground—the parks where men went to cruise after sundown, the clubs with the back rooms south of Market Street, the wild parties which mixed dancing, drugs and sex, and most of all, the indiscriminate and frenetic promiscuity of the city's bathhouses. When researchers first drew links between anal sex and AIDS, Shilts did not have to interview doctors or epidemiologists or bath owners or patrons to understand the significance of this discovery. He knew firsthand how baths encouraged easy and multi-partner anal sex. "If a group of people had gone out of their way to create a subculture in which a sexually transmitted disease could proliferate," Shilts wrote in 1984, "they could not have done a better job than gays in the 1970s." The baths themselves were a "petri dish" for disease, devastatingly effective in spreading the virus which in April 1984 was identified as the cause of AIDS (initially called HTLV-II). Shilts reached that conclusion about the baths long before the city's health department did. It was Shilts who reported in the *Chronicle* after an initial dip in attendance, "business is booming again in the bathhouses," and that "men, hundreds and hundreds of them can be found there every night, many under the influence of substances that make it doubtful they're pondering the Public Health Department's AIDS risk-reduction guidelines." Later, in 1985, Shilts disclosed that rectal gonorrhea among gay men was "surging again," an indication of unprotected anal intercourse. He profiled gay men who found themselves drawn to the baths, their sexual compulsions outweighing their fear of a fatal disease. Shilts reported that department officials were dismayed that some men with AIDS continued to patronize the bathhouses, and that they could not find a way to stop them. As 1984 began, Shilts had quoted James Curran, coordinator of the AIDS task force for the federal Centers of Disease Control in Atlanta, suggesting the time had come to close the bathhouses. "I'd like to see all the bathhouses go out of business," Curran said to Shilts. "I've told bathhouse owners they should diversify and go into something healthy— like become gymnasiums." After that story appeared, Curran told another reporter that Shilts had quoted him out of context; that he wouldn't be "disappointed" if the baths were closed down, but he didn't believe the government should be "legislating sexual behavior." Obviously, Curran said, Shilts disagreed. Shilts's critics seized on this. "He wants to shut down the bathhouses and tried to get someone to say that," Harry Britt, the gay supervisor who was appointed to replace Harvey Milk, told *The California Voice*, a gay newspaper.

Shilts's stories convinced many gay men that he was on a crusade. Shilts's reports were nearly as alarming—some of his detractors considered them closer to inflammatory—as the AMA's incorrect report that AIDS was spread through casual contact, and they were stampeding city hall into action. Shilts's coverage also provoked angry phone calls and street-corner confrontations that challenged him for even raising the subject of the baths. "I'm being crucified for the mere fact that I talk publicly about whether the bath houses should go out of business," Shilts told an *Advocate* reporter who questioned him about his coverage. "I don't see how anybody knowledgeable about the AIDS crisis can not talk about bath houses." In an essay that he wrote for the *Native* in the summer of 1984, Shilts said: "As far as I'm concerned, writing upbeat stories during the AIDS epidemic would be like writing about the party favors on the *Titanic*." Shilts had come under fire before, but he had never encountered attacks this intense. Shilts was vilified as a turncoat, a Nazi, a sexual fascist and an Uncle Tom who had put his career above his friends. His name appeared in a gay newspaper under a list of "traitors" to the community. He found himself scorned in his own world; he could not appear publicly without being confronted. Some of his friends refused to dine with him, weary of having their meals interrupted by loud attacks. When his image flickered on the screen during a Castro screening of the documentary *The Times of Harvey Milk* there were boos in the darkened auditorium. Shilts cringed in his seat. If he were straight, Shilts later said, he would have been honored for his work. Because he was a homosexual, his reporting was seen as betrayal. Explaining the attacks provided him little comfort. Shilts had always drunk too much—alcoholism ran in his family—and smoked a little too much marijuana. Now, he found himself drinking even more and adding cocaine to his daily mix. He felt lonely, sorry for himself and came to look at 1984 as the darkest year of his life. But it did not stop him from writing.

"A homosexual McCarthyism has descended on San Francisco's gay community," Shilts wrote in a first-person dispatch for the *Native* before the Democratic convention. "Even now, the thought police lurk in the sweet summer shadows of these balmy evenings. Hysterical inquisitors stand on the corners of 18th and Castro, ready to guillotine heretics from the True Faith."

Among those who believed bathhouses were not to blame for the epidemic, there was good reason to resent Shilts's stories. Public opinion appeared to be turning against what had once been the gay sexual underground:

A poll by the *San Francisco Chronicle* found 44 percent of respondents thought sex should be barred in bathhouses, and 36 percent thought the establishments should be shut completely.* Mayor Feinstein, who had always been uncomfortable with open displays of sexuality among gay men in her city, complained that the city health director, Mervyn Silverman, was moving too slowly against the bathhouses out of fear of offending politically influential homosexuals. "If this was a heterosexual problem, they would have been closed," Feinstein told the *Chronicle*. Silverman, who had agreed with the argument that closing bathhouses was an intrusion into civil rights that would drive unsafe sexual activity further underground, found himself under siege. Larry Littlejohn, a past president of the pre-Stonewall organization Society for Individual Rights, said the baths should be closed, and threatened to gather signatures to put before voters an initiative to bar sex in bathhouses if the health department did not act. "A lot of people in the straight community don't know what's going on in there," Littlejohn said. Faced with the possibility of a voter referendum on their sexual practices, most of the gay groups quickly fell in line behind a statement urging Silverman to crack down before voters did. "Bathhouses have long been important for gay people, but clearly now saving lives is of greater importance," a coalition of fifty political leaders wrote Silverman.

But rather than close the bathhouses, Silverman announced that he would seek regulations to bar sex in them. His tentativeness displeased Mayor Feinstein, and she voiced her complaints to Randy Shilts. "I don't like how political this has become," she said. "People are seeing hobgoblins where there aren't any, talking politics when people are dying." And even this hint of modest action by Silverman provoked a fury among gay men. Homosexual men, wearing white towels—and nothing else—showed up at a meeting to shout him down. Concern spread beyond San Francisco. Nathan Fain, who had provided some of the most clearheaded AIDS coverage in his *Advocate* column, described the fight as a struggle between the reality that this fatal disease was spread by sex and the perception that "having sex is presumably what the very identity of a gay man rests upon. Sexual freedom has been dearly won and won't be easily lost—even on the threat of death.

"What is shocking about the San Francisco news is the alacrity with which a significant number of gay men and lesbians acted to urge their city to make criminals of some of their own people," Fain wrote, adding: "Gay solidarity lay in ruins, shaken to shards by an ideological fault line that finally gave way. Else-

---

* Of the respondents who identified themselves as gay, 18 percent thought the baths should be closed, and 34 percent said sex should be barred. The poll was based on interviews with 554 people, 132 of whom said they were gay, a small and thus not very reliable sample of homosexuals.

where, people were wondering: Why San Francisco? Then: will it happen here?"

Fain's concerns reverberated across the country. "We're mistaken if we think this action will be confined to San Francisco," Frank Kameny told fellow board members of the Gay Rights National Lobby. The National Gay Task Force denounced Silverman's action, declaring "that personal behavior should not be regulated by the state, which historically has been an instrument of our oppression." (Both the Task Force and GRNL had, at various times used bath-houses as an inexpensive lodging for their male members during board meet-ings.) Thomas B. Stoddard, the openly gay legislative director of the New York Civil Liberties Union, suggested that any homosexual leader who advocated governmental intervention suffered from a "short memory" and had forgotten the way government had once routinely harassed such establishments. Silver-man's maneuverings created concern as the convention approached. At the last minute, the board of supervisors voted to delay dealing with the matter until after Democrats left. The bathhouse fight disappeared from the front pages just as the Democrats came into town, but it would return.

Nearly 100,000 homosexuals and their supporters marched up Market Street, from the Castro to the Moscone Center, on the Sunday afternoon be-fore the Democratic National Convention was gaveled to order in the second week of July. The march had been conceived the previous November as a "mass action," but it had evolved into a celebration rather than a demonstra-tion, a parade rather than a march. The walk had a festive air, with banners, balloons and soap bubbles glistening over the well-groomed crowd, notable for the absence of angry placards, extravagant drag queens or men in leather. The guests of honor were at the head of the line: the sixty-five openly gay men and lesbian delegates, alternates and committee members who would spend the next week inside the Moscone Center.* AIDS aside, the year had been filled with good tidings for gay activists, who had won one key test. An early contender for the Democratic nomination had categorically campaigned against gay rights, and he had not survived the primaries. "I would not advo-cate or promote homosexuality," said Senator John Glenn of Ohio, the Ma-rine Corps pilot who had fought in World War II and Korea, and was the first

---

* There had been seventy-seven in 1980. The decline was evidence of the relative lack of so-phistication in the movement. Senator Alan Cranston of California, an early candidate for the nomination, had aggressively courted homosexuals to run as his delegates, and gay activists had responded overwhelmingly. A more sophisticated movement would have fielded delegates sup-porting all the major candidates, to cover its political bases. The gay movement did not, and when Cranston dropped out, before the spring, forty-one gay activists running as his delegates were left without a ride to San Francisco.

American astronaut to orbit the Earth in 1962. Glenn said civil rights law should not cover "areas of personal behavior." He found himself in a firestorm. "It is an insult to everyone who believes in 'liberty and justice for all' to insinuate that this group of Americans should be excluded from that idea," Virginia Apuzzo said in a telegram. The issue dogged Glenn at every turn in New York. At a speech on the economy, Glenn was asked how old he was when he decided he was straight. Glenn's face flushed as he considered the provocative implications of the question. "I never made the choice," he finally replied. "I always presumed I was not gay and lived my life accordingly." Homosexual protesters picketed outside a fundraising dinner that night, and Glenn again stood fast. "What might be acceptable in New York and San Francisco might be quite different in other areas of the country," he said. The New York chairman of his campaign, Manfred Ohrenstein, the minority leader in the state Senate, who represented Manhattan's West Side, resigned in protest. Allen Roskoff, the former member of New York's Gay Activists Alliance who was now the openly gay president of the New York Chapter of Americans for Democratic Action, remarked: "I thought we had to do everything to get Reagan out. Now we have to do everything we can to keep Glenn out."

It soon became clear that this was not an unwanted controversy. "He has elaborated on his position and we're prepared for the political consequences," said Glenn's press secretary, Michael D. McCurry (who later became President Clinton's press secretary), and the reporters understood the meaning of the statement. Sam Nunn, who as chairman of the Senate Armed Services Committee would be instrumental in maintaining the Pentagon's policy barring homosexuals from the military in 1993, held up Glenn's opposition to gay rights as a badge of honor when the candidate went to Georgia. "John Glenn has the courage to give up his New York State campaign chairman rather than give up his strongly held moral belief that homosexuals should not be the role models for our children," Nunn said.

Glenn's views seemed particularly striking because one of his senior campaign officials was gay, and Senator Glenn knew it. The operative, who has never publicly declared his homosexuality, was fifty years old then. Like Paul Popham at the GMHC, he was not prepared to announce his sexuality, but he felt too old and established to try to hide his sexual identity at work. He had lived with the same man for nearly ten years, and politicians were frequently guests for dinner. When he began talking to the Glenn campaign, the operative came to Washington and told Glenn's campaign manager he needed a moment with the senator. Glenn invited his prospective employee to join him on the car ride back to the Capitol.

"I understand you had something you wanted to discuss with me," Glenn said, apparently expecting a demand for a favor in exchange for allegiance.

"Well, Senator," the man responded, "you've talked to me about playing a very important role in your campaign and I wanted to be sure you knew that I was gay."

There was a moment of silence. It was obvious that Glenn had not known the man was gay and, indeed, might never have been confronted with such a direct revelation from a homosexual before. Finally, Glenn responded, "I appreciate very much your candor in discussing this. I want to think about that." A week later the operative was hired.

The campaign official never spoke to Glenn about the senator's opposition to gay rights. He also never considered quitting. He had never expected to agree on every issue with the politicians he worked for, and while this difference of opinion disturbed him, he later said, he believed his presence as a quietly open homosexual could do more to change Glenn's thinking than any confrontation. Other gay leaders involved in the 1984 presidential race—notably David Mixner, who was a finance co-chair for Gary Hart—found it difficult to understand how any homosexual could support a presidential candidate who so actively opposed homosexuals. "We would rather die than support him," Mixner told the closeted Glenn aide. John Glenn placed third or lower in eleven primaries and caucuses on Super Tuesday, winning only thirteen of the 511 delegates at stake that day. And Larry Bush asserted in his column in the *New York Native,* "Glenn may, when it is all over, have made the strongest contribution to gay rights simply because he gave pro-gay supporters a focus."

Bush's observation seemed confirmed that summer as the gay delegates began the march down Market Street. Not only had Glenn lost, but the Democratic Party had been so accommodating to gay rights advocates that there was nothing left to fight about. The demands made in the original call for this march were largely incorporated in the gay rights plank in the Democratic Party's platform. The party was on record as opposing discrimination against homosexuals in employment, immigration and—for the first time—the military, and in support of an "enhanced effort to learn the cause and cure of AIDS and to provide treatment to people with AIDS." "This is not a protest, but a show of support for the Democrats," said Karen Clark, the lesbian state representative from Minnesota and member of the convention's rules committee. Apuzzo boasted of the gay movement's accomplishments on national television, telling ABC News, "We've gotten everything we could expect in the party platform." The chair of the platform committee, Geraldine A. Ferraro, a Roman Catholic representative from Queens who would be chosen by Walter Mondale to run for vice president, said: "Some people in my district might not like it very much. But I can't imagine they would expect me to favor discriminating against anyone."

The three Democratic candidates—Mondale, Jackson and Gary Hart—

had, like their party, become straightforward in their support for gay issues. Senator Hart, the only elected official in the race, had responded to pressure from gay supporters—including Mixner—and become a co-sponsor of the gay rights bill in the Senate. Mondale had, if uncomfortably, endorsed an end to discrimination against homosexuals in the military. And at the convention, glancing over a floor dotted with "Gay Vote '84" banners, Jesse Jackson showed no sign of the disapproval he had displayed in New York the previous fall. "The Rainbow Coalition includes lesbians and gays," Jackson declared from the podium, as gay delegates rose from their seats in appreciation. "No American citizen ought to be denied equal protection." Gil Gerard, a co-founder of the National Coalition of Black Gays, said, "It's the first time a major candidate has unequivocally spoken about us as being part of the Democratic Party."

What happened inside the convention hall was, arguably, irrelevant. People across the country instead heard about what was taking place on the streets of San Francisco. Jerry Falwell and Phyllis Schlafly organized a two-day "Family Forum" on the eve of the convention to discuss the "threat of homosexuality," while the more colorful members of the city's gay community demonstrated obligingly for the television cameras outside. "We didn't choose San Francisco—the Democrats chose San Francisco," Falwell said jubilantly. Unlike the marchers to the Moscone Center, the protesters outside were an assortment of men in drag, and some of the city's more colorful characters— including Sister Boom-Boom, a member of the Sisters of Perpetual Indulgence, who performed an "exorcism" of Falwell and Schlafly for the benefit of the cameras, as someone hoisted a banner which read, "Thank God I'm Gay." These were the camp antics San Francisco was known for, and they came to be a staple of the daily coverage of Democrats' meeting. "The media portrayed it as the land of fruits and nuts," David Goodstein noted in his *Advocate* column. "They concentrated on the most bizarre and the most outrageous characters they could find." Goodstein was irritated at the press, but he blamed homosexuals. "I want to go on the record that Sister Boom-Boom does not represent the gay community. Boom-Boom is no longer funny. Even the best jokes became stale after repetition by the same comedian for several years. When they first appeared, the Sisters of Perpetual Indulgence made an important point about the hypocrisy of religion. Now they are an embarrassment and a barrier to our being taken seriously. They are no more representative of our community than Amos and Andy were of the black community."

Jerry Falwell was as happy as Goodstein was not. "They played right into my hands," he boasted to his friend and ghostwriter, the Reverend Mel White (who, years later, would reveal his own homosexuality). "Those poor, dumb, fairy demonstrators gave me the best media coverage I've ever had. If they weren't out there, I'd have to invent them." Falwell left San Francisco with new material for new anti-homosexual rights mailings, taken from the demonstrations he inspired outside the Holiday Inn. He mailed them out in protective sealed envelopes marked "For Adults Only! Explicit photographs enclosed. Please do not let these photos fall into the hands of innocent, impressionable children." Inside were pictures of two men kissing, a demonstrator dressed as Christ and Sister Boom-Boom. Falwell told his followers that he saw two men "tongues intertwined, openly in public," and that there were men in "women's clothing," complete with makeup and hairstyles. "Homosexuals everywhere are doing these immoral acts. Blatantly, openly, in plain view of our children."

The mainstream backlash began before the summer ended. Morton Kondracke, the executive editor of *The New Republic*, complained that the Democrats had caved in to homosexuals. "Tacitly, but without any formal debate, the Democrats are backing the gay movement's goal of acceptance of homosexuality as a fully appropriate life style," he wrote. "What's wrong with this? What's wrong, in part, is that full acceptance of gays will lead to acceptance of the pathologies connected with the gay life style, including promiscuity and sadomasochism." "He's right, of course," Alexander Cockburn responded sarcastically in the next issue of *The Nation*. "After the Democratic Party accepted blacks you could hardly hear yourself think around the DNC offices, what with the noise of ghetto blasters and the screams of little old ladies having their purses snatched." Edward J. Rollins, who was Ronald Reagan's campaign manager, echoed Kondracke on *Face the Nation* the Sunday after the convention ended. "The Democrat party has been the party of quotas, the party of alternate lifestyles, the party of gay rights," he said.

There were no "GAY VOTE '84" banners on the floor of Rollins's Republican convention a month later in Dallas, where Jerry Falwell delivered the benediction the night Ronald Reagan was nominated for a second term. The rhetoric from the convention floor was filled with references to "family values," in obvious contrast to what television viewers had seen from San Francisco. But for Bruce Decker, the gay Republican from San Francisco who had quietly founded Concerned Americans for Individual Rights, there was some reason for hope. For the first time, three open homosexuals were alternate delegates. Decker's organization of gay Republicans was a presence as well, and even if he could not win recognition from the hierarchy—none of the gay events was ever listed on the official convention schedule—he believed that his organization was a means to convince Republicans to pay attention to homosexuals, and to convince homosexuals to pay attention to Republicans. "Somehow the term 'gay rights' has gotten a negative connotation," Decker said as he laid out for *The Advocate* his goals for the convention. "Gay rights is individual rights. We don't want special rights. We want the same and equal rights as anyone else." There would be no marches in Dallas—"That's not our style," he explained—but members of his gay Republican group would be around, attending caucuses and cocktail parties, making themselves and their modest demands known.

Decker considered Reagan perhaps the finest president of the century, and would, years later, proudly display a picture of himself shaking hands with the president—"With best wishes," Reagan scribbled across the bottom— taken during the president's visit to San Francisco in 1985. Reagan was more than tolerant of homosexuality, Decker argued, citing his opposition to the Briggs initiative and his refusal to support the Family Protection Act in Congress. Reagan had declined to endorse the gay rights bill in Congress, Decker acknowledged, but he hadn't torpedoed it, either. "Well, I just have to say I am opposed to discrimination," Reagan had said when asked about the measure. "Period." That was good enough for Decker and other Republicans, who weren't convinced that homosexuals needed any kind of special civil rights consideration, and were not then judging the response of politicians to the still new AIDS epidemic. It was obvious to Decker that Reagan was going to win reelection, and it made sense to get on board with the president.

Decker's main goal in Dallas was the opposite of what gay Democrats had set as their goal in San Francisco. He considered the convention a victory, he said, because the issue of gay rights did *not* come up, and was not explicitly referred to by Falwell and his supporters. The Republican Party was not about to endorse gay rights, and forcing the issue would only encourage the party's outright condemnation. "If you're going to get beat, don't get into a fight," he said.

"They are not fostering gay liberation," Mervyn Silverman announced on October 9, 1984. "They are fostering death in this city." Just three months after the end of the Democratic convention, and nearly eighteen months after the issue arose in San Francisco, the city's health director ordered fourteen gay bathhouses and sex clubs closed, asserting they promoted "disease and death," and displayed a "blatant disregard for the health of their patrons and of the community." Some of the city's gay leaders backed Silverman's decision. "It's very sad the AIDS epidemic has brought us to this point," said Carole Migden of the Harvey Milk Gay Democratic Club. "The bottom line is to save lives." But others did not. The announcement even produced something of a mass demonstration in the still largely unpolitical streets of the Castro: three hundred people turned out one night in protest, carrying signs that read, "Today the bathhouses—tomorrow our bedrooms."

November 1984, West Hollywood, California

There was little for gay rights advocates to celebrate with the election returns. In Texas, a representative named Phil Gramm, who had switched from the Democratic Party to the Republican Party two years earlier, was elected senator by an overwhelming 49 to 41 percent margin, after running an explicitly anti-homosexual campaign against Lloyd Doggett, a Democratic state senator from Austin. Doggett had accepted a $354 campaign contribution from a Texas gay rights organization, which he said he did not realize had been raised at a male strip show. Gramm—whose 1996 presidential candidacy would be compromised by disclosure that he had helped finance a soft-core pornography film—got wind of this and shared the information with voters in his radio and television ads, accusing Doggett of supporting gay rights and quotas for hiring gays. "On family issues," declared a woman narrator on a Gramm radio spot, "there's a sharp difference between Phil Gramm and Lloyd Doggett." That day Senator Jesse Helms, a sponsor of the Family Protection Act, was elected to a third term from North Carolina, in a contest in which he similarly criticized his Democrat opponent, Governor Jim Hunt, for taking money from gay groups.

Ronald Reagan also won that day. An effort by CBS News's election and survey unit to count the homosexual vote in the presidential election as part of its exit poll in California and New York—the first time that had been attempted—drew too small a response to be reliable; less than 2 percent of surveyed voters checked the box identifying themselves as gay or lesbian.* But there was anecdotal evidence that a sizable number of homosexuals, particularly middle-class men, had voted for Reagan. A candidate's position on AIDS would soon replace economics as an overriding deciding factor for many homosexuals, but not in the election of 1984. "My concern has always been that the country be strong economically," said Susan Jester, president of the San Diego County Log Cabin Republican Club, a gay Republican organization with chapters across the country. "If we're bankrupt, the last thing anyone's going to be thinking about is gay rights." As Bruce Decker had put it in an *Advocate* column endorsing Reagan: "A big, costly, and intrusive govern-

---

* In New York, 18 out of 1,894 identified themselves as homosexual; in California, it was 54 out of 2,000, in both cases far too small to be measured. The inclusion of the question was pushed by Murray Edelman, who had been with Henry Wiemhoff, one of the founders of Chicago Gay Liberation, and was now working, as an open homosexual, at CBS's polling unit. See also the essay by Associate Professor Robert W. Bailey of Rutgers University, "Estimating the Urban Gay Vote and Its Effect," Oct. 30, 1994, reprinted in his *Gay Politics, Urban Politics: Identity and Economics in the Urban Setting* (New York: Columbia University Press, 1998).

ment is no boon to gays or lesbians." Decker took satisfaction in Reagan's election, predicting it would be good for homosexuals.*

In the Democratic Party, homosexuals found themselves taking much of the blame for Walter Mondale's loss. Reagan's success at portraying Mondale as a captive of "special interests"—shorthand for blacks, labor, liberals, homosexuals, all symbolized by the choice of San Francisco as a place to hold a convention—became part of the conventional explanation for why Mondale had done so poorly. "According to the self-proclaimed experts, the thing that hurt Mondale *most* was his (snicker) support of rights for (can you believe it?) homosexuals," David Goodstein noted in a postmortem. "The election of 1984 may go down in history as a tremendous setback in the gay and lesbian community's fight for the rights of life, liberty and the pursuit of happiness." This accepted explanation of Mondale's loss became so widespread within the party that its so-called special interest caucuses, including the Gay and Lesbian Caucus, which had been created in 1983 and which consisted of two representatives to the Democratic National Committee, were purged. "Fringe issues and life style issues such as gay rights cannot be the priority in the dialogue of a major party," Paul Kirk, the new chairman of the party, announced in 1985.

But there was one unlikely victory for homosexuals and their supporters in the election of 1984, and it involved a 1.9 square mile spot of densely populated land, shaped roughly like a pistol, in the center of Los Angeles County. This was West Hollywood, which had been a refuge for homosexuals since the 1950s, when the first two gay bars opened there, out of the reach of the Los Angeles Police Department. Homosexuals and bohemians from across the Los Angeles basin were drawn to this unincorporated part of the county. By the end of 1985, there were close to a hundred businesses that catered to homosexuals in West Hollywood, including a gay bank that Sheldon Andelson had founded, and dozens of gay bars and dance clubs. Downtown West Hollywood became known as Boy's Town, for reasons that were obvious to anyone who took a drive down Santa Monica Boulevard on a Saturday night. The 1984 election presented the 20,000 registered voters in this part of Los Angeles with two ballot issues to consider. The first was whether to create a new city

---

* Decker went on to defend the Reagan White House when, in one of the first actions of the new term, the president chose as his director of communications Patrick Buchanan, the conservative columnist who had been among the first to suggest that AIDS was an appropriate punishment for homosexual coupling. That was a low-water mark for many gay activists, but not for Decker, who praised Buchanan's "impressive professional background" and dismissed the rumbling among other gay activists. "If the position to which he was appointed were dealing with civil rights or human rights, there might be some grounds to the criticism," Decker said. "But it sounds like the same old stuff that we always hear, that we'll be marched to the concentration camps if Reagan has his way. That's hogwash."

of West Hollywood. And the second was to select five people who would sit on the first council of this proposed municipality. On election night, West Hollywood became the eighty-fourth city created out of unincorporated Los Angeles County, but this was far from another municipal referendum. The vote in West Hollywood captured national attention, and the results that night were reason for celebration by homosexuals in West Hollywood and beyond. Seventeen of the thirty-seven candidates running for the five city council seats were openly gay or lesbian. On election day, 67 percent of the voters embraced the idea of creating this new city, and selected a council which included two gay men and a lesbian—a homosexual majority. Before this election there had been only thirteen openly gay elected officials in the country, and none in Los Angeles. In the space of a night, West Hollywood became known, if passingly, as a gay city.

Nearly a thousand people pushed their way into the auditorium of Fiesta Hall in Plummer Park on November 29, 1984, for the first meeting of the West Hollywood City Council. Someone had made a banner that read "West Hollywood City Hall," and hung it from the eaves of the building. By the end of the night, West Hollywood had adopted a gay rights ordinance: introduced, seconded, debated and passed in the single night. And the council selected from its members the first mayor of West Hollywood. She was thirty-one-year-old Valerie Terrigno, a lesbian, who had until recently run a job counseling service for the poor in West Hollywood. It was as if the Gay Activists Alliance had taken over city hall. The anti-discrimination ordinance passed on the first night was as sweeping as any in the nation; anyone who discriminated against homosexuals—in jobs, housing or public accommodations—faced a $500 fine. And as soon as that law took effect, Valerie Terrigno led a contingent of city hall officials and reporters to Barney's Beanery, the chili parlor with the "Fagots Stay Out" sign, where Morris Kight, Jim Kepner and Troy Perry had picketed fifteen years before. In truth, the owner had put up a new sign as soon as the Gay Liberation Front and the cameras had disappeared, a fact which Kight and the others knew but chose to ignore. Now it stood in violation of the laws of the new city of West Hollywood. Mayor Terrigno arrived not with a picket sign, but with a screwdriver. She climbed up behind the bar, and in less than a minute, removed the sign again. Barney's owner, Irwin Held, watched in disgust at what he considered a crude gambit for publicity, at his expense.

"The sign's always been part of Barney's," he protested.

"For the people of West Hollywood," Terrigno responded, "there has been nothing nostalgic about it."

35

FOR THE PUBLIC GOOD

May 1985

Sheldon Andelson and Bruce Mailman were both successful business-men, and business for both of them was the baths. Andelson's 8709 baths in Los Angeles and Mailman's New St. Marks Baths in New York's East Village were the nation's premier bathhouses in the mid-1980s, and they allowed Andelson and Mailman to live quite well, though money was not what they talked about when explaining why they kept the baths open even as signs of an epidemic swirled around them. Bathhouses, they said, were political establishments as much as they were commercial ventures—expressions of gay liberation. Until the middle of 1985, the bathhouses and sex clubs in Los Angeles and New York—and Shelly Andelson and Bruce Mailman personally—escaped much of the fury which had nearly consumed the gay sex industry in San Francisco. That was about to change.

Andelson was a public figure in Los Angeles, politically and socially of note. *Los Angeles Magazine* ranked him number 42 on its list of the fifty most powerful people in Los Angeles ("Very powerful because of his role in the gay community and as a Democratic fundraiser"). *The Advocate* said Andelson might be "the world's most powerful gay person," a description that did not seem exaggerated. And in May 1985, Andelson announced that he was closing the 8709, the most popular bathhouse in Los Angeles, famous for turning away patrons who were too old, too fat, too effeminate, or who smelled of cologne. Andelson said he was terminating the lease on 8709 in deference to the health crisis in the gay community. "It was a difficult decision," Andelson said. "I did what I think is correct." His action was applauded by the city's AIDS activists. Bill Meisenheimer, executive director of AIDS Project Los Angeles, termed it "courageous."

But Andelson's announcement was curious because to all public appearances he had removed himself from the bathhouse business more than three years before, when Governor Jerry Brown nominated him to be a member of the University of California Board of Regents, the job that Andelson had told Brown he wanted most of all. With his nomination, in February 1982, Andelson's public aspirations collided with his private tastes and business interests. There had never been an open homosexual on the Board of Regents, and certainly never one who owned a bathhouse.* Andelson knew that he faced an extraordinarily difficult confirmation battle in the Senate, and he turned to David Mixner and Peter Scott to guide him. Mixner had one piece of advice at their first meeting: "You can't go into these hearings owning that bathhouse." When they next met, Andelson informed Mixner that the bathhouse problem had been solved. "There's nothing in my name," Andelson said, choosing his words deliberately. The ensuing confirmation debate was, as Andelson put it at the time, a "conscious attempt to destroy me and make me go home." Senator H. L. Richardson, a Republican from Arcadia, denounced Andelson on the Senate floor for "pushing sick ideas and sick influences on the community. As the Lord says, 'They're an abomination.' " Andelson won his seat, 21–10, or one vote more than was needed in the forty-member Senate. When it was over, Andelson observed to a reporter that being a homosexual in public life extracts a "tremendous price," referring apparently not only to his confirmation fight but also to the money he had lost leaving the sex business. "Effectiveness and practicality dictate that sexuality be deemphasized in the public world," Andelson said. "There are a lot of sacrifices that public figures make. They must play by the rules." In fact, Mixner had understood what Andelson meant when he told him there was "nothing in my name": he had hidden his ownership, in this case, by transferring it to associates, including a former lover, and his brother and law partner, Arlen. He had maintained his financial interest in 8709; his name just wasn't on the public record, an ac-

---

* David Geffen, the music executive and another Brown benefactor, was also a regent when Brown nominated Andelson, but Geffen's homosexuality was not public at the time. Andelson took delight in needling Geffen about this. "I'm not the only gay regent on the board," Andelson pointedly told a reporter from a student newspaper. "I'm the only openly gay regent." When Andelson was nominated to be a regent, Geffen made certain, according to Brown's amused recollections, that the governor was aware Andelson was the owner of Los Angeles's biggest gay bathhouse, mentioning that fact more than once in conversation.

ceptable ruse in 1982 because Andelson's ownership of a bathhouse was a political problem but not an ethical one. All that mattered to Andelson and Mixner back then was making sure that Jerry Brown was not embarrassed in the state Senate for his gesture to the homosexual community.

But 1985 presented a wholly different climate. Gay bathhouses were no longer operating on the edge of society, ignored or unknown to most people. In San Francisco, after a long public battle, twelve bathhouse owners had convinced a judge to overturn health director Mervyn Silverman's order that they close down, but they were now operating under such restrictive conditions—doors off the cubicles, increased lighting, one sex monitor for every twenty patrons—that the bathhouses bore little resemblance to what they had once been. It was becoming difficult for Mailman and Andelson to defend their way of making a living, particularly given the amount of public attention the baths were drawing in the furor over AIDS. "Perhaps someone should comment on the civil rights of the rest of us, who must help pay for the medical care of the AIDS victims and risk catching the disease ourselves," wrote Guy Wright, a *San Francisco Chronicle* columnist. "The fast spread of AIDS is due almost entirely to the promiscuity of homosexuals. To the extent that they are willing to reduce their promiscuity, it is in their power to slow the spread of the disease. The gay bathhouses are crucial to the AIDS battle because they are warrens of promiscuity."

And AIDS was becoming a part of Andelson's daily life. Reports of AIDS deaths were beginning to show up in MECLA newsletters. Andelson's half brother, Roger Horwitz, the lover of the writer Paul Monette, was sick, a fact that was becoming known in Los Angeles, despite Andelson's initial efforts to keep it quiet, unflatteringly recounted in Monette's *Borrowed Time,* an account of Horwitz's death published in 1988. What Monette did not write about, and did not want to think about, was that Horwitz had probably become infected with the virus that would kill both of them in the gay baths of Boston or New York, which Horwitz had visited at the urging of Monette and some of the couple's close friends, who thought he needed to understand that part of the gay male experience. (And Mixner had even heard rumors that Andelson himself was sick, and wondered if he was noticing the first symptoms of AIDS in Andelson's wan countenance and tentative step. Andelson assured Mixner these were only a symptom of diabetes.)

It took more than an epidemic, personal tragedies or the urgings of Mixner, Scott and friends who knew of Andelson's hidden interest in 8709 to convince him that his bathhouse should be shut down. Notwithstanding his announcement that he was making this "difficult decision" for the public good, Andelson closed his bathhouse because he was faced with the embarrassment of a television exposé. His hidden role in 8709 had been unearthed by a KCBS producer, Michael Singer, and after learning that the story was about to appear, Andelson, still on the Board of Regents, went again to David Mixner, who told him that he had run out of options. "If it isn't closed, you will be destroyed politically," Mixner said. "And everything that we've worked for will be destroyed politically. And you will be responsible. And I will make sure everybody knows." Mixner, who knew Singer socially, arranged a meeting, and that evening Andelson told Singer that he was closing 8709.* The piece never aired.

Still, Andelson continued to believe the epidemic would end, even as evidence to the contrary gathered around him. As Roger Horwitz grew closer to death, Andelson informed Paul Monette that his powerful friends in government and medicine had assured him that a cure was imminent. "It's really nothing serious and it'll be over in a couple of years," Andelson said. He would change the topic when the subject of AIDS came up at MECLA board meetings, and in September 1985, when Elizabeth Taylor headlined the first "Commitment to Life" dinner to raise funds for the new AIDS Project Los Angeles, Andelson put off buying a ticket until the last minute, when it was clear this was turning into one of the bigger charity parties Los Angeles had seen, drawing 2,500 people and raising $1.3 million. Peter Scott, who was chair of APLA, was so irritated by Andelson's reluctance to attend that he assigned Andelson to a table at the back of the ballroom, by the kitchen, rather than his customary prestigious posting on or near the stage.

Unlike Shelly Andelson, Bruce Mailman preferred to remain unrecognized and undisturbed, even in his own establishments. Mailman was probably the most influential and imaginative gay business owner in New York in the 1980s, and he had a seminal effect on American gay male culture, since his bathhouse and discotheque were discussed and imitated across the country. Yet he shunned attention; when the *New York Native* featured him in a 1984 story, it billed the extremely rare interview as "exclusive." Mailman, unlike Andelson, did not have his image or public standing to consider, so the St. Marks Baths stayed open after 8709 closed. But the atmosphere in New York was changing even more rapidly than in Los Angeles. In 1983 postcards were distributed at the Gay Pride Parade addressed to Mailman, which demanded that he "voluntarily close the baths" because "unless we begin to police ourselves, government agencies will soon begin policing actions on their own." Mailman counted eighteen cards, a mail ballot which he found less than impressive. "If you close the baths," he argued at the time, in his piercing nasal voice, "the next question is, do you close the bars?" He bristled

---

* Arlen Andelson, Sheldon Andelson's brother, gave a different account than the one offered by Mixner and Singer. His brother acted only out of concern about the disease, he said, and took the action to Arlen's regret: "That sucker was lucrative," he said. Arlen Andelson said he had no knowledge of the impending television exposé.

when a Saint patron wrote a letter complaining that men were having sex in the darkened balcony over the club's dance floor, including one man the patron said had AIDS. "We designed the balcony as a viewing platform," Mailman wrote in a signed "editorial" that appeared in The Saint's in-house newspaper, *Star Dust,* in May 1983. "We cannot brighten the lights because it would destroy the dome lighting, and *we will not be put in the position of policemen.* If the balcony disturbs you, *DO NOT GO THERE,* but do not name those who do. This is FASCISM and we will close the Saint before we tolerate it." (Mailman's assertion that the balcony was "a viewing platform" was disingenuous; its designers expected from the start that the men would use the warm, carpeted, darkened area for sex.)

By 1985, it was getting difficult to shrug off the protests and the warnings. For Mailman, the evidence came in the number of undeliverable poster invitations sent out for his parties at The Saint. These were famous mailings, lurid and provocative: one, for a sado-masochistic themed Black Party, contained a series of sketches depicting a circumcision, mailed out with a needle and strand of black surgical thread. The invitations were beginning to return unopened, often stamped: "Addressee deceased." This anecdotal evidence was reflected at his club, too, where there were gaps on a dance floor that had once always been shoulder to shoulder. The club needed three thousand patrons to feel full; on some Saturday nights, the count at the door was as low as 1,200.

Mailman felt compelled to do something. He canceled the 1985 Black Party, The Saint's most popular event, a dark, marathon celebration which featured live sex acts and traditionally lasted from midnight to dusk the next day. And at his New St. Marks Baths, where business was down on some nights as much as 50 percent from its pre-AIDS heyday, began to hand out condoms and wallet-size cards listing safer-sex practices. The bathhouse posted warnings in every cubicle and invited the Gay Men's Health Crisis in to offer safer-sex seminars. "YOUR HEALTH AND SAFETY ARE OUR CONCERN," read the sign on the black tiled wall at the check-in counter. The lights were turned up in the club's darker corners, and what was euphemistically called the "dormitory" was closed to put an end to group-sex scenes. But the cubicles were another matter: Mailman would not remove the doors. He held fast when Baptist and Orthodox Jew pickets appeared at his door, wearing surgical masks and holding placards which read: "The Gay Baths May Spawn An Epidemic of A.I.D.S. That Will Devastate New York!" And he held fast when gay activists, including Jim Fouratt and Michael Callen, stopped customers at the door to ask them if they were aware of AIDS and that it was spread in places like bathhouses. It was clear to Mailman's friends that the New York bathhouse owner, like Andelson, believed gay men only needed to ride out a rough few years. Mailman's brash confidence was disconcerting to his associates, particularly as he—unlike Andelson—refused to agree to the blood test for the AIDS virus licensed that spring.* Mailman's friends began to call him "The Ostrich."

Rock Hudson made Bruce Mailman shut down the New St. Marks Baths. On July 25, 1985, a publicist announced from the American Hospital in Paris that "Mr. Hudson has Acquired Immune Deficiency Syndrome." That disclosure was followed by Randy Shilts's report detailing Hudson's secret life as a homosexual, substantiated with on-the-record quotes from the movie star's friends. "Rock had learned his lesson . . . in Hollywood," said the writer Armistead Maupin, who had frequented San Francisco's gay bars and restaurants with Hudson. "And he played by the rules. Those rules say that you keep quiet about [being gay] and everyone will lie about it." Hudson's diagnosis was a single moment in the history of AIDS. The White House announced that President Reagan called his friend in Paris to wish him well—the closest Reagan had come to publicly acknowledging the epidemic. Newspapers, magazines and television all focused on AIDS with a relentlessness that had more to do with Rock Hudson's celebrity than any public health concern.

With greater awareness of AIDS came a new spasm of fear about the disease and about homosexuals. "Now, No One Is Safe from AIDS," announced a *Life* magazine cover. Unfounded fears about AIDS transmission reemerged, as they had following the erroneous AMA report about casual contact in 1983; a *Newsweek* poll that summer found that 62 percent believed it was "very likely" or "somewhat likely" that AIDS would spread to heterosexuals.

The publicity surrounding Hudson's illness came on the heels of approval by the Food and Drug Administration, in March 1985, of a blood test for the virus associated with AIDS. The test was designed to protect the nation's blood supply from contamination, but its development hurled homosexual men into an agonized public debate about whether they should voluntarily submit to it. There was no sure medical gain from learning one was infected, since so little was known in 1985 about treatment. The presumed benefit would be that someone who tested positive for the HTLV-III virus, as it was then called, could limit sexual activity, although many men with AIDS had thus far not done so. But the prospect of a blood test alarmed gay activists, who foresaw what Paul Popham, the president of GMHC referred to in *The Advocate* as an "unprecedented threat" to the civil liberties of infected gay men. Would test results be confidential? Would they be made available to government so that it could compile lists of the diseased? Would insurance companies be allowed to use them in issuing health or life insur-

---

* Andelson took the HIV test as soon as it was available, in mid-1985. He had had a bout of shingles, a common disease associated with HIV infection.

ance policies? Could they be used in housing, employment or health care decisions?

Lambda Legal Defense and Education Fund with the support of the National Gay Task Force went to court to try to block the FDA from licensing the test.* In New York, the *Native*, whose coverage of AIDS had become less adventurous and more shrill—reflecting the panic among its readership—warned readers against taking the test in June 1984, a full year before it was licensed. "What if," an editorial asked, a reader took the test, turned up positive and was then asked by health officials to name all sex partners of the past five years, who in turn would be forced to submit to the test? And then, the editorial continued hypothetically, what if "those who test positive are ordered to report to quarantine centers around the country?" Stephen S. Caiazza, president of New York Physicians for Human Rights, a gay doctors group, was more blunt: "This is a pernicious test which will inevitably cause incredible personal and social pain and damage. *Stay away from it!*" Bruce Voeller made the opposite argument in an essay he wrote for *The Advocate* in the spring of 1985. "We need to be tested so we can medically protect ourselves and safeguard others with whom we are involved. Gay leaders have warned that lists of test-takers could fall into the wrong hands. Maybe so, but I'd rather be alive and on a list than dead because I'd been misled into believing I could get no value from knowing my test results."

As in the bathhouse battle, many men seemed to be placing their political and sexual interests ahead of the nation's health, and once again, homosexuals suffered for it politically. "They say that if they are found to have suspicious blood, they will suffer discrimination," the *New York Daily News* editorialized. "It's an amazing reaction. Of course there should be discrimination toward people with AIDS. They should be rushed straight to a hospital." The fear expressed by gay leaders of discrimination, and particularly quarantine, seemed to many outside the gay community to be more than a little paranoid, though it was not totally without cause. A fundraising letter from Jerry Falwell suggested the time had come to quarantine people with the AIDS virus "who, by continued irresponsible behavior, pose a threat to our public safety." During 1985, twenty states considered regulations directed at controlling the AIDS virus or people who were infected. Colorado health officials proposed a central registry of names of people who tested positive. The Texas

---

* Their argument on the blood test was a bit more convoluted: They suggested that sexually active gay men, who until now had refrained from giving blood and who wanted to find out if they were infected, would go to blood banks to donate blood, which would then be tested. In a few years, the result would be an increase in contaminated blood, and that would lead to a backlash against homosexuals. The FDA dissuaded the NGTF and Lambda, prompting them to drop their suit, by affixing a label on the test which read, "It is inappropriate to use this test as a screen for AIDS or as a screen for members of groups at increased risk."

Board of Health tentatively approved, but then rescinded, in response to criticism by doctors and gay leaders, a measure adding AIDS to the list of diseases requiring quarantine for infected people who continued engaging in sex.

By the fall of 1985, following Rock Hudson's death, the debate came to the floor of the U.S. House of Representatives. Representative William E. Dannemeyer, a conservative from Orange County, California, who was preparing to run for the U.S. Senate in 1986, declared that AIDS and homosexuals posed a threat to public health, and offered legislation to contain them. He hired on his congressional payroll a Nebraska psychologist, Paul Cameron, one of the nation's most dedicated opponents of homosexual rights, who had been expelled from the American Psychological Association in December 1983 for "misrepresenting and distorting the research of others" to support his positions on homosexuality. Cameron had prepared a series of leaflets attacking homosexuals; one, entitled "Child Molestation and Homosexuality," featured a sketch of a young boy being dragged by the arm into a men's room, and asserted that gay men were twelve times as likely to molest children as straight men, a fictitious statistic. Now, with the platform provided by Dannemeyer, Cameron called for quarantine. "They're getting what they deserve," Cameron said of homosexuals with AIDS. "Unfortunately, others are getting it too." On October 1, Dannemeyer went to the floor of the House and read into the *Congressional Record*: "God's plan for man was Adam and Eve, not Adam and Steve. And when a human male penis is inserted. . . ." The representative then offered a detailed account of anal intercourse. The next day the House approved a proposal by another conservative Orange County Republican, Representative Robert Dornan, to empower the surgeon general to close down bathhouses. Dornan called the measure a "tiny, small step forward to do something to help people who in many cases seem unable or unwilling to help themselves as far as stopping the transmission" of the disease. The legislation passed by an overwhelming 417–8; even Representative Gerry Studds, the openly gay representative from Massachusetts who ridiculed the measure as ineffective, voted for a bill that had become politically impossible to oppose.

In New York City that fall, Diane McGrath, a Republican who was challenging Mayor Edward I. Koch in the November election, went to the steps of city hall and called on the city to close its ten known gay bathhouses and to segregate people infected with the disease. McGrath was no threat to the entrenched New York mayor, but her criticism shook New York State's already nervous Democratic leadership. "Promiscuous, homosexual, aggressive sexual activity helps transmit AIDS," Governor Mario M. Cuomo said during a television interview. "Under those circumstances, shouldn't we consider discouraging an environment that clearly encourages that type of activity?" Cuomo ordered the state health department to study whether bathhouses should be closed, and Koch quickly followed by ordering his own health commissioner to review the city's bathhouse policy. Pressure mounted as election day approached. "The agonizing, foot-dragging, shuffling, buck-passing reluctance of Gov. Cuomo and Mayor Koch to move against the city's bathhouses in the face of the AIDS crisis is both a public health and a political scandal," wrote Ray Kerrison, a conservative columnist in the *New York Post*. "The politicians in this state have become utterly paralyzed at the prospect of having to take any action against the gay lifestyle . . . the elected Democratic party officials in this state appear to be political prisoners of the gay community." At the end of October, the state Public Health Council issued regulations barring high-risk sexual activity—defined as oral and anal intercourse—in commercial establishments.

The day after Koch won reelection, he called for the baths to be shut down. "What we are saying is that you can't sell death in this city and get away with it," Koch declared. Koch gave a one-word answer when a panel of editors and reporters, questioning him at a forum sponsored by the *New York Post,* asked when the city would begin enforcing the new state regulations: "Today." Koch would not disclose where the crackdown would begin, but by that point it seemed obvious: The Mine Shaft, a two-story, sado-masochist sex club at the far edges of New York's West Village, the sleaziest backroom bar in the city. A sign at the entrance read, "Don't let AIDS stop you from having a good time," and no one inside even went through the motions of trying to monitor behavior on its two black-walled floors filled with slings, simulated jail cells, cubicles, and glory holes. The Mine Shaft was so notorious that Jim Fouratt, on his picketing runs, didn't bother challenging patrons as he had at the New St. Marks Baths. Instead, he and others sprayed graffiti on the Mine Shaft walls reading, "Sleaze Breed Disease," and affixed posters reading, "AIDS lives here!" If the Mine Shaft functioned at the extreme edge of the gay male culture in the city, it operated on the far edges of the law as well. It registered with the state as a not-for-profit fraternal club, so it was exempt from most corporate taxes, and kept serving liquor past 4 a.m. the closing time for bars in New York. At 6:45 a.m. on November 7, 1985, a Thursday morning, a city health official nailed up a bright orange notice announcing "Closed by Court Order," and left behind a uniformed police officer to stand guard for the rest of the day.

There was no chance the shadowy ownership of the Mine Shaft would fight back. Bruce Mailman, however, attacked the new regulations on sex clubs, which were a direct threat to his bathhouse, as the "worst kind of sloppy, craven legislation," and said that while his New St. Marks Baths would guard against unsafe sex in public areas, there was nothing he could or would do about what men might be doing behind the closed doors of the cubicles. It took city inspectors another month to shut down Mailman's baths. Six months had passed since Andelson had closed 8709. "We're going to fight it," Mailman said, and he went to Thomas Stoddard at the New York Civil Liberties Union and the two men agreed the baths could be a test case to fight the regulations. Stoddard believed that the law was so broad that a police officer could break down the door of a hotel room and arrest a couple for engaging in anal or oral sex. He convinced the New York Civil Liberties Union to take the case, but he did not believe any judge in New York would be willing to endorse his argument—that there should be a presumption against governmental regulation of sexuality—in this political climate. Stoddard was right; Mailman was never able to find a court that would allow him to reopen the New St. Marks Baths. Mailman lost his biggest money-maker. The New St. Marks Baths was closed on December 6.

The legal skirmishing over the baths and sex clubs attracted a new kind of crowd to the establishments: city inspectors and members of the city's rambunctious tabloid press. When the city seemed to be dawdling in enforcing the state regulations, the *New York Post*—which referred to baths and sex clubs in headlines as "AIDS Dens"—dispatched a reporter on his own inspection tour. "The Case for Closing Bathhouses: Night Visit by *Post* Reporter Reveals Shocking Evidence," read the headline on this story:

> It is midnight and inside the atmosphere is dark, steamy and sad.
> It is the Skid Row of gay sex.
> And every form of sex—anal and oral and anonymous—that the
> city and state want to outlaw continues to go on.

The *Post* continued with a steamy, detailed account of the reporter's visit. Even the *New York Times* joined in introducing its readers to the Hell Fire Club, a club for bisexuals and straights known for "group-sex scenes and sadomasochistic exhibitions," which posted club rules including "no bull-whips, electric prods or animals." The crackdown in New York was feeding what was in many ways the darkest public portrayal of homosexuality since the McCarthy era. But it also triggered something else: the largest political gathering of gay men and lesbians in New York City since the founders of what would be the Gay Liberation Front showed up at Alternate U. sixteen years before.

November 1985, Los Angeles

When Larry Sprenger read the reports from New York, he could not help worrying about the future of MECLA, the first gay political committee in the nation, of which he was now a co-chair. MECLA was unique among homosexual organizations because it encouraged the involvement of heterosexuals; and that worked, in part, because the sex in homosexuality was not talked about. It was one thing for heterosexuals to see same-sex couples dancing at MECLA dinners.* And it was well-known, if not openly discussed, that Steve Smith, a MECLA co-chair, was involved in a three-way relationship, sharing a king-size bed with two other men, and had brought both his spouses to the head table with Edward Kennedy when the Massachusetts Democrat addressed the 1982 MECLA dinner. But the gritty details of what happened inside a gay bathhouse had been, for the most part, left unspoken to the heterosexual men and women of MECLA, and Sprenger was not alone in believing that that accounted for the ease with which heterosexuals fit into the ranks of MECLA.

The attention that first San Francisco and now New York were paying to sex clubs had been noted in Los Angeles, where health officials were talking about instituting their own rules that could lead to the closing of the county bathhouses. Sprenger had as a younger man spent many a night in the bathhouses. But now, older and plumper, he considered himself more pragmatic, and he decided that bathhouses, and the publicity they were drawing to a less-known side of male homosexuals, could destroy everything MECLA had fought for since its founding in 1977. The only way to quash the bathhouse issue, he decided, was to preempt it. On Sunday, three-days after the Mine Shaft was closed, MECLA called a press conference at its headquarters in West Hollywood. "Bathhouses are businesses which provide facilities for non-commercial sexual activity on the premises," Carol Childs, Sprenger's co-chair, said, reading from a statement. "While they are not solely responsible for the spread of this disease, we are calling for the owners of these businesses to close their doors for the duration of the AIDS epidemic." The statement did not invite a government crackdown on the baths. But the message was clear: if the club owners did not act on their own, MECLA would not use its influence to protect them.

The bathhouses of Los Angeles did not close, and the story disappeared from the front pages; and Sprenger always believed that was because of MECLA's statement. But that was not the real legacy of what MECLA did that day. Two weeks after the press conference, homosexuals threw up a picket line at a MECLA breakfast, led by John O'Brien, who had been one of the first members of the Gay Liberation Front in New York, denouncing MECLA as the "self-appointed power brokers of the gay community" who had come out in favor of closing "one of the few gay institutions in an anti-gay society.

---

* And same-sex dancing was only tolerable to a certain extent. Aides to Senator Kennedy had insisted, as a condition of his appearing at MECLA's 1982 black-tie fundraiser, that the senator leave before the dancing began, so he was not photographed against a backdrop of the same-sex couples twirling across the dance floor.

... What is NOT needed is for MECLA to add its voice to a rising tide of anti-sex, anti-gay hysteria." Morris Kight attacked MECLA as "apologists," and even Ivy Bottini dismissed them as arrogant, an assembly of people "playing God." The statement on bathhouses would prove to be the beginning of the end of MECLA. Attendance at MECLA events and its membership roles and contributions declined steadily and irreversibly. Like Steve Endean two years before, MECLA had fallen on the changing political terrain.

November 1985, New York

New York was permanently identified with the start of the modern gay rights movement because of Stonewall, but by 1985, there was still no gay rights ordinance in New York, as there was in nearly a dozen other cities, among them Boston, Washington, D.C., Dallas, Houston, Seattle, Minneapolis, Los Angeles and San Francisco. Since the day after Bruce Voeller broke away from the Gay Activists Alliance to form the National Gay Task Force in 1973, New York could claim no gay political organization of any influence. The California-based *Advocate* regularly ran stories deploring the absence of gay power in the city with the greatest concentration of gay men and lesbians. David Goodstein, who would die of bowel cancer at the age of fifty-three in June 1986—by all his friends' accounts, he did not die of AIDS, though given the climate, that was the speculation when news of his death became public—had devoted more than one column to mocking homosexuals in Manhattan.* "The affluent gay community there outrages me," Goodstein wrote in 1981. "Except for a few people, a more irresponsible, argumentative, arrogant, self-centered, parochial, closeted, paranoid, guilt-ridden, uncooperative, stingy group is impossible to find. Their outlook never extends beyond their individual selfish interests. These include some or all of the following: career, next vacation, drugs, sex, disco, country or beach house, gorgeous apartment and/or 'cultural' pursuits."

The first municipal gay rights ordinance in the nation had been introduced in the New York City Council on January 6, 1971, but almost fifteen years later, it still had not made it past the conservative Democratic majority leader, Thomas J. Cuite of Brooklyn, and the Archdiocese of New York. New York had yet to elect an open homosexual to public office. Mayor Koch had named a gay liaison to his staff, but this same person was also the liaison to the Orthodox Jewish community. New York had by far the largest number of reported AIDS cases in the country—more than one of every three cases, and

* Goodstein stepped down as publisher of *The Advocate* in the middle of May 1986. He died June 22, the day of the Christopher Street West Parade.

about 50 percent more cases than Los Angeles and San Francisco combined.* But the only AIDS organization in New York was the Gay Men's Health Crisis, a service organization, not a political one. The absence of political power was reflected in the city's poor handling of the health crisis. "It's so different in New York," said Mathilde Krim, an AIDS researcher at Sloan-Kettering Cancer Center, who had set up the AIDS Medical Foundation to raise money for research. "This is not San Francisco: We have not had the kind of coordinated, planned response to AIDS that has happened in San Francisco," she told Randy Shilts, writing a story for the *Native* on AIDS in New York.

Indeed, when it came time to critique New York City's response to the AIDS epidemic at a city council committee hearing in 1985, the case was presented not by a local gay organization, but by Virginia Apuzzo, a New Yorker, but the director of the National Gay Task Force. "There is in my community an overwhelming rage," she told the health committee, but the city government actions had been "lethargic, at best."

It took the sex club regulations to finally rouse gay men and lesbians in New York, but not in defense of the baths. Rather, it was a response to media coverage of the issue, typified by Charles Krauthammer's argument that "homosexuality is once again reverting to the status of public menace. It has quite simply come to stand for death." A Gallup poll in November found that 37 percent of those questioned had changed their opinions about homosexuals for the worse since the disease became widely publicized.† In November, a group of eight veteran New York activists and writers—including Jim Owles, the first Gay Activists Alliance president, and such former GAA officers as Vito Russo and Arnie Kantrowitz—met to consider what they saw as the most serious threat to gay civil rights since Stonewall. Homosexuals were being demonized, Kantrowitz thought; he felt a clutch of fear every time he read another story in the *New York Post*. There was no obvious way for activists to deal directly with AIDS, he thought, but society's reaction to AIDS, and to homosexuals, was something they could fight, and Russo suggested they create an organization modeled after the Anti-Defamation League of B'nai B'rith. It would monitor how homosexuals were portrayed, in the press and by the government, and would respond with letters, phone calls, meetings and demonstrations. They wrote a notice announcing its first meeting.

"AIDS is being used by both the government and the media to erode the basic rights for which we have struggled these past 15 years and more," the notice said. "Sensationalized accounts of gay activities, blatant scare tactics

---

* As of May 20, 1985, according to the Centers for Disease Control weekly surveillance report, New York had 3,836 cases and California, 2,411.
† The poll was taken November 11–18 of 1,008 Americans.

and outright misreporting of facts have produced an unnecessary panic and a new fear of gays in the minds of millions of our neighbors.

"Fight AIDS, not gays!"

On November 14, 1985, more than six hundred people filled the Metropolitan-Duane Methodist Church at the northern end of Greenwich Village for the meeting of what would be called the Gay and Lesbian Alliance Against Defamation, or GLAAD.* They sat in the pews and stood in the aisles and the choir loft upstairs, and spilled out onto the sidewalks on Thirteenth Street and Seventh Avenue. Kantrowitz hadn't seen so many people at a homosexual political event since his days at the GAA Firehouse. The air was filled with talk of Stonewall, and the audience included a substantial representation of men and women who had been part of that first wave after the uprising at the bar seven blocks away. Vito Russo told the crowd of the hand-scrawled leaflet that recruited him to his first gay march—on behalf of Diego Vinales—fifteen years ago. Russo, better known as an accomplished film critic and the author of *The Celluloid Closet,* defined what the meeting was about: "The AIDS epidemic is being used by right-wing fanatics and yellow journalists to create a witch-hunt mentality against lesbians and gays in this city." Russo was silenced by a roar and the first of many standing ovations; he responded by thrusting his hand in the air, his fingers parted in a V, the light from the church reflecting off his glistening forehead.

Another member of the eight who planned this town meeting was writer Darrell Yates Rist. "Tonight is the final notice to the bigots," Rist told the meeting. "Many of us had to live a lie too long. But in these years since Stonewall brought us out, we have learned the truth about ourselves, and it is good. *We will not go back*—not to closets, nor to shame, nor to fear, *not to celibacy,* not to letting heterosexual lies about us rule our lives. . . . In the name of all of our friends who have died and in the name of us who are still alive, we are putting out the warning: no more lies!" There was in Rist's speech a significant new sense of anger, drawn from the death around him, a suggestion that despair might not be the only response to AIDS.

GLAAD's inaugural action, two weeks later on December 1, was directed at the *New York Post.* Nearly five hundred people assembled at the paper's remote lower Manhattan offices on a cold, rainy Sunday. "As gays and lesbians, we are facing an unprecedented attack on our lives," the organizers had announced in the leaflet for the protest. "The *New York Post* whips up hysteria and defames us in a manner that no self-respecting community should have to bear." The demonstrators came with rags, and banners which

---

* The new organization was originally going to be called the Gay and Lesbian Anti-Defamation League, until a lawyer for B'nai B'rith sent a letter warning that it retained exclusive rights to the name and would go to court if necessary.

read, "Close the *Post,* not the Baths," and "Whips Don't Cause AIDS." Marty Robinson was another veteran among the leaders of this march. His hair and face were thinner than they were when he was organizing zaps for the GAA, and he seemed to have aged more than the fifteen years since then, but he was relishing his return to the spotlight, posing for a *Native* photographer in front of the Szechuan Cottage Restaurant, which filled the space that had once been the Stonewall.* "Who lies the most?" he declared, leading a crowd in a chant. "The *New York Post!*" Rist spoke again of the disease as a source of political anger rather than just grief. "We are suffering for our friends, we are mourning for the sick and the dead, and they are pushing this shit on us while we haven't the time to do anything but cry."

March 1986

New York's burst of vigor was in sharp contrast to a nationwide string of defeats for gay rights ordinances through 1985 and 1986, the most barren legislative record since the eighteen months after the Dade County vote in 1977. The issue of homosexual rights had by now become completely shaped by AIDS, and the epidemic had handed another sword to conservative leaders and clerics—Roman Catholics, fundamentalist and charismatic Christians, and Orthodox Jews—who were aligned in opposition to gay rights. Between 1982 and 1985 gay rights measures had been enacted by legislation or executive order in Houston, Philadelphia, Austin, Boston, Chicago and Laguna Beach, California. In 1982, Wisconsin became the first state to pass a gay rights law, sponsored by state Representative David Clarenbach, who ten years later would acknowledge his own homosexuality. The governors of Ohio and New York signed executive orders barring discrimination in hiring by state government. In all, by the start of 1985, three states, eleven counties, forty-seven cities and towns, and the District of Columbia had adopted some form of gay rights legislation.

In June 1984 the Houston City Council had approved two measures to extend civil rights to homosexuals, a tribute to the city's sophisticated Gay Political Caucus. But the measures stirred opposition from the city's religious community, who filled the chamber and sang "Onward Christian Soldiers" as the council narrowly approved the ordinances. They returned a month later, hauling paper boxes filled with petitions containing 60,000 signatures, demanding that the gay rights measures be put to the city's voters. The subsequent campaign reprised the tactics Anita Bryant used eight years before. Once again, voters were shown film clips from San Francisco. In November,

---

* A bar called the Stonewall has since opened in that space on Christopher Street.

Houston voters rejected the city gay rights measures by nearly 4 to 1. Three months later the Baltimore City Council voted down a gay rights bill, 11–7. In California, Assemblyman Art Agnos once again pulled back his anti-discrimination bill, which he had withdrawn after Anita Bryant's success, conceding in May that a brisk lobbying campaign by religious fundamentalists—which he said had made a "calculated distortion" to link job discrimination to AIDS—had defeated him.* That summer of 1985, the Providence (Rhode Island) City Council included sexual orientation in a city civil rights ordinance, but then deleted the reference in the final bill, a change that came at the urging of Bishop Louis E. Gelineau of the Roman Catholic diocese, who protested that "homosexual acts are contrary to God's command." The Massachusetts House of Representatives defeated a gay rights bill less than three weeks later, on September 23, despite the fact that it was nearly identical to a bill it had approved two years before; gay rights advocates blamed the reversal on the use of the epidemic by opponents of the proposal. "I guess they felt that just the mention of AIDS every 30 seconds would have the desired effect," said Peg Lorenz, the lobbyist for Massachusetts Gay Political Caucus. The trend continued in 1986. The Chicago City Council, which had a mayoral executive order but no gay rights law, defeated a proposed city ordinance after Joseph Cardinal Bernardin of the Archdiocese of Chicago urged lawmakers to "protect the rights" of "parents and their children, of those who are offended by gay lifestyles or advocacy."† The debate over a gay rights ordinance for New Orleans later that year was as raw as any homosexuals had encountered. "I was pinched by a homosexual teacher before I threatened to knock his teeth out," said the Reverend T. J. Smith, the leader of black ministers opposed to the bill.

All of this made what happened in New York City in the spring of 1986 extraordinary. On March 20—fifteen years, two months and fourteen days after it was introduced at the behest of the New York City Gay Activists Alliance—the city council passed a gay rights bill, by a margin of 21–14.

The vote in New York did not suggest any sudden shift in public sentiments about homosexuals, and it was not a tribute to any new sophistication or vigor in New York's gay community. The debate was still darkened by allusions to AIDS. ("Why should our city government encourage sodomy by treating it as a civil right?" the Family Rights Coalition demanded.) It had come about, mainly, for one reason: the council majority leader, Thomas Cuite, who had prevented the bill from being voted out of committee, had re-

---

* Agnos had managed to win approval of the bill the previous year, only to have it vetoed by the Republican governor, George Deukmejian.
† Gay rights activists said Cardinal Bernardin's statement cost them nine supporters in the 30–18 vote.

tired. New York's new gay rights bill was not particularly bold, and that was deliberate. It was drafted by New York Civil Liberties Union lawyer Tom Stoddard, with political advice from Ethan Geto. Stoddard had begun working on the bill while legislative director at the NYCLU. After the NYCLU declined to name him executive director—a decision he privately blamed on the organization's discomfort with his open homosexuality, though the NYCLU says his homosexuality had nothing to do with its decision—Stoddard became executive director of the Lambda Legal Defense and Education Fund, an organization that handled cases involving homosexuality. Geto, a political consultant and business lobbyist, had maintained close ties to city hall.

Following Cuite's retirement, Stoddard and Geto set out to draft legislation that would pass and that would discourage the kind of antics that had doomed earlier bills. Arthur Bell, the *Village Voice* columnist and Gay Activists Alliance member, had kicked Councilman Matthew J. Troy in the shins as the councilman explained his "no" vote to reporters in 1974 (the chunky Troy spun around and slapped Bell full force across the face). In 1981, David Rothenberg, an openly gay member of the city Human Rights Commission, opened his testimony by noting that it was the one-year anniversary of the night when a thirty-eight-year-old former transit policeman had opened fire with a machine gun in front of New York's gay bar the Ramrod, killing two gay men and wounding six others. A Hasidic Jew seated in the audience began applauding at the mention of the killings, embarrassing even opponents of the measure. In 1982 a leader of the Union of Orthodox Rabbis testified, in fairly direct language, that every unmarried member of New York City government—including the mayor—was homosexual and in sexual collusion with other government leaders or gay rights leaders. In 1985 rabbis and Catholic leaders showed up to testify wearing surgical masks so that they wouldn't be contaminated "by gay germs."

The bill that Stoddard produced was short and simple. The very first gay rights bill, Intro. No. 475, filed in January 1971 on behalf of the GAA, filled 182 lines of type and seven pages, listing every law that would be changed to protect homosexuals. The 1986 bill, Intro. No. 2, filled just forty-one lines and two pages, as sparse and concise as possible. There were more words devoted to what the bill would *not* do than to what it would do, exorcising all the ghosts that Stoddard believed had haunted the bill. The bill would *not* "endorse any particular behavior or way of life." It did *not* impose quotas on behalf of homosexuals and lesbians, or restrict employers from establishing "bona fide job-related qualifications," including dress codes, a reference to concerns by opponents that the bill would allow a male teacher to show up at work wearing a woman's dress. The bill also very narrowly defined who was covered. Sexual orientation meant homosexuality, heterosexuality or bisexuality, language Stoddard lifted from the Wisconsin state law. Transsexuals and drag queens, the men who had been identified with the start of the modern-day gay revolution, were not included.* Both Geto and Stoddard held to the same position: It was not politically feasible—"a deal-breaker," as Geto put it—to try to provide protections for drag queens. "Let me just explain this to you," Geto said to gay leaders who complained. "We can't do this. *We can't do this*. This is what we can do."

When Mayor Koch turned up to testify for the bill, fifty Hasidic Jews stood and turned their backs on the Jewish mayor. "Justice delayed is justice denied, too long denied," Koch declared, as the Hasidim booed and taunted the mayor with shouts of "Shame! Shame!" A representative of the archdiocese termed the bill "totally abhorrent to people of every religious persuasion." Paul Cameron, the former psychologist, showed up with a report to prove, he said, that child molestation by homosexuals was on the rise. And Rabbi Yehuda Levin, who had marched outside Mailman's bathhouse, denounced the "pro-sodomy" bill that he said was backed by the "corrupt mayor and his Greenwich Village buddies." Stoddard was struck even then by the intensity of the reaction, but he was coming to consider it a political advantage. He believed these raw emotions undercut the principal argument of opponents: here was vivid proof of the kind of discrimination gay men and women faced.

On the Sunday before the Thursday vote, John Cardinal O'Connor made one last effort to rally opposition to the bill, devoting his homily at St. Patrick's Cathedral, filled with worshipers and reporters, to the gay rights legislation. The bill, O'Connor declared in his even, reedy voice, was an affront to Judeo-Christian values, and would offer legal protection to sexual behavior that was a "sin" and "abnormal." That Tuesday the *New York Times* ran an op-ed piece by William F. Buckley asserting that AIDS was now threatening society at large. "Everyone detected with AIDS should be tattooed in the upper forearm, to protect common-needle users, and on the buttocks, to prevent the victimization of other homosexuals," Buckley wrote. But neither attack affected an outcome so certain that church leaders were already preparing to challenge the measure in court, and Andy Humm of the city's Coalition for Lesbian and Gay Rights was advising his activists to refrain from the angry displays that had

---

* Activists like Allen Roskoff and David Rothenberg questioned the decision to leave drag queens out of the New York City gay rights bill. They recalled that Sylvia Rivera had finally turned on the Gay Activists Alliance when it had eliminated transvestites from its gay rights agenda for the same reason fifteen years before. "It's not us they're afraid of—it's you," Rivera had proclaimed then, standing at the front of the Firehouse, wrapped in (what appeared to be) mink. "Get rid of us. Sell us out. Make us expendable. Then you're at the front lines. Don't you understand that?" Rivera exited, dragging the mink behind him, declaring: "Hell hath no fury like a drag queen scorned." It was a funny moment, but a poignant one as well, and it flashed through Rothenberg's mind as he watched the same act play out again.

hurt the movement in the past. "They can say anything they want," he said, "but we're going to win."

The moment the 21–14 vote was recorded, Stoddard headed for the men's room, where he collected his emotions and crafted a quote to give to reporters. It was the first day of spring, and Stoddard decided to invoke Shakespeare: "Today, the winter of our discontent is made glorious spring." But Stoddard's spontaneous "God, I can't believe it, after all this time" made its way into the next day's *New York Times.** Mayor Koch left his office and went to the chamber to proclaim: "The sky is not going to fall. There isn't going to be any dramatic change in the life of this city." On Sheridan Square the night after the victory, Jim Owles was among the thousand people who filled the streets near what was once the Stonewall, in a spontaneous celebration that closed the circle. "This is the best night of my life," said Owles. "This is really good news, and God knows, we need good news."

---

* When Stoddard found that his extemporaneous remark, and not the Shakespeare quote, had been printed, he called *Times* reporter Joyce Purnick to inquire why she hadn't used his carefully constructed quote. She explained, he said, that his spontaneous reaction more precisely captured the moment.

36

COP AT THE DOOR

June 1986, Washington, D.C.

The United States Supreme Court heard arguments in the case of *Bowers* v. *Hardwick* eleven days after the New York City Council passed the gay rights bill. Michael Hardwick, an Atlanta bartender, had been arrested by a police officer who came through his bedroom door one morning, and charged under a Georgia statute that outlawed sodomy, in this case, fellatio with another man. Michael J. Bowers was the attorney general of Georgia. Hardwick challenged the law as an invasion of his privacy; a federal appeals court agreed with him, and when the Supreme Court accepted the state's appeal, the stage was set for the single most anticipated court decision involving a homosexual rights case in American legal history.

The state and federal court systems had often been reliable allies for the civil rights movement in the 1950s and 1960s, and again—not invariably, but often—for the gay rights movement of the 1970s and 1980s. Appointed judges were better able to ignore the winds of public opinion than elected officials, and that fact had nurtured a distinct branch of gay organizing, activist lawyers who turned to the courts rather than the legislatures for relief. The Lambda Legal Defense and Education Fund was created in New York by a gay lawyer, William J. Thom, in 1973. Three years later in San Francisco, a law professor from the University of Southern California, Donald Knutson, helped found the nonprofit, public interest National Gay Rights Advocates. "Our criteria are very simple," Knutson explained at the time. "Will this case affect the civil liberties of gay persons in general and can we make a law that will have a general application?" Gay and Lesbian Advocates and Defenders was founded in Boston as a New England version of Lambda Legal Defense and Education Fund. The charge these organizations assumed took on a new urgency after Ronald Reagan's election, as the political turn to the right raised walls around city halls and state legislatures to gay activists pushing for legislative relief. In the 1984 presidential election, gay organizers trying to stir support for Walter Mondale argued that homosexuals should vote for the Democratic presidential candidate because he would fill judicial slots with liberal-minded judges. The next president would nominate forty-five federal judges for life, Virginia Apuzzo wrote in a column in *The Advocate* endorsing Mondale. The *New York Native* told its readers: "We suggest that you think seriously about the probable decisions of a Supreme Court dominated by the reactionary social biases of likely Reagan appointees to that body. Do not be complicit in your undoing! Do not put yourself at risk!"

To be sure, courts were far from unwavering in their support for gay rights. Courts had upheld sodomy laws, ratified the legality of the military's policy barring homosexuals, revoked custody of children from lesbian mothers and affirmed immigration laws prohibiting known homosexuals from entering the United States. Still, on balance, there had been many favorable rulings for homosexuals, on issues large and small, since the U.S. Court of Appeals in Washington ruled on July 1, 1969, that a federal budget analyst with NASA could not be fired solely because he was a gay. California's highest court had ruled in 1969 that the state could not refuse a teacher's license to someone on the grounds that he or she was homosexual. A judge in Los Angeles had ordered Police Chief Edward Davis and the Police Commission to grant Morris Kight and Troy Perry a permit for the first gay rights march in Los Angeles in 1970. New York's highest court directed the appellate division of the State Supreme Court to reconsider, and thus reverse, its unanimous rejection of an application by the Lambda Legal Defense and Education Fund itself for recognition as a legal defense and education fund (the lower court had asserted that Lambda was neither charitable nor benevolent, and thus didn't qualify). In July 1975, the United States Civil Service Commission dropped its ban on hiring gay men and lesbians, a lingering legal reminder of the McCarthy era, after several federal courts of appeals found that the government, in the words of a Ninth Circuit Court of Appeals ruling, could not disqualify a prospective employee "because that person is a homosexual or has engaged in homosexual acts." The California Supreme Court, in 1983, threw out the provision of the state's notorious 647(a) lewd conduct law that required people convicted under the statute—which in Los Angeles translated into gay men arrested for cruising in bars, on the streets or in the parks—to register as lifetime sex offenders. And sodomy laws in both Pennsylvania and New York were nullified by rulings by the two states' highest appeals courts.

The United States Supreme Court had been another matter. In May 1967 it upheld the Immigration and Naturalization Service's authority to prohibit homosexual aliens from entering the country, under a provision which closed the borders to people with "psychopathic personalities." For the next eighteen years, the Supreme Court avoided cases involving homosexuality, declining to accept them for argument, or dispatching them with terse, summary judgments that contained no analysis or opinion, and thus were almost useless as precedents. The most famous of these was a March 1976 ruling which affirmed, by a 6–3 vote and without explanation, a three-judge U.S. district court panel's decision that Virginia's sodomy law was constitutional. Similarly, the High Court declined to consider the appeal of a nineteen-year-old Eagle Scout, Timothy Curran, who had been expelled by a Boy Scouts of America troop in Oakland, California, for being homosexual. It did not take up the cases of a number of public school teachers who had been fired for being homosexual. By the same token, the court declined to weigh in when a lower court ordered Harris County to rehire its assistant treasurer, Gary Van Ooteghem of Houston, who had been dismissed for testifying in favor of gay rights.* It was not until 1985 that the Supreme Court accepted a substantial case involving gay rights, a challenge by the National Gay Task Force to an Oklahoma state law which gave public schools broad authority to fire homosexual teachers, and even their supporters. The Oklahoma law was passed in 1978 at the urging of Anita Bryant, and it was nearly identical to California's Briggs Initiative. The Tenth U.S. Circuit Court of Appeals overturned the statute, finding it a violation of the free speech protections in the Constitution. On appeal, the Supreme Court split 4–4, with Justice Lewis F. Powell Jr. abstaining. The tie vote affirmed the lower-court decision, and it was—once again—announced with a summary order, which set no precedent. Still, the Oklahoma ruling was embraced by gay activists and their supporters looking for even a whisper of judicial affirmation. Laurence H. Tribe, the Harvard Law School constitutional law professor who argued the case on behalf of the Task Force, termed it a "major landmark" because it was "the first time four members of the court are explicitly on record as agreeing . . . that laws of this kind are unconstitutional on their face and can be struck down."

Thus, the Supreme Court's decision to hear Hardwick's anti-sodomy challenge was greeted with both anticipation and anxiety by gay advocates now

---

* Van Ooteghem's firing led to the creation of the Houston Gay Political Caucus, and made him enough of a national gay figure that he served for a time on the board of both the National Gay Task Force and the Gay Rights National Lobby.

hoping to remove all the remaining state sodomy laws—the most widespread and explicit legislation directed at homosexuals, a codified instance of government animus toward gay men and lesbians—with one legal stroke. Before 1962, all fifty states and the District of Columbia had sodomy laws, dating back to theologically influenced sixteenth-century English common law and a decree issued during the reign of King Henry VIII. Between 1962 and 1986 almost half the states repealed their sodomy laws, either by legislative action or under court order. And by the time the Georgia statute came to the Supreme Court, only seven states retained sodomy laws which applied specifically to homosexuals: Arkansas, Kansas, Kentucky, Missouri, Montana, Nevada and Texas. The remaining states, including Georgia, prohibited sodomy regardless of sexual orientation, by statutes which usually applied even to married couples.

The facts in this case were not in dispute. On August 3, 1982, a police officer went to the home of Michael Hardwick, twenty-nine, to serve him a warrant for not paying a fine for public drunkenness. (Hardwick had been issued a summons for drinking a can of beer from a paper bag outside the gay bar in Atlanta where he worked.) A houseguest who answered the door at Hardwick's home told the officer he did not know whether Hardwick was there, but allowed him in to check. The police officer made his way to Hardwick's bedroom, cracked open the door, and saw Hardwick and another man engaged in oral sex on the bed. Hardwick looked up and demanded of the uniformed officer: "What are you doing in my bedroom?" The officer arrested Hardwick for violating an 1816 statute which prohibited oral and anal sex by homosexuals and heterosexuals, punishable by a prison term of one to twenty years. Hardwick spent a night in jail. Though prosecutors declined to press the charges, Hardwick decided to challenge the law under which he had been arrested.

It was hard to imagine a case better constructed to challenge a sodomy law. A coalition of gay lawyers orchestrating court battles against sodomy statutes—the Ad Hoc Task Force on Sodomy Reform was its formal name, but the lawyers called themselves the Sodomy Roundtable—determined to devote all their resources to this arrest, abandoning other cases that were advancing in other circuits. The Hardwick arrest involved two consenting adults having sex in private. There were no other issues—no minors, no suggestions of forced sex, no prostitution, no public displays of sexuality—that could clutter the issue of what authority government had to regulate private sexual behavior. A lower appeals court, the Unites States Court of Appeals for the Eleventh Circuit, had enthusiastically agreed with Hardwick's claim ruling that "the activity [Hardwick] hopes to engage in is quintessentially private and lies at the heart of an intimate association beyond the proper reach of state regulation." To justify the law, the state would have to prove a "compelling in-

terest in regulating this behavior," and this was the basis upon which Hardwick's lawyers built their final appeals case to the Supreme Court. Tribe, the
Harvard law professor who again took the lead in a major gay rights case, argued that "big brother" should not have the authority to regulate "sexual inti-
macies in the privacy of the home."

Privacy was not the issue the Georgia attorneys addressed in defending
the 170-year-old law. In their briefs and arguments to the High Court, they
offered as fundamental an attack on homosexuality as had ever been heard in
the courts, incorporating arguments that had been refined over a decade by
such opponents of homosexual rights as Anita Bryant, Jerry Falwell, William
E. Dannemeyer, Paul Cameron, John Briggs and Ed Davis, the Los Angeles
police chief. "In Georgia, it is the very act of homosexual sodomy that epito-
mizes moral delinquency," wrote Bowers. There was a public interest in barring sodomy by homosexuals, Bowers said, because "it leads to other deviate
practices, such as sadomasochism, group orgies, or transvestitism, to name
only a few." Homosexual sodomy, Bowers continued, is often committed in
"parks, restrooms, 'gay baths,' and 'gay bars,' and is marked by the multiplic-
ity and anonymity of sexual partners, a disproportionate involvement with
adolescents and indeed, a possible relationship to crimes of violence. Similarly, the legislature should be permitted to draw conclusions concerning the
relationship of homosexual sodomy in the transmission of AIDS.

"But perhaps the most profound legislative finding that can be made,"
Bowers concluded, "is that homosexual sodomy is anathema of the basic
units of our society—marriage and the family. To decriminalize or artificially
withdraw the public's expression of its disdain for this conduct does not uplift
sodomy, but rather demotes those sacred institutions to merely other alternative lifestyles."

It is usually pointless to attempt to forecast a Supreme Court ruling from
the justices' remarks during oral arguments, but some of the gay advocates in
this case did just that, drawing hopeful conclusions from the absence of the
kind of hostility that had been displayed during oral arguments in the Oklahoma teachers case. (When Tribe argued then that the Oklahoma law de-
prived homosexual teachers of their constitutional guarantee of freedom of
speech, Chief Justice Warren E. Burger cut him off, noting that homosexual
activity was a crime in Oklahoma and asking if Tribe thus believed that schools
should not be allowed to fire teachers who advocated murder, rape or the over-
throw of the government.) Reflecting the hopefulness of gay advocates, Abby
Rubenfeld, managing attorney of Lambda Legal Defense, told gay leaders
after the arguments that her overall feeling "was one of guarded optimism."

The Supreme Court handed down the *Bowers* v. *Hardwick* decision on
Monday, June 30, 1986, while municipal workers were still cleaning the

streets in cities where homosexuals had the day before celebrated the seventeenth anniversary of the Stonewall riots. The ruling was so unambiguous that the *New York Times* led its front page with a three-line headline over three columns: "High Court, 5–4, Says States Have the Right to Outlaw Private Homosexual Acts." Not only had the Court upheld the Georgia sodomy law, it had explicitly found that homosexuals in particular were not entitled to privacy, or to protection from governmental regulation in their bedrooms. The decision was so dramatic, and it so divided the Court, that the justices took the unusual step of reading portions of it from the bench. The majority decision was written by Associate Justice Byron R. "Whizzer" White, the University of Colorado football All-American and Rhodes scholar appointed by John F. Kennedy to the Court in 1962 after serving two years as the deputy attorney general under Robert F. Kennedy, the reward for his success as national chairman of Citizens for Kennedy in 1960. White noted that there had been a steady march by the Court toward recognizing the privacy of Americans when it came to sexual relations, marriage and conception, and abortion. Though the Georgia sodomy law applied to homosexuals and heterosexuals, married or not, White narrowed the issue only to whether homosexual sodomy was entitled to the blanket of privacy that the Court had established over the previous twenty-one years. And the notion that homosexuals were entitled to such consideration by the Constitution was "at best, facetious," White said.

"The issue presented is whether the Federal Constitution confers a fundamental right upon homosexuals to engage in sodomy and hence invalidates the laws of the many states that still make such conduct illegal and have done so for a very long time." The defendant, White wrote, was asking the Supreme Court to establish "a fundamental right to engage in homosexual sodomy. This we are quite unwilling to do." He would not even accept the argument that private sex should be shielded from government inspection. In that case, White said, it would be permissible to harbor stolen goods or narcotics in one's home.

In his dissent, Justice Harry A. Blackmun, who had been appointed by Richard Nixon in 1970 and who had written the majority decision in *Roe* v. *Wade*, responded to White's argument with language bordering on outright alarm. "This case involves no real interference with the rights of others," he wrote, "for the mere knowledge that other individuals do not adhere to one's value system cannot be a legally cognizable interest, let alone an interest that can justify invading the houses, hearts, and minds of citizens who choose to live their lives differently.

"I can only hope," Blackmun wrote, "that the court will reconsider its analysis and conclude that depriving individuals of the right to choose for themselves how to conduct their intimate relationships poses a far greater threat to the values most deeply rooted in our nation's history than tolerance of nonconformity could ever do. Because I think the court today betrays those values, I dissent."

The decision seemed to undercut homosexuals on almost every conceivable level. Sodomy laws were rarely enforced—Michael Hardwick had to bring suit to force his case into the courts—but the legal strictures against same-sex intercourse were invoked in court fights involving discrimination, child custody battles and immigration restrictions, and raised in legislatures debating gay rights statutes. "Sodomy laws have a much broader impact and scope than making gays *sexual* criminals," Arthur S. Leonard, a lawyer, had written in the *New York Native* earlier in 1986. "In the judicial sphere, they have provided justification for denying child custody and visitation rights, licenses to engage in the professions, naturalization as American citizens, and a host of other civil and human rights that most people take for granted." As Noach Dear, a councilman—and Orthodox Jew—who led the fight against a gay rights bill in New York City, observed, "No judge likes to be overturned by the Supreme Court, so this decision sends a very strong message to the lower courts." "The court has interpreted that a homosexual lifestyle is not a civil right and should not be exempted," Mr. Dear said. "It said they are not equal to heterosexuals."

The Supreme Court had now ruled that states could properly punish people for engaging in homosexual relations, an unambiguous finding that—as Jerry Falwell put it—"perverted moral behavior is not accepted practice in this country." Thomas Stoddard, the gay rights lawyer, told the *Washington Post* legal reporter Ruth Marcus that the most critical effect of the case "is not legal—it's social. The most important judicial body in the United States has expressed a certain distaste for gay men and women and suggested they may be treated differently from other Americans." Analyzing the decision in the *University of Chicago Law Review,* Stoddard later wrote: "The critical constitutional question in *Hardwick* was not what Michael Hardwick was doing in his bedroom, but rather what the state of Georgia was doing there." The decision represented "lawmaking by personal predilection—precisely the sort of judicial self-indulgence that the critics of the Warren Court most often decry." The Court, Stoddard argued, had gone out of its way to transform the case into one concerning only homosexual sodomy, raising issues that none of the lawyers had raised. "The majority was apparently so eager to hand down a ruling on sexual privacy that it either overlooked or deliberately disregarded the posture of the case before it," Stoddard wrote. "Given the importance of the ultimate constitutional question raised in *Hardwick,* the majority's zeal is more than improper; it verges on scandalous." He termed it "our *Dred Scott* case," a reference to the 1857 Supreme Court decision in which Negroes were found to be property, not citizens. Stoddard was generally not given to hyperbole, and his apocalyptic view of the decision was universally shared among gay activists. "We believed in the Constitution," Pat Norman, a California lesbian, told *Newsweek*. "Guess what? It doesn't mean us." A friend called Michael Hardwick in tears when she learned of the decision from television news. "It was all for nothing," Hardwick replied.

The *Hardwick* ruling stirred the deepest response among gay men and lesbians since the Dade County referendum nine years before. On the night of the decision, nearly three thousand homosexuals and their supporters gathered in Greenwich Village, blocking traffic on the broad avenues around Sheridan Square in what was by far the city's largest spontaneous gay political gathering since Stonewall. "The message is that we're second-class citizens," Joyce Hunter, a lesbian activist, told the crowd. "Nobody's going to tell me what I can do in the privacy of my home or hotel room." Later that week, in a demonstration on the Fourth of July, five thousand people turned out at the southern end of Manhattan to disrupt the centennial anniversary of the Statue of Liberty, an Independence Day ceremony attended by Ronald Reagan and Chief Justice Burger. In the wake of the decision, two dozen gay activists met to begin planning a second march by homosexuals on Washington, D.C. "This has been such a wretched time for all of us," said Steve Ault, who helped organize the 1979 march. "A march is needed for ourselves. We need to say that we're not going back into the closet, and we need an event that will be a self-affirmation." There was also a surge in fundraising for the national gay organizations, as there had been after Dade County. Jeff Levi at the National Gay Task Force asked Sean Strub to craft a fundraising letter keyed to the *Hardwick* decision, and it generated what he considered an astonishingly high 20 percent return rate, and $40,000 in contributions. Monthly contributions to Lambda Legal Defense in the two months after the ruling reached $90,000, compared to the typical $40,000, a few made in the name of Justice Byron White. "The time for gay rage is now!" The *Advocate* declared in an uncharacteristically strident editorial. "The time has come for gays to use massive, widespread, creative acts of civil disobedience to help win fair treatment and equal rights. Just as white society would never have voluntarily torn down the evil system of segregation without being pushed back by militancy, so too the [heterosexual] world will never give gays a fair shake unless it learns that there's a high price to pay for anti-gay violence and discrimination."

Yet for all the concern stirred by the case, no state ever reinstated a sodomy law, and some state courts—acting on state constitutions—actually overturned their sodomy laws (notably, Kentucky, whose sodomy law applied only to homosexuals). Byron White had framed the case as an appeal by homosexuals for special protections under the Constitution. But the public perception was that the nation's highest court had condoned the most far-fetched kind of governmental intrusion into private life. It was so shocking, and so reinforced the stereotypes that homosexuals had created of their opponents—sexual puritans peeping in through bedroom keyholes—that it produced a mocking defiance of the Court that swept up newspaper editorialists, legal commentators, cartoonists and talk show hosts. "A Government in the Bedroom" read the headline in *Newsweek*'s story on the decision. "I think that the *Hardwick* v. *Bowers* decision will go down as one of America's most shameful episodes," said the civil rights lawyer Alan M. Dershowitz. The *New York Times,* in a lead editorial titled "Crime in the Bedroom," called it a "gratuitous and petty ruling, an offense to American society's maturing standards of individual dignity." A Gallup poll for *Newsweek* found that respondents disapproved of the decision by 47 to 41 percent, and opposed, by an especially lopsided 57 to 34 percent margin, the suggestion that "states should have the right to prohibit sexual practices conducted in private between consenting homosexual adults."* When Tom Stoddard appeared on the Phil Donahue show, his television host made his brief for him, handing out flashlights to his audience and announcing he was deputizing them as members of the Supreme Court's sex police. When Donahue asked how many people agreed with the Court's decision, Stoddard counted a scattering of hands.

Four years later, Justice Lewis F. Powell Jr. told a group of New York University students, "I think I probably made a mistake" voting with the majority. Powell had voted with the majority in the *Roe* v. *Wade* ruling on abortion rights, so his decision to support White's narrow view of privacy in *Hardwick* was widely noted among Court observers, particularly as word filtered out that he had switched sides at the end of the deliberations to support the majority. He had second—or rather, third—thoughts when he read Blackmun's draft dissent, but he could not bring himself to reverse himself again so close to the end of deliberations. Some of the gay lawyers involved in the case knew one of Powell's clerks was homosexual, and they pleaded with him to come out to the justice in hopes that it might influence Powell, but the clerk declined, later saying he assumed Powell already knew.

July 1986, Los Angeles

Peter Scott, a founder and the first head of MECLA, David Mixner's consulting partner and most recently the chair of AIDS Project Los Angeles, entered the hospital one month after the Supreme Court ruled in the *Hardwick* case. Scott had been worrying about his health for nearly a year, and in that he was no different from most gay men in America in the summer of 1986, examining their skin for purple blotches in the shower, fingering the

* This was a telephone poll of 611 adults on July 1 and 2, with a 5 percent margin of error.

glands in their neck for signs of swelling. Scott convinced himself that he was infected with the AIDS virus before there was any reason to think it was true, and he shared his fears with David Mixner, to whom it was unthinkable that someone like Scott could get AIDS. Mixner didn't know many people who had become sick, and the few he knew had ridden the high-voltage sexual circuit that he and Scott had largely avoided. So when Scott called to report an AIDS-related opportunistic infection growing inside his mouth—"I think I have it," he said, crying,—Mixner just told his old friend, "Don't be silly," Scott's drawn and bloodless complexion notwithstanding. To himself, Mixner said: "*WE* don't get it." This delusion ended when an especially stubborn bout of summer flu Scott contracted turned out to be *Pneumocystis carinii*, the AIDS-related pneumonia. Scott's doctors said he might not make it even through the weekend, much less leave the hospital alive, but he did, and in fact survived another three years.

The AIDS diagnosis of such a socially and politically prominent figure (the *Los Angeles Times* sent a reporter to his hospital room to check the rumors that Peter Scott was sick; both the *Times* and the *Los Angeles Herald Examiner* published news of Scott's illness) sent a depressing tremor through the city's gay community, nearly obscuring even the *Hardwick* ruling. But it did not freeze the city's politically active gay community because it could not. The month that Scott learned of his illness, the California secretary of state certified for submission to voters the first voter initiative pertaining to gay matters in California since the Briggs initiative eight years before. Proposition 64, drafted and circulated by supporters of Lyndon LaRouche, the right-wing extremist, would give state authorities broad powers to contain AIDS, including the authority to quarantine those infected with HIV. LaRouche party members collected 683,000 signatures in support of its initiative, or twice the number needed. Mixner and Scott had handled the campaign against the Briggs initiative, and they were preparing to handle this one together before Scott's hospitalization. "We're busy burying our dead," Mixner told the *Los Angeles Times*, "and we have to defend our right to work."

The stakes, as always in California, seemed high. "If the initiative passes in California," said Jeff Levi, now the executive director of the National Gay Task Force, "it will be a signal for fanatics in other states to propose similar measures." What made this contest particularly frustrating was the realization that the only real reward of a win for gay activists was that it was not a loss. It would be hard to present the defeat of the LaRouche initiative—the first time the question of a state quarantine to deal with AIDS had been presented for public vote—as a surge in public sympathy or even tolerance for homosexuals, or people with AIDS. The campaign shaped up as the most unrewarding kind of contest imaginable: expensive, time-consuming, reactive and draining.

The LaRouche initiative designated AIDS as an "infectious, contagious and communicable disease," and provided that people with AIDS or the HIV virus be "subject to quarantine and isolation statutes." The measure would prohibit HIV "carriers" from working in schools or as food handlers. The overwhelming number of signatures filed, the opinion polls and the mood of the country all suggested sympathy for the kind of strong measures contained in the LaRouche initiative. In the conservative *National Review,* Joseph Sobran wrote an essay on "The Politics of AIDS," asserting that homosexuals deserved more blame and less sympathy for AIDS, and quoting personal ads in the *Native* ("Sordid and desperate, the ads make it impossible to idealize gay life"), to dramatize his argument that "the obvious carrier of AIDS is the 'gay lifestyle'—promiscuous homosexuality.

"Nobody died at Three Mile Island, but an accident there brought down strict control—and moral opprobrium—on the nuclear-power industry," Sobran wrote. "Thousands have died of AIDS, and more thousands are going to die of it, but no serious restraints or even censure has been placed on sodomite promiscuity. It's up to the rest of us to pay the bills, find the cures, and take the risk."

In California, the committee behind the initiative was called PANIC— Prevent AIDS Now Initiative Committee. "We start as an underdog," said Bruce Decker, the Republican chairman of the California AIDS Task Force and finance chairman of the opposing Stop LaRouche campaign. The "voting public is dreadfully afraid, and if they have the sense that any measure will make it safe for them, they'll vote for it, civil liberties be damned." But it soon became clear that this was not going to be a replay of either the Briggs or Bryant initiative. The gay movement was more sophisticated and influential. The image of Mixner and Scott riding off to a hidden corner of Los Angeles for a secret meeting with a political operative to plead for Ronald Reagan's endorsement seemed almost farcical now. The gay movement in California could raise money, produce a media campaign and enlist as allies nearly every established political figure in the state, which is what it did now. Even Governor George Deukmejian, who had blocked a gay rights bill in Sacramento, called Proposition 64 "wholly unnecessary and unwarranted." What's more, class frictions in California's gay community were put aside. Ivy Bottini, the most prominent of the state's grassroots lesbian leaders, joined forces with the members of MECLA, and the two sides shared office space on Wilshire Boulevard. Mixner and Torie Osborn oversaw fundraising and planned the commercial that marked the gay movement's final arrival in the modern age of politics. The LaRouche initiative lost by a huge margin—71 percent to 29 percent, dwarfing the 58 percent to 42 percent result of Briggs eight years before.

"It sends a very powerful message to any other politician, to any other cheap demagogue, that there is absolutely no political advantage to messing around with this community any longer," David Mixner said. Ever-optimistic, often self-congratulatory, Mixner overstated the case somewhat. The vote did not prove that the gay community had been embraced. Still, the idea of a governmental quarantine of AIDS patients was never considered seriously again.

February 1987, Atlanta

This is a historic moment, thought Urvashi Vaid, the dark and intense public information officer for the National Gay and Lesbian Task Force, as she settled behind the microphone next to Tom Stoddard, the executive director of Lambda Legal Defense, who was thinking the same thing. They were among fourteen men and women dressed in business suits and wearing name tags, assembled in two orderly lines, seated and standing, stiff and serious, like high school students posing for their yearbook picture. It was unusual to get fourteen gay and AIDS movement leaders together for one press conference, much less united behind one position, but that they had done on the second and final day of the Disease Control and Prevention conference in Atlanta to discuss the AIDS epidemic. Nearly every major gay and AIDS organization was represented: the National Gay and Lesbian Task Force,* National Gay Rights Advocates, the Human Rights Campaign Fund, the AIDS Action Council, People With AIDS, the Gay Men's Health Crisis from New York, Mobilization Against AIDS from San Francisco, and Gay and Lesbian Advocates and Defenders from Boston. "We have never been this organized," Urvashi Vaid said in the days leading up to the conference. They had spent weeks preparing for this, with four telephone conference calls, and meetings in California, New York and Washington, after learning that the Centers for Disease Control was considering a regulation mandating HIV testing at hospitals, sexually transmitted disease clinics and prenatal clinics. A mandatory testing policy would scare away the very people who needed medical attention, they said. They had found a consensus of support for their position at this meeting in Atlanta, and the press conference was intended to marshal public support by highlighting the opposition of medical professionals to the proposed regulations. "We came here organized to present an alternative case, to demand attention for real solutions," Vaid announced. "And we have succeeded. The message of this conference to the CDC is loud and clear: spend money on more education and research, expand anonymous testing centers and end the discrimination experienced with people with AIDS."

Vaid's audience was primarily reporters, sprinkled with a handful of gay activists not associated with the leaders holding this press conference. During the past two days these activists had made their presence known by wearing

* The National Gay Task Force voted Nov. 2–3, 1986, to add the word "lesbian" to its title.

replicas of Nazi concentration camp uniforms—gray shirts stenciled with prisoner numbers and painted with the pink triangle that Nazis used to distinguish known homosexuals. They called themselves the Lavender Hill Mob, for the 1951 British comedy with Alec Guinness about an aging, mild-mannered and loyal bank auditor who lived in a rooming house on Lavender Hill in London and organized a £1-million gold heist of the bullion shipment that he was in charge of safeguarding. The Lavender Hill Mob's view of activism was quite different from that of the gay leaders who mingled easily with the doctors and state and federal health officials at the Marriott Marquis Hotel that last Tuesday and Wednesday of February. A debate on the ethics of HIV blood testing meant little to the Lavender Hill Mob, or to the frightened constituency they were coming to represent.

Marty Robinson, the originator of the political zap—organized chaos and theater, calculated to attract press attention—from his years with the GAA, had suggested they dress as concentration camp prisoners. A member more recently of the Gay and Lesbian Alliance Against Defamation, he wanted to protest anti-homosexual sentiment spurred by AIDS. But Robinson found GLAAD timid and conservative, and had quit to help form the more subversive Lavender Hill Mob. This small organization had been an intermittently disruptive force in the months leading up to the conference in Atlanta, employing political zaps. "Who cares that the issue is mandatory testing of people going into hospitals?" Robinson said, broaching the idea of the Centers for Disease Control zap to Michael Petrelis, a young, loud and impressionable admirer he met at GLAAD. "We're going and we're going to demand drugs." Two of the five members of the Mob dressed in the concentration camp outfits and sat in the front row so CDC officials could see them. They interrupted the proceedings by raising a banner which read "THE LAVENDER HILL MOB," and shouted the conference into a premature end.

"We're tired of the genocide!"

"Where's the funding?"

"Why are we talking about testing *now?*"

"What about saving people's lives?"

"STOP KILLING US!" Michael Petrelis yelled, stretching out the word "us," his voice cutting through the ballroom.

Members of the Lavender Hill Mob saw little difference between the health professionals they had been haranguing and the homosexuals who now were talking into the television lights. They fumed at their smugness, and viewed their claims of victory as hollow. As Urvashi Vaid began the press conference she had spent so much time planning, Michael Petrelis rose from his seat at the back of the hall.

"You've sold out the gay community!" Petrelis bellowed, his loud voice overwhelming Vaid.

"We should be yelling, we should be screaming about this issue!" shouted Bill Bahlman. "We shouldn't be sitting, talking rationally about this!"

"I think you guys are really out of touch with the gay community," Petrelis declared, as the gay leaders behind the microphone exchanged uncertain glances. "The anger, the frustration—you're all up there with your nice little suits and ties on and you really don't know what the hell we're going through and the frustration. After six years there has been no action. And you guys are coming in here and acting as though what has happened today is something to be applauded."

It was like the summer of 1969 again, when Jim Fouratt of the Gay Liberation Front stood in the audience to shout down Dick Leitsch of the Mattachine Society; the gay movement was turning on its parents again. This time, though, the announcement of the campaign to defeat the mandatory testing proposal had boasted of a new unity among homosexual groups. "The gay and lesbian community has a lot to be proud of in the manner in which we responded to this proposal," Jeff Levi proclaimed in a press release. "The level of coordination indicates that our movement has matured and coalesced in a powerful manner." That early display of confidence, along with the television cameras and newspaper reporters who came alive at this man-bites-dog spectacle of gays zapping gays, only made the moment more excruciating. Urvashi Vaid was familiar with what she called direct-action protests from her years in Boston, but had never considered that she might be a target of such attacks: She could not believe that a group of men who struck her as opportunists would be willing to ruin this moment just for a few minutes of their own in the spotlight. Vaid sensed—correctly—that this was a turning point in gay activism. "I feel your anger," Vaid finally responded. "It's hard to be on the receiving end of it." But, Vaid continued tentatively, "you do us a disservice," by suggesting that she and the others did not appreciate the urgency of the epidemic. "I feel that we're pushing for the same end and that you're taking a different strategy—and this is equally viable to the strategy we're taking."

The press conference crumbled to an end, and the *New York Times* the next day took note of the "split among homosexual groups." The targets of the attack were shell-shocked. "That sort of stridency and anger and rage can do a lot to paralyze our supporters as well as mobilize them," Tim Sweeney of GMHC told *The Advocate*. The disruption, Jeff Levi said to a reporter after the conference, "demonstrates that just as the CDC has to deal with Dannemeyer, we have to deal with the Lavender Hill Mob."

Indeed, the Lavender Hill Mob presented quite a contrast to the established gay leaders. Their base of operations was not a suite of offices in Washington, D.C., but Bill Bahlman's cramped, one-bedroom apartment in New York City's West Village. And although they had boasted at times of a membership of fifty, the Mob really came down to a handful of men. Bahlman was a string bean, thirty-seven years old, half German, half Norwegian, a disc jockey who played New Wave music at the Anvil, a packed, triangular after-hours gay club by the Hudson River. Bahlman had met Marty Robinson at the GAA in the early 1970s, and in recent months had spent so much time working on the Lavender Hill demonstrations that he was now practically broke. Michael Petrelis was twenty-eight years old, sloppy and roly-poly, with black curly hair and a voice that was impossible to ignore. He did not care what people thought of him and seemed incapable of embarrassment. Petrelis grew up in the suburbs of New Jersey and commuted to New York City as a teenager, searching for sex. He soon discovered the Ninth Circle on Tenth Street, where he could satisfy his sexual cravings and make money in the process. If those $20 encounters with the older men who drank in the bar's basement weren't physically satisfying enough Petrelis would go down to the West Side piers where he enjoyed, as he later put it with characteristic direct-ness, "lots and lots of unsafe sex." Eighteen months before the Atlanta news conference, Petrelis, then twenty-six, had been diagnosed with Kaposi's sar-coma, and he had leaned back in his doctor's office and put a match to a cig-arette. I don't care if this is a doctor's office, Petrelis thought. That cigarette turned out to be the kind of brash and impolite gesture which would charac-terize Petrelis's next frantic eighteen months. He scrapped with members of Congress, city officials and even the board of directors of the GMHC. Petrelis was upset that the GMHC board did not include a person with AIDS, or more accurately, as Petrelis knew and would soon become publicly clear with the death of board president Paul Popham, no *openly* sick person. Petrelis acted more out of instinct than thought—he considered himself undereduc-ated and intellectually inadequate, and more than once lost his train of thought in the midst of a careening attack in a public forum—but what he lacked in intelligence he often made up for in volume.

The Lavender Hill Mob was dauntless because its members knew, or as-sumed, that most of them were infected with the AIDS virus. Petrelis, who made a trademark of screaming, "We're dying!" was the most open about it. He even agreed to allow a *Newsday* society reporter, James A. Revson, who would turn out also to die of AIDS, to chronicle his struggle with the disease in a series of stories that began April 9, 1986. By contrast, Marty Robinson would put off anyone who inquired about his health, or deny flat out that he was sick, though his increasingly ragged appearance and desperate air belied him. Indeed, Robinson insisted he was healthy right into his hospital room two years later, even as doctors discussed how to treat his *Pneumocystis carinii*.

When the epidemic emerged, gay leaders had responded by approach-ing it as a civil rights issue or an issue of governmental funding. It was, for most of them, familiar ground to argue that quarantine was wrong, or that mandatory testing was wrong, or that discriminating against people with

AIDS was wrong. It was even relatively easy to push for more money for AIDS research and treatment. It was quite another matter to try to comprehend the complex medical issues emerging around AIDS, the thicket of governmental agencies and regulations that dealt with, for example, speeding new drugs onto the marketplace. The Lavender Hill Mob's urgent agenda stood in contrast to the unhurried and uncluttered civil rights agenda that had dominated the gay rights movement for so long. The ground was shifting again. Faced with the AIDS epidemic, many homosexuals had initially turned in anger on doctors, the health system and the government. As the confrontation in Atlanta made clear, many of them were now turning on the homosexual rights movement itself.

37

REQUIEM

March 1987, New York

The AIDS Coalition to Unleash Power was founded on Tuesday, March 10, 1987, at the New York City Lesbian and Gay Community Services Center on West Thirteenth Street, with a bone-rattling speech by Larry Kramer, for whom this was an act of frustration (and to a certain extent, revenge) against his former associates at the Gay Men's Health Crisis, who had expelled him four years before. In the sobering and indelible climax of the evening, Kramer—unleashing what was by now a familiar stream of harangue and intimidation, drama and breathless hyperbole—instructed two-thirds of the audience to stand and then informed them they would probably be dead in five years. Fourteen days later, 250 members of this new organization surged through the streets of New York's Financial District, where they burned in effigy the commissioner of the Food and Drug Administration, chanted "Release the Drugs!" and blocked rush-hour traffic. This brought them seventeen arrests and a mention by Dan Rather on the *CBS Evening News*.

It all made for a compelling story for the reporters who came in the months ahead to reconstruct the birth of the AIDS activist movement. There was Larry Kramer as the lead player, whose warnings had been largely discounted for nearly a decade, and who now embraced the role of redeemed prophet. (*"Oh my people,"* Kramer said repeatedly as, later in 1987, he accepted an award at a Human Rights Campaign Fund black-tie dinner. "Oh my people, I beg you to hear me.") Kramer's audience at the Lesbian and Gay Community Services Center was an intense and eclectic group, mostly men, mostly young professionals who worked in public relations, government, communications, writing, design, journalism and the arts. ACT-UP, as the organization would be called, would be hip, stylish, informed and sexy activism, and it defied type. Homosexuals were not supposed to be this way.

It was a seductive and accurate story line, but it was incomplete. The birth of ACT-UP—as springing full-blown from that meeting in March 1987—was reported in a way that reflected the media savvy of its leaders in its extraordinarily successful early years. What was lost was context. The anger that gave rise to ACT-UP had been churning for almost two years in New York, Boston, San Francisco and elsewhere, stoked by the government crackdown on bathhouses, the demonization of homosexuals in the media, the *Hardwick* ruling, the reports of random assaults of homosexuals on the streets (often by attackers yelling about AIDS),* and most of all, by the quickening and unrelenting pace of illness and death. Larry Kramer's speech lit the match, but the gasoline had already been spilled.

The evidence of this could be seen in a series of small eruptions over the previous two years. In San Francisco, on October 24, 1985, nine people attended a demonstration sponsored by Mobilization Against AIDS and then, in an unplanned and poignant act of frustration, planted themselves on a plot of grass at the old Federal Office Building on United Nations Plaza, where they spent much of the next six months stubbornly encamped. Two protesters, already showing the first signs of AIDS-related opportunistic infection, chained themselves to a door and announced they would not leave until the government allocated $500 million for AIDS research, and the Food and Drug Administration approved experimental AIDS therapies that were already available in France and Mexico. On some nights the vigil attracted as many as a hundred people, who huddled under plastic sheets and slept in weather-beaten tents. At the same time in San Francisco, Arthur Evans, the Gay Activists Alliance founder from New York—who had long absented himself from any kind of activism—began to rally friends with the argument that AIDS was the greatest political crisis gay people had ever faced. In twenty

---

* At a hearing Nov. 22, 1986, before the House Judiciary Subcommittee on Criminal Justice, David Wertheimer, executive director of the New York City Gay and Lesbian Anti-Violence Project, testified that the project counted 351 incidents of violence in the first nine months of 1986, compared to 167 the previous year. In 28 percent of New York incidents in 1985, Wertheimer said, assailants taunted victims with comments about AIDS. "We're in the middle of an epidemic of violence against gay men and lesbian," he noted. A San Francisco group, Community United Against Violence, reported a 23 percent increase in reports of anti-gay violence over the year before.

years, he said, it would not be enough to look back and say that they had nursed friends who were dying. And so he began showing up at scattered demonstrations protesting the government and media's response to the epidemic.

The Lavender Hill Mob had disrupted the press conference of gay leaders in Atlanta in February 1987, but it had been working for almost eight months by then, orchestrating a campaign of demonstrations and zaps against government and church officials in New York City and Washington. Its members had stormed the offices of Senator Alfonse M. D'Amato in New York, brandishing mock "arrest warrants," camera-ready props which read: "Charge: mass murder by indifference, 15,345 dead."* When the Vatican issued its October 1986 "Letter to the Bishops on the Pastoral Care of Homosexual Persons," in which Joseph Cardinal Ratzinger, the Vatican prefect for the doctrine of the faith, found in homosexuals "a more or less strong tendency to behavior which is intrinsically evil from the moral point of view, and should therefore be considered objectively disordered itself," Bill Bahlman had dressed as a priest and joined seven other men in the first pew of St. Patrick's Cathedral. When Archbishop John J. O'Connor began his sermon, Bahlman and his associates stood up, holding hands, in a quiet but unmistakable gesture of protest. The Lavender Hill Mob picketed William F. Buckley's *National Review* after Buckley aired his proposal in the *New York Times* about tattooing people with AIDS. "While Buckley's *National Review* has the right to spew forth such venom," the Lavender Hill Mob declared in a leaflet, "we have the right and duty to respond and fight back." William J. Bennett, the secretary of education, encountered the Mob when he spoke about AIDS at Georgetown University. Michael Petrelis showed up with a Lavender Hill Mob banner, loudly asking why the Reagan administration had been so slow in responding to the AIDS epidemic. "YOU'RE KILLING UHSSS!" Petrelis shouted from the audience.

The anger boiled through the gay press as well. Eleven months before the first ACT-UP meeting, *The Advocate* ran a cover story headlined, "The AIDS Slur: Why Gays Should Stop Taking the Blame and Start Fighting Back." Written by Darrell Yates Rist, a founder of GLAAD and a man who would die of AIDS, the piece bristled with the kind of rage that would soon become familiar to much of the world. "We're assaulted in the legislatures, courts, the media, the churches and the street—not just because of AIDS, but because we're *queer*. We are meek and niggardly," Rist wrote, and he railed against the "hideous lies" being spread. "These lies sneered that we are sinful,

---

* They misspelled the senator's first name as Alphonse, but they stayed long enough to win attention to their demands for federal legislation prohibiting discrimination against people with AIDS, and money for AIDS research and treatment.

we are moral blights, we are sick, we are desperate . . . that we recruit young children *and* innocent adults, that we cannot love, that we're unlovable, that we're sexually obsessed, that we're all promiscuous, and our relationships don't last. That we spread disease, emotional and physical. That good, clean folk can catch perversion or a deadly germ by simply being near us in a room.

"We've taken in the lies that are, more surely than is AIDS itself, destroying us," Rist concluded. " . . . We'll survive only if we stop apologizing—for AIDS, our love, our lives. We'll survive," he said, " . . . if we let loose our rage." It was a challenge to homosexuals to defy the way society had typecast them, to affirm themselves the way gay activists had in the months after Stonewall. Eric Rofes took it the next step in an essay published in May 1986. Rofes, a product of Harvard University and the *Gay Community News* collective in Boston, was executive director of the Gay and Lesbian Community Services Center in Los Angeles. A teacher and essayist, he had spent ten years in gay organizing, and had a participant's appreciation of the evolution that had produced organizations like MECLA. Rofes argued that playing by the rules no longer worked. "If you are a gay man or lesbian in America today, your rights are threatened more than they've ever been during the past 15 years," Rofes wrote. "Large sectors of society are demanding your forced screening for HTLV-3 antibodies, the closing of gay bars and organizations, restrictions on your rights to assemble and freedom of speech. *How much are you willing to take before fighting back?*" Rofes argued that the time had come for a revitalized movement that would "apply the militancy of the 60s to the issues of the 80s.

"It must inspire us to creative forms of militancy, including passive resistance, high-visibility zaps and outrageous street dramas," Rofes wrote.

Finally, there was another group of men meeting in New York in the months before ACT-UP formed. The Lavender Hill Mob would lend to ACT-UP much of its tactical armament, but this collective would impart an artistic and marketing sensibility, which would prove equally distinctive to this new activism. Avram Finkelstein was one of its organizers. He was a trained artist, raised on Long Island, the son of two Russian Jews who had met at a Communist summer camp. Uneasy with the notion of selling his art for money, Finkelstein became an art director and hairstylist at Vidal Sassoon. He loved the reaction he got when he told the journalists who came to interview him about ACT-UP what he did. They were invariably startled by the notion that someone like him—poised, masculine, verbal, intense—could work as a hairdresser. Hairstyling was a blue-collar profession, Finkelstein would respond when challenged about his career choice. He said it with a touch of irony sometimes lost on his listener (after all, he was charging $100 for a haircut).

The first man Finkelstein knew who contracted AIDS was his lover, whom he met in 1979 and who died in 1984. It was a searing experience for

Finkelstein, who was just thirty-two. He fell in with several other men facing similar tragedies. They met every week for dinner, each inviting one friend to join in what came to be a consciousness-raising group. At the start, the six men would talk about surviving the trauma of AIDS, but invariably the talk became political as the evenings wore on, and shared grief turned to frustration at the government's lack of response to AIDS. Surely, Finkelstein thought, they were not the only young gay men in the country who were struggling with such grief and anger, and he made this point one night. "Every week we break into a political discussion," Finkelstein said. "As far as I'm concerned, the political crisis surrounding AIDS had not been addressed, and there is one." Finkelstein had studied at the School of the Museum of Fine Arts in Boston. He had visited there with his mother during the student strikes at Harvard Square, when the school had been transformed by its students into a round-the-clock poster factory. He remembered that the posters had worked as political circulars—flares to attract the eye of potential political allies—and he suggested that they use the same tool to stir organizing in New York around AIDS. They should produce posters: bold, glossy, provocative and polished—like music videos—so the political mainstream and the city's gay community would believe there was a large, organized and wealthy political movement afoot, even if there was not.

The first poster was designed in December 1986, as the men in the collective, gathering for a pre-holiday celebration, divided their evening between gift-giving, drafting the words that would appear on the poster, and dealing with the recent news that one of their members had Kaposi's sarcoma. By the time the poster was completed, it was the dead of New York's winter—the cold, gray and windy months of January and February, when there were few people on the street who might stop to read something on a wall. They put off the posting until the beginning of March. They printed almost 2,000 posters in the first run, each one two feet wide and three feet high. They cost $1,200 to produce, and another $1.50 apiece for the professional snipers, who wheat-posted them on the sides of Manhattan buildings and fences at night, with a three-week guarantee that no one would paste over them. Finkelstein financed the first run from his salary at Vidal Sassoon.

Michael Petrelis noticed the collective's posters as soon as he returned from the CDC protest in Atlanta. They seemed to be everywhere. They were unsigned (Finkelstein was worried that if the posters encouraged a riot, as he hoped they might, the collective could face indictment as the Chicago 7 had in 1968.) The final product was all type and design. To depict a person would have inevitably provoked debate: should it be a man or a woman? Black or white? The collective did not want to portray this as another white male movement (even though it was so far). The posters were white text on a black background, and they were stamped with a pink triangle, the increasingly familiar symbol of gay liberation. The collective picked it over the Lambda, the gay liberation symbol Tom Doerr had designed for the GAA, which Finkelstein thought was clunky. They punched up the pink triangle with a splash of fuchsia, flipped it on its head like an upside-down flag of distress and floated it in the center of a stark black background. The small text on the poster, meant to be read by passersby, asked: *"Why is Reagan silent about AIDS? What is really going on at the Centers for Disease Control, the Federal Drug Administration and the Vatican?"* (It should have read the Food and Drug Administration, an error that Larry Kramer pointed out to Finkelstein on their first meeting, when Finkelstein asked Kramer what he thought of their effort. "Well, if you're going to do it, you're going to have to get your facts right," Kramer responded testily.) *"Gays and lesbians are not expendable. Use your power. Vote, boycott, defend yourselves. Turn anger, fear, grief into action."* The poster was anchored by six-inch-high letters, designed to be read from a passing bus or taxi, and to sum up the new political spirit the collective hoped to inspire: *"SILENCE=DEATH."*

By now, Larry Kramer, who had briefly disappeared to write his play *The Normal Heart*—a project that had brought him fame and a platform from which he could denounce the GMHC founders—was back full-time on the public stage. Both feet planted, he was lobbing grenades at the GMHC— "Auntie GMHC," Kramer called it, in provocative imitation of the subtle feminine put-down favored by male homosexuals from Dick Leitsch's time. "I cannot for the life of me understand," Kramer wrote the executive director of the GMHC, in a letter Kramer then had published in the *Native,* "how the organization I helped to form has become such a bastion of conservatism and such a bureaucratic mess. The bigger you get the more cowardly you become; the more money you receive the more self-satisfied. No longer do you have to fight for a living; you have become a funeral home. You and your huge assortment of caretakers perform miraculous tasks helping the dying to die. . . .

"I am ashamed of the whole lot of you," he wrote. "I did not spend two years of my life fighting for your birth to see you turn into a bunch of cowards. I did not spend two years of my life fighting to establish Gay Men's Health Crisis to use it to turn into the organization it now is. . . . Get off your fucking self-satisfied asses and fight!"

Kramer was not involved in the Lavender Hill Mob, and would not have been welcome, even if he had had the time or interest, for one simple reason: Marty Robinson detested him. "His is a divisive voice of the movement," Robinson told Petrelis. It was an obvious point, though Robinson's view of Kramer was probably colored by bitterness at what he considered the lack of recognition for his own accomplishments. Kramer's celebrity-activist status, meanwhile, soared in a way that none of the first generation of post-Stonewall and pre-AIDS activists could have ever imagined. He was a writer whose rhetoric could promote his cause with unique power and public energy. Yet Kramer was intrigued with the Lavender Hill Mob after reading of its demonstration in Atlanta, and arranged to meet Michael Petrelis on his return. The questions that Kramer put to Petrelis in that first meeting suggested that the two activists shared much in common. Kramer wanted to know what Petrelis thought of GMHC and the state of activism in New York. Kramer was brimming with ideas. Why not ring the White House with protesters? Why not disrupt Congress? Why not block public highways, bridges and tunnels in New York City? Why not close down Wall Street? Why not, Kramer suggested, emotional terrorism: throwing bottles filled with a thick red liquid into public thoroughfares, yelling, "This is AIDS blood!" as they smashed on the pavement?

The main meeting room of the Community Center was crowded on March 10, 1987, but not packed. Every one of the folding chairs, about seventy-five of them, was filled. After the organizers of the center's second-Tuesday lecture series asked him to fill in for Nora Ephron, Kramer had turned to his telephone to assure himself as large an audience as possible. ("I'm speaking at the center on Tuesday night and you're coming," he told Andy Humm at the Coalition for Lesbian and Gay Rights. When Humm protested that he had heard Kramer speak the previous week, Kramer responded: "*You* are showing up at the center," and hung up the phone.) Members of the Lavender Hill Mob and Finkelstein's Silence=Death collective decided to bring their weekly dinner group to the center after hearing that Kramer was going to talk about the same issue they had been struggling with for months. The result was an unusual assembly. The few elders who were there—Jim Fouratt, Arnie Kantrowitz, Vito Russo, Larry Mass and Marty Robinson, among them—surveyed a room filled with faces they had never seen before. Many of the young men in the room were sick, or feared they were. They were caring for, and burying, friends and lovers. They were being chased from the closet by disease, and the precautions they had once taken to hide their sexual identity now seemed empty and even hypocritical. AIDS was a singularly radicalizing experience, the kind of shared trauma that other members of their generation had not experienced. Most of the men at the center, like the smaller group which formed the Gay Men's Health Crisis five summers before, were people who had never displayed an interest in gay causes before. They would never think of going to city hall for a hearing on the gay rights bill, or of writing a check to the Human Rights Campaign Fund, or of considering gay rights while inside the voting booth. The beginning of ACT-UP marked another new era in gay activism, at once a step forward and a repudiation of the past. Its birth, in many ways, was like the riots that grew from the raid at the Stonewall bar, less than five blocks from the center where they were meeting: another threshold had been reached on the evening in 1987 when Larry Kramer took the floor.

"If my speech tonight doesn't scare the shit out of you, we're in real trouble," Kramer announced at the start of the meeting, his eyes blazing at the men in the room. "If what you're hearing doesn't rouse you to anger, fury, rage and action, gay men will have no future here on earth." The speech was delivered four years, almost to the day, after the *Native* published "1,112 and Counting," and Kramer read whole passages of his first article to his audience. Kramer quoting Kramer seemed as relevant in 1987 as it had in 1983, except that there were now twenty-nine times as many cases of AIDS—32,000. Kramer, pointing at the right-side audience, rolled his arm across the room, as he commanded two-thirds of them to rise. "At the rate we are going, you could be dead in less than five years. Two-thirds of this room could be dead in five years.

"How long does it take before you get angry and fight back?" Kramer asked them. "I sometimes think we have a death wish. I think we must want to die. I have never been able to understand why for six long years we have sat back and let ourselves literally be knocked off man by man—without fighting back. I have heard of denial, but this is more than denial. It *is* a death wish." Some of the people in the room who were familiar with Kramer's style knew that his perspective was sometimes distorted, his rhetoric flat-footed, didactic or alienating. There were times that Kramer undercut himself by sacrificing objectivity for drama. This was not one of those moments. "How many dead brothers have to be piled up in front of your faces in a heap before you learn to fight back and scream and yell and demand and take some responsibilities for your own life?" He was bellowing at them.

When Kramer asked who would be willing to participate in a new organization, nearly every hand went up. "We need people," Petrelis shouted from the floor. "We have all got to get arrested." They determined that the obvious targets for protest were the Food and Drug Administration and drug manufacturers, who were restricting the release of drugs and marketing them at exorbitant prices. (Kramer referred to the FDA in a subsequent op-ed piece in the *New York Times* as "the single most incomprehensible bottleneck in American bureaucratic history that is actually prolonging this roll call of death.")

The new group formed by the men in the room that night knew what it wanted to do before it knew what to call itself. Avram Finkelstein's notes from the second meeting spoke of it passingly as the AIDS Action Committee, but he devoted most of his note-taking to the civil disobedience ideas shouted from the audience: stopping subways, blockading bridges and tunnels, darkening the skies above Manhattan with black balloons, throwing tacks under the tires of *New York Times* delivery trucks, taking over the Statue of Liberty. It was not until the third meeting that the group determined it needed a name for the leaflets announcing the Wall Street demonstration it had decided upon. Petrelis suggested calling it CAN, as in Cure AIDS Now, a suggestion that drew guffaws from the audience. Social worker Steev Borher, a volunteer at GMHC, suggested the acronym ACT-UP, or AIDS Coalition to Unleash Power. Belligerent, sexy and as cutting edge as the group it described, it also did not contain the word "gay," "lesbian" or "homosexual." This was not to obscure the group's goals, as had been the case with the Mattachine Society and the Daughters of Bilitis, nor to protect the identity of its members, as in the early years of MECLA. The founders of ACT-UP had come up with a name that suggested action, but that also made clear that gay lobbies, gay task forces and gay alliances were incapable of responding to a political agenda being forced on them by an epidemic. Until now, AIDS activism had been another faction in the gay rights movement. That changed with ACT-UP.

March 1987, Los Angeles

Duke Comegys was ashen when he arrived in David Mixner's living room for the March meeting of the Book Study Group. This was a small group, fewer than ten people, lapsed members of the Municipal Elections Committee of Los Angeles. They were all familiar players in the city's gay politics over the past decade, among them Mixner, Peter Scott, Diane Abbitt, Roberta Bennett, Larry Sprenger and Rob Eichberg. Jean O'Leary, the former NGTF co-chair and founder of Lesbian Feminist Liberation in New York, who was now executive director of National Gay Rights Advocates and living in California, had also been invited to attend. The Book Study Group was exclusive and deliberately secretive, starting with its ambiguous name, chosen so its members could escape the notice of the rest of the city's gay community. They were attempting to prevent the infighting that they believed came with opening the floor to democratic procedures. For that reason, there was no board of directors, no organization, bylaws or constitution. Membership was by invitation only, and important decisions—to whom to write checks—were made by consensus. Inevitably, the news that this group was meeting in David Mixner's living room became public, and Marylouise Oates ran an item on it in her society column in the *Los Angeles Times*. It was hard to maintain, as Mixner briefly tried to, that this particular group of people was really spending evenings sharing their thoughts on books. The true function of the Book Study Group was a familiar one: to funnel money from wealthy homosexuals to candidates sympathetic to gay causes. In the spring of 1987, the cause was AIDS.

Comegys had not been part of this circle when it launched MECLA a decade earlier. He had made his own name in Los Angeles as a fundraiser for the Los Angeles Gay and Lesbian Community Services Center. Comegys (pronounced KAH-meh-jis) was a man of inherited wealth, independent and politically involved. Like the other members of the Book Study Group, he enjoyed the competitive cross-fertilization between activism and socializing that the Book Study Group in Los Angeles—and, in another way, ACT-UP in New York—exemplified. He was a Harvard Law School graduate who grew up in Texas. But Comegys lived, as his parents had, off the successes of two generations of Texas real estate and banking investments. After a brief early involvement with the Gay Activists Alliance in New York, he spent the early 1970s traveling the world, then settled in San Francisco. He soon grew restless and bored, and moved south to Los Angeles. It was there, in a therapy group made up of wealthy gay men like himself, that Duke Comegys met Sheldon Andelson. Andelson had begun his own work at the Los Angeles Gay Community Services Center, which was always struggling for money, and at Andelson's urging, Comegys volunteered to help in fundraising. He started with the names of twenty-five people who donated $500 a year, and proceeded to expand the list to three hundred people who could be counted on to contribute or raise $1,200 annually. Luncheon invitations to the Hollywood Hills home of Duke Comegys were coveted, and Comegys would alternate social invitations with fundraisers, so his contributors felt they were getting their money's worth. His parties, like Andelson's, were certain to boast good food, a stocked bar and handsome men by the pool. These were people, he later observed, who were "buying access to a social lifestyle that they really wanted to live themselves, and they were seeing things that they could not afford." Comegys soon became known as one of the best fundraisers in Los Angeles.

Comegys, like the leaders of MECLA, believed in making the political system work for him. A registered Republican, he had not felt much enthusiasm about any Republican since Barry Goldwater ran for president in 1964, and tended to vote Democratic. He enjoyed his wealth. He liked displaying it, and he was used to being in charge, to having people defer to him, to getting his way. That all changed when Duke Comegys learned he was infected with HIV. Comegys was pale and agitated when he showed up at Mixner's living room for an evening meeting of the Book Study Group because he had just learned from his doctor that his T-cell count, a measure used to track the effect of HIV on the immune system, had dropped to an alarmingly low 167.* Comegys was not the only man in the room worried about his health: Scott and Eichberg had equal reason for concern. But Comegys brought a certain personal indignation and anger to his predicament, and it shook this group.

---

* The normal range is 1,200 to 1,600. The 167 count turned out to be an aberration; Comegys's T-cell count returned to more acceptable levels and his health remained stable.

They were supposed to be highly influential with government, Comegys said that day, yet nothing was happening.

"I'm just scared to death," Comegys said flatly. The edge in his thin voice, which still had traces of a soft Texas accent, frightened everyone in Mixner's quiet living room. These were men and women of considerable power in Los Angeles who had argued for years that influence came with contributions, who had worked resolutely to make the system work for them. The helplessness and fear that Comegys captured—and that others in the room felt, or had felt—called everything they had done into doubt. There were murmurs in the room—"Everybody's dying, everybody's sick," someone said—and confusion about what to do next. There were a few directions this particular group could have gone: they could, for example, redouble their efforts to work within the establishment. But Comegys and Mixner and the rest of the group had another idea: they could break the law. They could take the same course that the black civil rights movement had begun to take some thirty years before.

Comegys noted that many of the people in the group were planning to go to Washington for an international conference on AIDS that was convening there in June. Why not protest in front of the White House? Why not, said a man who liked to boast that he had the largest and most lavish bathroom in all of Los Angeles, get *arrested* in front of the White House? It was one thing for some young street activists—for a bunch of kids—to get led away in handcuffs. It would be quite remarkable for a group of upper-middle-class professionals—the same men and women who now attended and hosted fundraisers for some of the better-known politicians in America—to suddenly find themselves in jail.

The notion that came bubbling out of Mixner's living room got public airing when Comegys spoke, five days after the ACT-UP demonstration on Wall Street, at the eighth annual National Lesbian and Gay Health Conference, at the end of March 1987, in Los Angeles. Taking a certain pleasure in his performance, Comegys, the co-chair of the national Human Rights Campaign Fund, the leader of the Gay and Lesbian Community Services Center, speaking to an audience that included his local congressman, announced that in light of the crisis at hand, he was ready to go out and break the law.

"There have been several times in American history where civil disobedience has been appropriate," Comegys, a short block of a man with a mustache, declared. "I believe that now is one of those times." He began to paint a picture of a movement of people sickened and desperate, but also disciplined and ready for jail.

"Our own system of government is killing us and it will continue to kill us until we all act together to expose them," he said, his voice at once weary and angry. "We have tried rational discourse for six long years and it simply hasn't worked. I believe it will be enormously constructive to our cause for this president [Reagan] and this nation to learn how truly desperate we are. If reason alone can't do the job, then radical action—such as sit-ins and demonstrations with hundreds, even thousands of us going to jail—is our only recourse. I believe the time has come to follow the footsteps of Dr. Martin Luther King. We must begin a coordinated, carefully planned nationwide campaign of nonviolent civil disobedience. It is time that we challenge this president directly. I know that I am personally ready to go to jail to save my life and the lives of my family and friends. I just cannot take any more death."

As he spoke, Comegys—he was the keynote speaker that day—noticed Congressman Henry Waxman staring at him. Comegys was one of Waxman's regular contributors, and now the Los Angeles representative, who had been the first member of Congress to push the issue of AIDS there, was looking at Comegys as if he was out of his mind.

The worlds of ACT-UP and the Book Study Group—of the new street activism and the now shaken establishment gay leadership—came together on Pennsylvania Avenue, in front of the White House, on June 1, 1987. Word of the planned White House protest had spread quickly from Los Angeles and across the nation, from the establishment leaders in Washington and California to the members of ACT-UP in New York. They came to Washington for the conference and to get arrested. And they produced, for one afternoon, on the streets of Washington and later in its jail cells, an assembly of men and women who had been involved with the gay liberation movement for twenty-five years: Steve Endean, Troy Perry, Jean O'Leary, Larry Kramer, Virginia Apuzzo, Sean Strub,* David Mixner, Leonard Matlovich, Urvashi Vaid. They gathered in Lafayette Park and then moved on to Pennsylvania Avenue, in front of the White House, where they dropped in the street and refused to move. The police snapped on pairs of protective yellow rubber gloves as they moved in to arrest sixty-four of the men and women there, a reminder of how homosexual men had come to be seen by now. But in the cathartic atmosphere that day, the reaction was more humor than indignation, and a new gay liberation chant was coined at the sight of the police officers: *"Your gloves don't match your outfits!"* they shouted. Duke Comegys, Larry Kramer and David Mixner all proudly kept pictures of their White House arrests and displayed them prominently in their offices and homes. They shared stories

---

* Sean Strub, who tested positive for the virus in 1985 and whose medical charts indicate he may have seroconverted as early as 1978 or 1979, went on to create a large gay direct mail consulting business, ran unsuccessfully for Congress from New York in 1990, produced *The Night Larry Kramer Kissed Me* off-off-Broadway in 1992, founded *Poz*, a magazine about living with the virus which is now published in Spanish as well as English language editions, and since 1992 has lived with his lover, Xavier Morales in the Village.

about their hours spent in jail: singing and chanting, enjoying their few hours as misfits in the district's jail system.

Still, it was a searing image, all these men and women offering themselves up for arrest, acting on the frustration that was being heard from the New York City Lesbian and Gay Community Services Center in Greenwich Village to Mixner's living room. "Under normal circumstances, we could survive and live with some of the delays," Mixner told *The Advocate* at the time. "But time is not on our side in this crisis. We can just accept that—or we can do something dramatic and powerful." The arrest docket that day included a growing number of gay men, some well known, some not, who were either sick or learning they were infected. Dan J. Bradley, the former president of the Legal Services Corporation under Presidents Carter and Reagan, who had quit his job in 1982 and then come out with a letter to friends and an interview with the *New York Times*, was at the head of the march, carrying a white and yellow floral wreath laced with a large black ribbon to commemorate the 20,000 Americans who had so far died of AIDS: "I've been in bed for two days resting up for this," Bradley said. He still looked weary. Assembled on Pennsylvania Avenue at the same spot where Frank Kameny had twenty-two years before kept a lonely picket in front of the White House were a generation of homosexual leaders, representing nearly every chapter since Stonewall, who had come to Washington for one more protest. For many of them, it would be their last.

December 1987, Los Angeles

In another time, Sheldon Andelson might have been in Washington, too. But he was not, and Marylouise Oates took cryptic (and informed) note of why this was so in her *Los Angeles Times* mention of the Book Study Group. "Conspicuously missing from the sessions," Oates confided, was Sheldon Andelson, "who because of illness has been absent from the political front for months." The rumors were widespread: California's wealthiest and most influential gay activist had AIDS. Andelson denied it when asked, lying to even his closest friends, still insisting that his only illness was diabetes. But he, too, was betrayed by his appearance, since most people by now knew how to make their own diagnosis: the unsteady gait, the sallow complexion, visits to the doctor and rumored hospital stays, and the weight loss, which escaped Andelson's efforts at concealment—he bought ever-smaller dress shirts so they would appear snug around his withering neck. And there was the reclusiveness. Sheldon Andelson was such a relentlessly public figure—always at the front of the social and fundraising circuit, eating lunch every day at a prominent table at Trumps, the restaurant he owned—that people noticed when he started staying home. He took days to return calls, and then sounded weary. After a while the calls were not returned at all, as his brothers and sister-in-law fended off a steady stream of inquiries from friends, business associates, gay activists, politicians and reporters. The publisher of *The Advocate*, Niles Merton, couldn't get through. Rob Eichberg, who had guessed Andelson's situation from almost the start—"I know something is going on," he told Andelson. "I'm here if you want to talk"—couldn't get through.

Andelson told few people he had AIDS, intent on keeping the news contained for the duration of his life. He did not tell his former lover, Waldo Fernandez, until the final months of his illness, and then only because he needed help at his bedside. He did not share his diagnosis with his half brother, Roger Horwitz, himself in the last stages of the disease.* Andelson would insist he was healthy when confronted directly, which is what Beverly Thomas, his close friend, confidante and personal assistant, had done one morning in 1986. She had noticed how weak Andelson had seemed the evening before at a Trumps fundraiser for Ted Kennedy, and had spent the night crying. Thomas asked Andelson directly whether he had AIDS, and he insisted that he did not. Andelson even denied he was sick when challenged in the privacy of his therapy group, as Duke Comegys badgered him to be honest. "Sheldon," Comegys said, his voice verging on ridicule, "we *know* you have AIDS!" But Andelson again said he did not. Finally, he stopped showing up at therapy. More than anything, Andelson was not going to discuss his health with other members of the city's gay elite, with whom he had always remained a distant and more than a little superior comrade. And those friends who eventually were told the truth, including Bev Thomas, carried out Andelson's wishes, even when it seemed pointless. Mixner ran into Bev Thomas while visiting Peter Scott in the hospital. He had heard that Andelson was having a relapse, and was back in the hospital.

"How is Sheldon?" Mixner asked with concern.

"Oh Sheldon's in a board meeting," Thomas responded, moving quickly to change the topic. "How's Peter?" she asked.

"Oh, Peter's in a board meeting," Mixner said.

Andelson's secretiveness stirred resentment among Los Angeles gay leaders, who wanted someone as socially and politically prominent as Andelson—

---

* That was because Andelson considered Horwitz's lover, the writer Paul Monette, who also was infected, an untrustworthy gossip who would consider the news of Andelson's condition the highest form of gossip currency (Arlen Andelson to AJN). Indeed, when Horwitz and Monette called Sheldon Andelson after Roger Horwitz was diagnosed with AIDS, Andelson's instant advice had been not to tell anyone, not even their father. (For Andelson's reaction to Roger Horwitz, see Paul Monette, *Borrowed Time*, pp. 78–79.) Monette was initially furious with Andelson for having pressured them into that decision. But later, when Monette recounted Roger's death in *Borrowed Time*, he decided that Roger had enjoyed six peaceful months because they had followed Andelson's counsel.

a member of the Board of Regents, a friend of both Edward M. Kennedy and Edmund G. Brown Jr.—to come out for a second time as it were. Andelson was, after all, the same man who in October 1979 discussed his homosexuality at a roast for the Los Angeles Gay Community Services Center attended by elected officials, President Jimmy Carter's mother, Lillian, and his family. His refusal to announce publicly what everyone knew reinforced the impression that Andelson's primary interest was in himself, and his silence would ultimately tarnish his reputation. In truth, there was no political consensus, even among gay leaders in 1987, over whether there was any obligation to disclose an AIDS diagnosis. Some men made a point of discussing it: "I don't want to do a Sheldon Andelson," Peter Scott told David Mixner when a *Los Angeles Times* reporter was checking reports that Scott was ill. But for every person open about his illness—the singer Michael Callen, Dan Bradley of Washington or Leonard Matlovich, who announced his HIV diagnosis on *Good Morning America*—there were others who went to any extreme to safeguard their health from public scrutiny. Bruce Mailman would not discuss it even as he walked unsteadily down Lafayette Street, near the shuttered-up building on St. Marks Place that had been his bathhouse. Randy Shilts, who learned he was HIV positive on March 16, 1987, the day he finished writing *And the Band Played On,* did not share the information with the public for five years, until he finished his third and last book, *Conduct Unbecoming: Gays & Lesbians in the U.S. Military.* By then, his health had deteriorated so much he could not board an airplane for a promotion tour. The publicity interviews with Shilts inevitably portrayed him as walking around his Russian River home tethered to an oxygen tank.

Since Andelson never spoke publicly about his health, there is little public record of why he kept his silence. But Andelson's handling of his illness was not surprising, viewed in the context of his times and his personality, and in many ways it was typical of men of his generation. The epidemic sprang from an underground world of promiscuous gay sex from which Andelson had prospered, which he took care to shield from his straight circles. And it was now clear that AIDS was primarily contracted by being the receptive figure in anal intercourse, a passive sexual role, which ran counter to the image that Andelson had always tried to project of himself. Andelson told his brothers more than once that he did not want to become a symbol of an epidemic: he did not want to become one more AIDS poster boy, sacrificing his privacy so reporters or a television camera crew could document the gritty details of his final years. Andelson had made a career of accumulating power, and was certain that AIDS would turn him into just another weak and vulnerable dying gay man. Indeed, he paid vigilant attention to his political stature, even to his death. Jerry Brown visited him at home a week before he died. The former governor was taken aback when he approached the house on Stradella

Drive. He was used to seeing the driveway and street overflowing with cars, the thirty-two-foot-high living room echoing with voices and the sounds of clinking ice. But there were no cars in the driveway, the living room was empty, and the only people there were a nurse and a few family members. "I'm here and I want to see Sheldon," Brown announced. Brown walked into Andelson's second-floor suite, with its window overlooking his pool and Los Angeles, the same suite where Brown had joined Andelson to watch the 1982 election returns, and saw it was now a hospital room, with an IV pole and oxygen tent at Andelson's bedside. Andelson looked up from his pillow, his eyes glistening in recognition.

"The governor of California!" Andelson declared, announcing the visitor to his bedside. Brown stopped, suddenly feeling sorry for this wasted man. Brown was there not as a former governor of California, but rather as a friend, paying tribute to a man he had particularly respected. Brown had hoped that Andelson in his hour of death would be "getting down to basics," as Brown later put it. But even now—so emaciated that he slept on an air mattress to cushion his bones, struggling to breathe and speak—Andelson defined his importance not by who he was, or what he had accomplished, but by who had come to see him on his deathbed.

Andelson began to share the news of his impending death in the summer of 1987, selectively choosing his confidants and acting primarily because he needed help in planning one more party, in this case, his own funeral. He would not leave the details of such an important event to even his most trusted aides and family members. Andelson had still not actually told Bev Thomas that he had AIDS, though, of course, she knew. She had noticed how, at Roger Horwitz's October 1986 funeral, Andelson had leaned on his brothers and sister-in-law, who were standing stiff-legged to make sure that Andelson didn't tumble at Horwitz's graveside. (Andelson had been at Cedar-Sinai Medical Center, and had pressured the doctors there until they agreed to sign him out early for the funeral.) When Andelson finally told her he had AIDS, she just whispered under her breath, "No shit, Sheldon."

Even so, she was taken aback when he instructed her to pull up a chair and began dictating specific details of how his memorial service should be conducted. It would be at UCLA's Royce Hall, so people would recall his service on the state's Board of Regents. The list of invitees would be prepared in advance, so invitations could be mailed promptly upon his death to assure a proper turnout. The music would include "Song on the Sand," the love song from *La Cage aux Folles*, and he wanted among the speakers his two favorite politicians, Ted Kennedy and Jerry Brown. Kennedy had been the keynote speaker when the American Jewish Committee gave Andelson its first Social Concern Award in May 1984 at the Beverly Wilshire, and it was Kennedy's tribute which had helped make Andelson a national figure. "The story of Shelly Andelson is the story of America at its best," Kennedy had said then, which was, as it turned out, as ideal an epitaph as Andelson could have hoped for. Andelson's insistence on arranging his own memorial service required him to lift the curtain around his sickbed, at least a bit, since Bev Thomas needed to inquire quietly whether Brown and Kennedy would speak. They would.

Thomas found the process a little macabre, but eventually decided to just enjoy it. It was like planning another Sheldon Andelson roast, except the guest of honor wasn't going to be able to attend. Andelson's brother Sherman, thirteen years his senior, finally confided to Sheldon that he was uncomfortable with this whole exercise. "Sherman, you don't understand," Andelson responded, with a weak wave of his hand. "If you're going to have a good affair, you've got to plan it."

Andelson died at home on December 29, 1987, with his family gathered around his bed. "Don't be sad," he told them. "I've lived a wonderful life." News of his death drew together the gay community of Los Angeles in a particularly poignant moment of shared grief: the founders of MECLA and the Gay and Lesbian Community Services Center, the first members of the city's GLF, and people like Morris Kight and Ivy Bottini, who despite public differences had all formed private alliances with Andelson. He was buried, in a plain pine box, alongside his mother and father, on December 31, 1987. The official press release issued by Andelson's public relations firm included in the first sentence the fact that he had died from AIDS.

The *New York Times* noted Sheldon Andelson's death with a ninety-four-word article on its obituary page. The *Los Angeles Times* devoted a full thirty-three paragraphs to it, in a story that began on page one, under the headline, "Andelson Dies of AIDS; Gay Regent, Activist," and that captured Andelson's unique contribution to political activism: "In gay circles," the obituary noted, "the image of the nation's top Democrats sitting down to dinner unashamed with Andelson lifted him to the status of treasured role model." The memorial service at UCLA was set for twelve days after Andelson's death, to allow time for the engraved invitations to be delivered, and the turnout no doubt exceeded even Sheldon Andelson's expectations. There were 1,500 people by the time the service began at 11 a.m. on January 10, 1988, a Sunday, or five hundred more than the press release announcing the event had promised. Even the balcony was filled, Arlen Andelson noticed, thinking how much this would have pleased his brother. Bev Thomas, anticipating a big crowd, had roped off the front of the room for special guests, worried that Andelson's relatives and close friends might otherwise find themselves in the balcony. For those who had always disdained Andelson's elitist ways, this was the final indignation: even at his own funeral, there appeared to be an A-list and B-list, with someone posted at the ropes, checking prospective guests against a clipboard.

The mourners included U.S. Senator Alan Cranston, California Attorney General John K. Van de Kamp, Controller Gray Davis, Los Angeles mayor Tom Bradley and state Senator Richard Katz. Ted Kennedy was there, cutting short a vacation to attend. Jerry Brown flew back from Thailand to speak at the funeral and returned to the Far East the next day. The event flowed gracefully, moving as Andelson had intended with the rhythm and efficiency of a well-planned black-tie political dinner. People applauded after speakers. There were two podiums, each overflowing with long-stemmed white tulips and amaryllis, at least two video cameras, and a large screen at the back of the hall that would broadcast Andelson, in black tie, addressing the crowd at his center roast in 1979. "If I am any sort of role model at all, it is to prove that being an open gay person is not inconsistent with financial success, personal happiness and family love," he had said then. Ted Kennedy described Andelson as a "pioneer in national politics" on gay and lesbian rights. "Today," Kennedy said, "it is no longer regarded as a singular act of bravery for a national political leader to speak at a MECLA dinner. Twice now the Democratic national platform has pledged a commitment to lesbian and gay rights. These were Shelly's fights.

"Sheldon Andelson should have been a public figure in his own right— perhaps a senator," Kennedy said, adding, "In a different and better America, he might well have held one of the highest offices." Jerry Brown gave a slightly more earthy tribute to his benefactor: "With me, he always talked image," Brown said. "I like to talk theories and some would say deep subjects. But Sheldon would always say, 'What do the polls say? What do your image-makers say? Can't you fix your image up?' To him, a black-tie function, a good fundraiser, this is what politics is about. And he raised funds. At such a serious occasion, I'm not going to mention the amount. It would be indecent." Brown laughed at the memory. But, he added: "When we think of Sheldon Andelson, we have to sense the power of the force of life itself. Because that is what he manifested."

It was left to Rand Schrader to capture the moment of this particular man dying of this disease at this time. Schrader, the second openly gay judge appointed in California, had been one of the early members, with Morris Kight, of the Gay Liberation Front of Los Angeles. He had witnessed the police department's long years of persecuting gays, and he had watched and participated as the city's gay movement evolved, from the GLF, to the Community Services Center, to MECLA—and now, to this. Schrader was balding, with owl-rimmed glasses, and a neat, white carnation pinned onto a gray suit that fit snugly on his trim body. He seemed to glow with health as he sketched how Andelson's life tracked the gay liberation movement, a coming of age during the McCarthy era, when he found his hopes and career jeopardized by his sexual orientation. Andelson, like most gay men and lesbians, was a "million miles from the angry patrons" of the Stonewall riots, Schrader said. But Andelson had awakened to gay rights, first as a lawyer defending arrested homosexuals, then at the center, and then as the city's premier fundraiser. Schrader shared what Andelson had told him, more than once, was the mission of his life: " 'Randy,' he would say, 'I want to open the closet door of this embarrassed, tongue-tied, uncomfortable establishment,' " Schrader said. " 'They need liberation by seeing that we are confident in ourselves. We have to free them.' That is Sheldon's legacy."

Andelson had turned out to be typical of gay men of his generation for another reason: He was fifty-six years old and dead. "Sheldon's fate was to die of this plague that is taking the lives of a generation," Schrader said. "Some fear that the civil rights gains of gays and lesbians will be a victim of AIDS as well. During Sheldon's illness, and at his death, I felt this despair. Will we lose our freedoms as we lose our friends and lovers? But to despair, to be afraid, would be to deny the meaning of Sheldon's triumph.

"There is only one memorial worthy of Sheldon and all the others lost to this disease," Schrader said. "And that is to go forward with courage and spirit; to claim the ultimate victory of human freedom." Rand Schrader had been one of those distressed that Andelson had not publicly discussed his fight with AIDS, and at his memorial, delivered the speech that he had, no doubt, wished Andelson had delivered before his death. Within the year, Rand Schrader would also learn that he, too, was dying.

Epilogue

May 1992, Los Angeles

It fell to David Mixner to introduce Bill Clinton. It was May 11, 1992, a little more than four years after the memorial service for Sheldon Andelson, and Clinton, a Democratic candidate for president, was speaking at a fundraiser—a gay fundraiser—at the Palace Theater in Hollywood, a few miles east of the UCLA hall where Andelson's death had been observed. It was dark and crowded inside the theater, and the atmosphere was charged with anticipation. Nearly five hundred people, mostly men in their twenties, thirties and forties, a coat-and-tie crowd, many of whom had been at the Andelson memorial—were gathered on the dance floor beneath an arc of red, white and blue balloons that rustled against the ceiling of the old hall. Many of them had that distinctive California look of tan and beauty. Some of them looked not so well.

Even four years earlier many of these people—including the candidate—would never have attended an event as public as this one: a speech by a man running to be president, three weeks before the California primary, at a fundraiser that would raise $100,000 for the Clinton campaign, organized by homosexuals. There were risers and bright lights for the television news crews, and the audience included a dozen reporters from across the country. This was, of course, not the first time a candidate for president had spoken in a public forum to an audience of homosexual supporters—Jerry Brown had done the same thing in Washington, D.C., in 1979—but few people in the theater knew that, except perhaps for Mixner, who had helped arrange Brown's appearance as well. Still, this was different. Brown's speech was a bold moment, to be sure, but in the end it was only symbolic, since no one had ever expected him to win the 1980 Democratic presidential nomination. There was little doubt that the speaker whom Mixner introduced—"Bill," as he still called him—would be the Democratic challenger to President George Bush. Clinton knew that he was the presumptive Democratic nominee when he accepted the invitation to speak from Mixner, his old friend in the peace movement and one of the first openly gay men Clinton had known. Clinton's audience, including many of the founders of MECLA, which had first seriously pursued the idea that gay money could be translated into political authority, realized that, too. And so did the press corps. The simple fact of Clinton's appearing before an audience of gay men and lesbians, and giving, as it turned out, one of the most evocative speeches of his entire 1992 campaign, would earn a front-page story in the *Washington Post*, and stories in papers across the country, including the *New York Times* and *USA Today*. If the promise of this night was met, and it would be, its images would play across gay America, all through the general election campaign.

Much had happened in the four years since Andelson had fallen to AIDS. By the time Clinton's motorcade pulled up outside the Palace Theater that Monday evening, the gay rights movement had been overwhelmed and subsumed by the epidemic. Its leadership—the gay male leadership—had sickened and died at a staggering rate. One by one, in clusters and networks, many of the best-known figures in the movement, its founders, its organizers and financiers, its pamphleteers and chief personalities, its priests and politicians succumbed to the epidemic. Sheldon Andelson was only one of scores of men who are the subject of a history—this history—they will never have a chance to read. In cities like San Francisco, where the epidemic became as legion as Randy Shilts had warned in his early stories for the *San Francisco Chronicle*, young and middle-aged men, Democrats and Republicans, men from different schools of the movement—men as different from each other as Jim Foster and Bruce Decker and Cleve Jones—all discovered that they had the virus. For those who fell ill, AIDS and its attendant diseases became the obsession and distraction of their days, and for many, it meant their demise. A number of the original members of the Gay Activists Alliance, the organization founded in New York six months after Stonewall, would not live to see the twenty-fifth anniversary of the uprising: Jim Owles, Marty Robinson, Arthur Bell, Vito Russo, Morty Manford and Tom Doerr, among them. Carl Wittman, who had written *A Gay Manifesto* in San Francisco early in 1969, foreshadowing what would happen in New York later that year, quit taking the medications which seemed so useless to him and died in January 1986. Jim Foster, the first gay power broker in the Democratic Party, who spoke at its national convention in 1972, died in 1990. Others, increasingly debilitated, survived into the 1990s, but not for long: Steve Endean, the former director of the Gay Rights National Lobby and the founder of the Human Rights Campaign Fund, died at home in his basement apartment on Capitol Hill in Washington, D.C., in 1993, with his mother at his side. Nauseated, half-blind but determined to be in charge, he stopped eating and starved himself to death. Bruce Voeller, the founder of the National Gay Task Force, died where he had moved to live out his final years, in the hills north of Los Angeles. Mel Boozer, who had been nominated for vice president at the Democratic National Convention in New York in 1980, died of complications of the virus, as did Jerry Berg, the San Francisco lawyer who had been the first male co-chair of the Human Rights Campaign Fund, and Dan Bradley, the former president of the Legal Services Corporation and friend of Hillary Rodham Clinton. Randy Shilts died. So did Nathan Fain, Paul Popham, Peter Scott, Rand Schrader, Leonard Matlovich, Bill Kraus, Bruce Mailman, Paul Monette, Rob Eichberg, Darrell Yates Rist, Bruce Decker, Duke Comegys, Niles Merton and Henry Wiemhoff. Thomas B. Stoddard, the executive director of the Lambda Legal Defense and Education Fund, died, and so did Michael Hardwick, the man who was the subject of one of Stoddard's most famous cases after he was arrested in his bedroom on sodomy charges. The list was— is—exhausting but not exhaustive; it will no doubt be outdated by the time this book is published.

In psychological, political and historic terms, the reach of the disease was immense. It engulfed not just the gay community, but American society, so that by the time the future president took the stage in Hollywood, the gay rights movement was really in eclipse, overtaken by the ruder and more urgent AIDS movement. It would return later, and by the end of the 1990s, the Human Rights Campaign, as it renamed itself, and the National Gay and Lesbian Task Force would reemerge as forces working to pass gay rights legislation and to counter the rising influence of the religious right in state and national politics, and in Congress. But in 1992 the goals and battles that had been so critical to the young activists who emerged in New York, Minneapolis, Boston, Los Angeles and San Francisco in the months and years after Stonewall seemed irrelevant. The energy many had focused on gay rights had given way to fighting, literally, for life, and to fighting for public attention and money for AIDS research, treatment and care. The major gay organizations had given way to groups like ACT-UP, whose members were, as it happened, waiting for Clinton outside the Palace that afternoon. The disease disrupted the gay rights movement in other ways that could never have been expected. The major gay rights organizations found themselves starving for contributions. And lesbians, yet again, found their public identities shaped by men and their sexual habits, as public attention came to equate homosexuality with AIDS.

Still, the elements of Clinton's appearance at the Palace Theater that day—the crowd, the television cameras, the man who was speaking and the very direct and specific speech he gave—suggested that a profound change had taken place amidst the sorrow and tragedy of the past decade. It was not obvious at first, but as the years passed, the AIDS epidemic had become a source of political energy in the way that Stonewall was in 1969, the way Anita Bryant was in 1977. It had accomplished, cruelly and brutally, what pioneers of this movement—starting with Harry Hay and Frank Kameny and Barbara Gittings—had always tried to accomplish: it had forced many gay men and lesbians to live their lives openly. If there was one belief shared by all the different gay rights organizations and leaders over the past generation, it was in the need for homosexual men and women to live openly: in political terms, it was the best way to gain acceptance in society; in more personal terms, an open life was the ultimate expression of gay liberation. So it was that the name of the very first post-Stonewall newspaper for homosexuals, published by the Gay Liberation Front in New York in 1969 and 1970, was *Come Out!*

There was a brief period in the late 1980s and early 1990s when gay activists took to publicly identifying closeted homosexuals, forcing them into the open as a political gesture. But it was a passing moment, and the practice of outing was quickly overtaken by a mass phenomenon that occurred regardless of any organization or leader's plan. By 1992, it had become almost absurd—disrespectful—for men or women engulfed in the epidemic to pretend they were not homosexual. Young homosexuals felt an identity born of anger at what they saw as the Reagan and Bush administrations' inaction in the face of AIDS. And some of the movement's middle-aged leaders, in their illness, found a way to dramatize what it meant to be gay. Paul Monette turned from Hollywood screenplays to write *Borrowed Time: An AIDS Memoir,* the story of his lover Roger Horwitz's death. Then, before he died of AIDS himself, he wrote his autobiography, *Becoming a Man,* which won the National Book Award. Cleve Jones, in San Francisco, where so many men died so fast, lived to become the founder and keeper of The Quilt, a vast patchwork of cloth images sewn together by family members and friends in remembrance of lives lost.

Conversely, in mainstream, heterosexual America, some of the alarm and revulsion of the mid-1980s about AIDS and homosexuals had begun to fade as the public became more aware of how the disease is transmitted. As more and more homosexuals publicly acknowledged their sexual identity, a certain tenderness and respect for the victims had begun to emerge. AIDS had thus accomplished what none of the gay activists or their organizations had been able to do over the past twenty-five years: It made some parts of society at least sympathetic, if not empathetic, to gay men and women, as it prodded homosexuals to live their lives more openly. AIDS forced an emergence of homosexuality that could never have been foreseen, at least on this scale, by an Arthur Evans, or a Martha Shelley, or a Steve Endean, or a Morris Kight, or a Virginia Apuzzo, or any of the organizations they helped to create. It seemed only fitting that two weeks after Clinton spoke at the Palace, one of his environmental advisers who accompanied him there, a gangly young Californian named Bob Hattoy, called the future president and first lady to tell them he had just returned from the doctor and learned he, too, was infected with the HIV virus. The Clintons were saddened, but it was a diagnosis which would allow Bill Clinton to fulfill one of the promises he made at the Palace Theater in Hollywood that May night.

The theater was dark and the men on the dance floor stood silent while a biographic video tribute to the Arkansas governor played on the screen. Then the houselights went up, the sound of "Seventy-six Trombones" romped through the room, and a cluster of men and women walked onstage. Two of them, Diane Abbitt, a lawyer and one of the first women members of MECLA, and Dr. Scott Hitt stopped behind the podium, which had a big, blue and white "Bill Clinton" sign on it. Abbitt, a slim, graceful woman with a sunny face and a tailored rose coat, announced that this was "the biggest presidential rally ever held by the gay and lesbian community." It was right that it should be held here, she said, because it was in Los Angeles fifteen years ago that the nation's first gay and lesbian political action committee had been formed.

"And you know what?" she told the crowd. "When it was started, we couldn't raise money out of our own community. We were too scared. And when we did raise money, the politicians wouldn't accept it." Abbitt smiled as she spoke about the early days of MECLA, a future president of the United States at her elbow. "But times have changed," she said.

The audience cheered at that, and then David Mixner took the stage. He kissed the tall, blond Scott Hitt and then Diane Abbitt, and stood at the microphone with a grave smile, relishing the moment. "My brothers and sisters," he said solemnly, "we've all together come a long way to this place. No one handed us this event tonight. And no one did us a favor. We earned it, inch by inch, step by step and moment by moment. It is ours." The crowd applauded and Mixner quieted them with a look. "The last twelve years, especially, for this community, has been a long, hard and difficult road. We've buried thousands of our dead." His voice was quavering, and across the room his friends thought of Peter Scott. "We've cared for tens of thousands of our sick. We have marched in the streets against the indecent veto of AB101 [a gay civil rights bill] by Governor Wilson. We have laid in front of cars. We have marched on the capital. We have opened hospices, food centers, care-taking centers—

everything imaginable. We have done it in anger. We have done it because we had to. But don't forget, most of all, we have done it as a community, together. With dignity, and nobility, and we have every reason to be very, very proud tonight."

Mixner then recalled his early meetings with Clinton, when the governor of Arkansas promised he would sign an executive order that would ban discrimination against gays and lesbians in the military, as he courted the support—electoral and financial—that Mixner could provide. "And I started dreaming," Mixner said, "of all of us standing like this on the lawn of the White House next March, and there's a big table, with the president of the United States. And he picks up his pen, and with the stroke of a pen, we're so much freer. So much freer. . . ." The audience, which at first had tittered at the idea of all of them standing on the White House lawn, began to cheer. "It is this man!" Mixner shouted over the roar, "who is going to be our Harry Truman and sign that executive order! It is this man who is going to be our John Kennedy and include us in the vision of a greater America!"

By the time Clinton walked on, the crowd was ecstatic. "Thank you," he said twelve times before they quieted. "Thank you." His eyes looked bagged and crinkled from the campaign, and his voice was soft and a little hoarse from the allergies he suffered each spring. It was not an exuberant entrance. He was careful, contained, very deliberate. He had not hugged "my longtime friend" Mixner. He had shaken his hand and made a joke. "He's been giving speeches in his mind for thirty years," Clinton said with a little smile. "He's about to get good.

"Tonight I want to talk to you about how we can be one people again," he said, "without regard to race or gender or sexual orientation or age or region or income." For a moment, as he went on, it seemed Clinton might do what Walter Mondale had done at the Human Rights Campaign Fund dinner in New York in 1982, and talk around, rather than about, what had brought them together in one room. But he did not.

"Those of you who are here tonight," he said quietly, "represent a community of our nation's gifted people whom we have been willing to squander. We cannot afford to waste the capacity, the contributions, the heart, the soul, and the mind of the gay and lesbian Americans." He had cut to the quick so suddenly that the applause was stunned and grateful. The surprises continued. Clinton pledged to act on the Pentagon policy against homosexuals, a promise he would come to regret. He called them "My fellow Americans." He said he wanted the people in the theater that day to join him in his administration, and he promised to have "someone who is HIV-positive, but also has a positive attitude, come before the American people at the Democratic National Convention to speak about this issue."

Clinton told them he wanted to crack down on those who practice hate crimes against homosexuals and others. "This is not an election—or it should not be—about race, or gender, or being gay or straight, or religion, or age, or region, or income," he said. "What kills a country is not the problems it faces. There will be problems even until the end of time. What kills a country is to proceed day in and day out with no vision, no sense that tomorrow can be better than today, no sense of shared community."

He paused, and when he looked up, his eyes seemed damp. "If I could—if I could wave my arm for those of you who are HIV-positive and make it go away tomorrow, I would do it, so help me God I would, if I gave up my race for the White House and everything else, I would do that. Let us never forget, there are things we can and cannot do, but the beginning of wisdom is pulling together and learning from one another, and being determined to do better."

It was an extraordinary performance, daring and intimate at the same time. The men and women in the room that night had been prepared for something less personal. But Clinton that night spoke as a leader who seemed to understand. "What I came here today to tell you in simple terms," he said, "is, I have a vision, and you're a part of it."

To homosexuals who watched the Democratic National Convention on television three months later, it seemed clear, as they listened to Bob Hattoy speak about AIDS from the podium, and saw the teary eyes and gay placards on the convention hall floor, that gay men and lesbians were a visible, even desirable part of the Democratic coalition. It was equally clear to those who afterward watched the Republican National Convention, and listened to speakers like Pat Robertson and Pat Buchanan declare a cultural war of family values, that homosexuals were the enemy they had in mind. When The Quilt was spread on the Mall in the nation's capital that fall, the names and images of the dead covered acres between the White House and the Washington Monument. The tens of thousands who came to pay their respects each day looked very much like Middle America, but President George Bush did not emerge from the Oval Office to see The Quilt.

Bill Clinton would win the election that November, and while it is difficult to measure such things exactly—exit polls are particularly imprecise when used to count homosexuals—it seems fair to say that in that one year, in the presidential election of 1992, there was something approaching a unified gay vote. It could be heard gathering in the conversations of gay men and lesbians, particularly those who had gravitated to the Republicans in the economic boom of the early Reagan years, and who now were feeling angry and exploited. It could be seen in the political bustle on the streets in gay neighborhoods in New York and California and Georgia, in the checks that Mixner helped to deliver to the Clinton campaign and ultimately in the scope of

Clinton's victory that November. And it could be seen in the way the new president reached out to homosexuals—with appointments and with his ultimately abandoned attempt to change the military policy in the months ahead. This gathering of a gay vote was a direct response to an epidemic, and to the radically different ways that the two major parties—one, the host party of the gay rights movement, the other the party of the religious right—reacted to it. It had never happened before. It has not since. Whether it ever does again will almost certainly depend on the acceptance or rejection homosexuals find in the rest of the American political culture. For this is a movement whose members are, in the end, invisible, whose energies always seem to flow to other interests in untroubled times, but gather under attack.

Cast of Characters
and Interviewees

What follows is a log of taped interviews conducted by the authors in preparation of this history, combined with a list of all the major characters who appear in these pages. Some of the men and women who granted us interviews do not appear in the text itself; their names thus appear only in the following list, along with a brief description of their role in the movement.

Some of the people who appear in our history were not interviewed, most often because they were deceased or too ill when this research began in 1992, or, in a handful of cases, because they chose not to discuss their experiences. Their names appear here with a brief description of their roles. The characters in this book who died of AIDS are noted here as well.

The interview numbers correspond to the notations contained in the endnotes. In a few cases, the exact dates of the interviews were not recorded, as is noted below.

ABBITT, DIANE: Los Angeles. Among first women on MECLA. June 21, 1993 (Santa Monica, Calif.).

ABZUG, BELLA: New York. Former member of Congress. Nov. 11, 1994 (New York). Deceased.

ADDLESTONE, DAVID. The American Civil Liberties Union attorney for Sgt. Leonard Matlovich in his defense against discharge from the military in 1975. Jan. 12, 1996 (phone).

ALEXANDER, DOLORES: New York. Former executive director of New York NOW. Apr. 26, 1995 (phone).

ALTURO, LUIS: Los Angeles. Gay and Latino activist. June 9, 1994 (Silverlake, Calif.).

ANDELSON, ARLEN, MICHELLE, SHERMAN AND MIMI: Los Angeles. Siblings and in-laws of Sheldon Andelson. June 5, 1994 (Beverly Hills).

ANDELSON, SHELDON: Los Angeles. Major contributor to California and national political candidates, appointed by Governor Jerry Brown to California Board of Regents. Owner of 8709 Baths. Died of AIDS.

ANDERSON, CRAIG. University of Minnesota gay activist, leader in fight against the 1978 repeal of St. Paul's gay rights ordinance. (1) March 1993 (St. Paul); (2) September 1993 (St. Paul).

ANDERSON, LARRY. Former U.S. Naval Academy cadet who became Black Panther and Boston gay male liberationist. (1) Sept. 6, 1995 (phone); (2) Sept. 13, 1995 (Baltimore).

ANDERSON, SCOTT: Washington, D.C. Chief financial officer of National Gay Task Force in early 1980. Aug. 11, 1995 (phone).

APUZZO, VIRGINIA: New York and Washington, D.C. Former head of National Gay Task Force. (1) Nov. 13, 1992 (phone); (2) Aug. 17, 1993 (New York); (3) Oct. 15, 1993 (New York); (4) Sept. 13, 1995 (phone).

ARDERY, BRECK: New York. Early member of Gay Activists Alliance. Oct. 9, 1993 (New York).

BAHLMAN, BILL: New York. Member of Gay Activists Alliance, ACT-UP and Lavender Hill Mob. (1) Apr. 26, 1994 (New York); (2) Nov. 23, 1995 (phone).

BAKER, JACK: Minneapolis. First open gay elected to public office—as president of the University of Minnesota student body in 1971. Lover of Mike McConnell, whom he married in a public ceremony. Declined interview.

BARDEN, SHERI. See Johnson, Lois.

BARON, ALAN: Washington, D.C. Democrat, political newsletter publisher, closeted host of gay political salon in Washington. Produced first fundraising letter for Human Rights Campaign Fund in 1981. Aug. 17, 1993 (Washington); Baron memorial service, Dec. 5, 1993. Deceased.

BASTOW, THOMAS: Washington, D.C. Gertrude Stein Club president, co-chair of National Convention Project to get a gay rights plank in 1980 Democratic platform. (1) Oct. 6, 1993 (Washington); (2) Apr. 18, 1994 (Washington); (3) Apr. 28, 1994 (Washington); (4) Jan. 12, 1996 (phone).

BAUMAN, ROBERT. Former Republican U.S. representative from Maryland, chairman of Young Americans for Freedom and American Conservative Union, indicted in 1980 for buying sex from male prostitutes in Washington, D.C. (1) Sept. 26, 1994 (St. Petersburg Beach, Fla.); (2) Apr. 12, 1995 (St. Petersburg Beach); (3) Jan. 4, 1996 (phone); (4) Apr. 14, 1996 (phone).

BEAN, TERRY: Eugene, Oregon. Gay bar owner and businessman, leader of effort to pass a local gay rights ordinance in 1977. Sept. 5, 1996 (phone).

BEARD, JOSEPH: Washington, D.C. Conservative gay North Carolina Republican, came out in Washington in early Reagan years. Nov. 13, 1994 (Washington).

BELL, ARTHUR: New York. Early member of Gay Activists Alliance, *Village Voice* columnist, lover of Arthur Evans. Deceased.

BENNETT, ROBERTA: Los Angeles. Among first women on MECLA, partner of Abbitt. June 21, 1993 (Santa Monica, Calif.).

BERZON, BETTY: Los Angeles. A founder of Los Angeles Gay Community Services Center. June 9, 1994 (Los Angeles).

BLACKBURN, ED. Former sheriff of Hillsborough County, Florida. Founder of Florida Sheriffs' Boys Ranch. Oct. 21, 1993 (phone).

BOOZER, MELVIN: Washington, D.C. President of District's Gay Activists Alliance, addressed 1980 Democratic convention. Served shortly as Washington representative for National Gay Task Force. Died of AIDS.

BOTTINI, IVY: New York and Los Angeles. Former president of New York NOW. (1) May 28, 1993 (Greenwich, Conn.); (2) June 29, 1993 (Greenwich); (3) Dec. 21, 1994 (Greenwich).

BOYD, MALCOLM: Los Angeles. Openly gay cleric. June 14, 1994 (Los Angeles).

BRADLEY, ALEXA: Minnesota. Lesbian lobbyist, one of three co-chairs of campaign to pass Minnesota gay rights bill in 1993. March 1993 (St. Paul).

BRAKE, ROBERT: Dade County, Florida. Organizer of Anita Bryant's campaign in 1977. Apr. 27, 1995 (phone).

BRIGGS, JOHN: California. State senator who pushed referendum in 1978 that would have prohibited open homosexuals from serving as public school teachers.

BRITT, HARRY: San Francisco. 1970s Castro activist, appointed to Milk's council seat by Mayor Dianne Feinstein after Milk's murder in 1978. (1) Oct. 29, 1997 (phone); (2) Oct. 31, 1997 (phone); (3) Dec. 8, 1997 (phone).

BROMAN, LOUIS: New York. Companion to *New York Times* reporter Jeffrey Schmalz in the last year of Schmalz's life. May 11, 1994 (New York). Died of AIDS.

BROWN, CHUCK. Conservative Minnesota state representative, upset with the tactics of the religious right, voted to pass gay rights bill in 1993. March 1993 (St. Paul).

BROWN, EDMUND G., JR. Former governor of California and presidential candidate. (1) June 20, 1993 (phone); (2) June 30, 1995 (phone).

BROWN, HOWARD: New York. Appointed by Mayor John V. Lindsay in 1965 as head of the Health Services Administration. Announced he was homosexual in story on front page of *New York Times* on October 3, 1973. First chairman of the National Gay Task Force. Deceased.

BROWN, RITA MAE: Washington, D.C., and New York. Feminist writer, early member of NOW, Gay Liberation Front and Radicalesbians. (1) Jan. 5, 1995 (answers to written questions); (2) Oct. 20, 1995 (phone).

BRULETT, GREG, and lover. Retired older gay Republicans from conservative Cobb County, Georgia. June 2, 1993 (Cobb County).

BRYANS, RALEIGH: Atlanta. Former *Atlanta Journal* editorial writer and state political reporter. (1) June 6, 1995 (phone); (2) June 9, 1995 (phone); (3) June 13, 1995 (phone).

BRYANT, ANITA: Dade County, Florida. Leader of successful effort in Miami in 1977 to overturn gay rights ordinance. Miss Bryant, in response to requests for an interview, said she wanted to pray on the question and consult Jerry Falwell, the religious right leader. She then declined, saying she did not believe it would "be productive."

BRYDON, CHARLES: Seattle. Founder of Dorian Group in Seattle, executive director of National Gay Task Force. (1) June 21, 1994 (Washington, D.C.); (2) Aug. 11, 1995 (phone).

BUNCH, CHARLOTTE: Washington, D.C. Member of Furies, National Gay Task Force and Lesbian Feminist Liberation. (1) May 2, 1994 (New York); (2) Nov. 22, 1994 (New York).

BUSH, LARRY: Washington, D.C. Influential gay political reporter and columnist for *The Advocate* and other gay papers. JDC interviews: (1) Feb. 15, 1994 (phone); (2) Mar. 7, 1994 (San Francisco); (3) Mar. 8, 1994 (San Francisco). AJN interviews: (1) Aug. 6, 1995 (phone); (2) Aug. 16, 1995 (phone).

BYE, LARRY. Student radical at University of Minnesota, worked with Endean against repeal of St. Paul's gay rights ordinance in 1978; later drafted plan for Human Rights Campaign Fund. (1) Jan. 25, 1994 (phone); (2) Feb. 4, 1994 (phone); (3) Mar. 8, 1994 (San Francisco); (4) Jan. 11, 1997 (phone); (5) May 23, 1997 (phone).

CAIAZZA, STEPHEN: Chairman of New York Committee of Concerned Physicians and president of New York Physicians for Human Rights, two organizations that dealt with legal and medical rights for AIDS patients. Died of AIDS.

CALL, HAROLD. President of San Francisco Mattachine, publisher of the *Mattachine Review* after he and others forced out founder Harry Hay. Oct. 8, 1996 (phone).

CALLEN, MICHAEL: New York. A singer and early AIDS activist who, starting in late 1982, drew attention to sexual promiscuity among gay men. Died of AIDS.

CAMPBELL, JACK: Miami. Founder of Club Baths chain, first major financial supporter of the gay rights movement. (1) Nov. 3, 1993 (Miami); (2) Nov. 4, 1993 (Miami); (3) Nov. 5, 1993 (Miami).

CAMPBELL, TIM: Minneapolis-St. Paul. Radical gay activist ally of Jack Baker, enemy of Steve Endean. N.A., 1993, Minneapolis.

CANFIELD, BILL: Boston. Early member of Student Homophile League, Homophile Union of Boston. (1) June 18, 1994 (phone); (2) Sept. 2, 1994 (phone).

CANNON, CARL: California. Journalist who covered Briggs initiative. Sept. 15, 1993 (Arlington, Va.).

CARTER, ROBERT S.: Washington, D.C. Co-chair (1976) and chair (1980) of Republican National Conventions. Helped elect Washington mayor Marion Barry by persuading gay men to register as Democrats. Feb. 27, 1996 (phone).

CASTILLO, OLGA. Rick Castillo's mother, a Roman Catholic Republican. Sept. 21, 1992 (Tampa).

CASTILLO, RICK. Dancer and choreographer. First-time voter in 1992, for Clinton, because he was sick with AIDS and saw no compassion in Reagan and Bush administrations. (1) Sept. 6, 1992 (Baltimore); (2) Sept. 7, 1992 (Baltimore); (3) Sept. 8, 1992 (Baltimore). Died of AIDS.

CERVANTES, MADOLIN: New York. The heterosexual woman treasurer and later head of the Mattachine Society of New York.

CHALGREN, JIM. Early activist from Mankato, Minnesota. Became first campus counselor for gays in state university system. (1) March 1993 (Minneapolis); (2) March 1993 (St. Paul); (3) March 1993 (St. Paul).

CHESNUT, SARALYN: Atlanta. Member of Atlanta Lesbian Feminist Alliance in 1970s. Later director of lesbian, gay and bisexual student affairs at Emory University. June 1995 (phone).

CHURCH. JOK. Rode the Gay Freedom Train from California for 1979 National March on Washington for Lesbian and Gay Rights. Co-produced event album. Jan. 20, 1997 (phone).

CLARK, KAREN: Minnesota. Lesbian-feminist elected to Minnesota House of Representatives in 1980. (1) March 1993 (St. Paul); (2) March 1993 (St. Paul).

COLEMAN, CHARLOTTE. Prominent lesbian bar owner in San Francisco. Sept. 8, 1998 (phone).

COLEMAN, MILTON. Former Montgomery County reporter, now senior editor of the *Washington Post*. Feb. 29, 1996 (phone).

COMEGYS, DUKE: Los Angeles. Early gay fundraiser and member of MECLA and Los Angeles Gay Community Services board. (1) July 14, 1993 (Los Angeles); (2) Dec. 19, 1993 (phone); (3) Jan. 11, 1994 (phone); (4) June 8, 1994 (Los Angeles). Died of AIDS.

CONLEY, JEFF. Friend of Gerald Stacy's in Atlanta. Oct. 21, 1993 (phone).

COORS, DALLAS. Gay conservative, first cousin of Joseph Coors, the John Bircher who financed much of the New Right. The only Republican on the first Human Rights Campaign Fund board. Feb. 14, 1994 (Bethesda, Md.). Deceased.

CORDOVA, JEANNE: Los Angeles. First editor of the *Lesbian Tide,* member of Daughters of Bilitis–Los Angeles and Gay Liberation Front of Los Angeles. (1) Jan. 19, 1994 (Los Angeles); (2) June 13, 1994 (Los Angeles); (3) Feb. 1, 1995 (phone).

COSTANZA, MIDGE. First woman to be assistant to the president, under Jimmy Carter; became close to Jean O'Leary. (1) Feb. 24, 1994 (Newport Beach, Calif.); (2) Mar. 5, 1994 (San Diego); (3) May 13, 1995 (phone).

CRANHAM, BILL: California. Former chief of staff to Republican U.S. Senator John Seymour, defeated by Dianne Feinstein in 1992. Apr. 2, 1994 (Washington, D.C.).

CRONIN, BONNIE: Boston. The former program station manager who created *Gay Way* on Boston University radio station WBUR. Aug. 4, 1995 (phone).

DALY, JO: San Francisco. Early organizer, vice chair of the Alice B. Toklas Club and openly gay delegate to the 1976 Democratic convention. The first full-time paid liaison between the city's Human Rights Commission and the gay community. Deceased.

DANIELS. DON. New Orleans native, was bartender at the Stonewall Inn the night of the 1969 raid. (1) July 15, 1993 (Baltimore); (2) July 21, 1993 (Baltimore). Deceased.

DAVIS, ED: Los Angeles. Former chief of Los Angeles Police Department from August 1969 to January 1978. Apr. 23, 1994 (phone).

DAVIS, LANNY. Democratic candidate for Eighth Congressional District seat in Bethesda, Maryland, in 1976, with secret support of the new Gertrude Stein Club. Mar. 6, 1996 (phone).

DAVIS, MADELINE: Buffalo. With Jim Foster, addressed the 1972 Democratic National Convention in Miami.

DAWSON, GREG: New York. A founder of National Gay Task Force. (1) Dec. 30, 1993 (New York); (2) Feb. 25, 1995 (phone).

DEBAUGH, ADAM. The first Washington, D.C., lobbyist for homosexual issues, for the Metropolitan Community Church. Helped found the Gay Rights National Lobby. JDC interview: Apr. 21, 1994 (Maryland); AJN interview: Apr. 3, 1995 (phone).

DECKER, BRUCE: San Francisco. First prominent avowed gay Republican in California in the '70s, led effort to create a public gay GOP AIDS support group in Washington, D.C., in early '80s. June 28, 1994 (Fire Island Pines, N.Y.). Died of AIDS.

DECRESCENZO, TERRY: Los Angeles. One of the first women board members of Los Angeles Gay and Lesbian Community Services Center. (1) Jan. 19, 1994 (West Hollywood); (2) June 13, 1994 (West Hollywood).

DELISA, JOSEPH: New York. Early Gay Activists Alliance member. (1) Dec. 2, 1993 (phone); (2) Dec. 4, 1993 (phone); (3) Dec. 23, 1993 (phone).

DEVENTE, JEAN: New York. One of the Gay Activists Alliance's few women members. Oct. 2, 1993 (Stamford, Conn.).

DEYTON, BOPPER: Washington, D.C. Public health and early AIDS prevention worker. Apr. 14, 1994 (Washington).

DIAMAN, NIKOS: New York and San Francisco. Gay Liberation Front member. (1) Dec. 9, 1993 (phone); (2) Dec. 10, 1993 (phone); (3) Dec. 21, 1993 (phone); (4) Dec. 23, 1993 (phone).

DOBBS, BILL: New York. Member of ACT-UP. Apr. 12, 1995 (New York).

DOERR, TOM: New York. Early member of the Gay Activists Alliance. Designed the Lambda symbol, the early mark of the gay liberation movement. Deceased.

DOLAN, MARIA HELENA: Atlanta. Prominent lesbian-feminist from the late '70s. (1) Nov. 2, 1994 (Atlanta); (2) June 3, 1995 (phone).

DONALDSON, HERBERT: San Francisco. First gay attorney to fight security clearance denials and charges of soliciting in the San Francisco courts in the 1960s and 1970s. Appointed a municipal judge by Gov. Jerry Brown. Oct. 6, 1996 (phone).

DONNELLY FAMILY. Three gay brothers and three sisters who came for the spreading of The Quilt in Washington, D.C., because one brother has AIDS. Oct. 11, 1992 (Washington).

DONOVAN, BILL: Washington, D.C. Mattachine member in the 1960s. Apr. 10, 1995 (phone).

DUANE, TOM: New York. First openly gay New York City councilman elected in 1991. May 17, 1994 (New York).

DUBERMAN, MARTIN: New York. Gay historian. Mar. 23, 1995 (New York).

DUBOIS, DR. RICHARD: Atlanta. One of the first private physicians to treat AIDS in Atlanta. Feb. 26, 1993 (Atlanta).

DUCHENE, DANIEL JOSEPH: Minneapolis. Gay whose ashamed father wanted him to change his last name. Oct. 13, 1993 (phone).

DUNLAP, DAVID. One of the first *New York Times* reporters to tell his editors that he was gay, in 1984. Feb. 16, 1994 (phone).

DUNN, DR. JAMES. Prominent Southern Baptist minister, instrumental in getting Baptists to help Jimmy Carter win Texas in 1976. Aug. 8, 1997 (phone).

EDELMAN, MURRAY: Chicago. Organizer of early post-Stonewall movements in Chicago and later in San Francisco. Feb. 26, 1994 (New York).

EICHBERG, ROB: Los Angeles. Advocate Experience organizer and member of MECLA. (1) Apr. 15, 1994 (Washington, D.C.); (2) May 9, 1994 (New York). Died of AIDS.

ELIASER, ANN. Democratic Party fundraiser and liberal in the '60s, '70s and '80s in San Francisco. (1) Feb. 28, 1994 (San Francisco); (2) Mar. 10, 1994 (San Francisco).

ENDEAN, ROBERT. Steve Endean's father. March 1993 (Minneapolis).

ENDEAN, STEPHEN. University of Minnesota student, founded state gay rights lobby, left after repeal of St. Paul's gay rights ordinance in 1978 to direct the Gay Rights National Lobby in Washington, D.C.; founded the Human Rights Campaign Fund, forced out by *Advocate* owner David Goodstein. Died of AIDS. (1) Oct. 21, 1992 (phone); (2) Oct. 28, 1992 (Baltimore); (3) Oct. 28, 1992 (Baltimore); (4) Dec. 4, 1992 (phone); (5) Dec. 5, 1992 (phone); (6) Jan. 2, 1993 (phone); (7) Jan. 16, 1993 (phone); (8) Jan. 27, 1993 (phone); (9) Mar. 9, 1993 (phone); (10) Apr. 20, 1993 (phone); (11) May 13, 1993 (phone); (12) May 14, 1993 (phone); (13) May 22, 1993 (phone); (14) Date N.A. (Washington, D.C.); (15) May 27, 1993 (phone); (16) May 28, 1993 (phone); (17) June 4, 1993 (phone); (18) June 4, 1993 (phone); (19) June 5, 1993 (phone); (20) June 17, 1993 (phone tape message); (21) June 21, 1993 (phone tape message); (22) July 1, 1993 (phone tape message); (23) July 4, 1993 (phone tape message); (24) Date and place N.A.; (25) July 12, 1993 (Washington); (26) July 19, 1993 (Washington); (27) Aug. 2, 1993 (Washington). Endean-JDC Minnesota 1–3: a series of conversations over two days at the state capital in St. Paul (March 1993). Endean Memorial 1: speeches at memorial service in Washington, August 1993. Endean Memorial 2: speeches at memorial service in Minneapolis, September 1993.

EVANS, ARTHUR: New York and San Francisco. A founder of Gay Activists Alliance–New York. (1) Jan. 20, 1994 (San Francisco); (2) Jan. 21, 1994 (San Francisco); (3) Mar. 13, 1995 (phone); (4) July 8, 1995 (phone).

EVANS, JODY: Los Angeles. Chief political aide to Jerry Brown and aide to Sheldon Andelson. June 6, 1994 (Santa Monica, Calif.).

FAIN, NATHAN: New York. An organizer of Gay Men's Health Crisis who chronicled the early years of the AIDS epidemic for *The Advocate.* Died of AIDS.

FALWELL, THE REVEREND JERRY. Baptist televangelist, founder of the Moral Majority, leader of the religious right. Mar. 24, 1997 (phone).

FERNANDEZ, WALDO: Los Angeles. Former lover of Sheldon Andelson. July 15, 1993 (Beverly Hills).

FICKER, ROBIN. Bethesda, Maryland, lawyer, independent candidate for Congress against candidate secretly supported by the Gertrude Stein Club in Washington, D.C. in 1976. Feb. 26, 1996 (phone).

FIFIELD, LILLENE: Los Angeles. Los Angeles Gay Community Services Center member. Jan. 17, 1994 (Los Angeles).

FINKELSTEIN, AVRAM: New York. Early member of ACT-UP. (1) Apr. 24, 1994 (New York); (2) June 27, 1994 (New York); (3) June 25, 1995 (phone).

FISHER, PETER. Partner of Marc Rubin. New York. Early member of Gay Activists Alliance. Sept. 11, 1993 (New York).

FISKE, SALLIE: Los Angeles. Newspaper publisher in West Hollywood. June 9, 1994 (West Hollywood).

FONTANA, LORRAINE. Founding member of Atlanta Lesbian Feminist Alliance. Nov. 20, 1994 (phone).

FOSTER, JIM: San Francisco. Founded nation's first gay Democratic political club, the Alice B. Toklas Club. Addressed the 1972 Democratic convention. Political Director of Society for Individual Rights. Died of AIDS.

FOURATT, JIM: New York. Founder of Gay Liberation Front–New York, early member of Gay Activists Alliance and ACT-UP. (1) July 23, 1993 (New York); (2) Sept. 2, 1994 (phone); (3) May 10, 1994 (New York).

FRANK, BARNEY. First Boston politician to seek gay votes. Elected as closeted homosexual to state legislature in 1972, to U.S. House of Representatives in 1980. June 7, 1994 (Washington, D.C.).

FRANZ, TYLER. Young Republican, Log Cabin Club member, the only openly gay member of the Bush-Quayle 1992 reelection organization; forced out in Spring 1992. August 1992 (Washington, D.C.); (1) Aug. 27, 1992 (phone); (2) Oct. 19, 1992 (phone); (3) Oct. 22, 1992 (Washington); (4) Dec. 15, 1992 (Washington); (5) Jan. 21, 1993 (Washington).

GAIN, CHARLES. San Francisco police chief from January 1976 through January 1980, appointed by Mayor George Moscone. Was chief when Moscone and Harvey Milk were murdered by Dan White in 1978. Oct. 29, 1997 (phone).

GALVIN, EARL: New York. Early member of Gay Liberation Front. May 22, 1994 (San Francisco).

GETO, ETHAN: New York. Early member of Gay Activists Alliance, New York press secretary to George McGovern in 1972, director of gay effort in Dade County, Florida, in 1977. (1) Aug. 19, 1993 (New York); (2) Nov. 13, 1993 (New York); (3) May 16, 1994 (New York).

GILL, THE REVEREND ELDER JOHN. First Metropolitan Community Church pastor in Atlanta, went to New Orleans after the 1973 fire in the UpStairs bar. June 2, 1995 (phone).

GITTINGS, BARBARA, AND KAY TOBIN LAHUSEN. Leading spirits for forty years in the homophile and also modern gay rights movements, particularly in Daughters of Bilitis, in the struggle with the American Psychiatric Association in the early 1970s. (1) May 6, 1994 (Wilmington, Del.); (2) May 19, 1994 (Wilmington); (3) Sept. 9, 1993 (phone); (4) Sept. 13, 1993 (phone).

GOLD, RONALD: New York. Early member of Gay Activists Alliance and National Gay Task Force, and leader in fight to overturn psychiatric diagnosis on homosexuality. (1) July 30, 1993 (New York); (2) Aug. 6, 1993 (New York); (3) Feb. 25, 1995 (phone).

GOLDMAN, DAVID: Chicago and San Francisco. Member of Mattachine Society and Bay Area Gay Liberation. Dec. 10, 1994 (phone).

GOODSTEIN, DAVID: California. Publisher of *The Advocate* from Jan. 1, 1975, through June 25, 1985. Deceased.

GORDON, JIM. Diarist of the 1970s Castro generation of gay immigrants to San Francisco. (1) February 1994 (San Francisco). Note: tapes and notes of interview stolen in street mugging of JDC after interview. (2) Mar. 6, 1994 (San Francisco); (3) Dec. 10, 1997 (phone); (4) Jan. 7, 1998 (phone).

GRAVES, JOHN. First out gay professor at Massachusetts Institute of Technology in the early 1970s. Involved in Boston Homophile Community Health Services Center. July 28, 1994 (Provincetown, Mass.).

GREEN, BOB: Dade County, Florida. Former husband of Anita Bryant. Apr. 28, 1995 (phone).

GRIPP, BILL: Atlanta. Took over the Atlanta Gay Center in the mid–late '70s and turned it toward AIDS service. Oct. 31, 1994 (Atlanta).

HALFHILL, ROBERT. Graduate student at University of Minnesota and member of FREE, the gay organization there, in June 1969. (1) September 1993 (Minneapolis); (2) Dec. 24, 1994 (phone).

HAMLIN, CLAIRE. AIDS volunteer who conceived an AIDS absentee vote for Clinton in 1996. (1) May 25, 1993 (phone); (2) June 1993 (Atlanta).

HARRIS, DAVID. Former owner of Regency Baths in Washington, D.C. Supported Frank Kameny's campaign for Congress in 1971. Agreed to only one brief conversation: Apr. 7, 1995 (phone).

HART, LOIS: New York. Founder and early force in Gay Liberation Front in New York. Deceased.

HATTOY, BOB. Los Angeles gay leader, addressed 1996 Democratic convention. (1) Oct. 22, 1992 (Los Angeles); (2) Apr. 14, 1993 (Washington, D.C.); (3) May 26, 1993 (Washington).

HAY, HARRY: Los Angeles. Founder of Mattachine Society. May 1, 1994 (Los Angeles).

HELD, IRWIN: Los Angeles. Owner of Barney's Beanery. Nov. 3, 1994 (phone).

HIGGINS, THOMAS: Minnesota. Later changed his first name to Thom. Early Minneapolis activist with Jack Baker. Deceased.

HOFFMAN, AMY. Former staff member, editor of lesbian journal *Sister Courage* and then *Gay Community News* in Boston. Sept. 18, 1993 (Boston).

HOLDGRAFER, GEORGE. Student, supporter of FREE and gay rights movement at the University of Minnesota in 1969–70. December 1994 (phone).

HOLLOWAY, GENE. Black drag performer and activist who came to Atlanta in 1973, earlier performed at a fundraiser for victims of New Orleans fire. June 10, 1995 (phone).

HONGISTO, RICHARD. San Francisco policeman who became sheriff in 1971 and credited the gay vote with his election. (1) Sept. 9, 1997 (phone); (2) Oct. 25, 1997 (phone).

HOOSE, JERRY: New York. Early member of Gay Liberation Front. (1) Nov. 20, 1993 (New York); (2) Nov. 27, 1993 (New York).

HORMEL, JAMES: San Francisco. Meatpacking heir. Founding board member and financial backer of Human Rights Campaign Fund. (1) Feb. 26, 1994 (Los Angeles); (2) Mar. 10, 1994 (San Francisco); (3) May 5, 1994 (Washington, D.C.); (4) May 5, 1994 (phone).

HOWARD, JUDGE WILLIAM R. Hubert Humphrey's nephew, knowledgeable about Minnesota politics. March 1993 (Minneapolis).

HOWELL, DEBORAH. Former reporter for the *Minneapolis Star,* fiancée, later wife of Nick Coleman, deceased, the state Senate president who introduced gay rights bill in legislature in 1973. (1) May 8, 1996 (phone); (2) May 9, 1996 (phone tape message).

HUMM, ANDY: New York. Member of Coalition for Lesbian and Gay Rights. Apr. 10, 1994 (New York).

HUNTER, JOYCE: New York. Lesbian, gay rights figure and co-coordinator of the 1979 March on Washington. (1) Jan. 19, 1997 (phone); (2) Jan. 25, 1997 (phone).

JACKSON, DON: Los Angeles and San Francisco. Founder of Gay Liberation Front–Los Angeles. Nov. 3, 1994 (Los Angeles).

JACKUBOSKY, TONY. Treasurer of Kameny campaign for Congress in 1971, member of Washington, D.C., Gay Activists Alliance and Gertrude Stein Club. Apr. 18, 1995 (phone).

JARMIN, GARY: Washington, D.C. Founder of Christian Voice in October 1978, the first conservative Christian lobby on Capitol Hill. Jan. 29, 1997 (phone).

JENKINS, RAY. Deputy press secretary to President Jimmy Carter from September 1979 to January 1981. Jan. 31, 1997 (phone).

JOHNSON, DEAN. GOP minority leader of Minnesota state Senate, spoke out against the religious right and in support of gay rights legislation in 1993. March 1993 (St. Paul); (2) September 1993 (Minneapolis).

JOHNSON, LOIS, AND SHERI BARDEN. Early prominent lesbian couple in Boston, financial supporters of Elaine Noble in her first campaign. July 26, 1994 (Boston).

JOHNSTON, DAN: Iowa. Lawyer, former state legislator, announced himself as gay while county attorney in Des Moines. (1) Jan. 18, 1993 (phone); (2) Jan. 19, 1993 (phone).

JONES, BILLY (AKA PHYLLIS KILLER). Leading drag queen and chief personality in Atlanta gay male bar culture in 1960s and 1970s. Nov. 1, 1994 (Atlanta).

JONES, CLEVE: San Francisco. Aide to Harvey Milk, leader of Castro marches in 1978–79, founder of The AIDS Quilt. Mar. 9, 1994 (Sonoma County, Calif.).

KAMENY, DR. FRANKLIN: Washington, D.C. Harvard-trained astronomer, first federal court litigant for civil rights, founder of Washington Mattachine chapter, the first to organize repeated public demonstrations, the first to testify before Congress, the first open homosexual to run for federal office—in many ways, the father of the modern movement. (1) Aug. 18, 1993 (phone); (2) Aug. 23, 1993 (phone); (3) Sept. 12, 1993 (phone); (4) Apr. 19, 1994 (phone); (5) Jan. 16, 1995 (phone); (6) Mar. 8, 1995 (phone); (7) Apr. 30, 1995 (phone); (8) Oct. 13, 1995 (phone); (9) Nov. 20, 1995 (phone); (10) Jan. 4, 1996 (phone); (11) Mar. 7, 1996 (phone); (12) Jan. 13, or 14, 1997 (phone); (13) Sept. 6, 1998 (phone).

KANTROWITZ, ARNIE: New York. Early member of Gay Activists Alliance and AIDS activist. (1) June 4, 1993 (New York); (2) June 18, 1993 (New York); (3) June 26, 1993 (New York); (4) Mar. 25, 1995 (phone).

KELLEY, BILL: Chicago. Member of Mattachine Society of Chicago and National Gay Task Force. June 24, 1994 (New York).

KENNEDY, ALFRED, AND DR. BILL KENNEY. Socially prominent Atlanta gays who tried and failed to stage a black-tie Human Rights Campaign Fund dinner in 1982. Feb. 18, 1994 (Atlanta).

KEPNER, JIM: Los Angeles. Early member of Mattachine Society, Gay Liberation Front–Los Angeles, Los Angeles Gay Community Services Center, founder of International Gay and Lesbian Archives. (1) May 19, 1993 (West Hollywood); (2) July 15, 1993 (West Hollywood); (3) July 27, 1994 (phone); (4) June 5, 1994 (West Hollywood). Deceased.

KESHLEAR, BRAD: Atlanta. Friend of Gerald Stacy's. Oct. 21, 1993 (phone).

KESSLER, LARRY. Founding director in 1983 of AIDS Action Committee of Massachusetts, largest AIDS support organization in New England. (1) June 11, 1993 (Boston); (2) about June 12, 1993 (Boston).

KIGHT, MORRIS. Early Los Angeles gay leader, a founder of Gay Liberation Front and LA Gay Community Services Center. (1) May 19, 1993 (West Hollywood); (2) May 22, 1993 (West Hollywood); (3) June 8, 1993 (phone); (4) July 13, 1993 (West Hollywood); (5) July 16, 1993 (Los Angeles); (6) Dec. 4, 1993 (phone); (7) Dec. 26, 1993 (phone); (8) June 7, 1994 (West Hollywood); (9) June 14, 1994 (West Hollywood); (10) June 30, 1994 (phone); (11) Nov. 1, 1994 (phone); (12) Nov. 4, 1994 (phone); (13) Feb. 16, 1995 (phone); (14) March 10, 1995 (phone); (15) May 25, 1995 (phone); (16) October 5, 1995 (phone).

KIKEL, RUDY: Boston. Gay journalist who introduced the writer Paul Monette to his lover, Roger Horwitz. Sept. 18, 1993 (Boston).

KILHEFNER, DON: Los Angeles. Member of Gay Liberation Front and a founder of the Los Angeles Gay Community Services Center. June 1, 1994 (Los Angeles).

KIMBERLY, SUSAN: St. Paul. President of the St. Paul City Council 1976-78, Bob Sylvester then left his job and marriage, formed a new identity, had surgery and became Susan Kimberly, a transsexual who helped persuade the legislature to pass the only gay rights law in the nation that protects transsexuals, in 1993. (1) Oct. 9, 1993 (phone); (2) Oct. 10, 1993 (phone); (3) Oct. 16, 1993 (phone); (4) Nov. 13, 1993 (phone).

KING, GREGORY: Washington, D.C. Congressional page, apprentice to Alan Baron, spokesman for Human Rights Campaign Fund. Sept. 14, 1992 (brief phone conversation); Aug. 17, 1993 (brief phone conversation); (1) May 17, 1994 (Washington); (2) May 31, 1994 (Washington); (3) May 1997 (taped phone message); (4) May 7, 1997 (phone); (5) June 14, 1997 (phone).

KING, MEL. MIT professor, former Massachusetts state representative. Supporter of Elaine Noble and gay rights bills in the legislature. Sept. 20, 1993 (Cambridge, Mass.).

KNOWLTON, ELIZABETH. Lesbian-feminist active in Atlanta Lesbian Feminist Alliance. June 3, 1995 (phone).

KOCH, EDWARD: New York. Former mayor. May 19, 1994 (New York).

KOHLER, BOB: New York. Early Gay Liberation Front member. (1) Nov. 27, 1993 (New York); (2) early 1994 (New York).

KRAMER, LARRY: New York. Gay novelist, playwright, filmmaker and essayist; founder of Gay Men's Health Crisis in New York and of ACT-UP. (1) May 15, 1993 (phone); (2) Oct. 7, 1993 (phone).

KUNST, ROBERT: Miami Beach. Maverick gay personality, organizer, spokesman during the 1977 Dade County gay rights ordinance battle. JDC interview: Nov. 3, 1993 (Miami Beach); AJN interview: May 22, 1995 (phone).

KUNTZLER, PAUL. Member of Washington, D.C., Mattachine since 1963, manager of Franklin Kameny's 1971 congressional campaign, founder of Washington Gay Activists Alliance and Gertrude Stein Democratic Club. (1) Feb. 10, 1994 (Washington); (2) Apr. 14, 1994 (Washington); (3) Apr. 27, 1994 (Washington); (4) Mar. 18, 1995 (phone); (5) May 8, 1995 (phone); (6) Jan. 11, 1997 (phone).

LACHS, STEPHEN. A founder of MECLA, first openly gay judge in Los Angeles. (1) May 21, 1993 (Los Angeles); (2) June 3, 1994 (Los Angeles).

LAHUSEN, KAY. See Gittings, Barbara.

LAIDIG, GARY. Republican state senator in Minnesota. (1) March 1993 (St. Paul); (2) September 1993 (St. Paul); (3) Date N.A. (phone).

LANCE, BERT. President Jimmy Carter's closest friend and adviser, director of Office of Management and the Budget and liaison to Pat Robertson. (1) June 27, 1997 (phone); (2) Aug. 7, 1997 (phone).

LAURENCE, LEO. Midwest Republican radio reporter fired for being gay, moved west, created more radical brand of gay activism in San Francisco just prior to Stonewall. (1) Feb. 14, 1995 (phone); (2) Feb. 17, 1995 (phone); (3) Feb. 25, 1995 (phone).

LAURITSEN, JOHN: New York. Early member of Gay Liberation Front and writer for *Come Out!* Dec. 18, 1993 (New York).

LAVERY, MICHAEL: New York. Helped form Lambda Legal Defense and Education Fund in 1973. Dec. 31, 1993 (New York).

LEITSCH, DICK: New York. Mattachine Society leader at the time of Stonewall. (1) Oct. 27, 1993 (New York); (2) Mar. 12, 1994 (New York).

LEVI, JEFF: Washington, D.C. Member of Gay Rights National Lobby, National Gay Task Force and Gay Activists Alliance of Washington, D.C. Mar. 23, 1994 (Washington).

LEWIS, ANN FRANK. Barney Frank's sister, assistant to Boston mayor Kevin White, urged Elaine Noble to run for office. Encouraged lesbians in National Women's Political Caucus. Later served as White House Communications Director for Bill Clinton. Sept. 18, 1993 (Washington, D.C.).

LIEBMAN, MARVIN. Closeted homosexual who became prominent anti-Communist Republican in the 1950s and 1960s, close associate of William Buckley's, came out as gay in early 1990s. (1) Oct. 13, 1992 (phone); (2) Feb. 1, 1996 (phone); (3) Feb. 1, 1996. (phone). Deceased.

LINDSAY, JOHN: New York. Former mayor. Answered questions by letter, April 12, 1996.

LITTLEJOHN, LARRY. Early San Francisco figure. President of the Tavern Guild and the Society for Individual Rights. (1) Sept. 26, 1996 (phone); (2) Sept. 26, 1996 (phone); (3) Sept. 27, 1996 (phone); (4) Sept. 30, 1996 (phone).

LOVE, BARBARA: New York. Member of NOW, Daughters of Bilitis, Radicalesbians and Gay Liberation Front. Jan. 9, 1995 (New York).

LUCAS, DONALD. Harold Call's partner in Pan-Graphic Press, early gay activist in San Francisco, chairman of Committee on Religion and the Homosexual. (1) Oct. 8, 1996 (phone); (2) Oct. 9, 1996 (phone); (3) Oct. 18, 1996 (phone); (4) Nov. 13, 1996 (phone); (5) Nov. 14, 1996 (phone).

LYON, PHYLLIS, AND DEL MARTIN: San Francisco. Founders of the Daughters of Bilitis in 1955, authors of *lesbian/woman,* prominent in San Francisco and national movement for forty years. (1) Mar. 4, 1994 (San Francisco); (2) Aug. 28, 1994 (phone); (3) Sept. 18, 1996 (phone); (4) Dec. 7, 1997 (phone).

MCATEER, EDWARD. Conservative Christian who used his network of business contacts to become the circuit board of the religious right, the connection between strategists in Washington and preachers and laity across the country. (1) Mar. 9, 1997 (phone); (2) Mar. 14, 1997 (phone); (3) Apr. 14, 1997 (phone).

McCARTHY, VINCENT. Gay Boston lawyer and Democrat, adviser to 1988 Democratic presidential nominee Michael Dukakis. (1) June 16, 1993 (Boston); (2) June 29, 1993 (Boston); (3) Sept. 17, 1993 (Boston).

McCONNELL, JAMES MICHAEL. See Baker, Jack. (1) May 11, 1993 (phone); (2) Sept. 28, 1993 (Minneapolis); (3) by phone, 1998.

MACCUBBIN, DEACON. Owner of Lambda bookstores, Washington, D.C., and Baltimore. Jan. 8, 1996 (phone).

McFEELY, TIM. Gay Democratic Party activist in Boston in late 1970s and 1980s, then executive director of Human Rights Campaign Fund in Washington, D.C. (1) Sept. 9, 1993 (Washington); (2) Sept. 9, 1993 (Washington); (3) Sept. 21, 1993 (Washington).

McGOVERN, GEORGE. South Dakota and Washington, D.C. Former senator and 1972 presidential candidate. Mar. 3, 1995 (phone).

McILVENNA, TED. Young minister at Glide Memorial Church in San Francisco, helped found Committee on Religion and the Homosexual. Sept. 26, 1996 (phone).

McKENZIE, ANN: Baltimore. Attorney who represented homosexuals charged with sex crimes in North Carolina from about 1955 to 1975. May 3, 1995 (phone).

McMURRY, LAURA. Harvard doctoral student and secretary of Boston Daughters of Bilitis. (1) July 25, 1994 (Boston); (2) Feb. 18, 1995 (phone).

McNAUGHT, BRIAN: Boston. Roman Catholic Church journalist fired for being gay, became active in Dignity, then Mayor Kevin White's link to gay community. (1) Jan. 21, 1992 (phone); (2) Aug. 18, 1994 (phone).

MacPHERSON, MYRA. *Washington Post* reporter in 1976 who wrote about Ruth Carter Stapleton and her story of brother Jimmy Carter's becoming born again. July 23, 1997 (phone).

McWHORTER, CHARLES. Retired Republican Party figure from the 1950s to 1960s. Feb. 27, 1996 (phone).

MADDOX, THE REVEREND ROBERT. Southern Baptist minister, Carter family friend, served in Jimmy Carter White House as liaison to the newly emerged religious right. (1) Oct. 26, 1994 (phone); (2) June 16, 1995 (phone); (3) Jan. 31, 1997 (phone); (4) Apr. 16, 1997 (phone).

MAGUIRE, ANN. Lesbian political operative and later city official in Boston, campaign manager for Elaine Noble in 1974. July 1, 1993 (Boston).

MAILMAN, BRUCE: New York. Owner of St. Marks Baths and The Saint. (1) June 11, 1993 (New York); (2) June 21, 1993 (phone). Died of AIDS.

MANFORD, MORTY: New York. Early member of Gay Activists Alliance of New York. Died of AIDS.

MANKIEWICZ, FRANK: Washington, D.C. Political adviser to George McGovern in 1972. Mar. 21, 1995 (phone).

MARTIN, DEL. See Lyon, Phyllis.

MASS, LARRY: New York. A founder of Gay Men's Health Crisis and first writer to report early outbreak of what would become AIDS epidemic. (1) Apr. 29, 1994 (New York); (2) May 4, 1994 (New York); (3) July 17, 1995 (phone); (4) Sept. 18, 1995 (phone).

MASSELL, SAM. First Atlanta mayor to negotiate with newly organized gays and to appoint them to city boards. (1) May 22, 1995 (phone); (2) June 4, 1995 (phone).

MATLOVICH, LEONARD: Washington, D.C. Air Force sergeant discharged in 1975 after admitting his homosexuality. Died of AIDS.

MAULSBY, RICHARD: Washington, D.C. Worked in 1971 Kameny for Congress campaign, a founder and first president of Gertrude Stein Club in Washington, D.C. (1) May 4, 1994 (Washington); (2) Jan. 5, 1996 (phone); (3) Jan. 8, 1996 (phone).

MERTON, NILES: Los Angeles. Former publisher of *The Advocate.* June 1, 1994 (Los Angeles). Died of AIDS.

METZGER, B. J., AND D. J. MUNRO. Leaders of a lesbian-feminist separatist group in St. Paul, Minnesota, that failed to stop repeal of St. Paul's gay rights law in 1978, but helped repass it in 1991. 1993 (St. Paul).

MEUNIERE, JOHN. U.S. Representative Gerry Studds's driver at time of congressional page scandal, and Mayor Ray Flynn's second liaison to Boston gay community. (1) June 30, 1993 (Boston); (2) July 1993 (Boston); (3) Date N.A. (phone).

MILLER, DENNIS. University of Minnesota student, in 1977 part of team that threw a pie at the Roman Catholic archbishop for opposing the gay rights bill in the state legislature. Sept. 29, 1993 (St. Paul).

MILNE, BOB: New York. Member of Mattachine Society in the late 1960s. May 17, 1994 (New York).

MINDT, CAPT. PAM. Minnesota National Guard officer and state prison system social worker who acknowledged her homosexuality publicly in 1993. March 1993 (St. Paul).

MITZEL, JOHN: Boston. Gay sex liberationist, writer for *Fag Rag* and *Gay Community News,* porn theater manager, manager of Glad Day Bookstore. (1) Sept. 19, 1993 (Boston); (2) Date N.A. (phone).

MIXNER, DAVID. Gay rights leader from Los Angeles, a founder of MECLA; openly gay friend and supporter of President Clinton. AJN interviews: (1) Oct. 30, 1992 (phone); (2) Mar. 16, 1994 (Washington, D.C.); (3) May 31, 1994 (West Hollywood); (4) June 13, 1994 (West Hollywood); (5) Dec. 5, 1994 (Washington). JDC interviews: (1) Jan. 20, 1993 (Washington); (2) Apr. 26, 1994 (New York).

MOGULSON, JACK. Vice president and state lobbyist for the Teamsters Union in Minnesota who testified for the gay rights bill. March 1993 (St. Paul).

MONETTE, PAUL. Novelist and screenwriter who became famous for nonfiction memoirs about AIDS. His lover, Paul Horwitz, was the half brother of Sheldon Andelson. (1) Aug. 13, 1993 (phone); (2) Aug. 18, 1993 (phone); (3) Aug. 25, 1993 (phone); (4) Sept. 22, 1993 (phone); (5) Date N.A. (phone); (6) Feb. 26, 1994 (Los Angeles). Died of AIDS.

MORGAN, FRANK: Boston. Started the Homophile Union of Boston. (1) Aug. 17, 1994 (phone); (2) Sept. 2, 1994 (phone).

MORGAN, TRACY: New York. ACT-UP member. June 20, 1994 (New York).

NESTLE, JOAN: New York. Founder of Lesbian Herstory Archives; member of Lesbian Feminist Liberation and Gay Activists Alliance. Dec. 16, 1994 (New York).

NEWSTROM, MARY: Minnesota. A lesbian phone bank and polling strategist for gay political causes. March 1993 (St. Paul).

NICOLA, MICHAEL: Los Angeles. Fundraiser and MECLA member. (1) Dec. 5, 1993 (phone); (2) Mar. 12, 1994 (phone).

NOBLE, ELAINE: Boston. First openly gay candidate elected to state office in the United States, in 1974. (1) Nov. 10, 1992 (phone); (2) Nov. 13, 1992 (phone); (3) June 30, 1993 (Boston); (4) Aug. 4, 1994 (phone).

OATES, MARYLOUISE. Former columnist at *Los Angeles Times* and associate of MECLA founders. (1) May 5, 1993 (Washington, D.C.); (2) June 24, 1993 (Washington, D.C.).

O'BRIEN, JOHN: New York and California. Early member of Gay Liberation Front in New York. (1) Nov. 24, 1993 (phone); (2) Nov. 25, 1993 (phone); (3) May 6, 1994 (West Hollywood); (4) Dec. 10, 1993 (phone); (5) June 6, 1994 (West Hollywood).

O'LEARY, JEAN: New York and Los Angeles. Leading figure in lesbian-feminist separatist politics, co-chair of National Gay Task Force and friend of Midge Costanza. (1) Nov. 16, 1992 (phone); (2) Nov. 18, 1992 (phone); (3) Feb. 22, 1994 (Los Angeles); (4) Feb. 25, 1994 (Los Angeles); (5) May 5, 1995 (phone); (6) Jan. 14, 1997 (phone).

OFFEN, HAL: New York and San Francisco. Early member of Gay Activists Alliance of New York. Jan. 20, 1994 (San Francisco).

OSBORN, TORIE. Former leader of National Gay and Lesbian Task Force. (The Task Force voted to add the word "lesbian" to its name in November 1985.) (1) Apr. 30, 1993 (Washington, D.C.); (2) June 14, 1993 (Washington).

OSTROW, DR. STOSH. AIDS doctor, the first out gay physician in Atlanta. (1) Feb. 17, 1994 (Atlanta); (2) Feb. 18, 1994 (Atlanta).

OWLES, JIM: New York. First president of the Gay Activists Alliance of New York. Died of AIDS.

PALENCIA, ROLAND: Los Angeles. Gay/Latino activist. June 23, 1994 (New York).

PERRY, THE REVEREND TROY. Founder of the Metropolitan Community Church. Ordained southern charismatic preacher cast out for homosexuality. One of the few early leaders of gay culture and rights movement to remain alive and prominent through the 1990s. Feb. 21, 1994 (Los Angeles).

PETERSON, DAVID: Boston. Involved in the first gay political organizations in Boston and in *Gay Community News*, which he conceived. (1) June 26, 1994 (phone); (2) July 25, 1994 (Cambridge, Mass.).

PETRELIS, MICHAEL: New York. Lavender Hill Mob member. Apr. 21, 1994 (Washington, D.C.).

PHELPS, KOREEN. A founder of FREE at the University of Minnesota, in April–May 1969. (1) Dec. 25, 1994 (phone); (2) Dec. 26, 1994 (phone); (3) Jan. 2, 1995 (phone); (4) Jan. 11, 1995 (phone).

PHILLIPS, HOWARD. Appointed by Richard Nixon as Director of the Office of Economic Opportunity, conservative Republican figure who became part of the religious right network. Apr. 2, 1997 (phone).

PILLARD, DR. RICHARD. Boston University professor of psychiatry, founder of Homophile Community Health Services Center, the first group of gay mental health professionals to give positive counseling to homosexuals. Nov. 18, 1995 (phone).

PLATH, BILL. San Francisco bar owner, a founder of both the Tavern Guild and the Committee on Religion and the Homosexual. Oct. 3, 1996 (phone).

POPHAM, PAUL: New York. First president of the Gay Men's Health Crisis. Died of AIDS.

POU, MARY SPOTTSWOOD: Washington, D.C. Member of radical Furies in Washington, lover of Rita Mae Brown, producer of women's music, co-chair of National Convention Project in 1980. (1) Mar. 2 or 3, 1994 (these were among the notes stolen in JDC mugging) (Berkeley, Calif.); (2) May 12, 1994 (phone); (3) May 16, 1994 (phone); (4) May 21, 1994 (phone).

POVILLE, ELLEN: New York. Daughters of Bilitis member. Apr. 9, 1994 (upstate New York).

POWELL, BETTY: New York. National Gay Task Force member. (1) Dec. 29, 1994 (New York): (2) Feb. 16, 1995 (New York).

POWELL, JODY. Press secretary to President Jimmy Carter, 1976–80, and fellow Southern Baptist. May 1, 1997 (phone).

RAFSHOON, GERALD. Campaign advertising message manager to Jimmy Carter in gubernatorial and presidential campaigns. June 27, 1997 (phone).

REDMAN, MATT: Los Angeles. A founder of AIDS Project Los Angeles. Aug. 27, 1997 (Fire Island Pines, N.Y.).

REDMOND, LARRY. Lobbyist for arts community in Twin Cities, worked on passage of gay rights legislation there. March 1993 (St. Paul).

REEVES, KENNETH. Harvard College graduate, black, gay mayor of Cambridge, Massachusetts. September 1993 (Cambridge).

REINHOLD, ROBERT. National correspondent for the *New York Times* in Boston in the early '70s; then a closeted homosexual, he wrote a front-page story on the emergence of the gay rights movement on the nation's college campuses. (1) Feb. 26, 1995 (phone); (2) Apr. 30, 1996 (phone). Deceased.

RICCHIAZZI, FRANK: Los Angeles. A founder of gay GOP Log Cabin Club in the mid-1980s. (1) June 14, 1994 (phone); (2) June 17, 1994 (Washington, D.C.); (3) June 18, 1994 (phone).

RIVERA, CORA (NÉE PEROTTA): New York. Early member of Gay Activists Alliance and Radicalesbians. June 22, 1994 (San Francisco).

RIVERA, SYLVIA: New York. Early member of Gay Activists Alliance in New York; a popular drag queen.

ROBERTSON, THE REVEREND PAT: Virginia Beach, Va. Southern Baptist minister, host of *The 700 Club;* founder of Christian Broadcasting Network, chairman of Christian Coalition. Two interviews, the first by telephone, the second in his hotel suite, in the mid-1980s, for the *New York Times.* In these conversations Robertson first volunteered the story of Jimmy Carter's supposed promise to appoint an evangelical to his cabinet in return for Robertson's support in 1976 (dates of interviews N.A.).

ROBINSON, MARTY: New York. A founder of the Gay Activists Alliance and architect of many of its early political tactics. Died of AIDS.

ROCKHILL, NATHALIE: New York. Member of Gay Activists Alliance, Lesbian Feminist Liberation and National Gay Task Force. (1) Mar. 4, 1995 (phone); (2) Mar. 5, 1995 (phone).

RODWELL, CRAIG. Pre- and post-Stonewall gay activist, founder of first New York City Gay Rights Parade. (1) May 7, 1993 (New York); (2) May 15, 1993 (New York). Deceased.

ROFES, ERIC: Boston and Los Angeles. Founder and chair, Boston Lesbian and Gay Political Alliance; later executive director of Los Angeles Gay and Lesbian Community Services Center; executive director of Shanti Project, San Francisco. Sept. 15, 1993 (Provincetown, Mass.).

ROLAND, JOHN SID. Gay Atlanta prostitute. (1) February 1994 (Atlanta); (2) May 16, 1994 (phone); (3) May 30, 1994 (phone); (4) May 31, 1994 (phone); (5) June 16, 1994 (phone).

ROSENTHAL, RON. Visiting from Atlanta in 1973, he was in the UpStairs bar in New Orleans with his boyfriend when the fire was set which killed thirty-two people. Escaped. Sept. 9, 1998 (phone).

ROSKOFF, ALLEN: New York. Early member of Gay Activists Alliance. (1) Sept. 9, 1993 (New York); (2) Sept. 10, 1993 (New York).

ROTHENBERG, DAVID: New York. Early member of National Gay Task Force. May 7, 1993 (New York).

ROUSY, JAMIE. Gay southern fundamentalist, former Bob Jones University student who became sexually active and got AIDS virus. Ran AIDS absentee voter campaign for Clinton. June 1993 (Atlanta).

RUBIN, MARC: New York. Early member of Gay Activists Alliance. Partner of Peter Fisher. Sept. 11, 1993 (New York).

RUSSELL, DAVID: Los Angeles. Former lover of David Goodstein. (1) Jan. 28, 1994 (phone); (2) June 1, 1994, day (Los Angeles); (3) June 1, 1994, evening (Los Angeles).

RUSSO, VITO: New York. Early member of Gay Activists Alliance. Wrote *The Celluloid Closet.* Died of AIDS.

RYAN, PHILIP: New York. Member of Gay Activists Alliance and National Gay Task Force. Apr. 11, 1994 (New York).

SARRIA, JOSÉ. Waiter and cabaret performer at the Black Cat bar in North Beach, San Francisco, who became the first open homosexual in the nation to run for public office, for city board of supervisors in 1961. (1) Sept. 26, 1996 (phone); (2) Sept. 27, 1996 (phone).

SCHEUREN, FRANK. President of Atlanta Gay Center; spokesman for the gay bars in the 1970s. (1) Nov. 1, 1994 (Atlanta); (2) Nov. 16, 1995 (phone).

SCHIETINGER, HELEN: San Francisco. Nurse involved in early AIDS work; also Lesbian Feminist Liberation–Atlanta member. Mar. 6, 1994 (Washington, D.C.).

SCHNEIDER, WILLIAM. *National Journal* columnist, American Enterprise Institute scholar and CNN commentator. May 11, 1997 (phone).

SCHULTE, STEVE: West Hollywood. Executive director of the Los Angeles Gay and Lesbian Community Services Center, on first city council of West Hollywood. (1) Sept. 12, 1993 (Baltimore); (2) June 7, 1994 (West Hollywood).

SCONDRAS, DAVID. First openly gay candidate elected to Boston City Council, 1983. June 28, 1993 (Boston).

SCOTT, PETER: Los Angeles. A founder of MECLA. Partner with David Mixner in a political consulting firm. Died of AIDS.

SEELY, AL. At sixteen, in 1969, committed to Atlanta mental hospital by his parents to cure his homosexuality; married and divorced, held first openly gay political fundraiser in Virginia, in Norfolk in 1992, for Bill Clinton. (1) Sept. 4, 1992 (phone); (2) Sept. 15, 1992 (phone); (3) Sept. 23, 1992 (Norfolk); (4) Oct. 29, 1995 (phone).

SHACK, DICK: Dade County, Florida. Former agent of Anita Bryant. May 3, 1995 (New York).

SHACK, RUTH: Dade County, Florida. Commissioner who introduced gay rights ordinance in 1976. May 7, 1995 (phone).

SHANLEY, FATHER PAUL. Headed the Ministry to Alienated Youth on the Streets in Boston under Richard Cardinal Cushing in the early 1970s. Only Catholic priest in the nation authorized to minister to gays, until Humberto Cardinal Medeiros abolished his ministry. Sept. 17, 1996 (phone).

SHEATS, THE REVEREND MORRIS. Baptist minister present at Rock Church meeting with the Reverend Bob Maddox in 1979, and at White House breakfast with Jimmy Carter in January 1980. Feb. 3, 1997 (phone).

SHELDON, THE REVEREND LOU. Religious leader from California. (1) Apr. 30, 1993 (phone); (2) July 28, 1993 (Washington, D.C.).

SHELLEY, MARTHA: New York. A founder of Gay Liberation Front. (1) Jan. 21, 1994 (Berkeley, Calif.); (2) Dec. 30, 1994 (phone).

SHILTS, RANDY: California. Author and journalist. (1) July 5, 1993 (Guerneville, Calif.); (2) July 15, 1993 (phone); (3) July 17, 1993 (phone). Died of AIDS.

SHIVELY, CHARLEY: Boston. Radical gay activist, poet, editor of *Fag Rag*, college professor who in 1977 burned a Bible on the Boston Common to protest Anita Bryant's campaign. (1) Sept. 17, 1993 (Cambridge, Mass.); (2) June 15, 1994 (Cambridge); (3) June 18, 1994 (Cambridge).

SHULTIS, THE REVEREND CANDACE. Metropolitan Community Church minister in Washington, D.C., a friend of Stephen Endean's who assisted at his memorial service. Feb. 10, 1994 (Washington).

SHUMSKY, ELLEN: New York. Founding member of Gay Liberation Front and of the Radicalesbians. Feb. 11, 1994 (New York).

SHRUM, BOB: Washington. Democratic political consultant. May 5, 1993 (Washington, D.C.).

SIMPSON, RUTH: New York. Former president of Daughters of Bilitis–New York. Apr. 9, 1994 (upstate New York).

SINGER, MICHAEL: Los Angeles. CBS television producer. Oct. 18, 1995 (phone).

SMITH, BOBBY: Los Angeles. Black and White Men Together member. June 13, 1994 (Los Angeles).

SMITH, DAN: New York and California. Gay Liberation Front member. June 25, 1994 (phone).

SMITH, EMORY: Los Angeles. Black and White Men Together member. June 7, 1993 (Los Angeles).

SMITH, STEPHEN: California. Early member of MECLA, adviser to David Goodstein, supporter of Edward Kennedy's 1980 presidential campaign. (1) Oct. 11, 1993 (Washington, D.C.); (2) Oct. 26, 1993 (Washington); (3) Nov. 15, 1993 (Washington); (4) Jan. 12, 1993 (Washington); (5) June 16, 1995 (phone); (6) Oct. 27, 1995 (phone).

SOCARIDES, CHARLES: New York. Psychiatrist who held that homosexuality is a disease that can be cured with therapy.

SOCARIDES, RICHARD: Washington, D.C. The son of Charles Socarides, he later became gay liaison for President Clinton. (1) Dec. 15, 1993 (Washington); (2) Sept. 1, 1994 (Washington); (3) Sept. 3, 1994 (East Hampton, N.Y.).

SPEAR, ALLAN: Minnesota. Second openly gay state legislator in United States, president of the Minnesota Senate. (1) May 2, 1993 (Minneapolis); (2) May 1993 (St. Paul); (3) Sept. 28, 1993 (Minneapolis); (4) Jan. 25, 1997 (phone).

SPITZER, DR. ROBERT. Heterosexual psychiatrist and American Psychiatric Association member who in 1972 and 1973 became a leading figure in the effort to remove homosexuality from the APA's list of mental illnesses. Nov. 19, 1995 (phone).

SPRENGER, LARRY: Los Angeles. Leader of MECLA when it recommended in November 1985 that county bathhouses close down. May 21, 1993 (Los Angeles).

STACY, GERALD LEON. Gay, formerly married Appalachian hillbilly who became active member of Atlanta leather scene in 1970s and 1980s. (1) Oct. 13, 1993 (phone); (2) Oct. 21, 1993 (phone); (3) Oct. 23, 1993 (Atlanta); (4) Oct. 25, 1993 (Atlanta); (5) Oct. 27, 1993 (Atlanta); (6) Nov. 18, 1993 (phone).

STAFFORD, RICK: Minnesota. The only openly gay, HIV-positive Democratic state party chairman in the nation. Sept. 30, 1993 (Minneapolis–St. Paul).

STALEY, PETER: New York. Early member of ACT-UP. (1) Feb. 18, 1994 (New York); (2) Mar. 3, 1994 (New York).

STEWART, CHARLES: Los Angeles. Black and White Men Together member. June 15, 1994 (Los Angeles).

STODDARD, JACK: New York. Manager of the New St. Marks Baths and The Saint. Aug. 4, 1994 (phone).

STODDARD, THOMAS B. Lawyer, gay rights and civil rights activist and litigator in New York City. (1) Oct. 9, 1992 (New York); (2) Apr. 17, 1993 (New York); (3) Apr. 30, 1993 (Washington, D.C.); (4) Sept. 3, 1993 (New York); (5) Nov. 20, 1995 (phone); (6) Dec. 29, 1995 (phone). Died of AIDS.

STOKES, RICK: San Francisco. Prominent gay lawyer, bath owner. Ally of Jim Foster in the 1970s who opposed Harvey Milk for the Board of Supervisors. (1) Mar. 7, 1994 (San Francisco); (2) Sept. 18, 1996 (San Francisco); (3) Sept. 5, 1997 (phone); (4) Oct. 17, 1997 (phone); (5) Dec. 6, 1997 (phone).

STRUB, SEAN. Political prodigy from Iowa; as apprentice to Alan Baron, got Tennessee Williams to sign fundraising letter for the Human Rights Campaign Fund. Direct-mail specialist. Later became AIDS activist and publisher of *POZ* magazine. (1) Dec. 7, 1993 (New York); (2) Dec. 8, 1993 (New York); (3) Apr. 24, 1994 (New York); (4) Date and place N.A. (5) June 28, 1994 (The Pines, Fire Island, N.Y.); (6) May 29, 1997 (phone); (7) June 2, 1997 (phone).

TAFEL, RICH. National president of gay Republican Log Cabin Club. (1–3) week of June 20, 1993 (Boston).

TAYLOR, JUDGE HARRIET R. Active in Democratic Party politics in Washington, D.C., in the 1970s. Apr. 18, 1995 (phone).

TEMPLETON, THE REVEREND JOHN. Director of education and counseling for AIDS clinic at Grady Hospital, Atlanta. (1) Sept. 3, 1992 (phone); (2) Sept. 14, 1992 (phone); (3) June 1993 (Atlanta); (4) Nov. 1, 1994 (Atlanta).

THAIS-WILLIAMS, JEWELL: Los Angeles. Early activist in black-white gay relations. June 2, 1994 (Los Angeles).

THOMAS, BEV: Los Angeles. MECLA member. June 6, 1994 (Los Angeles).

THOMPSON, MARK: Los Angeles. Staff writer and editor at *The Advocate.* June 14, 1994 (Los Angeles).

THOMPSON, MIKE: Dade County, Florida. Organizer of Anita Bryant's 1977 campaign. Apr. 27, 1995 (phone).

THOMSON, CANDY (CANDUS) FRANK. Boston college student who worked in Elaine Noble's campaign and legislative office. Feb. 7, 1994 (Baltimore).

TILLOTSON, STAN: Boston. Started Student Homophile League at Massachusetts Institute of Technology in Fall 1969; it evolved into Boston Gay Liberation Front. (1) June 21, 1994 (phone); (2) Aug. 18, 1994 (Baltimore); (3) Feb. 24, 1995 (phone).

TOBIN, KAY. See Gittings, Barbara.

TRETTER, JEAN: Minnesota. Recruited by Steve Endean for the new gay rights lobby in Minnesota, worked for a gay rights law in the '70s. (1) Sept. 27, 1993 (St. Paul); (2) Apr. 25, 1996 (phone); (3) May 13, 1996 (phone).

TSONGAS, PAUL: Washington, D.C., and Massachusetts. Former senator and 1992 presidential candidate. Jan. 26, 1994 (Washington). Deceased.

TUCKER, NANCY. Washington, D.C., Mattachine member from 1967 to 1970, first editor of the *Gay Blade* (later the *Washington Blade*). (1) May 3, 1995 (phone); (2) May 9, 1995 (phone).

TYLER, ROBIN. Prominent California lesbian comedian and speaker, conceived the idea of the 1979 National March on Washington for Lesbian and Gay Rights. Jan. 19, 1997 (phone).

UPTON, ROY. Don Daniels's lover of fifteen years. July 18, 1994 (phone).

VAID, URVASHI. Member of feminist collective publication *Sister Courage* in Boston, became executive director of the National Gay and Lesbian Task Force. JDC interview: Sept. 16, 1993 (Provincetown, Mass.). AJN interviews: (1) Nov. 19, 1992 (phone); (2) Dec. 8, 1995 (phone).

VALESKA, LUCIA: Albuquerque. Feminist and short-lived co-chair of the National Gay Task Force. Declined interview.

VAN OOTEGHEM, GARY: Houston. Former Houston county treasurer, a founder of Gay Political Caucus; National Gay Task Force board member. June 24, 1994 (New York).

VIDA, GINNY: New York. Member of Gay Activists Alliance, Lesbian Feminist Liberation and National Gay Task Force. Nov. 25, 1994 (New York).

VINCENZ, DR. LILLI. Member of Washington Mattachine since 1963. Editor of *The Homosexual Citizen* from January 1966 to May 1967; founder with Nancy Tucker of the *Washington Blade*. (1) Feb. 19, 1995 (phone); (2) Mar. 16, 1995 (phone); (3) Mar. 20, 1995 (northern Virginia).

VOELLER, BRUCE: New York. Third president of Gay Activists Alliance, founder of National Gay Task Force. (1) May 19, 1993 (Topanga Canyon, Calif.); (2) June 9, 1993 (phone); (3) June 11, 1993 (phone); (4) July 14, 1993 (Topanga Canyon); (5) Dec. 28, 1993 (phone). Died of AIDS.

WADLEY, DENIS. President and lobbyist for Americans for Democratic Action in Minnesota, an early ally and tutor of Steve Endean. March 1993 (Minneapolis). Deceased.

WALLACE, HOWARD. Labor organizer, Socialist Workers Party member, organizer of Bay Area Gay Liberation, supporter of Harvey Milk, organizer of Coors Beer boycott. (1) Feb. 27, 1994 (San Francisco); (2) Mar. 2, 1994 (San Francisco); (3) Mar. 7, 1994 (San Francisco); (4) Jan. 23, 1997 (phone).

WANDEL, RICHARD: New York. Second president of Gay Activists Alliance and New York City gay archivist. Aug. 13, 1993 (New York).

WEINSTEIN, MICHAEL: Los Angeles. AIDS activist. June 14, 1994 (Los Angeles).

WESTMORELAND, TIM: Washington, D.C. Aide to Representative Henry A. Waxman, chair of the House subcommittee on health. (1) Jan. 4, 1994 (Washington); (2) Feb. 2, 1994 (Washington).

WEXLER, ANNE. Replaced Midge Costanza as assistant to the president for public liaison in March–April 1978. Feb. 27, 1997 (phone).

WEYBORNE, WILLIAM. Texas journalist and developer, active in gay organizing in Texas, who became executive director of Victory Fund. Apr. 28, 1993 (Washington, D.C.).

WEYRICH, PAUL. Founder of Heritage Foundation and Committee for the Survival of a Free Congress; among founders of what is known today as the religious right. (1) Mar. 7, 1997 (phone); (2) Mar. 11, 1997 (phone); (3) Mar. 14, 1997 (phone).

WHITE, GREGG. Twin Cities businessman, supporter of Steve Endean and gay rights in the 1970s. May 1993 (Minneapolis).

WICKER, RANDY: New York. Mattachine Society member. Oct. 14, 1993 (New York).

WIEMHOFF, HENRY: Chicago. Founder of Chicago Gay Liberation. (1) May 4, 1994 (New York); (2) May 6, 1994 (New York). Died of AIDS.

WILSON, DR. ALAN. Norfolk, Virginia, AIDS doctor, Al Seely's partner, co-hosted gay fundraiser for Clinton after becoming angry with the indifference of the Reagan and Bush administrations to AIDS. (1) Sept. 23, 1992 (Norfolk); (2) Oct. 15, 1992 (phone); (3) Oct. 22, 1992 (phone).

WILSON, PHILL: Los Angeles. Member of Black and White Men Together and Los Angeles Gay Community Services Center. Apr. 30, 1994 (New York).

WITT, CLIFF: Washington, D.C. Assistant manager of 1971 Kameny congressional campaign, member of Washington Gay Activists Alliance and a founder of Gertrude Stein Club. (1) May 12, 1995 (phone); (2) Nov. 20, 1995 (phone); (3) Jan. 4, 1996 (phone).

WOLFE, MAXINE: New York. ACT-UP member. Apr. 27, 1994 (New York).

WOODWARD, KERRY: Minneapolis. Worked with Stephen Endean in Minnesota, was officer of Gay Rights National Lobby and first woman co-chair of Human Rights Campaign Fund. (1) Nov. 11, 1992 (phone); (2) Nov. 18, 1992 (phone); (3) Feb. 28, 1993 (phone); (4) Sept. 28, 1993 (Minneapolis); (5) Jan. 11, 1997 (phone); (6) May 13, 1997 (phone).

WOOLARD, CATHY. Atlanta native, lesbian and southern regional organizer of Human Rights Campaign Fund effort to get out the gay vote for Clinton in 1992. Nov. 9, 1992 (phone).

WYNNE, CLAUDE: New York and San Francisco. Early member of New York Gay Activists Alliance, moved to San Francisco and helped form Bay Area Gay Liberation. Mar. 7, 1994 (San Francisco).

Notes

AJN refers to Adam Nagourney and JDC refers to Dudley Clendinen

PART ONE: AWAKENING

1: A Fight at a Bar

Page

21   paddy wagon pulled up at Stonewall: Craig Rodwell interview nos. 1 and 2 with AJN, and his oral history at Columbia University.

22   Rodwell had not read a single book: Rodwell interviews.

22   *New York Post* in 1969: The *New York Post* was in almost every way a different newspaper than it is today. Published by Dorothy Schiff, it was liberal and respected, particularly for its coverage of politics.

22   Rodwell reading the *Post:* Rodwell's recollection, in his oral history, was that the story was headlined something like, "Homosexual Unrest in Village." The actual headline on June 28, 1969, was "Village Raid Stirs Melee."

22   the second night of Stonewall rioting: see *Mattachine Report,* August 1969.

22   arrests, number of nights of riotings: Duberman, *Stonewall,* pp. 202, 209, and "Police Again Rout 'Village' Youths," *New York Times,* June 30, 1969, p. 22.

23   Even the *Village Voice:* Lucian Truscott IV, "Gay Power Comes to Sheridan Square," *Village Voice,* July 3, 1969, p.1.

23   signs painted on the door of Stonewall: Vito Russo interview with Eric Marcus, courtesy of Marcus; wording of the sign is from Duberman, *Stonewall,* p. 202; however, Duberman says that second sign appeared by Sunday.

23   Leitsch cared little for the talk about civil rights: Dick Leitsch interview nos. 1 and 2 with AJN.

23   Leitsch wrote personal letters to Lindsay: Leitsch was enamored with Lindsay and made no effort to hide it in his correspondence. "You are extremely handsome and radiate virility," the Mattachine director told the mayor in a June 18, 1969, letter that praised his gay rights record and expressed his "sadness" that Lindsay had lost the Republican primary. Leitsch letters to Lindsay, courtesy of Leitsch papers.

24   "Well, Dick, they call me the father. . . .": Leitsch interview no. 1. Wicker's reaction: interview with AJN, Oct. 14, 1993.

24   King photo on Leitsch wall: *Village Voice*, March 19, 1970.

24   "We're turning out. . . .": Leitsch interview no. 2.

25   Wicker's outfit and the scene at the Electric Circus: "Lige and Jack," "N.Y. Gays: Will the Spark Die?" *Los Angeles Advocate,* September 1969; and their slightly different account in *Screw,* July 1969. Lige Clarke and Jack Nichols were lovers who then wrote a gay column for Al Goldstein's *Screw* magazine. Wicker's remarks from his interview.

25   Wicker would come to regret remark condemning throwing rocks: Wicker interview.

25   first-year anniversary of Stonewall marches: *The Advocate,* vol. 4, no. 11 (July 22–Aug. 4, 1970).

25   "Where do we go from here?": leaflet, July 3–4, 1969, courtesy of Leitsch papers.

26   "Hairpin Drop" leaflet: As was Mattachine's custom, the leaflet and the *Mattachine Newsletter* were without a byline. The leaflet was reprinted in the *Los Angeles Advocate,* September 1969, with Leitsch's byline.

26   Michael Brown: Toby Marotta, *The Politics of Homosexuality,* pp. 77–78. Efforts to find Brown were unsuccessful.

26   Leitsch expressing concern about starting another group: Martha Shelley and Leitsch interviews with AJN.

26   "Who opened the tuna fish?": Shelley interviews with AJN and Marcus; and Leitsch interview no. 2.

27   2nd Gay Liberation Meeting: Tom Burke, "The New Homosexuality," *Esquire,* December 1969. It was confirmed and elaborated upon in Jim Fouratt and Leitsch interviews with AJN.

27   held at a church on Waverly Place: Brown's role in moving the meeting is taken from Marotta, *The Politics of Homosexuality,* p. 78.

28   Shelley at the rim of the fountain speaking without any amplification: Shelley interviews with AJN and Marcus. Details on demonstration from Shelley, Leitsch and other interviews with AJN, as well as from Jonathan Black, "Gay Power Hits Back," *Village Voice,* July 31, 1969.

29   on Shelley's early relationship and fallout with DOB: interview no. 1 with AJN for fallout, and interview with Marcus for first meeting with Joan Kent.

29   accused Shelley of being a Communist: Shelley interview no. 1. Kent is dead.

29   LSD trip: ibid.

30   "non-violent vigil. . . .": That is the name, with some variations, that the Mattachine Society/Daughters of Bilitis called the Washington Square Park action in their leaflets, courtesy of Leitsch papers.

30   Robinson's European vacation: Robinson interview in Kay Tobin and Randy Wicker, *The Gay Crusaders.*

30   Robinson and Bloomingdale's: *Gay* newspaper, no. 21 (June 29, 1970), with later interview with Robinson.

30   "DO YOU THINK HOMOSEXUALS ARE REVOLTING? . . .": Toby Marotta credits the idea for the leaflet to Charlie Pitts, a commentator on the public radio station WBAI.

31   Alternate U. ("Harvard Diplomas: Take One"): Shelley interviews with AJN and Marcus.

31   Alternate U. and the room for the first meeting: John O'Brien interview no. 4 with AJN.

31   the founding GLF meeting: Shelley, Fouratt, Jerry Hoose, O'Brien and Earl Galvin interviews with AJN, among others.

31   the name Gay Liberation Front: Shelley interview no. 1 and Galvin interview with AJN, May 22, 1994.

31   "use the word 'homosexual'": Galvin interview.

32   the GLF Statement of Purpose: printed in both the October 1969 inaugural issue of *Come Out!,* the GLF newspaper, and in the revolutionary newspaper *Rat,* Aug. 12, 1969; reprinted in John D'Emelio, *Sexual Politics,* and Marotta, *The Politics of Homosexuality.*

2: Los Angeles

34   Los Angeles Police Department sex arrests: A survey by two law students, Barry Copilow of USC and Thomas Coleman of Loyola University, in 1972, concluded that the 647(a) law was discriminatory, invidious and arbitrarily enforced. The study of arrests was from June to September 1972: of 663 "lewd conduct" arrests studied, 17 were women and 12 of those were prostitutes. Just 5 of the arrests came after civilian complaints. Fifteen were made by uniformed police and 642 by plainclothesmen. The report was funded by HELP (Homophile Effort for Legal Protection) and by the Whitman-Radclyffe Foundation, both homosexual advocacy groups. The report was reprinted in full in *The Advocate*, no. 105 (Feb. 14, 1973), and cited in the *Los Angeles Times*, March 25, 1973.

34   Valentine Day's raid on Little Cave: *Los Angeles Advocate*, vol. 3, no. 3 (March 1969).

35   stomping death of gay man at Dover Hotel: *Los Angeles Advocate*, vol. 3, nos. 3–5 (March–May 1969).

35   "You're goddamn right. . . .": Marsha Ross, "Once a Cop, Always a Cop: Joe Wambaugh Is Still on the Case," *New West*, July 19, 1976, p. 65.

35   locations of public bathrooms known for sex and arrests: Jim Kepner interview no. 4 with AJN.

35   Newman arrest and thinking, "I'm going to lose my job.": "Gays Fight Discrimination, Uncertain Laws," *Los Angeles Times*, March 25, 1974.

35   "Something in here stinks. . . ." and ". . . how Anne Frank must have felt.": P. Nutz, "Terror in the Tubs: The Raid That Wasn't," *Los Angeles Advocate*, vol. 3, no. 6 (June 1969), p. 3.

35   "bush queens and tearoom aunties.": "How to Cause a Riot," *Advocate* editorial, Vol. 4, no. 8 (June 10–23, 1970).

35   Joachim letter on not cruising: *The Advocate*, vol. 1, no. 1 (September 1967), p. 7.

36   "If there is any large city in the country. . . .": letter to the editor, *Los Angeles Advocate*, vol. 2, no. 6 (May 1968).

36   first meeting of GLF: Morris Kight, Don Jackson, Jim Kepner and Harry Hay interviews with AJN. Kepner went to the first GLF meeting to report on it for *The Advocate* (the reporters in the early gay newspapers usually were activists as well), to find out, as he later put it (interview no. 2 with AJN), "what the Commies were doing." Both Kight and Kepner claimed they first suggested the Barney's Beanery protest; Jackson, whose memory seemed sharper than both, and who appeared unbiased on the question, remembered it being Kight.

37   Don Jackson and GLF: Kepner, Kight and Jackson interviews.

37   *Examiner* demonstration: *San Francisco Chronicle*, Oct. 31, 1969; *The Advocate*, vol. 4, no. 1 (January 1970); and Jackson interview, Nov. 3, 1994.

37   notice for the first GLF meeting: reprinted in the *Berkeley Barb*, Dec. 18, 1969, from the *Los Angeles Free Press*.

38   "Barney has a right. . . .": Ken Gaul, "Yesterday's Pioneer with Tomorrow's Vision," *Gay Newspaper of New York*, vol. 1, no. 14 (May 11, 1970).

38   Jackson letter to Dick Michaels: undated, but stamped "received" by *The Advocate* on Jan. 5, 1970, courtesy of L.A. Gay and Lesbian Archives.

38   Perry rally in downtown L.A.: "Rev. Perry Leads 200 in Protest Against Sex Laws," *The Advocate*, vol. 4, no. 1 (January 1970).

39   Held–Perry conversation: Troy Perry interview with JDC, Feb. 21, 1994.

39   Held's reaction to demonstrations at his restaurant: Irwin Held interview with AJN, Nov. 3, 1994.

39   the Barney's Beanery demonstration: *The Advocate*, vol. 4, nos. 4 and 5 (April and May 1970); Kight, Perry, Kepner and Don Kilhefner; and Douglas Key, *Gay Liberation News Roundup, Los Angeles Free Press*, Feb. 13, 1970.

39   Schrader designated spokesman for the demonstrators: Kight interview no. 9 with AJN, and Schrader interview with Robert Dallmeyer for 1989 IMRRU-KPKF Public Radio documentary on 1969 Gay Day celebration.

39   tore the signs off the wall: Held, in an interview in 1994, insisted he never took the signs down then, and did not until the West Hollywood City Council passed legislation ordering him to do so. However, accounts in *The Advocate* and *Los Angeles Free Press,* as well as interviews with four people there—Kight, Perry, Kilhefner and Kepner—all say he did take down the signs, no matter how briefly.

3: New York

40   prohibited the posting of leaflets: John O'Brien described the difficulty in interview nos. 2–4 with AJN.
40   the *Voice* refused to print the word "gay": Mike Brown, Mike Tallman and Leo Louis Martello, "The Summer of Gay Power and the *Village Voice* Exposed!" *Come Out!,* vol. 1, no. 1 (Nov. 14, 1969), pp. 10–11, courtesy of New York Gay and Lesbian Archives.
41   How different this is: O'Brien interviews.
41   "root evil of our society. . . .": Red Butterfly Cell position paper, Nov. 15, 1969, courtesy of Jerry Hoose personal papers.
41   Kohler and Marxist theory: Bob Kohler interview no. 1 with AJN.
41   "five foot four on the outside . . .": Martha Shelley interview no. 2 with AJN.
42   Fouratt growing up: his interviews with AJN. Reaction to Fouratt, particularly to his clothes, comes from numerous colleagues during this period, including Jerry Hoose, Bob Kohler, Pete Fisher, Marc Rubin and Mike Lavery, in interviews with AJN. In his interview with AJN, Fouratt himself bragged about his "big dick," suggesting that was the reason people were resentful of him.
42   Shelley growing up and losing her virginity: Shelley interview.
42   men found Shelley fearsome: Kohler interview.
42   But Shelley kept yelling: Shelley interview no. 1 with AJN.
43   Fouratt showed up in a dress: Hoose and Kohler interviews confirmed by Fouratt.
43   "Wearing a dress is a revolutionary act.": Nikos Diaman interview no. 3 with AJN.
43   Shelley challenged Kohler to slug it out: Kohler and Hoose interviews. Shelley didn't recall that incident, but found it completely consistent with her general memory of the time.
43   Lois Hart (who is dead), her background, style and feeling on cells: Hoose, Shelley, Fouratt and Kohler interviews; also her writings in *Come Out!* Her spirituality and drug use are from Ellen Shumsky interview with AJN, Feb. 11, 1994.
43   Lauritsen could barely contain his contempt: his interview with AJN, Dec. 18, 1993.
43   consciousness-raising sessions: Diaman interviews with AJN.
43   "It is not a technique for dilettantes.": Martha Shelley's paper "Gay Liberation Front, A Liberal Tea Party," undated, courtesy of Lesbian Herstory Archives.
44   "no single editor. . . .": *Come Out!* staff box in vol. 1, no. 2 (Jan. 10, 1970).
44   GLF dances: Hoose and Kohler interviews.
44   dancing in clubs: Shelley interviews with AJN and Marcus, and Ruth Simpson interview with AJN, April 9, 1994.
45   "Who wants to go to a bar . . . ?": Kathy Braun, "The Dance," *Come Out!,* vol. 1, no. 3 (April/May 1970), courtesy of New York Gay and Lesbian Archives.
45   little difference between the *Voice* and the *Daily News:* Brown et al., "The Summer of Gay Power," on *Village Voice* demonstration.
45   the *Voice* was changing the ad to omit the word "gay": ibid.
45   almost a hundred people turned up at the *Voice*'s offices: Lauritsen interview.
45   *Village Voice* demonstration and negotiation: "Lige and Jack," "New York Notes," *Los Angeles Advocate,* November 1969; Brown et al., "The Summer of Gay Power"; and Kohler and Hoose interviews.
46   "investigating why we are gay.": Kohler interview.
46   a drug dealer could reliably be found during GLF meetings: Kohler and Hoose interviews.

46   psychotic behavior: O'Brien interview no. 4. Description of O'Brien at back of room from Hoose and Kohler interviews.

46   Fouratt demanded to know what right they had to even be there.: Barbara Gittings/Kay Tobin interview with Eric Marcus, courtesy of Marcus.

46   Robinson-Owles relationship: principally Arthur Bell, *Dancing the Gay Lib Blues*, p. 16, and Arthur Evans interview nos. 1 and 2 with AJN; also Robinson and Owles interviews in Kay Tobin and Randy Wicker, *The Gay Crusaders* and John O'Brien and Arnie Kantrowitz interviews with AJN.

46   Owles's disenchantment with the GLF: his interview in Tobin and Wicker, *The Gay Crusaders.*

46   The GLF was crumbling: Evans interviews, and Bell, *Dancing the Gay Lib Blues,* a particularly valuable book of the time because Bell, who is dead, was involved in the early planning.

46   Fouratt and Shelley disrupted homophile conference in Philadelphia: Fouratt interview no. 2 with AJN.

47   calling Fouratt "Vinegar" and "Goldilocks": Austin Wade, report to Mattachine Society of New York, courtesy of Lesbian Herstory Archives.

47   Mattachine delegation report: "ERCHO Fall Meeting," *New York Mattachine Newsletter,* December 1969, pp. 16–17.

47   Robinson and Owles's decision to create a new group: Michael Lavery interview with AJN, Dec. 31, 1993; he was in the van with Robinson and Owles.

47   "I am so frustrated. . . .": Evans interview, no. 1.

4: Climbing the System

48   Evans in New York: Arthur Evans interview nos. 1 and 2 with AJN.

49   Evans and civil rights march and Freethinkers at Brown: Evans interview no. 1.

49   Evans's first GLF meeting: ibid.; and Arthur Bell, *Dancing the Gay Lib Blues.*

50   "hitting the system below the belt. . . .": 1970 Robinson interview with Breck Ardery for the 1970 commemorative record marking the first year of the gay liberation movement, "June 28, 1970 Gay and Proud: A Living History of the Homosexual Rights Movement."

50   "just an old Eugene McCarthy liberal": Jim Owles interview in Kay Tobin and Randy Wicker, *The Gay Crusaders.*

50   Evans's views that led to the creation of the GAA: Evans interviews.

50   "Everybody has his or her say. . . .": "The GAA Alternative," a discussion and explanation of GAA organizing precepts sent out to gay activists around the country, undated, unsigned, courtesy of Hal Offen papers.

51   analysis of GAA constitution: Evans, the author of the constitution, gave AJN a line-by-line analysis of the document.

51   Kohler's reaction to gay rights bill: Bob Kohler interview no. 1 with AJN.

51   Greitzer and GAA gay rights petitions: text of petition in *Gay*, vol. 1, no. 6 (Feb. 16, 1970).

51   Kohler had been wary of the GAA: Kohler interview no. 2 with AJN.

52   the political calculation behind gay rights bill: Evans interviews and Rich Wandel interview with AJN, Aug. 13, 1993.

52   nudge homosexuals out into the public: "Intro 475: What Really Happened?" *The Gay Activist* (GAA newsletter), vol. 1, no. 10 (March 1972).

52   Metropolitan Museum of Art confrontation: Evans interview no. 2; also *Gay*, vol. 1, no. 13 (May 4, 1970); Robinson interview in Tobin and Wicker, *The Gay Crusaders;* Bell, *Dancing the Gay Lib Blues,* pp. 50–53i; Arnie Kantrowitz interviews with AJN; Kantrowitz, *Under the Rainbow.*

52   "I've never heard. . . .": Tom Doerr in Tobin and Wicker, *The Gay Crusaders.*

52   Lindsay's executive order on entrapment: "No Public Complaints Reported Since NY

Gay Harassment Ended," *Los Angeles Advocate,* vol. 2, no. 7, (July 1968), p. 2. Dick Leitsch interview nos. 1 and 2 with AJN.

53   Lindsay claiming no prior knowledge of Stonewall: Lindsay letter to AJN, April 12,1994. Because of Lindsay's poor physical and mental health at the time of this correspondence, he might have forgotten any prior communication with the police department.

53   the Snake Pit raid: *Village Voice,* March 19, 1970; Craig Rodwell oral history at Columbia University; *Gay,* vol. 1, no. 10 (April 13, 1970); Bell, *Dancing the Gay Lib Blues,* pp. 39–47, particularly for information on Diego Vinales jumping (Bell interviewed him for *Gay Power* newspaper); and *New York Times,* March 9, 1970.

53   Attendance at GAA meetings surged: Kantrowitz interview nos. 1 and 2, and Vito Russo and Morty Manford interview with Eric Marcus, courtesy of Marcus.

53   Robinson vowed to never again waste time on introductions: interview in Tobin and Wicker, *The Gay Crusaders.*

53   disturbance at taping of Lindsay's TV show: Sandra Vaughn, "Lindsay & Homosexuals: An Edited Encounter," *Village Voice,* April 23, 1970; *Gay,* vol. 1, no. 14 (May 11, 1970); Evans interview; Bell, *Dancing the Gay Lib Blues.*

54   Lindsay quietly endorsing legislation barring on-the-job discrimination against homosexuals: *New York Times,* May 15, 1970.

54   petitions urging passage of a gay rights bill: Bell, *Dancing the Gay Lib Blues,* pp. 69–73.

54   "icy cold. . . .": ibid., p. 69.

54   GAA confrontation of Greitzer: *Gay,* vol. 1, no. 17 (June 1, 1970), courtesy of New York Gay and Lesbian Archives; Bell, *Dancing the Gay Lib Blues* (Bell was there as a member of GAA and reporting it for the newspaper *Gay Power*); Kantrowitz interview no. 2.

54   Greitzer capitulation: Kantrowitz interview nos. 1 and 2, and his book, *Over the Rainbow.*

55   GAA alerted reporters in advance of upcoming protests: Ron Gold interview no. 1 and Bruce Voeller interview no. 1 with AJN.

55   Geto urged Abrams to lobby for gay rights bill: Ethan Geto interview nos. 1 and 3 with AJN.

55   Geto sketched map of city hall: Cora Rivera/Perotta interview with AJN, June 22, 1994; and Hal Offen interview with AJN, Jan. 20, 1994; handcuffs anecdote from Rivera.

55   Lambda or other symbol for the GAA: Bell, *Dancing the Gay Lib Blues* and Kantrowitz interview no. 1.

56   "symbolizes a complete exchange. . . .": GAA leaflet, undated, Arthur Evans papers.

56   Doerr chose the Lambda: Evans interview no. 1 and Voeller interview no. 4 with AJN.

56   "it's too bland.": Evans interview no. 1.

56   no real consultation with the other members of the group: Koreen Phelps in interviews nos. 1–4 with JDC remembered no collaboration. In interviews nos. 1 and 2 with JDC, Robert Halfhill said there was no with him. McConnell said there was not in interview no. 3, and Jack Baker declined several requests to be interviewed for this history.

56   McConnell-Baker applied for a marriage license: Mike McConnell interview with JDC.

56   "Well, thank you for telling me.": ibid.

56   The county attorney refused to grant the license: Jack Star, "The Homosexual Couple," *Look,* Jan. 26, 1971, p. 69ff.

57   the furthest thing from their minds: Phelps and Halfhill interviews.

57   "a terrible thing. . . .": *Minneapolis Star,* July 10 and Aug. 5, 1970.

57   Judge Neville's ruling on hiring of McConnell: *Minneapolis Star,* Sept. 9, 1970; and *New York Times,* Sept. 20, 1970.

57   services at the 385-seat Encore Theater: Edward B. Fisk, "Homosexuals in Los Angeles, like Many Elsewhere, Want Religion and Establish Their Own Church," *New York Times,* Feb. 15, 1970, p. 58.

58   Kight–Perry discussions on first Stonewall parade: Morris Kight interviews with AJN and Troy Perry interview with JDC, Feb. 21, 1994.

58   Perry would make the case: ibid.

58   gloss over exactly what this parade was about: Perry interview.
58   L.A. gay leaders resented attention to New York: ibid.; Harry Hay interview with AJN, May 1, 1994; and Kight interviews.
59   Judge Schauer issued the permits: *The Advocate*, vol. 4, no. 10 (July 8–21, 1970).
59   train young homosexuals in activism: Kilhefner interview with AJN, June 1, 1994.
59   Kepner and letters from Gainesville and Billings: Jim Kepner interview nos. 1 and 2 with AJN.
60   Noblesville, Indiana, letter to Gay Liberation Front of Los Angeles: L.A. Gay and Lesbian International Archives.
60   "A waste of time. . . .": Kight interview no. 10.
60   levitation attempt on Rampart's police station: Kight interviews.
61   "It's his place": The Los Angeles *Advocate*, vol. 1, no. 2 (October 1967).
61   "touch-in": *GLF Newsletter*, vol. 1, no. 1, leaflets and documents, and Kilhefner interview.
61   owners of The Farm relented: for details of the agreement, "GLF Wins Touch Privileges at Bar," *The Advocate*, Oct. 28–Nov. 10, 1970, p. 5.
61   waiting nervously off Sixth Avenue: Craig Rodwell interview no.1 with AJN.
61   two hundred gay men and lesbians: Kantrowitz, John O'Brien, Jean DeVente and Mike Lavery interviews with AJN; also "Thousands of Homosexuals Hold a Protest Rally at Central Park," *New York Times*, June 29, 1970.
61   Kantrowitz reaction to the small turnout at march: Kantrowitz interview no. 1.
61   Kantrowitz-Robinson conversation at march: Kantrowitz, *Over the Rainbow.*
62   radical demands at ERCHO conference: *Come Out!*, vol. 1, no. 2 (Jan. 10, 1970); also Bob Martin, "ERCHO Meeting Adopts Radical Manifesto," *The Advocate*, vol. 4, no. 1 (January 1970), p. 23.
62   concern of older delegates: "ERCHO Fall Meeting," *New York Mattachine Newsletter*, December 1969, p. 16.
62   on choosing the name Christopher Street Liberation Day: Rodwell, whose roots were in the homophile movement, later insisted that he had chosen such an unrevealing name only because he couldn't decide whether to use the word "gay," "homosexual" or "queer." There was never any doubt about what it was about; even the *New York Times* called it "The Gay Liberation Day parade."
62   Hot dog story and Rodwell: Rodwell oral history.
62   "You'll get stoned. . . .": Bob Milne interview with AJN, May 17, 1994.
62   marshals trained by the Quakers: Bob Kohler, Jerry Hoose, DeVente and Rodwell interviews with AJN.
63   DeVente description of crowd reaction: DeVente interview no.1.
64   stood and cried: Kantrowitz, Rodwell and Lavery interviews; also editorial proclaiming the day in *Gay* newspaper, no. 23 (July 13, 1970).
64   1,165 people at West Hollywood gay march: Rob Cole, the *Advocate* news editor, in telephone interview with Ardery for his 1970 LP.
64   L.A. Gay Pride parade: *The Advocate*, vol. 4, no. 11 (July 22–Aug. 4, 1970).
64   Davis letter: May 23, 1975, to Sharon Cornelison, president of Christopher Street West Organization, courtesy of Lillene Fifield papers.
64   A whole school year: The first meeting, Tillotson said (in interview no. 2 with JDC), was at the MIT Student Center in October 1969, in a room he had gotten by claiming that it was for the "Foreign Students Association."
64   more liberal campuses: ibid. Also the *Liberation SHL News*, published by the Student Homophile League of Boston, vol. 1, no. 5 (April 4–10, 1970), courtesy of Stan Tillotson.
64   He asked five heterosexual friends: Tillotson interview nos. 2 and 3 with JDC; and Alex Makowski, "GA to Consider Gay Mixer," *The Tech*, Sept. 22, 1970, p. 1, courtesy of Tillotson.
65   big campuses: "World News," *Liberation SHL News*, vol. 1, no. 5.
65   He consulted with: Makowski, "GA to Consider Gay Mixer"; Drew Jaglom, "GA Stalls Vote on Gay Rights," *The Tech*, Sept. 22, 1970, p. 1; and "Nyhart Explains Stand on Gay Mixer Request," *The Tech*, Sept. 29, 1970, all courtesy of Tillotson.

65   "thousands of college students. . . .": *New York Times,* Dec. 15, 1971, p. A-1.
65   Reinhold and *Times* story on gays on college campuses: Robert Reinhold interview nos. 1 and 2 with JDC.
66   But when the time came: Drew Jaglom, "GA Takes Final Stand in SHL Mixer Debate," *The Tech,* Nov. 20, 1970, p.1; Duff McRoberts, "Dissolution Tops Agenda for Tonight's Meeting," *The Tech,* Dec. 1, 1970, p. 1; and "Chisolm Wins GA Approval: Assembly Grants $500 to Homophile League for Education," *The Tech,* Jan. 13, 1971, p. 1. All courtesy of Stan Tillotson.
66   reasons for Fidelifacts demonstration in New York: Ernest Peter Cohen, "A Gay Odyssey," a history of INTRO 475 (the fair gay employment bill), *The Gay Activist,* vol. 1, no. 10 (March 1972).
66   Fidelifacts demonstration ("walks like a duck"): Pete Fisher, "Fidelifacts: Sex-Snooping Agency Draws Fire," *Gay,* vol. 22, no. 44 (Feb. 15, 1971). Also Ruth Simpson interviews with Eric Marcus, courtesy of Marcus, and with AJN, April 9, 1994.
66   Epstein article: "Homo/Hetero: The Struggle for Sexual Identity," *Harper's* magazine, September 1970.
67   *Harper's* raid: Arthur Bell, *Dancing the Gay Lib Blues* pp. 131–33; Arthur Evans 1970 interview in Tobin and Wicker, *The Gay Crusaders;* Pete Fisher interview with AJN, Sept. 11, 1993, and O'Brien interview no. 3 with AJN; *Gay* newspaper accounts.
67   Decter-Evans exchange: Bell, *Dancing the Gay Lib Blues* p. 134; Evans in *The Gay Crusaders;* Fisher interview.
67   Board of Examiners zap: Arthur Bell, "The 'Bedroom Busybodies' Meet Alias Richie X: Gay Fair Employment Zap," *Village Voice,* April 22, 1971; also Wandel interview.
67   the Lindsays and Evans at *Two by Two:* Evans interview no. 2; Bell, *Dancing the Gay Lib Blues;* "Lindsay and Wife Zapped by Gay Activists. Mrs. Lindsay Obviously Shaken," *Gay,* no. 38 (Nov. 23, 1970). Mayor Lindsay, in correspondence with AJN of April 8, 1994, had no recollection of the event.
68   Owles was aloof and distant: Rivera/Perotta interview; also Breck Ardery interview with AJN, Oct. 9, 1993.
68   Owles's arrest at city hall: *The Gay Activist,* vol. 1, no. 4 (August 1971).
68   Talk of sado-masochism or fetishism made him uncomfortable: "Where the Action Is: An Interview with Jim Owles," *Gay,* no. 31 (Sept. 7, 1970). Kantrowitz spoke of Owles's similar discomfort with use of the word "faggot" at Owles's memorial service, Sept. 18, 1993.
68   Owles wearing his oversized jacket to shoplift: Evans interview no. 2.
68   Owles ran into the bathroom and began to sob after losing GAA election: Geto interview no. 1 with AJN, and Evans, interview no. 2.
68   Robinson bio material: Robinson interview in Tobin and Wicker, *The Gay Crusaders;* also Evans interview nos. 1 and 2.
69   Robinson's estrangement from his family over gayness/drugs: Evans interview no. 2; Evans said Robinson confided in him repeatedly on this score.
69   "a cat who would fly off the handle. . . .": Bell, *Dancing the Gay Lib Blues,* p. 14.
69   Robinson and speed: Sources are numerous, including Arthur Evans, who said he knew firsthand from Robinson, including how it led to alienation from his father, and how he shot it up; Kantrowitz, Allen Roskoff, Kohler, Hoose and Lavery interviews with AJN.
69   Robinson was bitter at being ignored and did not want a memorial service: Evans interview no. 2; Bill Bahlman (in interview no. 2 with AJN) discussed Robinson's intense bitterness in the last year of his life.

5: First Stirrings

70   "The Homosexual Couple": *Look* magazine, Jan. 26, 1971.
71   "I hate him. . . .": Robert Halfhill interview no. 1 with JDC.
71   Baker's campaign posters: Mike McConnell, Larry Bye, Halfhill and Steve Endean

interviews with JDC. The second poster is from a photograph in Kay Tobin and Randy Wicker, *The Gay Crusaders.*

71   "His posters were great.": Dennis Miller interview with JDC, Sept. 29, 1993.
71   "In Minneapolis, an admitted homosexual. . . .": Tobin and Wicker, *The Gay Crusaders*, pp. 135–57.
71   from twenty cities: *The Advocate*, no. 58 (April 28–May 11, 1971). "planned for and by gays": first Gay Liberation National Conference invitation letter, Feb. 21, 1971, signed "Love in Struggle, Austin Gay Liberation," courtesy of L.A. Archives.
72   saluting the Black Panthers: *Gay Flames: A Bulletin of the Homofire Movement*, no. 2 (Sept. 11, 1970), courtesy of Lesbian Herstory Archives.
72   no difference between the Black Panthers and the Nazi Party: Martha Shelley, "Subversion in the Women's Movement," *Come Out!*, vol. 1, no. 4 (June/July 1970), pp. 8–9.
72   "a straight man's trip. . . .": *Come Out!*, vol. 1, no. 5 (September/October 1970), p. 5.
72   "Get out of here, you freaks! . . .": "Gay Man in Philadelphia," *Come Out!*, vol. 1, no. 7 (December/January 1970).
72   "Open Letter to Jerry Rubin": Step May, "What's Wrong with Sucking," *Gay Flames Pamphlet No. 3*, undated, courtesy of Lesbian Herstory Archives.
72   GLF banner was ripped to shreds: Nikos Diaman interviews with AJN; *Come Out!*, vol. 1, no. 4 (June/July 1970).
73   "The march was so full of liberals. . . .": Earl Galvin, "Washington Moratorium: Three Views," *Come Out!*, vol. 1, no. 2 (Jan. 10, 1970).
73   "Homosexuality is part of the problem. . . .": Rob Cole, "The Leftists They Woo Call Them 'Faggot,' " *The Advocate*, vol. 4, no. 5 (Sept. 16–29, 1970).
73   Communist Party threatened: *Come Out!*, vol. 1, no. 5 (December 1970–January 1971).
73   The Austin conference: Fouratt, Arthur Evans and Dan Smith interviews with AJN; also *The Advocate*, no. 58 (April 28, 1971).
74   Fouratt would not let Evans take over: Jim Fouratt interview no. 3 with AJN.
74   "This convention was originally called. . . .": Evans's report to the GAA "concerning the national gay conference held in Austin, Texas," March 30, 1971, courtesy of Hal Offen papers.
74   Kight was shoved and doused with beer: *Gay*, vol. 1, no. 27 (Aug. 27, 1970), editorial and news story, p. 3; also *The Advocate*, vol. 4, no. 11 (July 22–Aug. 4, 1970).
74   FREE was forced by radicals: Erik Larsson, "Radicals Split Direction of Mid-Western Conference," *Gay*, vol. 1, no. 38 (Nov. 23, 1970), p. 12. Also Lars Bjornson, "Experts Frozen Out at FREE Convention," *The Advocate*, vol. 4, no. 19 (Nov. 11–24, 1970).
74   Wiemhoff became the subject of a divisive debate: Henry Wiemhoff interview no. 2 with AJN. For Chicago Gay Liberation split, see also Murray Edelman interview with AJN, Feb. 26, 1994.
74   "destruction of the nuclear family": "Lesbian Demands," *Come Out!*, vol. 1, no. 5 (September/October 1970), p. 16.
75   "we no longer want. . . .": Chicago Gay Liberation, "Working Paper for the Revolutionary People's Constitutional Convention," published as *Gay Flames Pamphlet No. 13*, courtesy of Lesbian Herstory Archives.
75   The L.A. GLF Statement of Purpose: courtesy of L.A. Gay and Lesbian Archives; and *Come Out!*, vol. 1, no. 3 (April/May 1970).
75   "It becomes more and more apparent. . . .": *The Advocate*, vol. 4, no. 16 (Sept. 30, 1970).
75   "If the Gay Liberation Movement founders. . . .": letter of Jan. 5, 1970, courtesy of L.A. Gay and Lesbian Archives.
75   "now that the revolution. . . .": *Gay*, no. 36 (Oct. 26, 1970).
75   "the endless involvement. . . .": Kameny interview with *The Gay Activist*, vol. 1, no. 3 (June 1971).
76   "The problem is that. . . .": Jim Fouratt, "Word Thoughts," *Come Out!*, vol. 1, no. 2 (Jan. 10, 1970). Quotes added.

76   "Why are we going . . . ?": Barbara Gittings interview no. 1 with JDC and interview with Eric Marcus, courtesy of Marcus.

76   banned marijuana: Mike Lavery, in interview with AJN, discussed the policy of "do your drugs before you arrive." Also Randy Wicker, "The Wicker Basket," *Gay,* vol. 2, no. 54 (May 26, 1971), p. 4.

76   "heaven's cross between Woodstock. . . .": Arthur Bell, *Village Voice,* July 1, 1971.

77   "Gay Power Challenges . . .": Randy Wicker, *Gay,* vol. 2, no. 53 (June 21, 1971).

77   dances became a huge source of income: GAA Lambda (its business organization) profit and loss statement, March 31 to Nov. 1, 1971, courtesy of Offen papers.

77   attention of the local police precinct: *The Gay Activist,* vol. 1, no. 3 (June 1971).

77   Owles spoke at the opening of the Firehouse: "Militant Homosexuals to Stage March on Central Park Today," *New York Times,* June 27, 1971.

77   the group's political agenda would be trampled: Arthur Evans interview no. 1 with AJN.

77   Robinson brooded: interview with Tobin and Wicker, *The Gay Crusaders.*

77   "all you people. . . .": Arthur Bell, *Dancing the Gay Lib Blues* p. 89.

77   Robinson and Evans were battling: Arnie Kantrowitz, *Over the Rainbow,* and Evans and Kantrowitz interviews with AJN.

78   a mural: Kantrowitz, *Over the Rainbow.*

78   resentment from the remnants of other homosexual rights groups: John O'Brien interviews with AJN, particularly no. 3.

78   "To charge that this campaign. . . .": Dick Leitsch, "The Snake Pit Raid: Some After-thoughts," *Gay,* vol. 1, no. 10 (April 13, 1970), p. 13.

78   The GAA responded: *Gay,* vol. 1, no. 12 (April 27, 1970).

78   HELP raid and *Advocate* editorial: *The Advocate,* no. 94 (Sept. 13, 1972).

78   Abzug took her campaign to the Continental Baths: Peter Ogren, "Bella at the Baths," *The Advocate,* no. 72 (July 5, 1972). Bella Abzug interview with AJN, Nov. 11, 1994, and her letter read at Jim Owles's memorial service, Sept. 18, 1993.

79   GAA and gubernatorial candidates: "Gay Activists Confront Politicos," Kay Tobin, *Gay,* vol. 1, no. 7 (March 1, 1970), p. 3.

79   transcript of Goldberg demonstration: from tape recording on Breck Ardery record marking the first year of the gay rights movement called "June 28, 1970 Gay and Proud. A Living History of the Homosexual Rights Movement." It has interviews and live tape of the standoff.

79   Goldberg's statement endorsing gay rights: Evans/Manford unpublished paper on zapping.

79   "I've got no problem. . . .": Ethan Geto interview no. 1 with AJN.

79   backlash against the GAA's brash tactics: story on bill's defeat, *New York Times,* Jan. 26, 1972.

79   "Lindsay is an honest man. . . .": Dick Leitsch, *Gay,* vol. 1, no. 16 (May 25, 1970), p. 144.

79   "We do not doubt. . . .": *Gay,* vol. 2, no. 34 (Sept. 28, 1970).

80   Owles responded to the *Gay* editorial: *Gay,* vol. 2, no. 40 (December 1970). Owles later noted, in an interview with Tobin and Wicker, in *The Gay Crusaders,* that some gay leaders were smitten with Lindsay.

81   "Many of the goals. . . .": "Veteran Warrior Sees Light at the End of the Tunnel," *The Advocate,* no. 68 (Sept. 1–28, 1971), p. 8 (Kight interview announcing the GLF's suspension).

82   "It would mean gay territory. . . .": text from *San Francisco Examiner and Chronicle,* Oct. 18, 1970.

82   Kight and Kilhefner issued press releases: Don Jackson interview with AJN, Nov. 3, 1994; also Kilhefner and Kight interviews with AJN and Troy Perry interview with JDC, Feb. 21, 1994.

82   The people of Alpine County: Dan Collins, "Gay Nationalism in the High Sierras," *Gay,* vol. 2, no. 39 (Dec. 7, 1970).

83   Gay Community Services Center: Betty Berzon interview with AJN, June 9, 1994, and unpublished paper on founding of center, courtesy of Berzon.

83   "like a neon billboard. . . .": Rand Schrader at Sheldon Andelson memorial service, January 1988.
84   The center even incorporated: Gay Community Services Center Article of Incorporation, Jan. 4, 1972, filed with Secretary of State Edmund G. Brown, Jr., courtesy of Betty Berzon papers.

6: Sisters and Brothers

85   Shumsky took in the scene: her interview with AJN, Feb. 11, 1994. Also Martha Shelley interview no. 1, Bob Kohler and Jerry Hoose interviews, and Barbara Love interview, Jan. 9, 1995, with AJN.
85   "Women were lost to each other. . . .": Ellen Shumsky, "Radicalesbians," original unedited draft, 1970, courtesy of Shumsky. Describes the birth of the Radicalesbians.
85   "The oppressive ambiance. . . .": Ellen Shumsky, undated leaflet for the Radicalesbians, courtesy of Shumsky.
86   "Mafia guardsmen at the door. . . .": Kathy Wakeham, *Come Out!*, vol. 1, no. 4 (June/July 1970).
86   Hoose exchanges with women about GLF dances: Hoose interview nos. 1 and 2.
86   "environment of women rapping. . . .": Shumsky interview.
86   women demanded half the revenue: Ellen Bedoz, "Afraid of What?," *Come Out!*, vol. 11, no. 5 (September/October 1970), p. 7. Ellen Shumsky was then known as Ellen Bedoz.
86   Hoose quit: Hoose interview.
87   "Come on. . . .": *The Advocate*, no. 30 (Jan. 30, 1974).
87   "What the hell . . . ?": Elaine Noble interview with JDC nos. 2 and 3.
87   goodbye statement of the last lesbian: Nancy Tucker interview nos. 1 and 2 with JDC. Her exit speech was also reported in the DOB *Ladder* of the time.
87   one of the most influential lesbians at the GLF: Rita Mae Brown, *A Plain Brown Rapper*, p. 93; also Ivy Bottini interview no. 3 and Love interview with AJN.
87   gay men were *less* sensitive to women: *The Advocate*, no. 142 (July 17, 1974). (Brown said, "Gay men don't understand the emotional body language of women.")
87   "Gender is a stronger behavior. . . .": Jeanne Cordova, "Lesbianism Redefined," *Los Angeles Free Press*, March 29, 1974.
88   Perotta would bristle: Rivera/Perotta interview with AJN, June 22, 1994.
88   Brown compared men calling each other Mary to blackface: Sasha Gregory, "Rita Mae Brown: Keeping Equilibrium Through Humor," *The Advocate*, no. 232 (Jan. 11, 1978, p. 37.
88   "I am, without doubt, . . .": Bob Kohler, "Right On," *Come Out!*, vol. 1, no. 3 (April/May 1970), p. 5.
88   preached against cruising: Perry Bass, "Games Male Chauvinists Play," *Come Out!*, vol. 1., no. 5 (September/October 1970).
88   a man's deep voice: Rivera/Perotta interview. This theme is repeated in many other interviews, including with Shelley and Shumsky.
88   Kohler was chastised for holding the door open: Kohler interview no. 1.
88   "no man is free until. . . .": Bob Kohler, *Come Out!*, vol. 1, no. 2 (Jan. 10, 1970), p. 16 (italics added). Bob Kohler confirmed, in an interview with AJN, that the line "looking for male chauvinism, Bob?" was added by Lois Hart, one of the women putting out *Come Out!*
88   Cordova would interrupt Kight: Cordova interview no. 2 with AJN.
88   "Stand TALL and PROUD, *girls*": *DOB-LA Newsletter*, January 1971, with italics added, courtesy of L.A. Gay and Lesbian International Archives.
89   "a dumb redneck": Rita Mae Brown interview no. 1 with AJN.
89   Brown at her first NOW meeting: Bottini interview no. 3; also Love interview. "I'm your token lesbian.": Brown, *A Plain Brown Rapper*, pp. 86–88.
89   "dreary until death": Brown interview nos. 1 and 2 with AJN.

89   encounter groups: Brown, *A Plain Brown Rapper,* p. 94.

89   "Once a woman becomes clued in. . . .": Rita Mae Brown, "Those Little Things You Notice. . . ," *The Advocate,* July 17, 1974.

90   "Funny people are dangerous. . . .": Judy Klemesrud, "It's Hard to Hate People When They're Funny," *New York Times,* Oct. 13, 1977, reprinted as "Growing Up Gay—and Happy," *San Francisco Chronicle.* Profile of Rita Mae Brown.

90   LAVENDER MENACE demonstration: Shelley, Love and Ginny Vida interviews with AJN; also Sidney Abbott and Barbara Love, *Sappho Was a Right-on Woman;* "Lavender Menace Strikes," *Come Out!,* vol. 1, no. 4 (June/July 1970), p. 14; Toby Marotta, *The Politics of Homosexuality,* pp. 248–49; photograph of event taken by Ellen Shumsky, courtesy of New York Public Library exhibit, Summer 1994.

90   statement of LAVENDER MENACE women from stage: Marotta, *The Politics of Homosexuality.* There was no identification of which women said that, but photos from the time, and interviews with Martha Shelley, suggest it was Shelley.

90   "I know what these women. . . .": Abbott and Love, *Sappho Was a Right-on Woman,* p. 114.

90   irresistible force, with a sexual charge: Cordova interview no. 2 and Ivy Bottini interview no. 3.

90   Shelley had suggested that the women draft a paper: Abbott and Love, *Sappho Was a Right-on Woman,* p. 113.

91   preparation of "The Woman-Identified-Woman": Shumsky, Love and Brown interviews. Brown said the final document was put together by four women, with March Hoffman actually assembling it.

91   "What is a lesbian?": Radicalesbians, "The Woman-Identified-Woman," May 1, 1970.

92   "We are against hierarchical structures. . . .": Ellen Bedoz, "Radicalesbians," *Come Out!,* December 1970.

92   flier attacking Millett: Marotta, *The Politics of Homosexuality,* p. 248. Details of meeting at which she was attacked and the book party from Love interview.

92   Rolling Stones were a sexist band: Rivera/Perotta interview.

92   mistake for the women to try to separate: Shelley interview.

92   Wiemhoff, Tosswill and Dr. Socarides at AMA convention in Chicago: Henry Wiemhoff interview no. 2 with AJN.

93   Brown's visits to two New York bathhouses dressed as a man: Brown interview no. 2.

93   Washington bathhouse night for women: Mary Spottswood Pou interview no. 2 with JDC and Brown interviews.

93   considered promiscuity a badge of honor: Troy Perry interview, Feb. 21, 1994, and Steve Endean interview with JDC; Allen Roskoff, Arnie Kantrowitz, Bruce Voeller and Arthur Evans interviews with AJN.

94   the "cock-a-pillar" at the L.A. parade and reaction: *The Advocate,* no. 64 (July 21–Aug. 3, 1971); and Don Kilhefner and Morris Kight interviews with AJN; "Schism Splits California Parade Makers," *Gay,* vol. 3, no. 78 (June 12, 1972).

94   "As far as I know. . . .": "Long Well-rounded Entry Clouds Parade Aftermath," *The Advocate,* no. 64 (July 21–Aug. 3, 1971), p. 4.

95   "exploited as sex objects. . . .": Redstockings Manifesto, July 7, 1969, courtesy of Lesbian Herstory Archives.

95   "Goodbye my alienated brothers. . . .": "Female Gay Blasts Men, Leaves Movement," *The Advocate,* vol. 4, no. 18 (Oct. 28–Nov. 10, 1970), p. 21.

96   The NOW demonstrations: Toni Carabillo, Judith Meuli and June Bundy Csida, *Feminist Chronicles: 1953–1993,* p. 57.

96   "Gay women today are identifying. . . .": Rob Cole, "Collision in San Francisco: Old, New Ideas Tangle at NACHO Conference," *The Advocate,* Sept. 30–Oct. 13, 1970.

96   "anti-male hostility": Jim Bradford of Mattachine Midwest, letter to the editor, *The Advocate,* no. 54 (March 3–16, 1971).

97   Bottini's early history and joining NOW: Bottini interview nos. 1–3 with AJN.

98   NOW Statue of Liberty action: Bottini interview no. 1, and Carabillo, Meuli and Csida, *Feminist Chronicles*.

98   Bottini on lesbian circle in NOW: Bottini interview no. 3.

98   Friedan feared that lesbianism was discrediting the women's movement: Abbott and Love, *Sappho Was a Right-on Woman*, p. 112.

98   Friedan and the CIA: Elaine Noble interviews nos. 2 and 3 with JDC; also Klemesrud, "It's Hard to Hate People When They're Funny."

98   Brown's resignation letter from NOW: *New York NOW* (newsletter), January 1970, cited in Marotta, *The Politics of Homosexuality* pp. 234–35.

98   Shelley had to shove her way onto the platform of a women's rally: Shelley interviews with AJN and with Eric Marcus.

98   "We're your sisters. . . .": *New York Times,* Dec. 18, 1970.

99   "The Politics of Sex": "Who's Come a Long Way, Baby?" *Time,* Aug. 31, 1970.

99   marriage of Millett and Fumio Yoshimura: "The Liberation of Kate Millett," *Time,* Aug. 31, 1970, pp. 18–19.

99   "Women's Lib: A Second Look": *Time,* Dec. 14, 1970, p. 50; for details on exchange at Columbia University, "The Lesbian Issue and Women's Lib," *New York Times,* Dec. 18, 1970; Carabillo, Meuli and Csida, *Feminist Chronicles,* p. 57, and Abbott and Love, *Sappho Was a Right-on Woman,* pp. 119–20.

99   Millett response to story on lesbianism: Love and Bottini interviews; also Carabillo, Meuli and Csida, *Feminist Chronicles,* p. 57; *New York Times,* Dec. 18, 1970; "Kate Millett: Picked Out of Happy Obscurity," *The Advocate,* no. 223 (Sept. 7, 1977), p. 13.

99   women's press conference in response to *Time:* Love interview and Judy Klemesrud, "The Lesbian Issue and Women's Lib," *New York Times,* Dec. 18, 1970.

99   "Women's Liberation and homosexual liberation. . . ." and "'Lesbian' is a label. . . .": *New York Times,* Dec. 18, 1970.

99   Hernandez deploring *Time*'s "sexual McCarthyism": Carabillo, Meuli and Csida, *Feminist Chronicles*.

100   discourage NOW women from attending and "a terrible mistake. . . .": Judy Klemesrud, "The Disciples of Sappho, Updated," *New York Times Magazine,* March 28, 1971.

100   mainstream issues of NOW: "Bill of Rights for Women," passed in November 1967 at second national conference of NOW; see Carabillo, Meuli and Csida, *Feminist Chronicles,* p. 50.

100   Bottini had not been open about her own lesbianism: Abbott and Love in their book *Sappho Was a Right-on Woman,* published in 1972 and from which some of the details of the purging meeting are taken, describe Bottini only as "a New York chairwoman of NOW," and never directly say she is a lesbian. Love, in an interview, acknowledged that the woman in question was Ivy Bottini.

100   in NOW's interest to embrace the lesbianism movement: Bottini interview no. 1.

100   "been carried on the backs of lesbians. . . .": quoted in Marotta, *The Politics of Homosexuality,* p. 259 fn.

100   Bottini's and Friedan's remarks at Gracie Mansion after march: Abbott and Love, *Sappho Was a Right-on Woman,* pp. 121–22.

101   Friedan cast her armband: Bottini interview no. 1 and Love interview.

101   Friedan cab ride with Bottini: Bottini interview no. 1.

101   Love called with the urgent advice that she round up supporters: Love interview.

101   "hard hats in white gloves": attributed by Abbott and Love in *Sappho Was a Right-on Woman,* p. 127 to a woman who complained to NOW national officials about the purge.

101   "The house has been cleaned. . . .": Carol Turner, "On and About Lesbian Purges," *Now and Then,* Feb. 12, 1971; Abbott and Love, quoted in *Sappho Was a Right-on Woman,* p. 128. *Now and Then* was a publication for NOW dissidents.

101   Bottini's last NOW meeting: Bottini interview nos. 1 and 3.

102   "This had to happen. . . .": quoted in Abbott and Love, *Sappho Was a Right-on Woman,* p. 130.

102   Lyon/Martin and NOW meeting in L.A.: Lyon/Martin interview no. 2 with JDC.

102   Brown's move to Washington: Brown interview no. 1.

102   Bunch's background: Charlotte Bunch interview nos. 1 and 2 with AJN.

102   Brown's seduction of Bunch: Bunch interview no. 1.

103   "Heterosexuality as an institution. . . .": Bunch speech describing the creation of The Furies to the Socialist Feminist Conference, Antioch College, Yellow Springs, Ohio, July 5, 1975.

104   "to develop a lesbian feminist politics. . . .": ibid.

104   "The Furies" name: *The Furies*, vol. 1, no. 1 (January 1972).

104   "We call our paper *The Furies*. . . .": Ginny Berson, ibid.

104   the women in The Furies: ibid.; Brown, *A Plain Brown Rapper;* and Ginny Z. Berson, "The Furies, Goddesses of Vengeance," *Serials Review,* Winter 1990.

104   steps to level the economic class differences, and auto and home repair classes: Bunch interview no. 1; also *San Francisco Chronicle,* profile of Rita Mae Brown, Oct. 16, 1977. For their graduated income tax system, "Details," *The Furies*, vol. 1, no. 5 (June/July 1972).

105   "Our self-righteousness. . . .": Brown, *A Plain Brown Rapper,* p. 14.

105   ridiculing the notion of "man-hating": Rita Mae Brown, "Women Who Love Men Hate Them; Male Supremacy Versus Sexism," *The Furies*, vol. 1, no. 7 (Fall 1972), p. 15.

PART TWO: A PLACE AT THE TABLE

7: Kameny for Congress

109   rented for $100 a year: Washington Mattachine balance statements for January–June 1970 and 1971, courtesy of Dr. Lilli Vincenz.

109   shrunk to ten or twelve people: Paul Kuntzler interview no. 5 and Nancy Tucker interview no. 2 with JDC.

110   the room behind the furnace: Tucker interview no. 1 with JDC.

110   the occasional social gatherings were predictably well behaved: Dr. Lilli Vincenz interview no. 2 with JDC.

110   Hoffard, his career and meeting Kuntzler at the dance: Kuntzler interview nos. 1 and 3 with JDC; photograph of Hoffard in Kuntzler's study; and his obituary in the *Washington Post,* Dec. 1, 1977, p. B-14. Hoffard died at forty-five, apparently of a heart attack, in November 1977.

110   political history of Washington, D.C.: Frank Kameny, Kuntzler, D.C. counsel Tom Bastow and other interviews with JDC; campaign coverage researched in the *Washington Post* and *Evening Star.* The dates, specific details and quotations are from Harry S. Jaffe and Tom Sherwood, *Dream City: Race, Power, and the Decline of Washington, D.C.,* except in one or two cases where other sources seem more reliable.

111   moribund Washington Mattachine: Kuntzler interview nos. 1 and 3, Tucker interview no. 1; also Kameny interview nos. 1, 2 and 4.

111   Phillips was anti-gay: Kuntzler interview nos. 1 and 3.

111   Democrats outnumbering Republicans in the District: *Dream City,* p. 96.

111   *Washington Post* might refuse to accept an advertisement or notice: It was still common practice for major metropolitan newspapers to refuse to accept such ads at the time, and this was one of the arguments used in Kameny's leaflets to try to rally the gay community to the campaign. From campaign leaflet, courtesy of Dr. Lilli Vincenz.

112   Hoffard saw just how it would work and selection of Kameny to run for Congress: Kuntzler interview nos. 1–3 and Cliff Witt interview no. 1 with JDC.

112   Kameny had been arrested: Kameny interview no. 7, Kuntzler interview no. 4. Kuntzler recalled Kameny's telling the story in Mattachine circles. The arrest is mentioned without detail by John D'Emilio in *Sexual Politics, Sexual Communities.*

112   homosexuals a threat to national security: *Employment of Homosexuals and Other Sex Perverts in Government,* interim report submitted to the Committee on Expenditures in the Executive Departments by the Subcommittee on Investigations pursuant to Senate resolution 280 in the 81st Congress, Dec. 15, 1950.

113   believed to have monitored Mattachine meetings: Bill Donovan interview with JDC, April 10, 1995; and Kameny interview no. 1, in which he recounted the attendance of Washington morals squad officer at initial meeting of Mattachine.

113   made him unemployable: Kameny said he could never get another job in astronomy after his firing. His arrest record, he said, was expunged at his request when such arrests "for investigation" were held to have been illegal. Kameny interview nos. 1 and 7.

113   sent the Mattachine newsletter: Kameny interview no. 1.

114   "If society and I differ on something. . . .": Kameny in Kay Tobin and Randy Wicker, *The Gay Crusaders,* p. 89.

114   Kameny treated *everyone* with equal disdain and the membership generally put up with it: Tony Jackubosky interview with JDC, April 18, 1995; Vincenz and Tucker interviews.

114   At brunch the day after the dance: Kuntzler interview nos. 3 and 5.

114   The police pressure had begun to relax: Kameny, in an article comparing police practices in New York and Washington, D.C., in the Spring 1966 issue of *Res Ipsa Loquitur,* the Georgetown University Law Center journal, noted that the police did not "harass" gay bars in Washington, that dancing and even kissing inside were permitted, that the police had begun using more uniformed officers instead of plainclothesmen in the parks, and that arrests for solicitation in the previous year were down by 50 percent.

114   "Homosexual Revolution": Nancy L. Ross, *Washington Post,* Oct. 25, 1969, p. C-1.

115   Pier Nine: *Gay Blade,* vol. 1, no. 8 (May 1970).

115   the Guild Press and the Potomac News Company: Kuntzler interview nos. 2 and 4.

115   the *Blade*'s first issue: reprinted in the October 18, 1984, anniversary issue of the *Washington Blade,* courtesy of Dr. Lilli Vincenz.

115   why gay bars agreed to carry the *Gay Blade:* Tucker interviews.

116   campaign for Kameny: various Kameny, Kuntzler, Witt, Tucker, Dr. Vincenz and Richard Maulsby interviews with JDC.

116   only two were women: Dr. Lilli Vincenz's copy of the campaign telephone list, courtesy of Dr. Vincenz.

116   Hoffard's and Livingston's roles: Kuntzler interview no. 1; and the Mattachine telephone list and money from the Mattachine chapter statement prepared by Treasurer Otto Ulrich for January–June 1971, courtesy of Dr. Lilli Vincenz.

117   "Fairness for Homosexuals": *Washington Post* editorial page, Feb. 2, 1971.

117   "Dr. Frank Kameny, a well-known campaigner. . . .": Kameny news release and candidate statement, from original copies, courtesy of Dr. Lilli Vincenz.

118   "A new candidate swished. . . .": Kuntzler interview no. 1.

118   probably not a good idea to tell people they asked to sign Kameny's petition that he was a homosexual: Kuntzler interview no. 4, Dr. Vincenz interview, and Witt interview no. 1.

118   Marching orders: "Kameny for Congress, Guide for Petition Circulators," courtesy of Dr. Lilli Vincenz.

118   The flier they handed to voters: "!!! Let Another Good Man Be Heard!!!," courtesy of Dr. Lilli Vincenz.

118   "With Kameny on the ballot. . . .": "WE NEED YOU," courtesy of Dr. Lilli Vincenz.

119   Mattachine members few and shy: Kameny, Kuntzler, Witt, Tucker and Vincenz interviews.

119   New York's GAA role in Kameny campaign in D.C.: Paul Kuntzler and Cliff Witt, who acted as manager and assistant manager of the Kameny campaign, respectively, both remembered the GAA members coming down twice to gather signatures. Witt also recalled their coming to help with the leafletting during the campaign itself. Kuntzler recalled one bus each time.

Kameny spoke of two busloads. Witt remembered three or four, and his memory is more specific. Kuntzler interview nos. 1 and 2, Kameny interview no. 1, and Witt interview no. 1.

119   Troy Perry arrived in Washington: *Washington Post*, Feb. 15, 1971, p. A-26.

119   Hoffard watching from behind a tree: several Kuntzler interviews, including no. 4, and Witt interview no. 1.

120   David Harris and the Regency Baths: Kuntzler interview no. 4, Witt interview no. 1 and David Harris interview with JDC, April 7, 1995. Harris talked briefly about the baths, the police raids and collecting signatures for the campaign, but said he had left the business more than ten years ago and preferred not to be interviewed more about a time he remembered as painful, full of conflicts with the police and other difficulties.

120   Kuntzler paid $400 or $500: Kuntzler interview nos. 1, 3 and 4.

120   "This will place me on the ballot. . . .": campaign news release "FOR RELEASE 11am Monday, Feb. 22—KAMENY SERVES NOTICE," courtesy of Dr. Lilli Vincenz.

121   the most exhausting schedule: Kameny interview no. 1.

121   said nothing about homosexuality: prepared statements from which he spoke at those events, courtesy of Dr. Lilli Vincenz.

121   "the Neanderthals who make up the State Department. . . .": news release issued by the Kameny campaign, courtesy of Dr. Lilli Vincenz. It was Kameny who had first made an issue of the Defense Department ban on homosexuals serving in the military.

121   attacked the District's sodomy and solicitation laws: from speech delivered outside the District Building after a requested meeting with the Police Administration, Tuesday, March 16, 1971, from the Kameny campaign news release giving prepared remarks, courtesy of Dr. Lilli Vincenz.

122   The *Washington Post* led with Kameny: Joseph D. Whitaker, "Candidates Aim Talks at Women," *Washington Post*, March 14, 1971, p. B-1.

122   Fauntroy added something to his speech about gay rights: Witt interview no. 1.

122   about Womack, the pornographer: Kuntzler interview no. 5, Tucker interview no. 2, Witt interview no. 1 and James Lardner, "The Sex Industry: A Pornographer's Rise, Fall," *Washington Post*, Jan. 12, 1978, p. A-1.

122   Supreme Court had overturned Womack's obscenity conviction: "High Court Upsets Ban by Post Office in Obscenity Case," June 26, 1962; "Womack Arrested Again as Obscenity Publisher," April 25, 1970; "Publisher Is Convicted in D.C. Obscenity Trial," July 23, 1971, and "The Sex Industry: A Pornographer's Rise, Fall," Jan. 12, 1978; all from *Washington Post*.

122   Kameny's fliers and posters: Kuntzler interview no. 4 and posters on Kuntzler's library walls. Pink and green cards courtesy of Dr. Lilli Vincenz.

123   Campaign contributions: Kuntzler interview nos. 1 and 2, and Jackubosky interview.

123   Kameny's letter for Nixon: *Washington Post*, March 21, 1971, p. D-1.

123   Kameny received about 1,841 votes: *Washington Post* election story, March 24, 1971, p. A-1.

124   Kameny didn't go to New York: Kuntzler interview nos. 1 and 2.

8: A Voice in the Statehouse

125   Shively's background: Charley Shively interview no. 1 with JDC.

126   Shively had appeared before the DNC in a dress: *Boston Gay Line*, vol. 3, no. 2 (March/April 1973); Shively interview no. 3 and Larry Anderson interview no. 2 with JDC.

126   "Cocksucking as an Act of Revolution": Shively, *Fag Rag*, vol. 1, no. 1, courtesy of Charley Shively.

126   Boston lesbians and gay men and Father Paul Shanley: *Gay Community Newsletter*, vol. 1, no. 1 (June 17, 1973).

126   *Gay Way* radio show reach: Bonnie Cronin, Elaine Noble and other interviews with JDC.

126   "Gay People and the Law": Laura McMurry interview no. 1 with JDC and flier for "Gay Pride Week '72, June 17–25," courtesy of McMurry.

127   Frank introduction at meeting: McMurry interviews, Barney Frank interview, June 7, 1994, and Noble interview nos. 2–4 with JDC.

127   Frank wouldn't have told them the truth about himself: Frank interview.

127   Frank and Lewis growing up: ibid. and Ann Lewis interview with JDC, Sept. 18, 1993.

127   White won the election and hired Frank: Frank interview. Also Dudley Clendinen, "Profile in Politics: Boston Mayor's Reformist Style Faded with His Fortunes," *New York Times*, Dec. 30, 1982, A section.

128   Lewis went to Boston: Lewis interview.

128   organizing the National Women's Political Caucus: ibid. and Toni Carabillo, Judith Meuli and June Bundy Csida, *Feminist Chronicles: 1953–1993*, p. 59.

128   established a Massachusetts chapter of the caucus: Lewis interview.

128   Noble was elected co-chair of caucus: DOB *Focus;* Lewis, Noble and McMurry interviews. Noble said one hundred or two hundred lesbians. McMurry reported about ten from DOB in *Focus.*

128   Ward 5: Lewis and Frank interviews.

128   Noble was the best-known lesbian personality in Boston: Lewis, Cronin, Noble, Ann Maguire, Lois Johnson, Sheri Barden and other interviews with JDC.

128   how Frank got to the meeting: Frank and Lewis interviews, Noble interview nos. 2–4 and McMurry interview no. 1.

129   Frank's early history as gay: Frank interview.

129   Noble wanted Frank's support: ibid. and Noble interview nos. 1–3.

130   Frank marching in the Gay Pride Parade: Frank interview.

130   Boston GRA candidate questionnaire: *Focus;* also McMurry interview.

130   "What do you think you're doing? . . .": McMurry interview no. 1.

130   Frank had an easier time of it: As it turned out, in New Bedford, Massachusetts, on the South Shore and on Cape Cod, in the Twelfth Congressional District that fall, another hard-working bachelor Democrat and anti-war activist, former teacher Gerry E. Studds, who was also gay but would not say so, won a seat in the U.S. House of Representatives.

130   "Who's that guy . . . ?": Frank interview.

131   "I'll get this one": Lewis interview.

131   Frank's first gay rights hearing: Frank and McMurry interviews; also *Focus,* March 1973, and Shively interview no. 3.

131   "You know, I think this is the first time in my life. . . .": Cronin interview with JDC, Aug. 4, 1995.

9: The Fifth Column

132   Foster at the DNC: *The Advocate,* no. 91 (Aug. 2, 1972). For other details on the scene there, on Foster's personal history and his thinking that night, see Randy Shilts, *The Mayor of Castro Street,* pp. 63–65; *Conduct Unbecoming,* pp. 166–167, 169–170; and *And the Band Played On,* p. 278. Shilts conducted extensive interviews of the late Jim Foster for his books, and covered Foster for *The Advocate* at the time.

133   "Nobody in their right mind. . . .": quoted in Shilts, *The Mayor of Castro Street,* p. 63.

133   McGovern's five-point edge: *Presidential Elections Since 1789,* 5th ed. *Congressional Quarterly,* c. 1991.

133   history of fight over gay rights plank: John Herbers in *New York Times:* "Democrats Agree on Unity Planks but Fight Looms," June 26, 1972, p. 1; "Democrats Assured of a Platform Fight," June 28, 1972; and "McGovern Forces Shape Planks to Suit Candidate," July 13, 1972, p. 1. Also Guy Charles, "Democratic Convention Debate Due," *The Advocate,* no. 90 (July 19, 1972).

133   text of Foster speech: transcript courtesy of L.A. International Gay and Lesbian

Archives; description of his speaking style from Shilts, *The Mayor of Castro Street,* pp. 64–65; and *Conduct Unbecoming,* pp. 166–67.

133   chatter from the delegates: Troy Perry interview with JDC, Feb. 21, 1994; Barbara Love and Morris Kight interviews with AJN.

134   Perry wept: Perry interview.

134   "It was downright patronizing. . . .": Kight interview no. 9.

135   text of Wilch's speech to the delegates: *The Advocate,* no. 91 (Aug. 2, 1972).

135   "No! No! No!": ibid.

135   a gay man's frustration at convention: Love and Nath Rockhill interviews with AJN.

135   a tiny lifeboat: Rockhill interview no. 2.

136   the hostile delegate reaction: Love and Perry interviews. Love felt suffocated by defeat: interview with AJN, Jan. 9, 1995. "All we want. . . .": Perry interview.

136   the United Methodist Church: Kight interview nos. 7 and 9.

136   nearly two hundred gay activists represented eighty-six homosexual rights organizations: There is a conflict between the *Gay* and *Advocate* accounts, but *The Advocate*—which said two hundred people and eighty-six groups—is closer to contemporaneous recollection of attendees, among them Kight, William Kelley, Rich Wandel and Frank Kameny.

136   Abney and logistical details of meeting in Chicago: Morty Manford, "Gay American Plans for '72 Election," *Gay,* vol. 3, no. 72 (March 6, 1972).

136   Fouratt challenged group about the lack of minorities: Rich Wandel e-mail to AJN, Dec. 14, 1994.

137   rumors that Fouratt was an agent: ibid. and repeated in stronger forms in a number of interviews; for example, Steve Endean with JDC and Bill Kelley with AJN. Fouratt (in interview no. 3 with AJN) had few memories of the Chicago conference (and repeatedly denied the rumors that he was some sort of agent).

137   a "very destructive" meeting: Endean interview no. 5.

138   "I see no reason. . . .": *Gay,* vol. 3, no. 73 (April 3, 1972).

138   "This is no laughing matter. . . .": quoted in *The Advocate,* no. 80 (March 1, 1972).

138   results on GAA questionnaire to presidential candidates: *GAA Newsletter,* no. 11 (April 1972).

139   "Since Lindsay has not lived up. . . .": leaflet courtesy of Marty Robinson papers.

139   "We are going to trash. . . .": "Intro 475 May Dog Lindsay Campaign," *The Advocate,* no. 78 (Feb. 2, 1972), p. 1.

139   Lindsay letter to Voeller: *Gay,* vol. 3, no. 73 (April 3, 1972).

140   "No matter what the more conservative elements. . . .": ibid.

140   Geto's involvement in McGovern's New York campaign: This entire section, including his involvement with McGovern and Abrams, his reaction to Kathleen Wilch and what went on in McGovern headquarters is based on Ethan Geto interview no. 3 with AJN.

141   McGovern had no idea that Geto was a homosexual: George McGovern interview with AJN, March 3, 1995.

141   oblique reference to Geto: Guy Charles, "Not His Fault," Lindsay Tells *Advocate," The Advocate* no. 80 (March 1, 1972).

141   "It is entirely possible. . . .": "Democratic Convention," *The Advocate,* no. 90 (July 19, 1972).

142   text of Kathleen A. Wilch apology of July 13, 1972: courtesy of L.A. International Gay and Lesbian Archives.

142   "We are shocked. . . .": *The Advocate,* no. 90 (July 19, 1972).

142   New Jersey Gay Political Caucus: "Activists Suspend McGovern Support," *Gay,* vol. 3, no. 84 (Sept. 4, 1972), p. 3.

143   Endean on McGovern protest: Endean interview no. 3.

143   the issue of homosexuality never came up: McGovern interview. His account is credible, though there is one newspaper account of a reporter from an Oregon gay newspaper asking him about homosexuality at an event in late October.

143   "What the hell . . . ?": Frank Mankiewicz interview with AJN, March 21, 1995.

143   McGovern expressing sympathy to the homosexual demonstrators: Geto interview no. 3. McGovern, in his interview, had no recollection of discussion about homosexuality in his campaign.

144   the GAA raid on McGovern HQ: "GAA Occupies NY McGovern Office for Five Hours," *The Advocate,* no. 94 (Sept. 13, 1972); John LeRoy, "Activists Invade McGovern Hq.," *Gay,* vol. 3, no. 85 (Sept. 18, 1972), p. 1; "Gay Activists in Protest Occupy McGovern Office," *New York Times,* Aug. 22, 1972.

145   Offen on Geto/Roskoff: Hal Offen interview with AJN, Jan. 20, 1994.

145   Roskoff/Geto were inseparable at Firehouse, gay bars and bathhouses: Allen Roskoff interview no. 1 with AJN.

145   McGovern's senior advisers joking about the "prancing" homosexuals: Mankiewicz and Geto interviews.

145   GAA takeover plans: Geto referred to himself as a "fifth columnist" in interview nos. 1 and 3 with AJN on the takeover; other details on what Geto did and thought are from these interviews.

146   "Say something to show we're sympathetic. . . .": Mankiewicz interview.

146   gay efforts at RNC: Morty Manford, "Republicans Avoid Gay Issues: Ridicule Democrats for Involvement," *Gay,* vol. 3, no. 86 (Oct. 2, 1972), p. 3.

146   "We didn't consider it . . .": *The Advocate,* no. 94 (Sept. 13, 1972).

146   "cunning and vicious. . . .": *"Gay* Raps with the Stonewall Nation's Madeline Davis," *Gay,* vol. 4, no. 98 (March 26, 1973), p. 6.

10: San Francisco: Coming to Power

148   Ritch Street Baths: Rick Stokes interview nos. 3 and 4 with JDC.

149   Stokes had quit his job teaching: Stokes interview no. 4.

149   about David Clayton, and Stokes's reasons for going to law school: Stokes interview nos. 1, 2 and 4 with JDC.

149   Stokes had been at or near the center: Stokes interview; also Herbert Donaldson, William Plath, Phyllis Lyon and Del Martin, Larry Littlejohn and Donald Lucas interviews with JDC.

150   description of Stokes: Stokes, Harry Britt and others in San Francisco interviews with JDC, and pictures of him at the time in the *San Francisco Chronicle.*

150   "Gay Is Good" sermon: Herbert Donaldson interview with JDC, Oct. 6, 1996. He was there.

150   Stokes had become president of the Council on Religion and the Homosexual: "Homosexuals Elected by S. F. Family Service," *San Francisco Chronicle,* Jan. 27, 1971.

150   Stokes's law practice: Stokes interview no 4.

150   Police would rather that gay men have sex with each other in the privacy of the Ritch Street Baths than in places like the city's parks: Stokes said that people wondered if he paid the police off to keep them out of the baths. Stokes interview no. 3.

151   Tavern Guild: Jerry Carroll, "S. F. Homosexuals' Political Machine," *San Francisco Chronicle,* Oct. 13, 1971, p. A-1.

151   Stokes could make a credible run for public office: Stokes interview nos. 3 and 4, Richard Hongisto interview no. 1 and Charlotte Coleman interview, Sept. 8, 1997, with JDC. Also Randy Shilts, *The Mayor of Castro Street,* pp. 60–61; and Frances FitzGerald, *Cities on a Hill,* pp. 49–50.

151   Kinsey Institute had chosen San Francisco for survey of what homosexual life was like in 1969: Dick Halgren, "A Bay Area Study of Homosexuality," *San Francisco Chronicle,* June 20, 1969, p. A-3. The *Chronicle* itself, by the following year, was describing the city as "considered by some the gay capital of the United States."

151   the pulpit of Grace Cathedral: Peter Stack, "An Unusual Plea at Grace Pulpit," *San Francisco Chronicle,* Dec. 15, 1969, p. A-3.

152   issue was whether the company would allow SIR to place an advertisement in the Yellow Pages: "Homosexuals vs. Phone Firm Again," *San Francisco Chronicle*, April 15, 1969.
152   Berkeley police had killed one man: Charles Howe, "Berkeley Killing: Police Picketed by Homosexuals," *San Francisco Chronicle*, April 26, 1969.
152   middle-aged man had died of a stroke after being roughed up: "Homosexuals Seek to Bar Decoys," *San Francisco Chronicle*, June 26, 1969.
152   size of homosexual population: Earl C. Behrens, "Brown to Try Again on Sex Bill," *San Francisco Chronicle*, Dec. 17, 1969, p. A-10. The range of 50,000 to 90,000 in the city itself comes from that and other articles during 1969–72.
152   "Change the law. . . .": Hongisto interview no. 1 and Stokes interview no. 3.
152   aggressive when it came to Democratic Party politics: Ann Eliaser interview nos. 1 and 2 with JDC.
152   support liberal politicians who would then be obligated: Hongisto interview no. 1.
153   "crime against nature" statute: Shilts, *The Mayor of Castro Street*, p. 59.
153   Brown's district: notes on Brown in the program of "Harvey Milk's Birthday 1982" dinner, held by the Harvey Milk Gay Democratic Club in San Francisco. Courtesy of Jim Gordon, from his personal archives.
153   Pacific Heights: Hongisto interview no. 2 with JDC.
153   "as they do blacks. . . .": "Bill to Legalize Homosexuality," *San Francisco Chronicle*, March 14, 1969.
153   Brown's remarks at SIR meeting: "Brown Says Everyone Can Enjoy His Sex Bill," *San Francisco Chronicle*, April 17, 1969, p. A-40.
153   failed to endorse Brown's bill: "Board Won't Back Sex Law Reform," *San Francisco Chronicle*, April 22, 1969.
153   the board voted to endorse Brown's bill and Alioto vetoed it: Judith Anderson, "The Battle of the Sex Law," *San Francisco Chronicle*, Aug. 20, 1971, p. A-21.
154   the changing economy of San Francisco: See FitzGerald, *Cities on a Hill*, pp. 44–45.
154   By 1971, an average of 2,800 gay men: Shilts, *The Mayor of Castro Street*, p. 62.
154   The police in San Francisco had made eighty-eight such arrests in 1970: Anderson, "The Battle of the Sex Law."
154   a conviction could destroy a person's ability to work: Stokes interview no. 4.
155   politics had been dominated for decades by Irish and Italian Roman Catholic males: Eliaser interview no. 1.
155   Feinstein credited the gay vote with making the difference: Carroll, "S. F. Homosexuals' Political Machine."
155   "Many of us quite frankly. . . .": ibid.
155   "why are gay men . . . ?": Stokes interview nos. 3 and 4. Their session with Feinstein was probably in 1971 or 1972.
155   Feinstein's appearance at the SIR clubhouse: *The Advocate*, no. 62 (June 23–July 6, 1971).
156   Feinstein went on that summer: Feinstein introduced an amendment to the city's anti-discrimination ordinance in August 1971. The language would have effectively added women and homosexuals to the groups already protected by law. Maitland Zane, "Anti-Sex Bias Law Is Urged," *San Francisco Chronicle*, Aug. 20, 1971, p. A-2.
156   Feinstein had a goody-two-shoes quality: Hongisto interview no. 1 and Stokes interview no. 3.
156   Hongisto made a gay friend and became a policeman: Hongisto interview no. 1.
157   Officers for Justice: from an article by Derek Shearer which appeared in the summer issue of *Working Papers for a New Society*, reprinted as "San Francisco's Hongisto: A New Breed of Sheriff," *Gay Community News*, Oct. 23, 1976, p. 7.
157   Hongisto began to spend time hanging out at SIR meetings: Hongisto interview no. 1.
157   Hongisto drew close to Foster: Hongisto interview no. 1 and Stokes interview no. 2.
157   about Foster: Plath interview with JDC, Oct. 3, 1996.
157   "You see that guy. . . .": Hongisto interview no. 1.

157   Carberry's incompetence and heavy drinking: Hongisto, Coleman, Stokes and Charles Gain interviews with JDC. For that and also reference to criticism of him by a citizens' commission, see Shearer, "San Francisco's Hongisto."

157   Foster's intriguing proposition: Shearer, "San Francisco's Hongisto." Hongisto said it was either Foster or George Mendenhall, editor of the SIR newsletter, *Vector.* Hongisto interview no. 2.

157   David Goodstein: Eliaser interviews and Hongisto interview no. 2.

158   "I don't care. . . .": Carroll, "S. F. Homosexuals' Political Machine."

158   "I wouldn't give him a job. . . .": Carberry comment and Hongisto platform from Shearer, "San Francisco's Hongisto."

158   Homosexuals were giving him money, and speculation about his sexuality: Hongisto interview no. 2.

158   the Rembrandt: Carroll, "S. F. Homosexuals' Political Machine." Hongisto (in interview no. 2) said this was at Goodstein's house.

158   Coleman's fundraiser for Hongisto at The Mint: Coleman interview and Hongisto interview no. 1.

159   *Chronicle* coverage of gay weddings and other such events: Michael Grieg, "The Boom in Gay Marriages," July 14, 1970, p. A-1; Grieg, "Gay Married Life," July 15, 1970, p. A-1; Steve Zousmer, "A Study of Furtive Sex," Aug. 24, 1970; Ron Moskowitz, "The Homosexual Pupil," Nov. 12, 1970, p. A-6; Moskowitz, "Two Men Take Vows: A Covenant of Friendship," March 22, 1971; Donovan Bess, "Listening to Gays: A Training 'Encounter' for Cops," May 10, 1971, p. A-1; Frances Moffat, "Homosexuals in the City's High Society," June 1, 1971; and Duffy Jennings, "A Glittering Gay Wedding: 'To Me She Is a Girl,' " Aug. 17, 1971, p. A-3.

159   "The stigma is gone. . . .": Carroll, "S. F. Homosexuals' Political Machine."

159   Hongisto came in first: Shearer, "San Francisco's Hongisto."

159   Hongisto's thoughts about the gay vote, its meaning for his future and San Francisco's role in gay America: Hongisto interviews.

159   the gold sheriff's star with a peace symbol in the middle: Hongisto interview no. 2.

160   Harvey Milk settled in San Francisco: Shilts, *The Mayor of Castro Street,* p. 65.

160   Harry Britt: Britt interview nos. 1 and 2 with JDC.

160   The three existing gay neighborhoods: Jim Gordon interview no. 2 with JDC. See also FitzGerald, *Cities on a Hill,* pp. 32–33.

160   Britt's first months off Polk Street: Britt interview no. 1.

161   Most Holy Redeemer Parish: FitzGerald, *Cities on a Hill,* p. 49.

161   gay hippies: Gordon interview no. 2. Also Cleve Jones interview with JDC, March 9, 1994. See also Shilts, *The Mayor of Castro Street,* p. 82.

161   Foster had created a new gay Democratic political club: from an article on San Francisco politics in *The Advocate,* no. 174 (Oct. 8, 1975).

161   arrested by the police: Stokes interview no. 2. Stokes was Foster's friend and lawyer.

161   gratifying to Foster to be the leading gay spokesman: well known, but from various sources, including Larry Bye, Howard Wallace, Paul Kuntzler, Steve Endean and James Hormel interviews with JDC.

161   new election that year of members to the local community college board: Stokes interview no. 3.

162   far from clear, in late 1972: Hongisto interview no. 2.

162   giving speeches in public: Stokes interview no. 4.

162   "a rejection of the oppressive role. . . .": Lincoln Kaye, "New Directors' Aims: The 'Different' Families," *San Francisco Chronicle,* Jan. 27, 1971.

162   "I know that in the beginning. . . .": ibid.

162   educate his fellow board members: Stokes interview no. 4.

163   ". . . men who wear dresses?": Shilts, *The Mayor of Castro Street,* p. 64.

163   the roles of Foster, Goodstein, Brown and Hongisto in Stokes's campaign: Stokes interview no. 4.

163   Hongisto gave Stokes money and his list of campaign contributors: Hongisto interview no. 1.

163 no mention of his management and part ownership of the Ritch Street Baths: Stokes interview no. 4.
163 surprised some of the city's political analysts: Shilts, *The Mayor of Castro Street*, p. 64.

11: In Our Mothers' Names

164 Cordova and West Coast Lesbian Conference: Jeanne Cordova interview nos. 2 and 3 with AJN.
164 *Lesbian Tide* Collective broke off from DOB-LA: Cordova interview no. 1 with AJN; also "Ebb Tide: The Publisher and Editor of the *Lesbian Tide* Discuss Beginnings and End-ings," *Gay Community News*, Feb. 28, 1981, p. 9.
164 preparations for lesbian conference: Cordova interview nos. 1 and 3.
165 description of Beth Elliott: Cordova interview no. 1, and Robin Morgan, *Going Too Far*, p. 171.
165 details of DOB meeting: "Transsexual Ban Splits DOB Unit," *The Advocate*, no. 102 (Jan. 3, 1973). editorial in support of Elliott: *Lesbian Tide*, vol. 2, no. 5 (December 1972), p. 21.
165 "We are disgusted. . . ." Editorial quoted in *The Advocate*, no. 102 (January 3, 1973).
165 disruptions at conference: Cordova interview no. 1; Jean O'Leary interview no. 1 with JDC; *The Advocate*, no. 11 (May 9, 1973); and Morgan, *Going Too Far*, p. 17.
166 vote on allowing Elliott to perform: Cordova interview nos. 1 and 3; and Morgan, *Going Too Far*.
166 Some women left: Morgan, *Going Too Far*, pp. 170–71.
166 Morgan rewrote her keynote address: ibid., pp. 171–72.
167 Cordova's reaction to Morgan's speech: Cordova interview no. 3.
167 decision to abandon their own conference: Cordova interview nos. 1 and 3.
168 Voeller response to lesbian complaints about outdoor gay sexual activity: Bruce Voeller interview no. 4 with AJN.
168 "Stalking": Boston DOB, *Focus: A Journal for Gay Women*, undated.
168 women's movement was an attractive outlet for a closeted lesbian: Kay Lahusen/Bar-bara Gittings interview with Eric Marcus, courtesy of Marcus.
168 "Often I have heard. . . .": Brenda Weathers, *Front Lines*, vol. 1, no. 1 (December 1970).
169 text of Lesbian Feminist Liberation constitution: courtesy of Lesbian Herstory Archives.
169 O'Leary did not quite grasp some of the dense theoretical arguments: In interview no. 4 with JDC, she referred to books by Jill Johnston, the *Village Voice* columnist known for writing in long, run-on sentences without punctuation or capital letters.
169 O'Leary's experience at Cordova's conference: O'Leary interview no. 1 with JDC.
169 Voeller supported most lesbian demands: his interview no. 1 with AJN. He was an early male member of NOW.
170 "Prejudice against transvestites. . . .": Arthur Evans, *The Advocate*, no. 112 (May 23, 1973).
170 City Hall problems with transvestites during New York gay rights bill hearings: *New York Times*, Nov. 16, 1971.
170 transvestites and the webbed-iron staircase: Joan Nestle interview with AJN, Dec. 16, 1994.
170 Washington Square Park statement: O'Leary interview no. 4.
170 "We've gone back to supporting. . . .": Arthur Bell, "Hostility Comes Out of the Closet," *Village Voice*, June 28, 1973, p. 1.
171 Rivera wore no shoes at Washington Square Park: Morris Kight interview no. 9 with AJN.
171 Washington Square Park fracas: videotape shot by David Sasser, courtesy of Arnie Kantrowitz; Randy Wicker, "Gays Pour Through New York," *The Advocate*, no. 116 (July 18,

1973); Bell, "Hostility Comes Out of the Closet"; and O'Leary interview no. 4 with JDC, Arnie Kantrowitz interview with AJN and Sylvia Rivera interview with Eric Marcus.

12. New Orleans: Fire UpStairs

174   Kight stood on a platform in Washington Square Park: *The Advocate*, no. 116 (July 18, 1973). Also Kight interview no. 9 with AJN.

175   Santa Monica roast and police helicopter: Perry interview with JDC, Feb. 21, 1994.

176   emergency call for Gill: the Reverend John Gill interview with JDC, June 2, 1995.

176   the only independent gay groups: Don Daniels interview nos. 1 and 2, and Perry interview with JDC.

176   thirty-five active members in the young congregation of the MCC: the Reverend Troy D. Perry, *Don't Be Afraid Anymore*, p. 81.

176   the MCC congregation sometimes gathered for services at the UpStairs bar: the Reverend Lucien Baril, MCC worship conductor, quoted in "Gay Leaders Plan Aid for Victims of Bar Fire," *Times-Picayune*, June 27, 1973, sect. 1, p. 14.

176   layout of rooms in the bar: Gill interview.

176   "We didn't care. . . .": Perry interview.

176   two-hour special of free beer: *Times-Picayune*, June 27, 1973.

176   the bar's furnishings: mainly from a description by Bill Rushton, managing editor of the *Vieux Carré Courier*, in *The Advocate*, no. 117 (Aug. 1, 1973); also Perry, *Don't Be Afraid Anymore*, p. 78.

177   Two men had to be thrown out of the bar that afternoon: Perry, *Don't Be Afraid Anymore*, p. 84. A report in the *Times-Picayune* of June 25, 1973, also spoke of two men in an altercation at the top of the stairs shortly before the fire. The angry hustler is from Ron Rosenthal interview with JDC, Sept. 9, 1998.

177   forty to sixty people remained: The number of patrons is averaged from estimates of police and various witnesses.

177   the bar's clientele right before the fire: account of a survivor, Andre, in Perry, *Don't Be Afraid Anymore*, and various *Times-Picayune* accounts.

177   those in the bar: Bill Rushton, "New Orleans Toll 32; Arson Evidence Cited," *The Advocate*, no. 117 (Aug. 1, 1973); also Gill and Rosenthal interviews.

178   Gary was playing the piano and the crowd was singing as the buzzer sounded from below: *Times-Picayune*, June 25, 1973; Perry, *Don't Be Afraid Anymore*, p. 82. Also Perry and Gill and Rosenthal interviews.

179   Perry and Kight learned of the fire: Perry and Kight interviews.

179   fires had been set in the MCC in San Francisco: *The Advocate*, no. 118 (Aug. 16, 1972).

179   thirty-six MCC congregations: Vincent Lee, "Gay Leaders Plan Aid for Victims of Bar Fire," *Times-Picayune*, June 27, 1973, sect. 1, p. 14.

179   MCC of L.A. was destroyed by fire: Perry, *Don't Be Afraid Anymore*, pp. 69–75; *Los Angeles Times* February 14, 1973, A-24; *The Advocate*.

179   police arrests at The Patch: Perry interview, Jim Kepner interview no. 1 with AJN and Perry, *Don't Be Afraid Anymore*, pp. 31–35.

180   Perry found his picture on the front page of *The Advocate*: Perry interview.

180   Perry and Valdez, Perry and God: Perry, *Don't Be Afraid Anymore*, pp. 34–35.

181   Reagan sent a telegram, and crowd of 1,200: Troy D. Perry and Charles L. Lucas, *The Lord Is My Shepherd and He Knows I'm Gay: The Autobiography of The Rev. Troy D. Perry*, (Los Angeles: Nash, 1972), pp. 202–204.

183   victims could be anybody: *Times-Picayune*, June 25 and 26, 1973.

184   "What tragedy? . . .": Perry, *Don't Be Afraid Anymore*, p. 8.

184   Perry's office in L.A. told him that the *Los Angeles Times:* Perry interview.

184   The *New York Times* that Monday: John Darnton, "Homosexuals March Down Fifth Avenue," *New York Times*, June 25, 1973.

184   "We don't even know these papers. . . .": *Times-Picayune,* June 26, 1973.

184   main gay establishment was made up of gay bar owners, and they were saying nothing: Perry, Gill and Kight interviews.

184   prayer service: Bruce Nolan and Chris Segura, "Memorial for Fire Dead Has Forgiveness Theme," *Times-Picayune,* June 26, 1973, sect. 1, p. 3.

185   the telegram to Edwards and his lack of reply: Perry, *Don't Be Afraid Anymore* p 94; Perry, Gill and Kight interviews.

186   national appeal for funds for the victims: *Times-Picayune*; Perry and Kight interviews; and Perry, *Don't Be Afraid Anymore.*

186   Perry-Crutchfield exchange: Perry interview and Perry, *Don't Be Afraid Anymore,* pp. 98–101. When the phrasing differs, it is taken from the interview.

186   about Bishop Finis Crutchfield. Perry interview. Also Emily Yoffe, "The Double Life of Finis Crutchfield," *Texas Monthly,* vol. 15, no. 10 (October 1987).

13: Ordinary People

188   Voeller's children threw snowballs in SoHo: Allen Roskoff interview with AJN.

188   some of Voeller's friends considered the honorific pretentious: Ginny Vida interview with AJN, Nov. 25, 1994, among others.

188   Voeller's reaction to the gay panelists on the Susskind show: Bruce Voeller interview no. 1 with AJN.

189   Everything about Voeller suggested "privilege": Jim Fouratt interview no. 3 with AJN.

189   Voeller scolded his fellow activists for making fun of Sondheim: Story is from Voeller int. no. 1; Sondheim, in response to a query, said in a phone message on March 14, 1995, that he had no recollection of the incident, "but if Bruce Voeller said that it happened, then assume that it did."

189   Voeller protest of incident with *Advocate* reporter at a fundraiser: letter of Feb. 27, 1972, to *Advocate* editor Richard Michaels, courtesy of Hal Offen papers.

189   abrupt, condescending and pedantic: Some of this description of Voeller came from Greg Dawson, a onetime friend turned foe; his perceptions are widely shared by interviewees who knew Voeller in GAA and early NGTF days.

189   Voeller was unpopular: Jean DeVente, Pete Fisher, Marc Rubin, Roskoff, Arthur Evans, Ethan Geto, Fouratt, Breck Ardery, Michael Lavery, Greg Dawson and Ron Gold interviews with AJN.

189   Voeller complained about having to pick up cans and bottles: Voeller interview no. 4 with AJN.

189   refer to his enemies as "the trolls": "Not Dead Yet: New York GAA Determined to Survive," *The Advocate,* no. 156 (Jan. 1, 1974).

190   Voeller enjoyed gardening and his swimming pool: Bruce Voeller, "My Days on the Task Force," *Christopher Street* (magazine), October 1979, pp. 55–65.

190   "STOP THE HOMOFASCISTS!! . . .": leaflet from Marty Robinson papers, courtesy of New York Gay and Lesbian Archives.

190   demonstration to Eagle's Nest: Voeller interview nos. 1 and 4, and "Gotham Cops to Be Nicer," *The Advocate,* no. 120 (Sept. 12, 1973).

190   meeting to discuss disciplining Voeller: John O'Brien no. 2 and Voeller no. 5 interviews with AJN.

190   "For God's sake. . . .": Gold interview nos. 1 and 3 with AJN.

190   "Stop complaining. . . .": Gold interview no. 1.

190   Voeller quit: O'Brien interview no. 2 and Voeller interview nos. 2 and 5. Also Geto and Roskoff interviews; memo to general membership of GAA from Wayne Sunday, secretary, GAA (Oct. 5, 1973); and *The Advocate,* no. 125 (Nov. 7, 1973).

191   "What are we going to do? . . .": Gold interview nos. 1 and 3.

191   "This is it. . . .": Nathalie Rockhill interview no. 1 with AJN.

191   "I'm afraid I'm going to be stoned. . . .": ibid.

191   Rockhill got along with men and was alarmed at division between the sexes: ibid.

192   "The whole gay movement is public relations. . . .": Ron Gold, "Gays and Public Relations," *It's Time: The Newsletter of the NGTF,* vol. 1, no. 1 (May 1974).

192   the name National Gay Task Force: Gold interview no. 3 and Dawson interview no. 2.

192   "We don't wish to be picky. . . .": editorial "Exciting News!" *The Advocate,* no. 125 (Nov. 7, 1973).

193   "With each fag joke. . . .": Voeller, "My Days on the Task Force."

193   Mayor Lindsay had no idea that Brown was gay: Brown believed this, according to his book, *Familiar Faces, Hidden Lives,* p. 4. And Lindsay, in an April 12, 1994, letter in response to written questions from AJN, said: "No. I did not know he was gay when I hired him." Lindsay also said he did not know about Brown's fears about Drew Pearson.

193   Brown's handling of his lover and other details of his life at city hall: Brown, *Familiar Faces, Hidden Lives,* p. 3. Much about Brown's coming out, hospital stay and years in the Lindsay administration is drawn from his book, which was published after his death.

193   Brown closed his shades whenever he cooked: Voeller's eulogy at Brown's mem. service, Feb. 12, 1975, reprinted in *It's Time,* vol. 1, no. 3 (May 1975).

193   Brown's dancing wildly and overexerting himself: George Whitmore, "An Appreciation of Howard Brown," *The Advocate,* no. 158 (Feb. 26, 1975). Also Larry Bye no. 1 interview with JDC.

194   Brown suffered a heart attack in June 1972: *Familiar Faces, Hidden Lives,* p. 23.

194   Brown roamed around his apartment "in high heels": Martin Duberman, *Cures: A Gay Man's Odyssey,* pp. 286–87.

194   "I knew many rich homosexuals.": Brown, *Familiar Faces, Hidden Lives,* p. 22.

194   Voeller's reaction to Brown's coming out: Bruce Voeller, "Second Birthday Reminiscing," *It's Time,* vol. 2, no. 1 (October 1975), p. 3.

194   Gold and Voeller's role in Brown's coming out: Gold interview no. 1 and Voeller interviews with AJN.

194   "I am publicly announcing. . . .": Brown, *Familiar Faces, Hidden Lives,* p. 28.

194   Voeller invited Brown to be board chairman: numerous accounts, including Voeller interview nos. 1 and 4, and histories he wrote for "Special Bonus Issue, 1976," *It's Time,* vol. 1, no. 3 (1975).

194   Brown's suit: "Homosexual Civil Rights Group Is Announced by Ex-City Aide," *New York Times,* Oct. 15, 1973.

194   first press conference of NGTF: "Heavyweight National Gay Group Formed," *The Advocate,* no. 125 (Nov. 7, 1973).

195   Duberman quote from his diary: Duberman, *Cures,* p. 291.

195   demise of the GAA: "NY GAA Burns," *The Advocate,* no. 140 (Nov. 6, 1974).

195   "aping high-class values": Arthur Evans interview no. 2 with AJN.

195   "If NGTF is going. . . .": Arthur Evans, "Do NGTF's Purposes Conflict?," *The Advocate,* no. 127 (Dec. 19, 1973).

195   Evans-Voeller correspondence: courtesy of Arthur Evans papers.

196   "A group of professionals. . . .": Morris Kight interview no. 12 with AJN.

196   Gold at the community center: "Gays Zap Media—and Each Other, Too: Kight, Gold in LA Clash," *The Advocate,* no. 126 (Dec. 5, 1973). Gold, in interview no. 3, acknowledged some details of the meeting, but disputed the *Advocate* slant that he was viewed as a carpetbagger trying to push his way in. Kight also disputed that slant. Both agreed that the incident spotlighted the differences between the traditional activists and the new professionals.

196   Kight at the L.A. meeting: Kight interview no. 12.

197 $125 weekly salary: Rockhill interview no. 2 with AJN.

197   "We need the help of the board. . . .": Bruce Voeller, fundraising letter to NGTF board members, April 20, 1974.

197   NGTF had little money: *The Advocate,* no. 126 (Dec. 5, 1973).

197   Bunch was pushing for a national board: Charlotte Bunch interview no. 2 and David Rothenberg interview with AJN, May 7, 1993.

197   assembling a national board in New York would deplete the treasury: Vida interview.

197   Kameny's letter warning of NGTF's disintegration: Kameny letter to NGTF board and staff, Dec. 25, 1973, courtesy of Marty Robinson papers.

14: A Question of Sanity

199   American Psychiatric Association and homosexuality: Ronald Bayer, *Homosexuality and American Psychiatry: The Politics of Diagnosis,* p. 40, and the APA's *Diagnostic and Statistical Manual, Mental Disorders* (Washington, D.C., 1952), p. 34.

199   "I see nothing wrong. . . .": *Off the Cuff,* April 4, 1964 (an unrehearsed two-hour television panel show on Chicago station WBKB-TV). The other panelists were the Reverend James G. Jones, director of development of Episcopal Charities in Chicago; Dr. Jordan Scher, director of psychiatric services for the Chicago Board of Health and editor of *The Journal of Existential Psychiatry;* Del Shearer, president of the Chicago Chapter of Daughters of Bilitis; and Randy Wicker, of the Mattachine Society of New York. Cited in W. Mitchell, "Special Report: *Off the Cuff,*" *The Ladder,* October 1964.

200   1962 study: Irving Bieber, *Homosexuality: A Psychoanalytic Study* (New York: Basic Books, 1962). Also Bayer, *Homosexuality and American Psychiatry,* pp. 30–34.

200   the GLF's confrontation with Bieber: Gary Alinder, "Confrontation I: San Francisco," *Gay Liberation Meets the Shrinks, Gay Flames* Pamphlet No. 6, courtesy of Bruce Voeller. Also Karla Jay and Allen Young, eds., in *Out of the Closets: Voices of Gay Liberation,* p. 141. Bieber died before research for this book began.

201   McConaghy's paper on aversion therapy: Alinder, "Confrontation I: San Francisco."

201   the APA session and disruption of McConaghy's presentation, including shouts by protesters and psychiatrists: Alinder, "Confrontation I: San Francisco"; Larry Littlejohn interview no. 4 with JDC; *San Francisco Chronicle* and *Washington Post,* May 15, 1970, *Washington Star,* May 24, 1970, as cited in Bayer, *Homosexuality and American Psychiatry,* pp. 103–104.

202   The session ended in heaving chaos and police: The description of the police comes from the remarks made the following year at the APA convention by Dr. Kent Robinson, as he introduced the gay and lesbian panel that the APA agreed to as a result of the 1970 disruptions. Transcript of that panel, "Lifestyles of the Non-Patient Homosexual," at the APA annual meeting in Washington, D.C., May 6, 1971, courtesy of Dr. Lilli Vincenz and Bruce Voeller.

202   denounced as barbarians: report of the GLF-LA disrupting the Oct. 17, 1970, Second Annual Behavioral Modification Conference in L.A.; the audience was watching a film by Dr. M. Phillip Feldman of the State University at Binghamton when GLF activists started shouting, "Medieval Torture, Barbarians." *The Advocate,* vol. 4, no. 19 (Nov. 11–24, 1970).

202   the Chicago protest: Step May of Chicago Gay Liberation, "Confrontation II: Chicago," *Gay Liberation Meets the Shrinks.*

202   the Los Angeles protest: *The Advocate,* vol. 4, no. 7 (May 27–June 9, 1970).

202   "We declare that we are healthy homosexuals. . . .": Chicago Gay Liberation, "A Leaflet for the AMA," *Gay Liberation Meets the Shrinks.*

202   "The Mattachine Society of Washington. . . .": *The Ladder,* July/August 1965, p. 15.

202   Robinson-Littlejohn conversation and how the idea for a panel of homosexuals at the next APA convention evolved: Littlejohn interview no. 4. Bayer, in *Homosexuality and American Psychiatry,* pp. 103–104, credits Littlejohn with suggesting the panel to Robinson, but Littlejohn said that the idea was Robinson's.

203   planning among Washington gay activists for APA convention in spring 1971: Richard Pillard interview, Nov. 18, 1995, Frank Kameny interview no. 9 and Cliff Witt interview no. 2 with JDC.

204   they would all rush the stage: Kameny and Witt interviews.

204   Clark speaking and therapists attacking protesters: Kameny interview.

204   the cowering psychiatrist and Witt's falling out the door: Witt interview. Other general description of the scene from Bayer, *Homosexuality and American Psychiatry,* p. 105.

204   "I'm seizing the microphone!": Kameny interview.

204   Kameny at the APA convention: *The Advocate,* May 26, 1971, p. 3; the APA publica-

tion, *Psychiatric News,* Sept. 15, 1971, reprinted in *The Advocate,* Nov. 24, 1971; and Pillard and Kameny interviews.

205   Dr. Pillard and Kameny: Pillard interview.

205   "Lifestyles of Non-Patient Homosexuals": Barbara Gittings/Kay Lahusen interview no. 2 with JDC.

205   Bieber was terrified of being hurt: Kameny interview.

206   "There are a number of homosexuals. . . .": transcript of "Lifestyles of Non-Patient Homosexuals" at the APA annual meeting in Washington, May 6, 1971.

206   "I tend to feel. . . .": ibid. Emphases are Kameny's.

207   Robinson had them meet with another APA official: Bayer, *Homosexuality and American Psychiatry,* p. 107.

207   the Gay-PA: The meetings of gay psychiatrists in bars after the convention sessions at night may have begun before 1971, but this account is from Dr. Richard Pillard, who was at the 1971 APA convention, and at the late night sessions in the Chesapeake House and other gay bars in Washington.

207   the hunt for a gay psychiatrist: Gittings/Lahusen interview.

208   testimony of anonymous gay psychiatrist: Bayer, *Homosexuality and American Psychiatry,* pp. 109–11.

208   Fryer revealed that he was Dr. Anonymous: from Kameny and Gittings interviews with JDC.

209   Seidenberg's and Marmor's comments: Bayer, *Homosexuality and American Psychiatry,* pp. 109–11.

209   "that homosexual behavior was not necessarily a sign. . . .": ibid., p. 113.

209   "Torture Anyone?": ibid., pp. 115–16.

209   Spitzer's background, training and reaction to the disruption: Robert Spitzer interview with JDC, Nov. 19, 1995.

210   Gold-Spitzer meeting: Ronald Gold interview no. 1 with AJN and Spitzer interview. Each said he approached the other, but both agreed that it was Gold who pressed for a hearing before the Nomenclature Committee. Gold said he fastened onto Spitzer after the woman introduced them and never let go until the policy was changed.

210   Committee on Nomenclature meeting, with Silverstein arguments: Boyce Rensberger, "Psychiatrists Review Stand on Homosexuals," *New York Times,* Feb. 9, 1973, sect. 1, p. 24; Bayer, *Homosexuality and American Psychiatry,* pp. 116–20; and Gold interview.

211   Hooker study: Bayer, *Homosexuality and American Psychiatry,* p. 5.

211   It might be difficult for her colleagues to accept: Evelyn Hooker, "The Adjustment of the Male Overt Homosexual," *Journal of Projective Techniques,* 21 (1957): 18.

211   eight committee members sat quietly after the rest of the GAA delegation left: Spitzer interview. Also Spitzer interview in *The Advocate,* no. 129 (Jan. 16, 1974).

212   Brill on APA policy: Rensberger, "Psychiatrists Review Stand on Homosexuals."

212   progression of Spitzer's thought: Spitzer interview. See also Bayer, *Homosexuality and American Psychiatry,* p. 124.

213   Stoller and "There is no such *thing* as homosexuality.": Robert J. Stoller, M.D., "Criteria for Psychiatric Diagnosis," speech delivered at the symposium "Should Homosexuality Be in the APA Nomenclature?" on May 9, 1973, abstracted in the *American Journal of Psychiatry* 130:11 (November 1973), pp. 1207–1208.

213   Gold speech to the APA: Ronald Gold, "Stop It, You're Making Me Sick!" delivered as part of the symposium "Should Homosexuality Be in the APA Nomenclature?" on May 9, 1973, abstracted in the *American Journal of Psychiatry* 130:11 (November 1973), pp. 1211–12. Also from original copy of Gold's speech, both from the personal archives of Bruce Voeller.

214   reaction of the psychiatrists to Gold, Bieber and Socarides: Gold interview and *The Advocate,* no. 113 (June 6, 1973). Also *Newsweek,* May 21, 1973.

214   Spitzer at the Gay-PA dinner: Gold and Spitzer interviews; and Bayer, *Homosexuality and American Psychiatry,* p. 12.

215   verbatim exchanges at the Gay-PA gathering, and the army psychiatrist: Gold inter-

view. Spitzer, in his interview, recalled being moved by the experience of the gay psychiatrists he encountered there, but did not remember details, or the army psychiatrist in particular.

215   the APA announcement: news release of the American Psychiatric Association, Dec. 15, 1973, in the private archives of Bruce Voeller, courtesy of Voeller.

216   the results of Socarides's referendum on APA vote: "Doctors Vote to Cut Stigma of Deviation," *Los Angeles Times,* April 9, 1974, sect. 1, p. 9; and *The Advocate,* no. 137 (May 8, 1974).

216   "The Earth Is Round!": *It's Time,* vol. 1, no. 1 (May 1974).

217   "I would have to say. . . .": Spitzer interview, *The Advocate,* no. 129 (Jan. 16, 1974).

15: Elaine

218   Noble was very public about her homosexuality. She was the daughter: Elaine Noble interview nos. 1 and 2 with JDC; and Andy Merton, "Nixon Would Have Died," *Boston Magazine,* December 1974, p. 22.

218   In the poor black areas of Boston's South End: Noble interview no. 2 with JDC.

219   Peterson's proposal for a community-wide newsletter: David Peterson interview no. 2 with JDC.

219   The first issues of the newsletter: *Gay Community News,* vol. 1, nos. 2–4, 6, 7 and others, courtesy of MIT library archives. Some of its first stories: *Gay Community News,* vol. 1, nos. 1–8 (June, July and August 1973), courtesy of MIT archives.

220   "Gay to Run": *Gay Community News,* Sept. 15, 1973; also Noble interview no. 3 and Ann Lewis interview, Sept. 18, 1993, with JDC.

220   Lewis and Noble met for breakfast: Lewis and Noble interviews.

220   Sixth District: *Boston Sunday Globe,* Sept. 8, 1974, courtesy of Candy Thomson; and Noble interview no. 3 to JDC.

221   "The Issue Is. . . .": proposed Noble fliers courtesy of Candy Thomson.

221   "You make sure your friends. . . .": Noble interview no. 3.

221   Noble's big fundraising party: advertisement for the "birthday gala" in *Gay Community News,* Jan. 19, 1974, p. 3; and later news report of the fundraiser in *Gay Community News,* Feb. 2, 1974; both courtesy of MIT archives.

222   the older lesbians were enthralled with Noble: Lois Johnson and Sheri Barden, interview with JDC, July 26, 1994.

222   The *Boston Globe* might describe her: Three references are taken from different news reports in different issues of the *Boston Globe,* of Nov. 6, 1974, the day after the general election.

223   "The fact that my. . . .": Joseph Cimino's "Dear Voter" letter courtesy of Candy Thomson.

223   Kozachenko's election: *Ann Arbor News* election stories of Jan. 24, March 19, April 2, 1974 and Feb. 5, 1975, courtesy of the library of the *Ann Arbor News.* The *Michigan Daily,* the campus newspaper, called it "a stunning upset victory in a photo-finish race" (*The Advocate,* May 8, 1974), but news of her election didn't carry far.

223   Noble carried every precinct: David P. Brill, "Analysis: Campaign 74," *Gay Community News,* Nov. 16, 1974, courtesy of MIT archives.

223   "extraordinary fact of gay rights legislation. . . .": *The Advocate,* July 14, 1974.

224   *Tomorrow* show producer on one line: Candy Thomson interview with JDC, Feb. 7, 1994, and Noble interview no. 3.

224   "I've got to say to some people. . . .": Merton, "Nixon Would Have Died."

16: Minneapolis: The Coat Check

225   the young Steve Endean: Steve Endean interview no. 1 and Robert Endean interview, March 1993, with JDC.

226   wrote a letter: Steve Endean interview nos. 1 and 4, and Robert Endean interview with JDC.

226   his Roman Catholic guilt: several interviews, especially Endean interview no. 1: "In growing up Catholic, I felt very repressed. I've said that if I'd grown up Unitarian, I don't know that I would have been an activist, because I don't know that I would have felt the intense guilt and pain and have felt the intense need to change things."

226   he got stoned: Larry Bye interview no. 1 with JDC.

226   "What the fuck do you mean by that?": Endean interview no. 1.

226   Baker-McConnell legal history: All from *Minneapolis Star:* "Wedding: 2 'U' Homosexuals Wed in Ceremony," Sept. 7, 1971, p. A-1; Gwenyth Jones, "Pair Seeks Same-Sex Marriage Approval in Top Court Test," Sept. 22, 1971, p. E-18; Jones, "Supreme Court Upholds Ban on Marriage of 2 Homosexuals," Oct. 15, 1971, p. A-1; "U.S. Appeals Court Rejects Demand 'U' Must Hire Admitted Homosexual," Oct. 19, 1971, p. A-1; "High Court Won't Hear Appeal of Homosexual," April 4, 1972, p. B-18; and lastly, on the marriage appeal, "High Court Won't Hear Gay Case," Oct. 10, 1972, p. Y-1.

227   If women, blacks and American Indians could be represented: For changes in the 1972 Democratic convention delegate selection process, Ann Lewis interview with JDC, Sept. 18, 1993.

227   gay caucus could send one of its own: Allan Spear interview no. 1 with JDC. The gay DFL caucus member, Lowell Williams, was elected an alternate, joining Madeline Davis from Buffalo and Jim Foster from San Francisco as the three openly gay delegates that year.

227   seven-point gay rights agenda: Denis Wadley interview with JDC, March 1993. Wadley, an active force in the party, was Minnesota chairman of Americans for Democratic Action that year.

227   state party's radical platform: Spear and Wadley interviews.

227   "There are a lot of crazy things. . . .": *The Advocate,* no. 89 (July 5, 1972).

227   Spear was running for the state Senate: Spear interview nos. 1 and 2 with JDC; and *The Advocate,* no. 110 (April 25, 1973).

228   the Gay Rights Legislative Committee, and Endean's two specific goals: numerous Endean interviews. Also Jean Tretter interview no. 1 with JDC and Wadley interview. "Coalition Won't Join in Selective Buying Campaign," *Minneapolis Star,* Oct. 6, 1972, p. A-9; and "Homosexuals Lobbying at Legislature, Tone Down Approach," *Minneapolis Star,* Feb. 19, 1973, p. A-5.

228   Coached in the method and manners of legislative lobbying: Endean interview nos. 1 and 4 and Wadley interview.

228   "Steve, look at what. . . .": Robert Endean interview.

228   sometimes provoked discomfort: various Endean interviews. Also Dennis Miller interview with JDC, Sept. 29, 1993.

228   Four Republicans helped sponsor a bill: "Republicans Back Minnesota Law Reform," *The Advocate,* no. 109 (April 11, 1973).

228   Coleman, his Irish Catholic background and Ghent Howell's influence on him: Deborah Howell interview no. 1 and Spear interview nos. 1 and 3 with JDC.

229   "They should have their rights respected. . . .": "Homosexuals Lobbying at Legislature, Tone Down Approach," *Minneapolis Star.*

229   "Sex is only one aspect. . . .": Jack Baker, "Defining Gayness Under the Law," *Minneapolis Star* editorial page, March 19, 1974, p. A-8. Baker withdrew from gay activism more than a decade ago and, through Mike McConnell, declined to be interviewed for this history. McConnell, in interview nos. 1 and 2 with JDC, the first he had agreed to in almost a decade, spoke of their joint experience.

229   "We're trying to legitimatize. . . .": *Gay,* March 11, 1973.

229   "The terminology is offensive. . . .": *The Advocate,* no. 112 (May 23, 1973).

229   passed in the subcommittee: "Legislative Update: Homosexuals' Proposal Cleared," *Minneapolis Star,* May 5, 1973.

229   Coleman's parents walked out: Howell interview no. 2 with JDC. For the effect of the bill, Spear interview no. 1, among other sources.

229   a more respectful treatment on the floor: Endean interview no. 24, Spear interview no. 1 and Wadley interview.

230   "If you want to have this movement. . . .": Larry Bye interview. Also numerous Endean interviews.

230   Endean began to talk quietly with candidates for city council seats: Endean interview nos. 1 and 2, and Spear interview no. 1.

230   "By the way. . . .": Spear interview no. 1. Deborah Howell, now editor of the Newhouse News Service in Washington, D.C., said (in interview no. 1) that Coleman, whom she married in 1975, probably did tell Spear that she would like to have the story, but she said that she told Spear the same thing in a later conversation.

231   "affectional or sexual preference": Jack Baker, "Defining 'Gayness' Under the Law," *Minneapolis Star* op-ed page, March 19, 1974.

231   The vote on the council: Eric Pianin, "Council Protects 'Gay' Rights, Picks Lake-Nicollet Developer," *Minneapolis Star,* March 29, 1974, p. A-15.

231   Ann Arbor, East Lansing and other cities with anti-discrimination laws: *The Advocate,* no. 136 (April 24, 1974).

231   The council's handling of the issue: stories in the *Minneapolis Star* and *Tribune,* Feb. 23–March 30, 1974.

231   Caught off guard: Miller interview.

231   "This is what the Communists want. . . .": leaflet quoted in "Council Gets Bid to Protect 'Gay' Rights," *Minneapolis Star,* March 22, 1974, p. B-11.

232   "The Minneapolis City Council today amended. . . .": Pianin, "Council Protects 'Gay' Rights, Picks Lake-Nicollet Developer."

232   Northwestern Bell dropped its ban on hiring them: "A Humanitarian Milestone," *Minneapolis Star* editorial page, April 15, 1974.

232   audience were perhaps 250 people: average drawn from the different reports of those who were there.

232   meeting at the Roman Catholic student center: Endean interview no. 24, and Spear, Bye and Miller interviews.

233   the inaugural meeting: Bye interview. Also from an account of the meeting and Lyon's remarks in *The Advocate,* June 5, 1974.

233   had made a deal: Endean interview no. 24.

233   the Roman Catholic Church in Minnesota: Larry Kessler and Sean Strub interviews with JDC, among others.

233   "was much more threatening. . . .": "Priest Says State, Not Church, Might Sanction Gay Marriages," *Minneapolis Star,* Sept. 25, 1971, p. A-13. Also "St. Paul Clergy, Homosexuals, Hold 2nd Forum," *Minneapolis Star,* Nov. 4, 1972, p. A-8.

233   vocal opposition: Endean interviews and accounts in the *Minneapolis Star.*

234   archbishop coadjutor sent a letter, along with an editorial: " 'Gay Rights' Foes Joined by Prelate," *Minneapolis Star,* July 16, 1974, p. B-1.

234   Endean had gotten to Mayor Cohen through Miller, and Miller enlisted Cohen's support: Miller interview.

234   Coleman appeared before the St. Paul City Council: Betsy Barry, "St. Paul Passes 'Gay-Rights' Rule After Emotional Pleas, Protests," *Minneapolis Star,* July 17, 1974, p. A-15. Also Endean and Miller interviews.

234   *The Catholic Bulletin* lamented: quoted in " 'Gay Rights' Action Deplored," *Minneapolis Star,* July 20, 1974, p. A-8.

234   Spear dared to think: Spear interview no. 3.

234   the second conference of the Gay Academic Union: See Karla Jay and Allen Young, eds., *Out of the Closets: Voices of Gay Liberation,* pp. xiii–xiv. Also John D'Emilio, *Making Trouble: Essays on Gay History, Politics and the University,* particularly Chapter 11, "Gay and Lesbian Studies," p. 160.

235   "When do you think this will run? . . .": Spear interview no. 3.

235   "I wanted to stop the tittering. . . .": Deborah Howell, "State Sen. Allan Spear Declares He's Homosexual," *Minneapolis Star,* Dec. 9, 1974, p. A-1.

235   Spear stayed at home that Monday: Spear interview no. 3.
235   number of supportive phone calls: "A Moderate Gay Rights Bill," *Minneapolis Star* editorial page, April 19, 1975.
235   The DFL Party had developed a huge majority: Spear interview no. 3 and Wadley interview.
236   "Despite concern expressed. . . .": private archives of Bruce Voeller, courtesy of Voeller.
236   the difference between Baker/McConnell and Endean: Kerry Woodward interview no. 3 with JDC and Endean interview no. 24.
236   A lobbyist: Endean interview no. 1.
236   "While Jack has done much. . . .": *The Advocate*, Nov. 21, 1973.
236   "As far as I'm concerned. . . .": ibid., Dec. 19, 1973.
236   *Tribune* published an editorial: on March 1, 1975.
236   Thomas Higgins: Like other activists in Minnesota and elsewhere, Higgins altered his name, becoming Thom Higgins as a mark of his new, gay radical identity. His given name is used in this narrative to avoid confusion. Jean Tretter interview no. 3 with JDC.
237   His testimony: Carl Griffin Jr., " 'No Compromise' Gay Coalition May Sink Rights Bill," *The Advocate*, no. 163 (May 7, 1975).
237   subcommittee in an uproar: Endean interview no. 24.
237   Endean tried to make the best of it: ibid.
237   editorials: *Minneapolis Star*, April 19, 1975; and *Tribune*, April 21, 1975.
237   "It's a problem for a man in a dress. . . .": Tim Campbell interview no. 1 with JDC.
238   killed the gay rights bill: "Gay Rights Bill Killed," *Minneapolis Star*, May 9, 1975, p. B-8.
238   after the vote Endean: Endean interview nos. 2, 24 and especially 28.

17: Ordinary Things

239   Abzug figuring out every morning: Abzug interview with AJN, Nov. 11, 1994.
239   "the fruits of society": March 25, 1975, press conference. "Bella's Bill: 'Time to Enjoy the Fruits,' " *The Advocate*, no. 162 (April 23, 1975).
239   "My *faygelehs!*": Bruce Voeller interview no. 1 with AJN.
240   Russo on Abzug's "coming to us": Russo/Abzug interview, "Bella! Bella! Bella!" *The Advocate*, Sept. 23, 1975.
240   Abzug and backlash for supporting gay measures: Asked if support for gay rights helped her politically, she responded in her interview, "No. It never had. It has hurt me."
240   Voeller on strategy behind introduction of gay rights bills: Voeller interviews no. 1 and 2; also Voeller, "Master Plan," *NGTF on Capitol Hill*, a special bonus issue of the NGTF newsletter *It's Time*, undated.
240   Voeller on being upset: Voeller interview. The "Frankly" quote is from "Rights Struggle Shifts to Capitol Hill," *The Advocate*, no. 143 (July 31, 1974).
240   Voeller was furious: Voeller interview nos. 1 and 2 with AJN.
241   "I don't want to talk to you. . . .": Voeller interview nos. 1 and 5 with AJN. Abzug, in an interview in 1994, said she had little memory of Voeller or any disagreements over the bill. Her quotes from the time, in *The Advocate*, suggest her public irritation with Voeller.
241   doubting Abzug's true commitment to gay rights: Voeller interviews; also Charlotte Bunch interview no. 2 with AJN and Abzug interview; and Abzug/Russo interview, "Bella! Bella! Bella!" *The Advocate*.
241   history and impact of Abzug bill: Sarah P. Collins, *Federal Legislation Pertaining to Homosexual Rights, 94th to 96th Congress*, Congressional Research Service, Library of Congress, April 17, 1980; also Collins, *Homosexual Rights: An Issues Overview*, CRS, April 18, 1980.
242   Voeller strategy on the bill, including use of the phrase "affectional preference": Voeller, "Master Plan."
243   Voeller's complaints about raising money: "My Days on the Task Force," *Christopher Street* magazine, October 1979. That story includes detailed accounts of the Matlovich

fundraiser on Fire Island and the problems Voeller encountered trying to find gay bars in New York to support the Task Force. Information on gay discotheques competing with Task Force fundraisers came from Voeller interview nos. 2 and 5, and "My Days."

244   "All across the country. . . .": Arthur Evans, "While Nation Retreats, We Must Keep Trying," *The Advocate*, no. 131 (Feb. 13, 1994).

244   Whitmore on New York rally: *The Advocate*, no. 169 (July 30, 1975).

18: Citizen Goodstein

245   Evans started writing for *The Advocate:* Arthur Evans interview no. 3 with AJN.

245   Bio on Dick Michaels, and some details on founding: Randy Shilts, *"The Advocate:* A Tense Past, A Bright Future," *The Advocate*, no. 227 (Nov. 2, 1977). Other details from Michaels interview in Kay Tobin and Randy Wicker, *The Gay Crusaders.*

245   details on *Advocate* founding: Dick Michaels in Tobin and Wicker, *The Gay Crusaders;* also introduction to Mark Thompson, *Long Road to Freedom;* and *Wall Street Journal,* Nov. 3, 1975.

246   *Advocate* circulation: *The Advocate*, Dec. 4, 1974, in story on sale of the newspaper to David Goodstein.

246   quote in *Advocate* advertising brochure: "Sign of the Times: A Homosexual Paper, the *Advocate*, Widens Reader Influence," Stephen J. Sansweet, *Wall Street Journal*, Nov. 3, 1975.

246   Evans correspondence with Preston and Goodstein: January 1975, courtesy of Evans papers.

247   "We have been assured. . . .": from the editorial "A Farewell," *The Advocate*, no. 155 (Jan. 15, 1975).

247   a Rembrandt hung over his bed: Troy Perry interview with JDC, Feb. 21, 1994.

247   Goodstein's taste in Italian sports cars and gold and jade: John Satark, "Building a Gay Empire," *San Francisco Chronicle,* May 8, 1977.

248   Goodstein's claim of firing: recounted in numerous profiles and obituaries; the name of the bank is from Ann Eliaser interviews no. 1 and 2 with JDC and David Russell interview with AJN.

248   personal information on Goodstein: Much of it is from Russell interview nos. 1–3 with AJN. Russell was Goodstein's longtime lover.

248   Committee for Sexual Law Reform: "San Francisco Meeting Maps Law Reform Drive," *The Advocate,* no. 79 (Feb. 16, 1972).

248   Goodstein bragged about having gay leaders on his payroll: Randy Shilts interview no. 1 with AJN. Shilts, who worked for Goodstein, said soon after he met him, he heard Goodstein brag about having Jim Foster and others on his payroll.

248   repealing sodomy law a waste of time: Jeanne Cordova interview no. 2 and numerous Morris Kight interviews with AJN.

248   Committee for Sexual Law Reform meeting: Kight interviews, Cordova interview no. 2 and "Ideological Battle Wrecks Conference on Gay Law Reform," *The Advocate,* no. 106 (Feb. 28, 1973).

249   "They regard us as freaks. . . .": This article by David Goodstein was published in at least two places: "Gay Subcultists and the California Senate," *Vector,* August 1973, p. 32; and "Snub by Salons Points up Law Reform Problems," *The Advocate,* no. 117 (Aug. 1, 1973).

249   "honestly, and perhaps. . . .": David Goodstein letter to *The Advocate,* Jan. 30, 1974.

250   Goodstein dyed his hair: Eliaser interviews no. 1 and 2.

250   Goodstein foamed at the sides of his mouth: Niles Merton interview with AJN, June 1, 1994, and Russell interviews. Merton was the former *Advocate* publisher.

250   Goodstein's personality: numerous sources, but sympathetic insights in particular came from Russell interview nos. 1 and 2 and Rob Eichberg interviews no. 1 and 2 with AJN. Eichberg was a therapist and close friend and business partner of Goodstein's.

250   Goodstein would refer to himself as a "troll": Eichberg interview no. 1.

250   gravity inversion machine: Russell interview no. 3 and Merton interview.

250   never fit in: Bruce Voeller interview no. 5 with AJN.

250   under the porch: Russell interview nos. 1 and 2.

250   put to rest the notion that "wealthy gay people are immune to discrimination": *The Advocate*, no. 156 (Jan. 29, 1975).

250   "I thought, if they can do that to me. . . .": *Wall Street Journal*, Nov. 3, 1975.

251   venereal disease, a topic that fascinated Goodstein: Shilts interview nos. 1 and 2 with AJN.

251   "flamboyant exhibitionists" and "media freaks": "Opening Space," *The Advocate*, no. 174 (Oct. 8, 1975).

251   no longer publish the names Goodstein considered enemies of the movement: numerous sources, but most credibly Jim Kepner, who was working for *The Advocate* at the time, in interview no. 4 with AJN.

252   Goodstein moved *The Advocate* closer to his home: Russell, Shilts and other interviews; also *The Advocate*, no. 159 (March 12, 1975).

252   "We were under. . . .": *Wall Street Journal*, Nov. 3, 1975.

252   "If the liberation fairies. . . .": Goodstein quoted in Shilts interview no. 1.

252   It was clear to the people at *The Advocate*: Mark Thompson interview with AJN, June 14, 1994.

252   Shilts resisted exposés and didn't dare send *The Advocate* to his parents: Shilts interview no. 2 and interview with Eric Marcus, courtesy of Marcus.

252   the beer story: Shilts interview no. 2 and Kight interview no. 10.

252   Shilts's questions to Kight: Kight interview no. 10. Shilts said he did not recall the conversation exactly.

252   "GOOZ-steen": numerous Kight interviews. It is pronounced GOOD-steen.

253   Rotary Club for homosexuals: Charles Brydon profile, *The Advocate*, no. 234 (Feb. 8, 1978).

253   the largest homosexual group in the Pacific Northwest: Randy Shilts, "Future of Gay Rights? The Emerging Gay Middle Class," *The Advocate*, no. 175 (Oct. 22, 1975).

253   "over the sill of the closet": Brydon interview no. 1 with AJN.

253   Goodstein speech and TV coverage: ibid.

253   We have moved quite a distance: Brydon interview with Marcus, courtesy of Marcus.

254   Brydon had put together the Dorian Group: Brydon interview no. 1.

254   "non-radical, conservative. . . .": Shilts, "Future of Gay Rights? The Emerging Gay Middle Class."

254   "I am incredibly middle-class. . . .": "Politics with a Quiet Passion," *The Advocate*, no. 234 (Feb. 8, 1978).

254   Brydon meeting with mayor as a gay demonstration was proceeding: Brydon interview with Marcus.

254   Goodstein's first-year anniversary column: *The Advocate*, no. 181 (Jan. 14, 1976).

256   activists who shared his vision: "Publisher Announces Planning Conference," *The Advocate*, no. 184 (Feb. 25, 1976).

256   in a city with a comparatively small gay activist community: Paul Kuntzler interview no. 2 with JDC.

256   guards at the door: Perry interview.

257   "The autocratic San Mateo millionaire. . . .": *Newswest*, "Goodstein's Power-Play," undated leaflet which reprinted the editorial.

257   history of *Newswest*: Kepner interview no. 3 with AJN.

257   Perry's press release on Goodstein conference: March 5, 1976, courtesy of Adam De-Baugh papers.

257   opponents as obstructionists: "Opening Space," *The Advocate*, no. 186 (March 24, 1976).

257   *The Advocate* Invitational Conference: from JDC/AJN multiple interviews with Charles Brydon, Charlotte Bunch, Steve Endean, Barbara Gittings, Frank Kameny, Bill Kelley, Paul Kuntzler, Jean O'Leary, Troy Perry, Gary Van Ooteghem and Bruce Voeller.

257   the Sweet Adelines: Barbara Gittings interview no. 3 with JDC.

258   "Who are those people . . . ?": "Opening Space," *The Advocate*, no. 255 (Nov. 29, 1978). *Advocate* publisher Peter Frisch heard the conversation.

258   Goodstein opened: Gittings interview.

258   "I don't intend to say much" and other direct quotes from the conference: handwritten notes Adam DeBaugh took that day and shared in interview with AJN.

258   the conference was aimed at knocking out the Task Force: Charlotte Bunch interview no. 2 and Voeller interview nos. 3 and 5 with AJN.

258   a national gay rights group could not work out of Manhattan: Russell interview no. 2.

258   Kameny's suggestion: Frank Kameny interviews with JDC and DeBaugh interview.

259   a script he had written and the results: "Complete Text of the Agenda, Position Papers and Ground Rules for The Advocate Invitational Conference," March 27, 1976. Also "OFFICIAL MINUTES of Advocate Invitational Conference," by Sasha Gregory-Lewis, conference secretary, April 6, 1976.

259   Aldridge offered a keynote speech: DeBaugh notes.

259   Goodstein openly expressed his disgust: "The Goodstein Brand of Activism: Making Gay Okay," *The Advocate*, no. 328 (Oct. 15, 1981).

259   vote totals on motions: DeBaugh notes. Minutes of the Advocate conference, on file in L.A. International Gay and Lesbian Archives, do not list vote totals.

259   O'Leary quotes at the meeting: *The Advocate*, no. 188 (April 21, 1976).

260   rancor, bitterness and clumsy power struggles: DeBaugh interview.

260   DeBaugh's press release: from draft in DeBaugh papers. DeBaugh said he did not have the final copy, but that it was not changed when it was issued several days after the conference.

19: Brothers and Sisters

261   Voeller and O'Leary got along: Bruce Voeller interview no. 4 with AJN; Jean O'Leary interview no. 3 with JDC.

261   "Are we going to practice what we preach?": O'Leary interview. Bruce Voeller told the story of the conversation slightly differently in interviews with AJN before his death, and in his writing ("My Days on the Task Force," *Christopher Street*, October 1979). He noted that it was he who made the proposal at the Task Force meeting at which she was appointed (which is correct), but also suggested that he deserved more credit for coming up with the idea.

261   O'Leary named co-executive director: *Gay Community News*, vol. 4, no. 1 (July 3, 1976), p. 3.

262   first meeting of Gay Academic Union, and Kantrowitz getting booed: Arnie Kantrowitz interview no. 2 with AJN. For early strife at GAU, see also Martin Duberman, *Cures*, pp. 274–78.

262   "Cocksucking causes cancer": Rudy Grillo letter to *The Advocate*, no. 197 (Aug. 25, 1976).

262   Hanover on bars: David Aiken, "Discrimination Exists in the Gay Community," *The Advocate*, no. 212 (March 23, 1977).

262   Continental Baths gave free admission to NGTF members: undated NGTF newsletter, courtesy of Lesbian Herstory Archives.

263   Friday night dinners of Task Force women: Betty Powell interview nos. 1 and 2, Ginny Vida interview, Nov. 25, 1994, and Charlotte Bunch interview no. 2 with AJN.

263   Kameny arguments against equal number of women on Task Force board: many interviews, including Bunch, and Duberman with AJN, March 23, 1995. Kameny told JDC he had no specific recollection of that argument, but didn't quarrel with it.

263   "Bullshit it is.": Ronald Gold interview no. 2 with AJN.

263   O'Leary came to consider Gold sexist: O'Leary interview with Eric Marcus, courtesy of Marcus.

263   Voeller supported equal representation: Bruce Voeller interview no. 4 with AJN.

263   Gold quit the board: Gold interview no. 2. Gold said he later came to regret his feelings at the time, and now thinks the board was correct.

263   Brydon on co-sexuality: Charles Brydon interviews with AJN and Eric Marcus.

263   particularly NOW: NOW came out in favor of a gay rights bill at its national conference in Washington, D.C., on Feb. 18, 1973. For more see *New York Times,* Feb. 18, 1973.

264   "It doesn't represent me. . . .": Powell interview no. 2.

264   *Advocate* questionnaire: "Opening Space," *The Advocate,* no. 163 (May 7, 1975). Although it wasn't a scientific survey, it was revealing of women's interest in the newspaper.

264   Women's Caucus met with Goodstein: Barbara Love interview with AJN, Jan. 9, 1995, Duberman interview and Bunch interview no. 2.

264   Goodstein on gay women being more closeted than gay men: *The Advocate,* no. 160 (March 26, 1975).

264   "I've just about had it. . . .": letters to the Editor, *The Advocate,* no. 199 (Sept. 22, 1976).

264   Goodstein on sex ads: Voeller interview no. 3 with AJN. Voeller said Goodstein told him in 1979 that he had put $1 million of his own money into the paper, and the only place he made money was from the sex ads.

264   Goodstein on Foster's remark: David Russell interview no. 2 with AJN.

264   Goodstein repeating that gay liberation was about men: Rob Eichberg interview no. 2 with AJN, recounting conversations with Goodstein.

264   Goodstein and the *Advocate* sex ads: Powell interview no. 2. Eventually, Goodstein's successor moved this section of the newspaper out and created a very successful publication, *Advocate Classifieds.*

265   Goodstein suggested the women were prudes: ibid.

265   Brown described Goodstein as loathing women: Rita Mae Brown interview no. 1 with AJN.

265   the "Chorientation Debate": Bunch interview no. 1 with AJN.

265   wording of Abzug's gay rights bill: Abzug interview with AJN, Nov. 11, 1994. Abzug thought it would be better if the word "orientation" was used, but she steered clear of what she recognized was a serious dispute.

265   on language used in congressional legislation (sexual preference vs. sexual orientation): Sarah P. Collins, *Federal Legislation Pertaining to Homosexual Rights, 94th Congress to 96th Congress,* Congressional Research Service, Library of Congress, April 17, 1980.

265   "The Brooklyn Mafia": Bill Kelley interview with AJN, June 24, 1994.

266   Van Ooteghem considered many of the women "hateful": Gary Van Ooteghem interview with AJN, June 24, 1994.

266   deliberative women and "If we came to you first. . . .": Bunch interview no. 2.

266   Powell on problems with Voeller: Powell interview no. 2.

PART THREE: THE BACKLASH

20: The Governor of Georgia

269   Carter was using his position as chairman of the DNCC to build a network: Peter G. Bourne, *Jimmy Carter: A Comprehensive Biography from Plains to Postpresidency,* pp. 242–47. Also Midge Costanza interview no. 1 with JDC.

270   "Can I call you back?": Costanza interview.

270   from the first moment she loved him: ibid.

270   the themes he stressed: Kenneth E. Morris, *Jimmy Carter, American Moralist,* pp. 202–203.

271   that Carter felt as she did about discrimination against homosexuals: Costanza interview.

271   O'Leary–Voeller letter to Costanza and her response: Costanza interview nos. 1 and 2, and Jean O'Leary interview nos. 2 and 4 with JDC.

271   Carter and Southern Baptists: Jules Witcover, "A Profound Event," *Washington Post*, March 21, 1976, p. A-1.

271   Discrimination against homosexuals was not an issue, and Carter didn't bring it up: Costanza interview nos. 1 and 2, Jody Powell interview, May 1, 1997, and Gerald Rafshoon interview, June 27, 1997, with JDC. Research in newspaper and gay newsletter files, and a search by the Jimmy Carter Library turned up only a handful of instances during the campaign in which Carter or Carter spokesmen addressed the subject, none of them in the South.

272   Carter-Perry exchange: Troy Perry interview with JDC, Feb. 21, 1994. Perry did not remember the date, but his memory of the event coincides with another report of Carter telling a Los Angeles audience on March 12 that he would sign an executive order banning discrimination against homosexuals.

272   "He's going to be the next president.": ibid.

272   Carter's statements in Philadelphia and San Francisco: Press release issued in his name on May 23, 1976, during the California primary, probably in San Francisco, and held by the Jimmy Carter Library in the file of Carter statements on the subject. Entitled "Jimmy Carter Speaks Out on Gay Rights," it lists the various Carter statements opposing discrimination against homosexuals, and names the gay paper as the *Philadelphia Gay News*. Courtesy of the Jimmy Carter Library, Atlanta. Those statements were also reported in the April 1977 issue of *Alice*, a monthly newsletter of the Alice B. Toklas Democratic Club in San Francisco, which said Carter made his statement to the Philadelphia Gay Raiders.

273   Carter didn't expect to win the California Democratic primary: Rafshoon interview.

273   appealing to every group of voters: Burt Lance interview no. 1 with JDC.

273   "I think my position. . . .": Carter press release of May 23, 1976, which noted that "Jimmy Carter has repeatedly expressed his support of gay people." Also transcript of *The Tomorrow Show* interview, courtesy of the Jimmy Carter Library.

273   Brown regarded the issue of gay rights as politically "threatening": Jerry Brown interview no. 2 with AJN.

273   "Rather than insult your intelligence. . . .": "Gerry Ford & Gays," *Gay Community News*, July 17, 1976, p. 2.

274   "Go on and have your own rally!": Douglas E. Kneeland, "Jackson Salutes 'Amigos' in East Harlem," *New York Times*, April 4, 1976, sect. 6, p. 58.

274   Wicker on Jackson: Tom Wicker, "Jackson on Rights," *New York Times*, April 6, 1976, sect. 1, p. 35. Wicker noted that Jackson's Colorado comments were reported to him by Americans for Democratic Action, and said that a Jackson spokesman stated that the senator did not recall making the remark.

274   Carter's reliance on his Southern Baptist faith: Myra MacPherson, "Jimmy Carter's Inner-Healing Sister," *Washington Post*, March 21, 1976, p. A-1. For a larger appraisal of the relationship of Carter's faith and his politics, see Bourne, *Jimmy Carter*.

274   "I don't consider myself one iota. . . .": It isn't clear where or when Carter said this, but the statement is contained in the Carter press release of May 23, 1976.

274   "There has been a great deal of concern. . . .": Bourne, *Jimmy Carter*, p. 327.

275   Costanza connection through Apuzzo: Virginia Apuzzo interview no. 2 with AJN.

275   organize support for a gay rights plank and Costanza's letter: Costanza interview nos. 1 and 2, and O'Leary interview nos. 2–4 with JDC.

275   the height of Carter's popularity: Morris, *Jimmy Carter, American Moralist*, p. 226.

275   Carter had prayed with Bailey Smith: Betty Glad, *Jimmy Carter: In Search of the Great White House* (New York: Norton, 1980), p. 384.

275   "a born-again man in the White House. . . .": William Martin, *With God on Our Side*, p. 157. Also from Myra MacPherson interview with JDC, July 23, 1997. MacPherson covered the event for the *Washington Post*.

275   the assembly condemned homosexuality: Kenneth A. Briggs, "Baptists, in Shift, Ask Members to Seek Antiabortion Climate," *New York Times*, June 18, 1976, sect. 1, p. 1. Also James Dunn interview with JDC, Aug. 8, 1997.

275   Chip Carter's picture, sitting grinning on a tricycle in San Francisco: *Gay Community News,* July 10, 1976, p. 6, reprinted from *The Advocate.* Memorial Day weekend. From Jim Gordon letter to Clendinen of June 3, 1999, with citations.

275   Carter and Democratic platform committee: O'Leary interview no. 3.

276   Chip Carter said his father "doesn't think homosexuality is right. . . .": *Human Events,* as quoted in the *Manchester Union Leader* and reprinted in the *Gay Community News,* July 10, 1976, p. 6. The thirdhand sourcing is an indication of the spotty nature of the coverage of such events at the time. Chip Carter's appearance and comments in the city's major annual gay celebration don't appear in the news index of the *San Francisco Chronicle* that year—or, for that matter, of the *Los Angeles Times* or *New York Times.*

276   about O'Leary and Costanza, Apuzzo: Costanza interview nos. 1 and 2, and O'Leary interview nos. 2–4.

276   the basic package of causes shared by feminist groups: Costanza interview nos. 1 and 2, and Apuzzo interview no. 2.

276   Abortion rights was the consuming issue: Apuzzo interview no. 1 with AJN.

276   four openly gay delegates: Neil Miller, "Gay Delegates Form Caucus at Convention," *Gay Community News,* July 24, 1976, p. 7.

276   "Your issue is not a priority.": Ginny Apuzzo, "Carter's Burden," a letter to the editor, *Gay Community News,* Sept. 4, 1976.

276   "Midge, listen. . . .": O'Leary interview no. 4 and Costanza interview no. 2.

277   drove that night from New York: ibid.

277   "Now. . . ." and those crazy liberals: Costanza interview no. 2 and O'Leary interview no. 2.

277   she told the other delegates: Costanza interview no. 2.

277   hostile reaction: O'Leary interview no. 4.

277   some sympathy from a lively discussion: Costanza interview no. 2.

277   "Midge," he pleaded: ibid.

277   bending over backwards to be agreeable: "Democrats, Apparently United for the First Time in Years, Adopt a Platform That Pleases All Factions," *New York Times,* June 16, 1976, sect. 1, p. 1.

277   It was tabled, 57–27.: Miller, "Gay Delegates Form Caucus at Convention," p. 7.

278   "We've made significant gains. . . .": Neil Miller, "Strategists Veto Putting Gay Up for Nomination," *Gay Community News,* July 17, 1976, p. 1.

278   nominate a gay candidate for vice president: ibid.

278   "The convention is so tightly controlled. . . .": ibid.

278   Helping Carter get elected was their best chance for progress: O'Leary interview nos. 3 and 4.

278   formation of a gay caucus: Miller, "Gay Delegates Form Caucus at Convention."

278   The petition, the gay caucus and Foster's comments: Jerry Burns, "Gays' First Delegate Caucus: A Party of 4," *San Francisco Chronicle,* July 14, 1976, p. B-5.

279   The Reverend Bob Maddox was almost beside himself: Maddox interview no. 1 with JDC.

279   advertisement in *Christianity Today:* Martin, *With God on Our Side,* p. 153.

279   Conlan made a worried telephone call: Edward McAteer and Paul Weyrich interviews with JDC.

279   not be such a bad thing: Weyrich interview no. 2.

280   Weyrich hadn't been interested in meeting Robertson: ibid.

280   Ford seemed insufficiently ideological: Weyrich interview nos. 1 and 2.

280   Weyrich's speech in Dallas: Weyrich interview no. 2.

280   Scheer was a probing, pushy interviewer: Patrick Anderson, *Electing Jimmy Carter: The Campaign of 1976* (Baton Rouge: Louisiana State University Press, 1994), p. 111.

281   at the end of their last interview: ibid., p. 112.

281   U.S. Supreme Court and Virginia sodomy law: "Gays Lose Key Ruling in High Court," *San Francisco Chronicle,* March 30, 1976, p. A-1.

282   "*I can't change the teachings of Christ....*": "Excerpts from Jimmy Carter's *Playboy* Interview," *Gay Community News,* Oct. 30, 1976, p. 1.

282   " 'Screw' is just not a good Baptist word.": Glad, *Jimmy Carter,* p. 384.

282   Falwell, who had never liked Carter's politics: Jerry Falwell interview with JDC, March 24, 1997.

282   "Like many others....": Martin, *With God on Our Side,* p. 158, quoting Myra MacPherson story in the *Washington Post,* Sept. 27, 1976, p. A-1.

282   granddaddy of the arch-conservative movement within the Southern Baptist Church: McAteer interviews no. 1 and 2.

282   "highly offended": Martin, *With God on Our Side,* p. 158, quoting Jules Witcover, *Marathon: The Pursuit of the Presidency, 1972–1976* (New York: Viking, 1977), p. 567.

282   Ford campaign television ad: Martin, *With God on Our Side,* p. 158.

282   ten-point lead over Ford evaporated overnight: Anderson, *Electing Jimmy Carter,* p. 113.

283   the narrow southern edge of victory: Morris, *Jimmy Carter, American Moralist,* p. 224.

283   Maddox wrote a proposal for an office of religious liaison: Maddox interview no. 1.

283   Carter had courted Robertson: Richard G. Hutcheson Jr., *God in the White House: How Religion Has Changed the Modern Presidency* (New York: Macmillan, 1988), p. 155, citing Wesley G. Pippert, ed., *The Spiritual Journey of Jimmy Carter* (New York: Macmillan, 1978), p. 100.

283   Robertson felt he had cut a deal: Weyrich interview no. 1. Also Pat Robertson interview no. 2, McAteer interview no. 1, Maddox interview no. 1 and Lance interview nos. 1 and 2 with JDC. Robertson's claim that Carter had promised to appoint evangelical Christians to his cabinet and elsewhere in his administration became widely known. Bob Maddox believed there was such an agreement. Bert Lance believed Robertson sincerely felt he had made such a deal. But Lance and Jody Powell both said they knew of no such promise, and that it was very unlike Carter to have made one. Powell interview.

283   Lance tried to mollify the offended Robertson: Lance interview nos. 1 and 2.

284   Carter didn't intend to set up any special listening post: Maddox interview nos. 1 and 2 with JDC.

284   list of all the promises Carter had made during the campaign: Bert Lance interview no. 2. Lance was reading through his copy as he talked.

21: A Voice in the White House

285   The Costanza appointment and the public reaction: Midge Costanza interview no. 2 with JDC.

286   O'Leary on preapproved list of White House visitors: Jean O'Leary interview no. 4 with JDC and ibid.

286   "Jean, who is David Goodstein?": Costanza interview no. 2.

286   "In good conscience we cannot recommend....": *Advocate* editorial, no. 201 (Oct. 20, 1976).

286   O'Leary on Goodstein and telling Costanza not to allow him to White House: O'Leary and Costanza interviews.

287   Costanza-O'Leary talks about White House meeting: ibid.

287   importance of meeting being held in Roosevelt Room: Costanza interview no. 2.

287   rehearsing their presentations before White House meeting: Bruce Voeller, "My Days on the Task Force," *Christopher Street,* October 1979.

288   Kameny's attempt to see President Kennedy: "White House Meeting: Concrete Results Soon?" *The Advocate,* no. 214 (April 20, 1977), p. 35. Frank Kameny interviews and Gittings interview nos. 1 and 2 with JDC; Randy Wicker interview no. 1 and Craig Rodwell interview no. 1 with AJN.

288   "Oh, I know all about Dr. Kameny....": Voeller, "My Days on the Task Force," and Troy Perry interview with JDC, Feb. 21, 1994.

288   details of meeting: *It's Time,* vol. 3, no. 7 (April/May 1977).
288   Kameny at White House meeting: Kameny interview no. 4.
288   Kameny on meeting with IRS: ibid.
288   Raya spoke on health care: Randy Shilts, "NGTF: Political Lion or Paper Tiger?" *The Advocate,* no. 242 (May 31, 1978).
289   "Rather than read my prepared statement. . . .": Perry interview.
289   Perry told of 1973 New Orleans fire and Costanza's reaction: ibid. and Costanza interview no. 2.
289   leaving the White House: ibid.
289   "We were all hiding in the bathroom. . . .": Costanza interview no. 2.
289   Costanza on CBS: *Lesbian Tide,* vol. 6, no. 6 (May/June 1977).
290   Costanza on her perception and reaction to the meeting: Costanza interview no. 2.

22: Miami: The Fundamentalists Awake

291   Perry's reaction to questions about Anita Bryant: Troy Perry interview with JDC, Feb. 21, 1994.
292   Voeller did not recognize Bryant's name: Voeller, "My Days on the Task Force," *Christopher Street,* October 1979.
292   Bryant biography: Anita Bryant, "ABC Biography," ABC radio network, April 8, 1959. Anita Bryant declined an invitation to be interviewed.
292   "met the creator of Stars . . .": Bryant quoted in "God's Crusader," *Newsweek,* June 6, 1977.
292   eight Orange Bowls: *People,* Jan. 24, 1977, p. 33.
293   standing ovation at the White House: *Daily Variety,* vol. 131, no. 51 (May 18, 1966).
293   Bryant's demand at political conventions and fees: Dick Shack interview with AJN, May 3, 1995.
293   Bryant made $700,000: Cliff Jahr, *Ladies' Home Journal,* December 1980, p. 62.
293   Campbell opened two bathhouses: "In the Gay Camp," *Newsweek,* June 6, 1977.
294   "Well, although we have only thirty churches. . . .": Jack Campbell interview no. 2 with JDC.
294   a silver-plated peanut: "In the Gay Camp."
294   Transperience sessions "better than a quaalude": Robert Kunst interview with AJN.
294   Coalition for the Humanistic Rights of Gays meeting: Campbell interview nos. 1 and 2 with JDC; also Kunst interview no. 1 with JDC; "Battle over Gay Rights," *Newsweek,* June 6, 1977, p. 16.
295   Shack on introducing gay rights bill: Ruth Shack interview with AJN, May 7, 1995.
295   Brake's background and his reaction to gay ordinance: Robert Brake interview with AJN, April 27, 1995.
295   Brake's early involvement in petition-initiative recall: ibid.
296   Bryant and influence from pastor: Mike Thompson interview with AJN, April 27, 1995.
296   You have a "mother's heart . . ." and Chapman and Bryant conversation at her home: Bob Green interview with AJN, April 28, 1995.
296   Text of Bryant's letter to the Metro Commission and her plans to go before the commission: "Gay Anti-Bias Bill Criticized," *Miami Herald,* Jan. 17, 1977.
296   Shack's conversation with Bryant: Ruth Shack interview; the gist of it was recounted by Bryant in numerous Miami-area interviews at the time.
297   Kunst was unprepared for the turnout at Dade County Courthouse and sat next to Bryant: Kunst interview no. 2.
297   Shack at the public hearing: Ruth Shack interview.
297   Bryant at the hearing: *New York Times,* Jan. 19, 1977.
297   Brake invited Bryant to join the coalition, and her checking with Green and Chapman: Brake interview.

297   Villa Verde: numerous sources, including Green interview, "God's Crusader," and "Being Born Again," *Florida Magazine*, Feb. 21, 1988.

297   Bryant's attraction to Green, with description of white T-bird: Bryant in *Playboy* magazine, May 1978.

298   Green was the first man Bryant went to bed with: Jahr, *Ladies' Home Journal*.

298   Green was less spiritual than the other people in the room, and was motivated by love for Anita Bryant in becoming born-again: Green interview.

298   There is a direct conflict here between Bob Green and Dick Shack. Green said he always opposed his ex-wife's getting involved with the dispute and warned from the start that it would destroy her career (which it did). Dick Shack said that Anita Bryant had told him six months earlier to stop booking appearances for her; that Green learned this from Shack and, Shack believes, started pushing his wife to do religious appearances, assuming she would never turn them down, because he saw the homosexual issue as a way to increase demand for her performances.

298   Brake invited Thompson to join the campaign: Thompson interview.

298   Bryant's statement and afterward: ibid.

299   petition gathering and Metro Commission decision: Morton Lucoff, "Voters to Decide Gay Rights in Dade County," *Miami News*.

299   "beaches, bushes, fun. . . .": Campbell interview no. 2.

299   Shack on being upset at lack of support from gay community: Ruth Shack interview.

299   debate at NGTF as to whether to get involved in Miami: Ronald Gold interview no. 2 with AJN.

300   Bryant was the "perfect opponent": NGTF "Action Report: Opportunities for Action/Report on Results," April/May 1977.

300   "If the orange juice cow. . . .": Goodstein, "Opening Space," *The Advocate*, no. 214 (April 20, 1977).

300   Campbell on need for outside political consultants: Lee Solomon, "Lessons from Losing: Four Perspectives on Dade County," *The Advocate*, no. 333 (Aug. 24, 1977).

300   "Anita Bryant is a fine Christian lady. . . .": Ted Stanger, "Fight for Homosexuals' Rights Didn't Start, Won't End, Here," *Miami Herald*, April 11, 1977.

301   Noble on Bryant going on to other states: "Battle over Gay Rights."

301   situation that Geto found in Miami: Geto interview nos. 2 and 3 with AJN; Geto to *Christopher Street*, September 1977; and Geto to *The Advocate*, no. 333 (Aug. 24, 1977).

301   on Kunst discussion of anal/oral sex and putting the community on the couch: Kunst interview no. 2; also Ruth Shack and Dick Shack interviews and Geto interview no. 3.

301   Askew supported the referendum: *Florida Times Union*, April 30, 1977.

301   Foster's political history: *San Francisco Chronicle*, April 30, 1977.

302   Geto's disdain for the Florida activists: Geto interviews. Also his interview with Charles Ortleb in *Christopher Street*, August 1977.

302   results of first poll by Save Our Children: Thompson interview.

303   "That commercial is just driving them nuts!": *San Francisco Chronicle*, June 7, 1977.

303   "Some of the stories I could tell you. . . .": *San Francisco Chronicle*, May 15, 1977.

303   "This recruitment of our children. . . .": *Miami Herald*, March 20, 1977, cited in *The Advocate*, no. 214 (April 20, 1977).

304   "THERE IS NO 'HUMAN RIGHT'. . . .": *Miami Herald* ad, June 6, 1977, p. B-7.

304   the May poll: Foster discussed poll results in post-election interview with Joe Baker, "Miami," *The Advocate*, no. 219 (July 13, 1977).

304   other details on poll: Geto to *Christopher Street*, August 1977, pp. 24–25.

304   "By making the campaign. . . .": Foster to *The Advocate*, no. 219 (July 13, 1977).

304   Geto's pessimism about the way the election was going and decisions to focus on opinion outside the state: Geto interview no. 2.

305   Geto's fear of associating homosexuals with child molesters: Geto interview no. 2 and Solomon, "Lessons from Losing."

305   Campbell wore a bulletproof vest. Campbell interview no. 2.

305   Foster and shotgun: Geto interview no. 2; also Geto to *Christopher Street*, September 1977.

305   The bomb squad blew up the envelope: "Battle over Gay Rights."
305   "This is really a sewer. . . .": Geto to *Christopher Street*, August 1977, p. 24.
305   on swastika ad: Geto interview no. 2; text of ad from *Christopher Street*, August 1977, p. 26.
305   Bryant striptease: "Amusement Business," *Chicago*, Sept. 4, 1971.
305   "We didn't want to get down in the gutter. . . .": *San Francisco Chronicle*, June 7, 1977.
306   "Every gay bar. . . .": *San Francisco Chronicle*, April 26, 1977.
306   Bryant roast at the Pier Nine disco: Tom Bastow interview no. 2 with JDC.
306   "campy defiance": "Battle over Gay Rights."
306   "Nothing has ever. . . .": *San Francisco Chronicle*, April 21, 1977.
306   "Don't you know who that is?": Campbell interview no. 2.
306   Bryant on fornication: Frank Greve and Gerald Storch, *Miami Herald Magazine*.
306   Bryant best when reading from a script: Thompson interview.
307   friends found Bryant's rhetoric extreme: Green interview.
307   Thompson-Hongisto exchange: "Absentee Ballots Heavy," *Miami Herald*, May 31, 1977.
307   Campbell-Geto tension: Geto interview no. 2.
307   Endean thought Campbell and Geto were naïve: Steve Endean interview no. 9 with JDC.
307   Tobin/Gittings wanted Troy Perry in Miami: Tobin/Gittings interview with Marcus, courtesy of Marcus.
308   sermons the Sunday before the vote and *Miami Herald* editorial: *San Francisco Chronicle*, June 6, 1977.
308   original *Miami Herald* editorial: "Metro in the Right on 'Gays' Decision," *Miami Herald*, Jan. 20, 1977.
308   election night: Kunst, Campbell, Geto, O'Leary and Green interviews; also "Margin of Victory Greater than 2–1," *Miami Herald*, June 8, 1977; "Decency Is a Winner, Anita Says," *Miami Herald*, June 10, 1977; Baker, "Miami," *Los Angeles Times*, June 8, 1977; and *San Francisco Chronicle*, June 8, 1977.
309   "all the evidence anyone could need. . . .": Jean O'Leary quoted in *Los Angeles Times*, June 8, 1977.
309   O'Leary's reaction to head shot in *Miami Herald*: O'Leary interviews with JDC and Marcus.
309   "one step backward. . . ." Campbell quoted in *Miami Herald*, June 8, 1977.
309   "We had an army of recruits": Goodstein quoted in Associated Press, June 7, 1977.
309   "While we might have. . . .": Geto correspondence with Ruth Shack, July 1, 1977, courtesy of Shack papers.
310   gays woke up Abzug at home: Abzug interview with AJN.
310   San Francisco post-Bryant demonstration: *San Francisco Chronicle*, June 8, 1977.
310   NGTF membership doubled in four months: *It's Time*, vol. 4, no. 3 (December 1977).
310   "Let Miss Bryant. . . .": William Safire, *New York Times* op-ed page, June 9, 1977.
311   "Democratic issues are won and lost. . . .": letters to the editor, *The Advocate*, no. 220 (July 1977).
311   Geto on referendum: *Christopher Street*, September 1977.

23: A Very Bad Year

312   Boston Gay Pride Parade and the scene at Boston Common: articles and letters to the editor in *Gay Community News*, July 2 and July 9, 1977. Also Charley Shively, "Speaking Out: Bible Burning as an Act of Illumination," *Gay Community News*, July 23, 1977, p. 5. Copies of *Gay Community News* are on microfilm purchased from the private archives of former Boston activist Bill Canfield, of East Hardwick, Vermont.

313 "Christianity Is The Enemy!": ibid. Also Charley Shively interview no. 1 and John Mitzel interview no. 1 with JDC, and numerous other Boston interviews. The *Fag Rag* contingent carried this banner in Gay Pride Parades for years afterward.

313 had been warned that Harvard: Shively interview.

313 *Fag Rag*: Charley Shively, "The History of *Fag Rag*," *Gay Community News*, Feb. 18–24, 1991, p. 10, and subsequent issues, courtesy of Shively. Also Shively interview nos. 2 and 3 with JDC.

313 found it enormously offensive: ibid. Also Amy Hoffman interview, Sept. 18, 1993, in McCarthy interview nos. 2 and 3, and Laura McMurry interview no. 1 with JDC; and particularly the letters to the editor in *Gay Community News*, July 2 and July 9, 1977.

313 draped in his faded, crimson Harvard doctoral robe: Mitzel interview.

313 Leviticus: King James Version of the Holy Bible (New York: Oxford University Press, 1948).

314 dropped the whole Bible into the burning wok: tape transcribed by John Mitzel and provided courtesy of Charley Shively; Shively, Brian McNaught, Elaine Noble, Mitzel and Rudy Kikel interviews with JDC; and articles and letters to the editor, *Gay Community News*, July 2 and July 9, 1977.

314 conflicted feelings, much of it rage: Nancy Walker letter to the editor, *Gay Community News*, July 2, 1977.

314 Under Cardinals Cushing and Medeiros: Paul Shanley interview, Sept. 17, 1996, Noble interview no. 3 and McNaught interview no. 2 with JDC. For the founding of Dignity, see John J. McNeill, *The Church and the Homosexual*, p. 5.

314 McNaught's background: McNaught interview nos. 1 and 2, and Neil Miller, "Brian McNaught—A One-Person Reformation," *Gay Community News*, Sept. 17, 1977, pp. 8–10.

314 McNaught was beside himself: McNaught interview no. 2.

315 Noble, Maguire and Frank speeches: Walker letter to the editor.

315 someone might try to kill Shively: Noble interview no. 1 with JDC.

315 "Go to Hell! . . .": Shively interview no. 1; *Gay Community News*, July 2 and 9, 1977; and Shively, "Speaking Out."

315 the members of Dignity were threatening to kill him: McNaught said the death threat was Noble's dramatic invention. But "kill" was the word that Noble and Shively both used in describing the event and their conversations. McNaught interview no. 2, Shively interview no. 1 and Noble interview no. 1.

315 McNaught pleaded with the crowd: *Gay Community News*, July 2 and 9, 1977, McNaught interview no. 2 and Noble interview no. 1. Also Rudy Kikel interview with JDC, Sept. 18, 1993.

315 the television news: Shively interview no. 1 and McNaught interview no. 2.

316 Bryant promised to bring her crusade to Minnesota: "Homosexual Bias Law Loses in Miami Area," *Minneapolis Star*, June 8, 1977, p. A-4.

316 Archdiocese of St. Paul and Minneapolis had engineered the defeat of legislation: "Catholic Bishops Fight State Homosexual Bill," *Minneapolis Star*, April 30, 1977.

316 thought that his arguments to the church were persuasive: Endean interview with JDC.

316 the establishment endorsed gay rights law: Endean interview no. 16 with JDC. See also "Gay Rights Bill OK'd by Senate Unit," *Minneapolis Star*, April 18, 1977, p. A-5; also an editorial, "State Should Adopt Gay Rights," *Minneapolis Star*, April 23, 1977, p. A-10.

317 "bigots," "Christians," Spear wept: Blair Charnley, "Bill Protecting Homosexuals Is Killed," *Minneapolis Star*, May 5, 1977, p. B-10. Also Spear interview nos. 2 and 3 with JDC, and Spear's speech at Endean Memorial 2.

317 Miller's conversations with Casey and Schwartz: Dennis Miller interview with JDC, Sept. 29, 1993. Schwartz would soon identify himself as a member of a new Jack Baker organization, the Target City Coalition. Endean (interview no. 16 with JDC) also remembered Father Casey's involvement.

317 preparation for pie-throwing, description of event and attempted getaway: ibid.

318 Schwartz was arrested and sentenced: Steve Johnson, "Pie Thrower's Punishment Is 80 Hours of Community Work," *Minneapolis Star*, June 17, 1977, p. B-6.

318   Casey's role in the pie-throwing plot was leaked to the *Minneapolis Tribune*: Miller interview. For some details, also Willmar Thorkelson, "Homosexual Takes Blame for Pie-Throwing, Clears Priest," *Minneapolis Star*, May 14, 1977, p. A-5, keeping in mind that Dennis Miller said he lied to the reporter in order to try to protect Casey, who had been outed by Thom Higgins to the *Minneapolis Tribune*. Higgins died in November 1994, at age forty-four, of hepatitis C. Jean Tretter interview no. 1 with JDC.

318   Casey disappeared: Miller interview and Endean interview no. 16.

318   opponents of Spear's anti-discrimination bill: Debra Stone, "State Senator Is Joining Bryant Drive on 'Gays,' " *Minneapolis Star*, June 10, 1977, p. A-11.

318   doubling the Twin Cities population of lesbians and gays: Randy Furst, "City Group's Miami Ad Offers Homosexual Haven," *Minneapolis Star*, July 7, 1977, p. B-10; and "3 Ask Miami Gays to Move Here," *Minneapolis Star*, July 29, 1977.

318   ambushing local public officials, twice throwing pies: "Pie Throwing Prompts Activist's Arrest," *Minneapolis Star*, July 8, 1977; and Mary Lahr, "Pie Toss Is Spoiled by Target," *Minneapolis Star*, July 29, 1977, p. A-1.

318   "We welcome the challenge. . . .": "Homosexual Bias Law Loses in Miami Area."

318   200,000 marchers in San Francisco: Jerry Roberts, "Gay Freedom Day in S.F.: 200,000 in Peaceful Parade," *San Francisco Chronicle*, June 27, 1977, p. A-1.

319   Hillsborough died: Larry Kramer, "Neighbors React to Arrests in Gay Killing," *San Francisco Examiner*, June 26, 1977, p. 1.

319   "My son's blood. . . .": William Moore, "Stirring Tribute to Slain Gay," *San Francisco Chronicle*, June 28, 1977, p. 5.

319   "Here's one for Anita": "Mother of Slain Gay Sues Anita Bryant," *San Francisco Chronicle*, July 1, 1977, p. A-2.

319   conservative Christian pressure on Mayor Maynard Jackson: "Jackson Pressured for Gay Pride Day," *Atlanta Constitution*, June 21, 1977, sect. B; Lyn Martin, "Mayor Afraid, Gay Leaders Say," *Atlanta Constitution*, June 22, 1977, p. A-1; and Lyn Martin and Ken Willis, "There'll Be No 'Gay Pride Day,' " *Atlanta Constitution*, June 24, 1977.

320   "That's a stereotype. . . .": Vicki Brown, "Publicity Swells Gay Pride Parade," *Atlanta Constitution*, June 26, 1977.

320   "Have you or have you not . . . ?": Ken Willis, "Eaves Rules Out Homosexuals as City Policemen," *Atlanta Constitution*, July 15, 1977, p. A-1. Also Jim Marko, "Atlanta Police Applicants Asked, 'Are You Gay?' " *Gay Community News*, Aug. 27, 1977, p. 1.

320   House of Representatives voted 230–133: "Another Vote to Bar Aid to Homosexuals," *San Francisco Chronicle*, June 28, 1977, p. 8. Also Tom Wicker column on the op-ed page of the *New York Times*, July 10, 1977; and David Brill, "Conferees Kill Gay Legal Aid Ban," *Gay Community News*, Dec. 10, 1977, p. 1. McDonald's John Birch Society membership in Michael Barone and Grant Ujifusa, *The Almanac of American Politics 1982* (Washington, D.C.: Barone, 1981), pp. 260–62.

320   Helms wrote to his constituents: reprinted in Anita Bryant, *The Anita Bryant Story*, pp. 138–41.

321   "Enough! Enough! . . .": *Atlanta Constitution Sunday Magazine*, Sept. 18, 1977.

321   "The Ku Klux Klan is not embarrassed. . . .": "Ku Klux Klan Calls for Execution of Homosexuals," *Gay Community News*, Sept. 24, 1977, p. 1.

321   "Gay used to be one of the most agreeable words": Schlesinger quoted in "Himself" column, Charles McCabe, *San Francisco Chronicle*, March 10, 1977.

321   owners of the *Gay Wind* wanted to rename it: "Legal Notice: Change of Vessel's Name," *Gloucester Daily Times*, Sept. 10, 1977.

321   "Having lived more than 73 years. . . .": *Montgomery Advertiser*, as reported in "Knoxville's 'Gay Street' Name Causes a Furor," *Gay Community News*, Sept. 24, 1977, p. 3.

322   Wichita gay rights ordinance: "Wichita Passes Gay Rights Law," *San Francisco Chronicle*, Sept. 28, 1977, p. A-3; and "Wichita Bishop to Defy Ordinance," *Gay Community News*, Oct. 22, 1977, p. 6.

323   It was not a civil rights issue: Terry Bean interview with JDC, Sept. 5, 1996. Also "A New Approach to Gay Rights Appeal," *San Francisco Chronicle*, May 9, 1978, p. A-5.

323   Anderson helped form the Gay Students Collective: Craig Anderson interview no. 1 with JDC.

324   Anderson took some forms home: ibid., and Jeffrey C. Kummer, "How the Gays Lost the Battle in St. Paul," *San Francisco Examiner,* April 30, 1978, p. F-8. Also B. J. Metzger and D. J. Munro interview with JDC, 1993.

324   Angwin and his group: Brenda Ingersoll, "St. Paul Petitioned to Repeal Gay Rights," *Minneapolis Star,* Jan. 18, 1978, p. A-2.

324   hard to find any gay men or lesbians in St. Paul willing to testify: Miller interview.

324   Endean asked Woodward to chair the group: Kerry Woodward's speech at Endean Memorial 2.

324   Both U.S. senators supported the ordinance: *GRNL/NGTF Report,* April 1980.

325   "Both the Christian tradition. . . .": "Roach Backs Basic Rights for Area Gays," *Minneapolis Star,* Feb. 3, 1978, p. A-1.

325   a Tri-Cities Fund: Bean and Anderson interviews.

325   poll by the *Minneapolis Star:* John Carman, "Most Think Same-Sex Acts Are Wrong," *Minneapolis Star,* Nov. 18, 1977, p. A-1.

326   Angwin had some outside help: Brenda Ingersoll, "Voices Get Louder in St. Paul's Debate of Gay Rights Issue," *Minneapolis Star,* Feb. 27, 1978, p. A-1; and Kummer, "How the Gays Lost the Battle in St. Paul."

326   Endean and his defense team worked long hours: Endean interview no. 1 with JDC. Also "6 Minnesota Protestant Leaders Back Gay Rights Ordinance," *Minneapolis Tribune,* March 3, 1978, p. B-15; and "St. Paul–Minneapolis Archdiocesan Priest Backs St. Paul Gay Rights Ordinance."

326   strong editorial support from the newspapers: editorials in the *Minneapolis Star,* Feb. 8 and April 21, 1978, and the *Minneapolis Tribune,* April 19, 1978.

326   Perry flew in: Troy Perry interview with JDC, Feb. 21, 1994; also Perry's speech at Endean Memorial 2.

326   Latimer campaigned door-to-door: *GRNL/NGTF Report,* April 1980.

326   they had let homosexuality become the issue: Endean interview no. 2 with JDC.

326   Baker and Kunst: Spear interview no. 3 and Miller interview. Also "Bob Kunst Predicts St. Paul Gay Rights Ordinance Won't Be Repealed," *Minneapolis Tribune,* March 31, 1978, p. B-3; and Kummer, "How the Gays Lost the Battle in St. Paul."

326   On the way home from the office: Miller interview and Kerry Woodward interview with JDC. Endean, in numerous interviews, spoke candidly about his active and anonymous sex life, and how compulsive he became when under stress or attack. Endean interview nos. 1 and 28 especially, also Larry Bye interview nos. 2 and 3, and Tom Bastow interview with JDC.

327   communities of gay people in their midst: Bean interview.

327   "I felt that as a father. . . .": Kummer, "How the Gays Lost the Battle in St. Paul."

327   "Hallelujah!": ibid.

328   personal effect of the St. Paul Repeal: Endean interview nos. 1 and 2, Woodward interview nos. 2 and 3, Bye interview nos. 2 and 3, Miller interview, Mike McConnell interview nos. 1 and 2, and Tim Campbell interview no. 1 with JDC.

328   Bryant had promised to appear in St. Paul: "Anita Bryant to Appear in St. Paul April 19—Help Fight Gay Rights Law," *Minneapolis Star,* April 7, 1978, p. A-9; and "St. Paul Furor: Pastors Feud over Gay Law," *San Francisco Chronicle,* April 25, 1978, p. A-5.

328   met by wave of protesters: Jim Chalgren interview no. 1 and Endean interview no. 16 with JDC; and "750 Gays Protest Anita Bryant's Appearance in Minneapolis," *Minneapolis Tribune,* May 22, 1977, p. A-1.

328   Hit with a strawberry rhubarb pie: "A Sticky Face for Anita," *Gay Community News,* Oct. 29, 1977, p. 1. Also Endean interview no. 24 for description of Higgins.

328   NBC was concerned about Bryant's safety: "Anita Bryant Flees New York After Death Threats," *Gay Community News,* Nov. 12, 1977, p. 1. Also *Time* magazine, Nov. 21, 1977.

328   "I am clearly a victim. . . .": "Anita Challenges Her Citrus Critics," *San Francisco Chronicle,* Oct. 28, 1977, p. 2.

329   "Rally for Decency" in Indiana: "Jeers and Cherry Bombs for Bryant," *San Francisco Chronicle*, July 10, 1977, p. A-3.
329   "Was the New York blackout . . . ?": Tom Shales, *Los Angeles Times*, Aug. 7, 1977.
329   Bryant and Hitler: Mary Susan Miller, "The *Journal*'s Teen Survey: Whom Do Your Kids Love and Hate the Most?" *Ladies' Home Journal*, p. 33.
329   "She has been threatened with violence. . . .": *New York Times* editorial, Nov. 18, 1977.
329   "This is exactly what happened. . . .": Nat Hentoff, *Village Voice*, Nov. 28, 1977.
329   The era of big-time television evangelism: Alice Murray, "James Robison to Bring Ministry to TV," *Atlanta Journal*, June 10, 1978.

24: An Uneasy Victory in San Francisco

331   Gordon's job, and note-taking habit: Jim Gordon interview no. 3 with JDC.
331   "Orange Tuesday," and details of the day: Jim Gordon's journal for 1977, pp. 175–77, from the private papers of Jim Gordon, courtesy of Gordon.
331   Gordon's "Gay Rap" group: ibid. Also Gordon interview nos. 3 and 4 with JDC.
332   There were no rules in place: "There are no rules in place. . . . We're the first generation to live openly as homosexuals," Randy Shilts said. "We have no role models. We have to find new ways to live." Quoted in Frances FitzGerald, *Cities on a Hill*, p. 47. Also Cleve Jones interview with JDC, March 9, 1994.
332   estimates of gays in San Francisco: In a July 13, 1977, article in *The Advocate*, Bill Sivert started by stating that the city's population of 700,000 people included between 100,000 and 150,000 gay men and women. An earlier *Advocate* story on the Castro neighborhood, published in the Feb. 9, 1977, issue, reported the mass migration of gay people to the city in the '70s, and that one San Francisco TV station had put the number at 120,000, but that 100,000 was probably closer. In the wake of the massive Gay Freedom Day Parade later that month, a *San Francisco Chronicle* reporter asked two dozen knowledgeable people around the city how large they thought the homosexual population was and got two dozen different answers, ranging from 70,000 to 150,000. Whatever the number, as the article makes clear, given that there were only about 516,000 adult residents of the city, the gay population was proportionately large. Jerry Burns, "Number of S.F. Gays a Puzzle," *San Francisco Chronicle*, June 28, 1977, p. A-5.
332   a gay village: In *Cities on a Hill*, FitzGerald (p. 46) cites Harvey Milk as estimating from his own precinct counts that 25,000 to 30,000 gay people had moved into the Castro by 1977.
333   as a graduate student Gordon asked the archbishop of Chicago for permission to read forbidden books and was denied: letter of Sept. 18, 1962, from James E. Gordon to His Eminence, Albert Cardinal Meyer, and letter of Sept. 24, 1962, to James E. Gordon from the Rt. Rev. Msgr. George J. Casey, Vicar General. Both from Gordon's private papers, courtesy of Gordon.
333   Gordon's first sexual experience: Gordon interview no. 2 with JDC.
333   about Harry Britt: Britt interview nos. 1–3 with JDC.
333   about Claude Wynne, and meeting Howard Wallace: Wynne interview with JDC, March 7, 1994.
334   about Wallace, and meeting Wynne: Wallace interview no. 1 with JDC. Also "Howard Wallace: Biographical Background," a flier printed about 1979, courtesy of Howard Wallace.
334   Britt's new habits: Britt interview no. 1.
334   J. C. Funky: Randy Shilts, *The Mayor of Castro Street: The Life and Times of Harvey Milk*, p. 86.
334   the hippie look was passing: Britt, Gordon and Jones interviews.
334   the Ritch Street Baths was a social center for the new crowd: Britt interview no. 2.
334   reactions to Foster's convention speech: Britt interview nos. 2 and 3, Wallace interview no. 1 and Jones interview.
334   "S. F. Is the Issue . . .": Jerry Carroll, *San Francisco Chronicle*, June 7, 1977, p. A-1.
335   The filmed footage: ibid.
335   police arrests and community reaction: *The Advocate*, no. 148 (Oct. 9, 1974); "Police Say Welcome to Gay Recruits," *San Francisco Chronicle*, Sept. 12, 1974, p. A-7; and Tim Cor-

bett and rama, "Practice Makes Powerful: Can Gays Get It Together in San Francisco? A Political Analysis of Bay Area Gay Liberation," *Magnus: A Socialist Journal of Gay Liberation*, no. 2 (Summer 1977), from the private papers of James E. Gordon, courtesy of Gordon.

335   mixed group of leftists: *Magnus;* also Wallace interview no. 1.

335   adopted the nickname "Bagel": Gordon interview nos. 2 and 3. Also Gordon's journal, Jan. 22, 1975.

335   Foster silent and envious: Wallace interview no. 1.

335   Bagel formed a neighborhood patrol: "C. B. Patrol Protects S. F. Gays," *San Francisco Chronicle*, Jan. 24, 1977, p. A-2.

335   Heakin's murder and the Butterfly Brigade: Gordon's journal entry for the Bagel meeting of Nov. 22, 1976, at which the Gay Action Committee was formed and a letter of protest sent to Tucson Judge Ben C. Birdsall.

335   Sheriff Hongisto's report to the bar owners: "Hongisto's Pledge on Rights," *San Francisco Chronicle*, June 8, 1977, p. A-2.

336   the look of the crowd at Market and Castro: photographs, *San Francisco Chronicle*, June 8, 1977, p. A-2; and "Miami Fallout," *San Francisco Sentinel*, vol. 3, no. 7 (June 17, 1977), p. 2, courtesy of James E. Gordon.

336   the march up Market: "Defiant Gays March in S. F.," *San Francisco Chronicle*, June 8, 1977, p. A-2; "Miami Fallout"; and Gordon's journal, June 7, 1977, pp. 176–77.

336   a large red banner: ibid.

337   the main speaker at the rally was Harvey Milk: Gordon's journal, June 7, 1997, p. 177.

337   climbed up a pole: ibid.

337   Stokes sold the Ritch Street Baths: Stokes interview no. 4 with JDC.

337   Stokes and the Castro: Stokes interview no. 3 with JDC.

337   Milk's store: Shilts, *The Mayor of Castro Street*, p. 65.

337   Andy's Donuts: Stokes interview no. 3.

338   passed the time working jigsaw puzzles: Shilts, *The Mayor of Castro Street*, p. 46.

338   What Stokes and Milk were each doing: Stokes interview nos. 1–5 with JDC and Shilts, *The Mayor of Castro Street*.

339   Milk organized gay businesses in the Castro: Shilts, *The Mayor of Castro Street*, pp. 89–90.

339   Foster and Milk's conversation, and their differences: ibid., pp. 73–75.

339   Foster was a former Republican: Sasha-Gregory Lewis, "Building a Gay Politics," *The Advocate*, no. 174 (Oct. 8, 1975).

339   politics was theater: Shilts, *The Mayor of Castro Street*, pp. 77–79.

339   the votes Milk drew in 1973: ibid., pp. 79–80.

340   Milk's Republican background: ibid., p. 75.

340   Harvey Milk benefit dinner: Gordon's journal, Oct. 6, 1975.

340   gay resentment and consumer campaigns against Coors: Dallas Coors interview, Feb. 14, 1994, and Howard Wallace interview no. 2 with JDC. Also "San Francisco Bay Area Gay Liberation General Meeting" notice, Feb. 10, 1975; "BAGL," *Gay Sunshine, A Journal of Gay Liberation*, no. 24 (Spring 1975); and "A Call for Labor Leadership and Action on Human Rights," issued by the Labor Committee of Bay Area Gay Liberation of San Francisco to the Delegates of the Eleventh Constitutional Convention of the AFL-CIO in San Francisco, Oct. 2, 1975. See as well *BAGL Bulletin*, vol. 1, no. 2, and "Howard Wallace, Biographical Background, 1979." All courtesy of Howard Wallace.

340   William Coors's statement in *The Advocate*: David B. Goodstein and Sasha-Gregory Lewis, "The Coors Controversy," *The Advocate*, no. 228 (Nov. 16, 1977).

340   Glide Memorial Church celebration: Gordon's journal, Nov. 30, 1975. For Coyote, also Phyllis Lyon/Del Martin interview no. 4 with JDC.

340   Alice B. Toklas endorsed Milk's opponent in the 1975 supervisor's race: Shilts, *The Mayor of Castro Street*, p. 103.

340   ". . . the largest liberal voting bloc in the city.": Philip Hagar, "Gay Power Emerging at Ballot Box," *Los Angeles Times*, Sept. 30, 1975, p. A-1.

341   early encounter of Harvey Milk and Cleve Jones: Jones interview.

341   Cleve Jones discovered San Francisco and settled there: ibid.

341   "Aw, c'mon. . . .": ibid.

342   about Jo Daly: *The Advocate,* Sept. 10, 1975, part of a series on gay workers. Also "Arbiter and Activist: Jo Daly," *The Advocate,* Feb. 7, 1980.

342   Daly drove with Michelle to San Francisco: Lyon/Martin interview.

342   Daly's appearance: Stokes interview no. 5.

342   lesbian mothers could lose their children: Lyon/Martin interview.

343   Feinstein was not a liberal: Almost everyone interviewed about Feinstein's political attitudes remarked on her prim, or even prudish, views on sexuality—heterosexual or homosexual. Lyon/Martin, Richard Hongisto, Britt and Stokes interviews with JDC.

343   Daly's Human Rights Commission job: Michael Grieg, "Gay Aide on City Staff," *San Francisco Chronicle,* March 27, 1975. Also Lyon/Martin interview.

343   Achilles was a financial backer of Feinstein: Stokes interview no. 5 and Lyon/Martin interview.

343   Feinstein's response to Daly and Achilles's decision about marriage: Lyon/Martin interview.

343   the wedding: ibid.

344   the power of the gay vote in San Francisco by 1975: Hagar, "Gay Power Emerging at Ballot Box."

344   "Peaches, peaches, fuzz . . .": ibid.

344   Moscone never appeared at the Alice Club: Stokes interview nos. 3–5.

344   Moscone and the dramatic Senate repeal of the sodomy law: Shilts, *The Mayor of Castro Street,* pp. 105–106.

344   Daly's inability to win the Alice endorsement for Feinstein or to keep it from Moscone, and what it meant: Stokes interview no. 5.

344   Moscone's gay support: Shilts, *The Mayor of Castro Street,* pp. 105–106.

344   the 1975 elections: ibid., pp. 106–10.

345   the Milk swearing-in to the Board of Permit Appeals: ibid., p. 128.

345   Milk's decision to run against Agnos for the Assembly seat and the result: ibid., pp. 129–34. Also "Milk Gets Canned but Keeps on Running," *The Advocate,* no. 187 (April 7, 1976).

345   "Harvey Milk and the Machine": Shilts, *The Mayor of Castro Street,* p. 134.

346   Foster and Goodstein tried to head off Milk: Stokes interview no. 5.

346   Foster and Goodstein seemed to have rehearsed what they said to Stokes: ibid.

346   Stokes wasn't voluble or funny: Lyon/Martin, Hongisto, Charlotte Coleman, Britt and other interviews with JDC.

346   Stokes hated the slipperiness of politics: Stokes interview no. 5.

346   the marches, demonstrations and mass meetings in the wake of the Dade County vote: Gordon's journal, June 7–14, 17, 19–20, 1977.

346   the parade: Jerry Roberts, "Gay Freedom Day in S. F.: 200,000 in Peaceful Parade," *San Francisco Chronicle,* June 27, 1977, p. A-1. Also Gordon's journal, June 26, 1977.

346   the sense of crisis led to the growth of gay identity in the Castro: Britt interview no. 3.

347   the Bagel split and the San Francisco Gay Democratic Club: Wallace interview nos. 2 and 3, and Gordon interview nos. 2 and 3 with JDC; and Gordon's journal, Sept. 19 and Dec. 14, 1976, Jan. 18 and Feb. 15, 1977. Also Jim Gordon letter to Clendinen of June 3, 1999, and citations.

347   straight politicians sent their wives to represent them at Alice meetings: Britt interview nos. 2 and 3.

347   only a tiny portion was politically active: "No more than 1,000 of San Francisco's gays are active, and that includes the royalty pageants and softball teams," Jo Daly told reporter Bill Sivert, *The Advocate,* no. 219 (July 13, 1977).

347   Britt wished it were No. 1 Castro Street: Britt interview no. 3.

347   Britt lusting for Milk's boyfriend: ibid.

347   the strategy to deny Stokes the Alice endorsement: ibid.

348   Milk had not liked the idea of trying to block Stokes's endorsement by Alice: ibid.

348   Alice endorsement vote meeting: Gordon's journal, Sept. 12, 1977.
348   Stokes was hurt: Stokes's pain about the night he lost Alice's endorsement was evident even in conversation with him twenty years later. In the election, Stokes ran third in a field of ten. Gordon's journal, Nov. 8, 1977.
348   "I've *never* liked you!": Gordon interview nos. 2 and 3.
349   "As the years pass . . .": Shilts, *The Mayor of Castro Street,* p. 185.
349   "Harvey was born to be a martyr.": Bill Sivert, "Divided They Stand: The Milk-Stokes Split," *The Advocate,* no. 219 (July 13, 1977).

25: Money in the Hills of Bel Air

350   Andelson's grandmother told him to buy land: Michelle Andelson interview with AJN, June 5, 1994.
350   cash flow at 8709 bathhouse: Waldo Fernandez interview, July 15, 1993, and Arlen Andelson interview, June 5, 1994, with AJN; and Paul Monette interview no. 6 with JDC.
351   size and description of Andelson's living room: Marylouise Oates interview nos. 1 and 2, Jerry Brown interview no. 1 and Steve Schulte interview no. 1 with AJN. Also *Los Angeles Times,* Aug. 30, 1982; Marylouise Oates, "Sheldon Andelson: A Bridge Between Two Diverse Worlds," and Paul Monette, *Borrowed Time,* p. 199.
351   snuggling up with a cup of coffee: Andelson to Oates, "Sheldon Andelson."
351   Andelson lived in a second-floor suite: Bev Thomas interview with AJN, June 6, 1994.
351   "Where are we going to put . . . ?": Rob Eichberg interview no. 2 with AJN.
351   Andelson's fundraisers: Eichberg interview nos. 1 and 2 with AJN.
352   "People spend more. . . .": Eichberg interview no. 1.
353   "Don't ask Morris Kight. . . .": Eichberg interview no. 2.
353   slave auction raid and subsequent reaction: *San Francisco Chronicle,* April 12, 1976; *Los Angeles Times,* April 11, 1976; Morris Kight no. 3 and Stephen Lachs no. 1 interviews with AJN.
353   "This is the gay political movement. . . .": David Mixner interview no. 3 with AJN.
354   Mixner on death of his first lover: Mixner interview no. 2 with AJN.
354   Mixner's lying about the sex of his lover: Mixner interview nos. 3 and 2.
354   Clinton on Mixner: Transcript of Bill Clinton interview with Jeff Schmalz, for article published in *New York Times,* Sept. 9, 1992, while Clinton was Democratic candidate for president, courtesy of Schmalz.
354   Mixner's remarks at Eichberg brunch: Mixner interview nos. 3 and 4, Lachs interview nos. 1 and 2, and Eichberg interview no. 1 with AJN. Mixer also suggested that day that the men use the money to undermine the city council president, John S. Gibson Jr., who had led an unsuccessful charge against awarding $305,250 in federal funds to the Los Angeles Gay Community Services Center the previous summer. Homosexuality, Gibson declared to his council colleagues, "can only add to the further destruction of American family life and the family unit." Gibson quoted MECLA letter to Mayor Tom Bradley, April 27, 1977, protesting Bradley's support of Gibson; also *Los Angeles Times,* Aug. 25, 1976.
354   Mixner left the brunch feeling despondent, and his own drug use: Mixner interview nos. 3 and 4.
355   contrasts between Lachs and Eichberg: Lachs no. 1 and Eichberg no. 1 interviews.
355   Lachs would be president of the men's club: Lachs interview no. 1.
355   meddling in city council races a little boring: Eichberg interview no. 2.
355   "That's the way you raise money": Lachs interview no. 2.
355   "Pretty Me, Pretty You!" parties: Michael Nicola interview nos. 1 and 2, and Eichberg interview no. 2 with AJN.
355   "Well, it would seem. . . .": Stephen Smith interview nos. 1 and 3, and Nicola interviews with AJN.
356   create an environment in L.A. gay world for making political contributions: Eichberg interview no. 2.

356   "I've just got to do this. . . .": Lachs interview no. 2. Eichberg's recollection was that he was the one who, from the podium, set the level of contributions; Lachs said that it was the shill from the audience.

356   The MECLA master list: *The Advocate,* no. 224 (Sept. 21, 1977).

356   "That sounds elitist. . . .": Robert McQueen, "The MECLA Model for Fundraising: Chutzpah and Hard Work," *The Advocate,* no. 224 (Sept. 21, 1977).

356   Business attire was encouraged, and other strategy decisions on dinners: Eichberg interview no. 2 and Lachs interview no. 1.

357   "I'm aware that many of us experience. . . .": Eichberg letter to MECLA members, Feb. 4, 1978, courtesy of L.A. Archives.

357   "PERSONAL AND CONFIDENTIAL": "Dear Friend" letter to MECLA supporters, March 15, 1977, courtesy of the International Gay and Lesbian Archives in Los Angeles.

357   "We don't demand instant acceptance. . . .": *Los Angeles Magazine,* July 1979.

357   "Politics runs on money. . . .": *The Advocate,* 213 (April 6, 1977).

357   "The time has come for the hundreds. . . .": "Dear Friend" letter to MECLA supporters, March 15, 1977.

358   Andelson-Eichberg lunch: Eichberg interview no. 1.

358   Andelson's contributions: Jody Evans interview with AJN, June 6, 1994; for other MECLA members irritated, Lachs interview no. 2.

358   Andelson roast: videotape of event, courtesy of Los Angeles Gay and Lesbian Community Services Center.

358   Andelson's childhood: AJN interviews with brothers, Arlen and Sherman, and sister-in-law Michelle.

359   ". . . gay only with us": Rand Schrader at Andelson memorial service, Jan. 10, 1988, videotape courtesy of Andelson family.

359   L.A. attorneys met to divide the cases: Arlen Andelson interview.

359   Kight sent an arrested young gay to Andelson: Morris Kight interviews with AJN.

359   the Andelson-Kight meeting and arrangement: Kight interviews; the Andelson family confirmed some details.

359   Kight was charmed: Kight interview no. 9.

359   "Send them over": Don Kilhefner interview with AJN.

359   Andelson-Kight relations: Kight interviews and Arlen Andelson interview; Andelson told David Mixner about paying money to Kight.

360   Kight-Andelson meeting that led to Andelson serving on center's board of directors: Kight interview nos. 2, 3, and 9.

360   Andelson's being queried by the judge: numerous sources. Andelson discussed being dazed and thinking, What do I do now? with the *Los Angeles Times,* and it was recounted in his front-page obituary there, "Andelson Dies of AIDS; Gay Regent, Activist," Dec. 30, 1987. Also *Center News* (newsletter of Los Angeles Gay Community Services Center), vol. 2, no. 3, undated 1982.

360   "How does he know I'm gay?": "Sheldon Andelson: The World's Most Powerful Gay Person?," *The Advocate,* no. 349 (Aug. 19, 1982).

360   Andelson-Kight phone conversation: Kight interview no. 2.

360   "ripe to be used by the movement": Andelson to *Los Angeles Times,* Jan. 1, 1984, Column One.

360   Kight had been married: Andelson told Mixner that he was aware of this. Kight acknowledged it, reluctantly, in interview no. 9. Ivy Bottini, in her interviews with AJN, spoke of his keeping the marriage secret.

360   Kight bragged that he made Andelson rich: Kight interview no. 9.

360   Andelson helped Kight with his rent: ibid. Kight acknowledged having received "several hundred" dollars from Andelson. Mixner, in interview nos. 3 and 4, said Andelson told him he paid Kight's rent, a believable story since Kight had no visible means of support.

361   "Manipulators. . . .": Kight interview no. 2.

361   Andelson's testimonial to Kight: from the brochure "A Tribute to Morris Kight," Stonewall Democratic Club, Nov. 9, 1979.

361   Andelson and family seders: Michelle Andelson interview.

361   on inviting Fernandez to Andelson seders: Arlen and Sherman Andelson interviews.

361   Andelson's discomfort with intimacy: Stephen Smith interview no. 2 with AJN.

361   "intimate mystery": Sherman Andelson at Sheldon Andelson memorial service.

362   helicopter buzzing Andelson's villa: Duke Comegys interview nos. 1 and 3 with AJN.

362   drugs and sex at Andelson's house: Fernandez no. 1, Bob Hattoy no. 2 and Schulte no. 1 interviews with AJN.

362   Andelson arriving at the center: Betty Berzon interview, June 9, 1994, Terry De-Crescenzo interview nos. 1 and 2, Kight interviews and Andelson family interviews with AJN; and Schrader at Andelson memorial service.

362   Lachs at Andelson bathhouse: Lachs interview no. 2.

362   hot-tub discussion at Lachs house: Eichberg interview no. 1.

362   By midsummer, contributions had reached $40,000: Feb. 4, 1978, Fact Sheet from MECLA to members; also McQueen, "The MECLA Model for Fundraising."

364   Why should women be awarded half the seats?: Lachs interview no. 2.

364   "social desirability" argument in keeping women off MECLA: Eichberg interview nos. 1 and 2.

364   Scott at the meeting: Diane Abbitt and Roberta Bennett interview with AJN, June 21, 1993.

364   MECLA's coming-of-age: Lachs no. 1, Eichberg no. 1 and Mixner no. 3 interviews.

364   demeaned homosexuals to bring heterosexuals onto the board: Mixner interview.

364   tried not to see straight people after seven o'clock: Mixner interview no. 3.

365   Shilts's encounter with Briggs: Randy Shilts interview no. 1 with AJN; dialogue is recounted in Shilts, *The Mayor of Castro Street*, pp. 153–54.

365   "into the lion's den": Lou Sheldon interview no. 1 with AJN.

365   scene at Briggs announcement: AP picture; *San Francisco Chronicle,* June 15, 1977; and *Los Angeles Times,* June 15, 1977.

365   "Who is John V. Briggs . . . ?": *Los Angeles Times* editorial, June 17, 1977.

26: A Black-Tie Affair

367   Steve Smith's background: Smith interview no. 1 with AJN.

367   "blowing Mixner out of the water": ibid.

367   first meeting of New AGE: Morris Kight's handwritten notes, courtesy of L.A. Archives.

368   "Los Angeles will be ready. . . .": Rob Eichberg, *Lesbian Tide,* July/August 1977.

368   "If we fight this, we're dead. . . .": Goodstein quoted in Troy Perry interview with JDC, Feb. 21, 1994.

368n.   hold off fast to coincide with *Advocate* deadline: Perry interview; "Opening Space," *The Advocate,* no. 226 (Oct. 19, 1977).

369   Mixner fundraising letter announcing his homosexuality: Mixner interview no. 1 with AJN.

369   Goodstein wary of Mixner as another power figure: Smith no. 1 and 2 and David Russell no. 1 interviews with AJN.

369   Lachs couldn't stop weeping: Stephen Lachs interview no. 2 with AJN.

369   Mixner's nervous breakdown: Mixner interview nos. 2 and 3 with AJN; also Rob Eichberg interview no. 2 with AJN for some details of what happened in Malibu.

369   Mixner's coming out to his parents: Mixner interview no. 2.

370   anti-depressants: Mixner interview no. 3.

370   Lachs on learning Mixner did not have cancer: Lachs interview no. 2.

370   Mixner-Bradley meeting: Mixner interview no. 3.

370   Mixner's phony cancer report embarrassed MECLA: Lachs interview no. 2.

370   Smith-Goodstein conversation about Mixner: Smith interview no. 1.

370   Mixner-Smith exchange: ibid. and Mixner interview no. 3.

371   Nicola on Mixner: Mike Nicola interview no. 1 with AJN.

371   "I don't think. . . .": Smith interview no. 1.

371   the Sept. 16, 1977, weekend at Pajaro Dunes: Eichberg interview no. 2.

371   Goodstein's dinner with Erhard: Goodstein, "Opening Space," *The Advocate*, no. 374 (Aug. 18, 1983).

371   the correct response to Anita Bryant: "The Advocate Experience: An Invitation to Transformation," *The Advocate*, no. 241 (May 17, 1978).

372   "be proud of themselves.": Goodstein interview "14th Anniversary," *The Advocate*, no. 328 (Oct. 15, 1981).

372   Erhard declined to set up est for gays: "Report on Advocate Experience's First Anniversary," *The Advocate*, no. 266 (May 3, 1979).

372   Goodstein's hopes for Pajaro Dunes weekend: Eichberg interview nos. 1 and 2 with AJN; also "Opening Space," *The Advocate*, no. 242 (May 31, 1978); no. 256 (Dec. 13, 1978); and no. 260 (Feb. 8, 1979).

372   "All of us. . . .": *The Advocate*, Oct. 15, 1981, "14th Anniversary."

372   lunch where Advocate Experience was planned and financed: Eichberg interview nos. 1 and 2.

373   first Advocate Experience sessions: *The Advocate*, no. 241 (May 17, 1978).

373   "Enriching the Gay Experience." Goodstein, "Opening Space," *The Advocate*, no. 241 (May 17, 1978).

373   Goodstein's impatience with tardiness and est's emphasis on doing what you say you will: Smith interview no. 3 with AJN.

373   write a letter disclosing homosexuality: David Russell interview no. 2 with AJN, along with dialogue; Russell was at a number of experiences, and organized the first one in L.A.

374   refusal to do physical attractiveness exercise: Russell interview no. 1 with AJN.

374   Voeller's dinner with Goodstein: Voeller interview no. 3 with AJN.

374   "mere name could cause me. . . .": Bruce Voeller, "My Days on the Task Force," *Christopher Street*, October 1979.

374   Kight had never forgiven Goodstein: Kight interview no. 9 with AJN.

374   Goodstein's meeting with Kight: Kight interview nos. 9 and 11 with AJN.

375   First Tuesday meetings: Kight interview no. 9.

375   Eichberg at First Tuesday: Kight interview no. 9 and Eichberg interview no. 2.

375   MECLA dinner and attendance: "MECLA Celebrates Its First Successful Year," undated MECLA newsletter, courtesy of Gay and Lesbian Archives.

375   "This is great. . . .": Eichberg interview no. 2.

376   Goodstein scurried out of first MECLA dinner: Eichberg interview no. 1.

27: California: The Main Event

377   Briggs sent out inscribed picture of himself with Anita Bryant: Jerry Burns, "Political Showdown in State: The Move to Ban Gay Teachers," *San Francisco Chronicle*, July 12, 1978, p. 10.

378   the state senator using the initiative: Louis Sheldon interview no. 1 with AJN.

378   "It's important to provide leadership": "Briggs Submits Signatures for Anti-Gay Initiative," *Los Angeles Times*, May 2, 1978, p. 22.

378   "We're going to have the main event. . . .": notes of Carl Cannon, the *San Diego Union* reporter who covered Briggs's announcement speech, courtesy of Cannon.

378   text of Briggs initiative: "Initiative Measure to Be Submitted Directly to the Voters. . . ," from petitions, courtesy of Carl Cannon.

379   "Believe it or not. . . .": *Los Angeles Times*, Aug. 25, 1977.

379   details on Briggs: Mary McGrory, *Washington Post*, June 8, 1978.

379   Briggs did not believe his rhetoric: Randy Shilts interview no. 1 with AJN.

379   Briggs's friendship with Shilts: Shilts interview nos. 1 and 2 with AJN, Shilts interview with Marcus, and Shilts, "A Gay Journalist's Friendship with Briggs," *San Francisco Chronicle*, Oct. 31, 1978.

380   Briggs made jokes about Bryant and "It's just politics.": Shilts interview no. 2.

380   "I simply knew a different John Briggs. . . .": Shilts, "A Gay Journalist's Friendship with Briggs."

380   "The Human Side of Hitler": approximately Oct. 30, 1978, courtesy of Arthur Evans papers.

381   "Do you want to protect your children . . . ?": Carl Cannon interview with AJN, Sept. 15, 1993.

381   Briggs's leaflets: Randy Shilts, *The Mayor of Castro Street*, p. 238.

381   "We can't accept you as normal people. . . .": *Newsweek*, Oct. 2, 1978.

381   "Deviants Threaten the American Family": John Briggs, "Homosexual Teachers: Two Views," *Los Angeles Times*, Oct. 23, 1977.

381   Milk did everything he could to oppose Briggs: See Shilts, *The Mayor of Castro Street*, pp. 22–23.

381   Gay Pride Parades: *San Francisco Chronicle* and *Los Angeles Times*, June 26, 1978, text and photos; also *New York Times*, June 24, 1978, and ibid.

382   "This is one of those times. . . .": Goodstein, "Opening Space," *The Advocate*, no. 243 (June 14, 1978).

382   Bradley's clients: Lenny Giteck, "Another General Bradley: Mastermind of Election Battle Victory," *The Advocate*, no. 257 (Dec. 27, 1978).

383   "I don't need to talk to you then": Troy Perry interview with JDC, Feb. 21, 1994.

383   "I wasn't concerned about my own sexuality": Don Bradley profile in *The Advocate*, no. 257 (Dec. 27, 1978).

383   the poll findings were a road map to potential victory: David Mixner interview no. 3 with AJN; also Perry interview.

383   people felt the law was unneeded: Sallie Fiske interview with AJN, June 9, 1994.

384   Seattle referendum: Charles Brydon interview no. 1 with AJN.

384   "For years many of us. . . .": Fiske interview.

384   hair clip-ins: *Los Angeles Times*, Nov. 6, 1978.

384   Mixner at Laguna Beach fundraiser: Bob Hattoy interview nos. 1 and 2 with AJN.

384   Costanza at fundraiser: *Lesbian Tide*, September/October 1978; *Los Angeles Times*, Aug. 28, 1978; and *Gaysweek*, no. 82 (Sept. 18, 1978), p. 2.

385   "Money has its limitations. . . .": Peter Scott quoted in Randy Shilts, "The New Gay Movement: Will It Work?" *The Advocate*, no. 226 (Oct. 19, 1977).

385   Bottini hired by No on 6: Ivy Bottini interview no. 2 with AJN.

385   Kight being angered that Bottini had joined Mixner: Bottini interview nos. 2 and 3 with AJN. Kight would not answer questions on this subject.

385   Kight's campaign received little notice: Bottini, Fiske and Mixner interviews.

385   "They're afraid they'll get put on a list": "Fear Stalks No on Six Drive," *Los Angeles Times*, Sept. 15, 1978, p. 1.

385   Campbell's arrest on pandering charges: "Campbell Hit in Vice Raid," *The Advocate*, no. 249 (Sept. 6, 1978).

386   Field poll: *San Francisco Chronicle*, Sept. 19, 1978.

386   "If we could get that message to Reagan. . . .": Mixner interview no. 3.

386   Livingston's role in meeting of Mixner and Scott with Reagan aide: Mixner interview nos. 2 and 3 with AJN. Livingston and Scott are dead.

386   Mixner and Scott's meeting at Denny's: Mixner interview nos. 3 and 4 with AJN.

387   account of Reagan-Scott-Mixner meeting: Mixner interviews.

387   Reagan's statement against Briggs initiative: *San Francisco Chronicle*, Sept. 23, 1978.

388   "That one single endorsement. . . .": John Briggs interview with Robert Scheer, *Los Angeles Times*, Oct. 6, 1978.

388   Briggs and Costanza: ibid.

388   Briggs's opponents could scarcely believe: Bottini interview no. 3.

388   Briggs-Milk debates: For a full discussion of Briggs-Milk debates, including transcripts and excerpts, see Shilts, *The Mayor of Castro Street*, pp. 229–32.

388   John Quinn called the initiative "perilously vague": *San Francisco Chronicle*, Oct. 12, 1978.
389   Davis opposed the Briggs initiative: Edward Davis interview with AJN, April 23, 1994.
389   Anita Bryant's decision not to come to California: *Los Angeles Times*, June 13, 1978.
389   the scene at the hotel when Briggs lost: Perry and Paul Monette interviews with JDC.
389   Bradley's comments on Briggs defeat: "Gay Teacher and Anti-smoking Initiatives Lose," *Los Angeles Times*, Nov. 8, 1978.
389   "If it gets down to a plebiscite. . . .": "Prop. 6 Battle a Bit Bizarre," *Los Angeles Times*, Nov. 5, 1978, p. 1.
389   Perry felt relief: Perry interview.
389   Milk was worried about complacency: Shilts, *The Mayor of Castro Street*, p. 249.
390   "You've heard of sore losers. . . .": *San Francisco Chronicle*, Nov. 8, 1978; also ibid.

28: A Friend in City Hall

391   Marion and Effi Barry's visit to the Eagle: Tom Bastow interview no. 1 with JDC. Also Paul Kuntzler interview with JDC; Tom Huhn, "Eagle Owner Speaks Out: An Interview With Don Bruce," *The Blade*, Feb. 1, 1979, p. 15; Larry Van Dyne, "Is DC Becoming the Gay Capital of America?" *The Washingtonian*, Summer 1980, p. 96.
392   the *Post* Poll: A. E. Acosta, "The D. C. Primary: Gay Clout Comes Through," *The Blade*, October 1978, p. 1. For a good account of the politics of the period, see Harry S. Jaffe and Tom Sherwood, *Dream City: Race, Power, and the Decline of Washington, D. C.*
392   By noon Sunday, the Barrys' visit to the Eagle was the talk of the day, and Effi Barry's wearing leather: Bastow interview.
392   "the New Hampshire" of his campaign: Lou Chibbaro Jr., "D. C. Elections Hailed as Milestone," *The Blade*, Nov. 20, 1978.
393   Barry's gay rights record: "Barry," a front-page interview in *The Blade's Pull-Out Supplement for the Sept. 12 D.C. Primary.*
393   Barry equated gay and black movements: Richard Maulsby interview no. 1 with JDC.
393   on TV, Barry volunteered his close alliance with the gay community: Jim Zais, "The D.C. Primary: From the Wings to Center Stage," *The Blade*, October 1978, p. 1.
393   Barry figured he had little to lose: "Barry," *The Blade*.
393   The size of the gay vote was an unknown: Larry Bush, "Will Gay Votes Count?" *The Blade*, September 1978, p. 6.
393   Don Bruce: "Eagle Owner Speaks Out: An Interview with Don Bruce," a long interview and photograph in *The Blade*, Feb. 1, 1979, p. 15. Bruce is deceased.
394   gay contributions to the 1978 mayoral and council campaigns: Milton Coleman, "Washington's Gay Vote: Homosexuals a Force in May Election," *Washington Post*, April 21, 1979, p. A-1; *GRNL/NGTF Report*, April 1980; and *Does Support for Gay Rights Spell Political Suicide?*, a 1981 study sponsored by the Gay Rights National Lobby and the National Gay Task Force, pp. 25–27, courtesy of Joseph Cantor.
394   friends prevailed on Haft to get Carter: Robert Carter interview with JDC, Feb. 27, 1996.
394   how Carter helped Barry: ibid. and Bastow interview.
395   a thousand young gay men: Bastow and Kuntzler interviews.
395   Barry's upset victory: Jaffe and Sherwood, *Dream City*, p. 122.
395   hadn't thought he could pull it off: Zais, "The D.C. Primary," p. 1.
395   Endean, the Gertrude Stein post-primary party and Kuntzler's analysis of the results: Bastow, Endean no. 1 and Kuntzler interviews with JDC; and Acosta, "The D.C. Primary," p. 1.
396   Barry's meeting with gay supporters: Bastow interview.
396   page one story in the *Washington Post*: Milton Coleman, "Washington's Gay Vote: Homosexuals a Force in May Election," *Washington Post*, April 21, 1979, p. A-1.

396   Barry's "Gay Agenda": Lillian Wiggins, *Afro-American*, Dec. 9, 1978, reported in "Journalist Cites Gay Agenda," *The Blade*, Jan. 4, 1979, p. 15.

396   "I will not allow. . . .": Larry Bush, "Barry Takes Office, New Council Set," *The Blade*, Jan. 4, 1979, p. 1.

397   how Endean came to head GRNL: Endean interview and Kerry Woodward interview no. 5 with JDC.

397   Hartman, Kameny and Kuntzler: Kuntzler interview no. 6 and Kameny interview no. 10 with JDC; and Mike Green and Lou Chibbaro Jr., "National Gay Lobby Regroups," *The Blade*, October 1978, p. 7.

397   "I don't want people joining GRNL. . . .": Green and Chibbaro, "National Gay Lobby Regroups." Also *The Advocate*, no. 254 (Nov. 15, 1978).

398   scrambling for money, "Crazy Alice" and leaving brochures in dirty-book stores: Endean interview.

398   pushing the idea of a gay rights march on Washington: Larry Bye interview no. 4, Woodward interview and Craig Anderson interview no. 1 with JDC. Also Lou Chibbaro Jr., "Plans Fizzle for March on D.C.," *The Blade*, Nov. 6, 1978, p. 8.

398   the idea of a march surfaced at a lesbian fundraiser at the University of Minnesota: Robin Tyler interview, Jan. 19, 1997, and Joyce Hunter interview no. 1 with JDC. Also flier for the April 21, 1978, benefit jointly sponsored by the Lesbian Feminist Organizing Committee and University Community Feminists, and Joan Lopotko, "Robin Tyler Fights Back," undated fragment of an LFOC newsletter, both courtesy of Tyler.

398   Milk was dismissive of the march idea: Bye interview. He and Kevin Mossier met with Milk in San Francisco.

399   Tyler had spread the seeds for the march in stage appearances in California: Tyler interview.

399   Tyler shared forums with Milk: Jim Gordon's journal, March 10, 1978, the gathering of the California Democratic Council in San Diego, courtesy of Gordon.

399   "great symbolic impact. . . .": ibid.

399   Endean to Woodward: Woodward interview.

399   the feelings of the other groups: ibid., Kameny interview no. 10, Jean O'Leary interview no. 4 and Hunter interview with JDC; numerous stories in *Gay Community News, The Blade* and *The Advocate*. Also draft of Joyce Hunter's history of the march, written for independent study credit as a political science undergraduate major at Hunter College, New York City, Fall 1979, courtesy of Hunter.

399   the new Board of Supervisors membership: Randy Shilts, *The Mayor of Castro Street*, p. 191.

399   Milk's walk with Jack Lira and the media crews to city hall: Gordon's journal, Jan. 9, 1978.

399   "This is not my swearing-in. . . .": Shilts, *The Mayor of Castro Street*, p. 190.

400   the Feinstein vote and Milk's introduction of the gay rights bill: Gordon's journal, Jan. 9, 1978.

400   "You shouldn't be rubbing. . . .": Harry Jupiter, "Board Debates Lifestyles: Gay Women An Issue," *San Francisco Chronicle*, Feb. 7, 1978, p. 3.

400   the debate and first vote on Milk's proposed gay rights bill: Gordon's journal, March 20, 1978. Also "S. F. Outlaws Bias Against Gays in Jobs and Housing," *Los Angeles Times*, March 22, 1978.

400   Moscone signed the gay rights ordinance: Gordon's journal, April 11, 1978.

400   Hongisto's escort: ibid., Nov. 8, 1977.

400   Moscone had made it plain he regarded Milk as the leader of the city's gays: Shilts, *The Mayor of Castro Street*, p. 193.

401   Gain was made fun of as a boy, and it made him a different kind of police chief: Charles Gain interview with JDC, Oct. 29, 1997.

401   "We will hire gays the same. . . .": Raul Ramirez, "Gain to Gay Cops: Come Out of Closet," *San Francisco Examiner*, April 18, 1976, p. A-1.

401   Moscone's wish: Gain interview.

401   a closed system: ibid.

401   the hostility on the force to Gain: ibid.

401   Dan White's appearance at Milk's fundraiser: Gordon's journal, Jan. 10, 1978.

401   Dan White's demeanor in council and on the field: Shilts, *The Mayor of Castro Street*, p. 197.

402   "What do you think of my new theater?": ibid., p. 189.

402   in San Diego, he went further: Gordon's journal, March 10, 1978.

402   profane, phony calls and jelly beans: Shilts, *The Mayor of Castro Street*, p. 196.

402   Easter events: Gordon's journal, Easter Sunday 1978.

403   the shooting of Moscone and Milk, and the reaction of Milk's friends and of the crowd afterward: Shilts, *The Mayor of Castro Street*, and Gordon's journal, Nov. 27, 1978.

404   the San Francisco Gay Democratic Club renamed the Harvey Milk Gay Democratic Club: from Jim Gordon journal of Nov. 28, 1978, Jim Gordon letter to Clendinen of June 3, 1999, including citations, and Howard Wallace interview no. 4 with JDC. He was at the meeting that night.

404   the call to the Coalition for Lesbian and Gay Rights in New York: Hunter interview nos. 1 and 2 with JDC.

405   Endean despised Milk: Endean interview. His feelings were shared by many others.

405   trying to persuade congressional aides that support for gay rights wasn't death on election day: Endean interview no. 1. For the conservative Christian view of congressional fears about being associated with gay rights in that period, Gary Jarmin interview with JDC, Jan. 29, 1997.

405   Endean and the CRO: Endean interview.

405   Endean's happy problem: Endean interview no. 1. Also Larry Bush, "Congress Gets One Gay Rights Bill, More Coming," *The Blade*, Feb. 15, 1979, p. 3.

405   forty-six co-sponsors: Among other printed reports, *The Advocate*, no. 275 (Sept. 6, 1979).

406   Costanza was a loose cannon: Maddox interview no. 1, and Midge Costanza interview nos. 1 and 2 with JDC.

406   a threat to Carter's support among Christian conservatives: Costanza interviews, Maddox interview nos. 1 and 2, Jarmin interview and Morris Sheats interview, Feb. 3, 1997, with JDC.

406   Costanza had resigned: Costanza interview no. 2 and Anne Wexler interview with JDC, Feb. 27, 1997.

406   Costanza's letter of resignation: *Lesbian Tide*, September/October 1978.

406   It assured leaders: Charlie Brydon, the new co-executive director of the Task Force, said in March 1979 that White House aide Sarah Weddington had promised to follow through on the aims of the meeting Costanza had held at the White House. "This reflects the President's continuing commitment," Brydon said, "although political realities may not allow Carter to be openly supportive." It was basically the same line Jean O'Leary had used eighteen months earlier, at the Denver leadership conference. "Brydon Named New NGTF Co-Director," *Gay Community News*, March 10, 1979, p. 1. O'Leary in "News from All Over," *The Advocate*, no. 223 (Sept. 7, 1977).

406   the movement no longer had a voice in the White House: Wexler interview.

406   "He has trouble with it. . . .": Ron Javers, "Ex-White House Aide Sounds Off on Briggs," *San Francisco Chronicle*, Oct. 20, 1978, p. A-13. Also Costanza interviews for ample discussion of Carter's feelings about homosexuality, abortion and the ERA.

406   Carter alienated homosexuals and evangelical Christians: Costanza interviews and Ray Jenkins interview with JDC, Jan. 31, 1997. Jenkins was deputy press secretary in the last year of the Carter White House.

407   the "Gay Freedom Train": Jok Church interview with JDC, Jan. 20, 1997. *The National March on Washington for Lesbian and Gay Rights*, a documentary album produced by Church and Adam Ciesielski, Magnus Records, Sacramento, 1979, courtesy of Church and Ciesielski.

407   lesbians vs. NAMBLA, and replacement of age of consent demand: Hunter interview no. 1. Also numerous articles in *The Blade* and *Gay Community News*. Album cover from the march, courtesy of Jok Church and Adam Ciesielski.

407   Woodward reported back to the Task Force board: Woodward interview.

407   march organizers had endorsements they needed: *The Advocate*, no. 276 (Sept. 20, 1979), and no. 288 (Oct. 4, 1979).

407   Tyler talked Perry into going on the march: Tyler interview.

407   the train trip: ibid. and Church interview.

408   the preacher on the tracks: ibid. Also *The Advocate*, no. 281 (Nov. 29, 1979).

408   75,000 strong: "How Many Were There?" *The Blade*, Oct. 25, 1979, p. B-10, among others.

408   checking travel reservations: Lou Chibbaro Jr., "March Leaders Say Problems Are Resolved," *The Blade*, Sept. 13, 1979, p. 1.

408   where the crowd came from: Hunter interview no. 1.

408   Pope John Paul II's visit, Falwell there, but not Robertson: Wexler, Maddox and Jenkins interviews.

408   the delegation met with Wales: "Monday: At the White House," *The Blade*, Oct. 25, 1979, p. B-10; and Wexler interview.

408   brief TV coverage, and *Time* and *Newsweek* ignoring it: David Goodstein, "Opening Space," *The Advocate*, Dec. 13, 1979.

408   visited 160 congressional offices: "Capitol Dispatches: Bill Gains Co-Sponsors," *The Blade*, Nov. 8, 1979, p. 4.

408   "Until now. . . .": *The Advocate*, no. 281 (Nov. 29, 1979).

409   "Adam and Steve": ibid.

409   the meaning became very clear: Church interview.

29: Colliding Forces

410   Jerry Brown's financial reports: John Fogarty, "Brown's Strong Stand on Gay Rights," *San Francisco Chronicle*, Oct. 13, 1979, p. 1. Includes Federal Election Commission filings.

411   Andelson fundraiser: ibid., and David Mixner no. 5 and Jerry Brown no. 2 interviews with AJN.

411   Andelson's ambition was to be chief of protocol at the White House: Waldo Fernandez, Mixner and Andelson family interviews with AJN.

411   If Brown had any doubts: At Andelson's memorial service, Jan. 10, 1988, Brown said, "There are a lot of people in politics who claim to raise large sums of money. But Sheldon Andelson delivered. He delivered."

411   Brown had been slow to oppose the Briggs initiative: Brown interview no. 2 with AJN.

411   Brown had appointed no openly gay people during his first term: Steve Lachs interview no. 2 with AJN.

412   Brown's inaugural address: *The Advocate*, no. 261 (Feb. 22, 1979).

412   Brown attended the MECLA dinner against the advice of some aides: Jody Evans interview with AJN, June 6, 1994.

412   *Advocate* interview with Brown, including description of the governor's house: Lenny Giteck and Scott Anderson, "Jerry Brown, the Candidate, Takes Future Stock," *The Advocate*, no. 288 (March 20, 1980).

412   Brown staff closed Portland event to press: "Brown Meets with Oregon Homosexual Activists," *New York Times*, Dec. 15, 1979, p. 39.

412   Brown felt that whenever he spoke to a gay group: Brown interview no. 2.

413   NGTF press conference announcing Brown's telegram: Fogarty, "Brown's Strong Stand on Gay Rights."

413   Brown's speech in Manchester: *The Advocate*, no. 281 (Nov. 29, 1979).

414   Endean at the DFL convention: *The Advocate*, no. 109 (April 11, 1973).

414   Endean on the difference a gay rights plank made in Minnesota: Endean to *The Blade*, vol. 10, no. 20 (Oct. 11, 1979).

414   "Until at least one party. . . .": "The Unconventional Delegates," *The Advocate*, no. 285 (Feb. 7, 1980).

414   Bastow's lunch with Kuntzler and Endean: Tom Bastow interview no. 1 with JDC.

414   the kind of prestigious position: Bastow interview no. 3 with JDC.

414   Spottswood Pou wouldn't take the job if O'Leary was involved: Mary Spottswood Pou interview no. 2 with JDC.

415   looked as if NGTF was being shut out: Bastow interview no. 2 with JDC.

415   "It made no sense. . . .": *Capitol Hill* (the GRNL newsletter), vol. 2, no. 1 (Jan. 30, 1980).

415   Endean had hepatitis: Steve Endean interview no. 5 with JDC.

415   the scene at The Pier: Larry Bush interview no. 2 with JDC and Brown interview no. 2.

415   Brown hadn't known any open homosexuals before he met Mixner and Andelson: Brown interview no. 2.

415   "I've sent neither a letter. . . .": *San Francisco Chronicle*, Nov. 28, 1979.

416   Chanin was jeered and "Where's Midge?": *San Francisco Chronicle*, Nov. 28, 1979, p. 1; and Michael Chanin to JDC.

416   Germond/Witcover column: "Gays Use Fundraising to Gain Political Clout," *Washington Star*, Nov. 28, 1979, p. A-3.

416   The gay rights plank: Bastow interview nos. 2 and 3.

416   did not call for an end to the military's ban against homosexuals: Bastow interview no. 2.

416   financing by Campbell and other bathhouse owners: Bastow, Campbell and Endean interviews with JDC.

416   Spottswood Pou could not hide her unhappiness: Spottswood Pou interview no. 1 with JDC.

417   text of fundraising letter from Barry/Feinstein: "Convention Project Gets Major New Supporters," *The Advocate* (May 1, 1980).

417   raised barely $40,000: Scott Anderson, "Stalking the Plank: Will Pro Gay Delegates Count?" *The Advocate*, no. 297 (July 4, 1980).

417   Semerad letter to National Convention Project: "A Dimmed Ray of Hope," *The Blade*, July 24, 1980.

417   "I'm going to do it" conversation: recounted by a Kennedy staffer (not for attribution) to AJN.

417   text of Democratic Party plank on gay rights: "Report of the Platform Committee to the 1980 Democratic National Convention," pp. 51–52. The full text stated that the party would "affirm the dignity of all people and the right of each individual to have, in the Civil Rights section of the document, equal access to and participation in the institutions and services of our society. All groups must be protected from discrimination based on race, color, religion, national origin, language, age, sex, or sexual orientation. This includes specifically the right of foreign citizens to enter this country."

418   the debate in Campbell's suite: Bastow interview no. 3.

418   "present the smallest target he could": *The Advocate*, no. 298 (Aug. 7, 1980).

418   "We are no longer an embarrassing issue. . . .": "Convention Chronology," *The Advocate*, no. 302 (Oct. 2, 1980).

418   Carter endorsed Cranston's immigration bill: *Los Angeles Times*, June 25, 1980.

418   gay delegates at the 1976 convention: John Fogarty, "Gay Activist Nominated for VP at Convention," *San Francisco Chronicle*, Aug. 15, 1980.

419   It took an extra measure of courage: *The Advocate*, no. 281 (Nov. 29, 1979). Boozer is deceased.

419   details on decision to nominate Boozer: "Convention Chronology of New Gay Politics," *The Advocate*, no. 302 (Oct. 2, 1980).

419   a name that would not suggest demeaning jokes: Jeanne Cordova interview no. 2 with AJN.

419   "Why don't you just shut up?": Boozer in *The Blade*, Aug. 21, 1980.

419   Cordova's experience gathering signatures for Boozer: Cordova interview.

419   Boozer had to keep a finger on the page and had a parched throat: Don Leavitt, "The Nation's First Openly Gay VP Candidate," *The Blade*, Aug. 21, 1980.

420   Boozer's remarks: "Text of Mel Boozer's Convention Speech," *The Blade*, Aug. 21, 1980.

420   Bastow was unexpectedly moved: Bastow interview no. 3.

420   Boozer gathered forty-nine votes: Neil Bickford, "Convention Chronology of Gay Politics," *The Advocate*, no. 302 (Oct. 2, 1980).

421   Falwell's tale in Anchorage: Dudley Clendinen, "White House Says Minister Misquoted Carter Remarks," *New York Times*, Aug. 8, 1980, p. A-16. Also Jerry Falwell interview, March 24, 1997, Maddox interview no. 1, Ray Jenkins interview, Jan. 31, 1997, and Anne Wexler interview, Feb. 27, 1997, with JDC.

421   "an anecdote. . . .": Falwell interview. Also Jim Castelli, "Religious News: Anecdote Hurts Falwell Credibility," *Washington Star*, Aug. 23, 1980, p. B-6.

421   "Since many people believe his was the most influential. . . .": David Goodstein, "Opening Space," *The Advocate*, no. 285 (Feb. 7, 1980).

421   Reagan on gay rights movement: *Los Angeles Times*, March 6, 1980; quoted in *The Advocate*, no. 290 (April 17, 1980).

421   Carter's use of the values issue against Ford and the White House Conference on Families: "Jimmy Carter, The White House Conference on Families, and the Mobilization of the New Christian Right," a paper prepared by Professor Leo P. Ribuffo of George Washington University for a conference on the Carter presidency held at the Jimmy Carter Library, Atlanta, Feb. 22, 1997, courtesy of Professor Ribuffo.

422   a smoke screen to legitimize the homosexual lifestyle: Paul Weyrich interview no. 3 and Maddox interview no. 3 with JDC.

422   NGTF sought to be included on the conference advisory committee, and recommendation that gays be listed as a "diverse" family form: Larry Bush, "Family Conference Drops Gays," *The Blade*, Sept. 13, 1979, p. 3, courtesy of the Dr. Martin Luther King Jr. Library, District of Columbia Library system.

422   Jim Guy Tucker and the Library Court meeting: Weyrich interview.

422   delegate action at the White House Conference on Families in Los Angeles: Russell Chandler, "Conference on Families Endorses ERA: Supports Government-Funded Abortions, Opposes Housing Bias Against Gays," *Los Angeles Times*, July 13, 1980, p. A-3.

423   The conference delegates: Erin Kelly, "7,000 Conduct Own Families Conference," *Los Angeles Times*, July 13, 1980, p. A-3.

423   Anderson's candidacy: Michael Barone and Grant Ujifusa, *The Almanac of American Politics 1982* (Washington, D. C.; Barone, 1981), p. xiv.

423   Anderson was a born-again Christian: Neal R. Pierce, "Gays: Out of the Political Closet," *Los Angeles Times*, Aug. 4, 1980, part II, p. 5.

423   Schneider's article: "Ethnic 'Gays Are the Cities' Emerging Political Power," *Los Angeles Times* "Opinion" section, Sept. 7, 1980.

424   Moral Majority leaflets: the leaflets; Falwell, Gary Jarmin and Weyrich interviews with JDC.

424   1980 election results: Barone and Ujifusa, *The Almanac of American Politics 1982*, p. xvii.

30: The Pink Invitation

425   The invitation was printed on pink paper: The invitation is courtesy of the private papers of Gregory J. King. The guest list from Sean O. Strub, who helped Baron put it together and prepare for the party. Strub interview nos. 1 and 6 with JDC.

426   Baron predicted the GOP sweep of the 1980 Senate races: Jane Mayer, "Report on 'The Baron': Political Guru Finds Opinions Pay," *Wall Street Journal*, June 27, 1984, p. 62.

426   watched the Democratic convention instead of going to camp: Baron interview, Aug. 17, 1993, and his mother, Zerline Baron, interview with JDC.

426   description of Baron: many sources, including Gregory King interview nos. 2 and 3, Strub interview nos. 1–4 and William Schneider interview, May 11, 1997, with JDC; and the transcript of remarks at the Dec. 5, 1993, memorial service for Baron in Washington, D.C.

426   executive secretary of the DNC in 1972: Tom Sherwood and Alfred E. Lewis, "Newsletter Editor Arrested in SE on Drug Charge," *Washington Post*, Aug. 22, 1979, p. A-1.

426   Carter was so phony: Baron interview.

426   neither a true liberal nor a true Democrat: Schneider interview.

426   led the "Anybody But Carter" movement: Tom Riehle of Peter Hart Research, quoted in "Remembering Alan Baron," a leaflet collection of stories and tributes put out by some of his friends in advance of the memorial service.

426   Fired by the embarrassed McGovern: Baron interview.

426   a charge which the *Washington Post* treated as front-page news: Sherwood and Lewis, "Newsletter Editor Arrested in SE on Drug Charge."

427   new brochure which quoted the paper: Mayer, "Report on 'The Baron.' "

427   Warren Beatty: Strub interview no. 1.

427   Viguerie, Dolan, Weyrich and Falwell: From Paul Weyrich, Ed McAteer and Jerry Falwell interviews with JDC.

427   Baron's friendships: Baron 2. Also Strub to JDC.

427   poker-playing buddies: King interview no. 5 with JDC; and Mayer, "Report on 'The Baron.' "

427   friends knew that Baron used cocaine: Schneider interview.

427   his use was heavy: Strub interview no. 1 and King interview no. 2.

427   "There's something stuck. . . .": Strub interview no. 1. The story of the cocaine-encrusted keyboard and repairman also appears in a short novel, *Pizza Face: or, The Hero of Suburbia*, by Ken Siman (New York: Grove Weidenfeld, 1991), pp. 156 and 169–70, about gay life and Washington politics in which a newsletter editor with the same eccentric habits as Baron is a character. Siman was one of a series of young men who served as Baron's assistants in the 1980s.

427   many other prominent Democrats and Republicans used cocaine: Strub interview no. 1, King interview nos. 1 and 4, and Schneider interview with JDC.

427   Baron had advised Kennedy in 1980: Baron interview.

427   John F. Kennedy Jr. was Baron's intern: Strub interview nos. 1, 6 and 7 with JDC. Also Schneider interview.

427   The "Pre-Inaugural Ball" and who was there and who was not invited: Strub interview no. 6 and King interview no. 5.

428   Breen lived with Baron: Strub interview no. 6.

428   sex in the upper rooms and a loft space: Strub interview nos. 1 and 6, and King interview no. 5.

428   Baron could not recall how he and Endean met: Baron interview and Strub interview no. 6.

428   the relationship between Endean and Baron: Baron interview, Strub interview nos. 1 and 6, and King interview no. 2.

428   Baron worried about what his traditional friends and colleagues would think if they knew he was gay: Barney Frank interview with JDC, June 7, 1994, and Strub interview no. 1.

428   proud to have John Kennedy Jr. as an intern: Schneider interview and Strub interview no. 1. William Schneider used to lunch with Baron and young Kennedy.

428   how big John Jr.'s penis was: Strub interview no. 1.

428   John Kennedy Jr. in his underwear: King interview no. 2 and Strub interview no. 1.

428   The party was a kind of breakthrough: Strub interview nos. 1 and 6, King interview nos. 2 and 5.

428   Baron's house as the center of gay political and intellectual life: Frank interview. Also James Hormel interview no. 2 with JDC.

429   Endean decided that homosexuals needed to have their own national PAC: Hormel interview.

429   only one man in Washington: Baron interview. Also Strub interview no. 6.

429   Bauman as ideologue, politician and drunken patron of gay bars: Bauman interview no. 1 with JDC. Also King interview no. 5.

429   Baron patronized The Chesapeake House: Siman, *Pizza Face,* p. 150. Also King interview no. 5.

429   Bauman had been buying sex, and his furtive life collapsed on him: Bauman interview.

429   reactions to the charge against Bauman and its effect on his reelection: Robert Bauman, *The Gentleman from Maryland: The Conscience of a Gay Conservative,* pp. 66–71, 77, 233; and Michael Barone and Grant Ujifusa, *The Almanac of American Politics, 1982* (Washington, D.C.: Barone, 1981), pp. 466–67.

430   Barney Frank had won his seat: *The Almanac of American Politics, 1982,* pp. 496–98.

430   Frank came to Washington determined to have a life: Frank interview.

430   Frank came out to Endean, and Endean was astonished: ibid. and Endean to JDC.

430   the Frank-Studds conversation: Frank interview.

431   sex lives which were either austere or furtive: ibid. and John Meuniere interviews with JDC. Meuniere, later the gay liaison for Boston mayor Ray Flynn, was Gerry Studds's assistant and driver on visits home to the Tenth District in the early 1980s.

431   how Frank heard that Studds was gay: Frank interview.

431   "I want to start living. . . .": ibid.

431   The next person at the bar: Robert Carter interview with JDC, Feb. 27, 1996. Endean (interview no. 28 with JDC) said he first realized Dan Bradley was gay when he ran into him at a Washington dirty-book store. The two then went together to the Eagle bar down the street to talk.

431   Frank was discovering gay Washington through Endean: Frank interview.

432   "What are you taking . . . ?": ibid.

432   Endean had an idea: The idea of a gay national political committee, Larry Bye said (interview no. 5 with JDC), had then been floating in conversation for a year or more. But it was Endean's idea and his project.

432   Endean had asked Bye: Bye interview nos. 3 and 5 with JDC.

432   a national political committee as effective as MECLA: Endean to JDC. Also Hormel interview nos. 2 and 3 with JDC.

432   he wasn't comfortable in Los Angeles: various Endean interviews.

432   need the support of Goodstein and Foster: Endean interview nos. 12 and 18.

433   Endean flew out to San Francisco: Bye interview no. 3, Endean interview nos, 5, 8, 12, 17 and 18, and Kerry Woodward interview no. 6 with JDC.

433   Endean's awareness of the wealthy contacts Goodstein had through the Advocate Experience: Endean interview no. 12.

433   one who found Goodstein arrogant and abrasive: Hormel interview no. 2.

433   Hormel's background: Hormel interview no. 1 with JDC.

433   The seed money: Endean interview no. 18. Also Hormel interview nos. 2 and 3, and Dallas Coors interview with JDC, Feb. 14, 1994.

433   Endean had met Coors: Coors interview.

433   inherited wealth: ibid.

434   Endean courted Coors, and then left it to Goodstein: ibid. and Endean to JDC.

434   meeting in Washington: Bye interview nos. 3 and 5, Woodward interview no. 6, Hormel interview nos. 2 and 3, and various Endean interviews with JDC.

434   packed the board with his friends and supporters: Endean interview no. 12.

434   Baron wrote direct-mail letters: King interview no. 2 and Strub interview no. 1.

434   Baron had never done anything professionally for the cause of gay rights: Baron interview.

435   Baron met King at the 1979 march and later persuaded him to move to Washington: King interview no. 2.

435   a pattern that some of Baron's other friends had noticed: Schneider interview.

435   some of those relationships: King and Strub to JDC. While Gregory King and Sean Strub, like most of Baron's close friends, remained devoted to him through his life, not all of Baron's former interns were considerate in later years. One of them, Ken Siman, who was with Baron in the 1980s, wrote the novel *Pizza Face: or, The Hero of Suburbia*. One of its main characters is a gay, half-closeted, cocaine-addicted political newsletter editor who hires male prostitutes and has a young assistant named Sean.

435   Strub, how he came to Washington and his relationship with Baron: Strub interview no. 1 and Strub email to Clendinen of April 7, 1999. Also King interview no. 2 and Schneider interview.

435   Endean came to Baron for a fundraising letter and mailing list: Baron interview and Strub interview no. 6.

435   about $10,000: In his interview Baron said he raised around $7,000 from friends in Washington and contributed about $3,000 himself.

436   the letter: private papers of Sean O. Strub, courtesy of Strub. Also Strub email to Clendinen of April 7, 1999.

437   Endean and Weaver: Endean interview no. 17. Endean said he had formed the Human Rights Campaign Fund in 1980, given Weaver $1,000 through it and drummed up the balance in individual contributions.

437   Endean believed in the power of endorsements: One of the long-standing projects Endean was still working on when he died was the National Endorsement Campaign, whose goal was to create a list of prominent, respected public figures in every city and congressional district of the country who would lend their names to the cause of gay rights. From numerous Endean interviews.

437   Not Steve Endean, Baron said: Strub interview no. 6.

438   some public figure who would be taking a risk: Baron interview.

438   Someone gay—but not threatening: King interview no. 2.

438   getting names from other gay papers and buying names from porno magazines: Baron interview. Getting names from straight liberal donor lists: Strub email to Clendinen of April 7, 1999.

438   ought to ask Gore Vidal: King interview no. 2.

438   "Well, what about Tennessee Williams?": Strub interview no. 1. Gregory King did not remember Strub being at the kitchen table, so this might have been in another conversation.

439   Strub could talk his way into anything: Baron interview.

439   Strub's sexual history: Strub interview nos. 1, 2, 3 and 6. Also Strub email of April 7, 1999.

439   Strub's first reaction to Endean: Strub interview no. 1.

439   If he could get Tennessee Williams: ibid.

439   the story of the negotiation and encounter between Williams and Strub: Strub interview nos. 1 and 6, Strub email to Clendinen of April 7, 1999, Baron interview and Endean interviews.

31: Until the Party Ended

441   Mailman saved money on air-conditioning units: Jack Stoddard interview with AJN, Aug. 4, 1994.

441   New St. Marks Baths was well lit and sparkling clean: Larry Kramer interview no. 1 with JDC.

442   sex factory and no music on the top three floors: Stoddard interview.

442   combine gay dance clubs and Studio 54: Brooks Peters, "The Sexual Revolution Mailman Delivered," *Out* magazine, July/August 1994.

442   planning, construction and cost of The Saint: Mailman interview nos. 1 and 2 with AJN.

442   "Since the beginning of recorded history. . . .": the first Saint poster/invitation, courtesy of The Saint.

443   Mailman's nights at the ropes of Studio 54: Stoddard interview.

443   cost overrun of The Saint: ibid.

443   description of dome: "Welcome to the Pleasure Dome," The Saint description brochure, undated, courtesy of National Archive of Lesbian and Gay History in New York.

443   The star machine alone cost $96,000: Steve Rubin interview with AJN.

443   "The outcome is not unlike the fantasy. . . .": "Welcome to the Pleasure Dome."

444   a "religious experience": Mailman interviews.

444   "Go until the party ended": Stoddard interview.

444   Mailman felt vaguely embarrassed at the excess: Mailman interview no. 2.

444   Evans's mood turned dark: Arthur Evans interview no. 2 with AJN.

444   Evans and the clone culture of the Castro: ibid., also Evans interview no. 4 with AJN.

445   bathhouse scene in pre-AIDS San Francisco: Mark Thompson interview with AJN, June 14, 1994.

445   "86 list": courtesy of Arthur Evans papers.

445   Evans picketed at Club Baths: Evans interview no. 2. The Club Baths was not part of Jack Campbell's chain.

446   taken aback at public sexual intercourse: Randy Shilts interview no. 1 with AJN.

446   Shilts considered the Castro inspiring: ibid.

446   the beneficiaries of this change: Arthur Bell, "Arthur Evans and a Buncha Gay Guys Sitting Around Talking (This is Based on the Reunion They Had)," *Village Voice*, June 24–30, 1981.

446   a depressing wasteland: Evans interview no. 2; also Brandon Judell interviews with Arthur Evans, "I Want a Gay World I Can Live In," *New York Native*, June 29–July 12, 1982.

446   "Afraid You're Not Butch Enough?": leaflet courtesy of Arthur Evans papers; Evans interview nos. 2 and 4.

447   Saint bylaws: "Membership Notes," *Star Dust*, The Saint newsletter, undated, c. 1981, courtesy of Gay and Lesbian Archives.

447   Voeller had left the Task Force: Bruce Voeller, "My Days on the Task Force," *Christopher Street*, October 1979; also Voeller interview no. 4 with AJN.

447   The publisher took despondent note: David Goodstein, "Opening Space," *The Advocate*, no. 286 (Feb. 21, 1980).

448   "tired of explaining to Middle Americans. . . .": M. A. Karr, "Wandering—and Wondering—on Future Ground," *The Advocate*, no. 286 (Feb. 21, 1980).

448   a "foolish, even stupid book.": *The New Republic*, Jan. 6, 1979, p. 30.

448   He expressed these sentiments: Duberman interview with AJN, March 23, 1995. Kramer's enmity from interview.

448   Kramer interview with *Advocate* reporter: "Larry Kramer: Mad About *Faggots*," *The Advocate*, no. 260 (Feb. 8, 1979).

449   friends stopped speaking to Kramer: Kramer's notes in *Reports from the Holocaust*.

449   Kramer-Rodwell exchange at Oscar Wilde Bookshop: Kramer interview with Eric Marcus, courtesy of Marcus.

449   "most oppressive, ugly . . .": *The Advocate*, no. 275 (Sept. 6, 1979).

449   "There is a consequence. . . .": Urvashi Vaid, *Virtual Equality*.

449   "CBS displayed enough footage. . . .": *Los Angeles Times*, May 1, 1980.

449   "doing a documentary on Italians. . . .": Feinstein quoted in *San Francisco Chronicle*, April 25, 1980.

449   group in Houston successfully used CBS clips: *San Francisco Chronicle*, Jan. 11, 1985.

449   San Jose referendum results: *Los Angeles Times*, June 5, 1980.

450   city coroner was holding classes for homosexuals: *San Francisco Chronicle*, March 12, 1981.

450   "Frisco Needs Another Quake": Charles McCabe, *San Francisco Chronicle*, May 1, 1981; reprinted from *Peoria Journal-Star* editorial.

450   Mass-Kantrowitz meeting: Larry Mass interview no. 3 and Arnie Kantrowitz interview no. 3 with AJN.

450   since 1979, Mass had written about health: Mass interview nos. 1–3 with AJN.

450   Shilts had written about contracting hepatitis B: *The Advocate*, no. 207 (Jan. 12, 1977).

450   two-thirds of the gay men in San Francisco exposed to hepatitis: Shilts, *And the Band Played On*, p. 18.

450   Goodstein's fascination with venereal diseases: Shilts interview.

450   by 1980s, diseases approaching epidemic proportions: *San Francisco Chronicle*, April 13, 1978.

451   figures on amebiasis: "The Insides Story: Alimentary Aliens: "What You Should Know About Intestinal Parasites," *The Advocate*, no. 278 (Oct. 18, 1979).

451   Mass was unhappy with headline on his first AIDS story: Mass interview no. 1.

451   "Rare Cancer Seen in 41 Homosexuals": *New York Times*, July 3, 1981, p. 20.

452   Mass understood the medical implications of a fatal disease: Mass and Kantrowitz, interviews with AJN.

Part Four: Out of Anger

32: *After Disco*

455   appointment of Lucia Valeska: NGTF announcement "Valeska is named NGTF Co-Executive Director," undated, courtesy of Lesbian Herstory Archives.

455   Valeska was barely known: Even Charlie Brydon had never heard of her. Brydon interview no. 2 with AJN.

456   "There is a new threat. . . .": The LFL resolution on NAMBLA, March 27, 1979, courtesy of Lesbian Herstory Archives.

456   "I don't care. . . .": Brydon to AJN and to Marcus.

456   Brydon graded Carter's performance C-minus: exchange of letters in *New York Native*, no. 6 (Feb. 23–March 8, 1981), between Charles Brydon and Lucia Valeska, with response by Larry Bush.

456   drop in the number of sponsors of the gay rights bill: Larry Bush and Richard Goldstein, "The Anti-Gay Backlash," *Village Voice*, April 8–14, 1981, p. 1.

456   "Now that the national power. . . .": Apuzzo address at Kennedy Institute for Politics, Harvard University, Dec. 4, 1980, reprinted in *New York Native*, no. 3 (Dec. 29, 1979–Jan. 8, 1980).

457   "a one-person operation. . . .": Valeska speech at opening session of annual conference of NOW in San Antonio, Oct. 4, 1980, reprinted in ibid.

457   "The climate in the present Congress. . . .": Valeska letter to McCloskey, reprinted in *New York Native*, no. 7 (March 9–22, 1981).

457   "I am once again writing. . . .": Endean quoted in *Gay Community News*, March 21, 1981.

457   "There tends to be a view. . . .": ibid.

457   "I think the relationship. . . .": Valeska quoted in Larry Bush, "Washington Desk Column," *New York Native*, no. 7 (March 9–22, 1981).

457   "You can understand our bewilderment.": *The Advocate*, no. 316 (April 30, 1981).

457   "We might revel. . . .": Kameny statement, "Strategy for the Capital: Play Ostrich for a While," *New York Native*, no. 7 (March 9–22, 1981).

458   "I feel very strongly. . . .": Larry Bush, "Crisis at the Gay Task Force: Demands for Resignation Increase," *New York Native*, no. 9 (April 6–19,1981).

458   "was once a major purpose of NGTF. . . .": *New York Native*, no. 7 (March 9–22, 1981).

458   "I think the current leadership. . . .": *New York Native*, no. 11 (May 4–17, 1981).

458   "Gay public sex. . . .": Valeska, NOW speech.

458   "heavier positions": Maureen Oddone, "Lucia Valeska: Leading Lesbian at NGTF," *The Advocate*, no. 296 (July 10, 1980), p. 19.

458   both Brydon and Valeska had to approve NGTF releases: Brydon interview no. 1 with AJN.

458   speak off the record with Larry Bush: Bush interview no. 1 with AJN. Valeska declined to be interviewed.

459   "at times been inaccurate. . . .": NGTF letter, April 7, 1981, cited in *New York Native*, no. 10 (April 20–May 3, 1981).

459   "The co-directors have chosen. . . .": Brett Averill, "Opinion," *New York Native*, no. 11 (May 4–17, 1981), p. 5.

459   "disease-ravaged body. . . .": Robert McQueen, "Goodbye to an Old Friend," *The Advocate*, July 23, 1982.

459   Harris's last months: Mark Thompson interview with AJN, June 14, 1994.

460   "I'm asked to sign petitions. . . .": Kramer interview with Robert Chesley, *Gaysweek*, Jan. 1, 1979, which Chesley recounted in letter to *New York Native*, no. 28 (Jan. 4–17, 1982).

460   "I am not a crying man. . . .": Kramer *New York Times* op-ed page, Dec. 13, 1978.

461   "straggling, pitiful marches. . . .": Kramer, *Reports from the Holocaust*, Introduction.

461   Kramer on reaction to *Faggots*: Kramer interview nos. 1 and 2 with JDC; Kramer interview with Eric Marcus, courtesy of Marcus.

461   "I see no one. . . .": *New York Native*, no. 27 (Dec. 21, 1981–Jan. 3, 1982).

461   Kramer met with Dr. Friedman-Kien: For details of meeting, Kramer to Marcus and JDC; Larry Mass interview nos. 1 and 2 and Andy Humm interview, April 10, 1994, with AJN; also Randy Shilts, *And the Band Played On*, pp. 84–85; Kramer, *New York Native*, no. 27 (Dec. 21, 1981–Jan. 3, 1982); Scott Anderson, "New Viral Cancer Stirs Gay Fears," *The Advocate*, no. 324 (Aug. 20, 1981).

462   "Each man swallowed their panic. . . .": Nathan's Fain, "A History of GMHC," GMHC Circus Benefit Program, April 30, 1983.

463   "A Personal Appeal from Larry Kramer": *New York Native*, no. 19 (Aug. 24–Sept. 6, 1981), p. 13.

463   Volunteers handed out article on Fire Island: Mass interview no. 1.

463   fundraising totals from Labor Day weekend: Kramer, *New York Native*, no. 27 (Dec. 21, 1981–Jan. 3, 1982); also Fain, "A History of GMHC."

463   people only more mistrustful: Mass interview no. 1.

463   "Basically, Kramer *is* telling us. . . .": Chesley letter, "A Hidden Message," *New York Native*, no. 22 (Oct. 5–18, 1981), p. 4.

463   Kramer's response to Chesley: *New York Native*, no. 27 (Dec. 21, 1981–Jan. 3, 1982).

464   Popham was a registered Republican: Shilts, *And the Band Played On*, p. 28.

464   Popham asked that his name not be used in mainstream articles: David Black, "The Plague Years," *Rolling Stone*, March 28 and April 25, 1985. Black quotes the GMHC president and notes that he did not want his name used.

465   "perverted act. . . .": Falwell quoted in Larry Bush, "House Kills DC Sex Laws as Gay Prospects Dim," *The Advocate*, no. 330 (Nov. 2, 1981). The vote count is from Congressional Record-House, Oct. 1, 1981, p. 22778.

465   "Biggest and most conclusive defeat. . . ." *The New York Native*, no. 23 (Oct. 16–Nov. 1, 1981). The vote count is from Congressional Record-House, Oct. 1, 1981, p. 22778.

465   "Not only will two-thirds. . . .": Endean interview no. 2 with JDC.

465   "The Christian right's attack. . . .": *New York Times* op-ed page, April 18, 1981.

465   "going to be a crossroads for us. . . .": Goodstein, "Opening Space," *The Advocate*, no. 335 (Jan. 21, 1982).

465   "fucking their brains out": Mass interview nos. 2 and 3 with AJN.

465   "We won't need to criticize each other. . . .": Kantrowitz letter, *New York Native*, no. 29 (Jan. 18–31, 1982).

465   "The current opinion. . . .": Mass interview no. 2. Early-warning brochure courtesy of Mass papers.

466   impact of Brent Harris's death: Thompson interview.

466   sex with 15,000 different men: Niles Merton interview with AJN, June 1, 1994.
466   *Advocate* editors disapproved of gay cancer stories: David Russell no. 3, Niles Merton and Thompson interviews with AJN.
466   anonymous person with gay cancer: Larry Mass, "Cancer as Metaphor," *New York Native,* no. 19 (Aug. 24–Sept. 6, 1981); identity of anonymous interviewee from Mass.
466   "Breaking the Taboos on Anal Pleasure": *The Advocate,* no. 326 (Sept. 7, 1981).
466   "As I encountered each new revelation. . . .": Goodstein, "Opening Space," *The Advocate,* no. 360 (Jan. 20, 1983).
466   *Advocate* editors wondered whether they had been too slow in reporting on AIDS: Russell and Thompson interviews; both *Advocate* editors defended the coverage. Criticism was widespread, most notably from Larry Kramer and Randy Shilts in *And the Band Played On,* p. 245.
467   "I want to be especially blunt. . . .": Transcript of Hearing of the Subcommittee on Health and the Environment of the U.S. House Committee on Energy and Commerce, April 13, 1982.
467   "Look at the epidemiologic data. . . .": Voeller quoted in Russell interview no. 3 with AJN.
467   "Whether we like it or not. . . .": Goodstein, "Opening Space," *The Advocate,"* no. 338 (March 18, 1982).
468   GMHC representatives seemed aggressive to non-New Yorkers: Bopper Deyton interview, April 14, 1994, Tim Westmoreland interview no. 2 and Helen Schietinger interview with AJN.
468   Kramer's objections to "Showers" poster: Mass interview no. 3.
468   "We had told ourselves. . . .": Fain, "A History of GMHC."
468   figures on Showers fundraiser: ibid. Also Mass interview nos. 1 and 2.
468   "I need to talk to you about my private life. . . .": Westmoreland interview no. 1 with AJN.
469   "It won't keep you in rhesus monkeys. . . .": Westmoreland interview nos. 1 and 2 with AJN; also Deyton interview.
469   audience sitting in embarrassed silence: Deyton, Bruce Voeller, Bush and Barbara Love interviews with AJN.
469   people quietly gathered their belongings and left: Deyton and Love interviews.
469   "What are we going to do about Lucia?": Deyton interview.
469   Voeller told the NGTF board to dump Valeska: Voeller interview nos. 4 and 5 with AJN.
470   "Terminal Illness at NGTF. . . .": *New York Native,* no. 47 (Sept. 27–Oct. 10, 1982).
470   GMHC celebrated the opening of its first office: Fain, "A History of GMHC."
470   Valeska and Apuzzo had a brief affair: Apuzzo interview no. 4 with AJN. Valeska declined an interview.
470   Apuzzo told Bush Valeska's real name: Bush interview no. 2 with AJN. Apuzzo says she does not recall the conversation.
470   Fain's letter: Fain to Westmoreland, Aug. 16, 1982, courtesy of Tim Westmoreland.

33: Swept Away

472   "Today it can be a political death wish. . . .": Colman McCarthy column, reprinted in *Minneapolis Star,* Oct. 7, 1982.
473   Mondale's previous encounter with a homosexual group: *San Francisco Chronicle,* June 17, 1977.
473   "As Mondale concedes. . . .": Broder's column reprinted in *San Francisco Chronicle,* June 23, 1977.
473   "You should realize that I'm very uncomfortable. . . .": James Hormel interview no. 2 with JDC.
473   To Endean's surprise, Mondale said yes.: Endean interview no. 5 with JDC.
473   "Put your money where your mouth is": *New York Native,* no. 45 (Aug. 30–Sept. 12, 1982).

474   The honorary committee was testimony: *New York Times,* Sept. 4, 1982.

474   HRCF leaders worried that Mondale would cancel: Hormel interview.

474   worry that the audience might jeer him: Endean interview no. 5 with JDC.

474   Mondale's language: text of his speech at HRCF dinner reprinted in *New York Native,* no. 48 (Oct. 11–24, 1982).

474   "You're going to be swept away. . . .": Westmoreland interview no. 2 with AJN.

474   "The one thing AIDS. . . .": Endean interview no. 3 with JDC.

474   He boasted of evenings at the baths: Endean interview no. 8 with JDC.

475   Endean viewed Apuzzo with awe and jealousy: Endean interview no. 2 with JDC.

475   Apuzzo on her own religious and sexual struggles: Apuzzo interview nos. 1–3 with AJN.

475   "Sister Virginia": Betty Powell interview no. 1 with AJN.

475   Apuzzo debated Falwell on *Donahue*: on Oct. 13, 1982.

475   "I have Potomac Fever": Peter Freiberg, "NGTF's New Directions and Director Virginia Apuzzo," *The Advocate,* no. 360 (Jan. 20, 1983). Also, for the same quote, another interview/profile of Apuzzo in *The Advocate,* no. 370 (June 23, 1983).

476   "Are you crazy?": Powell interview no. 2 with AJN.

476   "The strongest negative I've heard. . . .": Freiberg, "NGTF's New Directions and Director Virginia Apuzzo." On the day she was named NGTF director, Endean was even more gushing: "I look forward to a cooperative relationship and competent leadership, and that will be a refreshing change," quoted in *The Advocate,* no. 382 (Dec. 8, 1983).

477   Levi's background: Jeff Levi interview with AJN.

477   "We need to take over the AIDS issue. . . .": Apuzzo interview no. 2 and Levi interview.

477   APLA: Most from Matt Redman interview with AJN; also Steve Schulte interview nos. 1 and 2 with AJN. The APLA decision not to use the word "gay" was in obvious contrast to what the founders of the Gay Men's Health Crisis did, and it set off a shouting match between founders Schulte and Redman. This happened with growing frequency over the next five years; for a discussion of "de-gaying" AIDS, see Urvashi Vaid, *Virtual Equality: The Mainstreaming of Gay and Lesbian Liberation* (New York: Anchor, 1995).

477   Nancy Cole: "13 Random Victims of an Indiscriminate Killer—AIDS," *Los Angeles Times,* May 24, 1987. Her married name was Sawaya.

478   gay male sexual liberationists hijacked the movement: mostly from Kramer to Eric Marcus, courtesy of Marcus; also Kramer no. 1 to JDC.

478   "We know who we are. . . .": Michael Callen and Richard Berkowitz with Richard Dworkin, *New York Native,* no. 50 (Nov. 8–21, 1982).

479   "What is 'excessive' to some. . . .": Nathan Fain, "Coping with a Crisis: AIDS and the Issue It Raises," *The Advocate,* no. 361 (Feb. 17, 1983).

479   "the concept of recreational sex. . . .": Kameny quoted in "Gay America in Transition," *Newsweek,* Aug. 8, 1983, p. 30.

479   Kight felt disease had nothing to do with homosexual intercourse: many accounts, among them Kight interview no. 5 with AJN; also Ivy Bottini interview nos. 2 and 3 with AJN.

479   "The correlation in this case. . . .": *Los Angeles Times,* April 5, 1984.

479   "During the last sixteen months. . . .": Michael Lynch, "Living with Kaposi's," *Body Politic,* November 1982.

480   "Two hundred cases of a deadly disease. . . .": Vincent Galotti of San Francisco letter in *The Advocate,* no. 341 (April 29, 1982).

480   "borders on the hysterical": letter to the editor, *New York Native,* no. 51 (Nov. 22–Dec. 5, 1982).

480   "1,112 and Counting": Larry Kramer, *New York Native,* no. 59 (March 14–27, 1983), p. 1.

480   Kramer-Koch first meeting: Koch interview with AJN, May 19, 1994. Kramer's reaction to the mayor is from "1,112 and Counting."

481   Kramer's departure from GMHC: Kramer to Marcus; Larry Mass interview nos. 1–3 with AJN; Kramer, *Reports from the Holocaust,* pp. 57–59; 65–67.

481   "Larry, you can't have it both ways. . . .": Jim Fouratt interview no. 3 with AJN.

481   candlelight marches: "Fighting for Our Lives," *San Francisco Chronicle,* May 3, 1983.

481   "I and the editors of the *Advocate*. . . .": Goodstein, "Opening Space," *The Advocate*, no. 367 (May 12, 1983).

482   Shilts note to Kramer on "1,112 and Counting": *New York Native*, no. 61 (April 11–24, 1983); also Shilts interview no. 1 with AJN.

482   study by two researchers at the U of C: Shilts, "Startling Finds on 'Gay Disease,' " *San Francisco Chronicle*, March 23, 1983.

482   "They'll put barbed wire. . . .": Shilts, *And the Band Played On*, pp. 255–56.

482   "I don't get paid to not write stories.": Shilts to Marcus; also call from his book editor in New York.

482   "I'd estimate that business. . . .": Shilts, *San Francisco Chronicle*, May 2, 1983; also Shilts interview no. 1.

482   dark and under siege: Shilts interview no. 1.

482   "Isn't it something. . . .": "The AIDS Epidemic: The Change in Gay Life-Style," *Newsweek*, April 18, 1983.

482   "Like heterosexuals who have to contend. . . .": Arnie Kantrowitz, "Til Death Do Us Part," *The Advocate*, no. 363 (March 17, 1983).

483   "We've finally come down. . . .": George Whitmore, "A Crisis Transforms a Community: New York, Where Intimacy Is In," *The Advocate*, no. 373 (Aug. 4, 1983).

483   "Why are health officials. . . .": *Capitol Hill* (GRNL newsletter), vol. 5, no. 2 (Fall/Winter 1983).

483   report in the *Journal of the American Medical Association*: AMA press release, May 6, 1983, reprinted in Shilts, *And the Band Played On*, pp. 299–300. Also *New York Times*, May 6, 1983.

483   "If routine close contact. . . .": AMA news release: Evidence Suggests Household Contact May Transmit AIDS, May 6, 1983. Reprinted in Shilts, *And the Band Played On*, p. 299.

483   The study set off a furor: For full discussion of the medical problems with the AMA "household contact" study and press release, see Shilts, *And the Band Played On*, pp. 299–301; also Nathan Fain's health column, *The Advocate*, no. 370 (June 23, 1983).

484   "The sexual revolution. . . .": Patrick J. Buchanan, "AIDS Disease: It's Nature Striking Back," *New York Post*, May 24, 1983.

484   "There's the potential that AIDS. . . .": *San Francisco Chronicle*, May 27, 1983.

484   "it might be a good idea. . . .": *Tulsa World* editorial, quoted in *The Advocate*, no. 376 (Sept. 15, 1983).

484   Apuzzo on hate calls/mail: Apuzzo interview nos. 2 and 3.

485   more stories on AIDS after *Journal* study: David Shaw, "Hudson Brought AIDS Out of the Coverage," *Los Angeles Times*, Dec. 21, 1987.

485   "While the number of AIDS victims. . . .": Peter Collier and David Horowitz, "Whitewash," *California* magazine, July 1983, p. 52.

485   "fruits to vegetables": *Screw* magazine, Dec. 5, 1983; cited in Nathan Fain, *The Advocate*, no. 385 (Jan. 10, 1984).

485   "We are speechless.": Fain, *The Advocate*, no. 385 (Jan. 10, 1984).

485   "All we can do. . . .": *San Francisco Chronicle*, June 28, 1983.

486   mosquito bites in Provincetown: Vin McCarthy interview no. 1 with JDC.

486   ". . . people you know who are *non-gay*.": David Mixner interview no. 5 and Marylouise Oates interview no. 2 with AJN.

486   "kinkiest garage sale. . . .": Mark Thompson (interview with AJN, June 14, 1994) recounted running into Shilts at the Hothouse.

486   "Gay America in Transition": *Newsweek*, Aug. 8, 1983.

486   "Now—just as homosexuality. . . .": Charles Krauthammer, "The Politics of a Plague Revisited, *The New Republic*, Aug. 1, 1983.

486   A Gallup poll on AIDS: Gallup poll for *Newsweek* of 767 adults by phone, July 20–21, 1983, with a margin of error of four points, *Newsweek*, Aug. 8, 1983. For more analysis and details, *The Bush Report*, vol. 1, no. 3 (August 1983).

487   AIDS is the "most political disease. . . .": *San Francisco Chronicle*, June 11, 1983.

487   "direct attack on the social. . . .": Alice attack reprinted in Shilts, *And the Band Played On*, p. 317.

487   When Supervisor Carol Ruth Silver: Shilts interview with AJN; also *San Francisco Chronicle*, May 27, 1983.

487   "What a peculiar. . . .": courtesy of Collier and Horowitz, "Whitewash."

487   "There is a trend. . . .": Shilts, *And the Band Played On*, p. 317.

487   "an end run around": ibid., pp. 254–55.

487   Falwell's appearances against AIDS: *The New Republic*, Aug. 1, 1983; *Los Angeles Times*, July 12, 1983; and *San Francisco Chronicle*, July 4, 1983.

488   quarantine for men with AIDS: McCarthy interview, Bruce Voeller interview nos. 4 and 5 with AJN, Larry Bush interview no. 2 with JDC and interview no. 1 with AJN, and Mass interviews. Also Nathan Fain, *The Advocate*, no. 371 (July 7, 1983), and Craig Rowland, "The Call for Quarantine," *The Advocate*, no. 443 (April 1, 1986).

488   "It's happened before. . . .": "The AIDS Crisis May Spread Faster Through Fear Than Any Other Way," *New York Native*, no. 65 (June 6–19, 1983), p. 59.

488   "serious efforts:" National Hemophilia Foundation Medical and Scientific Advisory Council, Jan. 14, 1983, reprinted in *New York Native* no. 57 (Feb. 15–27, 1983). Also *San Francisco Chronicle*, Jan. 19, 1983, and "Ban on Gay Men as Blood Donors Urged," *Los Angeles Times*, Jan. 18, 1983.

488   "political solution to a medical problem": NGTF press release, undated.

488   "I don't have to tell you. . . .": *The Advocate*, no. 362 (May 3, 1983).

489   "People are dying. . . .": *The Advocate*, no. 361 (Feb. 17, 1983).

489   "I have three children. . . .": Voeller interview no. 4.

489   "The government's policy. . . .": "Apuzzo," *Los Angeles Times*, Aug. 2, 1983.

489   GRNL requested $50 million on AIDS in fiscal 1984: "Gay Rights Lobby Addresses Mayors Conference on AIDS," *Capitol Hill*, vol. 5, no. 2 (Summer/Fall 1983), p. 6.

489   Apuzzo and the Task Force: Voeller interview no. 5.

489   request for $100 million was unrealistic: Endean interview no. 4 with JDC and Voeller interview no. 5.

489   The HRCF had raised $588,000: David Goodstein, in *The Advocate*, no. 358 (Dec. 23, 1982).

490   "I don't care how much they support the opera. . . .": Goodstein, "Opening Space," *The Advocate*, no. 348 (Aug. 5, 1982).

490   "I just want you to be clear, Steve. . . .": Endean interview no. 4. Similar accounts came from David Russell, Voeller and Rob Eichberg interviews with AJN.

490   "Even with the glacial attitude. . . .": Larry Bush, "D.C. Desk: The Year Gone By," *New York Native*, no. 54 (Jan. 3–16, 1983).

490   divert him from writing more critical stories: Bush interview no. 2 with AJN.

490   "Why are you guys not asking questions . . . ?": ibid.

490   promised to produce tapes: Larry Bush, "Capital Report," *The Advocate*, no. 366 (April 28, 1983).

491   "The gay community raised the largest. . . .": Lou Chibbaro Jr., "Endean to Give Up HRCF Post; Will Retain Two Others," *Washington Blade*, March 11, 1983, p. 1.

491   "Dear David" letter: Endean to Goodstein, March 15, 1983, courtesy of L.A. Gay and Lesbian Archives.

491   a sign of weakness by Endean: Russell interview no. 1 with AJN.

491   impossible to work with: "Capital Report," *The Advocate*, no. 370 (June 23, 1983); also Endean letter to *The Advocate*, no. 369 (June 9, 1983).

491   "GRNL's current financial plight. . . .": Voeller letter to GRNL board members, Feb. 22, 1983, courtesy of L.A. Gay and Lesbian Archives.

491   "Even though it pains me to say so. . . .": Goodstein, "Opening Space," *The Advocate*, no. 370 (June 23, 1983).

491   "David has a Hollywood picture. . . .": *Washington Blade*, July 3, 1983.

491   letters to gay newspapers: reported and quoted from "The Gay Community Struggles to Fashion an Effective Lobby," *Congressional Quarterly*, Dec. 3, 1983, p. 2546.

491   "No medieval scene would be complete. . . .": Melvin Boozer, "Beyond the Endean Controversy: The Gay Press Is Part of the Problem," *Washington Blade,* July 15, 1983.

492   "movement's propaganda arm. . . .": Larry Bush, "The Challenge of Community," *The Advocate,* no. 370 (June 23, 1983).

492   "You can be very certain. . . .": David Goodstein, "Opening Space," *The Advocate,* no. 378 (Oct. 13, 1983).

492   A report on GRNL's fundraising: *The Advocate,* no. 381 (Nov. 24, 1983).

492   Endean's resignation: numerous accounts, including "Steve Endean Out as GRNL Head," *Bay Area Reporter,* Oct. 20, 1983; "Rights Lobby Director Resigns Amid Criticism," *Gay Community News,* Oct. 29, 1983; and *Chicago Update,* Nov. 2, 1983.

492   "I believe the attacks on me. . . .": *Gay Community News,* Oct. 28, 1983.

492   "We are uncomfortable with the Great White Father. . . .": *Philadelphia Gay News* editorial, vol. 7, no. 38 (July 29–Aug. 4, 1983).

493   "vendetta waged mercilessly. . . .": Frank Kameny letter to *Washington Blade,* Nov. 4, 1983.

493   "Goodstein and Bush do agree. . . .": Charles Stewart letter to *The Advocate,* no. 372 (July 21, 1983).

493   "The Gay Movement in the nearly 15 years. . . .": "GRNL After Steve Endean: Time for a Merger," *Washington Blade,* Oct. 21, 1983, p. 19.

493   surprised by how traumatized: Kameny interview no. 3 with JDC.

493   "They call me the father. . . .": Cory quoted in Dick Leitsch interview nos. 1 and 2 with AJN.

34: Little to Celebrate

494   For a discussion on complaints about black-tie activism, see Dennis Altman, "Gay Money, Gay Votes: Why Bother with Electoral Politics?" *New York Native,* no. 54 (Jan. 3–16, 1983), p. 15.

495   Studio One treated blacks rudely: Bobby Smith interview with AJN.

495   the Ice Palace sting: Henry Wiemhoff interview no. 2 with AJN.

495 $6,000 in punitive damage: *The Advocate,* no. 387 (Feb. 7, 1984).

495   "Let's face it. . . .": *Los Angeles Magazine,* July 1979.

495   BWMT leaflets: courtesy of New York Public Library Archives.

495   "There's a complacency. . . .": Charles Michael Smith, "Discrimination and Its Discontents: The Proper Response to Gay Racists," *New York Native,* no. 73 (Sept. 26–Oct. 9, 1983).

495   how alone Powell felt: Betty Powell interview nos. 1 and 2 with AJN.

496   Endean-Stewart exchange: Charles Stewart interview with AJN.

496   "It's not about race prejudice. . . .": ibid.

496   most black leaders had never welcomed homosexuals: Taylor Branch, *Parting the Waters,* p. 265, also pp. 196–97.

496   Powell found anti-homosexual sentiment in blacks: Powell interview no. 2.

497   "Mrs. King, your husband wasn't speaking to conservatives. . . .": Virginia Apuzzo interview no. 2 with AJN. For "Letter from a Birmingham Jail," see Branch, *Parting the Waters,* pp. 737–44.

497   description of Washington rally and Audre Lorde's remarks: "Audre Lorde Speaks and Gays Join March on D.C.," *New York Native,* no. 72 (Sept. 12–25, 1983), p. 1.

497   discrimination based on skin color: Powell interview no. 2, Stewart interview, Smith interview and Phill Wilson interview with AJN.

497   "rainbow coalition of the rejected": *Congressional Quarterly,* Dec. 3, 1983, which also discusses some of the black-gay tension.

497   Jackson's HRCF speech: *New York Times,* Sept. 28, 1983; also *New York Native,* no. 74 (Oct. 10–23, 1983).

498   Geto-Fierstein exchange on dais as Jackson spoke: Ethan Geto interview no. 3 with AJN.

498   "Sex is a thrill. . . .": *The Bush Report*, vol. 1, no. 3 (September 1983).

500   "If a group of people. . . .": Randy Shilts, "San Francisco: Traitor or Hero? Notes from the Plague," *New York Native*, no. 94 (July 16–29, 1984).

500   "business is booming again in the bathhouses": Shilts, "Of Course, Nobody Had Planned on This," *San Francisco Chronicle*, Jan. 14, 1984.

500   "I'd like to see all the bathhouses. . . .": Shilts, "AIDS Expert Says Bathhouses Should Close," *San Francisco Chronicle*, Feb. 3, 1984, p. 4.

500   Curran and Britt statements on Shilts's articles about bathhouses and AIDS: "New Controversy Erupts in San Francisco: Bath Houses: Scapegoat for AIDS Fear or Real Health Threat?" *The Advocate*, no. 390 (March 20, 1984).

501   "I'm being crucified. . . .": ibid.

501   "As far as I'm concerned. . . .": Shilts, "San Francisco: Traitor or Hero?"

501   put his career above his friends: Mark Thompson interview with AJN; also Shilts interview no. 1 with AJN.

501   If he were straight, he would have been honored: Shilts interview with Marcus, courtesy of Marcus.

501   Shilts's alcohol and drug use: Shilts interview no. 1.

501   "A homosexual McCarthyism has descended. . . .": Shilts, "San Francisco: Traitor or Hero?"

502   "If this was a heterosexual problem. . . .": *San Francisco Chronicle*, May 6, 1984.

502   "A lot of people in the straight community. . . .": Littlejohn quoted in *San Francisco Chronicle*, April 1, 1984.

502   "Bathhouses have long been important. . . .": "S. F. Planning to Close Gay Baths," *San Francisco Chronicle*, March 30, 1984.

502   "I don't like how political. . . .": Shilts, "San Francisco: Traitor or Hero?"

502   "having sex is presumably. . . .": Nathan Fain, *The Advocate*, no. 393 (May 1, 1984).

503   Kameny and the baths: "GRNL Board Promises Renewed Agenda," *Washington Blade*, April 6, 1984.

503   NGTF and GRNL had used bathhouses as lodging: Gary Van Ooteghem interview with AJN, June 24, 1994.

503   Stoddard on governmental intervention: "Hands Off Baths," from "Space Available" column, *New York Native*, no. 91 (June 4–17, 1984).

503   "I would not advocate. . . .": *The Advocate*, nos. 383–84 (Dec. 22, 1983).

504   "It is an insult. . . .": ibid.

504   how old he was when he decided he was straight: *Los Angeles Times*, Dec. 13, 1983.

504   "I thought we had to do. . . .": *New York Times*, Dec. 15, 1983.

504   "He has elaborated. . . .": *The Advocate*, no. 385 (Jan. 10, 1984).

504   "John Glenn has the courage. . . .": *Washington Post*, Jan. 21, 1984.

504   one of his senior campaign officials was gay: The account is from the man himself, in an interview with AJN. Although his homosexuality is fairly well known in Washington, he requested that he not be identified, out of fear that it could jeopardize his political career in Washington.

505   "We would rather die. . . .": David Mixner interview no. 5 with AJN.

505   "Glenn may, when it is all over. . . .": Larry Bush, "D.C. Desk," *New York Native*, no. 84 (Feb. 27–March 11, 1985).

505   "This is not a protest. . . .": *San Francisco Chronicle*, July 16, 1984.

505   "We've gotten everything we could expect. . . .": quoted in *Task Force Bulletin*, vol. 11, no. 4 (August 1984).

505   "Some people in my district. . . .": *Los Angeles Times*, June 21, 1984.

506   "The Rainbow Coalition includes lesbians and gays. . . .": *The Advocate*, no. 401 (Aug. 21, 1984).

506   "It's the first time. . . .": ibid.

506   "We didn't choose San Francisco": "Falwell's Family Forum Opposes '84 Democratic Agenda," *The Advocate,* no. 401 (Aug. 21, 1984).
506   "The media portrayed it as the land of fruits and nuts. . . .": Goodstein, "Opening Space," ibid.
506   "They played right into my hands. . . .": Mel White, *Stranger at the Gate: To Be Gay and Christian in America,* p. 295.
507   "Tacitly, but without any formal debate. . . ." Morton Kondracke, *Los Angeles Times* op-ed page, July 18, 1984.
507   "He's right, of course. . . .": Alexander Cockburn, *The Nation,* Sept. 1, 1984.
507   Rollins on *Face the Nation: New York Native,* no. 96 (Aug. 13–26, 1984).
507   gays at the Republican convention: Bruce Decker interview with JDC, June 28, 1984; and *The Advocate,* no. 401 (Aug. 21, 1984).
508   Decker-Reagan picture: published in *San Francisco Chronicle,* Sept. 13, 1984.
508   "Well, I just have to say. . . .": transcript from *The Advocate,* no. 399 (July 24, 1984).
508   Decker's main goal in Dallas: Decker interview.
508   "They are not fostering gay liberation. . . .": *San Francisco Chronicle,* Oct. 10, 1984.
508   bathhouses and sex clubs closed: *San Francisco Chronicle,* Oct. 10, 1984; also *The Advocate,* no. 407 (Nov. 13, 1984), and *New York Native,* no. 104 (Dec. 17–30, 1984).
508   "It's very sad the AIDS. . . .": Ibid.
508   something of a mass demonstration: *San Francisco Chronicle,* Oct. 30, 1984.
509   "My concern has always been. . . .": Peter Freiberg, "Presidential Race: A Watershed for Gays," *The Advocate,* no. 406 (Oct. 30, 1984).
510   Decker took satisfaction in Reagan's election: *The Advocate,* no. 313 (March 19, 1984).
510   "According to the self-proclaimed experts. . . .": David Goodstein, "Opening Space," *The Advocate,* no. 413 (Feb. 5, 1985).
510   "Fringe issues. . . .": Associated Press, May 28, 1985.
511   first meeting of the West Hollywood City Council: Andrew Kopkind, "Gay City on the Hill: Once Upon a Time in the West," *The Nation,* June 1, 1985.
511   "Fagots Stay Out" sign came down a second time: Irwin Held interview with AJN, Nov. 3, 1994.

35: For the Public Good

512   Andelson was one of the fifty most powerful people in L.A.: *Los Angeles Magazine,* September 1985.
512   "the world's most powerful gay person": *The Advocate,* no. 349 (Aug. 19, 1982).
512   8709 turned away people who were old, fat, effeminate: Paul Monette interview no. 6 with JDC, David Mixner interview no. 4 with AJN.
513   "It was a difficult decision. . . ." and "courageous": *The Advocate,* no. 424 (July 9, 1985).
513   Andelson told Brown he wanted Board of Regents job: Jerry Brown interview no. 1 with AJN.
513   "I'm not the only gay regent. . . .": Melinda Smolin, "UC Regent Andelson Adds Diversity, Individuality to Board," *The Daily Californian,* vol. 17, no. 43 (March 13, 1985).
513   "You can't go into these hearings. . . .": Mixner interview no. 3 with AJN.
513   "There's nothing in my name.": ibid.
513   "conscious attempt to destroy me. . . .": Andelson interview in the Los Angeles Gay Community Services *Center News,* vol. 2, no. 3 (undated).
513   "pushing sick ideas. . . .": "Senate Confirms Gay as UC Regent," *San Francisco Chronicle,* April 30, 1982.
513   "tremendous price" and "Effectiveness and practicality. . . .": "Sheldon Andelson: the World's Most Powerful Gay Person?," *The Advocate,* no. 349 (Aug. 19, 1982).

513 he had hidden his ownership: Andelson family interview with AJN, June 5, 1994.

514 "Perhaps someone should comment. . . .": Guy Wright, *San Francisco Chronicle*, Feb. 16, 1985.

514 What Monette did not write about: Rudy Kikel interview, Sept. 18, 1993, Monette interviews 5 and 6 and Tony Smith interview with JDC.

515 a cure was imminent: Monette interview nos. 3 and 4 with JDC.

515 "Commitment to Life" dinner: *Los Angeles Times*, Sept. 19, 1985; *The Advocate*, no. 432 (Oct. 29, 1985).

515 assigned Andelson to a table at the back: Mixner interview no. 5 with AJN.

515 rare interview as "exclusive": "Patron Saint: An Interview with Bruce Mailman," *New York Native*, no. 97 (Sept. 10–23, 1984).

515 postcards to Mailman: Peter Freiberg, "A Case for Closure? AIDS and the Baths," *The Advocate*, no. 375 (Sept. 1, 1983). Bruce Mailman interview nos. 1 and 2 with AJN.

515 "If you close the baths. . . .": "The Plague Years," *Rolling Stone*, March 28, 1985.

516 "We designed the balcony. . . .": Bruce Mailman, "*Star Dust* Speaks: An Editorial," *Star Dust*, vol. 2, no. 4 (May 1983).

516 use the warm, carpeted darkened area for sex: Jack Stoddard interview with AJN.

516 number of undeliverable invitations: Mailman interview no. 1.

516 as low as 1,200: Stoddard interview.

516 canceled the 1985 Black Party: ibid.

516 business at New St. Marks Baths was down: Mailman quoted in Peter Freiberg, "Should the Bathhouses Be Closed?" *The Advocate*, no. 415 (March 5, 1985).

516 early health measures at St. Marks Baths: Stoddard and Mailman interviews.

516 Fouratt asked baths customers if they knew about AIDS: *The Advocate*, no. 415 (March 5, 1985) and Fouratt interview no. 2 with AJN.

516 only needed to ride out a rough few years: Stoddard and Susan Tomkin interviews with AJN.

516 Mailman refused to agree to the blood test for the AIDS virus and was called "The Ostrich": Stoddard interview.

517 Shilts's report detailing Hudson's secret life: *San Francisco Chronicle*, July 24, 1985.

517 AIDS negative coverage: David Shaw, "Hudson Brought AIDS Coverage Out of the Closet," *Los Angeles Times*, Dec. 21, 1987.

517 *Newsweek* poll on AIDS: "Special Report: The Social Fallout from an Epidemic," Aug. 12, 1985.

517 "unprecedented threat": Popham letter in *The Advocate*, no. 408 (Nov. 27, 1984).

518 Lambda went to court: *New York Native*, no. 110 (March 11–24, 1985). See also Shilts, *And the Band Played On*, p. 540.

518 "What if": *New York Native*, no. 91 (June 4–17, 1984).

518 Caiazza on HIV test: "Space Available: Why You Should Not Be Tested for HTLV-III," *New York Native*, no. 99 (Oct. 8–21, 1984).

518 "We need to be tested. . . .": Bruce Voeller, "Piece of My Mind," *The Advocate*, no. 419 (April 30, 1985).

518 "They say that if they are found. . . ." *New York Daily News*, Feb. 26, 1985; reprinted in *New York Native*, no. 110 (March 11–24, 1985).

518 Falwell letter: reprinted in *New York Native*, no. 120 (July 15–28, 1985).

518 twenty states considered regulations: "The Politics of AIDS: A Tale of Two States," *U.S. News & World Report*, Nov. 18, 1985.

519 Texas quarantine: *The Advocate*, no. 438 (Jan. 21, 1986).

519 "misrepresenting and distorting the research of others": "Enter on Stage Right: Crusader Dannemeyer, Defender of His Faith," *Los Angeles Times*, July 6, 1986.

519 "They're getting what they deserve. . . .": *Los Angeles Times*, Aug. 20, 1985.

519 "God's plan for man. . . .": Fred Barnes, "The Politics of AIDS: A New Issue for the Right Wing," *The New Republic*, Nov. 4, 1985, p. 11. Also *Los Angeles Times*, Oct. 3, 1985.

519 "tiny small step forward. . . .": *The Advocate*, no. 433 (Nov. 12, 1985).

519 vote in House on bathhouse closures: Barnes, "The Politics of AIDS."

519 McGrath called on NYC to close gay bathhouses: *New York Post,* Oct. 2, 1985, p. 19.

519 "Promiscuous, homosexual, aggressive sexual activity. . . .": NBC Sunday show, quoted in *New York Post,* Oct. 7, 1985.

519 Cuomo ordered the state health department: *New York Daily News,* Oct. 7, 1985.

520 "The agonizing, foot-dragging. . . .": Ray Kerrison, *New York Post,* Oct. 17, 1985.

520 New York closing baths: Mailman, Jim Fouratt no. 3, Jack Stoddard and Tom Stoddard no. 4 (no relation) interviews with AJN; also "New York Officials Reconsider Closing Baths, *The Advocate,* no. 433 (Nov. 12, 1985).

520 "What we are saying is that you can't sell death. . . .": *New York Daily News,* Nov. 7, 1985.

520 "Today": quoted in *New York Post,* Nov. 7, 1985.

520 Fouratt and others sprayed graffiti on the Mine Shaft walls: Fouratt interview no. 3 with AJN.

520 Mailman attacked the new regulations: Mailman interviews.

521 Stoddard believed that the law: *The Advocate,* no. 434 (Nov. 26, 1985); and Tom Stoddard interview nos. 3 and 4 with AJN.

521 Even the *New York Times:* "At Homosexual Establishments, a New Climate of Caution," *New York Times,* Nov. 9, 1985.

522 Kennedy seated at table with Smith threesome: Steve Smith interview no. 6 with AJN.

522 Kennedy would leave before the dancing: Mixner interview no. 5 and Bob Shrum interview no. 2 with AJN.

522 MECLA press conference: *MECLA Newsletter,* January 1986; *Los Angeles Times,* Nov. 11, 1985.

522 "self-appointed power brokers. . . .": O'Brien leaflet courtesy of L.A. Archives.

523 Morris Kight attacked MECLA: "Bathhouse Bashing, from Germany to LA": *New York Native,* Dec. 8–15, 1985.

523 Bottini on the bathhouses: Ivy Bottini interview no. 2 with AJN.

523 "The affluent gay community. . . .": David Goodstein, "Opening Space," *The Advocate,* no. 317 (May 1, 1981).

523 AIDS cases in New York and California: *Congressional Record,* May 21, 1985, p. E2315.

524 "It's so different in New York. . . .": Krim to Shilts, "Horror Stories and Excuses: How New York City Is Dealing with AIDS," *New York Native,* no. 112 (March 25–April 7, 1985).

524 "There is in my community. . . .": *New York Native,* no. 106 (Jan. 14–27, 1985).

524 "homosexuality is once again reverting. . . .": Charles Krauthammer, "AIDS Hysteria Shows Gays Their Political Heyday Is Over," *Los Angeles Times,* Nov. 5, 1985.

524 A Gallup poll: George Gallup Jr., "AIDS and Public Attitude Toward Gays," *San Francisco Chronicle,* Dec. 12, 1985.

524 the most serious threat to gay civil rights since Stonewall: Arnie Kantrowitz interview no. 3, Hal Offen interview, Jan. 20, 1994, and Bill Bahlman interview no. 1 with AJN.

525 On B'nai B'rith's objection to the name Gay and Lesbian Anti-Defamation League: Kantrowitz interview and *New York Native,* Jan. 27–Feb. 2, 1986.

525 GLAAD meeting: Bahlman interview; also *New York Native,* Nov. 25–Dec. 1, 1985.

525 GLAAD's inaugural action: *The Advocate,* no. 437 (Jan. 7, 1986).

526 Wisconsin gay rights law and other local gay rights laws as of 1985: Charles V. Dale, "An Overview of Legal Developments in Homosexual Rights," Congressional Research Service, Library of Congress, April 16, 1985.

526 Once again voters were shown: *San Francisco Chronicle,* Jan. 11, 1985.

527 Providence bill and bishop's opposition: "Providence Bill to Aid Homosexuals in Doubt," *New York Times,* Sept. 1, 1985, p. 25.

527 Massachusetts House vote and "I guess they felt. . . .": *New York Times,* Sept. 23, 1985.

527 Chicago gay rights defeat: *New York Times,* July 30, 1986; and *The Advocate,* (Sept. 2, 1986).

527   "I was pinched by a homosexual. . . .": *The Advocate,* no. 463 (Jan. 6, 1987).

527   "Why should our city government. . . .": Family Rights Coalition press kit, "Referendum to Repeal Homosexual Rights Law," May 29, 1986.

528   Bell-Troy encounter: *New York Times,* May 24, 1974.

528   Rothenberg and Ramrod: David Rothenberg interview with AJN, May 7, 1993.

528   A Hasidic Jew seated in the audience: *The Advocate,* no. 334 (Jan. 7, 1982), and *New York Times,* Nov. 24, 1981.

528   every unmarried member of New York City government was homosexual: This was Rabbi William Handler of Union of Orthodox Rabbis, quoted (among other places) in *The Advocate,* no. 364 (March 31, 1983).

529   Activists questioned leaving drag queens out of the NYC gay rights bill: Rothenberg interview.

529   "a deal-breaker. . . .": Ethan Geto interview no. 3 with AJN.

529   "Justice delayed. . . ." *New York Native,* March 24, 1986.

529   Stoddard on how opponents' tactics helped gays: Tom Stoddard interview no. 3.

529   O'Connor's homily: *New York Times,* March 17, 1986.

529   "Everyone detected with AIDS should be tattooed. . . .": William Buckley, *New York Times* op-ed page, March 18, 1986.

529   advising activists to refrain from angry displays: Andy Humm interview with AJN, April 10, 1994.

530   "the sky is not going to fall. . . .": *New York Times,* March 21, 1986.

530   "This is the best night of my life. . . .": Owles in *The Advocate,* no. 445 (April 29, 1986).

36: Cop at the Door

532   "National Gay Rights Advocates: *San Francisco Chronicle,* Feb. 11, 1979.

532   "We suggest that you think seriously. . . .": *New York Native,* no. 101 (Nov. 5–18, 1984).

532   the 1969 U.S. Court of Appeals case: *San Francisco Chronicle,* July 2, 1969.

532   United States Civil Service guidelines on hiring: U.S. Civil Service Commission, July 3, 1975.

533   previous Supreme Court decisions on gay rights: Elder Witt, "Gay Rights Test Before High Court," *Congressional Quarterly;* reprinted in *San Francisco Chronicle,* Jan. 13, 1985, p. 12.

533   the Oklahoma ruling: *Los Angeles Times* and *New York Times,* March 27, 1985; Tribe's reaction: *The Advocate* no. 419 (April 30, 1985).

534   origins of sodomy law: see John D'Emilio, *Sexual Politics, Sexual Communities.*

534   only seven states retained homosexual sodomy laws: Tom Stoddard interview no. 6 with AJN.

534   "What are you doing in my bedroom?" and Hardwick's account of arrest: Michael Hardwick, *The Advocate,* no. 454 (Sept. 2, 1986).

534   the Sodomy Roundtable turned its attention to *Hardwick:* Stoddard interview no. 5 with AJN.

534   "the activity [Hardwick] hopes to engage in. . . .": *Hardwick* v. *Bowers* 760 F. 2d at 1210–13; see also Thomas Stoddard, *"Bowers* v. *Hardwick*: Precedent by Personal Predilection," *University of Chicago Law Review,* vol. 54, no. 2 (Spring 1987), pp. 648–56.

535   Supreme Court arguments in *Hardwick: New York Times,* April 1, 1986.

535   "was one of guarded optimism": Rubenfeld quoted in "Lenny" column, *The Advocate,* no. 446 (May 13, 1986).

536   White's background: Bob Woodward and Scott Armstrong, *The Brethren* (New York: Simon & Schuster, 1979), pp. 65–66.

537   "Sodomy laws have. . . .": Arthur S. Leonard, "Keeping the Cops Out of Michael Hardwick's Bedroom," *New York Native,* March 24, 1986.

537   "No judge likes to be overturned. . . .": *New York Times,* July 1, 1986.
537   "The Court has interpreted. . . .": *New York Times,* July 14, 1986. "Bid For Homosexual Law Referendum Is Dropped."
537   "perverted moral behavior. . . .": *New York Times,* July 1, 1986.
537   Stoddard told the *Post:* Ruth Marcus, "Sodomy Ruling's Implications Extend Far Beyond Bedroom," *Washington Post,* July 2, 1986, p. 1.
537   "The critical constitutional question. . . .": Stoddard, *"Bowers* v. *Hardwick,"* p. 655.
537   "lawmaking by personal predilection. . . .": ibid., p. 656.
537   "Given the importance. . . .": ibid.
538   "We believed in the Constitution. . . .": *Newsweek,* July 14, 1986.
538   spontaneous demonstration at Sheridan Square: Maxine Wolf, Bahlman interview no. 1 with AJN.
538   "The message is that. . . .": "Gays on Two Coasts Protest Sodomy Ruling," *New York Native,* July 14, 1986.
538   "This has been such a wretched time. . . .": *The Advocate,* no. 453 (Aug. 19, 1986).
538   surge in fundraising: Jeff Levi interview with AJN, March 23, 1994. Figures are from *The Advocate,* no. 457 (Oct. 14, 1986).
538   "The time for gay rage is now! . . .": *The Advocate,* no. 452 (Aug. 5, 1986).
539   "A Government in the Bedroom": *Newsweek,* July 14, 1986, p. 36.
539   Dershowitz's reaction to *Hardwick: New York Native,* July 14, 1986.
539   A Gallup poll for *Newsweek*: *Newsweek,* July 14, 1986.
539   Stoddard and Donahue: Tom Stoddard interview nos. 3 and 5 with AJN.
539   "I think I probably made a mistake": *New York Times,* Nov. 5, 1990.
539   Powell had switched sides on *Bowers:* see, among others, *Newsweek,* July 14, 1986.
539   Powell's gay clerk and discussions with him: Stoddard interview no. 5. The clerk was identified in an Oct. 20, 1995, *Washington Blade* article as Cabell Chinnis, and he said that although he hadn't specifically come out to Powell, his homosexuality was well known and he assumed the justice knew of it. He said Powell asked him questions about homosexuality and homosexuals, and that, "as the Powell biography states, I explained to him that gay people make up about 10 percent of the population, that gay men love other men like straight men love women, and that the right to love the person of my choice would be far more important to me than the right to vote in elections."
540   "Don't be silly." and *"WE* don't get it.": David Mixner interview no. 5 with AJN.
540   Peter Scott's HIV diagnosis: *Los Angeles Times,* Sept. 30, 1987; Mixner interview no. 5 and Marylouise Oates interview with AJN.
540   *Los Angeles Times* sent a reporter to Scott's hospital room: Mixner interview no. 4 with AJN. *Los Angelas Times* and *Herald Examiner* published news of Scott's illness: *Los Angeles Times,* Sept. 29, 1986.
540   "We're busy burying our dead. . . .": Mixner interview in ibid.
540   Levi on Prop. 64: *The Advocate,* no. 453 (Aug. 19, 1986).
541   In the conservative *National Review*: Joseph Sobran, "The Politics of AIDS," *National Review,* May 23, 1986.
541   Deukmejian on Prop. 64: *The Advocate,* no. 457 (Oct. 14, 1986).
541   the two sides shared office space: Ivy Bottini no. 2 and Mixner no. 5 interviews with AJN.
541   "It sends a very powerful message. . . .": *The Advocate,* no. 461 (Dec. 9, 1986).
542   This is a historic moment: Urvashi Vaid interview no. 2 and Stoddard interview no. 5 with AJN.
542   organizing to oppose CDC position on mandatory HIV testing: "Gay Groups Defeat CDC Mandatory Testing Proposal; Gain Support for Federal Anti-Discrimination Protections," NGLTF press release, Feb. 26, 1987.
543   Lavender Hill Mob's view of activism: Michael Petrelis interview, April 21, 1994, and Bahlman interview no. 2 with AJN.
543   "Who cares that the issue? . . .": Petrelis interview.
543   two dressed in concentration camp outfits: Bahlman interview no. 2.

543   yelling match at CDC conference: *The Advocate,* no. 469 (March 31, 1987).
543   little difference between health professionals and homosexuals at conference: Bahlman interview no. 2 and Petrelis interview.
544   quotes from the CDC press conference, and description of the scene: "In Depth: CDC AIDS Conference," *The Advocate,* no. 469 (March 31, 1987). Also "Homosexuals Applaud Rejection of Mandatory Tests for AIDS," *New York Times,* Feb. 26, 1987; Stoddard interview no. 5, Petrelis and Bahlman interviews.
544   "The gay and lesbian community has a lot to be proud of. . . .": NGLTF press release, Feb. 26, 1987.
544   Vaid saw her attackers as opportunists: Vaid interview no. 2.
544   reaction of Sweeney and Levi to the Mob: *The Advocate,* no. 469 (March 31, 1987).
544   membership of fifty: Petrelis interview.
545   Petrelis's early life: ibid.
545   Petrelis had been diagnosed with Kaposi's sarcoma: ibid.
545   Petrelis was upset that the GMHC board did not include a person with AIDS: ibid.; James A. Revson, *Newsday,* April 10, 1986.
545   Petrelis considered himself intellectually inadequate and lost his train of thought: Petrelis interview.
545   screaming, "We're dying!": Bahlman interview no. 2.
545   Robinson's health: ibid. and Petrelis interview.

37: Requiem

547   first ACT-UP meeting: Avram Finkelstein, Larry Mass, Andy Humm, Jim Fouratt, Michael Petrelis and Arnie Kantrowitz interviews with AJN; Vito Russo and Larry Kramer interviews with Eric Marcus, courtesy of Marcus.
547   Financial District demonstration: Petrelis interview with AJN, April 21, 1994; *The Advocate,* no. 471 (April 28, 1987); Larry Kramer, *Reports from the Holocaust,* pp. 137–39.
548   random assaults of homosexuals on the streets: *New York Times,* Nov. 23, 1986.
548   Mobilization Against AIDS protest in San Francisco: *The Advocate,* no. 446 (April 15, 1986).
549   D'Amato's office takeover: Bill Bahlman interview no. 1 with AJN.
549   Ratzinger's letter: *The Advocate,* no. 481 (Sept. 15, 1987).
549   The St. Patrick's protest: Bahlman interview.
549   leaflet attacking *National Review*: courtesy of Bill Bahlman.
549   Lavender Hill Mob and Bennett: Petrelis interview.
549   "We're assaulted in the legislature. . . .": Darrell Yates Rist, *The Advocate,* no. 446 (May 13, 1986).
550   "If you are a gay man or lesbian. . . .": Eric Rofes, "A Call to Resist: Gays Must Return to Activism," *The Advocate,* no. 447 (May 27, 1986).
550   Finkelstein's decision to become a hairstylist, and reaction: Finkelstein interview nos. 1 and 2 with AJN.
550   Finkelstein's group: Finkelstein interview no. 3 with AJN.
552   Kramer pointed out that poster should have read the Food and Drug Administration: Finkelstein interview no. 2.
552   Kramer on GMHC: "An Open Letter to Richard Dunne and Gay Men's Health Crisis," *New York Native,* no. 197 (Jan. 26, 1987). Also Kramer interview with Marcus.
552   Robinson on Kramer: Petrelis interview.
553   Petrelis-Kramer meeting: ibid.
553   Why not ring the White House?: Lenny Giteck, "The Anger and Anguish of Larry Kramer," *The Advocate,* no. 479 (Aug. 18, 1987).
553   first ACT-UP meeting: Finkelstein, Mass, Humm, Fouratt, Petrelis, Kantrowitz to AJN; Russo and Kramer to Marcus.
553   "*You* are showing up at the center.": Humm interview with AJN, April 10, 1994.

554   Kramer's remarks at the center: Kramer, *Reports from the Holocaust,* pp. 127–36.
554   perspective sometimes distorted; his rhetoric flat-footed: many interviews, including Finkelstein interview nos. 1 and 2 and Mass interview nos. 2 and 3.
554   "We need people. . . .": Petrelis interview.
554   Kramer referred to the FDA: *New York Times* op-ed page, March 23, 1987.
554   civil disobedience ideas at second ACT-UP meeting: Finkelstein interview no. 1, based on his contemporaneous notes of the meeting.
555   derivation of name ACT-UP: Petrelis interview; and Finkelstein interview no. 3, based on his contemporaneous notes of the meeting.
555   Book Study Group: David Mixner interview with AJN; Duke Comegys, Diane Abbitt, Marylouise Oates and Rob Eichberg to AJN.
555   ambiguous name: Larry Sprenger interview with AJN, May 21, 1993.
555   Oates column on founding of Book Study Group: *Los Angeles Times,* July 8, 1987.
556   "buying access to a social lifestyle. . . .": Comegys interview no. 1 with AJN.
556   A registered Republican: Comegys interview no. 3 with AJN.
556   used to being in charge: Comegys interview no. 1.
556   Comegys's T-cell count: Comegys interviews 1–3 with AJN.
557   "scared to death": Comegys interview no. 2.
557   Description of scene: Mixner interview no. 3 and Eichberg interview no. 2 with AJN.
557   "Everybody's dying. . . .": Comegys interview no. 2.
557   Comegys said to break the law: Comegys interview nos. 1–3; *Gay Community News,* April 26–May 9, 1987, p. 5; *The Advocate,* no. 471 (April 28, 1987); and text of speech, courtesy of Comegys.
558   Waxman looking at Comegys during civil disobedience speech: Comegys interview no. 2.
558   White House arrests: Mixner interview no. 5, Steve Schulte interview no. 2 and Comegys interview nos. 1–3 with AJN; Sean Strub interview no. 6 with JDC.
558   *"Your gloves* . . .": Comegys interview no. 2.
558   kept pictures of their White House arrests on display: Kramer to Marcus; also Comegys to AJN.
559   "Under normal circumstances. . .": Mark Vandervelden, "Civil Disobedience: Are We Entering a New Militant Stage in the Struggle for Gay Rights?", *The Advocate,* no. 482 (September 29, 1987).
559   The arrest docket that day: Strub interview nos. 2 and 6 with JDC, Mixner interview no. 3 with AJN, Comegys interview nos. 2 and 3.
559   White House march, and Bradley quote: *Washington Post,* June 2, 1987, p. 10.
559   "Conspicuously missing. . . .": Marylouise Oates, *Los Angeles Times,* July 8, 1987.
559   Andelson bought ever-smaller dress shirts: Arlen Andelson interview with AJN.
560   After a while the calls were not returned: Niles Merton interview, and Eichberg interview no. 2 with AJN.
560   "I know something is going on. . . .": Eichberg interview no. 2 with AJN.
560   "Sheldon, we *know* you have AIDS!": Comegys interview no. 1.
560   "How is Sheldon?": Mixner interview no. 3.
561   "I don't want to do a Sheldon Andelson.": Mixner interview no. 5.
561   Shilts was HIV positive: Randy Shilts interview no. 1 with AJN.
561   why Andelson kept his diagnosis quiet: Andelson family interviews, Beverly Thomas interview and Jody Evans interview with AJN.
561   Sheldon Andelson did not want to become one more AIDS poster boy: Arlen Andelson interview.
561   Brown's visit: from his speech at Andelson memorial service, Jan. 10, 1988, from videotape of the event, courtesy of the Andelson family; also Jerry Brown interview nos. 1 and 2 with AJN.
562   was now a hospital room: Waldo Fernandez interview with AJN.
562   "The governor of California!": Brown interviews.

562   tribute to a man he had particularly respected: Brown interview no. 1. "Sheldon was a special kind of guy. . . . He was very loyal to me."

562   Andelson defined his importance: Thomas interview.

562   didn't tumble at Horwitz's graveside and hospital release: Michelle Andelson interview with AJN, 1994, and ibid.

562   how Thomas found out about Andelson's diagnosis and "No shit, Sheldon": Thomas interview.

562   his two favorite politicians: ibid.

563   "The story of Shelly Andelson. . . .": *Los Angeles Times,* Oct. 28, 1984.

563   "Sherman, you don't understand. . . .": Sherman Andelson interview with AJN.

563   Andelson died at home: Andelson family interviews.

563   The official press release: Unger/Thomas, Dec. 30, 1987. "Obituary: Sheldon W. Andelson—UC Regent and Civic Leader).

563   *Los Angeles Times* obituary: Kevin Roderick, "Andelson Dies of AIDS; Gay Regent, Activist," *Los Angeles Times,* Dec. 30, 1987, p. 1.

563   1,500 people at Andelson memorial service: *Daily Bruin* of UCLA, Jan. 12, 1988; also *Los Angeles Times,* Jan. 11, 1988. Much of description of memorial service is from videotape of the event.

564   "Today it is no longer regarded. . . .": memorial service videotape.

564   Brown at Andelson memorial: *Los Angeles Times,* Jan. 11, 1988, and videotape.

564   details of Andelson memorial service: Ivy Botinni interview no. 2, Merton interview, David Russell interview no. 3 and Andelson family interviews with AJN.

Bibliography

Abbott, Sidney, and Barbara Love. *Sappho Was a Right-on Woman*. New York: Stein and Day, 1972.

Altman, Dennis. *Homosexual Oppression and Liberation*. New York: Dutton/Outerbridge and Dienstfrey, 1971.

Bauman, Robert. *The Gentleman from Maryland: The Conscience of a Gay Conservative*. New York: Arbor House, 1986.

Bayer, Ronald. *Homosexuality and American Psychiatry: The Politics of Diagnosis*. New York: Basic Books, 1981.

Bell, Arthur. *Dancing the Gay Lib Blues: A Year in the Homosexual Liberation Movement*. New York: Simon & Schuster, 1971.

Blumenthal, Sidney. *The Rise of the Counter-Establishment: From Conservative Ideology to Political Power*. New York: Times Books, 1986.

Bollier, David. *Liberty and Justice for Some: Defending a Free Society from the Radical Right's Holy War on Democracy*. Washington, D.C.: People for the American Way; New York: Ungar, 1982.

Bourne, Peter G. *Jimmy Carter: A Comprehensive Biography from Plains to Postpresidency*. New York: Scribner, 1997.

Branch, Taylor. *Parting the Waters: America in the King Years, 1954–63*. New York: Simon & Schuster, 1988.

Brown, Howard. *Familiar Faces, Hidden Lives: The Story of Homosexual Men in America Today*. New York: Harcourt Brace Jovanovich, 1976.

Brown, Rita Mae. *A Plain Brown Rapper*. Baltimore: Diana, 1976.

———. *Rubyfruit Jungle*. Plainfield, Vt.: Daughters, 1973; New York: Bantam, 1977.

Browning, Frank. *The Culture of Desire: Paradox and Perversity in Gay Lives Today*. New York: Crown, 1993.

Bryant, Anita. *The Anita Bryant Story: The Survival of Our Nation's Families and the Threat of Militant Homosexuality*. Old Tappan, N.J.: Revell, 1977.

Bunch, Charlotte. *Passionate Politics: Feminist Theory in Action.* New York: St. Martin's, 1987.

Carabillo, Toni, Judith Meuli and June Bundy Csida. *Feminist Chronicles: 1953–1993.* Los Angeles: Women's Graphics, 1993.

Chauncey, George. *Gay New York: Gender, Urban Culture and the Making of the Gay Male World, 1890–1940.* New York: Basic Books, 1994.

Cordova, Jeanne. *Kicking the Habit: An Autobiographical Novel.* Los Angeles: Multiple Dimensions, 1990.

Cory, Donald Webster. *The Homosexual in America: A Subjective Approach.* New York: Greenberg, 1951.

———. *Homosexuality: A Cross Cultural Approach.* New York: Julian, 1956.

D'Emelio, John. *Making Trouble: Essays on Gay History, Politics and the University.* New York: Routledge, 1992.

———. *Sexual Politics, Sexual Communities: The Making of a Homosexual Minority in the United States, 1940–1970.* Chicago: University of Chicago Press, 1983.

Duberman, Martin. *Cures: A Gay Man's Odyssey.* New York: Dutton/Plume, 1991.

———. *Stonewall.* New York: Dutton, 1993.

Evans, Arthur. *Critique of Patriarchal Reason.* San Francisco: White Crane, 1997.

———. *Witchcraft and the Gay Counterculture.* Boston: Fag Rag Books, 1978.

Fisher, Peter. *The Gay Mystique: The Myth and Reality of Male Homosexuality.* New York: Day, 1978.

FitzGerald, Frances. *Cities on a Hill: A Journey Through Contemporary American Cultures.* New York: Simon & Schuster, 1986.

Gentry, Curt. *J. Edgar Hoover: The Man and the Secrets.* New York: Norton, 1991.

Goodstein, David B. *Superliving: You Can Have the Life You Want!* Englewood Cliffs, N.J.: Prentice-Hall, 1983.

Halberstam, David. *The Fifties.* New York: Villard, 1993.

Hall, Radclyffe. *The Well of Loneliness, with a Commentary by Havelock Ellis.* New York: Anchor/Doubleday, 1990.

Hippler, Mike. *Matlovich: The Good Soldier.* Boston: Alyson, 1989.

Holleran, Andrew. *Dancer from the Dance.* New York: Morrow, 1978.

Hunter, Nan D., Sherryl Michaelson and Thomas B. Stoddard. *The Rights of Lesbians and Gay Men: The Basic ACLU Guide to a Gay Person's Rights* (3rd ed.) Carbondale: Southern Illinois University Press, 1992.

Jaffe, Harry S., and Tom Sherwood. *Dream City: Race, Power, and the Decline of Washington, D.C.* New York: Simon & Schuster, 1994.

Jay, Karla, and Allen Young, eds. *After You're Out: Personal Experiences of Gay Men and Lesbian Women.* New York: Pyramid, 1975.

———. *Lavender Culture: The Perceptive Voices of Outspoken Lesbians and Gay Men.* New York: Jove, 1979.

———. *Out of the Closets: Voices of Gay Liberation,* 20th anniversary ed. New York: New York University Press, 1992.

Kantrowitz, Arnie. *Under the Rainbow: Growing Up Gay.* New York: Morrow, 1977.

Katz, Jonathan Ned. *Gay American History: Lesbians and Gay Men in the U.S.A.,* rev. ed. New York: Meridian, 1992.

Kinsey, Alfred C., Wardell B. Pomeroy and Clyde E. Martin. *Sexual Behavior in the Human Male.* Philadelphia: Saunders, 1948.

Kramer, Larry. *Faggots.* New York: Random House, 1978.

———. *The Normal Heart.* New York: Penguin, 1985.

———. *Reports from the Holocaust: The Making of an AIDS Activist.* New York: St. Martin's, 1989.

Liebman, Marvin. *Coming Out Conservative: An Autobiography.* San Francisco: Chronicle, 1992.

Lucas, Charles L. *The Lord Is My Shepherd and He Knows I'm Gay: The Autobiography of the Rev. Troy D. Perry, as Told to Charles L. Lucas.* Los Angeles: Nash, 1972.

McDarrah, Fred W., and Timothy S. McDarrah. *Gay Pride: Photographs from Stonewall to Today.* Chicago: a cappella books, 1994.

McNeill, John J. *The Church and the Homosexual,* 3rd ed. Boston: Beacon, 1988.

Marcus, Eric. *Making History: The Struggle for Gay and Lesbian Equal Rights, 1945–1990.* New York: HarperCollins, 1992.

Marotta, Toby. *The Politics of Homosexuality: How Lesbians and Gay Men Have Made Themselves a Political and Social Force in Modern America.* Boston: Houghton Mifflin, 1981.

Martin, Del, and Phyllis Lyon. *lesbian/woman.* Calif.: Volcano, 1991.

Martin, William. *With God on Our Side: The Rise of the Religious Right in America.* New York: Broadway, 1996.

Mass, Lawrence D. *Confessions of a Jewish Wagnerite: Being Gay and Jewish in America.* New York: Cassell, 1994.

———. *Homosexuality and Sexuality: Dialogues of the Sexual Revolution,* vol. 1. Binghamton, N.Y.: Harrington Park Press, 1990.

Melson, James Kenneth. *The Golden Boy.* Binghamton, N.Y.: Harrington Park Press, 1992.

Miller, Neil. *Out of the Past: Gay and Lesbian History from 1969 to the Present.* New York: Vintage, 1995.

Millett, Kate. *Sexual Politics: The Classic Analysis of the Interplay Between Men, Women and Culture.* New York: Simon & Schuster, 1969.

Monette, Paul. *Becoming a Man: Half a Life Story.* New York: Harcourt Brace Jovanovich, 1992.

———. *Borrowed Time: An AIDS Memoir.* New York: Harcourt Brace Jovanovich, 1988.

Morgan, Robin. *Going Too Far: The Personal Chronicle of a Feminist.* New York: Vintage, 1978.

Morris, Kenneth E. *Jimmy Carter, American Moralist.* Athens: University of Georgia Press, 1996.

Nestle, Joan. *A Restricted Country.* Ithaca, N.Y.: Firebrand, 1987.

Perry, Rev. Troy D., with Thomas L. P. Swicegood. *Don't Be Afraid Anymore: The Story of Reverend Troy Perry and the Metropolitan Community Churches.* New York: St. Martin's, 1990.

Plant, Richard. *The Pink Triangle: The Nazi War Against Homosexuals.* New York: Holt, 1986.

Puccia, Joseph. *The Holy Spirit Dance Club.* Liberty Press, 1988.

Quest Staff. *Building Feminist Theory: Essays from Quest, a Feminist Quarterly.* White Plains, N.Y.: Longman, 1981.

Rutledge, Leigh W. *The Gay Decades: From Stonewall to the Present: The People and Events That Shaped Gay Lives.* New York: Plume, 1992.

Safire, William. *Safire's Political Dictionary: An Enlarged, Up-to-Date Edition of The New Language of Politics.* New York: Random House, 1978.

Schlesinger, Arthur M., Jr. *Robert Kennedy and His Times.* Boston: Houghton Mifflin, 1978.

Schumacher, Michael. *Dharma Lion: A Critical Biography of Allen Ginsberg.* New York: St. Martin's, 1992.

Shilts, Randy. *And the Band Played On: Politics, People, and the AIDS Epidemic.* New York: St. Martin's, 1987.

———. *Conduct Unbecoming: Gays & Lesbians in the U.S. Military.* New York: St. Martin's, 1993.

———. *The Mayor of Castro Street: The Life and Times of Harvey Milk.* New York: St. Martin's, 1982.

Signorile, Michelangelo. *Life Outside. The Signorile Report on Gay Men: Sex, Drugs, Muscles, and the Passages of Life.* New York: HarperCollins, 1997.

———. *Queer in America: Sex, the Media and the Closets of Power.* New York: Random House, 1993.

Siman, Ken. *Pizza Face, or The Hero of Suburbia.* New York: Grove Weidenfeld, 1991.

Simpson, Ruth. *From the Closet to the Courts.* New York: Viking, 1976.

Sullivan, Andrew. *Virtually Normal.* New York: Knopf, 1995.

Theoharis, Athan. *J. Edgar Hoover, Sex, and Crime.* Chicago: Dee, 1995.

Thompson, Mark. *Gay Spirit: Myth and Meaning.* New York: St. Martin's, 1987.

Thompson, Mark, ed. *Long Road to Freedom: The Advocate History of the Gay and Lesbian Movement.* New York: St. Martin's, 1994.

Timmons, Stuart. *The Trouble with Harry Hay.* Boston: Alyson, 1990.

Tobin, Kay, and Randy Wicker. *The Gay Crusaders.* New York: Paperback Library, 1972.

Vaid, Urvashi. *Virtual Equality: The Mainstreaming of Gay and Lesbian Liberation.* New York: Anchor/ Doubleday, 1995.

Vidal, Gore. *United States: Essays, 1952–1992.* New York: Random House, 1993.

White, Edmund. *States of Desire: Travels in Gay America.* New York: Penguin, 1991.

White, Mel. *Stranger at the Gate: To Be Gay and Christian in America.* New York: Simon & Schuster, 1994.

Acknowledgments

THE NICE THING about writing these acknowledgments is that they come at the end of everything else. The long work on the book is done. It is a grateful moment, and the proper time and space in which to thank all those people whose contributions, commitment, love, friendship and patience have made these pages possible. This history has been a collaborative effort of two authors, but also of many other people, some paid, most not. Some have helped in the fashioning of the book. Some have helped in the fashioning of our lives. A few have been critical to both.

As anyone who has spent years reporting and writing a manuscript knows, there is no real way to convey the importance of the intellectual, emotional and material support given at critical moments by colleagues and friends, and also by some of those who are the subjects of this work. But we know the difference that each made, and we will try to express our appreciation.

There may be literary agents with bigger minds and hearts than Kathy Robbins, but you would have to prove it to us. This book is what it is, as she would say, in large measure because it reflects her tough and sound advice. She challenged us at the very beginning to make it a more ambitious work than we had considered, and found us the publisher, the protection and the help we needed at every point of the way.

We are grateful to many people at Simon & Schuster, starting with Gary Luke, but most particularly to our editor, the legendary Alice Mayhew, who has shepherded some of the great narrative works of American history of the last three decades. We are in debt to her for her belief in this book, for sheltering and guiding it through the added years it took to produce, and for recognizing it from the beginning as an important work of understanding for the general American public. She ensured that it was treated that way. Her associate editor, Roger Labrie, has been patient, resilient, resourceful, and more organized and helpful, than we had any right to expect. Bill Goldstein, who bid on this book as an editor at Scribner when the proposal first went to auction in New York, was indescribably valuable as a friend and outside editor when it came to cutting the manuscript down from the massive size to which it had grown almost six years later. Its present shape owes much to his eye, and we owe much to him.

There are others whose help, in varying measures, has been extraordinary. Karen Avrich, our friend and colleague, showed brilliant talent, focus and intuition over the course of more than a year in the vast files of the Library of Congress, during which she methodically selected out and assembled the thousands of articles and items that formed the paper core of our research. We owe her more than we can say. In New York, friends Alex Jones and Susan Tifft, biographers of the Bingham and Sulzberger families, gave us priceless advice, counseling us to build a written chronology of events as we discovered them in interviews and archival research, a chronology that became the historical spine of the narrative. In Philadelphia and Baltimore, transcriber Robert Melton was astonishing, monitoring and typing hundreds of hours of tape-recorded interviews by day and night, producing thousands of pages of transcript with ferocious speed and precision over a three-year period. Leslie Jones, a lawyer of silver voice and manner, made the task of combing the manuscript for legal issues seem uncommonly civilized and precise. Charlotte Gross, who copyedited the manuscript for Simon & Schuster, did it with infinite courtesy and care. And at the Robbins office, David Halpern and Bill Clegg fielded our concerns over the years with inexhaustible aplomb.

Other, established authors in the field were generous beyond measure. Eric Marcus, the author of *Making History*, the oral history of the movement, voluntarily opened his interview files to us—an access that has enormously enriched this book. Randy Shilts, author of *The Mayor of Castro Street* and *And The Band Played On*, made the same offer before he died. Martin Duberman, one of the founders and most prolific historians in the field of gay studies, made us feel welcome and collegially supported, as did Charles Kaiser, the intellectually keen and witty author of *The Gay Metropolis*.

In our research and interview trips across the country, there were people whose support made the time far more cheerful and worthwhile. In Miami, Gene Miller, the *Miami Herald*'s celebrated investigative reporter and editor, helped locate essential material on Anita Bryant and other characters in the paper's files. In San Francisco, Dorothy Knecht, a Clendinen family friend, lent her warmth, guest room and car for weeks on end—and her nursing skills, too, when her houseguest, returning from an interview near the Castro, was assaulted by a street gang at night. In Los Angeles, Mark Miller gave up his apartment for a whole month of research in a city where hotels are anything but inexpensive, while Steve Smith, in the midst of serving up endless interviews and insights, showed up with a flashlight and an offer of a warm meal on the morning of the Los Angeles earthquake. Eileen Rhea Brown in Atlanta, and Sara Rimer in Boston gave direction, space, dinner parties, and endless hours of good humor and hospitality, as they have all the decades that they have been friends.

There are also a number of people who made vital contributions to the archival foundation of this work. At the beginning of this project, at the kind request of former U.S. Rep. Sam M. Gibbons of Tampa, George Walser, a researcher at the Library of Congress, compiled a single-spaced list of mostly obscure and forgotten journals, books and publications—all of which were potential sources for us—1,000 pages long. In New York, Richard Wandel—a past president of the city's Gay Activists Alliance, who today curates the National Archive of Lesbian and Gay History at the Lesbian and Gay Community Services Center in New York City—has been a remarkable resource: patient, knowledgeable and infinitely helpful, through many trips down to the basement to retrieve heavy cartons of old records. The Lesbian Herstory Archives in Brooklyn was a researcher's dream, and its founder, Joan Nestle, was gracious and accommodating. We are beholden to the late Jim Kepner, the founder of the International Gay and Lesbian Archives in Los Angeles, who, with John O'Brien, was enthusiastic and endlessly curious as he guided us through the wonderful, if dusty, old archives in West Hollywood. The late Thomas B. Stoddard provided us a tutorial in gay legal history that we could not have paid for, and Jim Herring, Archivist at the Jimmy Carter Library in Atlanta, was gracious and responsive beyond measure.

Many of the people interviewed for this history became archival sources for it, too, sharing the personal records of their lives—personal papers, tapes, documents, photographs—and their involvements as members or witnesses of the gay rights movement. Their generosity has shaped this history, and among those to whom we are gratefully indebted, for the substantial time and materials they shared, are Thomas Bastow, Adam DeBaugh, the late Stephen Endean, Barbara Gittings and Kay Lahusen, Jim Gordon, Paul Kuntzler, Donald Lucas, Laura McMurry, Dr. Richard C. Pillard, Sean O'Brien Strub, Candy Frank Thomson, Stan Tillotson, Jean Nicholas Tretter, and Dr. Lilli Vincenz. There were more: Charlotte Bunch, the late Bruce Voeller, Dick Leitsch, Allen Roskoff, Tim Westmoreland, Larry Mass, Hal Offen, Maxine Wolfe, Pete Fisher, Marc Rubin, Helen Scheitinger and Dick Shack.

Lastly, in terms of those who contributed directly and most poignantly to this book, are those who were interviewed for it, who gave willingly of their time and history, but who are not in it. It is a long and tender list. Research always produces more rich material than any book can hold. This manuscript was also cut by some 40 percent, in order to achieve a readable and reasonable structure. Readers will still find plenty of names to keep track of in this history, but they can also find the names that are not in the narrative in the list of characters and interviewees in the back.

That is not the end of the acknowledgments. There are the more personal kinds of support, and each author has his own list.

• • •

This is a book that began with an article in a newspaper, and newspapers, magazines, and the friends and colleagues on and off them, have counted enormously in this work. The germ grew originally from a piece I had suggested and written for Mike Levitas, the Op-Ed Editor of *The New York Times*, observing that Bill Clinton's open reach to homosexuals—and the Republican dismissal of them—might create, among people like me, a gay vote in the coming presidential election. That was on August 1, 1992. It was, when it ran, a kind of coming out piece for me, and it also began to seem, in the weeks afterward, like an idea for a book. When Jeffrey Schmalz, a friend and a much-loved reporter and editor at the *Times*, brought me together with his friend Adam Nagourney, the two of us began to work to make it one. Howell Raines, Editorial Page Editor of *The New York Times*—and the author of *My Soul Is Rested*, the oral history of the black civil rights movement—perceived the importance of this history of the gay rights struggle early on. He has been supportive in all kinds of thoughtful and telling ways, and in this last year and a half has allowed me to write editorials for the *Times* under contract, while working with Adam to finish this book.

In Washington, D.C., Ronald Steel, the historian and biographer of Walter Lippmann, has been a treasured friend, giving countless generous hours of encouragement and conversation, analyzing and commenting on the emerging discoveries and written work. At Emory University in Atlanta, Melvin Konner, the author, physician and anthropologist, has done the same, providing soulful perspective and humor at vital times. Nelson Aldrich, the editor of *Civilization* and *American Benefactor* magazines, and a man lively in all things, has been an enthusiastic and interested friend, commissioning me to write other essays from my changing life while an editor at *Lear's*. He and Caroline Miller, then editor of *Lear's*, and now of *New York*, were generous with their time and support. Katy Roberts, the present Op-Ed editor of the *Times*, Martin Beiser, managing editor of *GQ*, and David Finkel, an editor of *The Washington Post Magazine*, all commissioned essays that helped me to think aloud from life. John Carroll, the Editor of the *Baltimore Sun*, has been a compassionate employer and a supportive spirit of this book.

Sidney and Jackie Blumenthal have been fond and loyal friends, especially at trying times, for a decade. Nathalie Dupree, the television cook and author, has been a soulful partner, a sage friend and incomparable source of needed hilarity and confidence during those same years. Jack Skuce, a shepherd to his friends, has often provided shelter, inspiration and related stories from his own encyclopedic experiences in the American culture these last years. Liz Trotta, the author and former network correspondent, has been a devoted, strong and funny friend, more important and appreciated at crucial times than she may know. Lindsey Gruson and Jane Whitney, Norrie Epstein and Steve Wigler, John and Jane Payne, Trudy and Mickey Magarill, Hackey Clark, Pat Conroy, David and Jean Halberstam, Gary Cohen, Bill Kovach, Eugene C. Patterson—who first believed in my ability to write a book—Sally Jacobs, Rosemary Shields and Marion Greene have all meant more at many different points than they will probably understand. So has Andy Barnes. John Siegel and John Templeton were great examples of how to live, sanely and soberly—and also artfully—who became great, intimate and patient friends, and hosts on trips to Atlanta.

My cousin Florence Hosch gave me love, understanding, and intellectual and financial support. Robin Kennedy taught me a new way to live. Others, my old, close friends, have been the beams and rafters of my life during the personal remodeling of recent years, while I made the transition from traditional marriage to my present life: David Hall; Carla Kelly; Harriet and Phillip Plyler and Eileen Brown; as well as Nathalie Davis Wood; my sister, Melissa, and her husband, Brad Spring; my godson, Christopher, Marian and Hal Flowers and my adorable half-ass godparents, Emyfish and Ashby Moody; are all proof that it is impossible to be trying and difficult enough to drive the friends who love you away. They, along with my aunt Virginia; and my cousins Baya, Ginger and Lynn and their families; have all given me so much over the years that we feel like extensions of each other, and I am more grateful than I can say, as I am to the rooms in every city from which people like me draw serenity and strength.

I am sad that my mother, Barbara Clendinen, is a stroke victim, no longer able to read. But she will know, in her unaffected heart, what this book means when she sees it. I am also lucky. The work on this history has been an extension of my life, and I have been blessed the last five years, by the generous, patient, creative, loving and endlessly supportive company of Stephen Salny. He has been understanding to a fault, of both me and my work, and life with him has made this book far more possible than it would otherwise have been.

Nancy Barritt, my former wife, has shown more good humor, respect and understanding than I probably deserve. But I appreciate it, and I am grateful most of all for our daughter, Whitney Clendinen. Her intelligence, compassion, open mind and voracious appetite for the life ahead are all the reason a father needs to attempt a book which is intended to increase understanding in the culture in which she will live.

DUDLEY CLENDINEN
Baltimore
November 1998

THIS PROJECT began about the time that Bill Clinton was moving into the White House, and has imposed on the resources, humor and patience of friends, colleagues and employers ever since. It's probably impossible to adequately thank them, but allow me to try. At *USA Today*, Tom McNamara, David Colton and Bob Minzesheimer were patient and generous as I drifted from the newsroom to work on this project. Bill Nichols, the paper's other White House correspondent, graciously picked up my slack, and offered nothing but encouragement. At *The New York Times*, a series of editors and colleagues kindly permitted me to finish this book before coming on board, and then again allowed me to disappear to finish it again: in Washington, Johnny Apple, Andrew Rosenthal and Rick Berke, and in New York, Mike Oreskes and Joyce Purnick.

There were countless friends and colleagues who were generous in their counsel, intelligence and support. Mark Halperin was extraordinarily helpful, badgering and provocative and always a year ahead of anyone in his political insights. Gail Collins, Mike Kelly, Ron Brownstein, Dan Balz and David Maraniss are all writers who have been there, and unstintingly offered advice on everything from managing computers to editors. Marylouise Oates and Bob Shrum were the first to help us understand the unique role Los Angeles and money played in the gay rights movement; their guidance and perspective can be seen in this book. Adam Clymer generously volunteered his research on Edward M. Kennedy and the gay vote. Carl Cannon retrieved his twenty-year-old notes from covering the Briggs Initiative. David Groff, who as an editor also offered a bid on this project, was a constant and remarkably well-versed friend and colleague, always willing to help untangle some moment in gay history. And there were friends who proved loyal and helpful in too many ways to elaborate in these pages, but in ways I will always remember: Andrew Kirtzman, Wendy Schmalz, Michael Wilde, Kevin McCoy, Marcia Kramer, Maureen Dowd, Richard Meislin, David Dunlap, Frank Bruni, Ann Bramson, Harry Wolff, Stephen Crowley, Maralee Schwarz, Justin Blake, Dan Lansner, Bob Thomson, Richard Runes and Eddie Borges. My siblings, Beth, Eric, and Sam, and my parents, Ruth and Herb Nagourney, were supportive, proud and enthusiastic throughout.

I only wish that Jeff Schmalz were around to read this book, and, in fact, to share in everything that has happened in my life since his death. It is because of him that I have the opportunity to walk into *The New York Times* newsroom each day and was allowed this remarkable opportunity to join Dudley Clendinen in writing a book like this.

Finally, there is Benjamin M. Kushner, my companion and my very best friend, to whom I personally dedicate this work. We have been together for almost a quarter of a century. I simply cannot imagine a life without him.

ADAM NAGOURNEY
New York
November 1998

Index

sheriff campaigns of, 157–59, 162,
335–36, 342–43
in Stokes campaign, 163
Honolulu, Hawaii, APA convention in,
212–15
Hooker, Evelyn, 211
Hoose, Jerry, 44, 51, 63, 69, 78, 85
Hoover, J. Edgar, 113
Hope, Bob, 82, 292
Hormel, James C., 433–34
Horowitz, David, 485
Horwitz, Al, 359
Horwitz, Roger, 514–15, 560, 562, 569
Hothouse, 486, 499
housing, 422, 518
Frank's legislative campaign and, 130
gay rights legislation on, 228, 231, 242,
272, 295, 327, 400, 450, 511
and homosexuality as illness, 216
Houston, Tex., 407, 533
AIDS in, 481, 484
gay rights legislation in, 449, 523,
526–27
Howell, Deborah, 228–29, 231, 235
Hudson, John Paul, 171
Hudson, Rock, 385–86, 517, 519
Human Rights Campaign Fund (HRCF),
433–40, 548, 557, 568
African Americans in, 496
on AIDS, 474, 485–86, 488, 498, 542
finances of, 472–74, 489–91, 494–95,
497–99
in presidential campaigns, 472–74, 571
Humm, Andy, 529–30, 553
Humphrey, Hubert H., 26, 227, 324
presidential campaigns of, 133, 138,
302
Humphrey, Muriel, 324
Hunt, Jim, 509
Hunt, William, 233
Hunter, Joyce, 405, 538

Ice Palace, 463, 495–96
immigration, 290
gay rights legislation and, 423, 505
judiciary on, 532–33
presidential campaigns and, 137
presidential order on, 416, 418
sodomy laws and, 537
Integrity, 314, 399

Internal Revenue Service (IRS), 83,
288
Itkin, Michael, 200

Jackson, Alice, 398
Jackson, Debra Anne, 146
Jackson, Don, 37–38, 75, 82
Jackson, Henry M. "Scoop," 273–74
Jackson, Jesse:
HRCF speech of, 494–95, 497–99
presidential campaigns of, 494, 505–6
Jackson, Maynard, 319–20
Jarmin, Gary, 409, 424, 426
Jester, Susan, 509
Jews, 12, 234, 281, 380, 464–65, 477,
523, 550, 562–63
discrimination against, 304
gay bathhouses picketed by, 516
on gay rights legislation, 298, 301–2,
304–5, 309, 526, 528–29, 537
homosexual, 222, 227, 229–31, 317,
338, 351, 355–56, 361, 430
presidential campaigns and, 274, 277
Joachim, Jerry, 35
John Paul II, Pope, 408
Johnson, Lois, 222
Johnson, Lyndon B., 111, 293, 382–83
Jones, Cleve, 160–61, 332, 341, 404
AIDS and, 487, 567, 569
on gay rights legislation, 346–47, 403
Jones, Harry, 220
Jones, Jim, 340
*Journal of the American Medical
Association*, 209, 483–85

Kameny, Franklin E., 14, 31, 46, 74–75,
171, 197–99, 263, 419, 493, 497,
559, 569
on AIDS, 479, 503
arrest of, 288
background of, 112–13, 117–18, 123
congressional campaign of, 112–24,
203
in founding of GRNL, 258–59
in founding of Mattachine Society,
109–10, 113–14
in founding of NGTF, 197–98
on gay rights legislation, 397
on homosexuality as illness, 199,
202–8, 215–16